Praise for *Sorrow and Blood: Christian Mission in Contexts of Suffering, Persecution, and Martyrdom*

It is not only inside the Christian church but also in civil society and global foreign policy today that the question of religious freedom has made a comeback. What unites church and civil society is the challenge of how to enter a future where relations between religions will be even more tense. Followers of Jesus will now realize more and more that "with the message of the cross goes the cross of the message." In this situation I thank God for the new book *Sorrow and Blood*. After reading many books on persecution that deal with parts of the challenge facing the future I find here the best book I have seen as it goes into all the dimensions of the challenge but also gives good practical advice. This is a must for everyone that wants to be relevant in missions work or in religious freedom work in the days ahead.

*Very Rev. Johan Candelin, Finland, Goodwill Ambassador, World Evangelical Alliance*

The human cost of the Great Commission in hostile environments is something Christians too often overlook. In this important resource book, Taylor, van der Meer, and Reimer provide an encyclopaedic study of suffering, persecution, and martyrdom in global Christian mission. It combines survey, scholarship, and stories to speak to both head and heart about the cost of discipleship for many believers. This is a well-researched call to pray and advocate for our persecuted brothers and sisters around the world and to prepare believers to suffer for their faith. Every mission agency, seminary, and church should have a copy.

*Very Rev. Dr. Justyn Terry, Dean/President and Associate Professor of Systematic Theology, Trinity School for Ministry, Ambridge, PA, USA*

This book brings to us a vast research on its proposed theme. One will not only learn about the present suffering situation. But one will also become aware of the need to have one's mission practices based on the Scripture's teaching. As the Bible and reality come together, naturally the book emphasizes the need of proper training before sending missionaries. I am sure that the reader will be able to engage in mission aware of its danger, price, and eternal reward.

*Silas M. Tostes, President, Brazilian Mission Association, and President, Antioch Mission*

*Sorrow and Blood* is a priceless, comprehensive compilation of material providing practical, biblical, and theological grist for any discussion of Christian suffering. Advocates for religious freedom will be emboldened, missionaries will receive wisdom, and the persecuted will find a tangible support base that allows hope to be both credible and sustained. For all, dove-like innocence will be buttressed by reptilian shrewdness, as pragmatic and best-practiced initiatives are taken on behalf of those who suffer. Quite simply, the "learned obedience" of Gethsemane will provide greater richness to the glorification that comes from Calvary's pain.

*Robert A. Seiple, Ambassador-at-large (retired) for International Religious Freedom, USA*

*Sorrow and Blood* shows that we cannot properly conceive of mission apart from suffering and persecution, and its sixty authors consider every dimension of their relation. In no other book can we find such careful biblical and theological discussion combined with history, a range of case studies, and nuanced discussions of countries and trends in the modern world. To this it adds information and advice on training and preparation, and guides to a range of resources. Anyone involved in mission, or studying mission, will profit immensely from this excellent book.

*Paul Marshall, Senior Fellow, Hudson Institute's Center for Religious Freedom*

*Sorrow and Blood* is a powerful and comprehensive global study of persecution and suffering. Every follower of Christ who wants to be informed and inspired should read this book. It should be required reading for pastors, missionaries, activists, or any other Christian who wants to engage biblically in a complex world where millions of fellow believers are under great pressure or persecution for their faith.

*Dr. Geoff Tunnicliffe, CEO / Secretary General, World Evangelical Alliance*

For most of us it is incomprehensible the suffering that our sisters and brothers have endured in many places around the globe for the sake of the Gospel. *Sorrow and Blood* is the best effort done by evangelical reflective practitioners to provide a comprehensive description and a deep analysis of what Christian suffering and martyrdom mean and what the situation looks like today. This is not just another book produced by the Mission Commission of WEA, but one of the most profound and challenging to read, particularly if you do it with an open mind and a warm heart.

*Dr. Bertil Ekström, Executive Director, WEA Mission Commission*

I recently stood in Cairo at the spot where just days earlier sixteen Egyptians had lost their lives—because they were Christians. Indeed, as this book vividly describes, Christians are being brutalized and killed the world around because of their confession of faith in Christ. *Sorrow and Blood*, with rich insights provided by a breadth of writers, is a milestone of analysis. My hope is that it will do more than sober a few mission specialists, but that these pages will find their way into messages, articles, film, and video media, expanding an ever-growing awareness of heroic, Christ-like suffering, and also about what can be done to effectively advocate for persecuted people of faith.

*Brian C. Stiller, Global Ambassador, World Evangelical Alliance, President Emeritus, Tyndale University College and Seminary*

With a wonderful balance of insight and passion this volume addresses the most neglected mark of the true church: suffering. Readers will not only be enlightened, but also deeply moved and challenged listening to voices from around the globe reflect theologically, report accurately, and testify personally on this topic. *Sorrow and Blood* is a profound and vital contribution to our understanding of the church and mission.

*Dr. Craig Ott, Professor of Mission and Intercultural Studies, Trinity Evangelical Divinity School*

The motto of those in China's house churches responsible for the "Back-to-Jerusalem" vision today is "Sacrifice, abandonment, poverty, suffering, death"! I suppose they must know what they are talking about, given the phenomenal growth of the Chinese church since the 1970s. Although there will always be those whose ingenuity will help them find a way around it, those who are concerned about the advance of the Gospel know that the cross is always central. *Sorrow and Blood* powerfully makes the same point. Read it if you want to be serious about missions!

*Dr. Hwa Yung, Bishop, The Methodist Church, Malaysia*

In *Sorrow and Blood*, a chorus of trusted global voices share the most compelling and comprehensive historical, theological, and missiological overview of ministry in a context of suffering, persecution, and martyrdom ever compiled. This volume will push you to reflect anew on the true cost of discipleship and inspire a fresh commitment to stand in the gap for those living out their faith under the storm clouds of oppression in its various forms.

*Steve Moore, President, Missio Nexus, USA*

This is an essential, impactful, disturbing book: clear and forthright without denying the complexity of the matter. This book is close to my heart because I grew up in the state of Chiapas, southern Mexico, in a context of severe persecution of those who confessed their faith in Jesus Christ and read the Bible for themselves. But we were not alone. The editors are eminently qualified to compile this volume. The authors and case studies provide the reader with breadth of experiential familiarity coupled with depth and sensitivity of understanding. The structure of the book provides the reader with a broad and deep treatment of a very difficult topic, offering theoretical, biblical, historical, and practical reflections. This is essential reading for anyone involved in cross-cultural mission on every continent.

*Dr. Charles Van Engen, Arthur F. Glasser Professor of Biblical Theology of Mission School of Intercultural Studies, Fuller Theological Seminary, USA*

As I read this book and write these lines, I am aware that right now native evangelical Christians are forced to leave their land and their towns in southern Mexico because of their faith. The question of religious persecution has become all pervasive and urgent, both in the European post-Christendom societies as well as in countries dominated by Islam and other religions. This book is a most valuable compendium and it should become required reading for future missionaries and mission educators. The rich diversity of nationalities, perspectives, and styles represented is a good example of how Christian missiology is becoming truly global.

*Dr. Samuel Escobar, Facultad Protestante de Teología UEBE, Madrid, Spain*

The history of our church is one of suffering and martyrdom. While it's impossible to completely comprehend God's sovereignty in this, our role is to be ever aware of the growing difficulties of our brothers and sisters worldwide and to do our utmost to understand, assist, and intercede. We should each also be prepared to face both unexpected and expected challenges in our own ministry and life. In this light, *Sorrow and Blood* paints us a fuller picture of suffering through splendid biblical, theological, historical, missional, and pastoral insights.

*Chulho Han, Director, Mission Korea Partners*

*Sorrow and Blood* hit me in a powerful way before this book went to press. My friend, Artur Suleimanov was gunned down because of his bold witness for Christ. When I picked up this book I thought of Artur. I know he would be thankful for the wonderful research found in its pages. He would praise God for such solid biblical theology regarding suffering. He would rejoice that global mission will never be the same as a result of this work and its application to our teaching, preparation, and prayers.

*Rev. Bruce Huseby, Pastor of Global Ministries, Calvary Church, Grand Rapids, MI, USA*

It is with reverence that I touch *Sorrow and Blood*. The data, reports, witnesses, and biblical reflections open before my eyes allow me and push me to see the faces of people who tell me with their lives that in Jesus Christ they found the meaning of life and of history. The world is not worthy of them (Heb 11:38) nor am I. But in grace they minister to our lives and to our generation, calling us all into a deeper commitment to being agents of God's Kingdom in the corners of the world in which we live. I feel honored to be ministered by those who tell me, through suffering, that it is good and necessary to serve our Lord Jesus Christ and to live, or even die, for him. It's an amazing work. Gloria Deo.

*Dr. Valdir Steuernagel, Theologian-at-Large, World Vision International, Brazil*

As Latins in mission to the Muslim world, we receive this book with enthusiasm and gratitude. Reading it has been a consolation and personal encouragement because of the various perspectives of this challenging reality, whether theological, historical, pastoral, or through case studies. I have the impression that this text will become required reading for all of us who aspire to continue serving and honoring the Lord of the Harvest on mission. Our prayer is that this book will contribute to a better church and mission preparation as we face these disturbing challenges, and also as we cultivate the same attitude and spirit of Jesus.

*Allan E. Matamoros, International Director, PM International, Limassol, Cyprus*

This volume jolts us out of our complacency by reminding us that one-third of all countries have either no religious freedom or it is severely restricted; it looks at the implications of this reality in terms of experience, Scripture, theology, and history, and it draws us into the implications of what all this means for prayerful action, spiritual warfare, political advocacy, and human caring. Finally, it brings a fresh perspective on what it means to genuinely pursue "the fellowship of sharing in his sufferings."

*Dr. Rod Wilson, President, Regent College, Vancouver, Canada*

At a recent Mani (Movement for African National Initiatives) consultation, a Sudanese brother shared his heart on the suffering of our brothers and sisters in the Middle East and North African countries. This resulted in an outpouring of prayer as I have seldom experienced. We were informed and it touched us. This most comprehensive book on suffering and persecution will be of immense value to the global church, but especially to the African church. It will create an awareness that is often lacking. May we all be shaken out of our complacency. Every pastor, mission leader, and Bible school student should read this book.

*Peter Tarantal, Director of Wensa (World Evangelization Network of South Africa) and leadership team of MANI, South Africa*

*Sorrow and Blood* takes an unflinching look at the cost of Christian mission in a violent and hostile world. Contributors from around the world tell the awe-inspiring story of missionaries and local believers who have followed their Savior in faithful and sacrificial witness. Theologians help us reflect on the redemptive impact of their suffering for the faith. Advocates advise on how to help without making matters worse. Digesting this epic work will require uncommon fortitude, effort that will be richly rewarded. May God use this volume to rouse his church to take the baton from those who have so valiantly gone before us.

*Galen Carey, Vice President, Government Relations, National Association of Evangelicals, USA*

What a resource! I knew this book would be packed with information, but I did not anticipate how much it would provoke and challenge me in my own life as a disciple. If suffering and sorrow drive us to desperation, where Jesus transforms, then we have much to learn from the persecuted church about Christian devotion. This anthology serves not only as an outstanding theological, historical, and missiological resource, but also as a prophetic witness to consumer Christianity. It's a bracing reminder that there is only one way to Christ, the way of the cross.

*Rev. Clifton David Sims Warner, Rector, Christ Church-Anglican, Austin, TX, USA*

# SORROW AND BLOOD

# SORROW AND BLOOD

*Christian Mission in Contexts of*
*Suffering, Persecution, and Martyrdom*

William D. Taylor
Antonia van der Meer
Reg Reimer

Prefaces by Ajith Fernando
and Christopher J. H. Wright

**WILLIAM CAREY**
LIBRARY

Sorrow and Blood: Christian Mission in Contexts of Suffering, Persecution, and Martyrdom
Copyright © 2012 by World Evangelical Alliance Mission Commission
All rights reserved.

copyediting, Koe Pahlka, Brad Koenig
cover design, Kalun Lau
interior design and indexing, Koe Pahlka

William Carey Library is a ministry of the
US Center for World Mission
Pasadena, California.
Printed in the United States of America. 16 15 14 13 12   5 4 3 2 1 COU2000

Library of Congress Cataloging-in-Publication Data

Taylor, William David.
  Sorrow and blood : Christian mission in contexts of suffering, persecution, and martyrdom / William D. Taylor, Antonia van der Meer, Reg Reimer.
      p. cm.
 Includes bibliographical references and index.
 ISBN 978-0-87808-472-2

 1. Missions. 2. Violence--Religious aspects--Christianity. 3. Suffering--Religious aspects--Christianity. 4. Persecution. 5. Martyrdom--Christianity. I. Van der Meer, Antonia. II. Reimer, Reg. III. Title.

 BV2063.T323 2012
 266--dc23

                            2012015377

# CONTENTS

*To the "unknown ones"*
*who because of their witness for Christ have suffered, been persecuted, and even martyred.*
*Unknown to the broader world, they are known to their families and friends;*
*and their names are written in God's book.*
*They are fully known and cherished by the loving Father, the suffering servant Jesus,*
*and the comforting Holy Spirit.*

# TO BE READ

*William D. Taylor*

We welcome you to yet another volume in our *Globalization of Mission* series. We are grateful to the World Evangelical Alliance (WEA) Theological Commission and the Religious Liberty Commission for their strategic partnership with us in this seminal book.

As this long project comes to a close, we are careful to acknowledge our debt; first, to the living and triune God who invited and empowered us into his mission. The eternal Community knew the cost that the suffering people of God would pay through the biblical narrative, all through human history to the present day, until that Day. We owe a countless debt to our sisters and brothers who, as God's people on mission over the millennia, have suffered, been persecuted, and perhaps martyred. This treasure seems endless and overwhelming. The more we studied the themes of this book, the more we realized how vast, how powerful, and how relevant it is to our day and time.

We are thankful to the participants of the Iguassu Missiological Consultation of late 1999, convened by the Mission Commission of WEA to grapple with crucial issues at the turn of the century and millennium. The Iguassu participants charged the MC leadership to explore a diverse set of themes; out of that challenge many publications have emerged.

I am personally thankful to my co-editors, both published authors. Antonia (Tonica) van der Meer, is a Brazilian of Dutch extract and a servant of the living God with enormous experience of ministry in Brazil and Angola. She serves as development coordinator, teacher, and mentor at the Evangelical Missions Center in Brazil.

Reg Reimer is a veteran Canadian mission leader who began his career in wartime Vietnam. He maintained close connections with churches in Vietnam after the Communist ascendancy and is recognized as a foremost authority on Vietnamese Protestantism and religious liberty. He led World Relief Canada for a decade, and in recent years has tirelessly promoted partnering in Christian mission in mainland South East Asia.

Tonica and Reg were invited onto the editorial team because I sensed in them a passion for the themes that drive this book. But they also have personal experience in suffering and persecution, and they personally know martyrs of our faith.

We are profoundly grateful to our many writers, some sixty-eight of them from twenty-two nations. English is a second language for many of them, and we are thankful for their commitment to our project. They write from their experience and their passion, and they quote Scriptures from their mother tongue. They are all "reflective practitioners"; that is, women and men who think as they serve, who ask questions in the vortex of ministry, who serve from tested missiological presuppositions, and who do so with integrity. Without them this book would not exist.

Full gratitude goes to Robin Harris, who helped craft the artistic elements in the book while working on her doctoral studies in ethnomusicology. Robin and family served Christ for years in Siberia. She now leads ICE (International Council of Ethnodoxology). Matt Fries helped identify the Scripture texts we would use throughout the book.

Deep appreciation goes to Mrs. Koe Pahlka, our copyeditor and layout artist whose creativity and competence produces yet another MC publication. She does this while (with the full-time help of her husband) mothering a brood of eight children and raising (at current count) three Nubian goats, ten rabbits, nineteen hens, two pigs, one dog, and three cats on thirty acres! Kalun Lau, working out of his ministry base in Hong Kong, has once again produced a powerful cover, evocative of prison cells and torture chambers.

## THE READER'S CHALLENGE

During the final weeks of collecting and collating the chapters of the book, stitching it together, and crafting my own reflections, I have also been reading the powerful book *Bonhoeffer: Pastor, Martyr, Prophet, Spy* (2010). Writer Eric Metaxas magnificently narrates that twentieth-century dramatic story. Many of us have been shaped by Bonhoeffer's writings on discipleship and community. This biography emerged as a capstone to the final editorial work on the book you are reading. I commend it to you. Revelation 6:11 prophesied about Bonhoeffer and countless others. The number of the martyrs has not yet been completed. Prepare to be moved.

And now, good and thoughtful reader, ask the living God by his empowering Spirit to give you the passion of Christ as you engage this book, mull over our rich history, and consider our response today as witnesses to the truth. How can you best read this work? Start by perusing the table of contents, where you capture the structure of the book. You can then plunge in and read it from cover to cover. Or perhaps some of you will select some articles based on your personal interest. Be sure to balance your diet with the diverse offerings of this rich banquet.

Then, as you are captured by the themes, ask the Spirit of God how you can best pray, defend, advocate, and prepare the church of Christ for the future.

Remember the prophetic words of Jesus, pregnant with meaning:

> Blessed are the peacemakers, for they shall be called sons of God.
> Blessed are those who are persecuted for righteousness sake, for theirs is the kingdom of heaven.
> Blessed are you when others revile you and persecute you and utter all kinds of evil against you falsely on my account. Rejoice and be glad, for your reward is great in heaven, for so they persecuted the prophets who were before you.

—Jesus in the Mountain Manifesto, Matthew 5:9–11

**William Taylor** is a Third Culture Person, born in Costa Rica and raised in Central America until his last year of secondary school. Married to Yvonne since 1967, they have three married Gen-X children born in Guatemala and now have seven grandchildren. Bill lived in Latin America for thirty years, seventeen of them with Yvonne in Guatemala, based at the Seminario Teológico Centroamericano under CAM International. His ThM is from Dallas Seminary and his PhD in Latin American studies from the University of Texas, Austin. From 1986–2006 he was executive director of the World Evangelical Alliance Missions Commission; he now is its senior mentor, publications coordinator, and global missiology task force co-leader. Edited books include *Too Valuable to Lose: Exploring the Causes and Cures of Missionary Attrition* (William Carey Library, 1997) and *Global Missiology for the Twenty-first Century: The Iguassu Dialogue* (Baker, 2000). He served for twelve years as editor of *Connections: The Journal of the WEA Missions Commission*. He and Steve Hoke co-authored *Global Mission Handbook: A Guide for Crosscultural Service* (InterVarsity Press, 2009). Bill also serves as president of TaylorGlobalConsult, a ministry platform that allows him to invest more time in mentoring and apprenticing, consulting and writing, and speaking and teaching (http://taylorglobalconsult.org). Based in Austin, Texas, the Taylors worship at Christ Church-Anglican.

# PREFACES

## From Ajith Fernando

The globalization of mission is one of the most exciting developments in the contemporary church. However, to our people in the Majority World, globalization often means the imposing of a Western agenda upon nations with less resources. We must ensure that the church does not fall into that trap. Each segment of the globe should be contributing to the life of the body of Christ. As I think of the contribution from the Majority World, where the church is growing, the first thing that comes to mind is a theology of suffering, because growth is taking place in the midst of suffering.

Suffering, of course, is presented in the Bible as an essential element of the Christian life, especially of Christian ministry. All of us will face some sort of suffering if we are faithful to Christ. I want to focus on the stresses and strains of ministry that come from being committed to people, and then explore how accepting this is very difficult in our cultural milieu. Paul has a lot to say about this from his own life.

- Though outwardly we are wasting away, yet inwardly we are being renewed day by day (2 Cor 4:16).
- So death is at work in us, but life in you (2 Cor 4:12).
- As servants of God we commend ourselves in every way: in great endurance; in troubles, hardships and distresses;…hard work, sleepless nights and hunger (2 Cor 6:4–5).
- Besides everything else, I face daily the pressure of my concern for all the churches. Who is weak, and I do not feel weak? Who is led into sin, and I do not inwardly burn? (2 Cor 11:28–29).

We may look at these verses with academic interest as good descriptions of Paul's suffering, but there seems to be a cultural block today to accepting these as having much relevance to us. One reason for this is that contemporary middle-class and affluent society in both East and West have in the past been enslaved by a commitment to productivity and profit. People who speak like Paul did in those verses from 2 Corinthians are regarded as driven people who live unhealthy lives and whose families and colleagues suffer because of their insensitivity to their needs; people who are sure candidates for burnout.

Sadly, we have seen this kind of tragedy work itself out all too often in the lives of driven people. Biblical Christians are also driven, but their drivenness is fuelled by the love of God in them (2 Cor 5:14), which is renewed by lingering daily in the presence of God. That prevents the emptiness that causes burnout. This biblical drivenness works with the glory of God as its ambition. It is a "holistic" drivenness. To glorify God we must obey all of God's commands. So a person driven by the glory of God would strive to be a good parent, a loving spouse, an encourager to colleagues, and a visionary mover for the Kingdom. When you try to do all of those things you end up with the physical and emotional stresses and strains which Paul talked about. But if it is done holistically you do not end up burnt out, and your family members and colleagues don't end up mad at you for neglecting them.

I think, or perhaps I should say, I hope, poorer Majority World cultures are more able to embrace a holistic vision than more affluent cultures. Having not had the history of a scientific revolution which produced a culture that valued single-minded productivity, our people are more adept at being committed to a lot of things at the same time. For example, they may find it easier to combine contemplation with activism. So a holistic life, which includes not only suffering and strain but also joy in the midst of suffering, could be our contribution to world theology. Certainly this was the lifestyle Jesus recommended. Just before his death he said, "I have told you this so that my joy may be in you and that your joy may be complete" (John 15:11). Immediately after that he challenged his disciples to love each other so much that they would die for each other as Christ died for them (15:12–13). Dying for others and joy can coexist in the same person at the same time! Such a person would likely not suffer from burnout.

However we have a problem! Most of the training material read by people in the Majority World comes from the affluent West, and a lot of that training would look at the behavior I am recommending here as unhealthy drivenness. Those who commit themselves at cost to their call would be told that they are disobeying God and be challenged to change their lifestyle. Somehow there seems to be this idea that if you are suffering you are doing something wrong.

The problem is compounded by the mobility of affluent people today. As people keep changing from job to job, from neighborhood to neighborhood, and from church to church, long-term commitments are becoming a culturally rare phenomenon. It is when you stick to your call, however hard it is, that you encounter the type of suffering that contributes to great mission. However, people are used to moving from place to place based on convenience, on the opportunity to be more productive, and on escaping from suffering and unpleasant relationships. So they may move when they are confronted by suffering. Persevering through inconvenience, struggling to be productive against so many odds, taking on suffering, sticking to unpleasant relationships are what combine to produce great mission.

So we need to be careful that globalization of mission does not blunt the rich contribution that the Majority World can make to the world church. Let's teach people to embrace suffering because of their commitments. Books like the one you have in your hand can be used by God to help reverse the trends I've warned against.

*Ajith Fernando*
*Teaching Director, Youth for Christ, Sri Lanka*

## *From Christopher J. H. Wright*

My mother was not very pleased at the idea, though she could hardly contradict it. I was in my early teens and the renowned Romanian pastor who had experienced years of solitary confinement and torture under Communism, Richard Wurmbrand, was staying briefly in our Belfast home during a visit to Northern Ireland. Pastor Wurmbrand was urging me to go and serve God in the dangerous places of the world where I might have to give my life for Christ. "After all," he said, "you have martyr's blood in your family."

He was referring to my late Uncle Fred who as a young man in 1935 had followed his older brother (my father, Joe Wright) to Brazil to reach Amazonian Indian tribes with the gospel. On his first expedition up the River Xingu with two other missionaries (Fred Roberts and Fred Dawson—hence their nickname, "The Three Freds"), they were all clubbed to death by Cayapo tribesmen at the foot of Smoke Falls. It would be hard to claim that they were killed because of their Christian faith, since they did not apparently have any chance to share it. They were white men, and the only white men those tribesmen had encountered were violent rubber tappers who tended to shoot Indians on sight. Their reaction to this group of three pioneers was not beyond understanding. But they did die for the sake of their desire to share the gospel with those who had never heard it. By God's grace, later efforts to reach the Cayapo were blessed with success, and my father and mother met believers among that tribe during a visit in 1965, when my father preached from Uncle Fred's Bible.

So I suppose I have had a lifelong awareness that suffering and martyrdom is part of the story of God's people from Bible times to today, and I have had enough encounters with missionary stories not far distant from Uncle Fred's to feel some personal closeness to those who have gone through it. Our home also hosted some who had been through the horrors of the Simba rebellion in the Congo in the 1960s. Our family marvelled at the simple, unadorned testimonies from ordinary families and frail single women who had witnessed butchery beyond our imaginings, yet who spoke of the unfathomable resources of grace, peace, and strength that had sustained them in the midst of it.

But beyond that, I have to say that I often feel a fraud and a coward when it comes to the issues addressed in this book. I know virtually nothing of suffering for my faith in my own life (I did not follow Wurmbrand's urging), so who am I to talk about it? All I can do is to keep informed, aware, and prayerful for the increasing number of sisters and brothers in Christ all over the world for whom suffering in one way or another is simply the normal and expected Christian life, and others for whom extreme suffering and degrading death is the gateway to a martyr's crown. And if I feel tears in my heart for the Lord's people in such circumstances, what tears must there be in heaven and in the heart of God? May this remarkable encyclopedic book stimulate tears and prayers in due measure, and where appropriate, matching action.

*Christopher J. H. Wright*
*International Director, Langham Partnership International*

# PART ONE

---

# BUILDING THE FOUNDATION

## DISCERNING THE TIMES

This section of our book lays out the broadest overall scope: the global survey leads to personal reflections; a study of the different responses to violence, persecution, and possible martyrdom leads to two views on defining and counting martyrs; a clarification of persecution concludes with a personal story and a strong question—does persecution cause a church to flourish or to die? With these chapters we begin laying our foundation.

For many years, Christ's intriguing words in Matthew 11:1–19 have captured my attention, particularly the ambiguity of verse 12. From the passage's context we note that Jesus has finished a training component in the shaping of the twelve disciples and that he now starts his more public teaching and preaching ministry. As the crowds gather, a remnant of John the Baptist's disciples travel north from his prison to pose the hard question to Jesus: (in my words) "Well, are you or are you not the Messiah? And if you are, why are you not doing what we expected Messiah to do? Did John and those of us who followed him so totally misunderstand the prophets that we bet our lives on the wrong messianic aspirant?" The response of Jesus is remarkable in verses 4–6: "Go and tell John what you hear and see: the blind receive their sight and the lame walk, lepers are cleansed and the deaf hear, and the dead are raised up, and the poor have good news preached to them." He concludes with coded words for John: "And blessed is the one who is not offended by me."

John's few disciples begin the trek south; after they have left, Jesus offers his highest accolade for John. I am disturbed that neither John nor his disciples heard what Jesus truly thought of him. Why not encourage that woeful remnant band? I do not know.

Then comes the passage, both clear and enigmatic: "From the days of John the Baptist until now the Kingdom of heaven has suffered violence, and the violent take it by force" (v. 12). However, this reading from the ESV eliminates a crucial textual ambiguity.

Jesus then publicly comments on John's unique ministry. From Matthew 3:1–16 we hear of John, who has shaken the foundations and captured the limelight through his person and ministry. But it's all preparatory for Jesus. By 4:23–15, John is offstage and in prison, and Jesus has moved to center stage. The transition has taken place. The Kingdom of heaven has been forcefully advancing by both John and Jesus—through their persons, their preaching, their teaching, and the miracles of Jesus where he trumped the powers of illness, nature, and evil supernaturalism. The enemy was being assaulted forcefully.

But the second part of Matthew 11:12 is the puzzler, and different translators obviously have made different calls. Note how different they are from one another.

- ASV: "And from the days of John the Baptist until now the kingdom of heaven suffereth violence, and men of violence take it by force."
- 1984 NIV: "From the days of John the Baptist until now, the kingdom of heaven has been forcefully advancing, and forceful men lay hold if it."
- But the New NIV is very different: "From the days of John the Baptist until now, the kingdom of heaven has been subjected to violence, and violent people have been raiding it."
- The Message: "For a long time now people have tried to force themselves into God's kingdom."
- Phillips: "The kingdom of heaven has been taken by storm and eager men are forcing their way into it."

A careful study of the Greek seems to reveal a designed ambiguity by Jesus, and the older NIV allows for this nuance. The parallel passage in Luke 16:16 (ESV) gives additional insight, "The Law and the Prophets were until John; since then the good news of the Kingdom of God is preached, and everyone forces his way into it."

Three final thoughts. First, in the days of John and Jesus the Kingdom of heaven was advancing forcefully. The assault was on. The lines were cast. The price would be high.

Second, the response to this forceful even violent advance would be double. On the one hand, individuals and evil forces empowered by the demonic would attack it. But at the same time, bold, audacious believers could become players of this forceful, radical advance of the Kingdom of heaven, willing to pay the price.

Finally, this pregnant passage takes us to our present day when again we witness this complex combination of attack and bold action. We are living in the days of the greatest growth of the church, when multitudes are coming into the Kingdom of Christ. At the same time, these are days of some of the greatest persecution of Christians in all of human history. A supernatural paradox.

Welcome to the first section of our book. —*William D. Taylor*

# A CRUCIAL INTRODUCTION AND OVERVIEW

*William D. Taylor, Antonia van der Meer, and Reg Reimer*

Today, googling "persecution of Christians" revealed 8,570,000 hits in .24 seconds (October 25, 2011). What can we do with that kind of information overload?

We mention but some key sources that have informed us from different perspectives. The first comes from the recently released international report by The Pew Forum on Religion and Public Life, "Rising Restrictions on Religion."[1] This report states that one-third of the world's population is facing increased religious restriction, but the stark reality is that 75 percent of religious persecution is against Christians.

A second key source comes from the International Institute for Religious Freedom (IIRF). We point you to the summary statement, the Bad Urach Call.[2] The extensive Bad Urach Statement has a highly developed theological evaluation of our themes.

A third source is Open Doors USA.[3] A report here introduces their World Watch List—where persecuted countries are ranked according to their level of oppression. Of the top fifty nations with significant persecution, oppression, severe limitations, or some problems, thirty-eight are Islamic, eight are secular or Marxist, one Hindu (India), and one Buddhist (Sri Lanka).

The World Watch List is compiled from a specially designed questionnaire of fifty questions covering various aspects of religious freedom. A point value is assigned for how each question is answered. The total number of points per country determines its position on the World Watch List of countries that are the worst persecutors of Christians. Our mission is to use this extensive resource to spread awareness of the degree and severity of persecution around the world.

Yet another source comes from the Religious Liberty Partnership, a remarkable collaborative network of some of the most important Christian organizations serving in this field.[4]

---

1        http://pewforum.org/government/rising-restrictions-on-religion(2).aspx.
2        http://www.iirf.eu/fileadmin/user_upload/pdfs/the_bad_urach_call.pdf, appendix A.
3        http://www.opendoorsusa.org/persecution/world-watch-list.
4        http://www.rlpartnership.org.

The research and analysis team of WEA's Religious Liberty Commission is a member of the RLP and they periodically send out thoughtful news reports that call for understanding, prayer, and action. For more information, seek out owner-wea-religiousliberty@hub.xc.org. A daily prayer request resource is the iPhone "app" from Voice of the Martyrs, which can be downloaded for free.

One excellent publication that arrived late in our editorial process is Patrick Johnstone's *The Future of the Global Church: History, Trends and Possibilities* (Biblica/InterVarsity Press, 2011). No other book gives a more excellent "flow of persecution" through church history, though we have little statistical certitude until more modern times. Patrick's charts, diagrams, and narrative are well worth the book; his prophetic words and prognostications will sober all Christians in all nations.

At the end of this book you will find two more comprehensive resources for further study: the Select Annotated Bibliography (appendix B) and Persecution Information on the Web (appendix C). Together they will accompany you on your journey of information, intercession, identification, and action.

## HIGH RISK AND REREADING SCRIPTURE

Without a doubt, being a Christian today in many parts of the world is a high-risk commitment. But then, what's new? The historical norm is that it has always been this way. Few times in history have Christians lived in extended contexts of peace, prosperity, influence, and freedom to practice their faith to its fullest expression. This kind of freedom is an exception in Christian history. Today it is estimated that some 200 million followers of Jesus live in contexts where they face the spectrum of harassment, some facets of persecution, and/or the possibility of martyrdom.

Think of the Bible itself! Indeed, we challenge our readers to identify which books in the Bible were not written from realities of uncertainty, violence, exile, oppression, famine, and displacement. The fact is that sixty-five books of our canon have either been written from or to these contexts. The possible exception would be the Song of Solomon.

Take the first books of both the Old and the New Testaments. The Pentateuch was narrated, crafted, and then written for a people who had just ended four hundred years of slavery. They were an emerging nation on the move through the desert, where the Lord God was teaching them the true cosmology, life values, civil code, self-identity, and worship. The Gospels were penned during the first century of the Christian Era in the brutal context of military dictatorship, an emperor cult, powerlessness, exile, refugee flight, waves of persecution, and a Pax Romana. The Acts of the Apostles starts in Jerusalem and ends in Rome—from a rebellious province to the heart of the imperial power of its day.

So then, take the entire canon and capture its context and realities. Would it not behoove us today to consider Scripture in those original contexts, and then apply them to our times? What's more, who can teach us today how to live lives of transformational discipleship if not those who have lived, or who live today, in situations of unrest, harassment, and persecution? Both Global South and North have much to learn from God, his Word, and his people.

## PERSONAL THOUGHTS FROM THE EDITORIAL TEAM

I, Antonia (Tonica), have felt a special burden for the subject of suffering and persecution since my ten years spent serving in Angola, in a time of war with a Marxist government. I saw suffering and persecution. This led me to serve with great care, love, and wisdom in order not to cause more suffering to my Angolan brothers and sisters by unwise behavior. As I was committed to develop a student ministry, this was something especially difficult; my students faced strong opposition because of their faith. I was also concerned about other missionaries and their suffering because of the context in which they served and because of a lack of appropriate preparation and pastoral care. This led me to do my doctoral research on the theme of "Active Care for Missionaries Serving in Contexts of Suffering." My personal experience made me more sensitive to the suffering of others and I thank God for the privilege of being part of the production of this very important book. I trust that God will help his church to respond in grace and wisdom to the needs revealed in this book.

I, Reg, consider it a high privilege to contribute to this conversation. It is perhaps not accidental. I am the son of parents who were forced to flee the first Communist revolution in Russia. I was called to serve as a missionary in Vietnam, where I buried colleagues who had been martyred. After Vietnam fell to Communism, I was called by church leaders there to advocate for persecuted Christians, even as I ministered to the many refugees who fled abroad. My advocacy journey led me into a deep study of the phenomenon of Christian persecution, especially by Communism. This led to further biblical and historical studies of the long and widespread suffering and persecution of Christians. I trust and believe that our wide polling of the global church and my own small contributions to this book will be a timely tool for those called to pursue Christian world mission in an increasingly dangerous world.

It was just three years ago that I, Bill, discovered a very significant ancestor in my family lineage. I am a direct descendent of Reverend Dr. Rowland Taylor, Anglican rector of a country church, born in 1510 and died in 1555. A graduate of Cambridge University, he had served as chaplain to Thomas Cranmer. He was married to Margaret, William Tyndale's niece (yes, the Bible translator). Imprisoned several times for his Reformed faith, he was burned at the stake in Hadleigh, Suffolk, England, thanks to Queen Mary, who had much innocent blood on her hands. John Foxe wrote, "He found the prisons to be quite a fruitful ground for the gospel. Queen Mary put so many believers in Christ in prison that 'almost all the prisons in England were become the right Christian Schools and churches, prisons turned into churches and churches into dens of thieves.'"[5]

## THE OTHER WRITERS OF THIS BOOK

Together we write as confessing evangelicals, committed to the Scriptures and the gospel, to mission and justice, to proclamation and reconciliation, to creation and new creation. We are women and men who come from a rich diversity of backgrounds, cultures, nationalities, ethnicities, ministries, ages, and leadership roles. We write with passion to tell truthful

---

[5]      Read about Rowland Taylor's experiences in prison in Suffolk, England at http://rowlandtaylor.wordpress.com/2006/11/19/the-legacy-of-rowland-taylor.

stories. Some of the chapters are personal narratives; others are case studies rooted in life realities; others are more exegetical or historical in orientation; some are more scholarly and heavily documented. But they all resonate with authenticity.

We have attempted to provide a realistic balance of writers from the Global South and the Global North. This is not always easy, as many times in the maelstrom of violence and suffering there is little time to step back, reflect, and write. Those who have done so have written at great personal cost, and we are honored to hear their voices. It is wise to remember that many of our writers penned their words in their mother tongue, and these were translated into English. Scripture passages may sound different because many of our writers originally worked in another language. Though we provided documentation guidelines, the results may seem uneven. They don't always fit Western academic canons. We don't apologize for this. Let the authenticity rather than the form convince you.

## SIDEBARS, STORIES, AND ART

All the chapters include thoughtful questions for either individuals or small groups to respond to. You will discover a variety of additional features, each to enrich and further stimulate you. They act like a kind of "selah" of the Psalms. You will listen to a selection of the many biblical passages that deal with our themes. You will engage with the short scriptural reflections by six of Tonica's Brazilian students. Miriam Adeney has contributed a series of thirteen stories from her excellent book, *Kingdom without Borders: The Untold Story of Global Christianity* (2009), which we have interwoven into the book. We share key quotes from Dietrich Bonhoeffer, who at age thirty-nine was executed by Hitler. We insert relevant statements out of the Cape Town Commitment, a product of the 2010 South Africa Lausanne Congress. We have additionally attempted to illuminate the book with diverse art forms that creatively address our core topics.

## THE TITLE OF THIS BOOK

Our title, "Sorrow and Blood," speaks of the grief that suffering produces and the blood of the martyrs that has seeded the church throughout two millennia. It speaks of our Lord's own blood as found in Revelation 7:9–17. And it comes out of the cry of the martyrs in Revelation 6:10, "O sovereign Lord, holy and true, how long before you will judge and avenge our blood on those who dwell on the earth?" (ESV)

The subtitle places our discussion within the parameters of Christian mission in the specific contexts of suffering, persecution, and martyrdom. These three terms—suffering, persecution, and martyrdom—are interwoven throughout the entire book. Thus *Sorrow and Blood: Christian Mission in Contexts of Suffering, Persecution, and Martyrdom*. The title and the contents are heavy, dense, serious, true, biblical, historical, and very present with us today.

## A CHARGE TO OUR READERS

Thoughtful reader, prepare to be stretched and to weep. Grow your world and prepare yourself, your family, and your ministry for the future we will engage, a future whose only certainty is that God is and that he walks with us.

—*William D. Taylor, Antonia van der Meer, and Reg Reimer*

## SIDEBAR AND STORY REFERENCES[6]

Adeney, Miriam. 2009. *Kingdom without borders: The untold story of global Christianity.* Downers Grove, IL: InterVarsity Press.

Bonhoeffer, Dietrich. 1976. *The cost of discipleship,* rev. ed. New York: Macmillan.

———. 1986. Jugend und studium 1918–1927. In *Dietrich Bonhoeffer werke,* vol. 9, eds., Hans Pfeifer with Clifford Green and Carl-Jürgen Kaltenborn. Munich: Chr. Kaiser.

———. 1992. Barcelona, Berlin, Amerika 1928–1931. In *Dietrich Bonhoeffer werke,* vol. 10. eds., Reinhard Staats and Hans Christoph von Hase with Holger Roggelin and Matthias Wünsche. Munich: Chr. Kaiser Verlag.

———. 1996a. Illegale Theologenausbildung: Finkenwalde 1935–1937. In *Dietrich Bonhoeffer werke,* vol. 14, eds., Otto Dudzus und Jürgen Henkys with Sabine Bobert-Stützel, Dirk Schulz, and Ilse Tödt. Gütersloh: Chr. Kaiser / Gütersloher Verlagshaus.

———. 1996b. Konspiration und haft 1940–1945. In *Dietrich Bonhoeffer werke,* vol. 16, eds., Jørgen Glenthøj, Ulrich Kabitz, and Wolf Krötke. Gütersloh: Chr. Kaiser / Gütersloher Verlagshaus.

———. 1998. Illegale theologenausbildung: Sammelvikariate 1937–1940. In *Dietrich Bonhoeffer werke,* vol. 15, ed., Dirk Schulz. Gütersloh: Chr. Kaiser / Gütersloher Verlagshaus.

Reflections by students of Antonia van der Meer at the Center for Evangelical Missions, Brazil.

---

6    All quotes of Bonhoeffer from works referred to in German above have been selected and translated into English by Douglas Bax.

## "WHO WORSHIP AS THEY SUFFER"—SONGS CONTEMPLATING SUFFERING AND PERSECUTION

In nations where suffering and persecution are common, their songwriters often speak of it through songs of faith [three songs from three different countries can be found throughout this volume—from Soviet Russia, "I Will Follow after Christ"; from China, Xiao Min's "In the Midst of Severe Times"; and from Ethiopia, Tesfaye Gabbiso's "I Refuse, I Refrain"]. By comparison, the topics of suffering, persecution, and martyrdom have not received as much attention from songwriters from the United States and the United Kingdom. All the same, there are many moving examples of songs from these countries which have pondered the faith of martyrs and challenged the church to contemplate their example.

The English language has a number of older hymns that deal with these themes. In 1827, Reginald Heber wrote the poem that eventually became known as the hymn "The Son of God Goes Forth to War," which lays out the challenge to forgive persecutors: "The martyr first whose eagle eye / Could pierce beyond the grave, / Who saw His Master in the sky / And called on Him to save. / Like Him, with pardon on His tongue, / In midst of mortal pain, / He prayed for them that did the wrong / Who follows in his train?"

We rapidly move 176 years into the future, our world today.  On February 28, 2003, Graham Kendrick sang "How Long" outside the Chinese Embassy in London in association with Release International and Christian Solidarity Worldwide.[1]  The footage of that event[2] is particularly moving because of the context in which it was filmed. The first part of the song talks about how our lives are impacted by the example of those who suffer for their faith, those whose pain is an offering of worship to the One they love: "Lord, help us to live worthy of / Our sisters and our brothers / Who love you more than their own lives / Who worship as they suffer / To embrace the scandal of the cross / Not ashamed to tell your story / To count all earthly gain as loss / To know you and your glory."[3]

In 2005, Keith and Kristyn Getty wrote a modern hymn "When Trials Come,"[4] reminding us how suffering is a fire which refines our faith and reveals a story of God's faithfulness to a watching world: "When trials come no longer fear / For in the pain our God draws near / To fire a faith worth more than gold / And there His faithfulness is told"[5]

A very recent music video combines footage of persecution with the work of a collaboration of rappers from the UK[6] as they sing a tribute to the sufferings of the persecuted church around the world.  George Luke[7] writes, "'Coming for Me' is powerful and very compelling; it's a great example of rap music being used to raise awareness of a very serious issue."

These are just a few examples of English-language songs which help us to view our own sufferings with the eyes of faith and challenge us in moving ways to stand in solidarity with the persecuted church around the world. I hope that in years to come, even in response to this book, there will be more engagement with the persecuted church through these kinds of artistic expression.

Robin P. Harris

1    For a full set of lyrics, see http://www.grahamkendrick.co.uk/songs/lyrics/how_long.php.
2    See http://www.youtube.com/user/presscreative#p/u/21/zMGIwAgvySc.
3    Graham Kendrick, ©2002 Make Way Music, www.grahamkendrick.co.uk.
4    Keith and Kristyn Getty, ©2005 Thankyou Music.
5    See www.gettymusic.com/hymns.aspx?id=93 for the full lyrics and an audio sample.
6    Music Video by The Frontline (see http://tinyurl.com/OpenDoors-Coming-For-Me). Produced by Steven "G.P."Abramsamadu, ©2010 Preacher Boy Music / Open Doors Youth, featuring Armor, Guvna B, E Tizz, New Direction Crew, McGladius, Jahaziel, and S.O. The single is available from iTunes (http://tiny.cc/c45sp).
7    From personal correspondence, October 23, 2011. George Luke is a writer, music journalist, and radio producer in the UK. He blogs at http://georgeluke.wordpress.com/.

# CHAPTER 1

# A GLOBAL SURVEY

## Religious Freedom and the Persecution of Christians
*Christof Sauer and Thomas Schirrmacher*

## THE SITUATION OF RELIGIOUS FREEDOM

The Washington DC–based Pew Research Center, in a late 2009 study, has consolidated all available global surveys on religious freedom. Strikingly, their data and conclusions are very similar to those reported by the Center for Religious Freedom of Hudson Institute (Washington, DC) and the International Institute for Religious Freedom. In sixty-four countries around the globe—a third of all countries—there is either no religious freedom or it is very restricted. Unfortunately these sixty-four countries host two-thirds, or more precisely 70 percent, of the world population. Armed conflicts, where religion was a central factor and where there are more than one thousand dead, were found in twenty-four countries from which 18 million of the world's refugees have emerged (Pew 2009).[1]

Let us examine these sixty-four countries more closely in view of the two largest religions in the world: Christianity and Islam. The only large group of Muslims living in a non-Muslim country with restricted religious freedom is found in India. Likewise, Russia is the only country with restricted religious freedom that has a Christian majority population. Leaving these two countries out of the equation for the time being, the difference between the situation of Christians and Muslims is quickly becoming obvious: the remaining 700 million Muslims who are living in countries with restricted or no religious freedom live in Muslim-majority countries. In contrast, the remaining 200 million Christians who live in countries with restricted or no religious freedom are living in "non-Christian countries" (countries where Christians are a minority). They are mainly spread over predominantly Communist and Islamic countries (and India).

This means that Muslims overall are enjoying much less religious freedom than Christians. However, as they are living in countries where Islam reigns, they only realize this lack of religious freedom if they want to renounce Islam or if they belong to a tradition or sect of Islam not tolerated by their respective state.

---

[1]    Some aspects of this essay are discussed in more detail in Schirrmacher 2008.

## THE COMPLEXITY OF RELIGIOUS PERSECUTION

Obviously there are vastly differing situations of religious persecution. So how do you define real persecution or discrimination? When is there cause for concern? When the church where you worship might be torched during the service, or only when it is in fact burning? Should hostilities only be called "persecution" when religion is the only factor, or also when religion is only one factor among others?

Violence against Christians ranges from the murder of nuns in India to the torching of churches in Indonesia, from the thrashing of priests in Egypt or the torture of a resistant pastor in Vietnam, to the rejection of children by their own families in Turkey or Sri Lanka if they attend Christian church services.

Or take a country like India as an example: Should one say that all Christians are affected when individual churches are continually burned—as naturally everybody worries who attends church? Or should one say only those living in provinces like Orissa or Karnataka are affected, as they live in the closest vicinity to such terrible events?

Take China as another example. On the one hand, all Christians are affected by persecutions in some way or another. On the other hand, hundreds of thousands of church services are taking place in China every Sunday, and only a few dozen pastors are imprisoned.

## PERSECUTION OF CHRISTIANS WITHOUT PARALLEL

The question arises whether the frequency and the scale of global persecution of Christians justifies us to focus our attention on them. Is it correct that persecution of Christian minorities has globally reached such proportions that this issue is forced to the foreground by its numerical weight when religious freedom is considered?

Hindu fundamentalism indeed also turns against Muslims. But even on a global scale there is hardly a parallel to the fifty thousand Christians in the Indian state of Orissa driven from their homes between 2008 and 2009 and the five hundred people killed in these events.

Brother will deliver brother to death, and the father his child, and children will rise against parents and have them put to death, and you will be hated by all for my name's sake. But the one who endures to the end will be saved.
*Matthew 10:21–22*

There is equally no parallel to the 100,000 Christians driven away by force of arms on the Maluku Islands of Indonesia during 2000–2001, where several thousands died. In Sudan and Nigeria, very large numbers of Christians died—huge in scale, however complicated the situation may be in these countries which are divided between Islam and Christianity. The enforced removal of hundreds of thousands of Christians out of Iraq during 2007–2011 is currently without parallel in the world of religions.

In order to find something more dramatic than these twenty-first-century events, one has to return to the persecution of the Jews during the Third Reich or the bloody unrest between Hindus and Muslims during the founding of India and Pakistan. Within the framework of persecution of Christians, one would have to return to the mass murders by Stalin and Mao.

A further example of Christians being greatly affected by persecution has to do with people renouncing Islam. In many countries it is dangerous for Muslims to renounce Islam, no matter whether they become atheists, Baha'i, or whether they join a branch of Islam that is considered a sect by others. It just so happens that most often they become Christians.

## WORSENING TRENDS

There are currently three reasons behind the worsening global religious freedom scenario.

First, in the successor states of the Soviet Union, particularly in the Islamic states but also in some of the Orthodox states, initial enthusiasm about democracy, freedom, and religious freedom has given way to increasingly restrictive religious laws. After several years of freedom, the religious persecution and/or persecution of Christians once practiced by Communists in these former states of the USSR has returned; Christians are being oppressed by the respective majority religion or by the control of religion by the government.

Second, two very populous nations which have experienced comparative calm over several decades, India and Indonesia, are returning to oppression. While there was never comprehensive religious freedom in either nation, the adherents of various religions lived together relatively peacefully. In both countries the situation dramatically worsened during the first decade of the twenty-first century. Due to the large size of their populations (India has more than 1.1 billion inhabitants and Indonesia around 230 million), any worsening of the situation in these two nations statistically worsens the global religious freedom score.

Third, religious freedom developments in the Muslim world have not been for the better. The expulsion and emigration of non-Muslim minorities, among them ancient churches which existed there for 1,500 years, have increased. In addition, the Organization of the Islamic Conference is attempting to remove the right to change one's religion from the Universal Declaration of Human Rights. Pakistan and other countries have requested this change several times already. In recent years, the Human Rights Council of the United Nations has voted annually in favor of declaring defamation of religion an infringement upon human rights. However, Islam is the only religion explicitly mentioned in that text. Global pressure trying to forestall any criticism of Islam is effectively curbing religious freedom.

## TYPES AND STAGES OF PERSECUTION

The multitude of types of persecution and human rights violations know no bounds. The more "harmless" among them are common, including ridicule, marginalization, mobbing at work, and the vilification of Christians, their symbols, and their teachings by the media.

Paul Marshall described with insight the usual phases of religious persecution of Christians:[2]

## PHASES OF PERSECUTION

Phase 1: Disinformation
Phase 2: Discrimination
Phase 3: Violent Persecution

---

2      Also see the typology of disinformation, discrimination, and destruction from Godfrey Yogarajah (2008, 85–94).

Initially rumors and disinformation are propagated by the media, public opinion, or word of mouth, which turns public opinion against Christians. When Christians themselves do not have access to public and published opinion in order to rectify this, disinformation is slowly regarded as truth. One striking example is the conviction by the majority of Turks that Protestants in their country are working for the CIA and want to undermine Turkey.

After Phase 1 follows discrimination of Christians as second-class citizens, be it by the state, the bureaucracy, and/or through the community and neighborhood. For example, in China the education of the children of Christians might be obstructed. In Islamic countries the economic status of Christians is lowered, and in India social aid for the poorest Dalit is cancelled if and when they become Christians.

> The Government that denies protection to the Church in that way sets the Church all the more visibly in the protection of its Lord. The Government that abuses its Lord thereby witnesses all the more clearly to the power of this Lord who is praised in the martyrs of the Christian community.
>
> D. Bonhoeffer in "Theologisches Gutachten: Staat und Kirche" (1996b, 529)

From all of this emerges fully fledged persecution which uses various forms of violence, ranging from spontaneous attacks and arson to imprisonment, the death penalty, or murder.

## REASONS FOR PERSECUTION

What are the main reasons for the violent opposition Christianity is encountering in many countries? It might be problematic to try to reduce the actions and thinking of millions to a few principles. Nevertheless, we would like to set forth the following theses for discussion:

1. Christianity has by far the largest number of adherents. Therefore it is proportionally more often affected by human rights violations linked to religion.

2. The main growth of Christianity is currently happening in countries which do not respect human rights and particularly deny the right to religious freedom. The most striking example of this is the explosive growth of evangelical and Roman Catholic house churches in China.

3. The phenomenal global growth of Christianity (after all, Christianity by definition is a missionary religion), particularly in its evangelical and to a slightly lesser degree in its Catholic form, occurs in countries with non-Christian majorities. This reality is increasingly seen as a threat to the position of the majority religions and state ideologies.

A quick glance at the statistics reveals that a numerical growth rate larger than that of the population (>1.19 percent) is only found among the three major religions. Hinduism is growing at a rate of 1.33 percent, mainly due to a high birthrate; Islam is growing by 1.78 percent through a high birthrate, economic and political interventions, and in some cases by propagation.

Christianity as a whole is growing by 1.3 percent per year. Evangelical and charismatic Christianity, through its missionary activity, has an enormous growth of 2.9 percent, which counterbalances the reduction of Christianity in the Western world. Through a geographical perspective, it is to be noted that Christianity has doubled in Africa and Latin America since 1970 and tripled in Asia. In each of the "non-Christian" countries of China, India, and Indonesia, more people go to church on any given Sunday than in all of Western Europe taken together. This enormous growth of non-Western Christianity has led to tensions in these respective societies.

4.  Some countries which had been colonized in the past seek to strengthen their own identity through a revitalization or promotion of inherited religious traditions. They increasingly proceed legally and/or violently against religions considered as "foreign."

    For example, in India there is a renaissance of Hinduism rising against Islam, Christianity, and Hindu-Buddhism. In Sri Lanka and Nepal, Buddhism is invoked against Christianity and Islam.

5.  In many countries there is an increasing liaison between nationalism and religion, which leads to the oppression of undesired religions in the country.

    This is the case in India, Indonesia, Bangladesh, and Pakistan, which together make up one-third of the world's population. Christianity is seen as a block to nationalism in Turkey and elsewhere. This is an issue on which Islamists and proponents of secularism find a rare point of agreement. Because of such religious nationalism even in some Christian-majority nations, there is no full freedom and equality for all Christians.

6.  Christianity as a whole, and particular groups of its representatives, have become voices for human rights and democracy.

    Advocacy for the weak and for minorities is inherent to Christianity. While this has always and everywhere been very prominent, it has become a trademark of Christianity. In consequence, Christians have often become targets of opponents of human rights and of violent rulers. Classical examples are found in Latin America and in North Korea. In addition, Christians increasingly have global networks at their disposal, which can be mobilized against human rights violations and can trigger global press reactions.

7.  Christianity often jeopardizes established corrupt business interests and their religious toleration.

    Drug bosses in Latin America who commission the murder of Catholic priests or Baptist pastors certainly don't do this out of interest in the religion of their opponents. Rather, the reason is that these church leaders are often the only people standing up for the local farmers and indigenous people, thus getting in the way of mafia bosses.

8.  Christianity has experienced a significant transition towards the renunciation of violence and sociopolitical pressure towards content-related persuasion and peaceful mission.

    The peacefulness of Christian churches, often manifested as genuine pacifism, has the side effect of inviting violence, as no opposition needs to be feared.

    Muslims are globally afraid of US-American retaliation, but usually not at all of the reaction of local Christians. If the governments fail to protect Christians (who, based on their conviction of separation of church and state, have left the monopoly of power to the state), then believers become fair game. How should Christians in Indonesia protect their houses and families against heavily armed gangs of Islamic Jihadists? Individual Christians have indeed made use of force to protect their families. Which of us who lives in a safe environment would want to criticize them? The Christian churches in Indonesia have finally agreed on nonviolence, sometimes paying a high price for it.

9.   The West is hated by the rest, and Christians are often equated with the West.

The reality today is that the West is no longer overwhelmingly Christian, that "Mc-World" and pornography really have nothing to do with Christianity, and that churches in the Third World are almost without exception under local leadership. But prejudice and suspicion in these matters seem to have a stronger influence on public opinion than facts. Christians in China are regarded as agents of the USA or the Pope (as a representative of the West), and "Christians" in Palestine are taken as agents of Zionism, despite financial support for Palestine from the West.

10.   The international character of Christianity and the international relations of Christians are regarded as a threat.

Now who is there to harm you if you are zealous for what is good? But even if you should suffer for righteousness' sake, you will be blessed. Have no fear of them, nor be troubled, but in your hearts honor Christ the Lord as holy, always being prepared to make a defense to anyone who asks you for a reason for the hope that is in you; yet do it with gentleness and respect, having a good conscience, so that, when you are slandered, those who revile your good behavior in Christ may be put to shame. For it is better to suffer for doing good, if that should be God's will, than for doing evil. *1 Peter 3:13–17*

Christians, beyond the citizenship of their country, ultimately feel connected with all "citizens of heaven" as Paul calls them (Phil 3:20). The church in the footsteps of Jesus perceives itself as multicultural and transnational (Matt 28:18). This can be viewed as a threat, just as much as the enormous international linkages through personnel, ideas, and finances. Christians view it as an enrichment that theology has long been internationalized and Christian theologians are in discussion with their peers around the globe. Non-Christians might view the same as an incalculable risk and power factor.

## IN CONCLUSION

As this survey has shown, the lack of religious freedom and the prevalence of religious persecution are a widespread global phenomenon that seriously affect a large part of the world's population. Religious persecution is a quite complex and diverse phenomenon which demands a good understanding and careful use of language. The frequency and massiveness of persecution events against Christians nowadays goes way beyond what adherents of other religions suffer. One also has to revert to half a century ago to find events of the same magnitude. Overall, the global religious freedom scenario seems to be worsening. It is important to register and address disinformation and discrimination in their early stages before they lead to overt and violent persecution. Based on a good understanding of the variety of reasons for persecution, intelligent and decisive action by Christians is the call of the hour.

## QUESTIONS FOR REFLECTION
1. How would you define persecution and discrimination?
2. What is the trend in your context? Is religious freedom improving or decreasing?
3. Are you able to identify disinformation about Christians or discrimination in your context which have the potential to lead to violent persecution?
4. If there is persecution of Christians in your context, are you able to clearly identify the reasons for it?

## REFERENCES

Pew Research Center. 2009. *Global restrictions on religion.* Washington, D.C.: Pew Forum on Religion and Public Life. http://pewforum.org/docs/?DocID=491.

Schirrmacher, T. 2008. *Christenverfolgung: Die vergessenen märtyrer.* Holzgerlingen: Hänssler.

Yogarajah, G. 2008. Disinformation, discrimination, destruction and growth: A case study on persecution of Christians in Sri Lanka. *International Journal for Religious Freedom* 1:85–94.

**Christof Sauer,** German, is co-director of the International Institute for Religious Freedom (Bonn, Cape Town, Colombo) and an editor of the *International Journal for Religious Freedom.* From Cape Town, South Africa, he supervises doctoral students in missiology and religious freedom studies at the University of South Africa. He is an associate professor extraordinary of the department of Practical Theology and Missiology of the Theological Faculty at Stellenbosch University.

**Thomas Schirrmacher**, German, is director of the International Institute for Religious Freedom (Bonn, Cape Town, Colombo) and serves as chair of WEA's Theological Commission. Based in Germany, he holds extensive professorial and presidential roles across Europe as well as in Shillong, India, teaching sociology of religion, theology, global ethics, and international development.

## A WOMAN'S WORDS

"Take me with you."

Heads swiveled and eyebrows were raised. Faces scrunched up, perplexed. "Your husband was martyred in that Li village just a week ago," the group leader said kindly, "yet you want to join us on this very risky return trip?"

"Haven't I earned the right?"

The men looked at each other. First of all, Liang was a woman. Second, she was young. Third, she already had suffered severely with the loss of her husband. Fourth, she had no special Bible knowledge. Wouldn't she be an impediment rather than a help?

Still, when the team set out, Liang traveled with them.

Why had the tribesmen killed her husband? They associated Chinese missionaries with centuries of Chinese domination. When the missionaries had walked into their village, the tribesmen had rushed at them, brandishing hoes and rakes and other farm implements, and yelling, "The spirits of the mountains rule our land. You Chinese dogs have been here only five hundred years. You know nothing. You have stolen our land—and now you wish to steal our gods? You will pay!"

Liang's husband was beaten to death.

Now, several weeks later, the church was sending a second mission team. What would they encounter? Surly looks greeted them. But before anyone on either side could open their mouths, Liang took a few paces forward and said clearly, "I am the widow of the man you killed three weeks ago."

Shock appeared on the villagers' faces.

"My husband is not dead, however," she continued. "God has given him eternal life. Now he is living in paradise with God. When he came here to your village, he wanted to tell you how you could have that life too. If he were here now, he would forgive you for what you did. In his place I forgive you. I can do this because God has forgiven me. If you want to hear more about God, meet us under the big tree outside of town this evening."

People listened quietly. Nobody raised a hand against the missionaries.

The team members put their heads together. It was clear that God had given Liang an opening. Maybe she should continue to be the spokesperson.

"What do I know? I am not a teacher. I simply gave a witness," she exclaimed.

"We'll teach you," her father-in-law counseled. "Every day we'll prepare you for what to say."

So when villagers gathered under the tree at the end of the day, Liang passed on what she had been taught that afternoon. After a week and a half, many tribal people had believed. When the mission team departed, her father-in-law stayed to instruct the Christians and baptize them.

Two months later he showed up at the home church with three men from the new Li church. During the service, these young believers gave greetings.

"I am the man who murdered Wang," one began.

There was a hiss of indrawn breath, but the congregation listened as the Li man told how God had forgiven him. He asked forgiveness from God's people, expressed an eternal debt of gratitude, and brought a money gift from the new church to show thanks to the church that had sent them the good news.

Miriam Adeney, *Kingdom without Borders: The Untold Story of Global Christianity* (2009, 41–43)

# CHAPTER 2

# REFLECTIONS ON MISSION IN THE CONTEXT OF SUFFERING

*Beram Kumar*

We read in 1 Peter 4:12–14 (Amp):

> Beloved, do not be amazed and bewildered at the fiery ordeal which is taking place to test your quality, as though something strange (unusual and alien to you and your position) were befalling you. But insofar as you are sharing Christ's sufferings, rejoice, so that when his glory [full of radiance and splendor] is revealed, you may also rejoice with triumph [exultantly]. If you are censured and suffer abuse [because you bear] the name of Christ, blessed [are you—happy, fortunate, to be envied, with life-joy, and satisfaction in God's favor and salvation, regardless of your outward condition], because the Spirit of glory, the Spirit of God, is resting upon you. On their part he is blasphemed, but on your part he is glorified. (See also Phil 1:29 and 2 Tim 3:12.)

In a society dominated by consumerism, the church has also been infiltrated by a theology of "it's all about me," and "what do I get out of following Christ?"—robed in nice and warm Scriptures focused on "bless me." We have somewhat conditioned ourselves and members of our churches to measure God's goodness with how good things are for us. Just take a look at most of our Bibles. The Scriptures colored and underlined in our Bibles are often the ones dealing with his promises to us, relating to blessings.

With such a "me-centered" theology, is it really a surprise that the theology of suffering is now a *missing theology*? Today, the theology of suffering is often confined to our historical books—it couldn't happen to us! When we do read about suffering, or when it hits closer to home, we are often confused and bewildered in our responses. Why did that happen? Where is God? Why did God allow it to happen?

This me-centered theology impacts our missiology as well. Even our preaching in evangelism is often dominated by "what you will get." Rather than preach the gospel in its entirety, we hide suffering and bait nonbelievers with the blessings. Now there is nothing wrong with the blessings. God does desire to bless us and there are many promises of blessings that we can claim and share with nonbelievers. However, if we neglect to mention the other side of Hebrews 11—that while many performed great acts of faith, some lost their lives for the faith—we may very well end up drawing people to Christ with a gospel that, at best, is half true.

Theologically, we need to rediscover our heritage (1 Pet 4:14): "For to you it has been granted on behalf of Christ, not only to believe in him, but also to suffer for his sake" (Phil 1:29). If Jesus suffered, why do we treat suffering with such surprise and shock? Someone once aptly said, "We are the only army where the soldiers live like kings and the commander-in-chief says of himself, 'Foxes have holes and birds of the sky have nests, but the Son of Man has nowhere to lay his head' (Matt 8:20)."

On a practical level, we need to include in our theology and missiology instruction on what to do and how to respond when suffering comes knocking on our doors. I use the phrase "a stone-throwing church," which was used by a leader in Asia to describe the situation that he observed firsthand in his city. He used it to describe the lack of preparedness on the part of the church on how to respond *practically* when attacked. The stone-throwing church is a church that, unprepared for persecution, reacts and picks up the stones thrown into the church and throws them right back at the people instead of responding in a God glorifying manner. Thus, they perpetuate the violence. What started off as persecution spirals into an ethnic/religious conflict, where right and wrong is lost in the smog of fighting and the church loses its witness.

The media today has, by and large, failed to call attention to the persecution faced by Christians, instead often calling it "religious or racial conflict." I wonder if sometimes we are partly to blame for contributing to that misconception as well. When the church reacts in violence, what started as persecution may very well, to the eyes of the world, look like a conflict.

> Behold, I am sending you out as sheep in the midst of wolves, so be wise as serpents and innocent as doves. Beware of men, for they will deliver you over to courts and flog you in their synagogues." *Matthew 10:16–17*

What I am about to say here may be a bit unsettling and a little hard to swallow, but please consider it. I speak from the context of missions in South East Asia, of which I am familiar. Be guided by the Holy Spirit to determine whether or not it applies in your context.

Let me start by asking this question: Is all suffering necessary?

To answer this question, we need to ask ourselves more questions: Are our strategies (or lack of them) provoking suffering? Is our suffering self-inflicted? Let me elaborate with some examples.

**Child evangelism:** Is our evangelism of children provoking hostility against us? Have we ever stopped to ask how unbelieving parents would feel when their children are lured to Christianity with sweets and balloons and fun and games (especially if they themselves, due to poverty, are unable to provide these)? Is it really a surprise that they then turn against us? Our motives may be pure, but how would we feel if the situation were reversed? I am not suggesting we stop child evangelism, but I am saying that we need to critically evaluate our strategy—to ask whether our approach will provoke hostility and hatred towards Christ.

Would it not be better to love the children in a way that honors their parents (and the community)? Would that not be the better witness for Christ? And when we do share, to share with the family or the community instead of just the children. When we are perceived as taking advantage of defenseless children, would it not cause anger and maybe even persecution? Isn't such suffering self-inflicted?

**Cultural and social structure:** In most societies, whether visible or not, there is a social structure in place. This is not only true with respect to the position of parents, but also with respect to the role of village heads and community leaders. This is especially the case in South East Asia and much of the rest of Asia as well. Are we ignoring this structure when engaging a community for Christ? In the early 1990s I was involved in church-planting efforts in a country closed to Christianity that was just beginning to open up. Before beginning our work, we were required to meet with the mayor and the religious establishment of the town or village and introduce ourselves (and bring gifts!). In most societies, there are elders who we in mission are ignoring. Is this contributing to the increased hostility towards the church and our mission?

**Confrontational evangelism:** In most contexts, confrontational evangelism only breeds confrontation. A short-term mission team was holding a prayer drive in a closed country. We had warned them to just pray and not to engage in any evangelism or distribution of tracts (or worse, "tract-bombing"—the phrase itself scares me!). Against our advice and firm instruction, a member of the team threw tracts out of the open window of the van the team traveled in. She assumed that since it was dark, no one would know. Really? How difficult would it be for the authorities to follow the trail of tracts to the only foreigners in town? The team was promptly arrested and interrogated. They divulged the names of local church leaders, who were then confronted by the authorities. (The suffering faced by these leaders was for Christ, but they suffered because of the actions of the individual who threw out the tracts. Was this not self-inflicted?) As I pondered on why she threw the tracts, I wondered: was her action about a "need" to preach? Does our need push us to such foolishness?

> Self-denial is never just a series of isolated acts of mortification or asceticism. It is not suicide, for there is an element of self-will even in suicide. To deny oneself is to be aware only of Christ and no more of self, to see only him who goes before and no more the road which is too hard for us. Once more all that self-denial can say is: "He leads the way, keep close to him."
>
> D. Bonhoeffer in *The Cost of Discipleship* (1976, 97f)

**Contextualization ignored:** Are we unpacking (from our cultural bias) and repacking the message in a way that is culturally adapted to the listeners? I think the hostility towards the church is often not directed towards nor a rejection of the message, but the reaction to the provocation caused by the packaging! Let me share an experience: A few days after the 2004 tsunami I flew into a Muslim country that had just faced the brunt of it. Sitting at the airport I saw a group of Christians who were also on their way to serve. They were all wearing T-shirts with Bible verses. What troubled me most were the verses and pictures used on these T-shirts; they depicted spiritual warfare, with pictures of army boot-prints and bullet holes. Is this the kind of packaging we use for the gospel (to Muslims!)? At a time when hundreds of thousands of lives were lost and extremist Islamic groups were patrolling the streets of the town and the airport looking for Christians that may be trying to convert "the vulnerable," was this the way to share the love of Christ? I don't think so. It was neither the time, the place, nor the context for this.

**Creativity (or rather, the lack of it):** At a time when we can use a variety of approaches to make the case for Christ, are we stuck in an old paradigm, refusing to allow the Holy Spirit—who is creative—to give us creative presentation of the gospel and creative entries into closed-door communities; e.g., through sports, arts, economics, tentmaking, etc. I do believe that in our mission we need to look at a variety of ways in which we can preach Christ (in word and action). Is the lack of creativity and keeping to the approach of standing on a box in the street corner (with in-your-face preaching) causing the hostility towards Christianity?

When we do something wrong, we get what we deserve for breaking the law. For example, a famous church leader from a closed country was arrested and imprisoned because he was found to have multiple passports for his international travels to speak in churches and conferences around the world. Would this be considered suffering for Christ, or would it be self-inflicted? I found it hard to forward the e-mail on his "suffering" when I received it.

So, is all suffering … necessary?

These are just some examples. I do not mean to judge anyone. We have all been guilty of indiscretion in our mission at one time or another. The more important point I am trying to make is that we need to rethink, critically evaluate, and reflect on some of the ways we approach our mission efforts.

I am by no means reducing or excusing persecution and violence against Christians. Even foolishness on our part does not justify that. I am, however, saying that we do need to consider carefully whether or not we are provoking the suffering, unnecessarily, against which we cry foul! I am also not saying that we should always choose to walk the path of least resistance, looking to please man more than God. We will face persecution, we will suffer—just let us suffer for Christ's sake and not as a result of our own foolishness and indiscretion.

May the Lord give us wisdom and grace.[1]

## QUESTIONS FOR REFLECTION
1.  Can you think of examples where persecution and its resulting suffering were self-inflicted? What caused the suffering and could the issue have been handled differently?
2.  Call to mind cases in which local believers have suffered as a result of the lack of appropriate behavior from well-meaning foreigners. How can we prevent such unnecessary suffering?
3.  How can we prepare those who go for short- or long-term service to restricted-access countries to prevent unnecessary confrontation and suffering?

---

1      As presented by Beram Kumar at the plenary of the World Evangelical Alliance Mission Commission Conference (Pattaya 2008).

**Beram Kumar**, a Malaysian, is the founder-CEO of STAMP (Strategic Missions Partnerships—www.stamp-upg.org), a ministry focused on bringing God's love to the least evangelized people groups, primarily in South East Asia. He was one of the founding leaders of the South East Asia Unreached Peoples Network, called SEALINK, and serves as its co-facilitator. He is also a member of the board of Tentmakers International.

Glorious Church. Mannar. *Connections*, vol. 7, no. 1 and 2, 40 (July 2008).

(http://www.weaconnections.com/Back-issues/Missions-in-contexts-of-suffering,-violence,-perse.aspx)

## NO MORE THIRD CHEEK?

"No more third cheek! The time has come to retaliate. We were patient. We offered the second cheek, just as Jesus advised, and it has been slapped. Now it is time to fight back," Nahor's friends advised.

Nahor's church in Northern Nigeria had been burned down the second time. This time the senior pastor had been murdered.

But Nahor disagreed with his friends. "This cannot continue, cycle after cycle. Burning, killing, fleeing. What future is there in that? Our priority is to share the good news of God's love in Jesus with our Muslim neighbors. We can't do that in a setting of conflict, but only in a setting of peace. So I am going to support dialogue."

Where there has been religious violence, some Christians avoid witness for fear that it will fan flames. But Nahor believes witness is intrinsic to worship. Jesus' people testify. That is the most powerful way to love our neighbors. "The enemy is whatever stops Christians from loving and evangelism," Nahor says. He works for peace in order to develop a better milieu for witness. And grassroots peacebuilding can succeed, he believes.

Miriam Adeney, *Kingdom without Borders: The Untold Story of Global Christianity* (2009, 238–40)

# CHAPTER 3

# CHRISTIAN RESPONSES TO SUFFERING, PERSECUTION, AND MARTYRDOM

*Reg Reimer*

This chapter will describe Christians' reaction to persecution—biblically, historically, and currently. It includes some responses of the church at large, then how Christians in the trenches of persecution respond to their plight.

## RESPONSES FROM THE CHURCH AT LARGE

The global church has responded conceptually to the growing phenomenon of persecution. Globally instructive statements on persecution are periodically made by the World Evangelical Alliance (WEA), the Roman Catholic Church, the World Council of Churches (WCC), and the Lausanne Movement. A by-invitation meeting of international leaders on persecution at Bad Urach, Germany, in September 2009 produced a comprehensive statement entitled, "Developing an evangelical theology of suffering, persecution, and martyrdom for the global church in mission." An excerpted version of the Bad Urach Call can be found in appendix A.[1]

While strongly evangelical, the Lausanne Movement is broader and more inclusive than the other communions stated above. The Lausanne congresses are summarized in guidance statements for the church—as in the Lausanne Covenant (1974), the Manila Manifesto (1989), and the Cape Town Commitment (2010). These can readily be found at www.lausanne.org.

The Bad Urach Statement (2009) appears to have contributed to the Lausanne Cape Town statement, as the Cape Town Commitment includes explicit language integrating suffering, persecution, and martyrdom into the theology of mission under the title "The love of Christ calls us to suffer and sometimes die for the gospel." All three Lausanne statements endorse strategic advocacy for religious freedom as part of Christian witness. Significantly, the Cape Town Commitment, under the heading "Love works for religious freedom for all people," states, "There is no contradiction between being willing personally to suffer the abuse and loss of our own rights for the sake of Christ and being committed to advocate and speak

---

1    The full statement, of which I am a signatory, may be found in Sauer and Howell (2010, 21–106).

up for those who are voiceless under the violation of their human rights." The statements of these organizations reveal a current conceptual response to persecution and suffering in the church.

## PRACTICAL RESPONSES

The period of Christian suffering under Soviet Communism gave rise to a number of evangelical organizations whose main purpose was to support and advocate for persecuted Christians. A number of these trace their roots to the remarkable Romanian evangelical leader Richard Wurmbrand. He endured severe persecution during long prison sentences. He was released in an amnesty, and left Romania in 1964. He became an eloquent advocate for the persecuted, founding the Voice of the Martyrs, from which many other organizations have spun off. The Dutchman Andrew van der Bijl, much better know as Brother Andrew, founded Open Doors in the 1960s as well. It has several national branches.

These two prominent organizations are representative of dozens of organizations advocating for the persecuted church. Most of these major in supporting persecuted believers both spiritually and materially, though some have also developed advocacy arms. Many now participate in the Religious Liberty Partnership (see chapter 56 and appendix D). They can be seen as a major response of mainly the Western church (at least until recently) to widespread Christian persecution.

## RECENT SCHOLARSHIP

Recent and rising interest in the topics of Christian persecution, suffering, violence, and martyrdom has recently spurred evangelicals to produce a number of books on these topics.[2] Glenn Penner (2004) wrote a comprehensive biblical theological study of persecution and discipleship. Charles Tieszen's contribution (2008) looks at reevaluating how religious persecution is understood.

Three volumes edited respectively by Harold Hunter and Cecil Robeck (2006), by Keith Eitel (2008), and by Christof Sauer and Richard Howell (2010) together contain the contributions of forty-four separate authors, including important voices from the Global South. In 2008 the International Institute for Religious Freedom launched the *International Journal for Religious Freedom* (*IJRF*). Ron Boyd-MacMillan's *Faith that Endures* (2006) is, as the book's subtitle suggests, an essential guide to the persecuted church for popular audiences.

All of these works deal substantively with the topic of this chapter: how Christians respond to repression, especially persecution. Today these phenomena are a rising tide.

## THE RESPONSES OF THE PERSECUTED

What follows is an attempt at categorizing the main ways Christians respond to repression and persecution. This can help the presently persecuted understand what other believers have done before them and help churches who are able to support the persecuted to do so wisely.

---

2     See reference section of this chapter for full bibliographic information on these books.

A common and useful paradigm or taxonomy used to describe how Christians respond to persecution is to say they either (1) flee and escape it, (2) patiently endure it, or (3) stand up and advocate against it. Homiletically one could say the responses are flight, fortitude, and fight. Under these main category headings, I will more fully describe Christian responses to persecution.

It is necessary to understand that the persecution of Christians is almost never for religious reasons alone. Glenn Penner has pointed out that "when the kingdom of God invades the kingdoms of this world" (2004, 162), Christians are persecuted also for political, cultural, economic, social, and psychological reasons. Reasons for persecution are often complex and combined. Sadly, this leads some secular observers and political leaders, who have little understanding of the centrality of religion for most people in the world, to overlook the foundational religious reasons for persecution.

> But before all this they will lay their hands on you and persecute you, delivering you up to the synagogues and prisons, and you will be brought before kings and governors for my name's sake.
> *Luke 21:12*

The forms of Christian response to repression and persecution are also determined in part by the sources of the persecution. Main sources today are radical Islam, Communism, religious nationalism, and secular humanism (Boyd-MacMillan 2006, 123–42).

It is also important to consider that persecuted Christians belong to churches. In many situations, Christians will formulate their responses to persecution in concert with one another. It is my observation that too often persecuted Christians are thought of chiefly as individuals.

The common responses to persecution are to:

## FLEE OR ESCAPE

Understandably, Christians do not wish to suffer the deprivations, pain, or even death that result from persecution.

A case could be made for dealing with recantation under a separate heading, but I will deal with it here. That is, persecutors sometimes offer a way of escape in trying to persuade or force Christians to recant their faith.

For example, in Communist Vietnam, government-sponsored campaigns against ethnic-minority Christians demanded Christians sign a statement agreeing to return to traditional animistic beliefs and practices. Sometimes these Christians were forced to participate in animistic rites, such as drinking the blood of ritually sacrificed chickens to prove their sincerity in recanting. Converts from Islam are routinely pressured to return to that faith, and according to some brands of Islam, face death if they don't. In India, Dalits, who have sometimes converted to Christianity in large numbers, have been gathered by hostile Hindu leaders in mass meetings to reverse their conversions.

In Vietnam, anti-Catholic pogroms began in the seventeenth century and continued into the nineteenth century. During these, even those who succumbed to unimaginable pressure and did recant their Christian faith were branded on the forehead with the words *ta dao* (heretic). Though they avoided death, they were never able to escape the opprobrium of having been a Christian.

Forced recantations present serious theological and pastoral problems. Those who sign a statement or, under great pressure, indicate that they recant yet continue to believe in their hearts often suffer deep guilt for having publicly denied their faith. Is there space in the Christian family for those who must truly live as secret believers? Much wisdom and discernment is required of those who pastor people forced to make such choices. And those who observe from afar ought simply to withhold judgment.

In some extreme cases, it must be admitted, persecuted believers buckle. They deem the costs too high. They capitulate and stop practicing their faith.

Others escape by fleeing from persecution. From Bible times onward, some severely persecuted believers have deemed it necessary to flee for safety or at least to reduce persecution. This has happened countless times in church history and continues to the present day.

> On that day a great persecution broke out against the church in Jerusalem, and all except the apostles were scattered throughout Judea and Samaria.... Those who had been scattered preached the word wherever they went. *Acts 8:1,4*

The persecution of God's people has a long and venerable history in the Old Testament (Schirrmacher 2008, 37–39). But most well known is the persecution in the book of Acts and the dispersion of the church in Jerusalem. Persecution of the apostles and the scattering of the followers of Jesus resulted in bringing the gospel to new areas, adding to the believers, and multiplying churches.

When disciples were scattered they did not go underground but continued their bold witness. They accepted that their hardships were part of the grand strategic plan of God to grow his church and spread his Kingdom (Penner 2004, 155–67). The pattern of persecution leading to scattered Christians who then evangelized and grew the church, which in turn spawned more persecution and more scattering, has been repeated through the centuries. The apostles did not view their suffering of harsh persecution as a reason for pity, but rather as an opportunity to encourage the church. After being stoned nearly to death, Paul returns to town, strengthening the disciples and encouraging them to remain true to the faith. "We must go through many hardships to enter the kingdom of God" (Acts 14:22) [NIV 1984-unless otherwise noted].

As well, Old Testament prophets, Jesus himself, and New Testament apostles often fled persecution and danger with God's blessing. They found shelter until they could fight another day, or, in Jesus' case, until his "time had come."

For more on how persecution has often led to the flight and migration of Christians and the spread of the faith, there is no better source than Kenneth Scott Latourette's monumental seven-volume *A History of the Expansion of Christianity*, published between 1937 and 1945.

In recent years, heavy persecution of Christians in the Muslim Middle East and some North African countries has led to their steady flight to other lands and the depletion of the church in their homelands. This push was exemplified by graffiti seen in Libya. It read, "First the Saturday people and now the Sunday people." If present trends continue, it is feared that some countries in the region may become Christian-free within a generation.

In Vietnam, some thirty-five thousand Christian Hmong have fled persecution in the Northwest mountainous region during the last decade, moving 800 miles south to the Central Highlands. Some nasty persecution has followed them, but on the whole they deem their new location as somewhat better. At the same time some Montagnard minority Christians in the Central Highlands have fled persecution for neighboring Cambodia. In this case, Christians have fled both internally and across a national border to escape repression for their faith.

The most recent report "Persecuted and Forgotten?" (2011) by the British branch of the Vatican-endorsed organization, Aid to the Church in Need, calculates alarmingly that three-quarters of all religious persecution in the world is against Christians! It would be a worthy study to find out how much this extensive persecution contributes to the 45 million refugees recognized by the United Nations High Commission for Refugees (UNHCR). By any measure, the flight by Christians from persecution remains a major way they respond to their lot, and the numbers are growing.

How can the church respond to the needs of those Christians who flee persecution? In one example, organizations which help resettle refugees in Western countries look for sponsors. Using the "first to the household of faith" principle, Christians may in this way help fleeing brothers and sisters to resettle and start new lives. There are also a number of Christian agencies which specialize in service to refugees. While they usually serve all regardless of faith and are worthy of support for that reason alone, sometimes they also become aware of the special needs of fleeing Christians.[3]

## ENDURE PATIENTLY

By far, most Christians who suffer "for Christ's sake" would fit into the category of believers through the centuries who have had no choice but to stay put and endure persecution. And, not coincidentally, the New Testament Scriptures have much more to say on this topic than on fleeing persecution or advocating for the persecuted.

In sum, Scripture is clear on the inevitability of suffering for Christ's sake and the call for patient endurance in it. Jesus, in John 15:20 said, "Remember the words I spoke to you, 'No servant is greater than his master.' If

> Blessed is the man who remains steadfast under trial, for when he has stood the test he will receive the crown of life, which God has promised to those who love him. *James 1:12*

they persecuted me, they will persecute you also." And Paul, in 2 Timothy 3:12 says, "In fact everyone who wants to live a godly life in Christ Jesus will be persecuted." These unqualified statements make clear that persecution for the followers of Jesus is both inevitable and normative.

3    See part 3, chapter 41: "The Refugee Highway Partnership."

Further, the epistles have volumes to say about how to face the promised suffering and persecution. Paul, in Philippians 3:10, writes of "the fellowship of sharing in his sufferings." Peter speaks of "suffering for doing good" (1 Pet 3:17). James writes of "patience in the face of suffering" (5:10).[4]

As I have written elsewhere, "Mysteriously, it is sometimes through persecution, suffering, and martyrdom that God spreads his glory and his name, making them expressions of both Christian spirituality and mission" (Sauer and Howell 2010, 330).

Hebrews 13:3 clearly enjoins us to "remember those in prison as if you were their fellow prisoners, and those who are mistreated as if you yourselves were suffering." Such remembering calls us to risk-taking activity and is not a mere cognitive exercise.

As indicated above, a whole raft of agencies has emerged in the last half century to minister to the persecuted church.[5] This is as it should be. However, the relationship between the hurting and the helping members of the body is not a one-way street, as anyone who has worked with the persecuted church will attest.

An equal if not more pressing question is what the persecuted church has to teach the rest of us. The persecuted church is living in a very New Testament and early church context and has much to share with the overly rational and sometimes spiritually flabby churches of the West. Boyd-MacMillan (2006, 303–49) says the reservoir of experience of the persecuted is a huge and untapped resource to provide the church-at-large with models of risking faith and habits of holiness.[6]

## ADVOCATE AGAINST IT[7]

After the miraculous events during Paul and Silas' imprisonment in Acts 16 which led to the jailer's salvation, the apostles' release was ordered. But Paul is not content with mere freedom. He says, in effect, to the officer letting them go, "They slapped us around and stuck us in jail without a trial even though we are Roman citizens, and now you just want us to slip away? Don't you think those who abused us should face the legal consequences?" Acts 21–23 provides further examples of how a persecuted Paul appeals for his legal rights as a Roman.

And so today, many Christians are persecuted in violation of the laws of their own nations and in violation of international treaties signed by their governments. God has given governments the mandate to provide peace, justice, and order.[8] Those abused have every right to ask for and expect justice. If no one advocates for them, the persecutors will be emboldened to multiply their abuses.

---

4    The matter of suffering for Christ's sake is more fully covered in the opening chapters of part 3.
5    Lausanne Occasional Paper No. 32, "The Persecuted Church," has a chapter cataloging various kinds of ministry to the persecuted church (44–59).
6    Excellent excerpts from Boyd-MacMillan's book on this topic appear in part 4, chapter 57.
7    I have written an entire chapter on advocacy. See part 4, chapter 59. Also in part 3, chapter 38 I relate my personal advocacy experience.
8    See subsection "What are governments for?" in part 4, chapter 59.

Advocacy can take place on many levels. First, we can pray to our heavenly Father who advocates with the very highest authority. Second, the persecuted themselves or those closest to them can advocate on humanitarian and legal grounds, though most often this is not successful. Specialists or lawyers in the country of persecution can often speak up for the persecuted, but this too is often a risk.

International advocates who specialize in legal advocacy can often help because they know the particular vulnerabilities of persecutors in law. Such advocacy is most effective if advocates have ample and accurate information and they are well coordinated and connected in the advocacy network. In my opinion there is much need in the persecuted church support community for the development of advocacy specialists and for effective coordination.

There is another kind of advocacy that some find difficult to deal with. In some places where Christians and Muslims have coexisted peacefully for a long time, radical Muslims from afar have incited gratuitous violence against Christians. In some Nigerian and Indonesian locations where civil authorities have been unable or unwilling to defend them and halt the violence, Christians have defended themselves, and in rare instances even retaliated.

Faced with the wanton destruction of their churches and personal property, the kidnapping and rape of their wives and daughters, and the wholesale murder of their communities, they believe they are left with no other choice. I have spoken with burdened Christian leaders who survived such attacks and asked me the heart-wrenching question, "What should we do when they attack like that by night?" This question is worthy of serious theological and ethical reflection, and careful answers.

Advocating for the persecuted cannot be expected to end persecution. But it is an essential part of our witness to the gospel to stand up for those made in his image and abused for Christ's sake.

Between standing up for their rights and readiness to suffer for Christ's sake the persecuted sometimes choose but often have no choice in their response. Whatever that response is, they deserve the understanding and support of the rest of the body of Christ.

## QUESTIONS FOR REFLECTION
1. How can the conceptual responses of the global church (as, for example, in the statements of the Lausanne Movement) become much better known in local churches?
2. Are you familiar with some of the recent scholarship on the topic as described by the author? Can you add to the list?
3. Are the three main "responses of the persecuted" mainly descriptive of history or are they also prescriptive for the present and future?
4. Are there other appropriate responses to persecution not captured in the author's broad paradigm?

## REFERENCES

Boyd-MacMillan, R. 2006. *Faith that endures: The essential guide to the persecuted church.* Lancaster, UK: Sovereign World.

Eitel, K. E., ed. 2008. *Missions in contexts of violence.* Pasadena, CA: William Carey Library.

Hunter, H. D., and C. M. Robeck, eds. 2006. *The suffering body: Responding to the persecution of Christians.* Sparkford, UK: Paternoster.

Latourette, K. S. 1976. *A history of the expansion of Christianity,* 7 vols. Grand Rapids, MI: Zondervan.

Penner, G. M. 2004. *In the shadow of the cross: A biblical theology of persecution and discipleship.* Bartlesville, OK: Living Sacrifice Books.

Pontifex, J., and J. Newton, eds. 2011. *Persecuted and forgotten? A report on Christians oppressed for the faith.* Sutton, Surrey: Aid to the Church in Need.

Sauer, C., and R. Howell, eds. 2010. *Suffering persecution and martyrdom: Theological reflections.* Religious Freedom Series, 2. Johannesburg: AcadSA Publishing.

Schirrmacher, T. 2008. *The persecution of Christians concerns us all: Towards a theology of martyrdom.* Bonn: Culture and Science Publishers.

Sookdheo, P., ed. 2005. *The persecuted church.* Lausanne Occasional Paper No. 32. The Lausanne Committee for World Evangelization.

Tieszen, C. L. 2008. *Re-examining religious persecution: Constructing a framework for understanding persecution.* Religious Freedom Series, 1. Kempton Park, South Africa: AcadSA Publishing.

**Reg Reimer**, a Canadian, has worked internationally in evangelism, relief and development, reconciliation ministry, promoting collaboration, and advocating for religious freedom. He describes himself foremost as a missionary to Vietnam where he began ministry in 1966 and remains deeply involved. He is considered an authority on the Protestant movement there. His book *Vietnam's Christians: A Century of Growth in Adversity* was released in July 2011. Reg was president of World Relief Canada from 1984 to 1994. He then served as senior staff member of the World Evangelical Alliance. He currently serves as international partnership advisor with the Evangelical Fellowship of Canada and South East Asia coordinator for International Partnering Associates. He is regularly called on by organizations for advice on promoting religious freedom in Vietnam. Reg is a long-time participant in the WEA Mission Commission. He is married to LaDonna, a social worker. The Reimers live in Abbotsford, BC, Canada. Their two children serve in Cambodia and South Korea.

# CHAPTER 4

# THE DEMOGRAPHICS OF MARTYRDOM

*Todd M. Johnson*

Throughout Christian history, across all traditions of Christianity and in every part of the world, some 70 million Christians have been murdered for their faith, and hence are called martyrs.

## ORIGIN OF THE WORD "MARTYR"

The English word "martyr" is derived from the Greek *martys*, which carries the meaning "witness" in English. In New Testament usage it meant "a witness to the resurrection of Christ." This witness resulted so frequently in death that by the end of the first century, *martys* had come to mean a Christian who witnessed to Christ *by his or her death*. This enlarged meaning has become the accepted norm throughout church history.

## DEFINITION OF TERMS

For a quantitative analysis of martyrdom, Christian martyrs are defined as "believers in Christ who have lost their lives prematurely, in situations of witness, as a result of human hostility." This definition has five essential elements that can be stated as follows:

1. *Believers in Christ:* These individuals come from the entire Christian community of Roman Catholics, Orthodox, Protestants, Anglicans, marginal Christians, and independents. In AD 2010, over 2.2 billion individuals can be deemed Christians, and since the time of Christ over 8.5 billion have believed in Christ.
2. *Lost their lives:* The definition is restricted to Christians actually put to death, for whatever reason.
3. *Prematurely:* Martyrdom is sudden, abrupt, unexpected, unwanted.
4. *In situations of witness:* "Witness" in this definition does not mean only public testimony or proclamation concerning the risen Christ. It refers to the entire lifestyle and way of life of the Christian believer, whether or not he or she is actively proclaiming at the time of being killed.
5. *As a result of human hostility:* This excludes deaths through accidents, crashes, earthquakes and other "acts of God," illnesses, or other causes of death, however tragic.

It is important to note that this definition omits a criterion considered essential by many churches in their martyrologies—"heroic sanctity"—by which is meant saintly life and fearless stance. Those are certainly essential for a martyrology if it is to have compelling educational and inspirational value for church members under persecution, and in particular for new converts. Heroic sanctity is, however, not essential to the demographic definition because many Christians have been killed shortly after their conversions and before they had any chance to develop Christian character, holiness, or courage.

## MORE DETAILED DEFINITION

A more complex definition sees martyrs as Christians whose loyalty and witness to Christ (as witnesses to the fact of Christ's resurrection and also as legal witnesses to, and advocates for, the claims of Christ in God's cosmic lawsuit against the world) lead directly or indirectly to a confrontation or clash with hostile opponents (either non-Christians or Christians of another persuasion) as a result of their either (1) being Christians, (2) being part of a Christian body or community, (3) being Christian workers, (4) averring the truth of Christianity, (5) holding to some Christian tenet or principle or practice, (6) holding to different Christian tenets than those of their opponents, (7) speaking for Christ, or 8) refusing to deny Christ or their Christian convictions, which then results in violence and in their voluntarily or involuntarily losing their lives prematurely (shedding their blood; being put to death, executed, assassinated, killed, stoned, clubbed to death, beheaded, guillotined, garroted, strangled, stabbed, eaten alive, gassed, injected, electrocuted, suffocated, boiled in oil, roasted alive, drowned, torched, burned, massacred, crucified, lynched, hanged, shot, murdered, pushed under oncoming traffic, immured, buried alive, crushed to death, poisoned, drugged to death, starved, deprived of medication, chemically or electronically killed, killed extrajudicially, killed under torture, killed due to beatings, killed in custody, killed in prison, killed soon after release from prison, or allowed or left to die). Any of these may take place with or without prior demand or opportunity to recant.

Note that (6) above means that most Christians killed as alleged "heretics" down through the ages should correctly be included in demographic enumerations of martyrs. Item (3) above also includes vocational Christian workers killed while engaged in ministry, or who lose their lives because they happen to be in the path of violence (this includes workers killed by robbers, soldiers, police, etc.). Note also that the definition of demographic martyrdom includes those children and infants who lose their lives along with adult martyrs.

## COUNTING MARTYRS

The basic method for counting martyrs in Christian history is to list "martyrdom situations" at particular points in time. A martyrdom situation is defined as "mass or multiple martyrdoms at one point in Christian history." It is then determined how many of the people killed in that situation fit the definition of martyr outlined above. (This is explained in more detail in *World Christian Trends*). Note that in any situation of mass deaths or killing of Christians, one does not automatically or necessarily define the entire total who have been killed as martyrs, but only that fraction whose deaths resulted from some form of Christian witness, individual or collective. For example, our analysis does not equate "crusaders" with "martyrs," but simply states that during the Crusades a number of zealous and overzealous Christians were in fact martyred as defined under the definitions above. Likewise in Latin America in the 1980s we do not count as martyrs all Christians who became victims of political killings, but only those whose situations involved Christian witness. Typical illustrations of the latter include the vast number of cases of an entire congregation singing hymns as soldiers lock their church's doors and proceed to burn it to the ground with no survivors.

One adjustment to the total is to include "background martyrs" or those very small or isolated or individual situations. They cover cases where a Christian is killed as a result of human hostility but where the circumstances have nothing directly or immediately to do with organized Christianity.

## MARTYRDOM NOT EXCLUSIVELY AN EARLY CHRISTIAN PHENOMENON

Martyrdom comes about because of persecution and results in a death that is in itself a witness for Christ. In the early church, the idea developed that it was not enough to be called a Christian—one had to show proof. That proof was normally some kind of verbal acknowledgement ("witness") of identification with Christ, starting with the confession "Jesus is Lord." Baumeister writes: "Dying because one is a Christian is the action par excellence in which the disciple who is called to this confirms his or her faith by following the example of Jesus' suffering and through action is able once again to become a word with power to speak to others" (1972). Eventually confessors were distinguished from martyrs.

When most Christians hear the word "martyr" they tend to think of the Roman persecution of early Christians. The *Ecclesia Martyrum* or Church of the Martyrs often is thought to refer only to the earliest period of church history, the ten imperial Roman persecutions. This is not the case. Martyrdom is a consistent feature of church history and occurs in every Christian tradition and confession. One can see that all of the ten largest martyrdom situations in Table 1 occurred in the second millennium of the Christian faith. The rate of martyrdom across the world throughout the ages has been remarkably constant at 0.8 percent. One out of every 120 Christians in the past has been martyred, or in the future is likely to be so.

If the world hates you, know that it has hated me before it hated you. *John 15:18*

## WHY ARE THERE MARTYRS?

According to Latin American theologian Leonardo Boff they exist for two reasons: (1) Christians prefer to sacrifice their lives rather than to be unfaithful to their convictions, (2) people who reject proclamation persecute, torture, and kill (Metz 1983). This general presence of evil in the world, combined with Christian devotion, is at the root of martyrdom. When we examine a list of martyrs down the ages, as comprehensive as is known today, some startling findings emerge. Table 1 provides a list of the ten largest known martyrdom situations ranked by size. Note that over 20 million were martyred in Soviet prison camps and that well over half of the 70 million Christian martyrs were killed in the twentieth century alone. Even though state-ruling powers (atheists and others) are responsible for most martyrdom, closer examination of the entire list of martyrdom situations reveals that Christians themselves have been the persecutors responsible for martyring 5.5 million other Christians.

Table 2 reveals that over half of all martyrs have been Orthodox Christians. One partial explanation for this is the vast anti-Christian empires throughout history centered in Eastern Europe and Central Asia. Nonetheless, all Christian traditions have suffered martyrdom.

**Table 1. Top ten martyrdom situations in Christian history ranked by size**

| Situation | Martyred |
|---|---|
| 1. 1921–50, Christians die in Soviet prison camps | 15,000,000 |
| 2. 1950–80, Christians die in Soviet prison camps | 5,000,000 |
| 3. 1214, Genghis Khan massacres Christians | 4,000,000 |
| 4. 1358, Tamerlane destroys Nestorian church | 4,000,000 |
| 5. 1929–37, Orthodox Christians killed by Stalin | 2,700,000 |
| 6. 1560, Conquistadors kill millions of Amerindians | 2,000,000 |
| 7. 1925, Soviets attempt to liquidate Roman Catholics | 1,200,000 |
| 8. 1258, Baghdad captured in massacre by Hulaku Khan | 1,100,000 |
| 9. 1214, Diocese of Herat sacked by Genghis Khan | 1,000,000 |
| 10. 1939, Nazis execute millions in death camps | 1,000,000 |

**Table 2. Confessions of martyrs, totals from AD 33–2000**

| Tradition | Martyrs |
|---|---|
| Orthodox | 43,000,000 |
|    Russian Orthodox | 25,000,000 |
|    East Syrians (Nestorians) | 12,800,000 |
|    Ukrainian Orthodox | 4,000,000 |
|    Gregorians (Armenian Apostolic) | 1,200,000 |
| Roman Catholic | 12,200,000 |
|    Catholics (before AD 1000) | 900,000 |
| Independents | 3,500,000 |
| Protestants | 3,200,000 |
| Anglicans | 1,100,000 |
| Marginal Christians | 7,000 |
| Other and background martyrs | 7,000,000 |
| *Total all martyrs* | *70,000,000* |

## A POTENTIAL IMPACT OF MARTYRDOM

In some countries one finds that martyrdom was followed by church growth. A contemporary example is the church in China. In 1949 there were only 1 million Christians in China. Fifty years of antireligious Communist rule produced some 1.2 million martyrs. The result: explosive church growth to today's 100 million believers. Today major martyrdom situations continue in the Democratic Republic of Congo, Sudan, Indonesia, Nigeria, and other hot spots around the globe.

## LIMITATIONS OF THIS MODEL OF COUNTING MARTYRS

Defining and enumerating martyrs in the widest possible sense has both limitations and advantages over other methods. First of all, it is limited because it leaves out questions of quality, such as holy lifestyle (mentioned above) or theological persuasion of Christian martyrs. Second, it reports on martyrdom from a purely demographic lens, leaving out thousands of fascinating stories and anecdotes. Fortunately, these are not in short supply in other publications.

Two advantages can also be highlighted here. First of all, due to extensive coding of martyrdom situations (available in *World Christian Trends*), it allows for a selective approach to the data. Questions such as "How many Roman Catholic martyrs were there in South America in the nineteenth century?" can be answered. Second, this approach resists fragmentation by placing all Christian martyrs in the same global phenomenon.

## THE FUTURE OF MARTYRDOM

One might be tempted to believe that mankind will gradually grow out of its violent nature and that, perhaps one hundred years in the future, people will no longer be killing others, for whatever reason. However, this is unlikely to be the case. The future almost certainly holds more martyrdom situations, and the names of individual martyrs are likely to continue mounting year after year.

*Note.* This article was condensed from Part 4, "Martyrology," in Barrett and Johnson, *World Christian Trends* (WCT). The compilation of data on Christian martyrs in all countries over the twenty centuries of Christian history is found in two large tables in WCT: Table 4–10, describing 600 major martyrdom situations in 150 countries, AD 33–2000; and Table 4–11, "Alphabetical listing of 2,500 known Christian martyrs, AD 33–2000." Country-by-country statistics of martyrdom can be found at www.worldchristiandatabase.org.

## QUESTIONS FOR REFLECTION

1. The editors believe this brief but very full article will hold significant surprises for most readers. What are some implications of the information in the article for the modern mission movement?
2. Discuss the definition of martyrdom used in this article.
3. Does the article support the statement that the "result" of severe persecution of Christians in China was explosive growth?
4. Are there martyrs today which fit the "heroic sanctity" model described in the article?

## REFERENCES

Baumeister, T. 1972. *Martyr invictus*. Münster: Regensberg.

Chenu, B., C. Prud'homme, F. Quere, J. Thomas. 1988. *Livre des martyrs chrétiens*. Paris: Éditions du Centurion. English ed: 1990. *The Book of Christian Martyrs*. New York: Crossroad.

Metz, J., and E. Schillebeeckx, eds. 1983. *Martyrdom today*. Edinburgh: T. & T. Clark.

Wood, D., ed. 1993. *Martyrs and martyrologies*. Oxford: Blackwell.

Marshall, P., and L. Gilbert. 1997. *Their blood cries out: The untold story of persecution against Christians in the modern world*. Dallas: Word.

Barrett, D., and T. Johnson. 2001. *World Christian trends*. Pasadena, CA: William Carey Library.

**Todd M. Johnson** is director of the Center for the Study of Global Christianity at Gordon-Conwell Theological Seminary in South Hamilton, MA. He is co-author of the *World Christian Encyclopedia*, 2nd ed. (Oxford University Press, 2001) and co-editor of the *Atlas of Global Christianity* (Edinburgh University Press, 2009).

*"I have learned the secret of being content in ... every situation.... I can do all this through him who gives me strength"* Philippians 4:11–13

Paul was a man just like us, but he lived an extraordinary life because of his faith and total submission to his Lord. In his letters he writes about tribulation and suffering, like extreme tiredness, hunger, thirst, being often flogged, beaten with rods, in prison, in all kinds of dangers (2 Cor 11:23–28). But he learned to suffer for the name of Jesus (Acts 9:16).

In our service to the Lord we may go through some of such sufferings, especially on the mission fields, but we can learn with Paul to "be content in any and every situation," knowing that we can do "everything through him who gives us strength." Like Paul we can see our suffering as an opportunity to know and to trust God.

Reflection by: Gissele Kocznykowski, Brazil

# CHAPTER 5

# A RESPONSE TO THE HIGH COUNTS OF CHRISTIAN MARTYRS PER YEAR

*Thomas Schirrmacher*

For many years, one number has been provided every year to report on the annual number of Christian martyrs. This is provided by the "Status of Global Mission." The number is quoted by various institutions, but only produced by one institution. At present it is most frequently quoted by the papal missions agency, Aid to the Church in Need. It reports 130,000–170,000 martyrs per year but does not conduct any of its own investigations.

This number is released every year in the *International Bulletin for Missionary Research*.[1] In 2010 the number stood at 178,000; for 2009 176,000; and for 2011 it was corrected to 100,000 (Johnson et al. 2011, 28). The commentary provided with the Status of Global Mission itself indicates that this number is the most quoted figure from this table (IBMR 2011, 28). A number for martyrs of this magnitude is widespread through the books *World Christian Encyclopedia, World Christian Trends, Atlas of Global Christianity,* and the electronic *World Christian Database*.

I find it difficult to criticize this number on account of its widespread use, particularly due to the fact that it comes from reputable researchers and good friends. However, as an academic I have too often had to answer for such numbers before secular colleagues, politicians around the world, our German parliament, and journalists to just allow our institute (the International Institute for Religious Freedom) simply to assume them.

Since by many secular, Christian, and among them also evangelical[2] researchers and specialists the figure is (1) viewed to be too high, and (2) on the basis of numerous factors viewed to be a number that cannot even be collected, it would be desirable to have a precise account of the basis of comprehensive research upon which the number is compiled. Furthermore, it would be desirable to know which scientific standards are followed in the process and how research colleagues' conformity can be reviewed. All of this is not available—even the comprehensive presentation in *World Christian Trends* nowhere mentions the source of the

---

1    www.internationalbulletin.org.
2    E.g., http://www.persecution.net/faq-stats.htm.

data and which criteria were used in producing the estimates (Barrett and Johnson 2001, ch. 16).

Nonetheless, in the present media landscape in which we find ourselves, it is natural that someone with even a roughly estimated number has an advantage over an individual who says that the number cannot be reliably estimated at the present time.

## THE ROLE OF CIVIL WARS

According to the reports of its authors, the figure of 156,000–178,000 martyrs per year is an average number for the ten years between 1990 and 2000 (Johnson et al. 2011, 28). In the process one has to recognize—without its being expressly stated—that the vast portion of the 1.6 million martyrs over a period of ten years comes from the civil wars in southern Sudan and in Rwanda. Let us suppose one were to use even a broader definition of Christian persecution, "martyrs in the widest possible sense" (Johnson et al. 2011, 28). Still, the extent to which Rwanda can be included at all, and the share of deaths in southern Sudan that can be traced back to the persecution of Christians by Muslims and not seen either affecting animists or originating with brutalizing southern Sudanese parties to the civil war, is at least disputed.

For the ten-year period 2000–2010, southern Sudan and Rwanda no longer count. The mammoth share of the amount of 10 x 100,000 comes under the civil war in the Democratic Republic of the Congo (DRC). Admittedly there were many Christians who died there, but that they died *because* they were Christians is not something that is defended by anyone in the literature. Let us suppose that there were 900,000 martyrs estimated for the DRC. The remaining 100,000 over ten years would then move one far closer to an exceedingly lower number.

What I criticize above all is that nowhere is the composition of the figure presented according to country. This would allow the main countries to be recognized and discussed. It would then be especially easy to see the one or two countries to which the high number could be traced back. I also criticize the fact that no discussion about these one or two difficult-to-classify situations can occur.

Not every Christian who dies in a civil war like the one in the Congo can simply be counted. An estimate is made about which portion of the Christians killed actually died as martyrs. This number would need to be discussed and justified. However, it is impossible to find out which portion was estimated, much less how the estimate was made. All that is said is that "a substantial proportion" of the 5.4 million killed in the Congo were martyred. A 10 percent increase in the number of martyrs in the Congo, however, would translate into an increase of the total number of 100,000 by 54,000 martyrs, a jump of over 50 percent! If 10 percent less than the unknown percentage in Congo were to be estimated, that would be 54,000 fewer annually, which means that the figure would shrink by over 50 percent from 100,000 to 46,000! This means that de facto the entire number of martyrs worldwide is decided through the estimate of the share of martyrs found among the victims of unrest in Congo.

## REGARDING DEFINITION

I see a general contradiction between the definition given by the Status of Global Mission, that martyrs are "believers in Christ . . . in a situation of witness," and the statement of "defining and enumerating martyrs in the widest possible sense."

An intra-Christian, theological definition will always be much tighter than a sociological one. As a sociologist of religion, I definitely see that a very broad number may be chosen that does not take into account whether the murdered Christian is a baby, a poor excuse for a churchgoer, or a sectarian of some sort. I personally consider the "situation of witness" to be unnecessary. If a church is blown up in Egypt and twenty people are killed in the process, this is considered Christian persecution even if the twenty people killed were only interested guests.

> "When they deliver you over, do not be anxious how you are to speak or what you are to say, for what you are to say will be given to you in that hour." *Matthew 10:19*

My broadest political definition would be the following: "Christians who are killed and who would not have been killed had they not been Christians." However, even if this definition is used as a basis, I would by far not reach the 170,000 or 100,000 Christian martyrs per year.

## MORE THAN FIFTY MARTYRS A DAY?

Events where twenty or fifty Christians killed are nowadays not just widely reported on in the Christian world. Rather, in some countries such as Germany this would as a rule appear on the front page of newspapers. Experts who deal with the question of the persecution of Christians hear about this in any case. No one would say that this happens every day. However, even if we assume that there is an event with fifty murdered Christians every day, that would amount to an annual number of only 18,250. Twenty murdered Christians per day would be 7,300—a number which I consider to be more realistic.

It might be pointed out that there have been and are events that generate a higher yearly average than fifty per day. Indeed that is true, but these are individual events spread out over years. I know of the following countries for which this applies since 2000: Indonesia, India, Iraq, and Nigeria. The point is that these events hardly overlap with each other. Stated otherwise: in years past these horrible events have occurred selectively within a period of one to three years and in the years thereafter were superseded by other main events in other countries. Again stated alternatively: as a general rule, an event with more than one hundred Christian martyrs in a country occurs one time a year somewhere in the world.

The strange numbers that arise when one simply makes a rough estimate is demonstrated when a grading is made in the World Christian Database countries according to the annual number of martyrs, whereby the average over the last fifty years was taken (beginning in 1960).

In Denmark and Finland there are said to be 15 martyrs per year, while in Sweden there were 19; in Switzerland, 20; in the Netherlands, 39; in Australia, 45; in Canada, 76; in Great Britain, 149; and, believe it or not, in Germany, 192. In all of these Protestant countries, there are no known martyrs and under no circumstances fifty times the number given since 1960.

That the high numbers are difficult to comprehend and are traceable to liberal estimates of the share of Christian martyrs killed as a result of warfare and civil war also applies to the numbers for historic cases. Were there really 1 million martyrs at the hands of the National Socialists? No researcher of National Socialism (among whom I count myself with two dissertations) would attest to that. Admittedly there were millions of Christians who died in World War II, not, however, because they were persecuted. Among true Christian martyrs are those Christians who were killed on account of their Christian resistance or as clerics or representatives of religious communities. Their destiny has been thoroughly researched, their stories have been recorded in biographical encyclopedias, and a curriculum vitae is available for almost every such individual. This notwithstanding, there is still a total of only a few thousand and not 1 million.

## ARE THERE SO MANY MARTYRS AMONG THE DEAD IN CIVIL WARS AND OTHER WARFARE?

I want to make one further comparison which leads me to believe that both numbers, the 170,000 and the 100,000, can be questioned. According to statistics of the World Health Organization, there were 184,000 victims of warfare and civil war in 2004 (2008, 74).[3] And the number of martyrs is supposed to be just as large, without experts immediately being able to list the cases which comprise these numbers? One can list all warfare and civil war in a year and make it clear how this number of 184,000 victims is composed. If the number of martyrs is just as large, how can the events not be likewise listed and added together more or less in one's head? How does it happen that far too few large events come to mind, even to the experts, which would be able to explain the high numbers?

## ON THE ROAD TO RESEARCH: AN ACTUAL NUMBER FOR A PREVIOUS YEAR

How high, then, is the actual annual number of Christian martyrs? I have occupied myself with this for years and have probably discussed this with every existing expert from every denomination and beyond who has anything to say about it. Let me put to one side for the time being the sheer difficulty of producing a definition of "martyr." Even if a concrete definition is set, experts strongly differ with respect to individual countries. Were the "missing Christians" of North Korea killed decades ago or are they still living in camps and currently being killed?

If one asks for the total number worldwide, practically no one wagers an estimate. Additionally, everyone agrees that an average is confusing. Rather, the number of martyrs strongly fluctuates from year to year. For that reason the number has to be newly ascertained every year. Anyway, whoever hears a statistic for 2010 assumes that this is not an average value for 1990–2000, but rather that some institution has concretely researched the number for 2010 and has documented or at least has realistically estimated it on the basis of reports.

---

3        Compare the information of 171,000 for 2002 in the map among the atlas collection representing the actual world: http://www.worldmapper.org/display_extra.php?selected=484.

Overall, I am of the opinion that we are far from having a reliable report of the number of martyrs annually. The International Institute for Religious Freedom will continue to address this issue, and wants to contribute to a fair and open universal discussion.

What we need is a database in which for any year we could enter all the known, larger cases so that at the end of the year we not only have a usable estimate, but rather a situation where, given the list, everyone can investigate the estimate's resilience.

## QUESTIONS FOR REFLECTION

1. Should we try to verify the number of martyrs at all?
2. How should one evaluate civil wars with religious undertones and Christians involved? As part of persecution or as bad politics unrelated to the matter of persecution?
3. Is it better to work with the largest number of martyrs possible (with a very broad definition) to stir up interest, or with the lowest number possible (and a very narrow definition of martyrdom)?

## REFERENCES

Barrett, D., and T. Johnson. 2001. *World Christian trends*. Pasadena, CA: William Carey Library.

Gordon Conwell Theological Seminary. 2011. *Status of Global Mission*. http://www.gordonconwell.edu/resources/documents/StatusOfGlobalMission.pdf.

Johnson, T. M., D. B. Barrett, and P. F. Crossing. 2011. Christianity 2011: Martyrs and the resurgence of religion. *International Bulletin of Missionary Research* 35, no. 1: 28–29.

World Health Organization. 2008. *The global burden of disease*. Geneva: WHO. http://www.who.int/topics/global_burden_of_disease/en.

**Thomas Schirrmacher**, German, is director of the International Institute for Religious Freedom (Bonn, Cape Town, Colombo) and serves as chair of WEA's Theological Commission. Based in Germany, he holds extensive professorial and presidential roles across Europe as well as in Shillong, India, teaching sociology of religion, theology, global ethics, and international development.

## DOES DYING TAKE MORE FAITH—OR LIVING?

During the brutal regime of the 1980s in Ethiopia, one pastor was known throughout the country not only for his blessed ministry but also for his height. He was six feet and five inches tall.

Many Christians were martyred during this period. The towering pastor was thrown into prison. When the president of neighboring Tanzania heard about it, he decided to intercede. He hopped into his private jet and made a trip to Ethiopia to ask for the pastor's release.

President Nyerere's request was granted. The pastor was escorted out of jail into the custody of the Tanzanian embassy, to be whisked away to safety.

But the pastor declined the privilege. "No, sir," he told President Nyerere, "I am not leaving the country. My place is here. If I leave, it will discourage all those pastors who do not have the opportunity to go. It will also undermine all I have said when I urged Christians not to desert our country in its time of need."

A few weeks later this pastor was strangled to death by government soldiers.

Meanwhile, another Ethiopian named Assefa was imprisoned and released, imprisoned and released, and frequently threatened with death. For years he had no home. Sometimes he survived on food gathered from garbage dumps. Yet when political conditions loosened, Assefa became the national director of the student Christian movement. Throughout the 1990s, almost one-fifth of Ethiopia's university students participated, with five hundred trained Bible study leaders. Even ordinary villagers said, "Go to the God of Assefa. He can help."

"Which of these two Ethiopian brothers showed the greater faith: the pastor who was strangled or Assefa?" asks Lindsay Brown, who recorded their stories. "They both walked by faith, but the Lord saw fit to take one and to spare the other." Whether in life or in death, both these Ethiopians followed the God who suffers with us.

Miriam Adeney, *Kingdom without Borders: The Untold Story of Global Christianity* (2009, 80–81), citing Lindsay Brown, *Shining Like Stars: The Power of the Gospel in the World's Universities* (Nottingham, UK: InterVarsity Press, 2006, 162)

# CHAPTER 6

# REDEFINING PERSECUTION

*Charles L. Tieszen*

## INTRODUCTION

Along with Croatian scholar Peter Kuzmič, we must lament that "contemporary reference works on religion move remarkably easily from 'perfectionism' to 'perseverance'" (Kuzmič 2004–2005, 35). All too often, "persecution" simply remains untouched by the theological attention it so direly needs.

Even where some attention is given to the event, it frequently comes as truncated reflection. This is evident in studies that place a distorted emphasis upon the early church's persecution with the resulting notion that persecution simply does not happen anymore. In a similar way, the popular attention persecution receives as only an eschatological event pointing towards end-times activity pushes Christian awareness away from the present, isolating it to the unseen future. Other studies restrict persecution to violence and therefore have difficulty seeing the event if it does not include martyrdom. As a result, persecution is thought to only occur in the Majority World, not in the West, where freedom of religion is thought to be a widely accepted value. Still other studies extend the experience of persecution to all types of suffering (e.g., sickness, natural disasters, etc.). Any unfortunate experience befalling a Christian, therefore, is considered persecution (Tieszen 2008, 17–35).

These ways of thinking about religious persecution are unsatisfactory and surely contribute to our inability to adequately respond to and reflect upon genuine experiences of the event. In the study that follows, correcting these missteps begins by rethinking the way we define the religious persecution of Christians.

## DEFINING PERSECUTION

In the most general sense, we must understand persecution to occur within a broad spectrum ranging from unjust actions that are intensely hostile, to those that are mildly hostile. Intensely hostile actions, those most commonly associated with persecution, lie at one end of this spectrum and can be carried out physically, psychologically (mentally or emotionally), or socially. Such actions could include beating, torture, isolation, or imprisonment.

Mildly hostile actions lie at the opposite end of this spectrum. Such actions are less intense, not violent, and can also be carried out psychologically or socially. These would include ridicule, restriction, certain kinds of harassment, or discrimination. These sorts of actions are no less significant than more hostile ones, and should thus still be considered as persecution. With this in mind, we cannot define the event based on the level of pain it might cause, or the level of intensity in which it occurs. Instead, a definition of persecution encompasses actions spanning the full range of hostility.

Beyond this spectrum, it is important to note that persecution can be carried out with a number of different motivations. These motivations often overlap since, as Paul Marshall rightly asserts, persecution rarely has a single impetus (Marshall 1998, 2; Marshall 2004–2005, 27). For example, a Hindu couple marrying outside of their caste may be ostracized from the entire community by their parents. Such an action may be motivated by religion, but it might also be an issue of ethnicity, since one's caste may be tied to a particular indigenous group. In this light, many examples of persecution represent a mix of political, geographic, and economic concerns, among many other examples (Marshall 1998, 2).

It is of final importance, in our most general understanding of persecution, to recognize that its results are both negative and persecutory when viewed from the victim's perspective. Thus, negative results are harmful, understanding that harm must encompass the same span of intensity as our understanding of hostility does. Harm, then, can be physical, psychological, or social, and occurs within a spectrum of mild to intense hostility. Most important, however, is the recognition that this definition of persecution must be produced from the perspective of the victim, not that of the persecutor. In fact, persecutors may be unaware or even feel quite justified in their actions. In cases of nationalism, for instance, persecutors may feel it is their duty to deport, harass, discriminate, or even kill certain people in the name of national security. Yet as Marshall makes clear: "The motive is not, per se, the issue; the key question is, what is the result?" (Marshall 2000b, 17; Marshall 1998, 7; Schirrmacher 2001, 97–99).

> If you were of the world, the world would love you as its own; but because you are not of the world, but I chose you out of the world, therefore the world hates you. *John 15:19*

In general, then, a basic definition of persecution could be:

> An unjust action of varying levels of hostility with one or more motivations, directed at a specific individual or a specific group of individuals, resulting in varying levels of harm as they are considered from the victim's perspective.

## GETTING RELIGIOUS ABOUT PERSECUTION

Keeping this basic definition in mind, we cannot assume that all persecution is religious persecution. Moreover, religious people who are persecuted are not necessarily victims of religious persecution. The Rwandan genocide in the mid-1990s, for example, involved Hutus and Tutsis of various religious persuasions, but even so, this was primarily an ethnic conflict. Simply because religious people made up parts of both sides does not mean that the nature and motivation of such a persecution situation is to be understood religiously. Thus, a victim's religious identity cannot be the sole factor that determines the type of persecution involved. As Marshall suggests:

A possible demarcation point of religious persecution is to ask whether, if the persons had other religious beliefs . . . would they still be treated in the same way. If the answer is yes, we probably should not call it specifically religious persecution. (Marshall 1998, 5)

Of course, rarely is religion, or any other single motivation, the only one involved. Other factors often overlap. What distinguishes certain cases of persecution as religious in nature is the primacy of religion as the leading factor. In our example from Rwanda, religious people were involved, but religion was far from being the primary motivation of persecutory actions. Removing religion as a factor would not have eliminated the conflict, and so victims cannot be seen as having experienced *religious* persecution, though such a distinction in no way eliminates our responsibility to oppose such violence.

With this in mind, most definitions of religious persecution function on sociopolitical standards. In this way, religious persecution is, at the very least, "the denial of any of the rights of religious freedom" (Marshall 2000a, 21). These rights include the freedom individuals have to worship in accordance with the fundamentals of their religion, to change their religion, and to appropriately propagate their faith (Marshall 2000, 20–21; Stott 1975, 50). Furthermore, in most cases, sociopolitical definitions of religious persecution focus on the systematic violation of religious freedoms. We must add to this, then, cases where individuals, though perhaps not systematically persecuted, nevertheless must endure irregular or arbitrary harassment or even situations where individuals face religious discrimination in contexts where basic religious freedoms are otherwise upheld (Marshall 1998, 5). Such cases of persecution may occur, for example, if a state does not systematically prohibit the gathering of believers for worship, but arbitrarily disrupts them (harassment). Additionally, religious minorities may have the right to live and assemble in certain countries, but may still face civic or economic disadvantages as members of their minority faith (discrimination).

In light of these additional details, *religious* persecution should be defined as:

> An unjust action of varying levels of hostility directed at *a believer or believers of a particular religion or belief system through systematic oppression or through irregular harassment or discrimination which may not necessarily limit these believers' ability to practice their faith,* resulting in varying levels of harm as it is considered from the victim's perspective, *each action having religion as its primary motivator.*

## UNDERSTANDING RELIGIOUS PERSECUTION OF CHRISTIANS THEOLOGICALLY

Of course, Christians are not the only religious victims who are persecuted for their beliefs. Muslims in India are persecuted by radical Hindu groups. Baha'i communities are religiously persecuted in Iran. Tibetan Buddhists and Muslim Uighurs are persecuted in China (Marshall 2004–2005, 27). Other examples abound. Without mitigating the persecution of non-Christians and without suggesting that religious persecution is only a Christian interest (Blunt 2005, 54; El-Hage 2000, 3–19), we cannot describe the experience of Christians simply by referring to "religious persecution." Clearly, "Christian" must be added to most accurately describe the type of persecution on which the present study focuses.

Even more, we must understand "Christian" to mean "one who believes in, or professes or confesses Jesus Christ as Lord and Savior, or assumed to believe in Jesus Christ" (Barrett, Kurian, and Johnson 2001, 655). This comprises "Christians of all kinds" ("census Christians," including all types of Christians; e.g., Protestants, Anglicans, Roman Catholics, Orthodox), "affiliated Christians" ("member Christians"), "church attenders" ("practicing Christians"), and "Great Commission Christians" ("committed believers") (2001, 655, 651, 655, 662; Marshall 1998, 4). Of course, the level of one's Christian commitment may, in certain cases, determine their experience of persecution. For example, someone less willing to publicly profess Christ may, as a result, avoid certain kinds of persecution. What must be noted here, however, is the significance of a broad understanding of "Christian." Such an understanding is important to our definition because the relative absence of Christian commitment should not disqualify an experience of religious persecution. Neither should the presence of great commitment necessarily glorify or substantiate an experience of religious persecution.

It is of utmost importance to distinguish our understanding of the religious persecution of Christians theologically (Boyd-MacMillan 2006, 85ff.). In this, we cannot dismiss sociopolitical definitions like those described above. They are indispensable because they offer a concrete way of resisting easily identifiable and observable cases of religious persecution and advocating for religious freedoms in contexts where they are not upheld or simply violated. This is important to both the church and the international community.

Even so, a theological understanding of the religious persecution of Christians goes further, for it demands more of the church. A theological definition of the religious persecution of Christians distinguishes itself, in part, on a theological expectation of the event. This expectation is a biblical principle whereby all those who choose to follow Christ must anticipate persecution (Matt 5:11–12, 10:22; John 15:20; 2 Tim 3:12; 1 Pet 4:12). Biblical statements by Christ or his apostles that tell us to expect certain consequences for our faith are only accounted for in a theological definition because such an understanding considers aspects of persecution that sociopolitical definitions do not. Ridicule, for example, does not demand a response from the international community. Actions like this, however, are dealt to Christians as a result of their choice to follow Christ. In this theological sense, they are also religious persecution even though they do not violate international standards or represent systematic violations of religious freedoms. As a result, the church must reflect upon them as persecution so that it might appropriately respond to them as such.

> Then they will deliver you up to tribulation and put you to death, and you will be hated by all nations for my name's sake. *Matthew 24:9*

To illustrate this important point, consider the example of a young man who converts from the religion of his parents and family heritage to Christianity (Marshall 2000b, 16). After converting, his parents ostracize him from the community and disinherit him from his family. Considered from a sociopolitical perspective, however damaging such actions may be, they do not constitute religious persecution. The same might be said concerning a school girl who is ridiculed by classmates for being a Christian. According to international standards, such rights are allowed to be exercised, unless they are followed by subsequent physical attack. However, considered theologically, such actions come as a part of an expected consequence of following Christ. In this way, they do constitute persecution. This theological reality may not necessitate a reaction from the international community. It does, however, require a response from the church, perhaps not directed at the persecutors, but at least in support of the Christian victims.

To this end, the religious persecution of *Christians* can be theologically defined as ("expanded definition"):

> Any unjust action of mild to intense levels of hostility, *directed at Christians of varying levels of commitment,* resulting in varying levels of harm, which may or may not necessarily prevent or limit *these Christians'* ability to practice their faith or appropriately propagate their faith as it is considered from the victim's perspective, each motivation having religion, *namely the identification of its victims as "Christian,"* as its primary motivator.

For purposes of brevity, a "standard definition" understands the religious persecution of Christians to be:

> Any unjust action of varying levels of hostility perpetrated primarily on the basis of religion and directed at Christians, resulting in varying levels of harm as it is considered from the victim's perspective.

The advantage of this definition lies in that it is not limited by any epoch of church history or restricted to any one part of the world. Neither is it determined by the extent of violence, animosity, or damage that it causes. It does not limit the experience based on Christian commitment, and it recognizes the multiple factors and motivations present in persecution, acknowledging that it often occurs in situations of great complexity.

Furthermore, this definition has important ramifications because it recognizes that a consequence for following Christ is not determined by how violent the action is. In fact, it may be limited to ridicule or discrimination just as it may be extended to systematic or intense violence. Thus, one cannot ask *why* persecution seemingly does not occur in certain areas or to certain Christians. Rather, we must ask *how* indeed it does occur, for the presence of persecution, theologically speaking, is universal even if the experience of it may depend on context (Tieszen 2008, 51–55).

## CONCLUSION

With few notable exceptions, it seems that the current state of theological reflection on persecution suffers from malformed definitions of the event. By reconsidering a definition of religious persecution and offering the proposal above, we hope to correct the limitations of previous understandings and provide a stronger foundation for more robust theological reflection.

It is perhaps most important, in closing, to restate the necessary care required in placing religious persecution—intense and frequent for many, mild and infrequent for others—in the context of theological expectation and a spectrum of hostility. In doing so, we in no way wish to cheapen or glorify the experience of those most intimately familiar with the event. Neither do we want to deny the experience of Christians whose connections to persecution may be less familiar. Even so, we must recognize that those who might be best able to reflect theologically on religious persecution and fill in the gaps left by so many studies may be the Majority World Christians who are often most closely connected with persecution. It is frequently the case that Christians in this position are unable or, understandably, unwilling to give reflection to their painful experiences. May this study stimulate their reflection and bolster their endurance. May it help those whose experience of persecution is less frequent to give more attention, prayer, and support to those enduring it most. Finally, may our experiences and triumphs over persecution draw the global church closer together until that time when Christ makes it complete.

## QUESTIONS FOR REFLECTION

1.  In what ways do you experience religious persecution—be it frequent, infrequent, mild, or intense—where you live?
2.  How can you connect with Christians in other areas of the world in order to share experiences and support one another?
3.  How can your Christian community become a better advocate for religiously persecuted Christians worldwide?
4.  In what ways does the definition offered in this study challenge or support the ways you think (theologically or otherwise) about the religious persecution of Christians? What does it mean with respect to non-Christians?

## REFERENCES

Barrett, D. B., G. T. Kurian, and T. M. Johnson. 2001. *World Christian encyclopedia*, vol. 2, 2nd ed. Nairobi: Oxford University Press.

Blunt, S. H. 2005. The Daniel of religious rights. *Christianity Today* 49, no. 9: (September): 53–58.

Boyd-MacMillan, R. 2006. *Faith that endures: The essential guide to the persecuted church.* Grand Rapids: Revell.

El-Hage, Y. K. 2004. Human rights: A Western, Christian invention? *The Near Eastern School of Theology Theological Review* 25, no. 2, (November): 3–19.

Kuzmič, P. 2004–2005. To suffer with our Lord: Christian responses to religious persecution. *The Brandywine Review of Faith and International Affairs* 2, no. 3 (Winter): 35–42.

Marshall, P. 1998. Persecution of Christians in the contemporary world. *International Bulletin of Missionary Research* 22, no. 1 (January): 2–8.

———. 2000a. Present day persecution of Christians. *Evangelical Review of Theology* 24, no. 1 (January): 19–30.

———, ed. 2000b. *Religious freedom in the world: A global report on freedom and persecution.* Nashville: Broadman and Holman.

———. 2004–2005. Patterns and contexts of religious freedom and persecution. *The Brandywine Review of Faith and International Affairs* 2, no. 3 (Winter): 27–33.

Schirrmacher, T. 2001. *The persecution of Christians concerns us all.* Bonn: idea/VKW.

Stott, J. 1975. *The Lausanne Covenant: Exposition and commentary.* Minneapolis: World Wide Publications.

Tieszen, C. L. 2008. *Re-examining religious persecution: Constructing a theological framework for understanding persecution.* Kempton Park, South Africa: AcadSA Publishing; Bonn: VKW.

**Charles L. Tieszen** completed his doctoral work in Islam and Christian-Muslim relations at the University of Birmingham, UK. He has written extensively on matters of religious freedom, including *Re-Examining Religious Persecution: Constructing a Theological Framework for Understanding Persecution* (AcadSA Publishing, 2008). He is currently a researcher living with his wife, Sarah, and son, Brahm, in California, USA.

Suffering and rejection are laid upon Jesus as a divine necessity, and every attempt to prevent it is the work of the devil, especially when it comes from his own disciples; for it is in fact an attempt to prevent Christ from being Christ. It is Peter, the Rock of the Church, who commits that sin, immediately after he has confessed Jesus as the Messiah and has been appointed to the primacy. That shows how the very notion of a suffering Messiah was a scandal to the Church, even in the earliest days. That is not the kind of Lord it wants, and as the Church of Christ it does not like to have the law of suffering imposed upon it by its Lord. Peter's protest displays his own unwillingness to suffer, and that means that Satan has gained entry into the Church, and is trying to tear it away from the cross of its Lord.

D. Bonhoeffer in *The Cost of Discipleship* (1976, 96)

## THE LOVE OF CHRIST CALLS US TO SUFFER AND SOMETIMES TO DIE FOR THE GOSPEL

Suffering may be necessary in our missionary engagement as witnesses to Christ, as it was for his apostles and the Old Testament prophets.[69] Being willing to suffer is an acid test for the genuineness of our mission. God can use suffering, persecution and martyrdom to advance his mission. "Martyrdom is a form of witness which Christ has promised especially to honour."[70] Many Christians living in comfort and prosperity need to hear again the call of Christ to be willing to suffer for him. For many other believers live in the midst of such suffering as the cost of bearing witness to Jesus Christ in a hostile religious culture. They may have seen loved ones martyred, or endured torture or persecution because of their faithful obedience, yet continue to love those who have so harmed them.

A) We hear and remember with tears and prayer the testimonies of those who suffer for the gospel. We pray for grace and courage, along with them, to "love our enemies" as Christ commanded us. We pray that the gospel may bear fruit in places that are so hostile to its messengers. As we rightly grieve for those who suffer, we remember the infinite grief God feels over those who resist and reject his love, his gospel and his servants. We long for them to repent and be forgiven and find the joy of being reconciled to God.

[69] 2 Corinthians 12:9–10; 4:7–10
[70] The Manila Manifesto, 12.

*Cape Town Commitment, Part II, Section iii. Living the love of Christ among people of other faiths, Paragraph 2*

# CHAPTER 7

# PERSECUTION, MARTYRDOM, AND MISSION

## The Improbable Partners?

*David Tai Woong Lee*

When I was first approached to write this chapter on persecution and mission some time ago, I had numerous reasons to say no. Let me spell out a few major ones. First, after reading through Philip Jenkins' book *The Lost History of Christianity*, suffering and martyrdom took on new meaning for me; it bothered and disturbed me greatly. Because the suffering and martyrdom that he described are of such magnitude, all other suffering, my own included, seems insignificant and not worth mentioning. Second, as is the case with Jenkins' book (despite that he has done a marvelous job making sense of such diversity of incidents and widespread history), it is very difficult to draw universal lessons or principles to which we all would consent. Finally, I have two mingled thoughts; one is the fear of reliving my own trauma. Come to think of it, I have not had any real personal debriefing, although for more than half a century I have been affected by it, both consciously and unconsciously. The other thought is that my experience is so personal that it can hardly be significant to others who were not in my shoes. Nonetheless, I am about to tell my story, and hope that in some small way it will contribute to our understanding of what we shall only finally and fully understand in eternity.

## MY PERSONAL STORY

When the Korean War broke out in 1950, I was ten years old. A stroke had paralyzed my dad's legs and he was unable to walk. We were left behind the invading force twice, experiencing first the North Korean regime for three months and subsequently the occupation by the combined forces of the North Korean and Chinese armies. This lasted until United Nations troops and South Korean soldiers reoccupied the southern half of the peninsula. The painful armed truce resulted in what is now close to sixty years of division by 155 miles of the demilitarized zone (DMZ)—a strip of land (2 km on both sides, totaling 4 km) dividing North and South Korea. Through this war more than 10 million people were permanently displaced and separated from their loved ones, 3 million died; another 3.7 million became refugees; 20,000 lost their spouses; 32,838 were declared prisoners of war; with another 84,532 people taken to North Korea by force. The war left 10,000 orphans. The UN casualties were also heavy—178,569 lost their lives, including 54,000 American soldiers.

The whole city of Seoul burned over and over, lighting up the entire sky at night for a long period. The city was literally cremated. Nothing was left sound; all turned into rubble and ruin. There was no food, no running water, no medicine, no system whatsoever left to sustain lives.

Terror, hunger, and sickness from both wounds and disease reigned in those days. Corpses were found in almost every village. Uncovered mass graves were not uncommon; North Korean troops (most probably South Korean soldiers did the same thing to North Koreans) shot and killed large numbers indiscriminately as they retreated. At the time, Christian churches were mostly concentrated in North Korea. Thousands of Christian leaders, both pastors and lay leaders, were killed, though many escaped to South Korea along with their members.

Let me focus on my personal experiences. I mention two things in particular, as they had a profound effect on me. One is the suffering associated with fear and the other is the pain of hunger. Both are part of the struggle for survival. I still remember vividly how fearful it was when the allied troops abandoned Seoul for the second time; again the whole city was in flames. There was a flour company known as "Hai-Tae" (해태) some ten kilometers away from where I lived. My mother took me to this company, now on fire, to get a sack of flour. I remember crying and screaming over and over because of terror. I begged my mom not to drag me into the burning fire, and said: "Please don't kill me!" The red-hot flames reminded me of hell and it was if she was trying to pull me right into it. The flour that we took then sustained our family through many days, along with a bit of grain we were able to retrieve from digging into the horse dung at the village stables that were used by the Chinese soldiers. We would mix chaff and bits of grain and a small amount of flour together; we had just enough to keep us alive. On another day, a Chinese soldier came into our small room and sat there many hours demanding that we give him food. He could have shot us then as he had a rifle in his hand at all times. These two incidents are symbolic of the suffering we were going through then.

For my parents, the fact that their oldest son was taken captive to the North when the North Korean troops retreated was the most devastating thing that happened to them during the war. Tai Jin was about the age of sixteen or seventeen when he was separated from our family. For sixty years we have not heard anything from him. My mother wept secretly in her bed for more than twenty years for her son. He is one of the 10 million people who were violently separated from their loved ones.

Even after the war ended, the suffering for survival did not end for several decades. It was not until the 1980s that we were able to have a decent life and food to eat in our nation. Prior to that period we would go through "barley hill" (보리고개) each year when the rice crop had run out, and have to rely only on the barley crop. I remember that my mother went without lunch for many years.

The Korean War has had a devastating effect on the whole nation morally, culturally, and spiritually. The Korean people were once known as "The People of White Cloths" (백의의 민족). It was probably due to the influence of Confucianism that Korea's strict moral system was intact for close to two millennia. One writer said that "Koreans have grasped Confucianism more thoroughly than the country of its origin." After the war, the moral system that once held the society together was gone. It took a long time to reinstate a new moral system after that war. The war literally destroyed our culture as well; it took almost half a century to arrive at where we are now, the modern Korea people know today. Only recently have we finally become confident of our culture as an integrated and fully functioning system.

## EFFECT OF THE KOREAN WAR ON CHRISTIAN MISSION AND CHURCH AND MY PERSONAL GROWTH

When Christianity first came to Korea in the nineteenth century, there was a spiritual vacuum. Buddhism had lost its power by the fourteenth century when the Chosen Dynasty was founded because of widespread corruption. As a result, the founding political philosophy of the Chosen Dynasty became Confucianism. By the nineteenth century when Christianity came to Korea, Confucianism was also bankrupt due to continuous bitter fighting among rival camps. This is altogether a different situation from the context the Nestorians found themselves in the Middle East and Central Asia. Philip Jenkins speaks of this in his discussion of the fate of Eastern Christianity that had to face continuous persecution under Muslim strong warlords.

Significantly, the state of Christianity in North Korea during the last sixty years under the Communist regime could be a parallel to the cases that Jenkins mentions. The North Korean Communist Party identified all Christians and either executed them (especially if the person was in leadership, such as a pastor) or sent them to the political prisons where many died from the harsh living conditions or torture because they didn't recant their faith. For more than a half century, North Korean leaders have tried to wipe out all signs of Christianity and replace it with the deified worship of Kim Il-Sung, their first ruler. The brainwashing began from childhood; children were ordered to spy on the older generations who might have embraced Christianity. The regime succeeded so thoroughly that children even reported their own parents for signs of apostasy. If North Korea opens up more, we will determine how successful they were in exterminating Christianity in that land. One thing is certain, though. If this trend continues for another generation, it could well accomplish what the Communist regime had intended. Fortunately, even the North Korean regime cannot shut the hearts of the people, especially with South Koreans praying and doing all they can to reevangelize North Korea.

Meanwhile, the South Korean situation changed drastically as a result of the suffering and pain of the war. At one time, the North was evangelized and the South was unreached; after the war, due to an influx of Christians from the North, the South was suddenly evangelized. Let me give several cases where persecution and suffering has resulted in mission and exploding church growth.

## THE CASE OF THE FULL GOSPEL CHURCH

In the 1950s, Koreans were in despair, without the basic necessities for survival, and in the midst of the rubble and ruins of the war. The greater tragedy was the wounds and scars inflicted on their hearts and minds and the lack of hope for their future and their children's future. Dr. Young-Ki Cho's message of the "triple blessing"—the blessing of healed bodies, the blessing of healed hearts, and the blessing of material well-being—landed like a bombshell of hope on the Korean people. Thousands and thousands flocked to hear the message and received literal miraculous healings. Some may criticize that message for being prosperity oriented. As an insider, it is possible to see things differently. The only qualms that I might have would be that the Full Gospel camp did not contextualize their message to take them to the next in-depth phase in the maturing process by mentioning the inevitability of suffering, persecution, and martyrdom accompanying the mission of God.

## YOUNG-NAK PRESBYTERIAN CHURCH

North Korean Christians of Presbyterian roots were forced to abandon their home regions, landed in South Korea, and met in their newfound city of Seoul. Thousands flocked together to worship and share news of their beloved ones who were either left behind or lost among the crowds of refugees. In no time at all, this body became the world's largest Presbyterian church. This community did a tremendous amount of evangelism and social work. Quickly, similar churches sprung up all over South Korea.

These two church case studies are not coincidental. In fact they became like the churches in the book of Acts, in which a persecuted people's movement became a missional movement. South Korea is now close to 30 percent Christian (this figure includes Roman Catholics). The Protestant Church alone sends out more than 20,000 missionaries to some 177 countries, and the number being sent out is still growing. There are now around 100,000 Christian full-time workers and pastors within South Korea. There are approximately 6 million diaspora Koreans all over the world along with 5,500 diaspora churches in 175 countries.

> Jesus said, "Truly, I say to you, there is no one who has left house or brothers or sisters or mother or father or children or lands, for my sake and for the gospel, who will not receive a hundredfold now in this time, houses and brothers and sisters and mothers and children and lands, with persecutions, and in the age to come eternal life. But many who are first will be last, and the last first." *Mark 10:29–31*

Interestingly, everywhere Koreans go, they plant churches. First they plant Korean ethnic churches and then move on to become a center for mission to the people group around them. Where do they get this church-planting strategy? Most of all, where do they get their energy and stamina? There is a popular catch phrase in New York among Korean immigrants: "blood and sweat" (피와 땀). It means they work hard and are not afraid to suffer for their cause. This kind of spirit has been prevalent since the Korean War and continues in current diaspora movements, both in mission and in secular work. How could we not connect this kind of spirit to the suffering and persecution that they and their immediate ancestors experienced while the majority of the current younger generation have looked on? Korean missionaries over the past thirty years have gone out with this kind of mind-set which was formed and trained in an actual life situation of suffering and persecution.

## MY PERSONAL JOURNEY

I became a Christian on February 24, 1962; my country was still in ruins and barely making a living. We were economically lagging behind even North Korea at the time. Meanwhile, I was already trained to live in tough situations. At the age of ten, when the Korean War broke out, I began to earn bread for the whole family, doing literally anything that I could to earn enough to feed my family. I shined shoes, sold cigarettes, became a house boy for the GIs, which included carrying five-gallon cans of hot water on my tiny shoulders for them to wash every morning, making all the beds, polishing all their shoes, and cleaning the barracks that I was assigned to. By nights I began to go to school to earn a junior high school education. By the time I reached my sophomore year in university, I became a Christian through the ministry of the indigenous student mission movement known as JOY Mission. I was only twenty-two. Before I was thirty, I was the leader of that movement and began to prepare hundreds of young people for mission. When I look back, without the tough training that I received through suffering and persecution and war, could I have done what I did in those times? I wonder.

## CONCLUSION

Is there a direct relationship between suffering, persecution, martyrdom, and mission? I honestly cannot say yes, as much as I want to do so. Vice versa, is there no direct relationship between these two? Again I must withhold my answer. In the case of South Korea, I must say on the whole that suffering, martyrdom, and persecution resulted positively for mission. Can we say the same for North Korea? It is too soon to make any definitive evaluation, but for the time being, I am afraid that I must answer in the negative. If it has helped any cause for mission, it is accidental; it helped by pushing out their Christian population to South Korea where those who had training in suffering and persecution lay the foundation for the future missionary movement as well as the evangelization of the rest of Korea. As for me personally, I continue to draw lessons and energy from the hardships that I went through in the past.

So I leave it up to you to decide how true it is to say that persecution, martyrdom, and mission are the improbable partners.

## QUESTIONS FOR REFLECTION

1. Think about the personal suffering of Dr. Lee as well as that of his family. How did this hardship and his coming to Christ as a young man influence his life and make him ready for suffering in mission?

2. How did the great suffering and hardships of the Korean people and church influence their church growth and mission expansion? What kind of influence would this have on their present generation?

3. What can we learn from this very dramatic life story? How can we become more sensitive to share with and comfort those going through very hard times today? What does it mean in terms of mission challenges for us today?

**David Tai Woong Lee** has been training Korean cross-cultural missionaries for the past twenty-five years. He is the founding director of the Global Missionary Training Center and the former chairman of the WEA Mission Commission (1994–2002). His MDiv and DMiss are from Trinity Seminary. He is currently the director of the Global Leadership Focus.

The cross means sharing the suffering of Christ to the last and to the fullest. Only a man thus totally committed in discipleship can experience the meaning of the cross. The cross is there, right from the beginning, he has only got to pick it up; there is no need for him to go out and look for a cross for himself, no need for him deliberately to run after suffering. Jesus says that every Christian has his own cross waiting for him, a cross destined and appointed by God. Each must endure his allotted share of suffering and rejection. But each has a different share: some God deems worthy of the highest form of suffering, and gives them the grace of martyrdom, while others he does not allow to be tempted above what they are able to bear. But it is the one and the same cross in every case.

D. Bonhoeffer in *The Cost of Discipleship* (1976, 98–99)

# PART TWO

# REFLECTIONS FROM SCRIPTURE AND THEOLOGY

## BRIEF THOUGHTS ON THE BOOK OF REVELATION

And now, good reader, engage with our writers as they speak to you with insightful reflections from theology, Scripture, and culture. Ponder the challenges of the "prosperity gospel," the place that persecution has in the context of world evangelization, the examples of Paul and Peter, the comparison of African and Western perspectives on persecution, and rejoice in the visions of Revelation.

Again, I am deeply moved when I consider that 99.4 percent of Scripture was written either from or into contexts of uncertainty, violence, exile, poverty, and weakness. That places a unique lens, a "new but normal hermeneutic" before our eyes as we approach and read the Bible. It is in these historical and political realities that the people of God were to set their roots; build families, communities, and culture, bless the nations; and protect and steward creation wisely. There they were to demonstrate transformational discipleship as both the gathered (the local church) and the scattered (the church on mission) followers of Jesus the Christ.

It does not mean that those who live in contexts of peace, prosperity, power, and influence cannot interpret the text correctly. But it does mean that we need the historical and the fully global contemporary church to understand what the Holy Spirit intended as he supervised the writing of Scripture in those contexts.

We are grateful to Margaretha Adiwardana's salient insights into the book of Revelation. God is the absolute ruler who is in control of history. Nothing misses his sight and insight. And his people, both church invisible and local, throughout history have constantly faced the realities of suffering and violence, persecution, and even martyrdom. These realities come from a variety of sources but ultimately they are energized by demonic forces. Revelation is penned towards the end of Domitian's reign and is full of "portents and prototypes of present pressures and coming traumas in the world's assault on Christ's church" (*ESV Study Bible,* Crossway, 2008, 2453).

Years ago I began using Revelation as cornerstone to a course I have taught on the themes of this volume at Trinity Evangelical Divinity School, Wheaton Graduate School, and the Escuela Superior de Estudios Pastorales in Costa Rica. It is the core of countless sermons of mine. But it was an African student at TEDS years ago who became my teacher. I had asked the class to read Revelation in one sitting, assuming they were first-century believers either listening to or reading the manuscript which the old apostle, prophet, pastor, poet, and seer had smuggled out of his island prison. What would it have meant to those believers to have heard the words of the sage pastor? My African student the next morning exclaimed in class, "Dr. Taylor, this book is written in a code, and only Christians could have broken the code!" It was an illuminating piece of insight, and so true.

## WORSHIP AND THE MARTYR'S PROTEST

I comment on only two themes which have shaped me: worship and the martyr's protest. Depending on how you determine what this adoration looks like, I find some seventeen worship scenes in Revelation. They range from small streams all the way to massive cataracts beyond the marvels of Iguassu, Victoria, and Niagara. They come from just a few voices to the countless myriads; from four strange and marvelous creatures to the twenty-four elders; from angels and all creation; from all peoples, tribes, nations, and languages and to their combinations. What an incredible splendor of sound, color, creativity, reckless abandon, rich diversity!

Revelation and worship: 4:8–9; 4:10–11; 5:8–10; 5:11–12; 5:13–14; 7:9–10; 7:11–12; 11:15; 11:16–19; 12:10–12; 14:2–3; 15:1–4; 16:5–7; 19:1–3; 19:4; 19:5; 19:6–8

There is no room to comment on these passages, but let me suggest you read them, study them, mull them over and allow them to enrich and transform you.

Listen to the martyrs' protest:
> When he opened the fifth seal, I saw under the altar the souls of those who had been slain for the word of God and for the witness they had borne. They cried out with a loud voice, "O Sovereign Lord, holy and true, how long before you will judge and avenge our blood on those who dwell on the earth?" Then they were each given a white robe and told to rest a little longer, until the number of their fellow servants and their brothers should be complete, who were to be killed as they themselves had been. (6:9–11)

Discover the identity of this multitude that vehemently cries out:
> After this I looked, and behold, a great multitude that no one could number, from every nation, from all tribes and peoples and languages, standing before the throne and before the Lamb, clothed in white robes, with palm branches in their hands, and crying out with a loud voice, "Salvation belongs to our God who sits on the throne, and to the Lamb!" (7:9–10)

Imagine what it would have been to have heard these cries and know, "These are the ones coming out of the great tribulation. They have washed their robes and made them white in the blood of the Lamb" (7:14).

This is the shaking Word of the Lord! —*William D. Taylor*

# CHAPTER 8

# DELIVER US FROM EVIL

## Biblical-theological Reflections

*Rose Dowsett*

*Hand cut off ... killed by bomb under his car ... detained without trial and left in metal container till he died ... gang raped for being Christian ... church burnt down ... taken by armed gang and not seen since ... not allowed to register children in school or themselves for work ... Bibles destroyed ... shot in the head as he left prayer meeting ... children abducted for forcible conversion to majority faith....*

Reports such as these, well documented, are not tales from the distant past. They are all current and can be replicated over and over again. They come from all over the world, too, though overwhelmingly from Africa, Asia, and the Middle East. Europe and America produce their own chilling stories. For these our brothers and sisters, suffering, persecution, and even martyrdom are no abstract theories to be debated, but the immediate context within which every day they must bear witness to the Lord Jesus Christ.

*It's a normal Sunday morning in London. A service of one of the largest congregations in Europe is in full swing. Several thousand people, mostly African and Afro-Caribbean, listen enthralled as the senior pastor thunders out his message. "Bring your offerings! Make them big! Empty your pockets! If you give and give and give, then the Lord promises you that you will be rich, that you and your kids won't get sick, that you'll be driving a big car.... Give, and God will reward you a hundredfold!" The auditorium rings with "Praise the Lord!" and "Hallelujah!" and "Yes, Lord!" The stewards stagger under the weight of the money collected, though most of those present are, in fact, in very poorly paid jobs, or unemployed, or migrants and asylum seekers. Many of them have experienced the violence of war, rape, famine, or forced displacement from their ancestral lands. Many are HIV positive, or already have full-blown AIDS. Their stories are painful. "The pastor's message gives me hope," says one young man. "Jesus is going to deliver me from all my problems!"*

On the one hand, there is persecution, martyrdom, and great suffering; not simply the suffering that is endemic in a fallen, groaning world, but specifically suffering that is a direct consequence of faithful Christian discipleship. On the other hand, there are parts of the church which teach that God's promised *shalom* encompasses the here and now in such a way as to ensure health, wealth, and safety for any Christian walking in his will; to miss out on these things is evidence of lack of faith and obedience.

The fact is that there are vibrant believers who can be found in both these categories (and of course there are many between these poles). It is not easy to harmonize these very different beliefs and experiences. There are committed Christians who prosper (in every sense of the word), and there are committed Christians whose lives are lived entirely within the boundaries of acute poverty, chronic sickness, and unjust suffering.

## THE TEACHING OF JESUS

It is true that Jesus healed many sick people and that he expected his disciples also to be able to cast out demons and heal the sick as signs of the Kingdom (see, for instance, Mark 16:15–18). It is also true that in Matthew 6:28–34 Jesus links faith with provision of food and clothes: "Seek first [God's] kingdom and his righteousness, and all these things will be given to you as well" (Matt 6:33).

Yet a far stronger thread in Jesus' teaching is of a more sombre character. He insists that persecution will be inescapable for his disciples: "All men will hate you because of me.… When you are persecuted in one place, flee to another" (Matt 10:22–23). Or again, "They will lay hands on you and persecute you. They will deliver you to synagogues and prisons, and you will be brought before kings and governors, and all on account of my name. This will result in your being witnesses to them" (Luke 21:12–13). In both these instances, persecution and suffering are directly linked to testimony to unbelievers.

Even more fundamental, and integral to authentic discipleship, is the command to "take up your cross and follow me" (Matt 16:24); that is, identifying with, and sharing the experience of, the shame and unjust condemnation and suffering of the Lord in his death at Calvary is absolutely central to being a Christian.

## THE EXAMPLE OF JESUS

It is no accident that one of the most powerful messianic prophecies, found in Isaiah 52:13–53:12, is entitled, "The suffering and glory of the servant." Suffering and glory are inextricably intertwined. Today we are able to see that every last detail of that prophecy was fulfilled in his life, death, and resurrection. The Son of God did not come in wealth and power and earthly triumph, but in weakness, rejection, and suffering. "Light has come into the world, but men loved darkness instead of light because their deeds were evil. Everyone who does evil hates the light," says Jesus (John 3:19–20). The more his light shone, the greater the hatred of his enemies, and the more committed they became to destroy him.

Well, says Paul, the one who "was rich beyond all splendor" chose "all for love's sake" to embrace poverty and powerlessness and to submit to a cruel death; "Your attitude should be the same" (Phil 2:5–11). At the very heart of our faith is sacrifice, supremely of the "Lamb of God who takes away the sin of the world." Followers of Christ must also, in response to and imitation of that once-for-all perfect and complete sacrifice, voluntarily live in a mindset and practice of sacrifice, offering up our lives in the mundane and the extraordinary, in the love of God, and in service of our fellow human beings. If that leads to the literal laying down of our lives, so be it.

# THE EXPERIENCE OF THE CHURCH

Very soon after Pentecost, the first Christians entered the furnace of persecution. Stephen was the first among many who gave their lives as martyrs (Acts 7:54ff.), but already others had been beaten and suffered for bold witness to the identity of Jesus and to the significance of his death and resurrection. After Stephen's death, the whole of Acts has the recurrent motif of the persecution that disciples experienced wherever they went. It was consistent rather than sporadic, though not continuous in any one place. The Epistles, especially those of Peter, refer frequently to the prevalence and depth of suffering for the name of Christ. We know that many of Jesus' closest earthly friends died as martyrs. There must have been many more, names unknown to us but recorded in the Lamb's book of life.

> God did not spare his own Son; he also does not spare us; God's children must suffer, but eternal communion with God and with Christ awaits them, a glory in comparison with which all the sufferings of this time are nothing (Rom 8:17).
>
> D. Bonhoeffer in "Examenklausur: Wie urteilt Paulus über die irdischen Leben?" (1992, 356)

The first centuries rapidly produced a long list of those who died bravely because they refused to recant their faith or to give to Caesar the honor which belonged alone to Christ. Eyewitness accounts circulated—for instance, of the torture and death of the saintly old bishop Polycarp, of the martyrdom of the young mother Perpetua and her slave girl Felicitas—and these testimonies inspired many contemporaries and others down through the centuries to stand fast even in the face of diabolical treatment and finally death in the cruellest ways imaginable.

It was not always quite like that. There were many, too, who could not face the suffering, and turned away from Christ. That, too, has been the pattern down through the centuries. At times, as Tertullian wrote, "the blood of the martyrs is seed," and the harvest was many who came to faith. At other times, in the face of persecution the Christians became divided among themselves, or compromised, or returned to their old religions.

In the twenty centuries of the church, and wherever the gospel has been taken, there has been a similar story: hostility and violence against those who have brought the faith, and yet some whose hearts have been opened by the Holy Spirit and who have become believers; a beachhead for the gospel—the ebbing and flowing of faith. There are very few places indeed where the gospel has come to a people group without resistance or without messengers and early converts suffering. Some church traditions, especially the ancient churches, commemorate many of those who have suffered or died in the cause of the gospel as "saints," so that the annual calendar reminds their people over and over again of the cost of faithful witness to Christ.

# THE SUBVERSION BY CHRISTENDOM—AND THE NEW REALITY

When Constantine in the early fourth century fatefully adopted Christianity as the protected religion of the Roman Empire, the church became seduced by power, wealth, and ease. There were of course always those who retained their prophetic voices, and especially those pioneering at the frontiers who continued to lay down their lives. But from then onwards it became increasingly easy for Christians, of whichever tradition, to expect protection from the state from persecution. All too often, the example of the church was not that of sacrifice but that of protecting its own interests. It was a short step to sanctioning violence to achieve or maintain dominance in the name of the Christian faith.

For most of its history, the church expanded territorially by wielding power rather than righteousness, on the back of political empires. Yet, in the sovereignty of God, imperialism itself has always been an ambiguous phenomenon, and there is plenty of biblical testimony to God's willingness to shape and use even wicked empires for his own purposes of grace or judgment. So, especially when we look at the modern missionary movement of the past two hundred years, there have been pluses as well as minuses, as empires have opened up by force or commerce parts of the world previously untouched by the Christian faith. Further, the motives of huge numbers of missionaries are beyond dispute: they did not cross the world in the cause of empire, but genuinely in the cause of the gospel. In some cases, as in India, it was for a long time with Western power pitted against them, not enabling them. In other cases, as in China in relation to the opium trade, it was missionaries who led the fight against their own governments' appalling policy and practice. Large numbers sacrificed their lives, through illness or violence. Many suffered rejection by their own families "back home." Untold numbers buried their children in foreign soil.

Many of the churches of the Global South thus have an ambiguous heritage. On the one hand, there may have been a point in the past where Christianity sheltered under some foreign political power, or indeed may have become entwined with national political power. On the other hand, Christians have often been at the forefront of prophetic protest against the corruption of power within and beyond the church, and have suffered and given their lives as a result. Today, a growing percentage of Global South churches have no connection with past imperial powers, but have developed independently. Sadly, they do not necessarily dissociate from worldly power and patterns of leadership spawned by Christendom rather than flowing from biblical revelation. We all (not just Northerners!) struggle with fallenness.

Now, in the early years of the twenty-first century, the Northern churches, especially those of Europe, are discovering all over again what it means to live without state protection. Indeed, with secular humanism as the default position for European governments, administered with varying degrees of aggression, Christians in many European countries face persecution for their faith in a way that is more akin to the pre-Constantinian church than anything that has happened since. It is not likely that Europe will return to the bitter, bloody wars between rival sectors of the church that followed the Reformation, but increasingly European Christians will find themselves having to choose between following Christ and keeping the law. It has been suggested that in Europe evangelical Christians are the least protected religious community of all, with their so-called human rights and conscientious convictions consistently overruled by those of other groups. Once again, like the early Christians, we will face starkly the question: "Are you willing to suffer, and if need be go to prison or even die, in faithfulness to Christ?" And, in the face of injustice and suffering, how will we respond? Seeking to retaliate, insisting on our rights? Or, like the Lord Jesus, will we give ourselves to sacrifice rather than self-protection? Will we fight for the gospel rather than for ourselves?

# COLLISION WITH OTHER WORLD RELIGIONS

European problems, at least for the moment, are of course trivial in comparison with those of many other world situations.

The weight of the world's population lives in Asia, which is also the heartland of Hinduism, Buddhism, and Islam, as well as (today's) Communist regimes. Along with North Africa and the Middle East, the countries of Asia (apart from the Philippines) are dominated by faiths other than Christianity, and Christians are usually a small (though not necessarily insignificant) minority. In most of these contexts, Christians have always known the reality of persecution.

> But I say to you who hear, love your enemies, do good to those who hate you, bless those who curse you, pray for those who abuse you. To one who strikes you on the cheek, offer the other also, and from one who takes away your cloak do not withhold your tunic either. *Luke 6:27–29*

In some places, Christians have been able to live peaceably side by side with those of other faiths. Loving service and integrity of life have enabled genuine clear testimony to the uniqueness of Christ without leading automatically to general hostility. Nonetheless, in recent years, on the one hand, Christians have been seen as a threat to national identity (usually closed tied to the dominant religion, even in a country technically under secular administration) and, on the other hand, more militant forms of those other faiths have emerged. Few governments have the will or the ability to curtail the activities of the latter. Politicians, police, and military may all sympathize with the militants, and will do little to protect Christians even if their constitution requires it. In some countries, especially Islamic ones, conversion to Christianity (or another faith) is illegal.

It is for this reason that in some contexts, again especially in the Islamic world, Christians have been struggling with very deep and complex questions as to how they live out their faith. Christians are not called deliberately to court persecution unnecessarily. Just as the council of Jerusalem affirmed early on, led by the Holy Spirit, that Gentiles did not have to become Jews before they could become Christians, so Global South Christians are right to insist that they do not have to become European or North American in the way they express their discipleship. Faith in Jesus should not look "foreign" in a way that extracts people from their own culture without due cause. At the same time, the gospel will always be counter-cultural anywhere in the world as it collides with human fallenness and with the religions and worldviews that the Bible insists to be delusions stemming from the suppression of God's revelation (see, for instance, Paul's argument in Romans 1, or the majestic assertions of Isaiah 45:18ff.). If there is to be persecution and suffering, let it genuinely be through resistance to God's truth, not through our cultural clumsiness.

Especially difficult is the current debate as to how far believers within a very hostile environment can remain within their old religious and cultural observance in order to avoid persecution. For instance, how far along the C1–6 spectrum can believers in Jesus align and be authentic disciples? At what point do they need to be distinct from the Islam, or Judaism, Hinduism, or Buddhism, from which they come and within which culturally they are still embedded? How far is it possible to be a believer in one's heart without outward dissociation from former religious and cultural allegiance? Is it sufficient to see this as a pragmatic (and pragmatically very realistic) way of avoiding an otherwise likely martyrdom, or at the least the cost of being outcast by family and society? Some would argue that remaining an insider gives opportunity to witness to Christ and is therefore justified. Others believe that it involves a level of compromise that is not compatible with true faith.

The early church divided sharply, too, over an arguably parallel situation: whether or not, to preserve one's life, one could outwardly conform to observation of emperor worship while not worshiping him in one's heart. Far more recently, in the middle of the twentieth century, under Japanese military occupation, Korean Christians disagreed sharply over whether or not to obey edicts that they must comply with Japanese emperor worship. In China, Christians are still deeply divided over whether or not they should belong to government-sanctioned churches—the Three-Self Patriotic Movement churches—or whether authentic faith means they must belong to house churches. As it happens, Christians in both streams have experienced persecution and even martyrdom in the last half century, and that particular story has not yet ended. The divisions in the early church led to bitterness that shadowed centuries. Many Korean Christians are still not reconciled. If nothing else, this should remind us very soberly that Christians in the furnace of suffering may reach different conclusions, and that while sometimes, historically, persecution has produced a harvest of faith, at other times it has sown deep divisions and also led to defections from the faith.

No wonder that the Lord Jesus taught us to pray, "Lead us not into temptation (i.e., testing, trial), but deliver us from evil." In the face of the experienced reality of suffering of so many of God's people, the prosperity gospel looks obscene.

## CONCLUSION
The Apostle John, in his magnificent vision that we know as the book of Revelation, tells us that those who gather round the throne of the Lamb of God are those who have come through great tribulation. The final victory over sin and evil is secure. In the meantime, we need to pray for those around the world being called upon to suffer at the present time, that they may know the grace of God to be faithful. And for those of us whose experience is at present far more comfortable, pray that we may be willing to pay the cost of witnessing far more prophetically into our fallen cultures.

## QUESTIONS FOR REFLECTION
1. How would you respond to a friend who is convinced by prosperity gospel teaching?
2. In your culture, in what ways do you think Christians need to be more bravely countercultural? If they were, what might be the consequences?
3. Where persecution has caused deep and painful divisions between believers, what practical steps could be taken to bring about reconciliation?

**Rose Dowsett**, with husband, Dick, served forty years with OMF International before retirement. A Bible teacher and missiologist, as well as mother and grandmother, Rose continues to write and teach. She is vice-chair of the WEA Mission Commission and remains passionate about world mission. She lives in Scotland.

# CHAPTER 9

# FROM GENESIS TO REVELATION

## Persecution as a Central Topic of Scripture

*Wolfgang Haede*

It may be surprising for Christians in a Western context to realize that the Bible speaks about persecution and suffering[1] literally from Genesis to Revelation.[2] A great number of the books of the Bible are written in a context of suffering (e.g., Job, many of the Psalms, Jeremiah, Paul's letters from prison) or for people who face persecution (e.g., 1 Thessalonians, 1 Peter, Revelation). Of course in this essay it will only be possible to touch on a few of these many references to persecution.

## AFTER THE FALL

After Adam and Eve fell into sin, God not only announced human suffering as a punishment for sin (Gen 3:16,19); the immediate promise of a Savior who will crush the head (Gen 3:15) of the satanic serpent included an announcement of the pain the Savior would have to endure in connection with salvation: the serpent "will strike his heel." Yes, salvation would be accomplished, but for the offspring of the woman and for his people there would be a lot of pain on the way.

The first person who died in world history was a martyr: Cain killed his brother Abel because Abel was righteous (Matt 23:35) and Cain was jealous of the "better sacrifice" (Heb 11:4). When Jesus later spoke of "the blood of righteous Abel to the blood of Zechariah" (Matt 23:35; cf. Luke 11:51), he put Abel alongside the prophet Zechariah, who died for his message (2 Chr 24:20–22).

The detailed story of the righteous Job makes it very clear that suffering is not always a consequence of an individual's sin. People may suffer just because they are righteous, though the reason will not always be obvious.

---

1       Persecution is suffering for righteousness and suffering for obeying God. To show the broader picture I include some forms of sufferings in this essay which are not exactly "persecution."
2       Most of the thoughts in this essay I owe to Glenn Penner and his book *In the Shadow of the Cross: A Biblical Theology of Persecution and Discipleship* (2004). I had the privilege to translate this book into German while I was a witness of persecution in Turkey.

## THE SUFFERING PEOPLE OF GOD

When the people of Israel were oppressed and threatened with extinction in Egypt, a new aspect of persecution could be seen. The individual Israelite had to work as a slave or to watch how his or her son be killed (Ex 1), not because of what sins he or she had committed personally but just because he or she belonged to the chosen people of God.

Later the chosen king of the people of God had to live with persecution for years (1 Sam 19–31). The rejected King Saul tried to kill the anointed David.

David is the author of many of the Psalms. Some of them, even in their introductions, express the context of David's persecution (e.g., Ps 34; 52; 54; 57; 59), while the words of many others are written obviously in a context of suffering.

## PROPHETS PERSECUTED BY THEIR OWN PEOPLE

When the prophets started to call Israel back to their God and to the Law of Moses, they were persecuted because of their ministry. The prophet Jeremiah is the most striking example of God's messenger being persecuted for his message. Probably for about forty years, Jeremiah had to suffer because he was obedient to God's commission to preach his word. When he asked God for an explanation about the discrepancy between the wicked's prosperity and his own sufferings (Jer 12:1ff.), the only answer he got was that it would be even worse (Jer 12:5).

The God-given message of the prophet Isaiah added a new dimension to the question of suffering. Suffering is not only a consequence of sin or a method to discipline sinners. Suffering is not only caused by obedience to God or being a part of his people. The sufferings of the Servant of the Lord, as Isaiah announced them,[3] are God's method for bringing forgiveness and salvation: "The punishment that brought us peace was upon him" (Isa 53:5). Sufferings work salvation.

## GOD'S OWN SUFFERING

Speaking about the Suffering Servant of the Lord—Jesus Christ dying for the redemption of mankind—we may ask the question: does God suffer, even before he is incarnated in the man Jesus? Or (as philosophers would say) does suffering contradict the unchangeable nature of God?

Then they spit in his face and struck him. And some slapped him. *Matthew 26:67*

The Old Testament shows a God who could not have been forced by any outside power to suffer, but who chose to love (Penner 2004, 89), and by choosing to love took the risk of being rejected and of suffering. In the Old Testament God suffers because of rejection by men (Gen 6:6; Isa 63:10). Moreover, he suffers together with his beloved people when they are oppressed (Ex 2:24; Isa 63:9).

God suffers also when he has to punish and when he has to uproot what he has planted (Jer 45:2). That God himself suffers is a strong argument in preparing his people (e.g., Baruch, the servant of Jeremiah, Jer 45:5) not to expect an easy life for themselves.

---

3    Cf. the so-called "servant songs" in Isa 42:1–4; 49:1–6; 50:4–9,11; and especially 52:13–53:12.

## ANNOUNCEMENT OF ESCHATOLOGICAL SUFFERINGS

In the book of Daniel the Son of Man, "coming with the clouds of heaven," is given authority by God (Dan 7:13–14). Together with him "the saints of the Most High will receive the kingdom" (Dan 7:18). However, for a limited time they will be "handed over" to the beast as their persecutor (Dan 7:25). Again, we see the truth of Genesis 3:15: the way to triumph passes through trouble.

## JESUS AS THE SUFFERING SERVANT

When Jesus came as the Servant of the Lord, he was confronted with the expectations of the people waiting for a triumphant Messiah without suffering. Following the climax of Peter's confession of Jesus as "Christ, the Son of the living God" (Matt 16:16),[4] Jesus had to rebuke the same disciple with the words, "Get behind me, Satan!" (Matt 16:23), because Peter wanted to keep Jesus from the way of suffering.

Jesus spent time teaching his disciples that "he must go to Jerusalem and suffer many things" (Matt 16:21), culminating in the post-Easter lessons to his followers showing from all the Scriptures: "Did not the Christ have to suffer these things and then enter his glory?" (Luke 24:26).

> "See, we are going up to Jerusalem. And the Son of Man will be delivered over to the chief priests and scribes, and they will condemn him to death and deliver him over to the Gentiles to be mocked and flogged and crucified, and he will be raised on the third day." *Matthew 20:18–19*

## PREPARING HIS DISCIPLES FOR SUFFERING AND MARTYRDOM

Of course Jesus knew the Scriptures, like those about the "saints of the Most High" (Dan 7:18ff.) going through tribulation. As Son of God, he knew that Peter would die as a martyr (John 21:19), so he certainly knew what we learn from the early church history: probably all of the twelve disciples except Judas and John would die for confessing their faith in Jesus.

Therefore, when Jesus sent out the Twelve to preach and heal in Israel (Matt 10), preparing them for their worldwide ministry to come, a long passage in this teaching session was about persecution (10:16–42). Jesus taught mission and persecution in very close connection to each other. Suffering for ministry, directly at the hands of people, could be called persecution.

As Christians in the West, we are so accustomed to downgrade words of Jesus, in this speech and in other places, to directly apply to the challenges of daily life that *we* experience. However, when Jesus sent his friends out "like sheep among wolves" (Matt 10:16), he was aware that the wolves would seriously bite and hurt. When he encouraged his disciples saying, "Whoever loses his life for my sake will find it" (Matt 16:39), Jesus could imagine these men in front of him, literally dying as martyrs. And when he commanded each of his followers "to take up his cross and follow me" (Matt 16:24), those listening were certainly reminded of

---

4        I mostly quote from the Gospel of Matthew here. Of course, there are many parallels in the other Gospels as well.

criminals actually facing execution and they knew that Jesus did not just speak about coping with some minor hardships without getting angry with God.

## SUFFERING IN THE NEW TESTAMENT CHURCH

After they received the Holy Spirit at Pentecost, the apostles seemed to grasp what Jesus had taught them about suffering. When Peter and John faced their first serious persecution through the Sanhedrin in Jerusalem, they seemed not to be caught by surprise. Instead, they "left the Sanhedrin, rejoicing because they had been counted worthy of suffering disgrace for the Name" (Acts 5:41).

The court case against Stephen and his subsequent execution (Acts 6:9–8:1) demonstrated obvious parallels to the suffering and death of Jesus. The case of the first Christian martyr hereby set an example for the reliability of the word of Jesus: "If they persecute me, they will also persecute you" (John 15:20); and also for the validity of his promise: "The Holy Spirit will teach you at that time what you should say" (Luke 12:12).

## SUFFERING AND PAUL

On the very day of the Apostle Paul's special encounter with Jesus, the Lord said about him: "I will show him how much he must suffer for my name" (Acts 9:16). A short time after his conversion he had to flee from Damascus because of a conspiracy to kill him (Acts 9:23–25). Later in his ministry he presented a long list of his sufferings for Christ's sake to the church in Corinth (2 Cor 11:23–29).

In his apostolic ministry, Paul was an example of suffering for the new believers, and he expected them to follow this example (1 Thess 1:6–7). We get the impression that persecution and suffering belonged to the basics that Paul was teaching every church (e.g., Acts 14:22). To his young disciple Timothy he wrote very clearly: "Everyone who wants to live a godly life in Christ Jesus will be persecuted" (2 Tim 3:12). Five of his thirteen letters in our New Testament (Ephesians, Philippians, Colossians, 2 Timothy, Philemon) were written by Paul while he was a prisoner.

When Paul expressed his desire to the Colossians "to fill up in my flesh what is still lacking in regard to Christ's afflictions" (Col 1:24), certainly the apostle did not say that Jesus' sufferings at the cross for the salvation of the world were not enough. However, as Jesus had spoken to Paul on the road to Damascus (Acts 9:4: "Why do you persecute me?"), the sufferings of the church are the continued sufferings of Jesus. As Jesus suffered for salvation, he continues to suffer through his body, the church, for the proclamation of this salvation. And these sufferings are not complete yet.

In the letters to the Corinthians, it seems like Paul had to defend his ministry against others who attacked him saying that "God's work was done in strength and power, not in weakness and suffering" (Penner 2004, 178). As Jesus had to explain the place of his sufferings in God's plan, Paul had to teach that God's way of showing his glory was through "the lowly things of the world and the despised things" (1 Cor 1:28), that his "power is made perfect in weakness" (2 Cor 12:9).

## SUFFERING IN THE OTHER LETTERS

The letter to the Hebrews was written to Christians who had experienced some persecution (Heb 10:32–34). When the "heroes of faith" are introduced in chapter 11, there is an important turning point in verse 35: "Others were tortured and refused to be released, so that they might gain a better resurrection." God did not always rescue those who trusted in him. To persevere in sufferings might be the even greater success.

James called believers to "joy" in "trials of many kinds" (Jas 1:2). Peter's first letter was written to encourage followers of Jesus, in what is today Turkey, who "have had to suffer grief in all kinds of trials" (1 Pet 1:6).

## REVELATION: THE CHURCH TRIUMPHANT IN SUFFERING

The Revelation was given to John as he was a prisoner on the island of Patmos, and it was sent to churches in the Aegean region experiencing persecution (Rev 2:3,9) or even martyrdom (Rev 2:13). The call to all of the churches is to "overcome" (e.g., 2:11,26).

In chapter 12, the theme of Genesis 3:15 is repeated and further developed: the dragon, "that ancient serpent, called the devil" (Rev 12:9), fights the woman, her son, and "the rest of her offspring" (12:17). As in Genesis 3:15 it is clear who will be the final victor, but it is also true that the way to victory goes through persecution. Those who overcome will be those who "did not love their lives so much as to shrink from death" (Rev 12:11).

Yes, the story of God working salvation for mankind is a story of suffering, persecution, and martyrdom—throughout the whole Bible. In Revelation 6:9–11 we see the assembly of martyrs crying out to the Lord: "How long, Sovereign Lord, holy and true, until you judge the inhabitants of the earth and avenge our blood?" (6:10). They are "told to wait a little longer, until the full number of their fellow servants, their brothers and sisters, were killed just as they had been" (6:11). When will the judgment come? After the last martyr has been killed!

As Abel, the first man who died in human history, was a martyr for his faith, so we have reason to believe that the last person who will die on this earth before Jesus returns will be a martyr.

## QUESTIONS FOR REFLECTION
1. Which books in the Bible are written in a context of suffering and persecution?
2. What experience contributed significantly to the suitability of this German missionary to Turkey for writing this article?
3. Assuming the author makes a convincing argument about the centrality of suffering in the Scriptures, how is it that Christians in the generally affluent and peaceful West may be scarcely aware of it? And what is the effect of this?
4. If God's method to spread salvation is through suffering, how should this affect our style of evangelizing?

## REFERENCE

Penner G. 2004. *In the shadow of the cross: A biblical theology of persecution and discipleship.* Bartlesville, OK: Living Sacrifice.

**Wolfgang Haede**, German, graduated from FETA Basel, Switzerland as MTh. Together with his wife, Janet, who is from Antioch, Turkey and daughter Debora, he has worked in church planting and theological education in Turkey since 2001. Necati Aydin, one of the three Christians killed in Malatya, Turkey in 2007, was the husband of Janet's sister. Wolfgang authored a book about the life and death of the Turkish Christian Necati Aydin, published in German (*Mein Schwager: Ein Märtyrer—My Brother-in-law: A Martyr*) in 2009.

### COMMISSIONING ELISHAS

"Obey authorities" (Rom 13:1). "Be gentle as doves yet wise as snakes" (Matt 10:16), Chhirc Taing advised the younger men in the makeshift meeting in Cambodia. On the other side of the thin walls, the bloody Khmer Rouge were murdering with impunity.

"How can our leader be so calm?" Barnabas Mam wondered.

But Chhirc Taing had more to say. "Rise up as an 'Elisha generation'" (2 Kgs 2:13). Just as Elisha picked up responsibility for leadership after Elijah was taken, so Barnabas and his friends were being commissioned.

With that, Chhirc Taing got up, walked out, and began witnessing on the streets. He knew it was his death sentence. Barnabas saw Chhirc Taing arrested and assassinated.

"He became my Elijah," Barnabas says. Since then Barnabas has written more than four hundred hymns for the church, and trained many others.

Miriam Adeney, *Kingdom without Borders: The Untold Story of Global Christianity* (2009, 258)

# CHAPTER 10

# A BIBLICAL THEOLOGY OF PERSECUTION AND DISCIPLESHIP

*Glenn Penner*

## A WORD FROM REG REIMER:

Glenn Penner, who served more than twelve years with Voice of the Martyrs (VOM) Canada, died at the too-young age of forty-eight of chronic lymphocytic leukemia in January 2010. He was an indefatigable advocate for the persecuted church.

Glenn was a rare combination of a strong leader/administrator who contributed greatly to the building of VOM Canada. He was a thoughtful, scholarly practitioner, a Kingdom of God thinker, and an encourager of many. His 2004 book *In the Shadow of the Cross,* is considered a significant evangelical contribution to the theology of persecution and a major legacy. This article well summarizes his approach to writing the book, which we highly commend to our readers.

Glenn had a passion for understanding the phenomenon of persecution and a desire to share that with suffering believers so they could understand the big-picture biblical context for their trials. *In the Shadow of the Cross* is an intensive biblical study of the theology of persecution and discipleship which Glenn saw as absolutely combined. Already translated into several languages, it remains an invaluable resource to Christians worldwide who are suffering for Christ's sake. A gifted teacher, Glenn was able to share the findings published in his book with Christian leaders in religiously restricted and hostile nations in South America, Africa, and Asia, as well as in seminaries and colleges in Europe and North America.

Well aware that any theologizing was always a work-in-progress, Glenn was sometimes heard to say, "I wish I'd discovered that before I wrote my book." But his main thesis is crystal clear. It is that persecution and suffering are normal for the Christian life. His preface in *In the Shadow of the Cross* begins with this quote from Dietrich Bonhoeffer: "Discipleship means allegiance to the suffering Christ, and it is therefore not at all surprising that Christians should be called upon to suffer."

# A BIBLICAL THEOLOGY OF PERSECUTION AND DISCIPLESHIP

It is well recognized by those who work among persecuted Christians that few attempts have been made to develop a biblical theology of persecution. Most attempts consist of selected texts arranged thematically which, while helpful and better than nothing at all, fail to reveal the extent to which suffering for righteousness is addressed in the biblical text. Much of the problem, it seems to me, comes down to a failure to adequately consider many of the scriptural passages on suffering in their context. For example, it is rarely recognized that the New Testament authors are not overly concerned to answer the question of suffering in general (i.e., suffering due to living in a fallen world). That such suffering occurs is recognized, but most of the New Testament passages that address suffering do so in the context of suffering for righteousness and not because of sin or because one lives in a fallen world. But in many of the classic books on suffering, this type of suffering is hardly ever stressed.

This is to be expected, I suppose, since most Christians in the West have little or no experience with persecution per se. In our quest to make the biblical text applicable to daily life, the tendency is for Western preachers and teachers to misapply these passages to situations of general physical, psychological, and spiritual suffering because the biblical texts that speak to suffering for righteousness cannot readily be applied to a setting where there is little or no persecution. Unfortunately, this misapplication is subsequently turned around upon the text itself in future readings. Hence, the application influences future interpretations, resulting in the typical Bible student in the West never even suspecting that the biblical texts that deal with pain and suffering might be dealing with suffering for righteousness' sake rather than suffering because of sin. This also influences how Western Christians view and deal with those who suffer for their faith in other societies. We fail to recognize that persecution is normative for the follower of Christ historically, missiologically, and (most importantly) scripturally.

> ... that I may know him and the power of his resurrection, and may share his sufferings, becoming like him in his death. *Philippians 3:10*

There is a clear scriptural link between persecution and discipleship. Indeed, there can be no discipleship without persecution; to follow Christ is to join him in a cross-carrying journey of reconciling the world to the Father. That this journey is set in the context of conflict, self-sacrifice, and suffering is alluded to as early as Genesis 3:15 when the Lord affirms that Satan's judgment, accomplished through human instrumentality, will bring deliverance to the offspring of the woman, but it will take place in a process of bruising and pain. The deliverance will come through the bruising of the serpent's head, but in the process the heel that bruises him will be also be bruised. This truth is illustrated in the following chapter when the first murder takes place following an act of worship, as Cain's sacrifice is rejected by God while his brother's is accepted. In jealousy (a common reason given in Scripture for persecution), Cain kills his brother. It is obvious that the New Testament views Abel's murder as much more than the result of sibling rivalry or a family squabble that got out of control. Jesus clearly saw Abel's death as an act of martyrdom (Matt 23:35), as does the Apostle John (1 John 3:12). John explains that Abel's death was because Cain's acts were evil and Abel's were righteous. Abel's death is clearly set in a context of martyrdom, a result of the conflict between the world and those who belong to God (1 John 3:13).

Persecution is hardly an exclusively New Testament phenomenon. Numerous passages refer to the suffering inflicted on the people of God throughout the Old Testament historical narratives. It is likely that the psalms of lamentation address the issue of the suffering of God's people more clearly than any other portion of Scripture (including the New Testament). The imprecatory psalms cry out for God's justice on those who inflict the righteous without cause. The thrust of the book of Job is how a man of God suffers not because of the sinfulness of himself or creation but because of righteousness, and it calls for trust in God in the face of such a paradox. This train of thought is amplified by the call of the prophets to look ahead to the Day of the Lord, believing that history is under the control of an Almighty God who, from the foundation of the world, has set his plans in motion for reconciling the world to himself.

All of this comes into focus with the coming of Jesus Christ, the revelation of the triune God. Through Christ, we see, among other things, that sacrificial love is in the very nature of who God is. To suffer and die to accomplish his Father's purposes was not to be unexpected; Jesus could not be God and do anything but. Weakness, suffering, and sacrifice are God's modus operandi. This is how God accomplishes his work: not through strength or compulsion but through love and invitation. As so, the Servant of God suffers and dies, as do those who follow him. This is to be expected; this is God's way of reconciling the world to himself. A cross-centered gospel requires cross-carrying messengers. When Jesus declared, "If anyone would come after me, let him deny himself and take up his cross and follow me" (Matt 16:24), these words are to be taken much more literally than we are accustomed to doing. At stake is not so much a willingness to die for Christ but a readiness to do so due to one's unconditional obedience to the Crucified One.

The demand of Jesus on his followers is to tread the path of martyrdom. As he prepared to send his disciples out as sheep among wolves, he told them that they would likely die in the process of carrying out their ministry. In order to build his church (Matt 16:18), his death was necessary, as he points out in 16:21. This is the foundation. Without Christ's death there is no redeemed community. But just as Christ's cross was needed to establish his church, our crosses are needed to build his church (16:24). Both are needed. As Josef Ton observed, "Christ's cross was for propitiation. Our cross is for propagation." To be called to follow Christ is to receive a call to suffer (e.g., Acts 9:16; 14:22; 1 Thess 3:3; 1 Pet 2:21; 3:9,17).

It was this understanding that sacrifice, suffering, shame, and even death were the normal cost of discipleship that fueled the evangelistic efforts of the first-century church. They did not expect to experience all of the blessings of heaven in this world. They knew that by their faithfulness, even unto death, they were storing up rewards in heaven. Contrary to the Western belief that it is a blessing not to be persecuted, they knew that it was the persecuted who are blessed (Matt 10–12). Rather than following the common Western practice of thanking God for the privilege of living in a free country where we do not suffer for him, the early Christians thanked God for the honor of suffering for his sake (Acts 5:41). They knew that in order to bring life to others, they must die; to see others experience peace with God, they would have to suffer the violence of the world; to bring the love of God to a dying world, they would have to face the hatred of those whom they were seeking to reach. It is in this context that the biblical authors described spiritual warfare; not freedom over bad habits or psychological problems, but the brutal reality of witnessing to the faithfulness of God in the face of suffering, sacrifice, and death. It was only in this context that the purposes of God would be accomplished.

> And when they had called in the apostles, they beat them and charged them not to speak in the name of Jesus, and let them go. Then they left the presence of the council, rejoicing that they were counted worthy to suffer dishonor for the name. *Acts 5:40–41*

This is also the reality of persecution today. We continue the task of taking the gospel to the end of the earth, knowing that he goes with us and that we do not suffer alone. In all of our afflictions, God is afflicted, and just as Jesus demanded of Saul of Tarsus, so he asks of today's persecutors, "Why do you persecute me?" The knowledge that nothing can separate us from Christ's love (Rom 8:35), that the Spirit prays for us when we can only groan in agony (Rom 8:26, 27) and gives us his words in the face of our accusers (Matt 10:19,20) provides the help that the disciples of Jesus require to remain faithful witnesses. God has provided all that is necessary for the disciple to stand firm.

Yes, there may be fear, but by God's grace it need not control us. Yes, there may be terrible suffering, but suffering is not the worst thing that can happen to the child of God; disobedience to the Father is.

As we witness the testimonies of courageous persecuted brothers and sisters in person or through reports, it is worthwhile to reflect on the words of Peter, "For this is a gracious thing, when, mindful of God, one endures sorrows while suffering unjustly" (1 Pet 2:19 ESV). In these words, Peter defines grace as being enabled to endure suffering due to one's faithfulness to God. As we read the accounts of those who have suffered for the sake of Christ, we might be justified in saying that, from the world's perspective, those who endure persecution are heroic. But from God's perspective, Peter reminds us, they are recipients of grace. Peter stresses that enduring suffering is evidence that God is at work in one's life. There is no glory for the sufferer. No hero worship. No merit for those who are able to endure hardship, no boasting of one's achievements. It is evidence of God's grace. It is all a work of God, from beginning to end. Is it any wonder that near the end of his first epistle, written especially to instruct persecuted believers to stand firm in their faith, the apostle writes, "And after you have suffered a little while, the God of all grace, who has called you to his eternal glory in Christ, will himself restore, confirm, strengthen, and establish you. To him be the dominion forever and ever. Amen" (1 Pet 5:10,11 ESV).

This hope is solidified with the Revelation of John's vision of the victorious Lamb. Written to address the apparent discrepancy between the belief that God's Kingdom has come and that Jesus Christ is Lord and the reality that the forces of evil continued to exist, to dominate the culture, and even flourish, while oppressing Christians to varying degrees, Revelation provides the churches with what they most needed: a revelation of who Jesus Christ is.

God's priority is not so much to answer the questions that his people may have as to why they are persecuted as to give them a revelation of himself. In this final book of the Bible, Jesus is revealed as the One who is in the midst of the churches, as One who is in control of history and who will soon bring history to its conclusion. The believers to whom John writes face the challenge of witnessing for Christ in the midst of temptations to compromise with idolatry. John sees the persecution as increasing and his warning is meant to prepare the churches for that day, as well as for the challenges they presently face. He sees that not all of the churches are prepared; some are already well on their way to denying Christ. The Christian in Revelation is called to witness for Christ, even to the point of death, in the midst of compromising Christianity and a hostile world, knowing that his reward is coming. Revelation helps us to see that there is always hope. Defeat may seem imminent to those in the midst of persecution; the disciple needs to be reminded that so is victory. The victory is not, however, as some might suppose, the punishment and destruction of the wicked; the victory is the vindication of the church. Redeemed, triumphant in heaven, secure forever with the Lamb who has won the victory for himself and the church through his death and his conquest over it, the church participates in this victory with Christ as Bride and Bridegroom. By refusing to deny their allegiance to him and acknowledge the idolatrous claims of the world order (13:15; 14:9), enduring even unto death, the martyrs share in Christ's victory over it and in his triumph over all the powers of evil (12:11). God has determined to save the world by the foolishness of the cross of Christ and by the foolishness of the crosses of his children whom he has chosen and called for this very purpose. He will be consistent in using this unique method until he achieves his final goal. God will thus bring the nations to himself by the sacrifice of his obedient Son followed by the sacrifices of his other obedient sons and daughters.

## QUESTIONS FOR REFLECTION
1. Does Penner make a convincing case of a close link between persecution and discipleship?
2. The author defines and the article assumes a certain kind of suffering. What is that and why does not any kind of suffering fit?
3. Discuss the author's assertion that "persecution is normative."
4. Reflect on the statement that "a cross-centered gospel requires cross-carrying messengers."

*"This man is my chosen instrument to carry my name… I will show him how much he must suffer for my name"* Acts 9:15–16.

Looking at Paul's calling, it becomes clear that suffering for the gospel is biblical. We should stop asking "why" we suffer, and ask instead "for what purpose?" What is the meaning of our suffering?

Suffering in the lives of God's faithful servants is part of their ministry, their pilgrimage, something to be expected, the fruit of their zeal for the gospel, as happened in Paul's life. It is a privilege to be called worthy to suffer for his name (Acts 5:41). Such suffering brings no shame on a Christian but proves his obedience to God's calling.

Paul never sought suffering, but the joy in responding to his calling was much greater than any distress (Acts 20:22–24). Serving God's Kingdom is much weightier than any pain in a Christian's life (Acts 14:22).

Reflection by: Willame Bruno, Brazil

# CHAPTER 11

# THE PROSPERITY GOSPEL

## A Heresy with Northern Roots Goes Viral, with Reflections on Poverty and Suffering in Africa

*Grant LeMarquand*

I came that they may have life and have it abundantly. *John 10:10*

Has not God chosen those who are poor in the world to be rich in faith and heirs of the kingdom, which he has promised to those who love him? But you have dishonored the poor man. Are not the rich the ones who oppress you, and the ones who drag you into court? *James 2:5–6*

Any analysis of the "prosperity gospel" must hold the two biblical references cited above in tension. On the one hand, throughout the Scriptures God makes promises to his people, promises which include more than eternal life. In the words of Jesus, God's people are invited into abundant life. That abundant life includes innumerable blessings: the joy of marriage and family, health and long life, good food, peace, security, prosperity, the pleasures of the created world, and of human-produced art and music. In both Testaments, these blessings are held up as good and right, as things which all people, especially God's people, can be expected to experience and enjoy. Blessings are never deified in the Bible—idolatry is a danger to be avoided—but they are considered gifts of a loving Father.

On the other hand, we live in a world defaced by wickedness, and God's people are not exempt from the malevolence of this evil age. In fact, there are times and places in which God's people are those most embattled by the forces of sin and death. If, as the passage from James says, "the poor of this world [are] the rich in faith," it seems also true that those who are rich in faith often seem to be poor. Certainly this is true in the twenty-first century in which the majority of Christian believers come from the least economically developed parts of the world, and the richer parts of the world are more resistant to the message of the gospel.

This essay will briefly examine how the movement known as the prosperity gospel has affected those parts of the world most in need of "health and wealth," as well as some of the problems arising from that movement. We will focus on Africa, both because the prosperity gospel is growing there, and because it is the area this author knows firsthand.

## PENTECOSTALISM IN AFRICA

Pentecostalism in Africa can be divided into three distinct groups. For the sake of this essay we will not distinguish between Pentecostalism and the charismatic movement (Hollen-weger 1972; Hollenweger 1997; Cox 1995; Kalu 2008). Clearly both are part of the same movement, even if there are distinctive manifestations in their theologies and social formation. First, there is what we may refer to as classic Pentecostalism. These churches derive from the work of Western missionaries and have their origins in the holiness movement and in that explosive event known as the Azusa Street Revival.

Second, revivals in Africa throughout the twentieth century gave rise to movements which could not be contained within the mission-founded churches.[1] These African-instituted churches are ethnically based and more open to African culture than the mission churches. They are usually charismatic, including prophecy, dreams, visions, prayer for healing, and deliverance from evil spirits in their worship and practice (Barrett 1968; Daneel 1987).

The third form is called by various names. These churches usually call themselves "Word" churches, "Faith" churches, or "Word of Faith" churches. By others they have been described as teaching the health and wealth gospel, or faith and prosperity doctrines. This "word of faith" movement has elements in common with other forms of Pentecostalism (prayer for healing, use of gifts of the Spirit), but they should not be confused (Barron 1987; Hanne-graaff 1993; Shorter and Njiri 2001; Gifford 2004).

All three movements can be seen as responses to social change in Africa. The original conversion of Africans to classic Pentecostalism (and to other mission-founded churches) was a conversion from local religion to a religion which was universal in scope. The world had become larger than the tribe—a religion was needed which accounted for this enlarged world (Horton 1972). But the mission-founded churches, although promising a more global vision, often delivered a *Western* vision of the world. Africans found that to become Christian was to become foreign. African-instituted churches responded to a need to feel at home, to express the gospel in more indigenous ways.

Prosperity churches are also a response to new realities: urbanization and globalization. The population of African cities has exploded. Urbanization has created a new culture: Western dress and modes of transportation, television, the Internet, and cell phones are ubiquitous in African cities. The need to feel at home in one's own culture has given way to the desire to participate in globalized culture. African indigenous churches worshiped in the mother tongue of the ethnic group. African prosperity churches use all the trappings of modern society including electronic musical instruments, careful staging—and English. Prosperity street preachers not only preach in English, but with American accents, imitating the American preachers who can be seen twenty-four hours a day on the American-based Trinity Broadcast Network in some African cities.

---

1    The East African Revival which began in Uganda and Rwanda in the 1930s, was kept within the Protestant churches, although divested of some early charismatic manifestations. Many mainline churches in Africa have also accommodated the charismatic movement.

## THE WORD OF FAITH MOVEMENT

Although the word of faith movement is usually associated with American religious orga-
nizations and personalities, the movement is a global one. African Pentecostalism has bor-
rowed from the American versions, but also from leaders such as Korean pastor Yonggi Cho
(Yoo 1988), and African Pentecostalism is influencing other parts of the world (Wagner and
Thompson 2004). The flow is not just from America to the world. On the other hand, the
American roots of the prosperity movement are crucial for understanding the movement.

Most associate modern prosperity teaching with the name of Kenneth E. Hagin, the Texas
preacher who reasoned that just as God spoke the world into existence, so human beings
have the power to speak things into existence—believers
can speak a "word of faith" and what they speak will
come to pass. Although healing and prosperity receive
much of the attention, it is this idea of a word of faith,
also known as "positive confession," which lies behind the visible manifestations of both
health and wealth.

> For I consider that the sufferings of this present time are not worth comparing with the glory that is to be revealed to us. *Romans 8:18*

Hagin was influenced by E. W. Kenyon, a New England Bible teacher who argued that the
Abrahamic covenant with God guarantees his material blessings to people who have faith.
Others see similarities between the word of faith movement, Christian Science, and the
"power of positive thinking" of Norman Vincent Peale. At the base of much of this, however,
is a desire in American culture for a religion which works, for a utilitarian religion that will
help the believer in everyday life. Recent prosperity preachers include Hagin's son Kenneth
W. Hagin, Gloria and Kenneth Copeland, Oral Roberts, Joel Osteen, Benny Hinn, Creflo
Dollar, and many others. Their critics point out that Jesus was not rich, that he spoke against
those who trusted in riches, and that he said it was the poor who were blessed. Jesus' disciples
did not become prosperous but rather died martyrs' deaths. Critics also argue that not all
sickness or poverty is due to lack of faith, since there are rich, healthy sinners, and impoverished, sick saints. Some critics have focused on doctrinal irregularities in some prosperity
preaching, such as that believers are "little gods," an idea which appears to be Christologi-
cally heretical.

## THE PROSPERITY GOSPEL IN AFRICA

In Africa, the prosperity gospel is an urban movement. African cities are insecure. Although
many move to cities in hope of education and jobs, many city dwellers live in enormous
slums, have limited access to health care, live in fear of crime, and are often cut off from the
support of family and tradition. Success and security are elusive. Dreams that the city often
denies are promised by prosperity teachers to those that have enough faith.

African prosperity preaching is not dominant in those parts of Africa that are the poorest.
Although the crusades of Reinhart Bonnke, the German evangelist who is influenced by
prosperity ideas, made some impact in Sudan, these appear not to have had lasting results.
Pentecostal churches are active in South Sudan, but those churches are of the more classical
variety. Prosperity churches take root in Africa in places where there is insecurity but also the

possibility of generating wealth—in urban centers of more wealthy countries such as Ghana, Nigeria, and Kenya.

An African bishop related the case of his daughter, a university student. She was given the money to pay for tuition, but later returned to him and asked for more money for fees. He asked what had happened to the money and she told him that she had "planted a seed"—gave her money in the offering at the church in faith that it would come back to her multiplied. Another African friend told me of a woman who felt led to give the car her husband had recently given her to the pastor of her prosperity church in the hopes of cashing in on a bigger return. Many African Christians have similar stories. But this is anecdotal evidence.

A study of the prosperity gospel in Nigerian churches by Adekunle Dada, although admittedly not large enough to provide scientific results, points in the same direction as my own anecdotal evidence. Dada interviewed worshipers from ten different prosperity churches, fifty interviews in all, asking each person three questions:

1. What made you join your present church?
2. Are you satisfied with your present state, spiritually and physically?
3. Has the prosperity gospel made the desired impact in your life? (Dada 2004, 101)

Dada's subject group consisted of people who attend prosperity churches, not the disillusioned who have gone elsewhere. Although more than half joined their church because of the promises of "prosperity and peace of mind" (101), and although the vast majority were satisfied with their church experience, 75 percent admitted that they had not seen an improvement in their financial status. In fact, Dada reports, the number of those who could point to any improvement was minimal (102). Dada's conclusion is that most adherents were satisfied with their church, even though the promises made by the prosperity teaching had not been satisfied.

Dada hypothesizes that the gap between promise and fulfillment must lead to a certain amount of "cognitive dissonance" among church members. Prosperity preachers explain the gap through a number of rationalizations: sin in a person's life and failure to give generously enough to the ministry being the most prominent. That is, "members are blamed for not prospering" (103). Such tactics may delay disillusionment, but guilt and finally rejection are obvious problems for the future of the prosperity movement.

To the present hour we hunger and thirst, we are poorly dressed and buffeted and homeless, and we labor, working with our own hands. When reviled, we bless; when persecuted, we endure; when slandered, we entreat. We have become, and are still, like the scum of the world, the refuse of all things. *1 Corinthians 4:11–13*

Also problematic are increasingly reported cases of the deception and greed of pastors. The fact that pastors become wealthier but the parishioners do not, can only be sustained as long as people believe that the pastor is godlier or has more faith than the congregation. But when the pastor is caught in a scandal, or when it is realized that the leader is rich at the congregation's expense, disillusionment will spread. If prosperity preachers became, in Dada's words, "outspoken champions of the poor" they might be seen as less self-serving.

It is clear that prosperity teaching touches something within the African worldview. Just as some Americans accept the prosperity gospel because it connects with practical everyday life, so the acceptance of the prosperity message reveals that Africa needs a gospel that does more than save souls. Although many in the West are satisfied with a gospel which deals only with the conscience—with sin and forgiveness—the African worldview is more holistic. A message which neglects the needs of the community will be considered useless. Churches that pray for "daily bread" but have no answer to human hunger, or "deliver us from evil" but cannot deal with demonic activity, will be considered weak. Any gospel which does not address the needs of the poor is a truncated gospel.

Interestingly, we see here a point of contact between the gospel of prosperity and liberationist theologies. Both realize that poverty is not marginal to the gospel message. If evangelicals rightly complain about some versions of liberation theology, they must provide a biblical vision which takes into account the whole human person. Likewise, if the health and wealth gospel is seen as deficient, it should not be because we see poverty as good or sickness as God's will. The biblical message is clear that sickness, death, pain, poverty, and oppression exist in a fallen world that Christ came to redeem. Prosperity preachers have an overrealized eschatology, not appreciating that believers must participate in the same fallen world with nonbelievers. But other Christians come close to a gnostic view of reality, believing that the world itself is evil and must be endured until we can escape to heaven.

## RESPONSE

An African response to prosperity preaching must include the acknowledgement that there are dimensions of the African worldview which may leave African believers susceptible to the temptations of these preachers. Just as American believers can be hoodwinked by preachers promising money and healing that they cannot deliver because Americans desire a faith that works, a faith that is practical, even so African Christians may fall into the trap of prosperity preaching both because of the great need for security in Africa and also because the African worldview is (rightly!) holistic, including every dimension of life within its scope. African Christians, therefore, need to be vigilant and to test any new message against the entire witness of Scripture.

There must also be a Western response to the prosperity gospel as it is preached in North America and Europe—and especially as it is exported in "crusades" and on television to the non-Western world. It seems clear that although many have Africanized the health and wealth gospel, its primary point of origin is in the United States. As an exported American product it has met with a hungry market overseas, longing for, along with freedom from poverty, a freedom from sickness which African traditional and modern health care systems cannot provide. The seed of the prosperity gospel has landed on the fertile soil of countries filled with people who do not have enough and who know that they are poor and desire an escape from the cycles of destitution in which they so often find themselves. American preachers of this false gospel need to measure their approach to the non-Western world against that of Paul in 1 Thessalonians 2:3–10:

For our appeal does not spring from error or impurity or any attempt to deceive, but just as we have been approved by God to be entrusted with the gospel, so we speak, not to please man, but to please God who tests our hearts. For we never came with words of flattery, as you know, nor with a pretext for greed—God is witness. Nor did we seek glory from people, whether from you or from others, though we could have made demands as apostles of Christ. But we were gentle among you, like a nursing mother taking care of her own children. So, being affectionately desirous of you, we were ready to share with you not only the gospel of God but also our own selves, because you had become very dear to us. For you remember, brothers, our labor and toil: we worked night and day, that we might not be a burden to any of you, while we proclaimed to you the gospel of God. You are witnesses, and God also, how holy and righteous and blameless was our conduct toward you believers. (ESV)

In contrast to some other wandering preachers, Paul's ministry among the Thessalonians did not put a financial burden on his hearers—he worked with his own hands to support his ministry. His ministry did not spring from impure motives like greed. He did not flatter or deceive, but like a nursing mother always desired the best for those who became his children in the gospel. This is not the attitude often seen by prosperity preachers who promise returns that they cannot provide in exchange for gifts that they do not deserve.

Any response to prosperity gospel people must acknowledge that God wants to bless: we should pray for healing and that the hungry will have food, and we should expect answers to prayer. But we are also called to participate in the alleviation of poverty and the causes of poverty and to care for the sick by working for the eradication of disease. Churches should become communities that the world can look at and say not "look how wealthy the pastor is," but "look how much they love one another."

Most importantly, the global church must learn again that the true gospel is a gospel which puts God at its center. Unfortunately, like other heretical movements, the false gospel of prosperity is anthropocentric: "Everything is centred in the human being and his or her attitudes, not in God and his grace." Accordingly, the word of faith message "is a scandal" since "it focuses … on material things, showing Christ as Mammon, the god of riches, and his church in opulence, contrary to the values of humility, sacrifice, and abnegation which characterize the kingdom of God" (Saracco 2007, 324, 326).

## QUESTIONS FOR REFLECTION

1. In what ways is the prosperity gospel a heresy?
2. How can we reach out to Christians who have been influenced by the prosperity gospel, acknowledging the true things that they have been taught, but attempting to provide balance?
3. What biblical texts and themes would be important for this task?

## REFERENCES

Barrett, D. 1968. *Schism and renewal in Africa: An analysis of six thousand contemporary religious movements.* Nairobi: Oxford University Press.

Barron, B. 1987. *The health and wealth gospel.* Downers Grove, IL: InterVarsity Press.

Cox, H. 1995. *Fire from heaven: The rise of Pentecostal spirituality and the reshaping of religion in the twenty-first century.* Reading, MA: Addison-Wesley.

Dada, A. O. 2004. Prosperity gospel in Nigerian context. *Orita* 36 (1–2): 101.

Daneel, M. L. 1987. *Quest for belonging: An introduction to a study of African independent churches.* Gwere, Zimbabwe: Mambo Press.

Gifford, P. 2004. *Ghana's new Christianity: Pentecostalism in a globalising African economy.* London: Hurst and Company.

Hannegraaff, H. 1993. *Christianity in crisis.* Eugene, OR: Harvest House.

Hollenweger, W. 1972. *The Pentecostals.* London: SCM.

———. 1997. *Pentecostalism.* Peabody, MA: Hendrickson.

Horton, R. 1972. African conversion. *Africa* 41: 85–108.

Kalu, O. 2008. *Pentecostalism in Africa.* Oxford: Oxford University Press.

Saracco, J. N. 2007. Prosperity theology. In *Dictionary of mission theology: Evangelical foundations,* ed. John Corrie. Downers Grove, IL; Nottingham, UK: InterVarsity Press.

Shorter, A., and J. Njiri. 2001. *New religious movements in Africa.* Nairobi: Paulines.

Wagner, P., and J. Thompson, eds. 2004. *Out of Africa: How the spiritual explosion among Nigerians is impacting the world.* Ventura: Regal.

Yoo, B. W. 1988. *Korean Pentecostalism.* New York: Peter Lang.

**Grant LeMarquand**, Canadian, was professor of biblical studies and mission at Trinity School for Ministry, an evangelical Anglican seminary in Ambridge, PA. He is now the area bishop for the Horn of Africa in the Anglican diocese of Egypt with North Africa and the Horn of Africa. He is the author of *An Issue of Relevance: A Comparative Study of the Story of the Bleeding Woman in North Atlantic and African Contexts* (Peter Lang, 2004) and edits the *Trinity Journal for Theology and Ministry.*

## DADDY GETS THE PRIVILEGE OF SUFFERING

"Choose Jesus or choose your family!" Mannu's parents threw down the gauntlet. She chose Jesus, and never saw her parents again. The pain aches to this day.

Mannu had been living in India, but one year after her marriage she and her husband relocated to their native Nepal. At that time it was illegal to witness to Hindus. Evangelists faced a six-year prison sentence. In spite of the threat, they immediately began a church in their living room. Some of the first believers were neighbor women whom Mannu taught to sew. They believed, and brought their husbands. Today the church has more than two thousand members.

Mannu's husband was arrested but freed on bail while his case was pending. Eight years later his case finally came to court. He was sentenced to six years in jail, followed by banishment. His lawyer advised him to activate the banishment at once, rather than go to jail. He did.

But Mannu stayed, and appealed the case to the king. If the appeal lost, she would be imprisoned in her husband's place. She had peace about that. It was more important for her husband to stay out of jail, because his ministry was more pivotal, she felt.

She stayed because she felt God had given her Jeremiah 42:10–12: "If you stay in this land, I will build you up and not tear you down; I will plant you and not uproot you, for I am grieved over the disaster I have inflicted on you. Do not be afraid of the king … whom you now fear. Do not be afraid of him, declares the Lord, for I am with you and will save you and deliver you from his hands. I will show you compassion so that he will have compassion on you and restore you to your land."

Several months later a national revolution took place. Mannu's husband returned, and in time received awards from the Ministry of Education for Nepali textbooks which he had written in exile.

When Mannu first learned of her husband's arrest, their children were in boarding school in India. She traveled to the school, took the three apart into a corner, and talked to them about the joy and the suffering that comes with serving the Lord. Then she told them their father had been taken.

"How come Daddy gets all the privileges?" was her oldest daughter's response.

Since then, that girl has graduated from Vellore Medical School and returned to Nepal to provide medical care for her people.

Miriam Adeney, *Kingdom without Borders: The Untold Story of Global Christianity* (2009, 130–31)

# CHAPTER 12

# REFLECTIONS ON THE PROSPERITY GOSPEL

*Femi B. Adeleye*

## INTRODUCTION

The "prosperity" or "health and wealth" gospel is one of the fastest growing different "gospels" spreading across denominations. This gospel asserts that believers have the right to the blessings of health and wealth and that they can obtain these blessings through positive confessions of faith and the "sowing of seeds" through the faithful payments of tithes and offerings. Although the Bible affirms that God cares enough to bless his people and provide for their needs—and although there are legitimate ways to work for such needs to be met—this gospel often makes the pursuit of material things and physical well-being ends in themselves.

The prosperity gospel focuses primarily on material possessions, physical well-being, and success in this life: which includes abundant financial resources, good health, clothes, housing, cars, promotion at work, success in business, as well as other endeavors of life. The extent of material acquisition and well-being is often equated with God's approval.

## THE HERMENEUTICS OF THE OFFERING

I once asked my cousin why he had not gone to church on a Sunday. He answered by telling me that in response to his pastor's preaching he had donated his Volkswagen car to his church, expecting God to replace it with a Mercedes Benz. After some months, when his miracle car did not materialize, he thought God had disappointed him. He stopped going to church. I told him that God had not disappointed him. Instead, he had been misled. My cousin had been attending a prosperity preaching church and had been taken in by the offering time.

In the past, the worship hour (or two) in most churches has centered on the proclamation of the Word. The sermon is preached in all solemnity. Today in many churches, at least in the non-Western world, the focus is now the "offering time." It is popular to say, "Offering time is blessing time," not least because for many it is investment time. The offering is often regarded as sowing, which looks forward to significant returns. The Word itself is often twisted to back the centrality of offering time, and in some churches there is a minisermon to urge the congregation to give. One would not worry as much if this took place just once during the service. Sometimes there can be as many as five or six different collections taken in a single service.[1] One simply feels a sense of the flock being fleeced bare.

## SCRIPTURAL TWISTING

From this writer's observation, the most popular verse used in motivating or mobilizing the congregation to give is Luke 6:38, which says, "Give, and it will be given to you: good measure, pressed down, shaken together, and running over will be put into your bosom. For with the same measure that you use, it will be measured back to you" (NKJV). This verse is quoted with relish and often backed by a minisermon on the benefits of giving. The verse is, however, often quoted out of context. Luke 6:38 is found in the context of Jesus' teaching on love and mercy and how we relate to and treat others. The full paragraph begins in v. 37 with "Judge not, and you shall not be judged: condemn not, and you shall not be condemned: forgive, and you shall be forgiven" (KJV). Following in God's example, love and mercy should produce a hesitation in judging others as believers realize that God will treat them in the way they have treated others. The passage is therefore first and foremost about relationships—not treating others or judging them in the way we do not want to be judged, for in this regard, "with the same measure that we use, it will be measured back to us."

The text is neither about giving to God financially nor expecting returns for what we give. It has more to do with loving and forgiving as well as being of service without expecting anything in return. This has, however, been twisted to indicate that God will return in double or hundredfold whatever one gives in offerings. It is common for several collections to be taken in a single service. Songs like "I am a millionaire" and "Let the poor say I am rich" became popular in anticipation of God's reward with material blessings. Positive confession is encouraged for good health, wealth, and other blessings.[2]

Very few people who use this passage as a basis for collecting offerings refer to the unusually strong words of the Lord Jesus on wealth in the same chapter. For example in Luke 6:24–25 Jesus says, "But woe unto you that are rich! For you have received your consolation. Woe unto you that are full! For you shall hunger. Woe unto you that laugh now! For you shall mourn and weep" (KJV). Matthew 7:1–5 actually helps to throw more light on the Luke 6:36–39 text. Both passages focus on human relationships.

Some also use 3 John 2, which says, "I pray that you may prosper in all things," as a mandate for the prosperity gospel. However, what does the apostle mean by prosperity here? A careful study of the meaning of this text as intended by the writer would reveal that the word used for *prosper* in English comes from the Greek word *euodoo*, which means "good road, route, or journey." Hence what the writer actually says is, "I want you to have a good and healthy lifelong journey." The words do not necessarily refer to riches or wealth. Why would John, a witness of the life of Christ, say, "Above everything else, I want you to be rich or wealthy"?

---

1    I was in a church recently in Lagos, Nigeria (September 21, 2008), where there were six different collections for various purposes, including one for freedom from fear.

2    I have observed this in Gabriel Oduyemi's Bethel Chapel in Lagos, Nigeria, as well as in other churches.

The reference to abundant life in John 10:10 is also often used as a prop. However, the term used for life here is *zoe*, a word indicating "life in the spirit and soul," rather than *bios*, which is used to refer to physical, material life. When read as intended, Jesus is saying, "I want you to have an abundant life in spirit," not riches, cars, houses, designer clothes, etc., as is often emphasized in the prosperity gospel preaching.

The hermeneutics of this gospel raises more questions than it answers. For instance, does it affirm and point people to the cross? Is the lifestyle of those who benefit from the teaching consistent with the ethos of the cross of Christ? One thing is certain—Jesus did not preach or teach a prosperity gospel! All he taught that referred to earthly possessions came as warnings to us. For example, he very clearly says, "Take heed and beware of covetousness, for one's life does not consist in the abundance of the things he possesses" (Luke 12:15). Unlike our modern-day preachers, Jesus warned against the deceitfulness of riches (Matt 13:22). He in fact refers to it as "unrighteousness mammon" (Luke 16:9). As an end in itself, money has the tendency to compete for our loyalty that belongs to God. It has the tendency to become an idol that rules our lives. This is why Jesus warns against relating to money as we relate to God. "No servant can serve two masters; for either he will hate the one and love the other, else he will be loyal to the one and despise the other. You cannot serve God and mammon" (Luke 16:13).

> Beloved, do not be surprised at the fiery trial when it comes upon you to test you, as though something strange were happening to you. But rejoice insofar as you share Christ's sufferings, that you may also rejoice and be glad when his glory is revealed. *1 Peter 4:12–13*

One may ask if there is anything wrong with material prosperity. Not necessarily. Very often material prosperity is related to physical and emotional well-being, and this is largely God's will for most people. In the Old Testament, God blessed Abraham and several others and made them materially prosperous. God also gives the ability to produce wealth (Deut 7:16–18). We also serve a God who desires and promises to supply all our needs according to his riches.

The challenge is that many churches have not adequately addressed how we are to acquire material prosperity and to what extent. One would suggest that there are various approaches which may include through hard work ("If a man will not work, he shall not eat"—2 Thess 3:10); through advanced planning, which includes saving the rewards of hard work through investments and other good money-growing options. Other ways may include shortcuts such as stealing, gambling, speculating, begging, or borrowing. The church ought to provide adequate teaching on these matters. However, this is often not the case, as many churches only work hard at presenting shortcuts like the seed-faith principle, hundredfold blessing, "pressed down, shaken together," and the idea of "sweatless victory" or "sweatless success."

## TRACING THE ROOTS

The roots of the prosperity gospel are easily traceable to the televangelist culture in the United States. The same context which nurtured the rich Christian heritage dating back to the eighteenth-century revivals and twentieth-century evangelical tradition is the same that has spread the prosperity gospel to other parts of the world. Lamenting this development several years ago, Gordon Fee says:

American Christianity is rapidly being infected by an insidious disease, the so-called "wealth and health" gospel—although it has a very little of the character of the gospel in it. In its more brazen forms ... it simply says, "Serve God and get rich"…in its more respectable—but pernicious—forms it builds fifteen million-dollar crystal Cathedrals to the glory of affluent suburban Christianity. (cited in McConnell 1990, 170)

From its American roots, the prosperity gospel has today spread to virtually all parts of the world.

Through the health and wealth gospel, the church in many parts of the world—Africa, Europe, and even the Middle East, as well as nations within Eastern Europe and Asia that were once under the yoke of Communism—has been invaded by a celebrity culture that has little space or room for the cross of Jesus Christ. Many people in the church want to live for Jesus without renouncing material greed. The pressure from the world of celebrities and popular culture is so strong that many people in the church want to live for Jesus without renouncing material greed.

## SOME SHORTCOMINGS OF THE PROSPERITY GOSPEL

The shortcomings of the prosperity gospel include the tendency to distort the mission of Jesus from primarily coming to save us from our sins to coming to make us rich. While some preach that Jesus has come both to save people from their sin and make them rich, it is rare to hear preaching on repentance or salvation from sin in prosperity gospel circles. Furthermore, this different gospel fails to see that all forms of giving to God are primarily acts of worship. Instead it teaches that tithing or giving to God is an investment that must yield some returns. It pressures people to give with wrong motives, suggesting that we must have returns or rewards here and now in material form. Importantly, the gospel distorts the person of Christ and misleads people by teaching that Jesus was materially rich. While Jesus was not destitute, we know from Scripture that he was not as materially prosperous as the health and wealth teachers make him out to be. The prosperity gospel also often feeds on the greed of its teachers at the expense of the needs of their followers. There is further the tendency to spend more energy raising money than on working to present the true gospel or nourishing the spiritual health of God's people. This suggests that money is more important than people or the urgent task of evangelism.

## IS THE PROSPERITY GOSPEL GOOD NEWS FOR THE POOR?

While the prosperity gospel often wears the mask of advocacy for the poor, it is hardly good news when in most situations the shepherds are fleecing the flock. In response to diverse schemes of manipulation, the poor who sow the seed are not the ones that get richer. The leaders and pastors wear better suits, drive better cars, and acquire bigger homes.

There is a deep sense of injustice and immorality when one considers the severe plight and vulnerability of the poor. Some of those who keep sowing to the prosperity gospel can hardly afford regular meals or other basic essentials like shelter or school fees for children. Why should any follower of Jesus support a gospel that tends to align much more with celebrity culture in depriving the poor of the dignity and respect they deserve? Rather than appreciate their endurance of living, often in subhuman conditions, or working to redeem or improve their situation, some preachers connive with popular culture to dangle unrealistic shortcuts to prosperity. While advocacy for the poor and poverty alleviation has become a multi-billion dollar business, the poor in many contexts can hardly be said to be benefiting. This is not only an affront to the poor but to God as well.

The prosperity gospel is nothing less than seduction into a false delusion. It is an unrealistic solution to the challenges of daily life, at least in my African context, and it contradicts biblical teaching on work by offering shortcuts to material success. Besides, it reduces God to the "genie in the bottle," whose main task is to respond to human manipulation. To embrace it is to fall into the peril of the love of money that Paul warned Timothy against in 2 Timothy 3:1–5. To be indifferent to its impact is to be more earthly than heavenly minded. It is to forget that the Kingdom of God is not of this world and to assume that it is primarily meat and drink. A common argument is that the prosperity gospel works. The question is, who does it work for? For those giving or those receiving? Importantly, one must also ask what becomes of many who have become disillusioned with the real gospel as a whole because they have sown their faith-seed but have not seen the anticipated fruits.

## HOW THEN SHOULD WE RESPOND TO THIS GOSPEL?

It is important to recognize and take seriously the fact that the prosperity gospel is primarily about money and that it contradicts both the life of Christ and the purpose for which he died on the cross. This false gospel elevates money to compete for a space in our lives that only God deserves. If the love of money is the root of all evil, the love of material property, mansions, and other accumulations in the dragnet of money must follow closely after. We are increasingly defined, not by who or what we are, but by what we have or own. In very easy ways—more subtle that we often think—any of these can become idols that dim our view of God and diminish our passion for him.

The French theologian Jacques Ellul in his book *Money and Power*, argues that "money is power, a spirit, a would-be God, a rival master" (cited in Petersen 1987, 33). Furthermore, he distinguishes between money and wealth. For him, "wealth consists of those good things of God's creation that are meant for our enjoyment. Money is the world's way of amassing those things, hoarding them, assuring that you can have more tomorrow, dividing people according to its arbitrary rules. Money does not merely tempt, it engulfs. It spins its web around people, forcing them to its service" (33). Even if we don't agree with Jacques Ellul, his position is not too different from that of Jesus who summarily concludes, "You cannot worship both God and mammon" (Matt 6:24).

There are few people today who can speak as authoritatively as Jim Bakker on the prosperity gospel. In an interview with *Charisma* shortly after his release from jail, Jim Bakker admitted that he had been building a 1980s-style tower of Babel to make a name for himself (1997). His tower of Babel was a multimillion-dollar business that had a 30 million-dollar payroll and more than 2,200 employees. Bakker has since repented and apologized for the PTL scandal. In the interview with *Charisma*, Bakker says:

While I studied Jesus' words, I couldn't find anywhere in the Bible where he said anything good about money. And this started to prick my heart. Luke 6:24 says, "Woe to you who are rich," Jesus talked about the "deceitfulness of riches" in Mark 4:19. Jesus told us not to lay up treasures on earth in Matthew 6:24. In Luke 12:15, he said: "Watch out, be on your guard against all kinds of greed. A man's life does not consist in the abundance of his possessions." (1997, 33)

Secondly, I suggest that we need to take the plight of the poor seriously enough to reject this gospel and work at better ways of meeting their needs over offering false shortcuts. We all should be concerned enough to feel a sense of pain to see a part of the church drifting away from sound doctrine in this way. Instead of working to alleviate the plight of the poor, this group not only consents to their marginalization but manipulates Scripture to do so. Some have turned the sacred space of the pulpit into a shrine of mammon worship. The injustice and idolatry of greed is what made our Lord use such strong words against the rich. And when sacred territory was profaned by the same idolatry, we see the only record of the Lord expressing his anger physically in the temple.

Thirdly, it is worth taking seriously the truth from Uncle John Stott that "life, in fact, is a pilgrimage from one moment of nakedness to another. So we should travel light and live simply" (1990, 246).

## QUESTIONS FOR REFLECTION

1.  How has the prosperity gospel twisted Scripture related to giving and receiving, and what kind of fruit have you seen in your own context? How can we help those who have become disillusioned by these expectations?
2.  What advice has Jesus given about seeking material wealth? When is our attitude to material prosperity healthy and when does it become dangerous?
3.  What have the practical results of following this gospel been for the poor in Africa? What would be a better way of responding to the needs of the poor?

## REFERENCES

Bakker, J. 1997. Interview with *Charisma*, February: 48.

McConnell, D. 1990. *The promise of health and wealth*. London: Hodder and Stoughton.

Peterson, R. 1987. Modern voices: The Christian and money. *Christian History*, vol. 6, no 2.

Stott, J. 1990. *Issues facing Christians today*. London: Marshall Pickering.

**Femi B. Adeleye** has over thirty years of experience in student ministry within and beyond Africa. He currently is IFES associate general secretary for partnership and collaboration and a Langham Partnership scholar studying towards his PhD in Ghana. Adeleye is originally from Nigeria and has lived in Nigeria, the United States, Scotland, Zimbabwe, and Ghana, where he now resides with his wife. He wrote *Preachers of a Different Gospel* (2011) and *Let No Man Despise Your Youth* (2000).

# CHAPTER 13

# IN THE CONTEXT OF WORLD EVANGELISM

## Jesus, Persecution, and Martyrdom

*Marvin Newell*

It is costly to serve as one of Jesus' messengers. For some it is very costly. If one is not paying out much in terms of their personal well-being and comfort, likely neither are they impacting the world much. The gospel of Jesus is so countercultural that it stands as a threat to the prevailing worldview of every culture it encounters. Gatekeepers of those cultures threaten back as it makes inroads into their terrain. They instigate backlashes and resistance that are manifested in acts of opposition, persecution, and at times even in the taking of lives.

Andrew Walls reminds us that Jesus took for granted the rubs and friction accompanying our witness—not from the adoption of a different culture that the gospel can bring, but from the transformation of the mind of those who believe in Christ. Accordingly, the follower of Jesus inherits "the pilgrim principle, which whispers to him that he has no abiding city and warns him that to be faithful to Christ will put him out of step with his society; for that society never existed, in East or West, ancient time or modern, which could absorb the word of Christ painlessly into its system" (Walls 2005, 8). If that be the case generally, how much more then for messengers who are sent by him?

With this perspective in mind, when it came to sending his disciples out into this fallen and hostile world, Jesus made three things perfectly clear: (1) he would not send them out with carelessness, (2) he would not send them out comfortless, and (3) he would not send them out clueless about the types and depths of opposition they would encounter.

Opposition and persecution was something about which Jesus had a lot to say, because he knew his messengers would experience them a lot. Divinely discerning the times, he knew that in every age his ambassadors would encounter opposition as they engaged the world on his behalf. His mission would be conducted in the context of confrontation. Engaging the hearts of mankind would demand engaging an even greater power in the sphere of spiritual warfare. There are always casualties in warfare. It is always costly for those who participate in it.

The discourse of Jesus found in Matthew 10 is a benchmark for understanding opposition, persecution, and martyrdom in the context of world evangelization. By it Jesus candidly covers the topic rather exhaustively. Why did he so painstakingly focus on this topic? Because he wanted to make sure that the disciples who first heard it, and all his messengers who would follow after them, would know what they would face as they went forth. Consequently, this pointed instruction serves as a template on opposition for gospel-bearing messengers of all ages.

In Matthew 10 we see Jesus for the first time sending his disciples out on a mission—albeit a short-term assignment. This would serve as a "trial run" or "warm up" mission to the greater worldwide mission they would initiate after his ascension into heaven. Notice all that he says about the resistance they would encounter.

## GRIM REALITIES OF PERSECUTION
### DEGREES OF PERSECUTION

First, Jesus informs his followers that not all persecution is equally intense nor carries equal consequences. Believers experience various degrees of resistance, with martyrdom as the ultimate possibility. As he was sending them out, he explicitly cautioned that they could face up to six degrees of opposition.

Jesus used six phrases to describe the increasingly intense hostilities that opposition can take. He begins with the least severe form of hostility then progresses in ascending order to the ultimate experience. Christ shows that his messengers could expect to be: prevented outright from proclaiming the gospel ("does not receive you," v. 14 ESV); rejected if given opportunity ("nor heed your words," v. 14); detained ("deliver you up," vv. 17,19); physically abused ("scourge you," v. 17); pursued with intent to harm ("persecute you," v. 23); and finally martyred ("kill the body," v. 28). When viewed graphically, the incremental progression becomes clear:

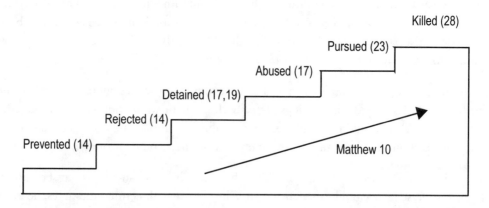

Notice that losing one's life as a result of human hostility in a situation of witness is the ultimate hostile experience. Less one be tempted to shy away from service because of the possibility of experiencing this ultimate trial—martyrdom—a word on this most severe form of opposition is needful.

Martyrdom is not something a person usually anticipates or to which one readily aspires. It is an experience that God in his providence bestows on select individuals for purposes ultimately known only to him. Yet, the premature death of a follower of Christ as a result of human hostility has an enduring impact on observant believers. It causes most to pause and ponder anew the extreme cost of discipleship. It forces many to question whether they themselves measure up to the highest standard of devotion to Christ and his cause. It motivates still others to abandon selfish plans and ambitions and turn to serve Christ in hard and difficult places. It creates a baseline for the church from which to measure its worth—whether its activities are meaningful and truly important in light of death and eternity. We need to be cognizant of the fact that martyrdom has multiple values.

> God does not call everyone to be a martyr.
>
> D. Bonhoeffer in "Aufsatz über den Protestantismus in den VSA. August 1939" (1998, 442)

## SOURCES OF PERSECUTION

Jesus did not want his messengers to be either surprised or naive about the sources from which opposition would come. He delineates four specific sources that messengers need to beware of and consider with guarded prudence. He cautioned that opposition would spring from *the community* ("Be on your guard against men; they will hand you over," v. 17); *the state* ("You will be brought before governors and kings," v. 18); *religious leaders* ("hand you over to local councils and flog you in their synagogues," v. 17) and even from those most dear to them—members of their own *family* ("Brother will betray brother to death, and a father his child," v. 21). In his foreknowledge of the global context of world evangelism, Jesus informs us that in reality there is no safe haven or refuge within a society and no level of authority within a community that should not be considered a potential oppressor.

## ATTITUDE BEHIND PERSECUTION

What is the underlying attitude that drives nonbelievers to oppose and oppress God's messengers? Jesus sums it up in one word—*hatred* ("All men will hate you because of me," v. 22). The form of the verb "hate" used shows this hatred to be ongoing, and can better read, "You will continually be hated because of me." Unqualified hatred has been the hardened heart's emotional response to Jesus through the ages. Why is this? Because his message is a threat to preferred lifestyles and orientations. Mankind hates the light (John 3:20) and the source of light (John 15:20). Thus, their ongoing disdain for bearers of the light.

Later, in a more sober setting, Jesus painted a fuller picture of this Satan-generated hatred. Fast-forward to the evening of his crucifixion. Jesus declared that the world's hatred of his emissaries was intricately tied to its hatred of him. In John 15 Jesus declared:

> If the world hates you, keep in mind that it hated me first. If you belonged to the world, it would love you as its own. As it is, you do not belong to the world, but I have chosen you out of the world. That is why the world hates you. Remember the words I spoke to you: "No servant is greater than his master." If they persecuted me, they will persecute you also.... They will treat you this way because of my name, for they do not know the One who sent me... He who hates me hates my Father as well. If I had not done among them what no one else did, they would not be guilty of sin. But

now they have seen these miracles, and yet they have hated both me and my Father. But this is to fulfill what is written in their Law: "They hated me without reason." (vv. 19–25)

## RESPONSE OF THE MESSENGER TO PERSECUTION

With these three realities clarified, how should Christ's messengers conduct themselves as they go forth heralding his message? Again in Matthew 10, Jesus mentions three appropriate responses.

### PRUDENCE

A messenger must exercise prudence in the context of opposition. Jesus warns his disciples to "be on your guard" (v. 17). He likely means that they should not naively entrust their well-being to anyone. Friends can quickly become foes, authorities become antagonists, and peaceful neighbors turn violent. Another prudent response is to "flee to another place" (v. 23). There are times when getting out of harm's way is the most appropriate course of action.

In their enthusiasm to serve Jesus, messengers should never wantonly waste their lives by courting martyrdom. The destruction of one's own life, by intentionally putting one's self in harm's way with the intent of being killed, cloaked in the excuse that it is for the cause of Christ, is selfish, self-serving, and sinful. Those who would attempt such a course are out for self-glory and the making of a name for themselves. It is their hope that others would applaud them for their "sacrificial" action and thus bring a degree of admiration to themselves that they could not achieve otherwise. These overly zealous acts differ little from that of a fanatical suicide bomber of another religion.

### COURAGE

Fear is a natural response to persecution, and Jesus was well aware of that. Three times in this passage he tells his disciples not to be afraid. He reminds them to look at the bigger picture. First, he reminds them that ultimately truth will prevail: "there is nothing concealed that will not be disclosed, or hidden that will not be made known" (v. 26). In the end, God will correct that which has brought harm and injustice to his messengers.

Secondly, he reminds them that no judgment which others may inflict upon a messenger can compare with the ultimate fate of those who do the inflicting: "Do not be afraid of those who kill the body but cannot kill the soul. Rather, be afraid of the One who can destroy both soul and body in hell" (v. 28). While it may be true that persecutors can kill a person's physical body, only God can condemn a man to the eternal death of his soul. That's even worse.

Thirdly, God's messengers should not be afraid because of God's loving and watchful care of them:

> Are not two sparrows sold for a penny? Yet not one of them will fall to the ground apart from the will of your Father. And even the very hairs of your head are all numbered. So don't be afraid; you are worth more than many sparrows. (vv. 29–31)

As already mentioned, God does not send messengers out carelessly. By these tender words he proves it! He is not capricious in his watch and care over his loved ones, no matter where they are sent. A person's worth, especially a redeemed person's worth, is more valuable to him than the sum total of all other creatures. God is genuinely concerned when messengers pay a high price for serving him.

## DISCRETION

Jesus colorfully draws from the animal world to bring to bear the necessity of his messengers to conduct themselves with discretion. He put it this way: I am sending you out like sheep among wolves. Therefore be as shrewd as snakes and as innocent as doves (v. 16).

If members of the animal kingdom can show discretion in survival, how much more should God's servants? The servant of Christ should conduct himself in a manner worthy of Christ even in the midst of persecution. He should be like a sheep, a snake, and a dove all at the same time. It is instructive to take a look at these three comparisons.

Sheep, when attacked, do not have the ability to retaliate—they are hopelessly harmless. In the same way Christ's messengers should exercise a demeanor of harmlessness even when under attack.

Then there is the snake, which has a reputation for its shrewdness and keenness. These two characteristics are recommended as human qualities, involving insight into the nature of things, and circumspection, common sense, and wisdom to do the right thing at the right time in the right manner.

Finally, Jesus mentions the dove, which symbolizes peace and innocence. This creature reminds us that neither wrongdoing nor questionable practices should mar the reputation of God's servant who is under fire. He is called upon to be discreet in his response, no matter how trying the situation, living uprightly in the midst of contemptuous circumstances.

## COMFORT IN PERSECUTION

Jesus has detailed the cost of serving as one of his messengers. He has made it clear that he would not send anyone out carelessly, nor clueless about the dangers they would encounter. These truths are evident up to this point. Finally, he explains that neither would he send them out comfortless. Comforting clauses are found throughout his discourse. Jesus knew these words of reassurance were important in giving peace of heart and fortitude in mind to those who would face opposition.

There is comfort in knowing that it is Jesus who puts us on mission with him: "I am sending you out" (v. 16). The double pronoun and choice of the word "send" can better read, "I myself am commissioning you." Granted, some may say that by their own free will they have chosen to serve or volunteered themselves to Christ's cause, and maybe to an extent that is true. But there is great comfort in knowing that it is ultimately Jesus who sends messengers to do his bidding, especially into hostile environments.

There is comfort in knowing that, if put in the position of having to defend one's ministry, one should "not worry about what to say or how to say it. At that time you will be given what to say, for it will not be you speaking, but the Spirit of your Father speaking through you" (v. 19). God will provide the words for a proper defense.

Finally, there is great comfort in knowing that in due course, "He who stands firm to the end will be saved" (v. 22). One way a person proves his redemptive relationship with God is evidenced by his unwavering loyalty to God to the very end. People don't allow themselves to be abused or lay down their lives for Jesus unless they really and truly believe in him. They prove their genuine belief in him by their willingness to suffer for him.

## CONCLUSION

It is *costly* to serve as a messenger of Jesus, and Jesus made this very clear in Matthew chapter 10. Some messengers pay a higher price than others. Some experience minimal opposition, whereas others are severely persecuted. Some serve with little discomfort, whereas others pay with their very lives. All are expected to be aware of the fullness that is theirs in following Jesus, no matter what the cost.

Messengers of Jesus are both vulnerable and valuable. David Sills, in his book *The Missionary Call*, helps keep Jesus' teaching on persecution and martyrdom in global perspective. He states, "The dangers that exist are real, but only illustrate the fact that men and women need Christ. The suffering and dying of missionaries advance the Kingdom as nothing else could and the blood of the saints has ever been the seed and fuel of gospel advance" (2008). Let us keep advancing, even in the face of hostility.

## QUESTIONS FOR REFLECTION
1.   What are the six progressive degrees of hostility that a Christian worker can experience?
2.   Persecution comes from a variety of sources. What are the four mentioned by Jesus?
3.   Why, through the ages, is unqualified hatred the hardened heart's emotional response to Jesus' message?
4.   What should be the three appropriate responses to persecution?
5.   In what ways can Christian workers find comfort in persecution?

## REFERENCES

Barclay, W. 1975. *The Gospel of Matthew*, vol. 1. Philadelphia: Westminster Press.

Hendriksen, W. 1975. *The New Testament commentary—Matthew*. Grand Rapids, MI: Baker Book House.

Newell, M. J. 2006. *A martyr's grace*. Chicago: Moody Publishers.

Sills, D. 2008. *The missionary call*. Chicago: Moody Publishers.

Walls, A. 2005. *The missionary movement in Christian history*. Maryknoll, NY: Orbis Books.

**Marvin J. Newell** is senior vice president of MissioNexus, a network of evangelical mission agencies, churches, and training centers in North America. Previously he served as a missionary to Indonesia, a mission administrator, a professor of missions, and director of a missions association. He is the author of two books: *A Martyr's Grace* and *Commissioned: What Jesus Wants You to Know as You Go.*

Translation, side of grave marker:
I am the resurrection and the life.
The person who believes in me, even if he dies, will live.
Jesus Christ

Written on the top of the marker:
Was martyred for the sake of Christ, 18.04.2007

Grave marker of Tillmann Geske.
Song and biographical information on following page.

## Sevgisin

Söz ve müsik:  Tilmann Geske

Görkemli (görkemli)
Muhteşem (muhteşem)
Şahane (Şahane)
Sağ elin korkunç güce sahiptir!

Hayatıma almaya
Layıksın, değersin.
Oğlunu bizim için verdin.
Hayatımı almaya

Layıksın, değersin.
Her şeyimi değiştir, ya Rab!
Her şeyime biçim ver, ya Rab!
Doldur beni, bur'dayım, ya Rab!

Sevgisin! Tanrımız Rab, Sevgidir.
Sevdin Sen. Sarıldım Sana Rab İsa.
Sevgisin! Tanrımız Rab, Sevgidir.
Sevdin Sen. Ben de seni seviyorum.

Sevgisin!

© Susanne Geske 2007
Used by permission

## You Are Love

Words and Music: Tilmann Geske

You are full of splendor! (Full of splendor!)
You are majestic! (Majestic!)
You are magnificent! (Magnificent!)
Your right hand has awesome power!

You are worthy to take my life,
You're worth it.
You gave your son for us.
You deserve to have my life,

You're worthy.
Change everything I have, oh Lord!
Form everything I have, oh Lord!
Fill me, here I am, oh Lord!

You are love! The Lord our God is love.
You loved me. I embrace you Lord Jesus!
You are love! The Lord our God is love
You loved me. And I love you!

You are love!

© Susanne Geske 2007
Translation: Doug Clark, Istanbul, used by permission[1]

Tilmann and Susanne Geske left Germany with their children to serve in central Turkey as missionaries in September 1997. They worked hard to master the Turkish language, and in 2003 they moved to Malatya in southeastern Turkey to continue their ministry there. On April 18, 2007, Tilmann was tortured and killed by men posing as "seekers," martyred along with Turkish co-workers Ugur Yüksel and Necati Aydin. Tilmann was buried in Turkey, and his grave marker remains a testimony to the world of this missionary's commitment to the cause of Christ. Before his death, Tilmann wrote the lyrics and music for a song expressing willingness to give his life for the Lord that he loved so much (see Sevgisin, "You Are Love"). The evangelical community in Turkey has declared April 18 as an annual Day of Prayer for Turkey. —*Robin P. Harris.*

1      Jonathan Carswell, with Joanna Wright, *Married to a Martyr: A Story of Tragedy and Hope: The Authorized Biography of Susanne Geske* (Colorado Springs: Authentic Media, 2008).

# CHAPTER 14

# THE TEACHING OF JESUS ON SUFFERING IN MISSION

*Antonia van der Meer*

What can we learn from the way Jesus prepared his disciples to deal with suffering in relation to our own missionary witness and ministry?

Why does suffering seem such a foreign concept to most Christians and churches today? Partly it is due to the widespread influence of prosperity theology and consumerism, related to a search for a comfortable lifestyle and our presumed right to more affluence. As Christians we have accepted many of the values and practices of our society. Our evangelical churches, in their effort not to lose out to more popular competing churches, seek to offer what people desire to hear and to receive. Few leaders have the courage to preach and teach unpopular messages. And there is too little emphasis on personal discipleship, on forming a Christian character, and on the need to deny ourselves, to be open to face suffering and follow Jesus on the way of the cross.

Another aspect of our present-day values is the need to protect ourselves from dangers: disease, violence, all kinds of threats. People feel insecure and seek ways to guarantee their safety. How will such people be ready to face suffering in mission?

Jesus taught the disciples through his attitudes towards suffering, not seeking his own comfort, being willing to pay the price for the fulfillment of his mission, seeking in all things to please God and to bless and restore fallen human beings. Jesus also taught them through his sermons, parables, and answers to their questions.

## SERMON ON THE MOUNT

Blessings are promised to disciples who give up everything to follow Jesus, who are ready to deny themselves (Matt 5:3–12; Luke 6:20–23).

"Blessed are the poor in spirit, for theirs is the kingdom of heaven" (Matt 5:3). The poor are those who are humbly dependent on God (Ps 34:6), who recognize that they cannot save themselves. The economically or socially poor are included as well (see Luke 6).

"Blessed are those who mourn, for they will be comforted" (Matt 5:4). This sadness refers to repentance, to an attitude of humble contrition. It includes weeping for a world of violence marked by moral degradation and oppression.

"Blessed are the meek, for they will inherit the earth" (Matt 5:5). The word for meek is *praus*, meaning gentle, humble, considerate, respectful (Thayer 1980, 534). The meek are gentle to others, renounce their own rights, and endure violence patiently.

"Blessed are those who hunger and thirst for righteousness, for they will be filled" (Matt 5:6). This hunger is related to living in conformity to God's will and includes social justice. Christian disciples hunger for a complete renewal of themselves and of the earth, with an irresistible love for the downtrodden and the outcasts (Carson 1994, 25).

"Blessed are the merciful, for they will be shown mercy" (Matt 5:7). The word is *eleêmones*, and means mercy, compassion to the miserable and afflicted, and a word that is related to pain, despair, and poverty (Esser 1986, 594–95).

"Blessed are the pure in heart, for they will see God" (Matt 5:8). This phrase refers to those who have a transparent relationship with God and with others. These qualities are indispensable for fellowship with God (Stott 1981, 41). It refers to the humble who seek forgiveness and grace.

"Blessed are the peacemakers, for they will be called sons of God" (Matt 5:9). Peacemakers are called "sons of God," because they renounce violence and endure suffering, rather than inflicting it on others. Peacemakers are a necessary gift for contexts of conflicts within families, societies, nations, and ethnic or religious groups.

"Blessed are you when people insult you, persecute you and falsely say all kinds of evil against you because of me" (Matt 5:10–12). Those who seek righteousness and follow Christ may be rejected for Christ's sake. Suffering in Christian mission should not be unexpected, but we need to stand together and to receive grace to face it.

Jesus was open about what he offered and about what he expected; he did not want "soft" disciples, willing to receive blessings but not to face suffering; he needed followers committed to service for his Kingdom, extending his blessings to others.

## THE MEANING OF JESUS' SUFFERING

The call to follow Jesus is associated with his suffering, so to follow him means to deny ourselves, take his cross, and share in his suffering.

Jesus died our death, enduring the penalty we deserved. The cross teaches that our sins are so serious that the only way out was for God to bear them himself, in Christ, in order to forgive us. The cross is the expression of divine mercy and justice, the place where, in holy love, Jesus paid the penalty for our sins (Stott 1986, 32, 60–61, 88).

God gave his Son, and Jesus gave his life to set us free, creating a new community which must learn to live according to his example and teaching. He knew that this would cost him everything, but he was willing to pay the price and to become the Suffering Servant of God. He brought new life through his death and suffering, and prepared the way for us to follow his footsteps, if we want to be instruments of God's restoring grace.

## THE PURPOSE OF THE DISCIPLE'S CROSS

The purpose of the cross of Jesus was the forgiveness of our sins and our reconciliation with God, a one-time event, never to be supplemented. But the salvation of the world consists of the suffering of Christ for the sins of the world, followed by the proclamation of his salvation to all nations. This salvation will not reach the nations without the self-sacrifice of the messengers. So, to take up our cross means that the main goal of our life will be witnessing about Christ to others, making disciples of them, and teaching them to obey Christ. This will cost money, it may cost our reputation, take us to the mission field, and may even mean death (Ton 2000, 102).

The cross of Christ is the symbol of suffering service, a stimulus to patient endurance and the path to mature holiness. It becomes clear that suffering is indispensable to effective service. The place of suffering in service and of passion in mission is rarely taught today, but the secret of missionary effectiveness is the willingness to suffer and to die. Suffering and service, passion and mission belong together, both in Jesus' experience and in that of his disciples (Stott 1986, 315–17).

We have to understand that the Great Commandment is about loving God and our neighbor. The verb used is *'agapaô*, which means self-sacrifice in serving others. We have to deny things which may not be wrong but which stand in the way of his will for us. Paul denied his rights to have a family and financial support. Christians today may be called to forgo married life, a good job, and a comfortable home (Stott 1986, 275–84).

James and John sought Christ's help to satisfy their ambition for thrones and power (Mark 10:35–45), while Jesus came to hang on a cross in weakness and shame. We are called to follow him, not to seek great things for ourselves. Lust for power is incompatible with the way of the cross. We are called to choose between comfort and suffering (Stott 1986, 285–93). Sadly, missions have often done wrongs to other peoples because of our ambition for power, dominating others through our service instead of humbly serving alongside them and respecting them.

Christ was able to face his trials because of "the joy set before him" (Heb 12:2). Suffering as Christ did is suffering with Christ. To share in his sufferings is to share in his glory, and the hope of glory makes suffering bearable. God's purpose is to present us before his glorious presence without fault and with great joy (Jude 24), as those who are conformed to the likeness of his Son.

## SERVING AND SUFFERING IN MISSION

Jesus prepared his disciples for mission, and whenever he spoke about their mission it became clear that the cost would be high. He told his disciples that some would listen and accept their message, while others would react with hatred, persecute them, arrest them, bring them before authorities in judgment. They should not fear and not be surprised, they had been forewarned. A very painful aspect of persecution would be the hatred of their own families. They were called to stand firm until the end (Matt 10:7–10,16–20,37,38; Mark 13:12–13; Luke 12:50–53).

Jesus explained that his disciples would be hated, persecuted, and killed because of him, but that the gospel of the Kingdom would be preached to all nations before the end (Matt 24:9, 13–14; Luke 21:12–19; Mark 13:9–11). Mission would lead to persecution, but persecution would be unable to hinder mission or to prevent people from coming to the light.

Jesus sent them to make disciples of all nations. The disciples understood that their way would not be easy. But they could go out and obey because of the Lord's affirmation that all authority on earth and in heaven had been given to him, and because of the promise of his presence, in all times and all places, to all who obey him. And they would receive the power of the Holy Spirit to enable them to be his witnesses (Matt 28:16–20).

Jesus sent his disciples as sheep among wolves, as those who, at the same time, need to be as shrewd as snakes and as innocent as doves. It is to be prudent and sincere, not seeking solutions through harmful ways (Luke 12:3–12; Matt 10:16–33). Jesus called them to be bold witnesses when brought before hostile leaders (Matt 10:17–18), and to use such occasions as opportunities to witness (Luke 21:13). Even today, Christians who have spoken with hostile authorities are amazed about the way they were enabled to speak. During persecution it is easy to lose one's self-control and provoke the authorities. Wisdom and innocence are absolutely necessary under persecution (Matt 10:34–39; Ton 2000, 70–81; Bonhoeffer 1967, 237–39).

> "A disciple is not above his teacher, nor a servant above his master. It is enough for the disciple to be like his teacher, and the servant like his master. If they have called the master of the house Beelzebub, how much more will they malign those of his household."
> Matthew 10:24–25

Jesus teaches his disciples not to resist evil men but to be ready to react with humility and a willingness to serve, and not in self-defense. The disciples must not only accept evil done to them, but love evildoers and bring them to God. They can behave like this because they are children of a Father who loves those who hate him (Matt 5:38–48, John 3:16; Luke 6:27–36; Ton 2000, 45).

## SUFFERING UNTIL THE END OF TIME

Jesus taught that wars, famines, earthquakes, false Christs, and persecutions would come, but that "by your endurance you will gain your lives" (Luke 21:5–37; Matt 24; Mark 13).

Christian mission provokes persecution and Jesus wants his disciples to continue to preach the gospel and to stand firm in their faith. The repeated order given by Jesus is to watch and pray, to be alert and watch out. The verbs used by Jesus (all are in the present imperative) define the attitude Christians should have:

*Blepete* – (Matt 24:4; Mark 13:5,9,23,33; Luke 21:8) to discern, to have understanding (Thayer 1980, 103), to pay attention to, to be careful (Dahn 1986, 515).

*Gnēgoreite* – (Matt 24:42; Mark 13:35,37), to watch, give strict attention to, to be cautious (Thayer 1980, 122).

*Agrupneite* – (Mark 13:33; Luke 21:36) be wakeful, ready (9).

*Prosechete* – (Luke 21:34) be attentive, give heed to (546).

Jesus knows all about our human weaknesses; he does not encourage speculation, but an attitude of watchfulness as we face situations of increased sufferings.

In conclusion, Jesus presented only one way to his disciples, of following him in humble service, total dedication to our missionary calling, suffering, and ultimate victory. To belong to him is to be hated by the world, to follow him is to follow the same pattern of dying in order to produce fruit and gain eternal life. He also promises his presence, his joy, his strength and wisdom, related especially to fulfilling the mission of preaching the gospel to all nations.

## QUESTIONS FOR REFLECTION

1. How do you react to Jesus' continuing emphasis on suffering as part of the lives of those who follow him? How did the first disciples react?
2. How does Jesus' model and his teaching prepare his disciples to face hardships in their missionary task?
3. How can a greater emphasis on Jesus' teaching in our church or Bible study group enable us to be better prepared for suffering in mission?
4. What kind of unhealthy teachings are we facing today, related to this subject?

## REFERENCES

Bonhoeffer, D. 1967. *The cost of discipleship*. New York: Macmillan.

Carson, D. A. 1994. *The sermon of the mount*. Biblical classics library. Carlisle, UK: Paternoster.

Dahn, K. 1985. See, vision, eye. In *The new international dictionary of New Testament theology*, ed. C. Brown, vol. 3, 511–18. Exeter, UK: Paternoster.

Esser, H. H. 1986. Ἔλεος (eleos), compassion, mercy. In *The new international dictionary of New Testament theology*, ed. C. Brown, vol. 2, 594–98. Exeter, UK: Paternoster.

Stott, J. 1981. Contracultura Cristã. In *A Bíblia fala hoje*, trans. Y. M. Krievin. São Paulo: ABU Editora. English ed.: 1992. *The message of the Sermon on the Mount: Christian counter-culture*, 2nd ed. with study guide. Downers Grove, IL: InterVarsity Press.

———. 1986. *The cross of Christ*. Leicester: InterVarsity Press.

Thayer, J. H. 1980. *A Greek-English lexicon of the New Testament*. Grand Rapids, MI: Baker Book House.

Ton, J. 2000. *Suffering, martyrdom and rewards in heaven*. New York: Romanian Missionary Society.

**Antonia Leonora van der Meer**, Brazilian with a Dutch background, served with IFES for many years in Brazil and Angola. Now at the Evangelical Missions Center in Brazil, she is development coordinator, dean, teacher, and mentor. She has a master's in theology at the Baptist Brazilian Theological Faculty in São Paulo and a doctorate in missiology at the Asia Graduate School of Theology in the Philippines. She has published several articles in *Connections: The Journal of the WEA Mission Commission*, in *Global Missiology for the Twenty-first Century*, in the Brazilian version of *Perspectives*, in *Doing Member Care Well*, in *The Dictionary of Mission Theology*, and in the *Atlas of Global Christianity*. She wrote several books in Portuguese: an inductive Bible study *(ABUEditora)*, a personal missionary story (*Eu, um Missionário?*), and a book on caring for Brazilian missionaries in contexts of suffering (*Missionários Feridos*).

CHAPTER 15

# BIBLICAL TEACHING ON SUFFERING AND PERSEVERANCE IN PAUL AND PETER

*Margaretha N. Adiwardana*

This study deals with perseverance in situations of adversity in the mission field, looking to the Bible for solid and absolute principles, especially as perseverance in suffering runs counter to contemporary culture. Most books of the Bible were written in a context where the servants of God were suffering, specifically from rejection by the people to whom they were sent, (e.g., Isaiah, Jeremiah, and even Jesus himself), and from persecution (e.g., Elijah, Paul, Peter, and John). This serves as a kind of warning of what is to be expected by those who serve God and an example of how they should react to persecution and suffering.

Biblical teaching on perseverance is considered in the following passages: 2 Corinthians 11:23–33, where Paul wrote about the suffering he underwent as missionary, and 1 Peter 4:12–16, where Peter exhorted Christians to rejoice in suffering.

## PERSEVERANCE IN THE LIFE AND TEACHING OF PAUL: 2 CORINTHIANS 11:23–33

From the very beginning of his calling, Paul was warned that he would suffer as he preached the gospel (Acts 9:15). Towards the end of his ministry, he said that if he had to boast of anything about himself, he would boast of being a servant of Christ who had gone through much suffering. He lived in constant danger: Danger in travels included traveling through rivers, enduring shipwreck, and facing the risk of being robbed. Dangers caused by man included opposition from fellow countrymen, Gentiles, false Christians, and the Roman government. Deprivations he faced involved physical labor, tiredness, and hunger.[1] Paul had "often gone without sleep" (2 Cor 11:27), not because it was deliberately shunned, but because sleep was impossible. He also faced cold, nakedness, and lack of money (Barret 1986, 300). Furthermore, he was worn down by his emotional concerns in the pastoral caring for the church. He faced death on many occasions and eventually died in Rome.

---

[1]     Bratcher mentions that toil and hardship implies working hard to make a living and to preach the gospel (Bratcher 1983, 126).

In Romans 8:17 Paul described Christians as children of God who are fellow sufferers with Christ and coheirs of his glory and sufferings. In verses 35–39 he affirms that no kind of suffering can separate us from Christ. From this, one might conclude that suffering could be used to try to separate us from God, but it need not prevail. In 2 Corinthians 1:3–11 Paul asserts that suffering makes us experience the comfort of God. Then we are able to comfort others when they are going through the same sufferings as we have. "Comfort" is translated from a Greek word which means not only consoling someone in trouble, but also helping and encouraging them. In verses 3–7 this word occurs ten times, which indicates the importance this letter gives to "comforting in trouble" (Barret 1986, 7). Verse 6 mentions that patience and the comfort of God in suffering are of equal measurement. As fellow sufferers with Christ, Christians experience the comfort of God. Verse 8 warns them not to be ignorant of the real reason and nature of hardships, even when it seems to be more than human strength can bear. The aim of suffering is to encourage Christians not to rely on themselves but on God, who gives life (resurrection) even after death. God who delivered Jesus will deliver them by faith. This is Paul's explanation for suffering.

Paul suffered even as he warned others. He was stoned, lashed, imprisoned (Acts 14:19; 16:22ff.; 20:23; 21:13,31ff.; 22:22; 23:21). Morris writes that Paul's understanding of suffering is that it is not aimless, nor inflicted by fate. Suffering comes only as God Almighty permits, and God's purposes are accomplished in the sufferings of his servants (Morris 1995, 26).

Perseverance (*hypomone*) in Paul's writing is a characteristic which is demanded from those who wish to live lives pleasing to God. "To those who by persistence *(kath' hypomone)* in doing good seek glory, honor and immortality, he will give eternal life" (Rom 2:7). The active meaning of firm persistence in doing good, as well as the passive patient resignation in difficulties, may be included here.

Paul shows in Romans chapter 5 that suffering can be used to transform the character of the righteous. Verses 3–5 state that suffering (*thlipsis*) produces perseverance (*hypomonen*) and experience and hope. Hope is waiting patiently for what one does not see yet (Rom 8:25). There is a relationship between *hypomone* and *thlipsis,* perseverance and suffering/affliction (Rom 12:12–13). *Thlipsis* has the meaning of "pressure" in the physical sense and "oppression" in the figurative sense. According to the *International Dictionary of New Testament Theology,* "The aim of the Scriptures is to promote *hypomone* which furthermore reflects the very character of God" (Brown and Coenen 1985, 360). Paul wrote in Romans 15:3–6, "For everything that was written in the past was written to teach us so that through endurance and the encouragement of the Scriptures we might have hope. May the God who gives endurance and encouragement (*ho de theos tes hypomones kai tes parakleseos*) give you a spirit of unity among yourselves as you follow Christ Jesus, so that with one heart and mouth you may glorify the God and Father of our Lord Jesus Christ."

In 1 Corinthians, *hypomone* is a characteristic of love: "It always protects, always trusts, always hopes, always perseveres (*Panta hypomenei*)" (1 Cor 13:7). In 2 Corinthians, Paul develops the theme of perseverance, especially relating to being in the service of Christ for the sake of the church (2 Cor 1:6). Paul mentions his own perseverance as a quality demanded of Christian workers (1 Tim 6:1; 2 Tim 3:10) and older men (Titus 2:2). Out of love for the elect it is necessary to endure all things (2 Tim 2:10) (Brown and Coenen 1985, 380–81). In 2 Corinthians 1:8–9 Paul says that "this happened that we might not rely on ourselves, but on God who raises the dead." Clements writes:

> Paul is convinced that his descent into abject despair was deliberately engineered by God's providence.… Doubt, uncertainty and intellectual insecurity are experiences we have to pass through to discover faith. The opposite of faith, according to Paul, is not doubt but confidence 'in the flesh'… that one can cope on one's own; … that one does not need the grace of God.… The people who are farthest from faith are … those who are all too sure of themselves.… God had to teach even him … not to rely on himself, but 'on God who raises the dead.'" (1994, 24–25)

## CONCLUSION: 2 CORINTHIANS 11:23–33

Paul is an example of a missionary whose suffering is a consequence of his desire to serve Christ in bringing the gospel to people. Persecution from man and suffering from poverty and dangers were to be expected. Yet Paul persevered. He recognized that troubles are part of the whole process whereby a Christian is conformed to Christ's image, the Suffering Servant. In his suffering he experienced God's comfort and grew in the hope of sharing in Christ's glory. Barnett concludes that while Paul had health problems and relationship conflicts like other people, faithfulness to Christ and to the ministry were the chief source of his trouble (Barnett 1988, 30). As Hauck asserts, Paul considered that Christians showed their faith by persevering in suffering (cf. 2 Tim 2:10). The ability to endure is given by God (Rom 15:5), and it is closely related to faith and love (1 Tim 6:11; 2 Tim 3:10), and in Titus 2:2, steadfastness in hoping. If hope focuses on the future, the steadfastness of hope is during the present affliction. Hope is based on the promise that those who die with Christ, if they endure, shall also reign with him (2 Tim 2:11–12, Hauck 1985, 583).

Carson makes the case that our society mirrors the church of Corinth in triumphalism. And Paul told the church of Corinth that when miracles, typical of the apostolic ministry, appeared, it was in the context of great endurance. "The 'endurance' in Paul's case refers to the beatings, the privations, and the thorn in the flesh" (Carson 1984, 157). Belleville applies this to the current church, affirming that the central theme of 2 Corinthians is divine power in weakness, a theme much neglected by the church in the West. It is considered appropriate only for Christians under oppressive political regimes. Health, wealth, and prosperity is a popular theme in many contemporary sermons. But Paul defines the role of gospel preacher in terms of trials and hardships. There God's power is seen and appropriated, his comfort experienced in suffering (1:6–7; Belleville 1996, 36). The model set by Paul before the church is pastoral care, self-sacrifice, and a lifestyle of weakness (45). Paul maintained that God's power is seen most effectively in ministerial hardship and distress: "Dying, and yet we live on; beaten, and yet not killed, … having nothing, and yet possessing everything" (6:9–10). In the very weakness of the ministers, Jesus is revealed. This is difficult to accept in today's current mind-set. People frequently want to be in control of their circumstances. And yet in Paul's opinion, weakness authenticates the true gospel minister (123).

Suffering is often part of missionary life. It brings God's comfort. With the experience of God's comfort, character is transformed, self-reliance is changed to dependence on God. This is the mark of real faith and the true gospel. It results in endurance, perseverance in good works, love, and steadfastness in faith. In the missionary's weakness, God's power is displayed. It shows human weakness and displays divine strength and human dependence on God. A missionary should endure in producing good works, with trustful hope, not necessarily for deliverance but for hope in God's promise that God, in the end, will give him eternal life. When Christians remain faithful amidst suffering, God who gives endurance, comfort, and encouragement is glorified.

## PERSEVERANCE IN RESPONSE TO SUFFERING IN THE TEACHING OF PETER: 1 PETER 4:12–19

According to Clowney, the heart of Peter's concern in writing his first letter is to assure Christians of their hope as they face trials (1988, 51). Ramsey Michaels considers this passage as an opportunity to reflect on the themes of 2:11–4:6, which show how one should "respond to one's enemies and how to face hostility and the prospect of suffering" (1988, 258).

Peter considered suffering for Christ as quite normal. There is nothing special in it. It is not strange or extraordinary. The clear message that is being conveyed in this passage is that suffering is part of the natural experience of Christians; it is not something foreign to them. It would be strange and unusual if they did not suffer because of their faith (Arichea and Nida 1980, 145–6). Christ suffered and it is an indication of identification with him when his followers suffer as he did. Verse 13 says that participation in Christ's suffering is a reason to rejoice, because those who share in his suffering will participate in his glory. Cranfield says that "this sharing is a two-way sharing. We share in his sufferings, and he shares in ours. We share his reproach…. To share Christ's shame is a glorious privilege—to have his fellowship though it be in the midst of the flames—is to have fullness of joy, and to partake of his humiliation in this world is the pledge of participation in his glory in the world to come" (Cranfield 1960, 120). To suffer on behalf of Jesus' name is a blessing because that is the sign that the Spirit of Glory is present in that person (cf. Matt 5:10–12).

The Christian has to glorify God in suffering (v. 16). Marshall comments, "Rather we should recognize that suffering because of our faith is a way of bringing glory to God…. He is glorified by the faithful witness of his people" (Marshall 1991, 155). The Spirit of Christ is in the person who suffers. From the point of view of the world, it is strange and uncommon when man has to suffer, as human beings seek a comfortable life. But persecution and rejection are to be expected by those who follow Christ's way of life which is against the world and the flesh. It is "against the characteristic of our age," according to Morris (1995, 330). Man has to force himself to appreciate suffering.

Suffering is part of the purifying process of the Christian life for those who obey the gospel of God. The "painful trial" in verse 12 is also translated as "the fiery ordeal" (cf. Prov 27:21). As Grudem comments, "The image of a refiner's fire suggests that such suffering purifies and strengthens Christians" (1988, 178). They should not be ashamed of suffering or shy away from it. Judgment is the sign of the end of times (cf. the great tribulation, Mark 13:20), which starts with the persecution of the church and ends with the divine fury against the rebellious (Rev 6:15,17; Isa 10:12; Jer 25:29; Ezek 9:6; Mal 3:1–6 (Shedd 1989, 280). It is God's own will which allows the Christian to suffer. "According to God's will" in verse 19 may be rendered as "because this is what God desires that they should experience" (cf. 2:15; 3:17). Christians should also "commit themselves to their faithful Creator and continue to do good." They should also "do good to others, and in this way trust themselves completely to their Creator" (Archea and Nida 1980, 153). Marshall's conclusion on the passage is as follows:

> Are we to say that God intends his people to suffer? Hard though it may seem, the answer to this question is affirmative. It was God's will that Christ should suffer to redeem his people, and Christ was obedient to that will. To be sure, the need arose only because of the evil in the world, but in a world where evil exists, its defeat is possible only through suffering.... It is right to say that God's will for us is suffering because there is no other way that evil can be overcome. When we suffer, it is not a sign of God's lack of love or concern for us....Those who suffer can confidently place themselves in the care of God. (1991, 157)

The Christian who suffers has to trust God, rely on his perfect will, entrust his life to his Master and Creator. Michaels translates "commit themselves" as "let (them) entrust their lives" and comments that "this phrase ... defines rather the attitude of mind that makes the glorification of God in a time of crisis possible." He compares it with Psalms 30:6, "Into your hands I entrust my spirit," and concludes that Peter wants his readers to entrust themselves continually to God's protecting care, whatever the circumstances. "Lives" (or "souls") is a favorite term in 1 Peter, either in connection with salvation (1:9,22; 3:20) or (as here) with divine care and guidance (cf. 2:25). *Psyche* is used throughout, not for an immaterial "soul" in distinction from the body, but for the whole person, especially with reference to the person's ultimate physical and spiritual well-being (Michaels 1988, 273). The attitude is of trust, "handing over something of value to the care of another," which "in our context is of handing over one's most valuable possession, one's very own self, to God" (Davids 1966, 159).

> Then Jesus, calling out with a loud voice, said, "Father, into your hands I commit my spirit!" And having said this he breathed his last. *Luke 23:46*

The Christian is to rejoice in suffering, as when it is on behalf of Christ's name it means participating with him and in his glory. "Rejoice" (*chairete*) in verse 13 is present tense, which according to Stibbs indicates the demand not for a single isolated response, but for a continuous attitude and activity. "For it means that they have a privileged share in the outworking of God's age-long purpose, according to which Christ enters his glory, through suffering" (cf. 1:10,11; Luke 24:26; Stibbs 1966, 159). Verses 14 and 16 refer to the sufferings that Christ endured and those we endure in his name. "As we suffer for Christ, we are linked to him. Our sufferings witness to his. Because he suffered for us, we can rejoice when we are counted worthy to suffer for him" (Clowney 1988, 191). We have to continue living virtuously and practicing good works. This is contrary to the normal acceptable human reaction towards suffering. Our first reaction in suffering is, "Why me?" and after a prolonged period of suffering, "Where is God?" Thus Peter had to exhort Christians to persevere and even be joyful in suffering instead of the normal automatic human reaction of aversion and bafflement. Clowney affirms that, "suffering for Christ leads to glory and tastes of glory; it also gives glory to God. When believers suffer because they are Christians, God is glorified" (1988, 192).

In 1 Peter 5:9, Peter mentions that sufferings are being borne by Christians all over the world and that Christians should resist the devil, standing firm in the faith. Verse 10 says that after they have suffered for a little while, Christ himself will restore them, making them strong, firm, and steadfast. Suffering is a blessing when it results from righteous action or persecution. In such circumstances, Christians need not be afraid of the danger of suffering (1 Pet 3:14). 1 Peter 1:6 says that one should rejoice in suffering because the final revelation is salvation. It is God's power which keeps the righteous through faith. Many tribulations sadden the believers, but their faith is proved to be more precious than gold which perishes. "The aim of suffering is to redound to the praise, glory, and honor when Jesus Christ will be revealed. Peter exhorts those who suffer to follow Jesus' example, an example of patience and perseverance on the cross, as a rebuke of unrighteousness (1 Pet 2:21)"; Morris says that we need to try to reproduce this attitude in our experience (1995, 322). Perseverance (*hypomone*) is mentioned twice in 2 Peter 1:6 as a virtue, producing Christian character (cf. Rom 5:3 Jas 1:3; Brown and Coenen 1985, 381).

## CONCLUSION: 1 PETER 4:12–19

Peter, the apostle who denied Jesus three times for fear of imprisonment when Jesus was being taken away to the crucifixion, later understood that suffering for doing what is right is part of the Christian life. One has to expect it and should not think it strange. It is a blessing and a reason to rejoice, as it means that one is taking part in Christ's suffering and therefore will also take part in his glory. The response towards suffering is to persevere. That will bring blessing. It will finally bring glory to God when by faith it is proven that God keeps one steadfast in suffering. To suffer because of evildoing is a shame, but to suffer because of righteousness is a blessing. It is an identification and participation with Christ, both in his suffering and in his glory.

Peter understood our human fears, "Do not fear what they fear; do not be frightened. But in your hearts set apart Christ as Lord" (1 Pet 3:14–15a, quoting Isa 8:12). As Cranfield comments on 1 Peter 3:13, "If we do not have to fear persecution, there is still fear of illness, of bereavement, of failure, of getting old, of the next war, and so on." He further comments on 1 Peter 3:14–15 with reference to Isaiah 8:12ff., "According to the Hebrew text, the prophet and his disciples are warned not to conform to the ideas of the people, nor to fear what the people are afraid of, but to fear the Lord God alone.... Christians must let the true fear—the fear of Christ their Lord—banish all false fears from their hearts" (Cranfield 1960, 99).

The sovereignty and initiative of God even in the suffering of his own people is considered to be the most striking feature of the passage by Michaels. Faithfulness and doing good makes it possible to rejoice even under slander and oppression, and to experience now in advance, through the Spirit of God, the glory of Christ for which we wait (Michaels 1988, 274–75).

# QUESTIONS FOR REFLECTION

1.  What can we learn from Paul's example in facing suffering and persecution which will help us to face these and to support those who suffer and are persecuted today?
2.  Adiwardana emphasizes persevering and endurance in Paul's teaching to the churches facing hard times. How can we recover this biblical teaching in our own churches and mission schools today? How will it help our missionaries going to hard places?
3.  Peter considered suffering for Christ as quite normal, not something foreign to them. He indicates that it would be strange if they did not suffer because of their faith. Christ suffered and so will his followers. Why has this teaching become so foreign to our churches today? How can we recover a more balanced Christian understanding?
4.  The Christian response towards suffering is to persevere. That will bring blessing. It will finally bring glory to God. How and why can Christians today rejoice under slander and oppression? What is our responsibility to our fellow Christians who suffer for their witness?

# REFERENCES

Arichea, D. C., and E. A. Nida. 1980. *A translator's handbook on the first letter from Peter.* New York: United Bible Societies.

Barnett, P. 1988. *The message of 2 Corinthians.* Downers Grove, IL: InterVarsity Press.

Barret, C. K. 1986. *The second epistle to the Corinthians.* London: A. C. Black.

Belleville, L. L. 1996. *2 Corinthians.* Downers Grove, IL: InterVarsity Press.

Bratcher, R. G. 1983. *A translator's guide to Paul's second letter to the Corinthians.* New York: United Bible Societies.

Brown, C., and L. Coenen. 1985. *Dicionário internacional de teologia do Novo Testamento.* São Paulo: Edições Vida Nova.

Carson, D. A. 1984. *From triumphalism to maturity.* Grand Rapids: Baker.

Clements, R. 1994. *The strength of weakness.* Rosshire, UK: Christian Focus.

Clowney, E. 1988. *The message of 1 Peter.* Downers Grove, IL: InterVarsity Press.

Cranfield, C. E. B. 1960. *1 and 2 Peter and Jude.* London: SCM.

Davids, P. H. 1990. *The first epistle of Peter.* Grand Rapids, MI: Eerdmans.

Grudem, W. 1988. *1 Peter.* Downers Grove, IL: InterVarsity Press.

Hauck, F. 1985. Hypomone. In *Theological dictionary of the New Testament,* eds. G. Kittel, G. Friedrich and G. Bromiley. Grand Rapids, MI: Paternoster.

Marshall, I. H. 1991. *1 Peter.* Downers Grove, IL: InterVarsity Press.

Michaels, J. R. 1988. *1 Peter.* Waco, TX: Word.

Morris, L. 1995. *The cross in the New Testament.* Carlisle, UK: Paternoster.

Shedd, R., ed. 1989. *A Biblia vida nova.* São Paulo: Edições Vida Nova and SBB.

Stibbs, A.M. 1966. *1 Peter.* London: Tyndale Press.

**Margaretha Nalina Adiwardana** is the president and CEO of AME (Associação Missão Esperança), working in international disaster relief and community development, and working to partner with and strengthen local churches. She is the founder and coordinator of REDE SOS GLOBAL, a Brazilian network for disaster relief. Ms. Adiwardana is a missionary trainer in several Brazilian organizations, seminaries, and training centers.

CHAPTER 16

# THE PROBLEM OF EVIL AND SUFFERING

## A Comparative Look at African and Western Views

*Isaiah M. Dau*

## INTRODUCTION

Who am I? I am a woman who dresses in rags, a woman who cannot speak a foreign tongue: I am blind, and I am unschooled. My survival has always relied on cattle, but now all our animals have been raided. My children have been bribed to come and torment me. My Nhialic, my Nhialic have mercy on me. It is (only) you who will raise me (up) out of this suffering. I endured ten days without eating and I lived on the water you brought me.[1]

Tell me yourself directly, I challenge you: imagine that you yourself are erecting the edifice of human fortune with the goal of, at the finale, making people happy, of at last giving them peace and quiet, but that in order to do it, it would be necessary and unavoidable to torture to death only one little tiny creature ... would you agree to be the architect on those conditions, tell me and tell me truly?[2]

The problem of human suffering puts faith under severe strain.[3] It understandably generates discussion across cultures and communities. That it touches all people everywhere and places their faith in a God of love under strain is undeniable. In recent times, the reality of evil and suffering in our world has been made visibly acute by globalization and rapid dissemination of information. Consequently, with this rapid growth of communication technology in our time, we are almost daily brought face to face with actual or potential victims of suffering and evil in our world like never before in human history. The gruesome

---

1     This is a prayer of a Sudanese victim of the war offered at a displaced people's camp in Uganda, February 1994. She narrates in prayer her suffering resulting from the war in which she has lost her family, cattle, and home. Her faith in Nhialic, or "the one above," as the Dinka of Sudan refer to God, is very real and is the only thing that has given her the strength to survive the brutality of the ongoing war (see Dau 2000). The prayer is quoted in Nikkel (1997, 61–78).

2     This is Ivan Karamazov's question to his brother Alyosha on the problem of suffering (Dostoyevsky 1993, 282).

3     John Hick has persuasively argued that "whilst the reality of evil undoubtedly challenges the Christian faith and sets it under a severe strain, it does not finally render that faith untenable by a rational person" (1973, 53).

images of the 1990s massive death and genocide in Rwanda and the Balkans are still fresh in our minds. The same is true of the horror of chopped off limbs of children as young as a few months old in Sierra Leone or images of man-made famine in Ethiopia, Eritrea, Sudan, Angola, and the Democratic Republic of Congo, to mention but a few examples. We gasp for breath as we ask in desperation and frustration: Why should there be suffering at all? What purpose and value does suffering serve in our human existence? Where is God when evil assails? Although these questions are easier to ask than to answer, they constitute what has traditionally been called the problem of evil. These questions belie our human quest for an answer to this troublesome problem. "The human heart cries out for an answer, which reaches down to the sorrowing and the sufferer with a word which brings hope in a world of despair" (Carson 1978, 13). Although such an answer does not come forth as humanity expects, God may still be experienced in suffering. As C. S. Lewis has astutely observed, "God whispers to us in our pleasures, speaks in our conscience, but shouts in our suffering; suffering is his megaphone to rouse a deaf world" (Lewis 1967, 10).

But the quest for an answer has never been a matter of consensus, inevitably resulting in diverse viewpoints and interpretations. This is what the above quoted statements, one from Africa and the other from the West, represent. Tokunboh Adeyemo has rightly classified this diversity in the way we view reality as a "clash of two worldviews" (1998, 369). Thus the above statements are essentially typical of the differences in the way the problem of suffering and evil is interpreted in Africa and in the West. The first is a prayer of a Sudanese woman who is struggling with the reality both of suffering and faith in the brutality of war and death in her country. The second is a classic Western protest against the apparent domestication of evil and suffering, espoused by the theodicy and theology of nineteenth-century Europe. This protest is personified in Fyodor Dostoyevsky's classic novel, *The Brothers Karamazov*, which challenges the traditional assumption that suffering is purposeful in the larger scheme of things, in the original divine plan. It protests in very strong terms the suffering of children and refuses any justification of suffering, not even the bliss of the hereafter. The prayer of the Sudanese woman expresses trust in the faithfulness and provision of God in war and suffering.

In this article, we attempt to analyze the African traditional understanding of suffering and evil, compared to the Western view. At the outset, we argue that the African view of reality is holistic, rarely distinguishing the sacred and the secular or the spiritual and the material. Then we examine some African traditional thinking on the origin of evil and suffering as we attempt to differentiate between natural and moral evil. We then move on to investigate prayers, dirges, protests, and laments expressed in the African traditional context as a way of facing the tragic reality of suffering and evil. We compare the African view with the Western view before we conclude with theological implications in relation to the problem of evil and suffering. These theological implications are drawn from the framework of the incarnation as the Christian answer to the problem of evil and suffering. We speak of the cross, community, hope, and character as the basis of transcending and transforming suffering and evil into the highest good possible in this life.

## A HOLISTIC COSMOLOGY

The African view of evil and suffering is a component of a complex but holistic cosmology. This cosmology, as John S. Mbiti and others have pointed out, hierarchically consists of God, spirits or divinities, ancestors, the living dead, the living, the unborn, the animals, and the plants, etc. In this worldview, reality is a coherent whole and unified. Good and bad, blessing and misfortune, comfort and suffering, joy and grief, success and failure, life and death are all part of the existential reality. Far from being fatalistic, the African worldview accepts that life is sometimes unfair and bitter. Although this worldview never domesticates or fatalistically accepts suffering and evil as normal, it still recognizes that these are realities of life that must be faced and resisted, unpleasant as they truly are. Thus, the African view recognizes suffering and evil as the unfortunate lot of humanity that God did not originally intend for it to experience but, nevertheless, do experience here in this world. Evil and suffering are regarded as realities that must be faced as part of a tragic existence.

African peoples are very much aware of evil in the world and they endeavor to fight it in various ways (Mbiti 1990, 199). But as K. A. Busia notes, the problem of evil as so often discussed in Western philosophy and Christian theology does not arise in the African concept of deity. The Supreme Being of the African is the Creator, the source of life, but between him and humanity lie many powers and principalities good and bad—gods, spirits, magical forces, and witches—to account for the strange happenings in the world (Busia 1998, 197). Equally, many African traditional thinkers, as it is the case among the Akan for instance, while recognizing the existence of moral evil in the world, generally do not believe that this is inconsistent with the assertion that God is omnipotent. In their view, evil is the result of the exercise by humans of their freedom of will, with which God endowed them (Gyekye 1987, 128).

## EVIL AND SUFFERING IN AFRICAN TRADITIONAL THOUGHT

In African traditional thought, the origin of evil is assumed, not explained. Many African tribes categorically reject the idea that evil originated from God. Some, like the Vugusu of Kenya, believe that evil originated from spiritual beings or divinities. The Dinka of Sudan believe the *jak,* or independent spirits, as opposed to *yieth,* ancestral spirits, cause destruction and suffering (Deng 1972, 122–23). These divinities or spirits were created by God but only became evil when they rebelled against God and began to do evil. Francis Deng observes that the *jak* in Dinka cosmology act as God's police, executing his prescribed judgment on those who do wrong.[4] Mbiti believes this concept is a personification of evil itself (1990, 199–210).

What is more, there is human responsibility in how evil came to be. Evil is supposed to have come about as a result of human transgression of a divine command, whose exact content varies from one tribe to another. There is a widespread notion in African traditional

---

4        Deng elaborates further that the jak or evil spirits do not act only when called upon. All the unexplained suffering is attributed to their malice, although the fatalistic and guilty disposition of humans often traces the chain of causation to some human fault, if only an error (Deng 1972, 123).

thought that in the beginning God and humans lived together on earth and communicated frequently. But owing to some misconduct on the part of man or woman, God left the earth and went to live in the sky, leaving humankind ever endeavoring to reach him in vain (Smith 1950, 7–8). A story of "the Fall," somewhat similar to the biblical one in Genesis 3, is thus given in different forms and flavors in African oral traditions to attempt to explain the origin of evil.[5] The Dinka of the Sudan, for instance, relate a myth in which the first human persons, a man and a woman, transgressed the divine command not to cultivate in a forbidden territory. The woman, who is regarded as the main culprit, while ploughing with a long pestle struck the divinity and he withdrew from the earth. Having been greatly offended, the divinity sent a sparrow or a finch called *atoc*, to sever the rope which had previously linked humans to God in heaven. Access to heaven, where humans were restored to vitality and youth when they became old was, thereby, denied. This is how things were "spoilt."[6] Hunger, sickness, suffering, and death were the results of this abrupt separation between humankind and God to this day (Lienhardt 1961, 32–55).[7]

Humanity had disobeyed God's command and chose to have its own way rather than the way of God; therefore, according to the Dinka, humankind has to accept suffering and death as logical consequences of its disobedience. Thus, God is not the origin of evil. To the Dinka and other African peoples such as the Ashanti, the Yoruba, the Nuer, and many others, evil did not originate from God; God does not do what is evil nor can he harm anyone. According to the Ila people, God is always in the right and cannot therefore be charged with an offense, cannot be accused, cannot be questioned (Smith and Dale 1920, 199–211). Rosemary Guillebaud reports that the Banyarwanda-Urundi peoples believe that Imana is surpassed by nothing. He gives life to all, does no evil, and there is nothing evil in him. All good comes from him and if prosperity should cease to be, it is because Imana has withdrawn himself from humans. They believe it is impossible that evil should occur if he is still there (Guillebaud 1950, 186). The Nuer people of Sudan share this view as well (Pritchard 1956, 21).

## THE ORIGIN OF EVIL

According to John Mbiti, in nearly all African societies the spirits are either the origin of evil or agents of evil (Mbiti 1990, 199). The living dead, who become detached from the living, are also believed to bring fear and evil to the living. If they are improperly buried, neglected, or disobeyed they take revenge and punish the offenders. The living, therefore, bear the consequences of their actions when they experience evil and suffering because they fail to accord the living dead the honor they deserve. Since God is always in the right, misfortune, suffering, and evil come to humans mainly by their own actions (Pritchard 1956, 19–21).

---

5       For further reference to the similarity of African worldview and the Hebrew worldview as shown in the Old Testament, see Desmond Tutu's "Some African Insights and the Old Testament" (1972, 16–22).

6       David Bosch rightly notes that the word used for sin in several African languages means to "spoil," especially to spoil or harm human relationships (see his "Problem of Evil in Africa: A Survey of African Views on Witchcraft and of the Christian Church Response" (1987, 50).

7       E. Bolaji Idowu tells the Yoruba creation story and the Fall in his book, *Olodumare: God in the Yoruba Belief* (1962, 18–29). There are striking similarities between this tradition and that of other African people, including the Dinka.

However, there are times when evil and misfortune are attributed to God. God, as the one who knows all things, may be held responsible for epidemics and afflictions. Mbiti reports that the Tilo people believe God has the power to kill and the power to give life (Mbiti 1971, 81). Although God is not to be rejected on account of evil, most African people believe he is the only one who can deliver them from evil and misfortune. The Nuer people believe God is the only one who can remove evil and misfortune from their path.

Thus, in African traditional thought, God may be exonerated of responsibility for evil, yet at the same time be implicated. Whichever the case, the traditional African will never reject God because evil, suffering, and misfortune afflict him. Rather, he will cling to God even more in spite of evil and suffering. People may, however, complain to God and ancestors for the suffering or evil that befalls them, but they will never accuse God of any moral wrong-doing. God is turned to as the last resort when all other helpers fail (Smith 1950, 30). He cannot be charged with wrongdoing because the moral culpability for this is always placed on the shoulders of humanity (Magesa 1997, 50).

## NATURAL AND MORAL EVIL

At this point, we must distinguish between the evil that a human person does to fellow humans and the evil that naturally occurs beyond human control. The first is in the context of communal relationships and it concerns matters of virtue and character. Among the Nuer and the Dinka people, as well as many other African peoples, conforming to the norms of behavior in the family and the community is paramount. Failure to adhere to these is a serious offense that may bring evil consequences, such as a curse or death. One's conformity to the customs and the norms of community largely determines if one is considered evil or good. If a person acts in ways that do not hurt communal relationships, he/she is good, and if he/she does otherwise he/she is evil.[8] People should be ready to reap the results of their conduct. Most African people generally believe that good always follows the right conduct and ill follows bad conduct. Consequences of one's actions, good or bad, always catch up with him/her sooner or later. This is the logic in the Nuer religion, and to some extent in that of the Dinka. If a person keeps in the right, does not contravene divinely sanctioned interdictions and injunctions, does no wrong to others but fulfills his/her obligations to divinities and to his/her kith and kin, he/she will avoid serious misfortunes.

That person may not, however, avoid misfortunes that come upon one and all people (Pritchard 1956, 17). No one can avoid suffering. God does not punish those who wrong others unknowingly; however, the consequences of one's actions, deliberate or not, are accepted when they are exposed.[9] Still, there is no concept of inherent personal sin that is not connected with one's conduct in the community. Suffering in any form in this category is always attributed to something or someone in the community. In Mbiti's words:

---

8    Compare Mbiti and his discussion of concepts of evil, ethics, and justice in his *African Religions and Philosophy* (1990, 199–210).

9    Being exposed when one is in the wrong results in both shame and guilt. It may not be entirely correct to say, as Van der Walt does, that shame plays a more important role than guilt in African communal ethics. Guilt seems to lead to shame and not the reverse. As in the case of the Dinka, this is true (see Van der Walt 1997, 33).

Every form of pain, misfortune, sorrow, or suffering; every illness and sickness; every death, whether of an old man or of the infant child; every failure of the crop in the field, of hunting in the wilderness, or of fishing in the waters; every bad omen or dream: these and all the other manifestations of evil that man experiences are blamed on somebody in the corporate society. (1990, 204)

Usually, that somebody may be a witch, a sorcerer, or a magician. "The witch," as David Bosch rightly notes, "is sinner par excellence, not primarily because of his or her deeds, but because of the evil consequences of those deeds: illness, barrenness, catastrophe, misfortune, disruption of relationships in the community, poverty, and so on" (1987, 50). In African traditional thinking, it seems, there is nothing that happens without being caused by something or somebody. It is true, as Laurenti Magesa correctly observes, that in typical African traditional moral ethics, sin and evil do not and cannot exist in human experience except as perceived in people. It is people who are evil or sinful, whether or not they are aided by invisible forces. For even when evil forces cause harm, it is because evil people use them to attain their own ends (Magesa 1997, 162). People are, nevertheless, not inherently sinful, but they are sinful because they do evil and destroy communal relationships. Thus, all that happens in African traditional society may be mystically or naturally explained, sometimes resulting in sustained communal suspicion and fragmentation. This is what constitutes moral evil in traditional thinking.

The second type of evil is what humans suffer as a result of natural causes. This may be in the form of droughts, epidemics, floods, and other natural disasters that may not be directly attributed to human activity. Suffering, evil and misfortune may be experienced as a result of these. But again, nothing in African society just happens without being caused by somebody or something. Consequently, possible explanations of whatever befalls humans are always sought or given. In this process, soul-searching or even a witch hunt inevitably ensues in the community, if only to find a scapegoat. The evil eye or the evil heart and the evil mouth, all due to jealousy, hatred and rivalry or even ancestral anger may be possible causes to examine whenever suffering and tragedy strike (Fortes 1987, 211–17). When that happens, every aspect of human conduct in the community may be considered as a possible cause for the suffering or misfortune that is now being experienced.

In some societies, it is thought that suffering results from God punishing the offenders who contravene his laws. For the Dinka, as Francis Deng explains, anyone who is plagued by an illness or a disaster explores the depth of his/her inner self or that of his/her close relatives in the hope of finding the sin that has brought on the discord. So when a Dinka suffers illness or injury, he/she is likely to attribute it to divinities that punish wrongdoers (Deng 1972, 128). For the Nuer and other African peoples, misfortunes ultimately come from God through human and spiritual agents (Pritchard 1956, 18).[10] Whatever explanation is given, human beings, not God, are primarily to blame for their own suffering which results from their actions.

---

10    The Dinka too believe that mankind, as a totality, is subject to the one supreme power of God, for it is God who creates and destroys all men (Deng 1972, 126).

# FACING EVIL AND SUFFERING

Wherever and however evil and suffering come to be, they must be fought and confronted. African people are never passive in the face of suffering. They try to do everything possible to alleviate suffering and restore health and harmony to the individual and the community. Sacrifices, libations, and prayers are offered to God and divinities to solicit their intervention and help at the time of suffering. Sometimes, this help is procured; at other times it is not. Ultimately, resignation to the mystery of evil and suffering prevails when answers are scarce. African traditional thought readily accepts that life is fraught with the unexplainable and the unknowable. Suffering and evil, life and death, God and humankind are all part of this mystery of human existence in the world. This being so, suffering is, nevertheless, not fatalistically accepted; it is wrestled with. It is this wrestling with suffering which boils down to the continual struggle and search for the real meaning of life as it relates to God and the origin of evil. In African traditional religion, God is the complete other, the absolute sovereign one, external to his creation, so far removed in his solitary glory so as to be unapproachable save through intermediaries. At the same time, he is also thought to be immanent in humans as expressed symbolically in creation stories (Smith 1950, 27). This tension in the traditional understanding of God is particularly manifest when suffering and adversity are encountered. It is clearly brought to surface in times of anguish, pain, and suffering. We explore this in the prayer-songs and funeral dirges of African religions, especially those offered at the time of anguish and suffering.

Prayer in African traditional thinking expresses what is deeply troubling or exciting the innermost being. Praying forms an integral part of African religious systems. Prayer is offered in life and death, in sickness and healing, in prosperity and poverty, at work and rest, in war, in adversity and peace, in traveling and settling down, in planting and harvesting, in offering, dedication, blessing, thanksgiving, confession, and all areas of life without exception. Prayer is primarily directed to God and secondarily to intermediaries. According to Mbiti, everyone prays in the sense that all present at the time and place of prayer are party to the contents of the prayers, and may sometimes participate by repeating prayer formulas (Mbiti 1975, 3). There are many kinds of prayers in African traditional religion.[11]

In prayers offered at the time of suffering and adversity, people basically wrestling with God and struggle with the reality of evil and suffering. Prayers are sometimes expressed in very strong language. Sufferers complain and quarrel with God for an alleged failure to intervene at the hour of dire need. God is addressed like a fellow human being. The expression of feelings forms an integral part of prayer. Praying is not only worship; it is also a rhetorical dialogue, a one-way dialogue in which human questioning and heart-searching in the presence of God and other spiritual realities occur (Mbiti 1975, 44). Heaviness of heart due to bereavement or emotional distress is openly expressed to God in a combination

---

11      John S. Mbiti has collected over two hundred such prayers in a book entitled *The Prayers of African Religion* (1975). The prayers cover a wide range of issues dealing with faith in God, life, and communal relationships. Suffering is one of these issues. I am very thankful to Professor Mbiti for drawing my attention to this rich source when I had the privilege of meeting him at a conference in Stellenbosch, South Africa, in May 1999.

of song and prayer. Rosemary Guillebaud, who worked as a missionary in Burundi for many years, recorded the following song-prayers. The loss of a loved one precipitated the first of these song-prayers and the bereaved, in a self-focused lament, charges Imana of treating him unjustly:

> As for me, Imana (God) has eaten me,
> As for me, he has not dealt with me as with others.
> With singing I would sing,
> If only my brother (or whoever the deceased was) was with me.
> Sorrow is not to hang the head mourning,
> Sorrow is not to go weeping (for that will not take away sorrow).
> As for me, Imana has eaten me.
> As for me, he has not dealt with me as with others;
> If he has dealt with me as with others, I could be Scorner-of-Enemies
> Woe is me! (Guillebaud 1950, 198–99)

Being eaten by Imana implies, among other things, having been dealt with unjustly by a God who is presumed to be good and just. It betrays the feeling that the loss of one's relation is like one's own death. But Imana is not a subject of rejection here. He is being indicted for not doing for the plaintiff what he has done for others. Imana has given to others what he has not given to the plaintiff. He has given them children, he has given them covered baskets or prosperity in land produce, and he has given them bulls and other blessings. Only the plaintiff has been forgotten and hence his protest and complaint. The ring of his complaint and protest is shared in the following song-prayer by another individual who is also suffering from some heart-heaviness due to a possible loss in the family, probably a loss of an only son.

> I do not know what Imana is punishing me for: if I could meet with him, I would kill him. Imana, why are you punishing me? Why have you not made me like other people? Couldn't you even give me a little child, Yo-o-o! I am dying in anguish! If only I could meet you and pay you out! Come on (Imana), let me kill you! Let me run you through with a sword, or cut you with a knife! O Imana, you have deserted me! Yo-o-o! (Woe is me!)

The heaviness of the heart due to an irreparable loss of an only son has prompted this individual to draw battle lines to fight Imana. Like suffering Job, the plaintiff demands to know what Imana is punishing him for. He goes further than Job, making his intentions clear that should he meet Imana, he would run him through with a knife. Strong words such as these express both faith in and anger with the God whose presence and absence are experienced at the time of pain and suffering. Faith in the fact that he is present even if his presence is not felt, but anger in the fact that he does not seem to intervene when he is needed most. Both the notions of faith and anger, in this context, denote a process of spiritual journey that leads to mature knowledge of God and freedom to express deep human feelings to him. A human person argues and dialogues with God as if he/she were face to face with him.

As Mbiti rightly points out, this is an outstanding dimension of African spirituality that should be carefully cherished, not ignorantly dismissed (Mbiti 1975, 44). We hasten to point out that there are no atheistic overtones in the prayer. In African traditional society, there is room for complaining, quarrelling, or even fighting with God but there is no room for atheism. Belief in God and other divinities is an inherent part of daily life for all. Religion is inseparable from the day to day activities of life. As Mbiti puts it, African peoples are "notoriously religious." It is thus virtually impossible, in a typical African traditional society, to be a part of the community and fail to be a part of its religious systems and beliefs. One is because his community is. He cannot be an atheist if his community is not and vice versa. There are, therefore, no practicing atheists in African traditional communities and there is no "death of God theology." This holds true even when suffering and adversity abound and when answers to the problem of evil and suffering lack. But wrestling with the problem of evil and suffering in relation to faith in God is a continual reality as shown in the prayer-song.

There is another area in which the African traditional society wrestles with evil and suffering. This is the area of the inevitable reality of death. When death strikes, dialogue between human beings and God is clearly heightened. In African traditional thought, death is regarded as the climax of evil because it takes away life. When a person dies, it is acknowledged that God has let him/her go. Although the belief that a person goes to another land when he/she dies is entertained, death is still a frightening experience. The prospect of dying, particularly dying childless, is the worst imaginable thing that could happen to a human person (for a man particularly). Dying at a good old age when one has raised a family is not such a bad thing. Indeed, there are communities which believe that such a death is not a serious blow since the deceased has left offspring to perpetuate his lineage. Nevertheless, death still generates very strong feelings, expressed through prayers and songs. Such prayers and songs, teeming in sorrow, pain, agony, bewilderment, and suffering, are uttered to register protest. Lament or even blame is vented on God and other spiritual realities for not sustaining life as they are supposed to. Consider the following prayer-lament from the Congo:

> O great Nzambi or God, what thou hast made is good, but thou hast brought a great sorrow to us with death. Thou shouldst have planned in some way that we would not be subject to death. O great Nzambi, we are afflicted with great sorrow.

This prayer is a thinly veiled rebuke to Nzambi for making people subject to death. It is, however, not a cause for doubting his goodness or that of his created order. Those are acknowledged already in the beginning of the prayer. The sorrow that death brings is the point made in the prayer-lament. The wish that God would have planned things better so that people were not subject to death is a universal desire that we express when suffering and tragedy strike.[12] The utterance of that wish is a sort of bewilderment in the face of the mystery of evil and suffering, especially heightened when tragedy assails. But the fact that one can pray at such a time at all is in itself an affirmation of faith in God, even if the mystery of evil still remains unresolved. Praying at this time is a relief to a heavy heart

---

12      This is my paraphrase of Mbiti's comments on the above prayer (see 1975, 91).

of sorrow. Strong language and anger underscored in the prayer are part of the process of coming to grips with the reality of suffering and grieving. This should not be condemned, but should be expressed and allowed to heal with time so that it may result in the relief and restoration of the bereaved.

Prayer-laments or songs associated with suffering and death include accepting that death shall ultimately overtake all people, but it should not call too soon. In the following song-lament we see this thought clearly spelled out with the idea that death is not the end of life but the beginning of another life.

> Would it were not today!
> God, you have called too soon!
> Give him water, he has left without food;
> Light a fire, he must not perish of cold;
> Prepare (the deceased is addressed) a place for us,
> In a little while we shall reach you,
> Let us reach each other.[13]

The pain of sorrow in losing a loved one brings out in us the universal feeling that death should wait a little while. We wish that it did not come at certain stages in life, especially if the deceased has not fulfilled life's vital obligations such as marriage and bearing children, or has not lived long enough to enjoy his "food." This is the reason why God is reminded that the departed "has left without food." He has not lived long enough to enjoy his life; he died young. But that is the nature of death, it comes when it is least expected, as a debtor or thief in the night. As the Akan people say, "Everybody is a debtor to death," and "To be in the hands of death is to be in the hands of someone indeed," for it is a matter of time before every "man will die and rot away" (Nketia 1954, 128). In this song-prayer, both God and the departed are addressed. God is told to give the deceased some water and food. Implied is the belief that a land of the dead exists beyond the grave, where people eat and drink. Hence, the deceased is not really considered dead, but gone to that land. This is the reason Got is asked to prepare a place where he is now going for those who are still alive. The hope of being reunited soon with the departed is expressed in the words: "In a little while we shall reach you, let us reach each other."

The conception of death as a journey to another world may also be expressed in funeral dirges. In these dirges, the departed is told not to give away secrets of this world to those in the other world:

> Do not say anything,
> Yaa Nyaako (the departed name), do not say anything.
> If you did your speech will be long.
> When you arrive, do not tell tales.
> Yaa Nyaako, do not tell tales.

---

13  This, as well as the above songs and prayers, are also recorded in Mbiti (1975, 88–100).

If you did your tales will be long. (Nketia 1954, 122)

The fact that death is not the end of life is brought out again. It is also implied in the dirge that life in this world is similar to the one in the other world. There, people are capable of talking and even letting out secrets as they do here. This belief neither minimizes the pain, suffering, and sorrow felt at the time of death nor explains the mystery of death. The sense of uncertainty and loss as to why death is here at all still fills the air. It is a cause of lingering wonder or even anger as expressed in yet another dirge:

When the Creator created things,
When the Manifold Creator created things,
How did he create?
He created bereavement.
He created sorrow,
The sorrow of bereavement.
Alas! Drinking vessels!
Alas! Drinking vessels!
Alas! Drinking vessels!
Anno Ofori (name of deceased) that spells death to others,
I could shoot myself on account of this event. (Nketia 1954, 199–231)

The reality of suffering and evil as manifested in death is as elusive as ever. It is a mystery, which is confronted, not explained, in African traditional religions. This is clearly shown in songs, prayer-laments, and dirges performed at the time of death. These are expressions of faith in and anger with the God whose presence and absence are experienced in the face of the reality of suffering.

## AFRICAN AND WESTERN VIEWS: A COMPARISON AND EVALUATION

In African traditional religions, both good and bad are accepted as a part of life. Life to an African is, therefore, a holistic reality. In the African view, unlike in the Western view, the dichotomy between the sacred and the secular, between the spiritual and the material, between the state and the cultic is virtually absent. As Bennie Van der Walt has correctly observed the African thought aims at holistic, integral knowledge of the totality (1997, 89). This totality of the traditional worldview is characterized by the multiplicity of spiritual beings, the essential connection and interaction between these beings, the virtual absence of dichotomy between the sacred and the secular, the religious interpretation of all life experiences, the cosmic struggle and the centrality of the human person in the community of the dead and the living (Adeyemo 1998, 373). The African view accepts living with the paradoxes of life such as good and evil rather than preoccupying itself with the search for a solution. Suffering and evil are not regarded as things to explain, analyze, or interpret, but as realities to face as part of a tragic existence. This is not the case in the Western view, which subjects reality to detailed scientific analysis and explanation.

But the African traditional view does not lack explanation. For although the African traditional world is not as mechanistic as that of the West, it tries to give cosmic and religious explanations to the events and calamities which upset and disturb it.[14] Natural disasters such as droughts, famines, epidemics, sickness, diseases, and other social and moral evils do not just happen; they are caused. Possible suspected causes of these calamities might include the sorcerer, the evil eye, the evil mouth, or even vindictive ancestral spirits punishing the community or individual for some neglected duty or honor due to them or God's judgment for some hidden evil. To ward off these cosmic and social evils, religious activities such as prayer, sacrifice, invocation, and exorcism are undertaken, if only to maintain the equilibrium of the community which the natural and social calamities constantly threaten. Thus, religion to an African, as Tokunboh Adeyemo observes, is not just a department of life disciplines; it undergirds and permeates all of life (1998, 374). Religion is the grid through which the African interprets his/her reality. African society is so impregnated with religion and ethics that it is difficult for it to exist without them (Parrinder 1976, 146).

Thus, the African view of suffering and evil is holistic and not dualistic, like the Western view. It accepts suffering and evil as realities of life that must be faced, fought, and overcome. It does not, primarily, view evil and suffering as issues to explain, nor does it accept them fatalistically. Suffering is an integral part of life as we experience in this world. Because life is an integral, holistic unit in African traditional thought, the distinction between orthodoxy and orthopraxis of liberation theology, the dialectic of the cross and the resurrection (Jürgen Moltmann), and other modifications of Western dualistic thought will be meaningless. The cross and the resurrection will not form a dialectic but two dimensions of one event. Orthodoxy and orthopraxis will not be possible to separate, for one cannot possibly exist without the other since belief and practice are two sides of the same coin.

Strangely, however, Karl Barth's understanding and explication of evil as being the shadow side of creation and his contention that creation consists of both Yes and No will fit in well with the African traditional view.[15] As Barth argues, creation consists of clarity and obscurity, growth and decay, progress and impediment, beginning and ending, success and failure, gain and loss, laughter and tears. There are both dark and bright sides to life (1976, 296). Moreover, Kwasi Wiredu has eloquently argued from the Akan saying, "The hawk says that all that God created is good," that there is a sense in which evil is involved in the good (1998, 198). Wiredu maintains that the sentiment that evil, although it is evil, is unavoidably involved in the good and is ultimately for the best. This would have warmed the heart of Leibniz because

14    Kwasi Wiredu has correctly observed that the principle of rational explanation or evidence is not entirely absent from the thinking of the traditional African. For no society could survive for any length of time without basing a large part of its daily activities on beliefs derived from the evidence. See his *Philosophy and an African Culture* (1980, 43).

15    Barth's interpretation of evil as the dark side of creation is fraught with difficulties. Closely examined, it may be understood to mean that the creation before the Fall was imperfect. While Barth does not deny the Fall, like Hick does, his discussion of evil as the shadow side of creation is problematic and remains the most difficult aspect of his theology (1932–1967, 296f; cf Hick 1987, 141 and Dau 2000, 126–29).

it would agree with his maxim of the "best of all possible worlds."[16] According to the Akan "if something does not go wrong, something does not go right," a saying which underlines the fact that one cannot really talk about good without the possibility of contrasting it with evil (Wiredu 1998, 198). Thus, Wiredu would seem to imply that Leibniz would find a place for his philosophy in African traditional thought. However, the extent to which this assertion might be sustained would be a matter of debate.

The African traditional view would also agree with Gerrit C. Berkouwer's argument that it is improper for creatures to try to justify the ways of God to man when the opposite should be the case (1983, 242). Equally, the African view, like Berkouwer's "Believing Theodicy," would refuse to discard God on account of the problem of evil and suffering, as has happened in Western thought in the form of atheism, but it would maintain protest in suffering as a means of mutual dialogue with God. It would, however, be very doubtful to say that the songs, prayers, laments, and funeral dirges of the African traditional religions that we examined are the same as the doxology of the church in the face of evil, which Berkouwer discusses.

Nevertheless, there are striking similarities between the African view and the biblical view. Both views see reality as a totality, as an integral whole. Both assume, not explain evil and suffering. Neither do away with God because of suffering and evil. Both maintain the language of protest against suffering and evil expressed in song, lament, prayer, and funeral dirges as we saw in the songs of African traditional religions and can see in the Psalms and

> O Lord, how long shall I cry for help, and you will not hear? Or cry to you "Violence!" and you will not save? *Habakkuk 1:2*

the Prophets (cf. Ps 10:1,13,17–18; 22:1,11; 13:1 and Hab 1:2–4,12–17). In very general terms, it seems that the African mode of thought is much closer to the Hebraic holistic, concrete way of thinking as contained in the Old Testament than to the Greco-Roman Western mode of thinking. This may be why many African people seem to be more congenial to the Old Testament literature than to the New Testament literature (Van der Walt 1997, 89). Although the language of protest is sometimes very strong in the prayers, songs, laments, and funeral dirges as well as in the Psalms and the Prophets, it is not the same as protest atheism, generated by the problem of evil in Western thought.

Having said this, it is conceded that there still exists in the African view an element of obscurity as to the origins of evil and suffering in relation to God. On the one hand, traditional views generally exonerate God for the existence of evil in the world, which are squarely placed on humanity's shoulders. But on the other hand, it ultimately indicts him as the Omnipotent One who can stop it altogether if he so wishes, as evidenced in the Nuer and Dinka religions. The African view in the context of cosmological reflection maintains a doctrine of the unqualified omnipotence of God in regard to issues with direct

---

16      Gottfried Wilhelm Leibniz (1646–1716) was a many-sided genius with vested interests in science, mathematics, politics, law, economics, theology, and philosophy. He argued that in creating the world, God chose between two possible systems the best possible world because he is a wise God. "Our world," he concluded, "is the best possible world despite the presence of evil in it" (1710, 123–35).

bearing on the fate of humanity on earth. But it also maintains a diminution of God's omnipotence, a reduction of God's omnipotence to the level of a human potentate (Wiredu 1998, 199). In one sense, the African traditional view of suffering and evil suffers from the same shortcomings that plague the Western view: neither reach the bottomless pit of the mystery of evil and suffering. But unlike the Western view, African traditionalism accepts this mystery as a reality to face rather than to explain.

## THEOLOGICAL IMPLICATIONS AND CONCLUSIONS

That the problem of suffering and evil generates diverse interpretations across cultures and communities presupposes its insolubility. Neither the African view nor the Western view offer a definite answer to this perennial problem. To be sure, there is no human system that adequately solves the problem of evil and suffering if by solving we mean total elimination of the problem so that we no longer suffer or die in this world. As we have seen, both the African and Western views either maintain an unqualified doctrine of God's omnipotence or a reduction of the same. The Western view is basically dualistic even as the African view is essentially holistic. From both of these views we may conclude the following: both discuss the problem of evil and suffering in relation to a supreme God, the Creator. Both struggle with the reality and the fact of evil as an existential problem. Neither adequately deal with the problem of evil and suffering as a problem that reveals the dark side of humanity, the human potential to perpetrate evil. In some African religions human beings are not inherently evil or sinful but they are only considered evil when and if their actions disrupt the harmony and tranquility of the community. Similarly, some Western philosophy relativizes human sin, declaring that what is called "sin" might be different in disposition or inclination, which varies from one culture to another or from one person to another. Finally, both draw from personal and communal resources to respond to the problem of evil and suffering. Whether in the form of prayer, lament, protest, or funeral dirge, this response entails an existential struggle with the mystery of evil, real but inexplicable.

From the biblical perspective, both the African and Western views fall short of admitting that suffering and evil are indications of something terribly wrong in our nature as human beings. The Bible calls this sin, an irresistible force capable of alienating us from God and from one another and so to miss the goal of life for which we were created. This is the force that moves us to do evil and inflict suffering upon one another. As such, we as human beings need to be delivered not only from the evil that may be visited upon us, but also from the evil that we have the potential to visit upon fellow human beings. From the biblical viewpoint, therefore, the answer to this problem is redemption provided in Jesus Christ. In that sense, "The ultimate solution to the problem of evil must lie in the fact that the God who created the world is also the God who redeemed it; the Creator is himself in Christ, the bearer of all creation's sin and suffering as he is the bringer of the redemption that shall be. But only the Christian can know that Christ has explained suffering in the act of defeating it" (Richardson 1983, 196).

Consequently, redemption through a suffering theophany is the only truly Christian response to the problem of evil (Surin 1982, 114). The incarnation as the Christian answer still does not explain evil and suffering, but it does provide a viable framework in which the believer may respond to the problem of suffering and evil and thereby transcend and transform it. God's coming to humanity in Jesus Christ and his identification with us in all that we may suffer is the basis of our positive response to evil and suffering. Thus, the theology of the cross, which is also a theology of suffering, is the basis of transforming and transcending the problem of suffering and evil without being destroyed by it. The cross does this by conveying to us the following:

First, the cross speaks of God's presence and participation in all that we suffer as human beings. Martin Luther King, Jr., has noted that God does not leave us alone in our agonies and struggles, but he seeks us in dark places and suffers with us in our tragic prodigality (1963, 16). Put another way, God does not observe our suffering from a safe distance, but he comes down to us and participates in it. Consequently, the cross is the supreme demonstration of God's solidarity with us is in this world of suffering. In the cross, we see God allowing him to suffer as we do, not because he was under pressure or obligation but because he willingly chose to do so out of his redemptive love for us. In that way, the cross of Christ will always stand as a powerful reminder that God was prepared to suffer in order to redeem the world and that he expects his people to share the same commitment as they participate in the task of restoring the world to its former glory (McGrath 1995, 15, 26). Thus, the problem of suffering and evil is deeply rooted in the divine mystery of the cross but at the same time, it is profoundly human. The essence of this mystery is that God's redemption of the world employed suffering in the form of the cross to enable humanity to acknowledge God and recognize its true self in a vital relationship characterized by love.

Second, the cross directs our gaze from contemplating our own anguish and suffering to the suffering and transforming God who shares in our suffering (Inbody 1997, 180). When we look at the cross, we realize at once that God suffered in a way that none of us has or will ever suffer. On the cross, God gave us his all and his utmost so that we may live. By so doing, he incredibly demonstrated his overwhelming love for us. Thus, the death of Jesus Christ on the cross brings us face to face with the wonder of God's sacrificial love so much that we are strengthened to deal with our suffering with courage and determination. As we direct our gaze to the cross, we find incredible power and courage to face the fear and terror of suffering. Suffering possesses what Alister McGrath has referred to as

> For the sake of Christ, then, I am content with weaknesses, insults, hardships, persecutions, and calamities. For when I am weak, then I am strong. *2 Corinthians 12:10*

"a double cutting edge: the sheer pain of experiencing it and the unbearable intensity of what it means or implies" (1995, 68). That is why the possibility of experiencing suffering frightens and intimidates all of us. But the cross reminds us that its power has been broken and its sting has been blunted. Although the presence and the fact of evil and suffering are still pertinent realities in this life, the cross clearly points to their ultimate defeat and elimination in the future when God shall usher in a new order of things where there will be no more suffering, tears, and death.

Third, the cross spurs us on to respond to the suffering of others as God has responded to our suffering. In the cross, we are provided with a stimulus for alleviating and healing the suffering of others. Because the suffering of any human being grieves the heart of God, those who have experienced the comfort of the cross need to reach out to those who suffer with the love and compassion of Christ. Attending to the practical needs of those who suffer clearly demonstrates the message of the cross. When we provide for the spiritual, emotional, and material needs of those who hurt in any way, we assure them that God has not abandoned them in their pain and misery. When we as the community of faith thus convey the message of the cross in practical love and compassion, we empower those who suffer to transcend and transform their hurt and suffering.

Finally, the cross reminds the believer that there is suffering involved in following Jesus. There is such a thing as "the fellowship of his suffering" for the disciples of Jesus. They are not only called to believe in Christ, but also to suffer for him. In that sense, both joy and suffering are an integral part of the Christian experience in the same way summer and winter are seasons of the year (Smith 1971, 92). Scripture makes it clear that the believer is not excused from suffering with the rest of humankind just because he/she is a follower of Christ. To be sure, Scripture asserts that the believer has been promised additional suffering and persecution for being a follower of Christ. There is, therefore, a strong sense in which Scripture has always insisted that the crown we wear precedes the cross we bear and that being a Christian involves taking up one's cross, with all the sufferings and the difficulties that go with it, and carrying it until it leaves its marks. Bearing that cross to that end redeems one to that more excellent way which only comes through suffering (King 1963, 25). Thus, the sufferings of the cross and the glories and the blessings of the cross are inseparable.

Within the framework of the incarnation, we not only find victory and comfort in the towering example of the cross but also in the unconditional love and the valuable support of the community of faith. The community gives us the capacity to transform and transcend suffering. In historical terms, as Stanley Hauerwas has rightly observed, Christians have not always had a "solution" to the problem of evil, but rather they have had a community of care that has made it possible for them to absorb the destructive terror of evil that constantly threatens all human relations (1990, 53). Within the warmth and the care of our community we come to know at the time of suffering what it means experientially to have our burdens carried.

Furthermore, suffering within the framework of the incarnation has the capacity to shape our character. Suffering produces perseverance and perseverance character. This shaping of a resilient Christian character through the things we suffer enables us to endure and to be steadfast in the midst of trials and testing. In addition, the Christian is inspired by a living hope that suffering and evil will be ultimately defeated when the redemption we have received in Christ shall be fully consummated. This hope is stronger than death and it is absolutely invincible in the face of evil and suffering. It participates in the presence as it anticipates the future.

Thus, within the assurance of God's presence and his suffering with us as the cross shows, as well as the love and the care that the community of believers provides, with the goal of shaping a resilient character in focus and the endurable hope of ultimate destruction of all that causes suffering set before us, we are empowered to transcend and transform suffering and evil into the highest good possible in this life. While the incarnation, in providing all this, may not necessarily be described as a theodicy, it still is the only system that assures humanity of the ultimate victory of goodness over evil, of life over death. With that in mind, however, we still acknowledge with Kenneth Surin that evil is a deep mystery. How God grapples with it and overcomes it is a mystery too. We must ponder over suffering in the context of God's infinite love, for it is therein that we have the assurance of victory. But we can neither use this as a pretext for indifference in the face of suffering nor as an easy consolation for the victims of suffering and tragedy (Surin 1982, 115).

## QUESTIONS FOR REFLECTION

1. Dau declares that "the African view of reality is holistic, rarely distinguishing the sacred and the secular or the spiritual and the material. In this worldview, reality is a coherent whole." How does this worldview help them to face suffering?

2. According to the African worldview, it is always important to discover who or what has caused the evil and suffering. Nothing in African society just happens without being caused by somebody or something. How can we seek to understand this worldview and at the same time help them to overcome this thought pattern?

3. The African response to suffering and evil is similar to the Old Testament response, according to Dau. How can we recover a biblical response to suffering? How can we remain open to learn from very destitute people?

## REFERENCES[17]

Barth, K. 1932–1967. *Church dogmatics,* 3:3. Edinburgh: T & T Clark.

Bosch, D. 1987. The problem of evil in Africa: A survey of African views on witchcraft and of the Christian church response. In *Like a roaring lion,* ed. P. R. C. de Villiers. Pretoria: C. B. Powell Bible Centre.

Dau, I. M. 2000. *Suffering and God: A theological-ethical study of the war in the Sudan.* A doctoral Dissertation, presented at the University of Stellenbosch, South Africa.

Deng, F. 1972. *The Dinka of the Sudan.* New York: Holt, Rinehart and Winston.

Dostoyevsky, F. 1993. *The brothers Karamazov.* London: Penguin Books. First published 1880.

Hick, J. 1973. *God and the universe of faiths.* London: Macmillan.

———. 1987. *Evil and the God of love.* San Francisco: Harper San Francisco.

Idowu, E. B. 1962. *Olodumare: God in the Yoruba belief.* London: Longmans.

---

17    A note from the editors: Dr. Dau has researched his chapter thoroughly, but due to his responsibilities in South Sudan is unable to send us the full documentation desired in scholarly work. Thank you for extending editorial grace in this case.

Lewis, C. S. 1967. *The problem of pain.* Ithaca, NY: Cornell University Press.

Mbiti, J. S. 1990. *African religions and philosophy.* London: Heinemann. First published 1969.

———. 1975. *The prayers of African religion.* Maryknoll, NY: Orbis Books.

Nikkel, M. 1997. Children of our fathers' divinities. In *Land of promise,* Andrew Wheeler. Nairobi: Paulines Publications Africa.

Nketia, J. H. 1954. *Funeral dirges of the Akan people.* Ghana: Achimota.

Tutu, D. 1972. Some African insights and the Old Testament. *The Journal of Theology for Southern Africa* 1: 16–22.

Wiredu, K. 1980. *Philosophy and an African culture.* Cambridge: Cambridge University Press.

**Isaiah M. Dau**, former principal of the Nairobi Bible College, was recently elected general overseer/archbishop of the Sudan Pentecostal Church, Republic of South Sudan. He is the author of *Suffering and God: A Theological Reflection on the War in Sudan* (Paulines Publications Africa, 2002) and *Free at Last: South Sudan Independence and the Role of the Church* (Kijabe, 2011). A pastor and theological educator, Dr. Dau conducts grassroots leadership training in South Sudan and other areas of Africa.

Ugandan martyrs of 1885.

# CHAPTER 17

# GOD'S PLAN OF PERSEVERANCE AND SUFFERING IN THE BOOK OF REVELATION

*Margaretha N. Adiwardana*

One main theme of the book of Revelation is "the absolute authority and supreme sovereignty of God over the whole creation" (Hughes 1990, 52). The Apostle John perceives God's plan of history and clearly God is in control. The practical result of knowing this fact enables Christians to view suffering in light of the ultimate reign of Christ (Wilcock 1991, 42).

Another theme in Revelation is suffering and perseverance in relation to God's plan for salvation. Suffering and death are seen as glorification because God is at the center of history. The emphasis is on victory, and suffering is viewed merely as a means of carrying out God's plan, allowed by God from the perspective of the cross. Thus Christians should understand suffering, as Christ's suffering on the cross brought salvation. This transforms our understanding of suffering and transforms the values of Christ's followers. Suffering is not mere evil. When it is correctly borne, it will bear fruit for the good (Morris 1995, 359). To follow Christ and become like him is to bear the cross (Luke 9:23). Christian service is sacrificial, costly as to bring the gospel to others is to walk the path of the cross (393).

John is a companion and brother who suffered for the Kingdom and patiently endured for God's word and testimony of Jesus (Rev 1:9). Patient endurance is the ability to endure persecution and suffering (Bratcher 1984, 13). He partakes "in the costliness of personal affliction which is inseparable from the true brotherhood of the faith,… in the tribulation and Kingdom and patience, in Jesus" (Hughes 1990, 23). Suffering is part of the calling of those who preach God's Word and are witness of Jesus (Acts 1:8). Tribulation and the Kingdom are closely connected. Sweet says, "The tension between them is expressed by endurance, a keyword (Rev 2:2,19; 3:10; 13:10; 14:12), with a flavor of expectancy, not stoicism" (1979, 67).

Jesus knows those who persevere and endure hardships for his name (Rev 2:2–3). "You have not grown weary," means God recognized the people had not given up nor become discouraged (Bratcher 1984, 20). Perseverance in hardship requires hard work, toil, and patience. Hughes writes that the Christians in Ephesus did not abandon the struggle under the stress of painful opposition and affliction because they were Christ-centered, not self-centered. Thus they expressed gratitude, and did not seek to accumulate merit. There was blessing in the endurance of hardship and indignity for the Lord's sake (Matt 5:11). Suffering is hard, but it is a path that leads to incomparable glory (Phil 2:8; Rom 8:18; 2 Cor 4:17; Hughes 1990, 34–35).

God knew of the tribulation, poverty, and the coming imprisonment, trials, and even death in the church of Smyrna, a poor church in a rich city (Rev 2:9,11). Mounce suggests their poverty may have been due to the antagonistic environment, which made it difficult for Christians to make a living. Smyrna Christians may have been the victims of mob violence and looting (cf. 1 Heb 10:34; Mounce 1977, 92). They suffered slander (v. 9). *Blasphemia* means defamation. Sweet comments that Christianity was considered an unauthorized cult, vulnerable to charges of antisocial behavior. The magistrate might order them to renounce their Christianity, and refusal would mean execution (cf. 1 Pet 4:12–16; Sweet 1979, 85).

Jesus exhorted them not to be afraid of the suffering which was to come, but to be faithful even unto death. Verse 10, "of what you are about to suffer," implies God's foreknowledge, sovereignty, and permission. It has overtones that their suffering and the devil's attack were within the divine plan (Sweet 1979, 85). God promised that to those who overcome tribulations, the crown of life will be given and they will not suffer from the second death (cf. Matt 24:13). Overcomers in Revelation are people who remain faithful to the Lord despite temptations and persecution, maybe unto death. The martyrs overcome the beast (15:2). They are winners and are given the crown of life, just as the winners in games and in wars (1 Cor 9:25). The crown of life symbolizes the eternal life given to the overcomers (Rev 4:4; 14:14; Josh 1:12; 1 Pet 5:4; Shedd 1989, 292).

> Do not fear what you are about to suffer. Behold, the devil is about to throw some of you into prison, that you may be tested, and for ten days you will have tribulation. Be faithful unto death, and I will give you the crown of life.
> Revelation 2:10

The church in Thyatira exhibited deeds, love, faith, service, and perseverance known to God (Rev 2:19). Deeds or works are defined by Beasley-Murray as the criterion of genuine faith in the last judgment and present judgment; the persistence demanded in works worthy of faith is related to the toil of maintaining true faith (1978, 73–74).

Revelation 2:24 affirms that the Lord knows the believers' strength in enduring suffering, not allowing them to suffer more than they can bear. Verse 25 exhorts believers to preserve in what has been given them until Jesus returns. The overcomer is the one who does God's will until the end comes (v. 26; Bratcher 1984, 31). They will receive authority, rule, and the power to destroy nations (v. 27).

Those who keep Jesus' command to endure patiently will be kept from the ultimate hour of trial that is to come upon the whole world (Rev. 3:10). They will not be exempt from suffering, but they are given the promise that they will be able to get through the period of distress and hardship (Bratcher 1984, 31).

God's plan and sovereignty allow Christians to be martyrs (Rev 6:9–11). It still happens today and will continue to happen "until the number will be complete." Sweet comments that "there the point is the fixity of the divine program—delay is not slackness or weakness. Here it is the divine program as embodied in Christ's sacrifice in which his people must share; cf. Col 1:24. Protection from 'the hour of trial' (3:10) does not give bodily immunity, as the Lord had warned" (Matt 10:28; 24:9; Sweet 1979, 142). They were martyred for being faithful, refusing to deny God, preaching God's Word. Now they rest, waiting for God's final judgment on the evil one who put them to death. White robes are given to the martyrs after the Great Tribulation (Rev 2:13–17). The Lamb himself will finally keep them from all suffering, be their shepherd, give them eternal life, and wipe their tears away (Rev 21:4,7). Hughes comments that martyrs are of special importance in the plan of God (cf. 1:9; 2:13; 3:8; 7:14; 11:3ff.; 12:11; 14:12,13; 20:4). A martyrdom silences by death one of the Lord's faithful witnesses. This looks like a defeat for God and a setback for the church. But it has been proven to lead to the progress of the gospel and power and blessing for God's people (Hughes 1990, 90). Ladd links the passage with Jesus' teaching that his disciple must take up his cross, which means not self-denial nor the bearing of heavy burdens, but the willingness to suffer martyrdom:

> The proclamation of the kingdom will be carried out effectively, but in a hostile environment which in spite of the presence of the gospel of the kingdom will be characterized by war, suffering caused by material and economic need, and death,… (a) fact that the church must face as it pursues its mission of proclaiming the gospel of the kingdom is persecution and martyrdom.… The souls of the martyrs are seen under the altar as though they had been sacrificed.… Thus Christian martyrs are viewed as sacrifices offered to God.… One of the repeated emphases of the New Testament is that it is the very nature of the church to be a martyr people. (Ladd 1972, 102–3)

The martyrs overcome Satan and his angels by the blood of the Lamb, by the word of their testimony (the witness of the gospel), and by not loving their lives even to death (Rev 12:11). Ladd writes, "their very martyrdom was their victory over Satan, not a physical victory preserving their lives or saving them from persecution, but a spiritual victory which proved that the accusations against the brethren were empty" (173).

The saints need to persevere and be faithful, heeding the warning about the beast which is to come (Rev 13:10). It encourages believers to obey God, even in imprisonment and death. Hughes comments that God assures the faithful servants that nothing happens to them that is not under God's control or contrary to his will:

> In all things God rides and overrules … in accord with his plan. It is in the acceptance of affliction that the endurance and faith of the saints are triumphantly demonstrated. Such testing gives proof of the genuineness of their faith and the unshakability of their hope in Christ. The suggestion of inevitability implies the supremacy of the divine will, which is always directed to the good and the blessing of the redeemed community. (1990, 150)

Revelations 14:12 emphasizes that to persevere is to keep God's commandment and faith in Jesus. Those who die in the Lord are blessed, as their works will follow them (v. 13, cf. John 15:16). Mounce says that faithfulness to Christ issues in martyrdom, but is a blessing and victorious entry into rest (1977, 277).

In Revelation 16:5–7 God Almighty, true and just, will judge those who persecute and kill his prophets and saints (cf. 18:24), all those from every nation who have been seduced by sorcery (19:2). God will clothe in white robes as a symbol of righteousness (19:7) those who are slain because of their witness of Jesus and of God's Word, who do not worship the beast nor his image and do not receive his mark. They will reign with Christ and live forever as his priests (20:4). Morris comments:

> None less than God will be the Consoler of his people. He will wipe away every tear. His concern is infinite.… Death has no final triumph and it is well that God's people see that it will ultimately cease to be.… So also sorrow and wailing and pain will cease. John sees a reason for this, namely that "the first things passed away" … Life as we know it is completely replaced by the new order. John had wept at the thought that there was no-one worthy to open the seals (v. 4). Is there no answer to the problem of earth's evil? His visions have answered that question. The Lamb has conquered. Now he finds that tears, too, have gone forever. (1995, 245)

Revelation reveals the design of God's plan for the salvation of man and history of this world. The Lamb opens the scroll because he has purchased by his blood people from every nation (Rev 5). An angel said salvation is to be preached to every nation, as judgment has come (14:6–7). John also saw under the altar the souls of those who have been slain because of the word of God and the testimony they maintained (6:9). Then John heard that the accuser has been overcome by those who did not love their lives so much as to shrink from death, by the blood of the Lamb and by the word of their testimony. The devil is filled with fury because his time is short (12:10–12).

The design is: salvation has come through the death of Jesus. This needs to be preached to all peoples, or else they are under the judgment of God. The end is the salvation of many from every people. But in-between, the devil shows his fury. Martyrdom happens to those who witness to the Lamb. But they overcome by maintaining their testimony of the Word of God.

John brings a warning of suffering, trial, and tribulation, which includes deprivation, slander, and even death. He also brings the assurance that God is in control, carrying out the divine plan of salvation for the whole creation. Wilcock applies this to the church today, where some Christians suffer while others live in relative comfort:

> The immediate prospect was one of suffering and even death. This was a certainty—a fact which has lessons for those of us who live in comparative ease. Would we be taken aback to find persecution knocking at our door tomorrow? Many a church has had to learn to live with that prospect and so ought we. For the great tribulation that John sees bringing

this age to an end he also sees in miniature, recurring constantly in the experience of God's people. And it is a test. It is the devil's action, but God's intention. (1991, 45)

The church today needs to take heed of John's warnings and encouragement. Beasley-Murray emphasizes the worth of the church to God and its destiny in the eternal ages. In witnessing to the world the church is to suffer. Heeding John's warning, the church will not be surprised by opposition in carrying out its mission to the nations. God knows but he refrains from intervening. He encourages Christians to endure. Suffering with its Lord, the church will share his glory in the Kingdom to come. "Suffering is permitted to ensure the approvedness of those for whom the kingdom is prepared" (Beasley-Murray 1978, 44–45, 81).

Revelation shows the whole eternal plan of God: salvation, judgment, preaching of the gospel to all peoples, the battle between Jesus' followers and Satan, and God's final victory. In the course of the fulfilment of God's purpose, Jesus' followers to whom the preaching of the gospel has been entrusted, will suffer. Somehow suffering is part of God's plan for the salvation of the believers. Exhortation repeatedly encourages to persevere to overcome. Even unto death.

## CONCLUSION

Suffering is to be expected by Christians, especially by those who preach the gospel. Sometimes God allows suffering in order to fulfill his divine plan of redemption, molding his people thereby and demonstrating his glory when they persevere and are triumphant by being faithful to him. Self-denial; the bearing of our cross; relinquishing our comfort and possessions; putting God even before our own family and home; facing hatred, rejection, and persecution are all part of the cost of true discipleship.

Perseverance is needed when we are faced by trials and suffering. Human beings are averse to suffering, yet Christians should not think it strange nor shy away from it. They are to rejoice in the certainty of God's final victory, considering themselves blessed when they suffer for Christ's name and for righteousness. Perseverance can be cultivated by understanding God's Word, by remaining within the Christian community, and by following Jesus' example as the Suffering Servant.

## QUESTIONS FOR REFLECTION

1. Why is it that suffering is of great importance in God's salvation plan?
2. How would we explain the definition Beasley-Murray sets forth that "deeds or works are … the criterion of genuine faith in the last judgment and present judgment. Persistence demanded in works worthy of faith is related to the toil in maintaining true faith," in connection with the church in Thyatira which exhibited deeds, love, faith, service, and perseverance, known to God (Rev 2:19)?
3. What are the implications for the church that suffering is directly connected to bringing the good news of salvation to all peoples who have been bought by the blood of the Lamb?
4. In the life of your church and friends, to what extent is suffering part of the cost of following Christ, leading a just life, and proclaiming the gospel?

## REFERENCES

Beasley-Murray, G. R. 1978. *The book of Revelation*. London: Oliphants.

Bratcher, R. G. 1984. *A translator's guide to the Revelation of John*. New York: United Bible Societies.

Hughes, P. E. 1990. *The book of Revelation: A commentary*. Grand Rapids, MI: InterVarsity Press / Eerdmans.

Ladd, G. E. 1972. *A commentary on the Revelation of John*. Grand Rapids, MI: Eerdmans.

Morris, L. 1995. *The cross in the New Testament*. Carlisle, UK: Paternoster.

Mounce, R. H. 1977. *The book of Revelation*. Grand Rapids, MI: Eerdmans.

Shedd, Russell, ed. 1989. *A Biblia vida nova*. São Paulo: Edições Vida Nova and SBB.

Sweet, J. P. M. 1979. *Revelation*. Philadelphia: Westminster.

Wilcock, M. 1991. *The message of Revelation: I saw heaven opened*. Leicester: InterVarsity Press.

**Margaretha Nalina Adiwardana** is the president and CEO of AME (Associação Missão Esperança), working in international disaster relief and community development, and working to partner with and strengthen local churches. She is the founder and coordinator of REDE SOS GLOBAL, a Brazilian network for disaster relief. Ms. Adiwardana is a missionary trainer in several Brazilian organizations, seminaries, and training centers.

*Pieta*. Emmanuel Garibay.

Filipino artist Emmanuel Garibay writes, "Pieta is an image of a woman with a picture of a loved one (son or husband) who is missing and presumed killed. When people disappear due to political or religious repression, it leaves their loved ones with deep pain and anguish, uncertain of the fate of the victim, clinging on to faint hopes that they are still alive. I used the title Pieta to associate it with the famous sculpture by Michelangelo, to suggest a contextual and contemporary version of the death of Jesus and the suffering it brought to his mother." Used with permission.

*Beloved*. Genocide site, Ntarama, Rwanda. Adella Thompson.

Photographer Adella Thompson writes, "Many genocide sites in Rwanda are left intact, with skeletal remains unburied in testimony to the horrors of the 1994 genocide. In this Catholic Church where over 5,000 were killed, someone—I presumed a loved one—took the time to wrap his or her beloved's head with a head scarf. When asked how he was able to cope with the death of more than twenty family members, one person told me: 'We learn to forgive, because we must. But we never forget, for if we forget, then this will happen again. We forgive, but we never forget.'"

*Genocide Journal.* Genocide site, Ntarama, Rwanda. Adella Thompson.

"At the genocide site a young guide took me to an outbuilding and simply said: 'This is where they burned people.' It was dark and lit only by a small window on the western wall. This journal and the bones of a man's fibula and foot protruding from his burned pant leg were the only things left in the soft, red Rwandan dirt." – Adella Thompson, photographer.

*Martyrdom* *always remains*

# THE SUPREME ENACTING

*and perfecting*

of Christianity.

## THIS GREAT ACTION

has been initiated **for us,**

done **on our behalf,**

exemplified **for our imitation,**

and inconceivably communicated

**to all believers**

by CHRIST

on Calvary.

—C.S. Lewis, The Problem of Pain

C. S. Lewis on martyrdom. James Harris.

*Qwiqwelstom* (Balance and Harmony). Don Froese.

In this wood carving, First Nations artist Don Froese depicts the Creator's sacrificial love for all his people. He says about this work, "The pierced hands on the upper rays and pierced feet on the lower ones depict the crucified Christ. The symbols where the rays begin to separate from the sun-face depict the ears of the Creator and Savior God. He is the careful Listener to the sufferings and cries of all people, from all directions, at all times. But He is not a passive listener. His deep listening to human suffering brings tears, not just drops of tears but great blue rivers of tears which flow down to and connect with the great canoe (a traditional motif of creation and redemption from the story related to the Biblical account of Noah's Ark). The rivers of tears also appear as paddles for the great canoe. The empathetic co-suffering of the Creator and Savior with His creation propels the great canoe, giving both power for and ultimate meaning to our human journey, including transport back to the Creator."[1] Used with permission.

---

1      The carving pictured here was commissioned for the World Christian Gathering of Indigenous Peoples in 2008. This image and Don Froese's expanded explanation of it were published in the March 2009 issue of *Mosaic*, a publication of StoneWorks International, and can be accessed online at http://stoneworks-arts.org/stoneworks/wp-content/uploads/2010/02/MOSAIC-Issue-3.pdf.

Chinese Christian just after arrest. *Connections* vol. 7, no. 1 & 2 (July 2008), cover.

(http://www.weaconnections.com/Back-issues/Missions-in-contexts-of-suffering,-violence,-perse.aspx)

A secret Uzbek Christ worshipping community. *Connections* vol. 7, no. 1 & 2 (July 2008), 37.

(http://www.weaconnections.com/Back-issues/Missions-in-contexts-of-suffering,-violence,-perse.aspx)

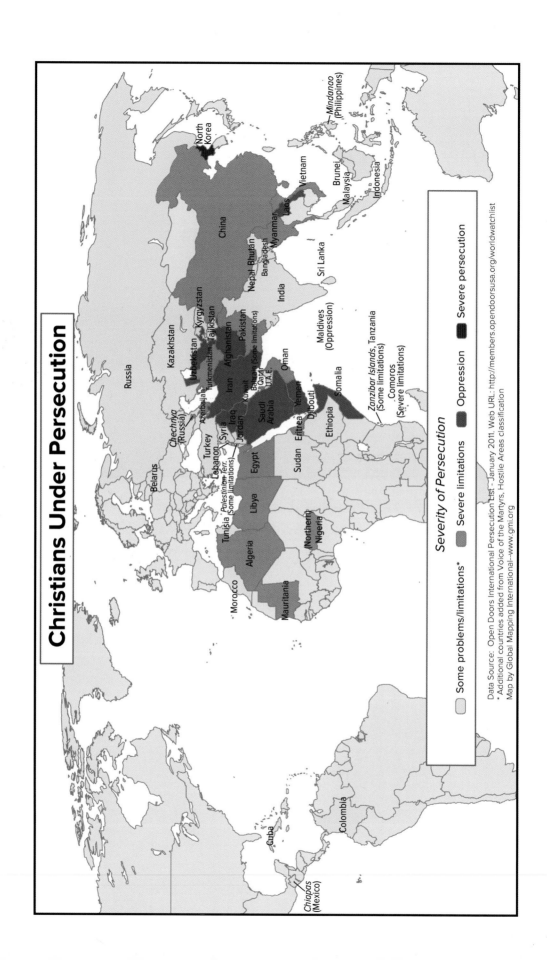

# Christians Under Persecution

North Korea

Vietnam

Brunei

Malaysia

Indonesia

*Mindanao (Philippines)*

China

Laos

Myanmar

Nepal Bhutan

Bangladesh

Sri Lanka

India

Kazakhstan

Kyrgyzstan

Tajikistan

Uzbekistan

Turkmenistan

Afghanistan

Pakistan

Bahrain (Some limitations)

Maldives (Oppression)

*Zanzibar Islands,* Tanzania (Some limitations)

Comoros (Severe limitations)

Russia

*Chechnya (Russia)*

Azerbaijan

Iran

Iraq

Kuwait

Oman

U.A.E.

Qatar

Saudi Arabia

Yemen

Somalia

Djibouti

Ethiopia

Eritrea

Sudan

Turkey

Lebanon

Syria

Jordan

*Palestinian Terr. (Some limitations)*

Belarus

Egypt

Libya

(Northern) Nigeria

Tunisia

Algeria

Morocco

Mauritania

Chiapas (Mexico)

Cuba

Colombia

## Severity of Persecution

Some problems/limitations*

Severe limitations

Oppression

Severe persecution

Data Source: Open Doors International Persecution List – January 2011. Web URL: http://members.opendoorsusa.org/worldwatchlist
* Additional countries added from Voice of the Martyrs, Hostile Areas classification
Map by Global Mapping International–www.gmi.org

PART THREE

# REFLECTIONS FROM HISTORY AND CASE STUDIES

## LESSONS FROM THE EARLY CHURCH

We now study our themes from the framework of history. We will read the narrative about Asia Minor from the first century to the present day. We listen to stories and case studies from around the world. We can picture persecuted believers. We get inside our writers and listen to their heartbeat. We wonder how "saintly" biographies ought to be. We travel to the Middle East, to China, to Japan, to Russia, to Sri Lanka and Nigeria, to Vietnam and Iran. We grieve the tragedy of Rwanda and the complicity of the church in the genocide, yet rejoice in new hope today. We visit prisons and refugees and travel to Angola with a Brazilian missionary. We listen to personal narratives of generations of persecution. We learn from Korean short-term missions to Afghanistan, and we sit with the poor of India.

As we engage this rich section, let us listen to the blunt and realistic Jesus and then consider our early Christian history.

> Behold, I am sending you out as sheep in the midst of wolves, so be wise as serpents and innocent as doves. Beware of men, for they will deliver you over to courts and flog you in their synagogues, and you will be dragged before governors and kings for my sake, to bear witness before them and the Gentiles. When they deliver you over, do not be anxious how you are to speak or what you are to say, for what you are to say will be given to you in that hour. For it is not you who speak, but the Spirit of your Father speaking through you. Brother will deliver brother over to death, and the father his child, and children will rise against parents and have them put to death, and you will be hated by all for my name's sake. But the one who endures to the end will be saved. (Matt 10:16–18, 22)

My reflections for this part of our book are shaped by Gerald L. Sittser's moving book, *Water from a Deep Well: Christian Spirituality from Early Martyrs to Modern Missionaries*. I cannot recommend this book highly enough for its rich, historical perspective on spirituality, with deep implications for believers, church, and mission.

I summarize two themes that Sittser develops in his first two chapters, the spirituality of both the early Christian martyrs and the early Christian community. "Persecution, suffering and death are at the heart of the Christian message" (29). He contrasts Christian martyrdom with modern suicide bombing, diametrical opposites. "The early Christian martyrs were victims of such hate, not perpetrators. They absorbed violence; they did not inflict it. They were called to martyrdom; they did not force it on innocent people, which is what suicide bombers do today" (31).

## SO WHY WERE THOSE EARLY CHRISTIANS PERSECUTED?

First, pagans looked with suspicion at Christians. Christianity was a new and strange religion, even a threatening foreign cult that was rumored to practice orgies, cannibalism, and incest.

Second, "Christians practiced a way of life that passed implicit judgment on Roman society" (26). For them, this world was neither the primary one nor the end of history. They were permanent aliens, citizens of Another World.

Third, "Christian allegiance to the lordship of Christ threatened Rome's hegemony" (39). Actually, the empire was relatively tolerant of religion, especially if it contributed towards civil order and affirmation of Rome's power. But when Christ was Lord (i.e., Caesar), and especially as emperor worship developed, Christianity became a threat to be eliminated.

Fourth, "the early Christians believed their faith as ultimately and exclusively true, which threatened the popular pluralism of the day" (41). For the Christians, all religions had failed and that explained the necessity for the incarnation of Jesus.

## AND WHAT WAS UNIQUE ABOUT THESE EARLY CHRISTIAN COMMUNITIES?

They held to the sanctity of life from the womb on. "The Christian worldview condemned infanticide, abortion, and incest, and it disapproved of marital infidelity, divorce, and polygamy" (57). They rescued unwanted, abandoned babies (especially little girls) found in the alleys of Rome and gave them Christian homes.

"Second, the Christian community provided a high degree of social stability, which caught the attention of people who lived in a world that seemed to teeter on the verge of chaos" (60–61).

This was particularly true of the cities, wracked by violence in their ethnic enclaves, and true of a very mobile, floating population. They became "family" to aliens and outsiders who flocked to the cities. Theirs was out-lived radical community and they were all "resident aliens," citizens of the Kingdom of God.

"Third, the church cared for people during periods of intense crises" (62). They modeled a new life of sacrificial service during the plagues (AD 165 and 250), serving their own sick as well as pagans. Perhaps 25 percent of the population died in each of the plagues. A significant percentage of Christians had recovered from the plague and became immune to it. They were considered miraculous healers. And they believed in a supernatural God of miracles, which they practiced and witnessed. Christians had a different worldview towards disasters and disease. For them this world was a mere earthly journey; they were headed to the Heavenly City and Revelation 21:1–4 was their assured future.

"Finally, pastors helped to create a sense of belonging by functioning as shepherds of the flock, providing pastoral care from cradle to grave." In a world with no secular nor religious counter to the pastor, Christian leaders "practiced the 'cure of souls' as it was called then, to help believers make progress in the faith" (65). Christians loved the unlovely, and treated strangers and slaves with unusual kindness. They cared for the widows and the orphans. By the year AD 250, the church in Rome had some 1,500 widows and distressed persons under its care (59).

Consequently, their lifestyle became public testimony and gradually people from all levels of society began to come to Jesus. It was the power of transformational discipleship and worldview that gave witness (*marturion*) of Jesus as Lord.

As I reflected over these lessons from our early church history, I was struck by their powerful application to Christians today regardless of our geography. Are we ready?

Read on to join our writers as they grapple with history and present the case studies that ring with authenticity. —*William D. Taylor*

# REFERENCE
Sittser, G. L. 2008. *Water from a deep well: Christian spirituality from early martyrs to modern missionaries.* Downers Grove, IL: InterVarsity Press.

# CHAPTER 18

# PICTURING THE PERSECUTED CHURCH IN THE ART OF THE EARLY CHRISTIAN CATACOMBS

*Kelley Magill*

## THE ORIGINS OF CHRISTIAN ART IN THE CATACOMBS

Christian art has a long history of communicating hope and salvation in the midst of suffering and persecution. The earliest known examples of Christian images from the late second and early third centuries appear in the Roman catacombs, a place intimately associated with death and mourning. The catacombs are a series of underground passageways and small rooms, called *cubiculi*, which held the tombs of Rome's early Christian community. In ancient Rome, cemeteries were only permitted outside the city walls. When the above ground cemeteries along the major Roman roads became overcrowded, the ancient Romans created an intricate maze of underground catacombs carved out of tufa, a soft volcanic rock that is easy to work with but hardens when you dig into it and expose it to air. Why would the early Christians in Rome choose to spend their time and money to create paintings and sculptures in these dark and secluded places? While it might seem like an unlikely choice, this was a setting that needed art to honor the lives and sacrifices of the deceased and to affirm the faith of the living.

Christianity is not limited to a particular culture, class, or ethnicity. Rather, the perseverance and hope found in Christ distinguishes Christians from their culture. These differences are most acute in contexts of suffering, mourning, and persecution. For this reason, it is not surprising that the first identifiable images of Christian subjects appear in the catacombs. While Christian burial practices may have looked similar to the rest of the ancient Roman world, the art adorning the Christian tombs in the catacombs distinguished the faith and hope of the early Christian church in times of persecution and mourning.

It has often been speculated that the early Christians gathered and worshiped in the catacombs to hide from their persecutors. Were the images adorning the walls of the catacombs meant to transform these underground tombs into modest chapels? This seems unlikely. While Christians may have sought refuge in the catacombs on rare occasions, these spaces could not hold large gatherings, and there is no evidence that members of the Roman church regularly worshiped here. The Christian community also did not exclusively use the catacombs. Pagans, Jews, and Christians were often buried side by side. Studies of the early Christian community in Rome have shown that Christians adapted to the culture of the Roman world in many respects. Following ancient Roman tradition, Christian families and communities gathered at the catacombs for funerary feasts to celebrate the memory of the deceased and to honor the martyrs. During these celebrations, the family and friends of the deceased shared a meal honoring the dead. The inscriptions and images adorning the Christian tombs, however, differentiated them from their pagan counterparts. While Christians adopted many of the cultural traditions of the Roman world, they often gave these customs new meaning.

Christian images in the catacombs reflected the unique beliefs and solidarity of the early church. Traditional Roman tomb decoration and sarcophagi relief sculptures often glorified the deceased's life, occupation, or cultural sophistication. In contrast, early Christian images in the catacombs portrayed biblical narratives that represented Christian beliefs about the afterlife, salvation, and resurrection. In the catacomb paintings, Old Testament stories of deliverance foreshadowing Christ's resurrection, such as scenes from the lives of Daniel or Jonah, are often paired with New Testament imagery of Christ performing miracles or Christ as the Good Shepherd.

Figure 1: Ceiling Fresco: Jonah (Wilpert 1903, 61).

For example, in the catacomb of Saints Peter and Marcellinus on Via Labicana, one room has a painting on the ceiling that depicts Christ as the Good Shepherd in the central roundel, framed by four scenes from the life of Jonah (see figure 1). The prophet Jonah was a popular and instructive subject for early Christian communities because the three days that Jonah spent in the belly of the fish foreshadowed the three days between Christ's crucifixion and resurrection. Portraits of men and women with their hands raised appear in the banners dividing the scenes from the life of Jonah. These figures are often referred to as Orans in descriptions of Christian art because they represent the posture of prayer and praise within the early church. Above the entrance to the same room, images of Daniel in the lion's den and Christ's raising of Lazarus also depict stories of deliverance (see figure 2). The types of scenes portrayed in the catacomb of Saints Peter and Marcellinus appear throughout early Christian art in the catacombs. These images of deliverance, healing, and resurrection affirmed the early church's faith in a context of grief.

The challenge facing the early Christian community in Rome is not unlike the work of global missionaries who hope to create art that will communicate the gospel across cultures.

During the second and third centuries, the early church in Rome was primarily made up of immigrants from the Middle East and Greece. When faced with the task of creating a new visual language to communicate the biblical narrative, the early Christian community hired Roman artists and adopted culturally familiar forms from traditional Roman art. They drew upon the artistic skills and familiar styles of the Romans but gave them a new meaning. Amidst the persecutions of the early church, art provided one outlet in which Christians could encourage their faith and community while also communicating in a way that would be accessible and familiar to the dominant Roman culture.

Figure 2: Catacomb panel: Daniel and the Lion's Den (Wilpert 1903, 62).

The martyrs' tombs in the catacombs make these sites an important memorial of the persecuted early Christian church. This history has inspired subsequent generations to return to the catacombs to honor and remember the martyrs and the sacrifices of the early church. Christians have the blessing and privilege of being in a local church body, but we are also connected to a global community of believers and to generations of Christians that reach back to the early church of the apostles. The body of Christ is not bound by geography or history! The catacombs are a powerful reminder of the church's roots and the faith of the persecuted. The paintings that adorn the walls of these modest tombs testify to the early church's faith in the resurrection and the power of art to communicate hope. How might missionaries and the global church create art and worship environments that embody a spirit of hope in the midst of persecution such as that found in the catacombs? How could art encourage local church communities to remember the legacy of the early church and the faith of the martyrs and support Christians experiencing persecution throughout the world?

## PICTURING THE CATACOMBS DURING THE REFORMATION

When the painted catacombs on Via Salaria were rediscovered in Rome in 1578, it inspired generations of Catholic historians and antiquarians to search for and explore the catacombs to learn more about the early church and its martyrs. This exciting discovery of early Christian art in the catacombs occurred in the wake of the Protestant Reformation, which began in 1517 when Martin Luther published the "Ninety-Five Theses." During the Reformation, the nature and function of Christian art was highly debated among Catholic and Protestant leaders. Protestant reformers identified ways in which religious images had contributed to superstition, false teachings, and irresponsible spending. Catholic and Protestant leaders both recognized that the church needed to reform Christian art to prevent abuses. During the reformation period, scholars and theologians supporting diverse arguments researched early Christian history and the lives of martyrs to inform their theological and liturgical reforms and to encourage missionaries. Because of the serious dangers and problems regarding the role of Christian art within Renaissance Europe, some Protestant theologians completely rejected Christian art and removed or destroyed the images in their churches. While legitimate concerns informed Protestants' hesitancy or outright denunciation of art in the church, the history of Christian art also presents countless examples of how art has taught, inspired, and encouraged faith. In response to these critiques of Christian images, sixteenth-century Roman Catholic scholars began to study early Christian art. The discovery of the painted catacombs in 1578 revealed that the history of Christian art had its origins in the persecuted, early Christian church, which defended the value of art within the church and particularly within contexts of persecution.

Inspired by the faith of the persecuted church in the catacombs, late sixteenth-century Catholic reformers commissioned images of early Christian martyrs to encourage their priests and congregations to relate their present suffering to those of the early church. For example, the Jesuit Order commissioned an elaborate fresco cycle in the early 1580s depicting early Christian martyrs at Santo Stefano Rotondo, a fifth-century church, which had become the site of a Jesuit seminary in 1579. The frescoes by Nicolo Circignani encircle the entire sanctuary: beginning with an image of *Christ Crucified Surrounded by Martyr Saints*, followed by *The Martyrdom of St. Stephen*, and continuing chronologically and thematically with images of martyrs from the first to the fourth century. Seen in relationship to the early Christian architecture of the sanctuary, the late sixteenth-century frescoes of martyrs create a liturgical setting that encourages reflection on the persecuted church. Circignani's frescoes also inspired a series of prints by Giovanni Battista Cavallieri in *Ecclesiae militantis triumphi* (1583, 1585). Jesuit missionaries used the print series based on Santo Stefano Rotondo's martyrdom frescoes as devotional images and took these prints with them into the mission field. The function and message of early Christian art in the catacombs and its revival by the Jesuits in the late sixteenth century present models for the contemporary church on how art can educate Christians about the nature of suffering and encourage meditation and prayer for the persecuted church.

Visiting the catacombs in Rome or reflecting upon the early Christian paintings found at these sites, enlivens one's memory of the persecuted church and its martyrs. The experience of visiting the catacombs today, however, is far removed from the journey of an early Christian. Many of the Roman catacombs have been carefully excavated and made accessible to the public with the additions of modern staircases and electric lighting. Exploring the winding underground pathways and rooms of the catacombs, one can imagine the experience of visiting the martyrs' tombs in the third and fourth centuries. What would it have been like to navigate these dark corridors by candlelight with a small group of believers in search of one special grave out of the hundreds lining the passageways and rooms? Finding the name of Christ on a tomb inscription or seeing an image of the Good Shepherd would have brought an overwhelming sense of peace and confidence to the early Christian pilgrims making their way through these dark corridors. In many ways, a mental picture of what a visit to the catacombs may have been like for the early Christians is much more powerful than what physically remains in these sites today. Generations of Christians have studied and meditated on the catacomb paintings to envision the spirit and faith of the early Christian church. The numerous artistic interpretations of the persecuted church by future generations of Christians, such as those commissioned by the Jesuits for Santo Stefano Rotondo, have continued to enliven the history and faith of the martyrs. By reflecting on the role of art in the catacombs, I hope that artists, missionaries, and ministers may be inspired to create work that encourages Christians to remember and to pray for the persecuted church and to proclaim the Christian message of the resurrection in contexts of suffering.

## QUESTIONS FOR REFLECTION

1.  Think about what it would have been like to visit the tombs of the martyrs in the early Christian catacombs. Try to engage all of your senses. What would it have sounded and smelled like to be in these cavernous spaces, surrounded by tombs? What would it be like to walk through these damp underground chambers, feeling your way through the dusty corridors? If you were to share a meal at the tomb, as was the Roman tradition, what would it have tasted like? What would it have been like to see the paintings of biblical scenes and symbols by flickering candle light? Having meditated on this imagined journey, how could you interpret or recreate this atmosphere through art?

2.  How might the history of the catacombs relate to your experiences of suffering and grief? How might the history of the early church compare to your local church community?

3.  What forms and symbols would effectively communicate the hope of the gospel in contexts of suffering and persecution to both your local church body as well as the broader culture?

## RELEVANT WORKS

*The Origins of Christian Art in the Catacombs*

Beard, M., J. A. North, and S. R. F. Price. 1998. *Religions of Rome,* 2 vols. Cambridge: Cambridge University Press.

Finney, P. C. 1994. *The invisible God: The earliest Christians on art.* New York: Oxford University Press.

Grabar, A. 1968. *Christian iconography: Study of its origins.* Bolligen series. Trans. Terry Grabar. Princeton, NJ: Princeton University Press.

Lampe, P., and M. D. Johnson. 2003. *From Paul to Valentinus: Christians at Rome in the first two centuries.* Minneapolis, MN: Fortress.

McCann, A. M. 1978. *Roman sarcophagi in the Metropolitan Museum of Art.* New York: Metropolitan Museum of Art.

Nicolai, V., F. Bisconti, and D. Mazzoleni. 2009. *The Christian catacombs of Rome: History, decoration, inscriptions.* Trans. C. C. Stella and L. Touchette. Regensburg, Germany: Schnell and Steiner.

Wilpert, J. 1903. *Die malereien der katakomben Roms: Tafelband.* Freiburg: Herder. http://diglit.ub.uni-heidelberg.de/diglit/wilpert1903/0063?sid=3236c08326ea627b557b0e67a6da10d6.

*Picturing the Catacombs during the Reformation*

Bailey, G. A. 2003. *Between Renaissance and Baroque: Jesuit art in Rome, 1565–1610.* Toronto: University of Toronto Press.

Gregory, B. S. 1999. *Salvation at stake: Christian martyrdom in early modern Europe.* Cambridge, MA: Harvard University Press.

Noreen, K. 1998. Ecclesiae militantes triumphi: Jesuit iconography and the counter-reformation. *Sixteenth Century Journal,* 29, no. 3 (Autumn): 689–715.

Osborne, J., and A. Claridge, eds. 1996. *Early Christian and medieval antiquities. The paper museum of Cassiano dal Pozzo. Series A: Antiquities and architecture,* part 2, 2 vols. London: Harvey Miller.

Scavizzi, G. 1992. *The controversy on images from Calvin to Baronius.* Toronto Studies in Religion 14. New York: Peter Lang.

**Kelley Magill** is a PhD candidate in Italian Renaissance and Baroque art history at the University of Texas at Austin. Her dissertation project argues that the exploration of the catacombs in the late sixteenth and early seventeenth centuries impacted the reform of Christian art in Rome and contributed to the development of archaeology and modern historical methods.

# CHAPTER 19

# FROM ASIA MINOR TO CONTEMPORARY TURKEY

## Suffering, Persecution, and Martyrdom in History and Geography

*Carlos Madrigal*

## THE CEMETERY OF THE CHURCH

The land, history, and peoples of Asia Minor remain to this day as extraordinary witnesses to the deep scars, challenges, and sufferings of the church throughout the ages. Outside of the Holy Land it is hard to find another place in the world where so many significant events of the Christian faith have converged. This is the land known as "the cradle" of the church. It is where the first Gentile church was founded, thus inaugurating the universal church. It is where the first missionary church began, hence initiating the church's global expansion. And finally, it is the home of all seven churches of Revelation which foreshadowed and today exemplify the glories and hardships of the earthly church.

However, this land that witnessed the extraordinary vitality which pioneered the church through the centuries has now become known as "the cemetery of the church." Unfortunately, Christianity has been virtually eradicated today from this soil. So, what exactly happened in this span of twenty centuries? What caused this decline? The answer: innumerable sufferings, persecutions, and martyrdoms.

Asia Minor is the home of the Tigris and Euphrates rivers which watered the garden of Eden; of Mount Ararat, where the ark rested; of Haran, Abraham's native land; of Tarsus, the birthplace of Paul; of Syrian Antioch, the first missionary church; of Patmos, where John was exiled; of Galatia, Bithynia, Iconium, Thrace, and Cappadocia; and finally, of the seven "candlesticks" of Asia Minor. At this point it would be good to remind ourselves that none other than the Lord himself can blow out the candlesticks of the church, and that no one but the community of believers has a responsibility to keep this flame alive. Nor must we forget that the Lord is the one who "will rebuild the ancient ruins," "restore the places long devastated," and "will renew the ruined cities that have been devastated for generations," bringing salvation, joy, and justice to all peoples (Isa 61:4,10).[1] As a worker with over twenty-five years of experience in the field, I believe great lessons must be learned from the devastation experienced in these lands. We must take them to heart and equip ourselves for the great spiritual restoration to come.

## AN EPISTLE FOR ASIA MINOR

What roles have adversities, persecutions, and massacres played in Asia Minor? What lessons stand out? I would not want to make a simplistic or cold review of all historical facts—which would not be possible—but rather tell some "inside" stories (i.e., the *Acta Martyrum*) of the suffering and therefore, the victorious church! What better stage to echo the words of the Apostle Peter and identify with "your brothers throughout the world [who] are undergoing the same kind of sufferings" (1 Pet 5:9). Peter wrote these words specifically to the "scattered" churches in Asia Minor: "Pontus, Galatia, Cappadocia, Asia and Bithynia" (1 Pet 1:1).

In the book of Revelation, the Lord speaks to the seven churches of Asia Minor which are threatened from both outside and inside forces. He speaks to them with words of warning or praise; but there are only two churches that he does not reproach: Smyrna and Philadelphia. He only uses words of approval and encouragement with these communities. Why? They are the only two churches that are trying to survive by engaging in efforts to overcome persecution. One church (Smyrna) suffers the persecution of their preachers and evangelists (i.e., speakers of the Word), and the other (Philadelphia) suffers a defamatory persecution against the proclamation of the gospel. The Lord has no words of reproach for those who are faithful in the midst of suffering. They are not perfect people or communities but they bear the "mark of Christ on their bodies," and this glory completely overshadows any of their defects. This gracious treatment towards sufferers was true then and has continued to be true throughout the entire history of the church.

> We are afflicted in every way, but not crushed; perplexed, but not driven to despair; persecuted, but not forsaken; struck down, but not destroyed; always carrying in the body the death of Jesus, so that the life of Jesus may also be manifested in our bodies. *2 Corinthians 4:8–10*

Today we live in a world and see a church that is ever more obsessed with the eradication of pain from everyday life in favor of its welfare. In contrast, the first churches lived to eradicate evil from the world regardless of sacrifice. Which of these two positions fits better with the purpose and message of the gospel? Ending suffering is one of the objectives of the gospel, but it is a collateral purpose, if I may say so, and not the central objective. Seeking healing, comforting the depressed, praying for provision, and pursuing happiness are all aspects of living the gospel, but if all we want is a life without diseases, without adversity, and of continued success are we not drifting somewhere else? If our desire of ending suffering makes us desist from any task that requires sacrifice, are we not imprisoned by ourselves and are we not shunning the major difficulties we face in proclaiming the gospel in the world's most challenging areas?

---

1    In places like Turkey, the spiritual application of such passages as "blessings for all peoples" is easily distorted by people that want to see a hidden imperialist agenda in these statements, as if our objective was to strip them of their land. Nothing is further from the truth! In reality, this type of commitment to add a political content to the gospel's message is another form of persecution. It is a way of exerting an intimidating pressure on the legitimacy and freedom of Christian thought.

In contrast, if we assume that the task of the church is fighting evil in the world regardless of the sacrifice required, then the words of Peter to the suffering believers in Asia Minor become very significant: "Therefore, since Christ suffered in his body, arm yourselves also with the same attitude, because whoever has suffered in his body is done with sin" (1 Pet 4:1). We must arm ourselves with the kind of mental attitude found in Hebrews 12:4 if we want to recover a worldview of our mission against "sin" and "evil," even if this means it will cost us suffering and maybe the shedding of our own blood. It is not that we should seek mortification and suffering as a goal itself, but it is time we rediscover the ultimate cost that we will face when pursuing the Kingdom legitimately. The aim is to overcome evil, the cost is sacrificial self-denial.

## THE SEEDS PLANTED BY DIOCLETIAN

During the first three centuries of church history, the Roman Empire led ten major waves of persecution against the Christian faith. Such was the state of persecution in the lands of Asia Minor that Ignatius Martyr, bishop of Antioch (AD 68–107), coined the following famous phrase: "I am God's wheat, and I need to be ground by the teeth of wild beasts [of the Roman circus] that I may be found the pure bread [of Christ]" (*Epistle to the Romans* VI,1). Polycarp, bishop of Smyrna (AD 74–155), said to his executioner: "Eighty and six years have I served him (Christ), and he never did me any injury: how then can I blaspheme my King and my Savior? You threaten me with fire which burns for an hour, and after a little is extinguished, but are ignorant of the fire of the coming judgment and of eternal punishment" (*Martyrdom of Polycarp*, ch. 9,11). Then came the famous statement of Tertullian (AD 160–220): "The blood of the martyrs is the seed of the church."

Persecution did not erase Christianity. However, in spite of persecution, or perhaps because of it, Christians survived the Roman Empire itself. Between AD 303 and 313, Emperor Diocletian ordered and approved (perhaps instigated by Galerius) the last and most devastating of the imperial persecutions which took place in Asia Minor. It is said that half of all the martyrdoms of the entire Roman era occurred between those dates.[2] Both Eusebius, in his *Ecclesiastical History* (n.d., 2–3), as well as Lactantius, in *Death of the Persecutors* (n.d., 1–5), report this same fact. This wave of persecution was so intense that Diocletian raised a column with the inscription: "The name Christian is extinguished."[3] Today, in the place of his palace in ancient Nicomedia, stands the city of Izmit in modern Turkey.

In 1998 the Lord led us to start work in Izmit (not to be confused with "Izmir" or Smyrna). After a year of church planting we decided to look for a building that we could use as a

---

2       The eighteenth-century historian Edward Gibbon reduced the number of casualties during the Great Christian Persecution to a maximum of 2,000 and suggested a total of 4,000 for the entire imperial period. Historians now say that you cannot determine an exact number, the numbers being considered range from 10,000 to 100,000 martyrs: "Judging from the calculation of L. Hertling one could estimate that during the second half of the first century (Nero, Domitian) the martyrs would be about 5,000; during the second century (Septimius Severus, Decius, Valerian, Aurelian) about 20,000; and the late third and early fourth century (Diocletian, Galerius, Maximinus Daja) some 50,000. This calculation would give us the number of approximately 100,000 martyrs during the persecution of the Roman Empire" (Gomez 2001, 104–5).

3       "Extincto nomine Cristianorum" (Harold 2008, 58). There is also talk that a coin was minted with the inscription: "Diocletian emperor who destroyed the Christian name."

church and would be affordable in our limited economic options. On August 17, 1999, an earthquake measuring 7.4 on the Richter scale devastated the city. More than thirty-five thousand people died within forty-five seconds! Our building immediately became a center of distribution for humanitarian aid sent by evangelical organizations around the world. The church was not damaged, but several of our neighboring buildings collapsed. Underneath these collapsed buildings appeared the remains of Diocletian's palace! Of all places in a city inhabited by over a million people, unbeknownst to us, we had planted the church on top of the palace that had shed the most blood of martyrs throughout the history of Rome. Was it coincidence or providential guidance? If we remember Tertullian's maxim—"the blood of the martyrs is the seed of the church"—the answer does not offer much doubt! This small, faltering church remains there today, struggling against all odds to succeed.

## THE FRUITS OF PERSECUTION

During the reign of Diocletian, a soldier of the emperor's personal guard named Georgios was ordered to participate in repression. Instead, he chose to publicly declare his Christian faith and oppose the imperial decision. An enraged Diocletian ordered his torture, and he endured it without uttering a single complaint. He was subsequently executed. Georgios was beheaded outside the walls of Nicomedia (Izmit) on April 23, 303. The testimony of his suffering convinced Empress Alexandra and an anonymous pagan priestess to convert to Christianity. They too would eventually join Georgios in martyrdom. Today this martyr is known as Saint George.

The history of persecution in places like Nicomedia and Cappadocia, though initially a seeming blow to the survival and expansion of the church itself, are illustrative of how persecution and martyrdom revitalized the church and were ultimately epic victories over all the powers of evil. It is through this history of suffering that the ultimate goal of the gospel was fulfilled.

On the one hand, these persecutions would prove to be the seeds of the great artistic heritage found in the churches carved into the caves of Cappadocia. On the other hand, these histories would bring about one of the most influential stories in popular consciousness: the legend of Saint George and the Dragon. Both of these cases, beyond their anecdotal and mythical aspects, make it clear that any sacrifice made by faith ends up being the seed needed for the restoration and revitalization of believers.

The last and bloodiest of all the persecutions in Rome soon led to the eventual recognition of the Christians in the empire. Gradually, however, a new and more terrible form of persecution ensued: that of Christians against Christians, and of Christians against other religions. This movement would reach its peak with the Crusades and the Inquisition. These new persecutions were even more terrible because they were done in the name of Christ! This is an episode that we cannot avoid if we want to understand the situation in Asia Minor following the fifteenth century. Although the Crusades may seem like an item that has nothing to do with our topic, we cannot nor should we ever stop mentioning them. The Crusades have left deep, unhealed scars throughout the Middle East. Moreover, this wound is not just in the historical memory of the Muslims, but also of our fellow Orthodox, Armenian, Nestorian, and Coptic Christians.

While my Turkish friends often mention the Crusades and the Inquisition as two sides of the same coin, I say that "we, the Protestants" were as much victims of this persecution as were Jews and Muslims (that is, by the Inquisition); we cannot ignore or walk away from these two scourges of "Christianity." Moreover we must acknowledge the atrocities done in the name of Christ and ask forgiveness for them. Only then will we have the authority to denounce any other injustice. If persecution causes humiliation and pain, forgiving and knowing to apologize—even if you are the victim—dignifies and heals. Ultimately, it makes us participants in his glory (1 Pet 4:14) and a herald of his fair trial to come (2 Thess 1:4–6).

The day we begin assuming that the role of persecution falls within the outcomes of divine providence, we stop being victims and become victors. This change in mentality, in turn, also helps us celebrate his liberation in advance. Several years ago the following words of the suffering Jeremiah taught me this valuable lesson: "It is good for a man to … offer his cheek to one who would strike him, and let him be filled with disgrace. For men are not cast off by the Lord forever. Though he brings grief, he will show compassion, so great is his unfailing love" (Lam 3:27,30–32).

Martyrdom has its most far-reaching effect when those who suffer persecution grant a full pardon to their persecutors. This, ultimately, helps to spread the seed so that it is truly effective: "Lord, do not hold this sin against them.… Those who had been scattered preached the word wherever they went" (Acts 7:60,8:4).

## TOWARDS CONTEMPORARY TURKEY

Following the rapid spread of Islam in the eighth century, in the late fifteenth and early sixteenth century the religious setup and map of the Mediterranean world drastically changed. While Constantinople, capital of the Byzantine Empire, fell into the hands of the Ottomans (1453), the last capital of the Umayyad Caliphate, Granada, was reconquered by the Catholic Kings (1492), and consequently Muslims were expelled from the Iberian Peninsula (1502). Luther nailed his ninety-five theses onto the door of Wittenberg (1517), while the Ottomans expanded their empire practically to the gates of Vienna (1529).

The Ottoman Turks grouped different populations according to their millet (i.e., ethnic nationalities). These "nationalities" were determined by religious denominations. Apart from the ruling Muslim millet, several other "nationalities" included the Jews, the Armenians, the Catholics (there was even a Protestant millet in the nineteenth century), and finally the Orthodox millet, the highest millet after the Muslims. These "nationalities" enjoyed a good degree of autonomy and were governed by their religious leaders. This system remained the same until the time when nationalism began its push for independence during the nineteenth century.

First, with the independence of Greece and later, with the wave of Balkan independence on the brink of World War I (i.e., former Yugoslavia, Albania, Hungary, Romania, Bulgaria), the Christian millet or "nationalities" began to be seen as treacherous forces eager to support the West and end the rule of the Ottoman Empire. This situation created waves of suspicion, and with it came a sense of urgency "to crush the enemies installed in our backyard."

In 1915, under the guise of preventing an uprising, the Armenians were forced to evacuate their lands in eastern Turkey and the consequence was that they suffered unprecedented destruction along with their exodus. The Armenians took the brunt of ethnic suspicion. This latest massacre had claimed 300,000 victims, according to some, and up to 1.5 million lives, according to others. What Turks remember, however, is the perception of "betrayal" of these millet groups towards their empire. These suspicions were confirmed when in 1919 the Ecumenical Patriarchate hailed the Greek army's invasion of Western Anatolia. From that moment onward, the Patriarchate and ethnic minorities became known for many Turks as the "fifth column";[4] that is, a group of infiltrated traitors.

Although we cannot delve into details here, this very rapid analysis will be useful to understand the trigger for what is remembered in modern Turkey as "black September" or "the events of September 5 and 6" in 1955. It was a time when public psyche was deeply disturbed by the conflict in Cyprus. Assaults, looting, murder, and rape ravaged the central districts of Istanbul where Christian and Jewish minorities and their businesses were concentrated. The events were triggered by a false story about a bomb explosion that supposedly had taken place the previous day in Thessalonica (Greece), in the house where Mustafa Kemal Atatürk, the founder of the Turkish Republic was born in 1881. As a result, a mob stormed and razed for nine hours straight more than five thousand premises of the Greek minority population. Jewish and Armenian minorities also suffered (Güven 2005). The mob was encouraged by some organized groups who were responsible for locating homes, businesses, churches, and cemeteries in these communities (Koçoglu 2001, 25–31). Some 11 to 15 people died (depending on sources), and there were 30 to 300 wounded; between 60 and 400 women were raped (Sword 2009). This further accelerated the emigration of ethnic Greeks (or *Rum*, in Turkish) from Istanbul, whose Greek minority population declined from 135,000 in 1924 to about 7,000 in 1978 (Kuyucu 2005, 361–80).

While these unjustifiable events were not acts perpetrated against Christians as a direct result of their faith, but rather due to chauvinistic and ultranationalistic reasons, they do provide us with a framework that aids us in understanding the reactions against Christians and attempts to spread the gospel in today's modern Turkey.[5]

## A NEW BEGINNING

Not until after the 1960s did evangelical work in Turkey restart, after a lapse of half a century trying to survive unnoticed. There was virtually nothing left of the revivals of the late nineteenth century. Turkey, or what was then the large area of Anatolia belonging to the Ottoman Empire, had at one point witnessed many revivals among ethnic minorities of Christian origin. The sons and daughters of these revivals either lost their lives in the events

---

4       In Turkish *besinci kol*; i.e., espionage and sabotage forces aiming to overthrow the Turkish state.
5       All evangelistic activity, or proclamation and defense of the Christian faith, is understood by some sectors as illegal proselytism and therefore as another strategic branch of the "fifth column."

of the century that followed or fled to other regions and continents. Today these remnants are still scattered throughout Europe and the Americas.

In the 1980s, however, an unheard-of phenomenon emerged: Turks of Muslim background began to convert to the Christian faith and started to form small "Turkish Protestant church-es," where the word "Turkish" meant "ethnic Turks" and not Christian ethnic minorities. In the 1990s they began trying to obtain legal recognition in a country that declared herself secular and unprejudiced to all religions, but in practice viewed Christians as a threat. By the late 1990s, these Turkish converts began to appear on television debate programs; they were courageous witnesses of their faith and suffered all kinds of criticism. In 2005, the State Security Commission identified what they called the three major threats against the Turkish state as the following: Kurdish terrorism, Islamic fundamentalism, and the proselytism prac-ticed by missionaries ("İç Güvenlik Strateji Belgesi" 2005). News articles began to emerge about "thousands" of hypothetical underground churches hidden in homes, which came to be called "pirate churches." Speculations that billions of dollars were used to buy land and recruit native missionaries by deceiving young misfits through promises of financial compensation created a climate of global fear and psychosis against Protestants. This fear culminated in the statements of the former first lady Rahsan Ecevit, of a secular-left party, in a press release in 2005: "Our religion is wasting away… In our country, churches have infiltrated apartment buildings. Some citizens become Christians due to various interests. Unfortunately, the authorities turn a blind eye to all this.… I do not want to be governed by camouflaged sects. I want my country back."[6]

In a culture where discourse about "invisible enemies that want to overthrow the state" cre-ated psychosis, children who were five or six years old in the mid 1990s grew to adulthood under the "threat" of "illegal" proselytism and under a state which identified missionaries as "public enemy number one" (declaring that it could not do anything to combat them). Some of these young men were literally indoctrinated with the need to save the homeland from the intrusion of Christianity and they became "cannon fodder" for ultranationalist sectors that incited them to murder.

## HARASSMENTS

According to the Pew Global Research on "Global Attitudes" dating from 2008, the country in recent years with the largest growth of hostility toward Christians has been Turkey.[7] This contrasts with the Turkish public opinion that there is complete religious freedom in this country. Is there an explanation for such a dichotomy?

On the one hand, freedoms are guaranteed on paper and the average Turk naturally accepts the presence of native Christians; their only real concern is to make ends meet, to pay their mortgage, and to pay for their children's schooling. On the other hand, both the educa-tional systems and much of the media transmit a worldview on international developments

---

6      *Radikal* newspaper, January 3, 2005.

7      "In 2004, about half (52 %) of Turks gave Christians an unfavorable rating; today roughly three in four (74%) hold this view" (http://pewresearch.org/pubs/955/unfavorable-views-of-both-jews-and-muslims -increase-in-europe).

in terms of a Christian crusade. This creates fear towards the idea that Christianity might be expanding in their homeland. This feeling causes both private and personal reactions as well as organized pressures, either by radical groups or sometimes by public authorities. This hostility can translate into a wide variety of actions, ranging from verbal abuse to physical assaults and arrests at the slightest complaint about anything "Christian." Molotov cocktails have been launched at churches, and death threats and murders have even taken place. But before we consider the specific cases of martyrdom, let's try to explore some of the environment that faces evangelical work on a day-to-day basis.

The most systematic of these harassments occur when authorities apply the "letter" of the law to Christians, while in other cases easily "turn a blind eye." Thus, pastors have been fined, according to a law banning religious manifestations in public (TCK 529), for leading the "public" worship service of their church, when many mosques on Friday often invade the streets and nobody objects to anything. Native Christians have been fined thousands of dollars for alleged violation of a data protection law for writing and visiting Bible correspondence course contacts. Sometimes places of worship are closed on the grounds that they are illegal because they are not registered in the zoning code. One church was raided because "there was a lead" that it had a hidden arsenal. The police sometimes request lists of church members or require the identification documents of new attendees. There are foreign families who are deported for "working illegally" when in reality they were voluntarily aiding the leadership of a local church in Turkey. A foreign pastor was threatened with deportation for going to another church outside of the one that employed him to preach. Through the usage of bureaucratic excuses, a church was penalized for hosting refugees lawfully in the country. One church building was threatened to be demolished for allegedly failing to comply with antiearthquake regulations. Anyone who tries to preach the gospel openly is stopped, claiming a breach of public order. These actions are always justified with explanations like "we only abide by laws," which makes it very difficult to prove that there is a systematic policy of attrition and assimilation.

Turkey remains a paradise of contrasts and contradictions, and we should not ignore that it is the only country with a Muslim majority which allows the presence of public communities composed of converts from Islam. It is also the only Muslim country that contemplates the legalization of church buildings, although the process is proving to be very arduous and costly.[8] Whenever a situation has been brought to the courts, although a lengthy process, the state has decided in favor of rights and freedoms. Turkey is also the only Muslim nation that sponsors debates on national television between Muslim and Christian theologians (that, of course, discuss the corruption of the Christian faith),[9] and yet it tolerates the presence of radio and television channels that proclaim the gospel. This land can be both a haven of peace and a powder keg ready to explode.

---

8        http://www.youtube.com/watch?v=7gCZ_Y9YcfA.
9        http://www.dailymotion.com/video/xd62l9_haberturkozel-subtitles-eng-93mb_lifestyle.

The emerging native church, however, is not wavering in its Turkish identity nor its desire to serve its country, and continues to persist today in its attempts to achieve an officially recognized place in society!

## TODAY'S MARTYRS

As we have seen above, every act of aggression has its period of gestation. We should not ignore the spiritual causes leading to persecution, but neither should we ignore those economic, social, cultural, or political causes that also have an impact on the spiritual, and vice versa. These have, in recent years, led to another black page in the history of Asia Minor.

Elsewhere in the world, Christians in many other circumstances live dramas that are much more tragic. But the Turkish case is unfortunate as it is a nation that prides itself on being an example of tolerance and freedom in the Islamic world, worthy of being imitated by others. In practice, however, Turkey is airing a message which states that "infiltrated enemies" are to be eliminated. Those who do not subscribe to this speech think that Christians should remain silent and not provoke the masses and instigate their prejudices. The prevailing idea in public opinion is that "the victims would not have encountered a tragic event if they had not sought after it." Unbelievably, the victims are the ones that end up being declared guilty of disturbing what some have called the "Pax Ottomana."

But who are the ones that are really disturbing the peace? Forgive me, for I cannot write dispassionately about these issues that have affected me so closely. The alleged disturbers of peace were actually messengers killed for preaching peace in word and deed.

Since 2006, seven Christians have been killed atrociously and there have been other failed attempts. I use the word "atrociously" because they were cruel, premeditated murders, including torture in some cases.

On February 5, 2006, Andrea Santoro, a Catholic priest in Trabzon (the Black Sea coast), died after being shot twice in the head while praying on the pews of his church. His crime? Trying to rescue some prostitutes from their ignominious life and annoying some individuals due to his integrity and enviable testimony. His murderer was justified on the grounds of the offensive Muhammad cartoons.

On January 19, 2007, a born-again believer and Armenian journalist, Hrant Dink, was shot dead in the entrance of the Armenian newspaper office in Istanbul. Why? Because he sought after ways to reconcile Armenians and Turks by courageously making both parties face the facts and not deny them systematically.

On April 18, 2007, three Protestants were tortured and murdered in a publishing house in Malatya (southeastern Turkey). Their throats were slit. Two of them were Turkish converts from Islam—Necati Aydin, 36, and Ugur Yüksel, 32. They were the first martyrs of the Turkish church (in the ethnical sense). The third—Tilmann Geske, 45—was a German citizen. Their crime? Distributing Bibles, celebrating Christmas in a hotel with friends and relatives, and preaching the gospel to those who were interested.

On December 16, 2007, Adriano Francini, a Catholic priest, was stabbed and injured in Izmir. Fortunately, he survived. The day before the event, the aggressor had called our church office in Eskisehir (Anatolia). The Turkish pastor in Eskisehir, who had been beaten a couple of years ago after attending a similar call, apologized and hung up the call. The aggressor then decided to call the following address in Smyrna. Apparently he had a list of church addresses from the Internet. His justification? He had been influenced by a Turkish TV series (*Kurtlar Vadisi—Valley of the Wolves*) that shows Christians as conspirators against Turkey.

On July 20, 2009, Gregar Kerkelink, a German tourist who left the Saint Anthony of Padua Catholic church in Istanbul, was stabbed in the middle of the street by an assailant who claimed to have woken up that morning wanting to kill a Christian.

On June 3, 2010, Bishop Luigi Padovese, apostolic bishop of Anatolia, had his throat slit by his driver in the city of Iskenderun (near Antioch, in southeastern Turkey). After the murder, the murderer climbed to the roof and cried, "*Allah'u ekber*" ("Allah is great"—this was also shouted by one of the gunmen mentioned above), and then shouted, "I've killed the devil!"

In a country where the immediate and predictable impulse is revenge, the relatives and Christian friends of the victims, in all of these cases, forgave the murderers and testified of Christ's love for them. I knew all of these victims either personally or through acquaintances, except for the German tourist. It is difficult to describe the emotions one experiences when these things happen to people that are close to you. It is a mixture of agony and exultation. Therefore, I want to honor the lives and deaths of these martyrs with three testimonies which have tearfully marked my life since then. All three testimonies illustrate the spiritual triumph that lies behind these earthly tragedies.

The first of these "testimonies" is the biblical text that was painfully read amidst praises to the Lord at the funeral of Father Santoro by his companions in the bishopric:

> I tell you the truth, unless a kernel of wheat falls to the ground and dies, it remains only a single seed. But if it dies, it produces many seeds. The man who loves his life will lose it, while the man who hates his life in this world will keep it for eternal life. Whoever serves me must follow me; and where I am, my servant also will be. My Father will honor the one who serves me. (John 12:24–26)

The second is the reflection of Hrant Dink's widow, Rakel—a believer committed to the Lord. On January 23, 2007, she read her text which still reverberates in the ears of people nationwide during the massive funeral held for her husband in Istanbul:

> I know there was a time in which the murderer was a baby. What force of darkness is it that can turn a baby into a murderer? This is what we have to question … because only love alone will enter heaven.

The third is a poem written by one of the martyrs of Malatya, Necati Aydin, in premonition of his own death:

I have given my address to death
So it finds me without distress;
Do not think that I feared it,
That I shy away from facing it…
Let death be close to us!
Is she not ever present?
I'm leaving without a farewell
To those who have loved me so well.
I leave without satiating my soul enough
With beauty, goodness, truth, and love…
So I run every moment,
To achieve at any moment,
The ultimate goal: eternity. (Aydin 2008, 12, 46)

## CONCLUSION

What do we learn about suffering, persecution, and martyrdom with respect to the specific case of Asia Minor and its long and complex cultural history? In my view, this lesson can be summarized in three brief thoughts:

From a cosmic perspective, the church is not of this world and cannot rely on a comfortable life, nor should it seek it. The church's central struggle should not be to avoid persecution, but to preserve the values of the gospel. When these central ideas disappear, sooner or later the testimony or "candlesticks" might disappear as well.

From a historical and sociopolitical perspective, no one is without fault and no one can cast the first stone. We should not form sides but learn to put ourselves in each other's shoes, like Jesus did in his incarnation. Despite all injustices, we must learn to love hostile societies and overcome all hatred with forgiveness; by this, I do not mean that we should remain silent or justify these hostilities.

From a missiological perspective, persecution is an unavoidable traveling companion. Jesus said, "If they persecuted me, they will persecute you also. If they obeyed my teaching, they will obey yours also." The church should not be sedated with a "feel good" theology centered on avoiding pain but should be awakened to bring the gospel to places of high risk; even if this means that a cross is waiting for us at the end of the journey.

## QUESTIONS FOR REFLECTION

1. What percentage of the text in the New Testament written in or for Asia Minor includes the themes of suffering, persecution, and martyrdom? Does this figure correspond to the interest given to the topic in theological circles and or in the daily practice of Christians?

2. Is the theme of "suffering, persecution, and martyrdom" an issue only for the early church or for those parts of the world facing persecution? Is it valid for the churches that have managed to settle down and earn a respectable place in society? According

to 1 Peter, how should these "settled down" churches act or how much should they get involved?

3. If this subject is equally valid and important for every church, Bible school, ministry, or contemporary Christian organization, how much should suffering, persecution, and martyrdom affect our cosmology, our participation in the sociopolitical arena, and our approach to missions?

4. How can one measure "success" in the context of suffering, persecution, and martyrdom? If in certain contexts there is no exponential growth taking place and we only witness adversity, is this an indication of failure? Should the missionary movement, in such cases, leave its mission field in favor of other regions or contexts that are more "productive"?

## REFERENCES

Aydin, N. 2008. *Benim adim göklerde yazili*. Istanbul: Gercege Dogru Publishers.

Eusebius. n.d. *Historia ecclesiastica*, VIII, iv. 2–3.

Güven, D. 2005. 6-7 Eylül Olaylari. *Radikal*.

Harold, J. S. 2008. *Why you can have confidence in the Bible*. Eugene, OR: Harvest House.

Internal Security Strategy Document. 2005. Iç Güvenlik Strateji Belgesi. October, 31. http://ikincicumhuriyet.org.

Koçoglu, Y. 2001. *Azinlik gençleri anlatiyor.* Istanbul: Metis Publishers.

Kuyucu, A. T. 2005. Ethno-religious unmixing of Turkey: 6-7 September riots as a case in Turkish nationalism. *Nations and nationalism* 11, no. 3 (July).

Lactantius. n.d. *De mortibus persecutorum* X: 1–5.

*Martyrdom of Polycarp*. Author and date unknown, c. AD 169. Text available at: http://www.earlychristianwritings.com/text/martyrdompolycarp-hoole.html.

Saint Ignatius. n.d. *Epistle to the Romans* VI, 1.

Sword, Ecevit. 2009. 400 Kadina Tecavüz Edildi. *Sabah Newspaper*. 26 Eylül.

**Carlos Madrigal,** of Barcelona, is married to Rosa Maria and is the father of three children. He is an art director, pastor, and writer. He has served the Lord in Turkey since 1985, where he has established the Istanbul Protestant Church and its Foundation, the first evangelical church officially recognized in Turkey. Carlos is also the author of more than a dozen Christian books in Turkish and in English, including *Explaining the Trinity to Muslims* (William Carey Library, 2011).

# CHAPTER 20

# HOW SAINTLY SHOULD BIOGRAPHIES BE?

*Miriam Adeney*

"Henry is one-fourth Jesus," Joel said soberly as he munched on a peanut butter sandwich. He had just returned from playing with seven-year-old Henry, the oldest child in a Christian family.

Now Joel is almost thirty, but that phrase has stayed with me. One-fourth Jesus. Over the years I have wondered: would anyone describe me like that?

Over the years also I have been nourished by Christian biographies. The life of Catherine Booth. Of Lilyas Trotter. Of Henrietta Mears. Without those stories of Christ's followers, my life would have been different. I would not have dared or persevered as much.

Yet today saintly biographies are criticized. If subjects sound like angels, with few doubts, pain, impatience, or anger, readers wonder, "Are these accounts real?"

All writing is selective, no matter how objective authors try to be. So why worry about accounts that emphasize the positive? For several reasons. First, human beings have shortcomings. Certainly the neighbors will know a person's faults. If a story acknowledges these, it will be more credible. Second, idealized accounts can be discouraging. Others who suffer may wonder, "Why do I keep hurting? Am I out of the will of God? Why am I not experiencing glorious confidence and serenity like this person I'm reading about?"

In light of those concerns, here are four suggestions that may help us write better biographies.

## GOOD BIOGRAPHIES INCLUDE CONTEXT

In 2007, twenty-three Korean short-term missionaries were bouncing through Afghanistan in a bus when they were abducted. For forty-two days they were held hostage. Two died. Although twenty-one were released, all were traumatized.

To achieve the release, the South Korean government bargained directly with the Taliban terrorists. Suddenly, instead of being seen as a marginalized rogue fringe, the Taliban were raised to the level of significant players on the world scene, worthy of international negotiation. As part of the agreement, the Taliban required all Korean Christian workers, aid workers, and noncombat troops to leave Afghanistan. Meanwhile, back in Korea, the sending church's senior pastor apologized to the nation, then resigned from his pastorate. While he was reinstated eventually, mission work was tarnished throughout the country (Lee 2008, 171).

Was this suffering simply the work of evil men and satanic powers? Or did contextual factors contribute? In this case, other Korean groups had sent thousands of short-term missionaries to Afghanistan during the preceding year. These short-termers conducted massive rallies in Kabul, threw tracts over courtyard walls, and confronted strangers in the marketplaces with their testimonies. Afghan media protested. So did long-term Christian workers in the country, including Koreans. Eventually the Afghan government deported the eager witnesses. But the damage had been done. The following year, others suffered the backlash.

Suffering does not occur in a vacuum. Geopolitics may motivate murderers to see their action as part of a "just war." Innocent people can be squashed in local land struggles, competition between factions, or ongoing struggle against an encroaching imperial power. Or perhaps the martyr himself has behaved in a risky way. An accurate story places the martyrdom in context.

To research the context, we must check the Internet and newspapers and magazines, missionaries' letters and churches' and Bible schools' archived publications and records, and general social, political, and economic data for the relevant time periods. We read novels, watch movies, and listen to songs from those eras. We talk to people who lived at that time and place.

We study the culture. What was the economic picture, for example? What was an average family meal? What was a rare luxury? What vehicles did ordinary people use—private cars, bikes, busses? What technology did they have? Who were people obligated to share with beyond their immediate family? Who could they turn to when they needed financial help?

Like the fabled blind men encountering an elephant, we approach our person of interest from multiple angles so that we can understand his life in a well-rounded way. For example, George Muller was a nineteenth-century British with a big social conscience who rescued street children and founded orphanages. Sometimes he would pray for six hours at a stretch. Then he would open the door and find fresh bread on the doorstep. This is true. But it is not the whole truth. Muller also made trips to North America to raise awareness about his orphanages. That data must be reported as well.

In one of his Quaker missionary biographies, Ron Stansell illustrates this many-angled approach when he asks, "What contributed to this early success? Was the Latino population disillusioned with Catholicism and seeking something more from God? Did a dogged persistence in church planting and leadership training begin to pay off? Was success the result of the leadership of an intelligent and aggressive superintendent? Was the work better suited to women? Or did the spiritual factors of prayer, holiness revival, and surrender to God's will bring growth?" Stansell also reports honestly about tensions, conflicts, and shortcomings. The nitty-gritty issues in transferring property and power are laid wide open (Stansell 2009, 99, 238).

"Triangulation" means studying a subject several times from several angles, perhaps employing different researchers, different methods, different time periods, different communities, or different theoretical grids. Writing under the pen name "Iliam," a missionary triangulated in time when she wrote *What Is That in Your Hand?* about Muslim-background followers of Jesus in Pakistan. She described several people at ten-year intervals. Some of the subjects blossomed over time. Others relapsed. Triangulation allowed her to present this community with layers of complexity, increasing the truthfulness of her account (Iliam 2004).

## GOOD BIOGRAPHIES INCLUDE SIN AND FAILURE

Biographers' subjects are not perfect. They snore and sweat and stink and sometimes lose their keys or their passports or their tempers. They jump to bad decisions, unleashing decades of difficulty down the line. They are finite and they are sinners. Remembering this protects us from the temptations of triumphalism.

One Sunday in Asia, as I was remarking on the loveliness of local Christians, my friend Amat threw cold water on my bliss. "For twenty years I've poured my life into students," he said. "I've discipled them, cried with them, celebrated with them. Then they graduate and take good jobs. Ten years later all they can talk about is the house and the car and the promotion and the vacation and the big church remodel. The poor are still everywhere around, but they no longer see them. This happens student generation after generation." He sat with eyes downcast and shoulders slumped—this gifted, dedicated leader.

> "And everyone who has left houses or brothers or sisters or father or mother or children or lands, for my name's sake, will receive a hundredfold and will inherit eternal life. But many who are first will be last, and the last first." *Matthew 19:29–30*

It was a helpful corrective to my rosy picture. Eugene Peterson says:

> The church is made up of sinners. The fleas come with the dog. We expect a disciplined army of committed men and women who courageously lay siege to the worldly powers. Instead we find some people who are more concerned with getting rid of the crabgrass in their lawns. We expect a community of saints who are mature in the virtues of love and mercy, and find ourselves working on a church supper where there is more gossip than there are casseroles. We expect to meet minds that are informed and shaped by the great truths and rhythms of Scripture, and find persons whose intellectual energy is barely sufficient to get them from the comics to the sports page.... Faith in Christ does not in itself make a person an interesting conversationalist or stimulating companion. (Sometimes you just have to) endure tedious relationships with unimaginative pilgrims. (Peterson 1988, 51, 55)

Missionaries sometimes fail to balance ministry and family well. Tensions here mark many Christian leaders' stories, occasionally recounted bitterly by one of their children. Rosalind Goforth pondered this dilemma when her extremely gifted husband, Jonathan announced his plan for evangelizing China following the Boxer Rebellion. Assistants would establish centers in several regions, he said. The family would live in each center for a month. Every night there would be a meeting. Then the Goforths would move on.

As Rosalind listened, her "heart went like lead." It was not suited to a family. Exposing their little ones to the infectious diseases that were so prevalent out in the villages was too risky, and she could not forget the "four little graves" they had already left behind on Chinese soil. Although she objected, he went ahead with his plan, convinced it was God's will (Tucker 2004, 204).

A fifth child died. But tens of thousands of Chinese turned to the Lord. How does a biographer interpret this? At least the author can record the facts.

Sometimes good preachers or writers or service workers are poor administrators or even poor colleagues. Consider Mary Slessor. Arriving in Nigeria in the 1880s, she rescued hundreds of babies and women from abandonment in the jungle. Because she ventured further into the interior than anyone else, she was appointed first woman vice consul of the British Empire. Because she viewed Africans as God's children just as much as Europeans, she lived, traveled, ate, slept, worked, and played right alongside them. They gave her the title "Mother of all the Peoples." Yet her missionary colleagues did not look forward to working with her. Mary did not suffer fools gladly. She was not a team player. To her colleagues, Mary was "difficult."

On the field, discernment of strengths and weaknesses is essential. For example, some people cannot handle money well. Their math is poor, or their judgment is impulsive. Someday they may change. We can be hopeful. Meanwhile, it would be a disaster to put them in charge of a team's funds. As in life, so in writing, biographies should not encourage blindness to faults.

In church history, idealizing a leader's teaching has led to many unnecessary quarrels and splits. Writers must recognize that no leader's teaching is perfect. We stand on the shoulders of others, but that means we can see a little further. There is progress still to be made. "Heirs need to be aware of errors," as one theology student quipped to me.

With celebrity culture so widespread, some readers would prefer books that idolize heroes. That is not Christian writing, however. Certainly the Holy Spirit causes us to triumph in wonderful ways. Still, Paul and Barnabas quarreled. Peter needed rebuke from Paul. All of us remain "jars of clay." Amid the praises, then, a sense of humility must be conveyed.

## GOOD BIOGRAPHIES INCLUDE HONOR AND DIGNITY

"We don't talk about parents like that," Elizabeth's friends told her.

Preparing to serve in South East Asia, Elizabeth had joined an Asian church in Seattle. One evening during testimony time, she shared how pain over her mildly dysfunctional family had propelled her to the Lord Jesus.

"That isn't a testimony. That's disrespect," her friends told her gently afterwards. "However crazy or unkind our parents have been, we never dishonor them publicly."

Similarly, in cultures where honor is emphasized, biographies do not dwell on shortcomings. Yet hints can be offered. Consider two cases, one Bedouin and one Japanese. In daily life, the Egyptian Bedouin admire toughness, self-control, and honor. They do not speak about their hurts. Only their *ghinnawa* songs pulse with vulnerability, feeling, and caring. The symbols in their songs convey what never can be stated plainly (Abu-Lughod 1988).

In the second case, anthropologist Takie Sugiyama Lebra argues that among the Japanese only an uncouth person needs a complete, frank verbal message. A person of any refinement will find a more indirect, nuanced, euphemistic, metaphorical way to make a point. Suppose, for example, a Japanese woman has had a hard day with her mother-in-law, who lives in the home. How would she communicate this to her husband? She might arrange the flowers in front of the door in a haphazard way. He sees the flowers disarranged, realizes that his wife is at her wits' end, and is more tolerant that evening (Lebra 1976, 47). In cultures like these, biographies will critique indirectly and obliquely.

Privacy is another issue. Who has the right to tell about a person's faults? In everyday life, ordinary Christians are not asked to disclose their sins and vulnerabilities for all the world to see. We make disclosures with trusted prayer partners, in small groups, or alone with God. Does that change when a person is martyred or thrust into a situation of intense suffering? Is full public disclosure suddenly required in the interests of truth when one has been part of a newsworthy event?

Surely persons can maintain a degree of privacy if they so wish, both for their own good and for the good of others who might be hurt by disclosures. The public does not have the right to know all personal details.

On the other hand, a person may choose to reveal a lot. When Dr. Helen Roseveare was raped in Congo, she included that in her biography. Alongside organizational and personal humiliations both early and late in her career, violent rape was one more shame. God used her disclosures for good, however. Herded into a prison camp, she encouraged nuns, especially a young Italian girl who had been paraded naked before she was gang-raped. Feeling she had lost her purity, the girl contemplated suicide. Helen helped her. In later years Helen was in great demand as a mission speaker because of her honesty (Burgess 1975).

## GOOD BIOGRAPHIES INCLUDE CHRISTLIKENESS

"I like hagiographies. They're just about my favorite kind of reading," Alvin confided.

"Why?" I wondered (as I remembered that "hagiographies" are very saintly stories).

The author of *Taking Your Soul to Work*, Alvin Ung is a Malaysian, a husband and father, and formerly an international reporter for the Associated Press. He was also the commencement speaker at Regent College where I teach. Alvin responded in an e-mail to my question, "Why?" He said:

> In our generation, we're appropriately skeptical about Christians who lead saintly lives. We assume everyone has a dark side. Even the most saintly people, such as Mother Teresa of Calcutta, has her share of critics, such as Christopher Hitchens who (unsuccessfully) tried to shred her reputation in his book titled, sneeringly, *Missionary Position*.... Fundamentally we believe that it's not possible to conquer habitual sin and addictions so that we can become the new human—a person clothed with

righteousness, a person who has "escaped corruption" and "participates in the divine nature" (2 Pet 1:4).

As well, Western readers usually assume that miracles and demons can't be real. Westerners are used to scientific facts, and attribute any kind of demonology to psychological activity. (Asian readers wouldn't make the same assumption.)

Yet if we can suspend our twenty-first-century lens of "hermeneutical suspicion" and read biographies appreciatively, in the style of *lectio divina*, we will learn the art of living well, the art of ongoing conversion, and the art of dying well, Alvin suggests. We will discover that living and dying are related. "To me to live is Christ" (Gal 2:29).

"Because we are too weighed down by sin and preoccupied by depravity, we think it's not possible to live in union with God on this side of paradise," Alvin continues. But consider the life of Antony, a fourth-century Egyptian who pioneered monastic life. As Antony struggled with financial fears, lust, anger, deep-rooted attachments, and demons,

> he discovered Jesus had always been present in his life, and especially during his darkest struggles. And this discovery of Jesus' presence led him into even deeper levels of conversion… He lived a life of ongoing relinquishment. And therefore he began to grow in virtue… Antony's life shows us how a flawed human being can become like Christ. At age 105 he embodied the spiritual innocence of my young son: a life of wonder, joy, and amazement at the gifts of life.

## WHO AM I?

Before he died in a Nazi prison, pastor Dietrich Bonhoeffer penned these lines.

> Who am I? They often tell me
> I stepped from my cell's confinement
> Calmly, cheerfully, firmly,
> Like a squire from his country-house.
> Who am I? They often tell me
> I used to speak to my warders
> Freely and friendly and clearly,
> As though it were mine to command.
> Who am I? They also tell me
> I bore the days of misfortune
> Equably, smilingly, proudly,
> Like one accustomed to win.
>
> Am I then really all that which other men tell of?
> Or am I only what I myself know of myself?
> Restless and longing and sick, like a bird in a cage,
> Struggling for breath, as though hands were compressing my throat,
> Yearning for colors, for flowers, for the voices of birds,
> Thirsting for words of kindness, for neighborliness,
> Tossing in expectation of great events,

Powerlessly trembling for friends at an infinite distance,
Weary and empty at praying, at thinking, at making,
Faint, and ready to say farewell to it all?

Who am I? This or the other?
Am I one person today and tomorrow another?
Am I both at once? A hypocrite before others,
And before myself a contemptibly woebegone weakling?
Or is something within me still like a beaten army,
Fleeing in disorder from victory already achieved?

Who am I? They mock me, these lonely questions of mine.
Whoever I am, Thou knowest, O God, I am thine! (Bonhoeffer 1953, 173)

## WELL DONE

In 2002 Dale Stock, a second-generation missionary in Pakistan, was relaxing at a lake with his family and some friends.

"Help!" someone shouted from the water. Dale dived in. He saved the swimmer. But he himself drowned.

As I write this, I am listening to a rich choral rendition of a song that Dale's brother Paul composed. It is titled "Well Done."

Eagerly I waited, knowing it was time.
All heaven raised a cheer as you crossed the finish line!
I reached down in the water, took you in my palm.
Now you're in my arms where you belong.

Don't worry about your loved ones: I will dry their tears.
In what will seem like minutes, they will join us here.
The throngs have come to greet you, loved ones gone before.
Listen to their welcome roar!

Well done, good and faithful servant!
You've completed all the work He gave you to do.
Well done! You have brought Him glory,
You will shine now like the stars and the sun.
The crown of life you're won, beloved.
Welcome home, Dale. Well done! (Stock 2002)

How saintly should our biographies be? How much should grief balance glory? Context, sin and failure, honor, and dignity all must be considered. And we can hope that in the end our subjects will be at least one-fourth Jesus.

## QUESTIONS FOR REFLECTION

1. "All writing is selective, no matter how objective authors try to be. So why worry about accounts that emphasize only the positive?" How could this discourage readers according to Adeney?

2. What picture do the Scriptures present about God's servants? How can we remain humble, transparent, and glorify only our Lord?

3. According to Adeney one might ask who has the right to tell about a person's faults: "In everyday life, ordinary Christians are not asked to disclose their sins and vulnerabilities." Why would that change when a person is in a situation of intense suffering? How can an honest presentation of weaknesses and fears help others to grow?

## REFERENCES

Abu-Lughod, L. 1988. *Veiled sentiments: Honor and poetry in a Bedouin society.* Berkeley, CA: University of California Press.

Bonhoeffer, D. 1953. *Letters and papers from prison.* London: SCM.

Burgess, A. 1975. *Daylight must come: The story of a courageous woman doctor in the Congo.* New York: Dell.

Iliam. 2004. *What is that in your hand?: Reaching village Muslims.* Reading, PA: Christar.

Lebra, T. S. 1976. *Japanese patterns of behavior.* Honolulu, HI: University Hawai'i Press.

Lee, D. 2008. The case of the Korean hostage incident. *Connections* 7, no. 1.

Peterson, E. 1988. *Reversed thunder: The Revelation of John and the praying imagination.* San Francisco: Harper and Row.

Stansell, R. 2009. *Missions by the Spirit: Learning from Quaker examples.* Newberg, OR: Barclay.

Stock, P. 2002. *Well done.* Distributed by Interserve International, www.interserve.org.

Tucker, R. 2004. *From Jerusalem to Irian Jaya: A biographical history of Christian mission.* Grand Rapids, MI: Zondervan.

**Miriam Adeney** is an anthropologist and missiologist based at Seattle Pacific University and Regent College. Since early service with the Philippine InterVarsity Christian Fellowship, Miriam returns regularly to South East Asia. Besides teaching in seminaries, she conducts "Writing for Publication" institutes for Christian writers working in their own languages in the Middle East, Latin America, Africa, and Asia. Her books include *Kingdom without Borders: The Untold Story of Global Christianity; Daughters of Islam: Building Bridges with Muslim Women; God's Foreign Policy: Practical Ways to Help the World's Poor; A Time for Risking: Priorities for Women;* and *How to Write: A Christian Writer's Guide.*

# CHAPTER 21

# AN INDUCTIVE APPROACH TO UNDERSTANDING PERSECUTION IN THE MIDDLE EAST

*Andrew Edward[1]*

During the decades I lived in the Middle East, I accumulated many stories. In relating some of these stories I am hoping readers can learn about persecution in an inductive way.

My approach will be to share an incident about a kind of persecution and then ask questions to help us think more deeply about the story. All names in the examples are fictitious, but the stories are true. It may be helpful for people working in difficult situations to go through this as a group exercise.

We often think of persecution in terms of religion only. However, people are also persecuted for their political, economic, educational, and social beliefs. Usually people face persecution for a combination of reasons.

A comprehensive definition of persecution is: "any unjust action of varying levels of hostility with one or more motivations directed at a specific individual or a specific group of individuals, resulting in varying levels of harm, as it is considered from the victim's perspective" (Tieszen 2008, 41).

Persecution occurs everywhere and in every country of the world. Many are involved in it. I have observed families, teachers, employers, coaches, preachers, scholars, civil service workers, business employees, and soldiers participating in persecution.

Sometimes persecution leads to death. When one dies for Christ, it is called martyrdom. On this I am in agreement with David Barrett in the *World Christian Encyclopedia* (Barrett et al. 2001) and Christof Sauer of the International Institute of Religious Freedom (Sauer 2008, 26–48). My focus in this paper will be on Christians facing persecution.

---

1   Pseudonym.

## RECOGNIZING MIDDLE EASTERN RELIGIOUS PERSECUTION

Persecution is used as a tool to influence behavior changes that will result in conformity to the society's group think. Persecutors use physical, social, psychological, and mental pressures to gain control of people. The goal is to force people to change towards the norms that the dominating group wants to be instilled in all citizens.

Persecution is carried out in the privacy of one's home, among neighbors, in the market place, and in government offices. Religious and political persecution in the Middle East is pervasive. A wind of change, however, is blowing around the Arab world as ordinary citizens press their governments to end the persecution and introduce democratic change.

## RAMI'S EXPERIENCE

Rami, not his real name, became a disciple of the Lord Jesus Christ early in his adult life. He and his wife and children loved and cared for one another. Rami worked in the city and was faithful in his responsibilities.

One day, several years after Rami began to follow Christ, someone in the city accused him of being an apostate. The police referred his case to the Sharia Court.

If he did not retract his commitment to Christ, the Sharia Court would declare him an apostate from Islam. This conclusion would empower the court to cancel his civil rights and make him a ward of the state. His marriage contract would be annulled. His children would be taken from him. He would be forbidden to sign any contracts for renting a house, buying a car, or taking out a loan. Any contract would have to be signed for him because as a ward of the state he would be considered a minor. The only religion he would be permitted to practice would be Islam.

The police and the court assumed that he would deny his faith in Christ and return to Islam. He refused to recant. As the Sharia law requires, he was declared an apostate and received the sentence stated above. He knew that as an apostate, others would also feel permitted to kill him.

Rami and his wife and children moved to another Arab country where they could live in freedom. Eventually, he and his family found asylum in a Western country and are living there today. His case is an open case of religious persecution, even by United Nations standards.

Rami's sentence has made it very clear to other followers of Jesus Christ that there is a sword hanging over their heads. If they are accused of being apostates and do not recant, they too will be sentenced like Rami and have to face the consequences.

Inviting Muslims to come to Christ is done in obedience to the Lord Jesus. Muslims coming to Christ in the Arab world face adversaries in their nuclear and extended families, from the police and courts, and from any person who might want to accuse them of apostasy before the Sharia Courts. Persecution and martyrdom are always a possibility.

*Questions for Reflection:* Knowing full well that they will face persecution, Muslims are coming to Christ for their salvation. What are some of the reasons they are willing to endure great losses for Christ? What does it mean for them to gain Christ?

## PRIVATE PERSECUTION

A troubled teenager came into contact with radio and satellite TV broadcasts that told about new life in Jesus the Messiah. He wrote to the address of one of the programs asking for a correspondence course. He did his lessons at home and kept the papers in a locked cabinet by his bed.

In his country he met Arabs who were able to help him with his correspondence studies. Several months later, he came to the realization that he wanted to receive the salvation from his sin available by Jesus. He received Christ as Savior and began to follow him as a disciple.

One day he came home and found a box of charred papers in his bedroom. He learned that his younger brother had somehow or other opened the locked drawer and showed his parents what his brother was reading. The parents were angry and burned the study papers and materials.

When the young man met his parents, they beat him and sternly warned him not to have anything to do with the Bible and Christian books.

Although his father was a lawyer and an official in one of the ministries of the government, the teenager continued to study the Christian materials, but outside the home. Eventually, life at home became impossible and he left.

As an eighteen-year-old he was free to travel outside of his country. He traveled to a nearby country where he was able to continue his discipleship studies at a postsecondary level.

Several years later he finished that program. While a student there, his father visited him.

His parents know that he now has the education to become a teacher of Christian religion. They know he has turned away from Muhammad and is following Christ. They are talking to him again and inviting him to come home. The young man now must contemplate the risk factor of moving back home.

*Questions for Reflection:* Will the young man be accepted as a follower of Jesus by his parents and siblings? Will a family member or former friend accuse him of apostasy and take him to Sharia Court? Should he risk losing his civil rights and his life? Is this God's timing for him to face heavy persecution and perhaps martyrdom?

## MIRACLE BIRTHS AND REBIRTHS

Ali is a man in his forties. He and his wife, let's call her Sarah, were a devout and happily married Muslim family. Their one regret was that they were childless. As a way to have children they had attempted in vitro fertilization with several hospitals. After spending more than $25,000 on the procedures, his wife did not conceive.

Ali and Sarah traveled to Cyprus. While there, they decided to ask a Christian priest to pray for them to have children. They went to a church and the priest prayed for them to have a baby. A short time later they returned to their homeland and Sarah conceived and bore a son.

Ali and Sarah were convinced this child was a miracle from God. The Christian priest had prayed in the name of Jesus. They began looking for information about Jesus.

They met some Arabs who told them where they could buy a Bible and other literature. Slowly, they began to realize that they wanted to follow Jesus. Ali's wife became pregnant again and they had a second healthy boy.

With their story of two miracle babies, they began to look for someone who could teach them about Jesus. They found an Arab couple who began to meet with them. Several months later they committed their lives to Christ. They changed. A confidence blossomed in them about the truth of the Bible and its story of Jesus the Savior. They began to grow in their faith and read more about their new discipleship.

One day a family member came into their apartment and found the Christian literature. Ali and Sarah acknowledged that it was theirs. The materials were taken to Ali's father for his examination.

When he questioned them, the father learned that Ali and Sarah were now followers of Jesus. He responded to the situation by telling Ali he needed to leave the apartment the father had given him and that Ali would no longer be able to work for him. Suddenly, Ali and Sarah were unemployed with nowhere to live.

For I consider that the sufferings of this present time are not worth comparing with the glory that is to be revealed to us. *Romans 8:18*

Sarah's sister's husband provided them with an apartment and gave them the use of his truck to do free-lance trucking and hauling. They live on the odd jobs that Ali can find. One day Sarah said to Ali, "The Lord promised us to give us our daily bread. He didn't say anything about meat. While we may have had lots of meat in the past, we will be content with the bread he will daily provide."

Early in 2010 one of Sarah's brothers called to tell her that her dad was very sick and needed to see her. When she arrived with her two sons, she learned that her dad was fine. Her brother just wanted to get her to their house. The brother was angry that she and Ali had become Christians. He separated her from her children and locked her in the bathroom. He kept her in the bathroom for several days. At various times he hit her and threatened her with a knife.

When Ali came home from work, he discovered Sarah was not home. He began looking for her. He learned that she was being kept as a prisoner with the children at her brother's house. After three days, he was allowed to bring his wife and children home.

Several more months passed. One day Ali's father confronted him and threatened to harm him if he did not leave the country. He made one of his other sons swear on the Qur'an that the brother would shoot Ali in the legs if Ali did not leave the country permanently. His father consented to give him a year to find a new country in which to live.

Ali realized it was useless to go to the police. All they would do would be to refer him to the Sharia Court. The Sharia Court would find out that he would not recant his faith and then they would declare him an apostate, remove his civil rights, annul his marriage, take away his children, and not let him practice any religion but Islam. The ultimate sentence for apostates is death. In neighboring Saudi Arabia, apostates are beheaded.

When Ali left his father's home, he began looking for a country to which he could flee with his family and be permitted to work. He began to contact embassies to see if someone might be able to help him.

He discovered one country that allows its officials to interview asylum seekers. Ali and Sarah have now visited that embassy twice. Their application for asylum is pending. Meanwhile, the clock ticks towards the one-year deadline that his father set.

If Ali does not leave the country, his brother will shoot him in the legs. As a diabetic, Ali's life will be threatened from blood loss. Martyrdom may be his lot. While he is prepared for that, who will care for his wife and children? Who will protect them from his father and his brothers when Ali is in the grave?

If the family accuses him of apostasy, the police will send Ali to the Sharia Court. The civil court authorities will not intervene. The judgment of the Sharia Court will be sent to the Sharia Appeals Court. The outcome is already known. There will be no escape as an apostate from Islam.

*Questions for Reflection:* What does one do when one's own family feels it is right to beat you, maim you, or kill you because you changed your allegiance from Muhammad to Jesus? Where does one go when the civil courts have abandoned you to the Sharia Courts? If you are married, how do you protect your wife and children from the inevitable sentence of the Sharia Courts?

## INSTITUTIONALIZED PERSECUTION

The main purpose of public schools is to provide a safe and accepting training ground for helping children grow into good citizens. From kindergarten through twelfth grade, schooling is teaching you how to become a responsible person and how to respect people who are different from you.

But if you are a follower of Jesus from a Christian or Muslim background, you will face intellectual, social, and academic challenges as a public school student. In privately run schools, the persecution may be less. You may face animosity from teachers, bullying from students, and sometimes grade changing by examiners. When children come home and tell parents about what is happening at school, many parents remain quiet. They are fearful that talking with the school will make more problems for them and their children.

One day in a private school during the Ramadan fast, Muslim bullies picked on a Christian child. They took him to the school bathroom and covered his mouth with chocolate because the Christian was not fasting at Ramadan. The harassment was reported to the teachers and administration. No action was taken against the bullies.

Quickly children recognize that this kind of treatment is overlooked by the school. Children grow up knowing that Muslim bullies will be an accepted part of their lives. And they learn that most other adults are not willing to engage these bullies. It is hard to keep hope alive when you realize there are different rules for different religions.

All Middle Eastern schools teach religion. All children whose identity papers say they are Muslims must take Islamic Education courses. Children of parents who now follow Jesus but were Muslims at birth are not permitted to choose what religion classes their children will take. The children and the parents are forced against their will to study Islam. Students are compelled to study what their parents at home teach is wrong.

## HIDDEN PERSECUTION

There is a place for Christians and Muslims in governmental systems that run on the principle of being loyal to the group's high ideals. When all are committed to the same things, unity can promote national growth and development. But when these high ideals are compromised by religious or party biases, the affect can be generational.

A young man applied for a job that was in line with his professional training. He was interviewed by the employer and found to be a good candidate for the job. Then his paper work was sent to the Internal Security Department of the Ministry of the Interior. The ministry response came back to the potential employer indicating that the applicant was not eligible for the job for security reasons. No further explanation was given.

The young man applied for a similar job. The same thing happened. The employer was favorable towards hiring the candidate. But the Internal Security Department declared him a security risk and not eligible for the job. In both cases, there was no opportunity to ask why the security clearances were denied.

One is left pondering why the rejection happened twice. Is it because the person's parent is an influential church leader and the government is trying to reduce the parent's influence? Is it because the person himself utilized his freedom of speech and the government felt that he went too far when he said something years ago? Is it because he is an independent thinker and not easily influenced by the pressure? All these questions go unanswered because no one is allowed to ask them of the authorities.

When the young man marries and has children and they are of employment age, they may go to some of the same places where their dad hoped to work and apply. They also will likely find acceptance from the employers but rejection from the security authorities.

If the father of the applicant in such a case has not yet applied for immigration to another country, he will soon do so, even if it takes twenty years. Islamic countries lose some of their best citizens, whether Muslim or Christian, when these seniors see their children rejected by the same system that rejected them when they were young people.

*Questions for Reflection:* What keeps people in a situation where they know they are likely to be discriminated against generation after generation? Is it their calling that keeps them from migrating elsewhere?

## BUILDING REPAIR LICENSES

In 1980 or so, a large church in Assuit, Egypt applied for a license to repair and renovate the church's restrooms. Application was made to the city of Assuit. The application was passed on to the governor of Assuit. Later the permit application went to the authorizing office in Cairo. Finally, the application arrived at the office of the president of the republic, Anwar Sadat. In Egypt, any repair permission for a church has to be approved by the president of the country. While it is possible for the president to find that all the papers are in order and that it is logical to give his approval, it rarely happens.

Hosni Mubarak became the next president of Egypt. Still no permission was given to repair the church bathrooms. The church waited fifteen years for a response.

One day, a new governor of Assuit Province was appointed. He called the pastor and said, "We will not notice you making repairs for several weeks." His message was to go ahead and fix the bathrooms as quickly as possible.

*Questions for Reflection:* What is the purpose of hindering repairs to church buildings? What does this say about the value the Muslim leadership places on Christians?

## LITERATURE-FOCUSED PERSECUTION

Sometimes attempts are made to turn people away from a religious faith by supporting acts of violence against the religion itself. One of the ways this is done is by destroying Bibles, song books, and other religious literature.

### Book burning

One of the tools used by persecutors to harm believers is book burning. If no one gets hurt, governments seem to regard them as harmless radicalism.

In May 2008 in Or Yehuda, Israel, devout Jewish citizens gathered for a bonfire. The kindling and fuel for the fire were New Testament books and related writings collected from homes in the community. The timing was two days before the holiday that remembers Rabbi Akiva from the Revolt of AD 135. One of the ways this holiday is celebrated is with the lighting of bonfires.

One of Israel's popular newspapers, *Maariv*, included a short article and picture of the event in Or Yehuda on their online edition of May 20, 2008. The article could still be accessed on their website in early December 2010.

Citizens from the town and its surrounding environs gathered at the appointed time for the fire lighting. Attendants, including the deputy mayor, fed the fire with the printed materials.

*Questions for Reflection:* What made leaders think that burning books about the Messiah would be a wise idea? What message were they trying to communicate to their children, to other Jews, to Muslims, to Christians, to their nation, and to the world? What fears might their act have stimulated with Messianic believers?

*Bible burning*

Upper Egypt was politically unstable in the 1980s. After President Sadat was murdered, supporters of his killers attacked the main police station in the city of Assuit. There was great loss of life. The Egyptian Army had to send in paratroopers to gain control of the situation. A new kind of Islamic radicalism was nurtured in the area.

One day in the late 1980s, a group of radical students and their leaders came to the city of Sohaj from Assuit. They were intent on causing anger and disarray in the city between Muslims and Christians. A group of these students came to one of the churches in Sohaj on a weekday with the goal of burning the Bibles that were there.

They entered the church and gathered all the Bibles and hymnbooks together in a pile. They poured an inflammable material on the books and lit the fire. They destroyed the books and some of the benches, and blackened the walls and ceiling with smoke.

In their fervor, the students ran upstairs to the pastor's apartment. Fortunately, the pastor had locked the door of the apartment. He and his wife and children were inside. The attackers screamed that they were going to kill the pastor and his wife and children.

The pastor got on the telephone and called the police station. Soon the police arrived. The attackers fled. Calm was restored.

Eventually, the police identified the attackers and jailed many of them. The church was repainted. Furniture was repaired. New Bibles and hymnbooks replaced the burned ones. The police recommended the church build a higher perimeter wall around it. A twenty-four-hour armed guard was posted at the door of the church.

*Questions for Reflection:* What is the message book-burning radicals wish to send? When governments rapidly intervene in religion-related tragedies, what is the message they wish to convey? What is the long-term affect of religion inspired terrorist attacks on families? What pastoral counseling and care would be needed for the family and pastor of this church or other churches that experienced similar attacks?

## PERSECUTION FROM THE VIEWPOINT OF THE PERSECUTOR

As we seek to cope with persecution, it might be helpful to try to state the steps that occur in persecution, a kind of taxonomy of persecution from the perpetrator's viewpoint. It is doubtful that the persecutor would be aware of the taxonomy. I am hoping that those who witness persecution might join the discussion and let me know which steps ring true to them and where they might add other factors.

Each section of the taxonomy is built on the preceding one. After the taxonomy has been introduced and explained, it will be illustrated from two of the persecution anecdotes that appear in this paper. My hope is that by explaining persecution from the perspective of the persecutor, we may gain ideas about the kind of interventions that may or may not be wise to introduce when persecution occurs.

## TAXONOMY OF PERSECUTION FROM THE PERSECUTOR'S VIEWPOINT

1. Persecution is conceived when a person feels their way of life is being threatened by another person.
2. Persecution starts with one person who transforms perceived threats into threats carried out against others.
3. Persecution increases when the person who feels their way of life is being threatened is able to influence others to his/her point of view.
4. Persecution expands when others begin to view persecuting actions as good ways to support their cause.
5. Government steps into persecution with a policy or rule that legalizes persecution.
6. People get used to persecuting others and keep it up because it feels good and they do not necessarily know why they started persecuting in the first place.
7. The will to maintain persecution dwindles.
8. The persecutor goes into hibernation until a new event occurs that casts someone or something as a threat.
9. An event occurs that awakens the persecutor from hibernation, and he redefines its parameters.
10. The persecutor begins to talk about a person who is threatening him and the process begins again.

It may be a help to those people who experience persecution to know in some small ways how persecutors act when they face problems. Let us experiment with one of the illustrations given earlier and see what we can learn.

| TAXONOMY | REACTION TO RAMI |
|---|---|
| *Persecutor's Perspective* | *Persecutor's Action* |
| 1. Our way of life is threatened. | A friend or family member viewed his convert status as an embarrassment and besmirching family honor. |
| 2. Persecutor takes the threat he/she feels and turns it around into a threat against the other person. | The friend or family member does something that Rami will view as threatening behavior. |
| 3. Persecutor helps others see that the person is a threat and needs to be dealt with as a person who is threatening their lives. | Several officials hear of Rami and begin to work against him in the community and family. |
| 4. We have a just cause. People like Rami should not be permitted to operate without facing negative consequences. | Persecutors begin to threaten Rami with things they will do against him. |
| 5. Government creates new policy or law on how to treat socially wayward citizens. | Internal police interview Rami and ask him what is happening in his relationships. |

| 6. Persecutors keep on persecuting because it feels good. | Refer Rami to the Sharia Court for a judgment. |
|---|---|
| 7. The will to maintain persecution wanes. | Rami is sentenced by the Sharia Court and is no longer a person of concern to the persecutor. |
| 8. Persecutor goes into hibernation. He's tired and wants to rest. He's not really interested in Rami anymore. | Rami is gone. We do not need to think about him anymore. |
| 9. Reemerges from hibernation. Redefines parameters of persecution. | Starts to talk about Rami's issues. |
| 10. Begins to talk about a persecution threat. | Starts to feel uncomfortable with someone. |

While the taxonomy may not fit every situation, at least it gives us a tool to help think about why the persecutor does what he does. It may also help the one being persecuted know what he or she might expect next and how to prepare for it. It might also help those who are praying for the one being persecuted to know how to be the most effective in prayer.

## CONCLUSION

Persecution is pervasive in the Middle East. Every country has it. Where there are Christians present, the people will find ways to persecute them. If there are no Christians in the community, people find other groups and other religious sects to persecute.

The challenge for Christians is to decide how they want to cope with persecution and at the same time maintain a credible witness for Christ in the Middle East. Some Christians will be called to immigrate to other countries. Others will be called to remain in the Middle East. Whether in the Arab world or a distant land, Arab Christians need to find ways to help reach the Arab world for Christ.

A great way to help is to pray regularly for friends and relatives in the Middle East. Pray that they will be loyal to their calling to stay in the area and serve. Pray that believers in the Arab world will act in loving kindness to their Christian and Muslim neighbors and workmates. Pray that Arabic-speaking believers will never grow weary of this kind of well-doing. God works through us in powerful and unseen ways when we do his will.

Pray for boldness. Pray that when Arab believers hear the voice of the Lord directing them to share their faith in a creative way that they will follow this leading and do it. Pray for a willingness to speak to officials when given the opportunity, with the view to possibly reducing the persecution and pressure that someone else may be experiencing.

Another way to support Christian witness in the Middle East is to visit. Visitors from outside are treated in a hospitable way by Muslims and Christians alike. These encounters can go a long way towards bringing out the best in everyone. The shared experiences that people have in the homeland with visitors from other cities and countries leave a lasting impression that can improve interreligious relationships long after the visitor is gone.

One of the things we can always count on is that persecution will continue until the Lord returns for us. We learn to live with both persecution and hope.

With the expectation of Christ's soon return and being confident of his presence here and now, we share his gospel with our families and neighbors. We believe that it is the gospel message that shines the light of God's truth everywhere. We pray that our words and lives will brighten the path to the Savior for many.

## QUESTIONS FOR REFLECTION

1. How might careful inductive thinking by the persecuted help them in their responses to persecution? How might such thinking help others in persecuted contexts? What if the persecuted do not have the luxury of carefully considering their response?
2. In a group setting, select two of the author's seven stories and discuss his "questions for reflection" at the end of the story.

## REFERENCES

Barrett, D. B., G. T. Kurian, and T. M. Johnson. 2001. *World Christian encyclopedia*, 2 vols., 2nd ed. Nairobi: Oxford University Press.

Sauer, C. 2008. Researching persecution and martyrdom. *International Journal for Religious Freedom* 1 no. 1, 26–48.

Tieszen, C. 2008. *Re-examining religious persecution: Constructing a theological framework for understanding persecution*. Kempton Park, South Africa: AcadSA Publishing.

**Andrew Edward** (pseudonym) is a follower of the Lord Jesus Christ, who was declared with power to be the Son of God by his resurrection from the dead. Andrew is a member of an Arab church and has lived in the Middle East for many years. His professional life has been invested in helping with the educational needs of the children, youth, and adults of the area.

## LOVE WORKS FOR RELIGIOUS FREEDOM FOR ALL PEOPLE

Upholding human rights by defending religious freedom is not incompatible with following the way of the cross when confronted with persecution. There is no contradiction between being willing personally to suffer the abuse or loss of our own rights for the sake of Christ, and being committed to advocate and speak up for those who are voiceless under the violation of their human rights. We must also distinguish between advocating the rights of people of other faiths and endorsing the truth of their beliefs. We can defend the freedom of others to believe and practise their religion without accepting that religion as true.

A) Let us strive for the goal of religious freedom for all people. This requires advocacy before governments on behalf of Christians and people of other faiths who are persecuted.

B) Let us conscientiously obey biblical teaching to be good citizens, to seek the welfare of the nation where we live, to honour and pray for those in authority, to pay taxes, to do good, and to seek to live peaceful and quiet lives. The Christian is called to submit to the state, unless the state commands what God forbids, or prohibits what God commands. If the state thus forces us to choose between loyalty to itself and our higher loyalty to God, we must say No to the state because we have said Yes to Jesus Christ as Lord.[78]

In the midst of all our legitimate efforts for religious freedom for all people, the deepest longing of our hearts remains that all people should come to know the Lord Jesus Christ, freely put their faith in him and be saved, and enter the Kingdom of God.

[78] Jeremiah 29:7; 1 Peter 2:13–17; 1 Timothy 2:1,2; Romans 13:1–7; Exodus 1:15–21; Daniel 6; Acts 3:19,20; Acts 5:29

Cape Town Commitment, Part II, Section iii. Living the love of Christ among people of other faiths, Paragraph 6

# CHAPTER 22

# SUFFERING AND PERSECUTION IN THE MIDDLE EAST

## *A Pastor from Egypt*

## INTRODUCTION

It is a fact of history that has been neglected by the body of Christ that Christianity was born in the Middle East. The church of Christ has been established in the Middle East since the first century and so it is important to recognize that we are addressing the situation of a people who have been in existence for two thousand years. Often there can be a tendency to view Christians in the Middle East as small minorities that have been planted into the Islamic community.

Although the church faced tremendous challenges in the seventh century from the invasion of Islam and subsequent aggressive attempts to disrupt the national identity of the country by imposing an Islamic culture, it has survived. In many Arab countries it is hard to find even a trace of the ancient Christian heritage, but to the glory of God there are seven Arab nations where the church is alive, acting as salt and light in the midst of the darkness. The church remains strong in Egypt, Sudan, Lebanon, Jordan, Syria, Iraq, and Palestine. Egypt enjoys the highest percentage of Christians, ranging from 8–12 percent of the population.

## THE CRUSADES

Fighting Muslims to regain Jerusalem was a traumatic experience for the Arab World, stemming back from the Crusades in the eleventh century until now. The Arab communities experienced the arrival of thousands of soldiers from the West and struggled to understand what they wanted. The result of this military approach fuelled the fire of antagonism against Christianity throughout the Islamic world as the pages of history clearly reveal. From an Islamic perspective the Crusades are viewed as an invasion by the Christian West against their country. Some Islamic propaganda claims that the Crusades were a means of planting Christians in the Arab World. It is important to be clear that Islam is a religion of intolerance towards all other religions.

The current climate that Christians throughout the Arab World experience is one where you can be "seen but not heard." There are two ideologies which exist within the Muslim mind-set; total eradication or peer pressure from the local community where Christians are treated as second-class citizens. In the latter, Christians are welcome to stay, but they are not given a voice and are discriminated against on a daily basis. However, Christians are becoming increasingly bold and refusing to accept this ideology. Evangelistic activity is growing steadily as the burden for Muslim people increases. The result of such endeavors has been persecution in an attempt to stop growth and eradicate new converts. More recently this has included the burning of church buildings and the prohibition of new buildings. Modern-day persecution in this sense demonstrates that the seeds of intolerance are planted deep within the ideology of Islam and show little sign of being uprooted.

## MIRIAM[1]

Though persecution is a very present reality, God is at work! Over the years we have seen many Muslims who have been exposed to the truth of the gospel and the claims of Jesus Christ. Many have seen dreams, experienced miracles, and walked the long journey into the light. Converts of this kind are the most targeted group of people for persecution and intimidation. Local Christians try to help them in a variety of ways. The persecution comes from their family, the community, and government authorities. Some may have families who are more tolerant, but they still face social stigma from their community and local authorities.

One particular story that stands out is that of Miriam. She was a bright bubbly law student with an infectious sense of joy and zeal for life. She met the Lord while she was at the university through reading the New Testament and subsequent discipleship from church leaders. She became a secret believer and learned to keep her faith in her heart while also attending a local church where she was able to fellowship with friends and other Muslim-background believers (MBBs).

As Miriam's graduation approached many had a genuine concern for her future, as they feared her family would insist upon her marriage to a Muslim man. The best advice they could offer was to seek work in another country where she could set up a new life and identity. Miriam listened carefully to the advice, but she decided in her heart that she could not leave Egypt without witnessing to her family. Her life had been so transformed by the reality that Jesus loved her enough to die for her and give her eternal life that she could not keep this from those who were most precious to her.

It must not be underestimated as to how big a step this in the life of an MBB. There is no guarantee that such a revelation will be well received; parents can go to extreme measures to bring a son or daughter back to Islam.

Shame and honor is very much the mentality of the Muslim world, freedom of belief does not feature. To desert the Islamic faith brings great shame and disgrace upon the entire family and community. There are many different techniques that can be used to make a believer recant including starvation, violence, imprisonment, and intervention by Islamic clerics to reinstruct the individual regarding the faith.

---

1   Name has been changed for security.

Miriam had calculated the risks and decided that she must share her testimony with her family before leaving Egypt. No one could have predicted how her family would react. Her mother's heart was thoroughly broken and so she sought counsel with the extended family. They decided that the only solution was to get rid of Miriam completely.

Several weeks passed and we had not seen or heard from Miriam. We became increasingly concerned and sent someone to inquire with her neighbors as to her whereabouts. There were several varying reports including that she had jumped off her balcony, also that she died in a diabetic coma. We were not convinced by these stories and sent some believers to a local police station to inquire further. They made the simple statement, "Oh yes, this is the young lady that became a Christian and her parents took care of her." It is believed that her uncle threw her from the seventh floor. She was just twenty-four years old.

> Indeed, I count everything as loss because of the surpassing worth of knowing Christ Jesus my Lord. For his sake I have suffered the loss of all things and count them as rubbish, in order that I may gain Christ and be found in him.
> *Philippians 3:8-9a*

## SALEH[2]

As Miriam's story demonstrates, life for the MBB often amounts to that of a castaway where the only option is to move location frequently. The government remains unwilling to change Christian ID cards, meaning they are still treated as Muslims and expected to conform to Islamic practices. This has a big impact upon the family as the children must still go to Muslim schools even though they are now a Christian family. They are often isolated and intimidated and undergo tremendous emotional, mental, and sometimes physical suffering.

Saleh was from a wealthy family; he grew up with privileges and financial liberty. He tried his best to hide his faith from his family for as long as possible, but they eventually found out. They abandoned him completely and cut him off from the family inheritance. Saleh left for another city and tried to begin work and integrate with a new community. He was soon reported to the secret police as he was becoming more active in his Christian life; witnessing, going to meetings, fellowshiping with other MBBs.

He was arrested, confined to a small cell, and subjected to inhumane torture for weeks on end. The charge for his arrest was blasphemy against the Qur'an and the Prophet Muhammad. The penalty for such a charge is three to seven years imprisonment with the only hope of release due to international intervention at the highest level. Saleh was put in a pitch-black cell so small that he could not even stretch his body to sleep at night. Often they would throw buckets of freezing ice over him through the watches of the night. During the day they would bring buckets of human excrement. Still Saleh would not renounce his faith in Jesus Christ. He was beaten and electrocuted repeatedly and still suffers physical defects to this day. We are reminded of the ancient words of Jesus in Matthew 10:

> I am sending you out like sheep among wolves. Therefore be as shrewd as snakes and as innocent as doves. Be on your guard against men; they will hand you over to the

---

2    Name has been changed for security.

local councils and flog you in their synagogues. On my account you will be brought before governors and kings as witnesses to them and to the Gentiles. But when they arrest you, do not worry about what to say or how to say it. At that time you will be given what to say, for it will not be you speaking, but the Spirit of your Father speaking through you. (vv. 16—20)

After Saleh's solitary confinement period ended he stated, "You either go crazy or you meet with God." The Lord was faithful and sustained Saleh throughout his nine-month stay in prison. Pray for the protection of his family as they live by faith each day.

## EFFECT OF PERSECUTION ON CHRISTIAN COMMUNITY IN EGYPT

Christians in Egypt remain under constant pressure and discrimination. There are many different levels, for example the lack of permission to build new churches. If you are seen to be engaging in direct Muslim evangelization you can face arrest or kidnapping. The root of this intimidation is largely irrational and based on hate without cause. Recent incidents in Minya show how a simple dialogue can escalate into aggressive mob action with no accountability.

One sunny Easter day a Muslim man was driving along in his car when he collided with an unexpected speed bump on the road. He got out of his car and tried to find out who was responsible. It transpired that a Christian had built the speed bump in front of his house to slow traffic down as a safety precaution. As soon as the driver became aware of this he started hurling insults at him. Because of the man's Christian faith, the speed-bump incident quickly faded into insignificance. Soon more people joined in the commotion and fighting broke out with shots of gunfire piercing the commotion. The violence escalated further and resulted in the burning down of houses across the neighborhood. Many lost their possessions due to fire damage and theft. The next day the thieves wore the Christian families clothing in order to taunt and intimidate them. One man lost all of his livestock; thirty cows and buffalo and now has no income.

In recent weeks the Christians have attempted to rebuild their homes, but every time they try to do so they face Muslim intervention and threats. They are left with no other choice but relocation.

## CONCLUSION

The Christian presence is getting smaller in the Middle East due to organized and escalating violence. In Iraq the Christian population has decreased by approximately 50 percent. Sadly this is a shadow that comes and goes all the time for those of us who remain long term in the Arab World. We must not overlook the reality and impact of the immigration and reallocation throughout the Arab world. This is a strategic battle from the enemy, which Christians in the West need to fully realize. The media neglects this fact; however, we take hope in that Christianity has survived thus far. It is our hope that one day there will be freedom of religion so that the Christian community can live, grow, and thrive. Nevertheless we take heart in the fact that the Lord has promised to build his church and the gates of hell will never prevail against it.

## QUESTIONS FOR REFLECTION

1. Reflect on Miriam's and Saleh's stories. What lessons may we learn from Miriam's decision to witness to her family at the risk of her own life? What lessons may we learn from Saleh's response to his torture?

2. What are the options for a church body whose plans for a building or meeting place are thwarted by the government?

3. Are there ways in which Christians around the world can raise awareness in the media and among church members about the long-standing Christian church in the Middle East?

This article was written by a pastor from Egypt who is strongly involved in ministering to Christians who are suffering and being persecuted in this region of the world.

To endure the cross is not a tragedy; it is the suffering which is the fruit of an exclusive allegiance to Jesus Christ. When it comes, it is not an accident but a necessity. It is not the sort of suffering which is inseparable from this mortal life, but the suffering which is an essential part of the specifically Christian life. It is not suffering per se but suffering-and-rejection, and not rejection for any cause or conviction of our own, but rejection for the sake of Christ.

D. Bonhoeffer in *The Cost of Discipleship* (1976, 97f)

*"But we have this treasure in jars of clay…"*   2 Corinthians 4:7–11

Paul writes that suffering has become part of his life as a consequence of his radical commitment to Jesus Christ. He creates a number of contrasts in his experience. He has been "hard pressed, but not crushed, perplexed, but not in despair, persecuted, but not abandoned" (vv. 8–9).

"But not" refers to God's power which supports him. His body is a fragile vessel of clay, facing persecution and suffering as a result of the proclamation of the gospel, creating the opportunity for God's power and the life of Jesus to become manifest.

Paul is willing to face any persecution and suffering or whatever loss for the cause of the expansion of God's Kingdom. The values brought about by an eternal perspective cause suffering for mission to become a privilege and a gain instead of a loss.

Reflection by: Edilson Ribeiro Gomes Filho, Brazil

# CHAPTER 23

# THE FIRST CHRISTIAN MARTYRS OF JAPAN

## An Asian Case Study

*How Chuang Chua*

From its earliest beginnings, the church has often faced the daunting prospect of having some of her members pay the ultimate sacrifice for keeping the faith. This is hardly surprising in light of the biblical truth that the church is founded on the very death and resurrection of Jesus Christ. The church as the body of Christ is indeed no less than the body of Christ crucified and raised. Jesus could not have been clearer in saying, when he exhorted his disciples to take up their crosses and follow him, that suffering, even to the point of death, is to be a hallmark of authentic discipleship (Mark 8:34–37). In a similar vein, the Apostle Paul taught that to be baptized with Christ is to be baptized into his death (Rom 6:3). Many Christians, especially in places where freedom of religion is guaranteed, interpret these biblical passages in an almost purely metaphorical sense. Exegetically this is not wrong since the metaphor of death does pertain to a spiritual reality that is central to what it means to be a follower of Christ. On the other hand, for many other Christians, in times past as well as today, the physical reality of persecution and death is a constant threat. Indeed, these believers draw strength and comfort from their reading of Jesus and Paul that the church is theologically a "martyr-church" (cf. Hovey 2008, 23–41). For these suffering brothers and sisters, suffering and death are a mark of identification with Christ and his church.

The paradox of martyrdom is that it unwittingly gives the seemingly powerless church a voice to bear the message of faith and salvation to the very people that seek to silence it. It is a powerful witness that transcends time and space, such that even today we can still hear the voices of these Christian martyrs reverberating not only from a distant past, but also from lands unfamiliar to us. Yet their message is a common one—one that testifies to the faithfulness of God and the truth of the gospel. In this chapter, we shall listen to one such voice from the martyr-church from Japan, a voice lifted up to God in unison by the historic crucifixion of the twenty-six martyrs of 1597. In particular, we shall listen to the last words of two of the martyrs—in the form of a sermon and a letter—and reflect afresh on what it means to bear the ultimate witness for Christ.

## JAPAN'S ENCOUNTER WITH CHRISTIANITY

Christianity came to Japan in 1549 with the arrival of three Jesuit missionaries and four lay companions, led by the Spanish-born Francis Xavier. It was Japan's very first encounter with Christianity, and a most dramatic one.[1] For by the time all-out persecution broke loose in 1614 under the Tokugawa government—less than seventy years after the launch of the Christian mission by Xavier—there were no fewer than 300,000 baptized Christians in the country.[2] Nagasaki, a city on the southern island of Kyushu, became so predominantly Christian that Luis Cerqueira, the second bishop of Japan, proudly referred to it as the "Rome of the Far East" (Fujita 1991, 9). Christian growth spread northwards along the populated coastal regions, both east and west, right up to the southern edge of what is today's Aomori prefecture. Historian C. R. Boxer was so impressed with the phenomenal growth of the church in Japan between 1549 and 1650 that he coined the phrase "the Christian century in Japan" of the title for his seminal work on the Jesuit mission to Japan (1967). Equally awed by the achievements of the Jesuits is Andrew Ross (1994, 87), who hails the Society of Jesus as "the creative force in the growth of the Japanese Church."

Yet in spite of the spectacular growth of the church, following Tokugawa Ieyasu's edict to expel all missionaries from the country in 1614, the church was ignobly persecuted, and thousands of Christians were martyred. For the next 250 years or so, during which Japan closed her doors to the rest of the world, the physical presence of the church would be all but eliminated.

## THE TWENTY-SIX MARTYRS OF NAGASAKI

While there had always been intermittent instances of local persecution, the Jesuits had by and large enjoyed free rein, even official patronage at times, during the first twenty-eight years of their ministry in Japan. Within just a quarter of a century, the church had grown to be a highly visible social and cultural institution, thanks to the Jesuits' top-down strategy of evangelizing the territorial samurai warlords.

"But be on your guard. For they will deliver you over to councils, and you will be beaten in synagogues, and you will stand before governors and kings for my sake, to bear witness before them." Mark 13:9

On July 25, 1587, without any prior warning, Toyotomi Hideyoshi, the supreme military commander of the newly unified nation, issued an edict to banish all foreign missionaries. While the edict took the church completely by surprise, it was never quite enforced, resulting in only three out of the 120 or so Jesuit priests leaving the

---

1       Some have suggested that the Nestorians' presence in Japan predated that of the Jesuits by at least three hundred years, but the evidence for that is ambiguous at best. It is true that Nestorian relics are found in Japan, but these were unearthed from the tomb of the envoys from Kublai Khan who were executed in 1280 (see Saeki 1951, 444–47) as well as from the tomb of five men captured and executed during the failed Mongolian invasion in 1281 (see Natori 1957, 12–16).

2       Exact figures are notoriously difficult to establish. C. R. Boxer (1967, 197), in all probability relying on the 1605 report of the missionary Fernão Guerreiro, reports the presence of "a Christian community of about 750,000 believers, with an annual increase of five or six thousand." Mark Mullins (1998, 12) suggests that the ratio of Christians to non-Christians then was "probably several times higher than what it is today." The population of Japan at that time was somewhere between 15 and 20 million.

country and an influential Japanese Christian samurai being forced to give up his land and property. In all probability, the anti-Christian edict was Hideyoshi's way of expressing his distrust of the church which he had come to view as the vanguard of Portuguese imperialist expansion. Ironically, six years after the issue of the edict, Hideyoshi allowed another missionary order, the Franciscans, to enter and work in Japan. It is obvious that the Franciscans, who came from Spain, were welcome as a means of counterbalancing what was perceived as the growing political influence of the Portuguese Jesuits.

However, a particularly significant event happened three years after the Franciscans' arrival in Japan, an event that would precipitate the first martyrdom in the Japanese church. On October 19, 1596, a Spanish vessel *San Felipe*, on its way from Manila to Acapulco, ran aground on the southern island of Shikoku after being driven by a storm. The ship was richly laden and well armed. When a high-ranking government official was sent to investigate the ship and confiscate its cargo, the officers of the ship protested and apparently invoked Spain's military might as a threat.[3] Whether an actual threat was meant or not, the encounter between the Japanese official and the Spanish crew yielded disastrous results, for when the official conveyed a report of the incident to the Japanese court, the incensed Hideyoshi promptly confiscated the ship and ordered the execution of all the Franciscans in Japan. However, for practical reasons, and also apparently because of the influence of the Christian warlords, Hideyoshi chose instead to display his sovereign power by executing twenty-six Christians right in Nagasaki, the heart of Japanese Christianity.

At first, twenty-four Christians were arrested, almost randomly: three Japanese Jesuits arrested in Osaka, six Franciscan missionaries in Kyoto, and fifteen Japanese Christians seized from the Franciscan hospital in Kyoto. Having their left ears cut off, the Christians were paraded through the streets of Kyoto and then sent off on a five-hundred-mile forced march in the cold of winter to Nagasaki. En route, two more Christian prisoners were added. The journey to the execution site took a whole month.

Among the twenty-six martyrs of Nagasaki—as they are famously known—were five teenage boys, the youngest of whom was barely twelve. There was also a father and his fourteen-year-old son. The prisoners were allowed to write letters, some of which have been translated and preserved. Thomas Kozaki, the fourteen-year-old, wrote this letter to his mother:

Dear Mother,

With the gracious help of God, I am writing this letter to you. According to the written sentence, we, twenty-four of us including the padres, will be crucified in Nagasaki. Please do not worry about father Michael and me, for we shall soon meet in Paradise. We will be waiting for you. Even if you are not able to find a padre before you die, as long as you feel deep remorse for your sins and be thankful for the abundant grace

---

3      There are at least two different accounts of what actually transpired: the Jesuit view and the Franciscan view (Fujita 1991, 133–39). But even in the more defensive Franciscan account, the ship's pilot was said to have shown the Japanese official a map of the world that depicted the vast territories colonized by Spain, and on this map the country of Japan appeared "smaller than a thumb" (134).

of Jesus Christ, you will be saved. As everything in this world will come to naught, please be diligent so as not to lose the perfect glory of Paradise. No matter how you are treated by others, please exercise great patience and treat everyone with love and kindness. Please make every effort to ensure that my little brothers Mancio and Philip are not handed over to unbelievers. I will pray to our Lord for you, dear Mother. Please give my greetings to everyone I know. Let me ask you again not to forget this one important matter, that you immerse your heart in profound contrition for your sins. For even Adam was able to be saved from his sin of turning against God because of his subsequent remorse. May God protect you.

Thomas.[4]

The party of twenty-six finally reached Nagasaki on February 4, 1597. The following morning, they were led to a small hill overlooking the city of Nagasaki, where they were tied with ropes on wooden crosses. Iron clamps were placed around their wrists and ankles, and a straddle piece was placed between the legs for weight support. Attached to the shaft of a lance planted before the twenty-six crosses was the written death sentence personally issued by Hideyoshi. The sentence read:

> I have ordered these foreigners to be treated thus, because they have come from the Philippines to Japan, calling themselves ambassadors, although they were not so; because they have remained here so long without permission; because in defiance of my prohibition they have built churches, preached their religion, and caused disorders. (Moffett 2005, 85)

Paul Miki, a thirty-three-year-old Japanese Jesuit brother preparing for ordination, and known for his eloquence of speech, converted his cross into a pulpit from which he delivered this stirring sermon:

> All of you who are here, please listen to me. I did not come from the Philippines. I am a Japanese by birth, and a brother of the Society of Jesus. I have committed no crime, and the only reason that I am put to death is that I have been proclaiming the teaching of our Lord Jesus Christ. For this I rejoice, and regard my death as a great gift of grace from the Lord. As I come to this supreme moment of my life, please believe me that I have no desire to deceive you. But I want to stress and make it clear that man can find no salvation other than through the Christian way. Christianity teaches us to forgive our enemies and those who have harmed us. I therefore forgive the Supreme General (Toyotomi Hideyoshi) and everyone who has had a part in my death. I do not have any ill feelings towards the General at all. On the contrary, I deeply yearn for the General and all my Japanese countrymen to become Christians.[5]

An eyewitness described Miki's cross aptly as "the noblest pulpit he had ever filled" (O' Malley 2007, 38).

---

4       The original letter did not survive, but a copy is kept in the Museum of the Twenty-Six Martyrs in Nagasaki. An early Portuguese translation of the letter is kept in the Vatican.

5       The transcribed Japanese sermon is kept at the Museum of the Twenty-Six Martyrs in Nagasaki.

As late afternoon approached, the executioners took up their positions, one on each side of every cross. The prisoners were given one last chance to renounce their faith, but all resolutely declined. On signal, the executioners pierced both sides of each person's body with a long spear up through the left and right ribs toward the opposite shoulder. Paul Miki was heard to have prayed, "Lord, into your hands I commit my spirit. Come to meet me, you saints of God" (Yuki 2002, 14). Most of the twenty-six martyrs died almost immediately. Those who did not were given another thrust to the neck to give the *coup de grace*. The bodies were left hanging on the crosses for nine months.

## FURTHER PERSECUTION AND THE CLOSING OF JAPAN'S DOORS TO THE WORLD

Thinking that the public spectacle that he made of the twenty-six Christians was sufficient to curtail the influence and growth of the church, Hideyoshi did not follow through with his original order to execute all the other Franciscans. In June the following year, Hideyoshi died unexpectedly of dysentery. In the respite that followed, the church saw remarkable growth. Bishop Cerqueira reported that Jesuit baptisms alone over the next two years numbered about seventy thousand (Moffett 2005, 85). The martyrdom of the twenty-six Christians obviously had the opposite effect of what Hideyoshi had intended, for it fueled the spiritual passion of the church to a new degree, inspiring many more to follow Christ.

The growth of the church was unfortunately short-lived. Civil war broke out in 1600, in which the Tokugawa family defeated the heirs of Hideyoshi. Ieyasu, a staunch Pure Land Buddhist, then established the Tokugawa shogunate that was to rule Japan for the next 250 years or so. Believing that Christianity was subversive to his government, Ieyasu issued his infamous anti-Christian edict in 1614 that outlawed Christianity. All missionaries were to be deported and all churches closed. Every Japanese person was to be officially enrolled with the local Buddhist temple. Christians who refused to renounce their faith were to be tortured and killed. Ieyasu's edict was mercilessly implemented by his son and grandson who succeeded him as shogun. On the hill in Nagasaki where the twenty-six Christians were martyred, many more were executed. Over the next thirty years, "the entire Christian population was systematically burned, strangled, starved, tortured, or driven underground" (Moffett 2005, 90). Things came to a head in 1637 when the farmers in the Christian province of Arima revolted against the religious persecution and economic deprivation imposed by the authorities. Fighting under banners with small red crosses in what is now known as the Shimabara Rebellion, the embattled villagers managed to hold out for three months until their supplies ran out. The Tokugawa forces, numbering some 120,000, then overran and slaughtered virtually all twenty thousand villagers, including women and children. Convinced that the rebellion was instigated and supported by the Portuguese in an attempt to take over the country, the Tokugawa government enforced a self-imposed policy of national isolation in 1639. With this, the Christian century in Japan came to a tragic end. And Japan was to remain a closed country until the middle of the nineteenth century.

## SOME MISSIOLOGICAL REFLECTIONS

Now that we have heard echoes of a voice from the martyr-church in sixteenth-century Japan, let us now reflect briefly on what we can learn from this episode in the history of the Japanese church.

In the face of ferocious persecution, the courage of the martyrs seems almost unnatural. Thomas Kozaki's letter to his mother and Paul Miki's sermon from the cross give us two pieces of insight as to the source of their indomitable spirit. First, both Kozaki and Miki held to the unwavering faith that salvation is to be found in Christ alone. The priceless treasure of salvation, when grasped and experienced personally, will not be exchanged or compromised, even in the face of death. If it is, as in the case of a theological pluralism that posits different paths to salvation, the church would only lose its martyr-witness. For who would be willing to die for what is only one way to salvation? The second point, related to the first, is a consuming vision of paradise. For both Kozaki and Miki, heaven is not an abstract doctrine, but an existential reality against which life in this world becomes a pale shadow. Here is a lesson for contemporary Christians, for many of whom the longing of heaven is blunted by the glittering distractions of the world.

Despite the severe suffering of the Japanese martyrs, missionaries have often wondered why their deaths did not bring about a phenomenal growth of the church, as would be the case later in China and Korea. Some have even gone to the extent of lamenting that the Japanese church, despite its promising start, died along with the thousands who were martyred for their faith. But is it theological to suppose that the church could die at the hands of its enemies? After all, did not Christ promise that he would build his church and that the gates of hell would not prevail against it (Matt 16:18)? In truth, Christ's church did not die in Japan, even though humanly speaking, it seemed to have all but disappeared. The church was not decimated as a result of the martyrdoms, for as Craig Hovey (2008, 34) puts it succinctly, "The dead saints are still members." Indeed, the church of Jesus Christ is a historic body that transcends space and time, comprising those who are living on this earth and "the cloud of witnesses" who have gone ahead (Heb 12:1), and in this sense it could never die. Moreover, in the case of Japan, the church, though relatively small, is still very much alive today; it has indeed outlasted the Tokugawa government that sought to destroy it. It may well be that we have yet to see the full flowering of the fruit of the Japanese martyrs.

However, an important lesson can still be gleaned as to why the gospel did not take root after the church was driven underground. Because of the decrees issued at the Council of Trent (1545–63) that stipulated Latin to be the language of the Mass, and the Latin Vulgate as the only authoritative Scripture for public reading and doctrinal expositions, the Jesuits did not make any serious attempt to publish and distribute Japanese translations of the Bible. Indeed portions of Scripture, including the Gospels, were translated for the use of public ministry, but these were all virtually destroyed in the fire on the island of Takushima in 1563. Ironically, the loss of these materials coincided with the closing year of the Tridentine Council. Consequently, when the missionaries were expelled from the country, Roman Catholicism would suffer a catastrophic blow simply because the church did not have a good, standardized Japanese translation of the complete Bible to nurture the faith of subsequent believers.[6] The vernacular principle as an integral part of the cultural translatability of the faith is something that we take so much for granted in missions today, but it proved to be a blind spot for the Jesuits.

Finally, it is interesting to note that the persecution of the Japanese church stemmed from the perception by the governing authorities of the church as a real political threat. This perception seems to be common in other persecution contexts as well. Ironically, the church that seeks to be faithful to Christ and his teaching would not have the slightest desire to usurp political authority from the state. Even Francis Xavier understood this, and early in his ministry, had in fact written a letter back home to plead with the Spanish monarch not to harbor any intention of colonizing Japan (Skoglund 1975, 464). Yet it cannot be denied that there is a political dimension to the gospel—and by extension to the missionary task—that is often not acknowledged but one that certainly needs to be explored. While most missionaries today consciously steer clear of any political agenda, their attitudes and actions are nonetheless shaped by certain political convictions in ways that they are not always aware of. In any case, missionary work, at the very least, calls for an acute sense of political awareness. There is also the great need to exercise wisdom, sensitivity, humility, and cooperation with other missions, especially when working in countries politically and religiously hostile to Christians.

## QUESTIONS FOR REFLECTION

1. Why do you think that persecution against the church is often politically motivated? Is it possible to carry out mission work in a way that has completely nothing to do with politics? Why or why not?

2. In the light of Tertullian's famous words celebrating martyrdom, "*Semen est sanguis Christianorum*" ("The blood of Christians is seed"), how do you make sense of the virtual disappearance of the Japanese church following its severe persecution by the authorities in the seventeenth century? Is there any necessary relationship between persecution and church growth?

3. How can the church help its members prepare for persecution, and even martyrdom?

4. Read again Thomas Kozaki's letter to his mother and Paul Miki's sermon from the cross. What can you learn from the last words of these two martyrs that will encourage you in your faith journey?

---

6    In contrast, the Chinese church of the twentieth century grew phenomenally despite the Communists' expulsion of all missionaries from the country in 1949 and the ensuing persecution of the church. This was due, in good part, to the existence of the Union Bible, a good and established translation of the whole Bible in the Chinese script that enjoyed wide circulation since its publication in 1909.

## REFERENCES

Boxer, C. R. 1967. *The Christian century in Japan 1549–1650*, 2nd printing, corrected. Berkeley, CA: University of California Press.

Fujita, N. S. 1991. *Japan's encounter with Christianity: The Catholic mission in pre-modern Japan.* New York: Paulist.

Hovey, C. 2008. *To share in the body: A theology of martyrdom for today's church.* Grand Rapids, MI: Brazos.

Moffett, S. H. 2005. *A history of Christianity in Asia, vol. 2, 1500–1900.* Maryknoll, NY: Orbis Books.

Mullins, M. R. 1998. *Christianity made in Japan: A study of indigenous movements.* Honolulu: University of Hawai'i Press.

Natori, J. 1957. *Historical stories of Christianity in Japan.* Tokyo: Hokuseido.

O' Malley, V. J. 2007. *Saints of Asia: 1500 to the present.* Huntington, IN: Our Sunday Visitor Publishing.

Ross, A. 1994. *A vision betrayed: The Jesuits in Japan and China 1542–1742.* Maryknoll, NY: Orbis Books.

Saeki, P. Y. 1951. *The Nestorian documents and relics in China,* 2nd ed. Tokyo: Maruzen.

Skoglund, H. 1975. St. Francis Xavier's encounter with Japan. *Missiology: An International Review* 3, no. 4: 451–67.

Yuki, D. R. 2002. *The martyr's hill Nagasaki,* 4th ed. Nagasaki: Twenty-Six Martyrs Museum.

**How Chuang Chua** was born and raised in Singapore. He and his wife, Kaori, serve as missionaries in Japan with OMF International. How Chuang is academic dean of Hokkaido Bible Institute in Sapporo and also serves as an adjunct lecturer at Japan Bible Seminary in Tokyo. His current research interests include cross-cultural theology and mission spirituality.

# CHAPTER 24

# TSARIST RUSSIA AND THE SOVIET AND POST-SOVIET UNION

## Persecution of Christians

*Mark R. Elliott*

At the beginning of the twentieth century, tsarist Russia banned or restricted all expressions of Christianity other than Russian Orthodoxy, the privileged state church. Among the Christian communions with no legal existence was Eastern-Rite Catholicism (worshiping according to the Orthodox liturgy and served by a married priesthood, while submitting to the authority of the Pope in Rome). Pejorativ

ely called the Uniate Church by Russians, it had been suppressed throughout most of the empire in 1839 and as well in the former Austrian Kholm District in 1875 (Elliott 1985, 212).

Tsarist Russia also denied a legal existence to Stundists—Slavic evangelicals hailing originally from Ukraine, who were named for the prayer hour (*stunde*) they borrowed from their German Mennonite mentors. Authorities came to label as Stundists any Protestants they chose to harass or arrest. Other evangelicals facing concerted state and Orthodox opposition included Slavic converts to Baptist faith (originating in the Caucasus and Ukraine), followers of Protestant convert Colonel Vasilii Pashkov, known as Pashkovites, and later, evangelical Christians (originating in St. Petersburg), Methodists, and Seventh-day Adventists (Sawatsky 1981, 34).

In 1900 Latin-Rite Roman Catholics, predominately Poles, Belorussians, and Lithuanians in Russia's western borderlands, had a legal existence but were being subjected to heavy-handed state policies of russification. In the nineteenth century thousands of Poles who had opposed tsarist rule had been deported to Siberia, giving Catholicism an unintended presence east of the Urals (Chaplitskii and Osipova 2000, lxi).

Working in tandem, the Russian state and its state church imposed numerous restrictions on another Christian community, the Old Believers. Also known as *Raskolniki* (Schismatics), they had rejected changes in the Orthodox liturgy and in the rendering of icons imposed by Patriarch Nikon in the late seventeenth century. By 1900 state executions, imprisonments, and harsh discriminatory taxation, countered by Old Believer flight, self-immolations, and predictions of the Apocalypse, had long since given way to a patchwork of bureaucratic carrots and sticks that nevertheless failed to cow this intransigent and increasingly prosperous religious opposition (Beeson 1982, 91; Robson 1995, 14–40).

As of 1900, German Baptists, German Mennonite colonists, and Lutherans, also mostly German in origin, came the closest to tolerated, non-Orthodox churches. However, they, as well, were subject to various bureaucratic impediments, and the latter were legally confined to the Baltic region and certain larger cities of the empire. In every case, non-Orthodox churches were legally proscribed from accepting converts from Russian Orthodoxy.

An ideological amalgam of xenophobia, nationalism, and Orthodox triumphalism served as the justification for the wide array of measures taken by the Russian state against non-Orthodox Christians—and other faiths as well. Nicholas II, the last Russian tsar (1896–1917), and his reactionary advisor, Konstantin Pobedonostsev, oberprokurator of the Russian Orthodox Holy Synod (1880–1905), personified the ingrained intolerance of the Russian state and its state church. Both men were passionately ethnocentric and anti-Semitic, fearing that non-Orthodox expressions of faith would undermine the viability of the Russian realm. Difficulties faced by evangelicals under the procuracy of Pobedonostsev included discrimination in employment, disruption of worship, inability to buy or lease land for prayer houses, fines, beatings, prejudicial passport identification as "Stundist," lack of state recognition of "stundist" marriages, deprivation of parental rights, exile abroad, and arrest and deportation to the Transcaucasus and Siberia (Brandenburg 1974, 123, 125; Hefly 1979, 227; Sawatsky 1981, 35–36).

In 1884, Alexander III had personally ordered the banishment abroad of Colonel Pashkov. Another prominent evangelical in the capital, Ivan Prokhanov, eluded Russian police by fleeing abroad in 1895. Prior to 1917 Baptist preacher Feodor Kostronin spent nine years in prison and sixteen years in exile, while Vasili Ivanov-Klyshnikov (later, secretary of the Baptist Union) was arrested thirty-one times and exiled twice (Brandenburg 1974, 130).

The 1905 Russian Revolution brought a momentary reprieve to the non-Orthodox via Nicholas II's Edict of Toleration (April 1905). For the first time in Russian history, all citizens of the empire were granted freedom of conscience, including the legal right to leave the Orthodox fold for another church. However, once the immediate threat to his throne passed, Nicholas II gradually reneged on his own 1905 October Manifesto with its provisions for representative government and civil liberties, including freedom of religion. Evangelicals suffered increasing harassment and discrimination, including censorship, limitations on youth work, and a requirement for police permission for Protestant meetings (frequently denied). An anti-Protestant climate fostered by the state, the state church, and the state-influenced press led to extralegal repression, namely mob actions, sometimes fomented by priests, leading to injuries and deaths (Brandenburg 1974, 152; Sawatsky 1981, 36). Only the inefficiencies of an inept bureaucracy spread over eleven time zones saved evangelicals and other non-Orthodox believers from more systematic persecution.

The coming of World War I brought new trials to evangelicals who were correctly accused of pacifist leanings but incorrectly accused of pro-German sympathies. Wartime authorities subjected evangelical services to police surveillance, closed meeting houses, and arrested and deported pastors. The president of the Baptist Union went into hiding in Central Asia while evangelical Christian leader Ivan Prokhanov faced trial in 1916, but was acquitted. Russian German Baptist pastors Walter Jack and Karl Fullbrandt were exiled to Siberia and northern European Russia, while William Fetler was deported abroad (Brandenburg 1974, 150, 157–58, 173).

On the eve of the revolutionary upheavals of 1917, it should be noted as well that the favored Russian Orthodox Church also suffered its own crippling disabilities. From Peter the Great to Nicholas II the state church languished in velvet chains imposed upon it by a Holy Synod that was forced to function as a branch of government. Its civilian oberprokurators—even including military generals—thwarted all attempts at internal church reform and renewal.

Communist victories in the October 1917 Revolution and the Russian Civil War (1918–21) brought to power a determinedly atheist regime that would be responsible for the most comprehensive and deadliest persecution of Christianity—and of all religions—in history to that date. Dwarfing in size, intensity, and thoroughness the intermittent persecutions of the Roman Empire, the Soviet antireligious campaign of 1917–89 appears to have been surpassed in lethal consequences by only one other, that of Communist China from 1949.

The Russian Orthodox Church, perceived by the new Marxist state to be a major source of opposition, was subjected to an especially unrelenting assault during the first two decades of Soviet power. The 54,147 Orthodox churches and 25,593 chapels as of 1914 were reduced to between 100 and 300 by August 1939 (Beglov 2008, 68; Davis 2003, 12–13; Ellis 1986, 4, 14; Emel'ianov 2004, 3; Hefly 1979, 270; Newton 1990, 83; Pospielovsky 1988, 66; Tsypin 1994, 107). By 1939 Moscow had only 15–20 functioning parishes from over 600; Leningrad, 5 from 401; Tambov, 2 from 110; and the Kiev Diocese, 2 from 1,600 (Davis 2003, 12–13; Pospielovsky 1988, 66; Tsypin 1994, 107).

Of 1,025 Orthodox monasteries and nunneries functioning in 1914, with some 95,000 monks, nuns, and novices, not a single one remained open in 1929 (Beeson 1982, 58; Davis 2003, 164, 166; Emel'ianov 2004, 3; Shkarovskii 1999, 67; Stroyen 1962, 9). Likewise, from 1914 to 1939, all 57 Orthodox seminaries and 4 theological academies were suppressed (Beeson 1982, 58; Shkarovskii 1999, 67). In addition, by 1939, Soviet authorities had closed or nationalized 37,528 Orthodox parochial schools, all 1,131 of its homes for the aged, and all 291 of its hospitals (Beeson 1982, 58).

Of roughly 300 Orthodox bishops in 1914, less than 20 were alive by 1943. Only 4 bishops enjoyed some degree of liberty, while living in fear of imminent arrest or worse (Davis 2003, 11, 64; Hefly 1979, 27; Zugger 2001, 247). Of some 51,000 priests in 1914, no more than 300 to 400 were still serving parishes in 1939 (Beeson 1982, 58; Davis 2003, 129). Of the 1,000-plus priests in the vicinity of St. Petersburg in 1917, only 15 were free to conduct services in the renamed Leningrad Region in 1937. German forces advancing through Ukraine in 1941 found only 2 remaining Orthodox priests in 2 open churches in the Kiev Diocese, down from 1,435 priests in 1917 (Davis 2003, 11, 13).

Orthodoxy's staggering institutional and human losses must also, of necessity, be calculated in terms of arrests, executions, and forced labor terms, with mortality rates in confinement as high as 85 percent (Pospielovsky 1984, 177). Patriarch Aleksei II estimated that by the late 1930s Russia's Communist government was responsible for the deaths of some 80,000 Orthodox clergy, monks, and nuns (Davis 2003, 11; Hefly 1979, 270). Executions of priests in 1918–19 and 1930–31 alone have been estimated at over 15,000 and 5,000 respectively, not counting deaths in prisons and labor camps (Emel'ianov 2004, 2–3). In addition, the number of Orthodox parishioners who perished for their faith in the interwar decades must have run at least into the hundreds of thousands (Shkarovskii 1999, 93).

Before World War I the population of tsarist Russia included over 5 million Roman Catholics, with the heaviest concentrations in western Ukraine, partitioned Poland, Belorussia, Lithuania, and Latvia (Chaplitskii and Osipova 2000, xxii; Zugger 2001, 21–22, 36, 42, 45, 264). Wartime territorial losses saw Russia shorn of sizeable portions of its western frontier with its large Catholic populations, such that by 1917 the new Soviet state was home to a much-reduced 1.4 million Catholics. Unwavering Kremlin hostility toward the Vatican and fear of fifth columnists in its vulnerable western borderlands led to the nearly complete institutional demise of Catholicism on Soviet territory in two decades. Communist repression reduced the number of functioning Catholic churches from 980 in 1917 to 2 showcase parishes in Moscow and Leningrad in 1939 (Beeson 1982, 23; Solchanyk and Hvat 1990, 53). Likewise, the number of priests fell drastically from 912 in 1917 to 2 in August 1939. By 1934, Soviet Russia had not a single serving Catholic bishop, from 21 in 1917, not a single functioning parochial school or social institution, from 300 to 500 in 1917, and no functioning seminaries, of the 4 previously in operation (Beeson 1982, 123; Hefly 1979, 232).

Therefore let those who suffer according to God's will entrust their souls to a faithful Creator while doing good. *1 Peter 4:19*

Protestants initially benefited from the fall of the Romanovs and Bolshevik fixation on the perceived threat of Orthodoxy. The new regime's relatively benign neglect permitted dramatic evangelical growth in the 1920s. Baptists and evangelical Christians, who together numbered just over 100,000 members in 1905, grew to 250,000 by 1921, and to 500,000 members with up to 1–2 million counting children and adherents by 1929 (Elliott 1981, 17; Elliott 1992, 192; Elliott 2003, 26; Sawatsky 1981, 27; Sawatsky 1992, 240).

The 1930s, however, brought crushing repression in the form of wholesale church closures, arrests, prison and labor camp sentences, and executions. The ruthless, indiscriminate antireligious campaign of that decade led to the total elimination of institutional life for Baptists, Lutherans, Mennonites, Methodists, Pentecostals, and Seventh-day Adventists. In the Leningrad Region in 1937–38 alone, 34 evangelical Christian and Baptist pastors and activists lost their lives (Nikol'skaia 2009, 105). A single evangelical Christian church in Moscow may have been the only Protestant congregation still legally functioning in 1939, down from over 7,000 in 1928 (Elliott 2003, 26; Sawatsky 1981, 48; Sawatsky 1992, 243).

The 1930s also witnessed a crescendo of state-sponsored antireligious propaganda directed against all faiths. The Soviet regime went to extraordinary lengths and committed prodigious resources in this effort, for example, in its League of the Militant Godless, whose membership reached 5.5 million in 1932. While the antireligious campaign obviously succeeded in closing churches, it failed to make atheists of millions of believers, so many that results of the 1937 census were suppressed on this account (Powell 1975a, 35, 134).

The partitions of Eastern Europe precipitated by the Nazi-Soviet Pact of August 1939 included Red Army occupation of eastern Poland (1939) and the Baltic states of Estonia, Latvia, and Lithuania (1940). These territorial gains temporarily brought into the Soviet Union many millions of Latin- and Eastern-Rite Catholics and Protestants, including Lutherans, evangelical Christians, Baptists, Pentecostals, Moravians, Methodists, Churches of Christ, and Reformed. Religious repression quickly commenced in these newly annexed lands but was cut short by the German invasion of the Soviet Union in June 1941. In most respects Nazi occupation policies were as draconian as the Kremlin's, but the Germans did permit thousands of churches to reopen.

In 1943 Stalin made a surprising about face, granting concessions to believers that seem to have been motivated by a desire: (1) to facilitate the war effort; (2) to counteract the enthusiasm that accompanied church revival in German-occupied territories; (3) to utilize the Orthodox Church in the suppression of Eastern-Rite Catholicism in lands to be annexed at the end of the war; and (4) to employ the church in the furtherance of Soviet foreign policy. Following Metropolitan Sergei's summons to a late-night meeting with Stalin in September 1943, Soviet authorities, on Stalin's orders, actually expedited the convening of an Orthodox Council a month later that elected Sergei patriarch.

By 1950 Stalin had permitted the Moscow Patriarchate to reopen over 14,000 churches led by some 12,000 priests (Davis 2003, 126, 130). In addition, the Russian Orthodox Church was able to reestablish 67 monasteries and nunneries, 8 seminaries, and 2 theological academies (Beeson 1982, 58). For convenience of control Stalin also engineered a merger of evangelical Christians and Baptists in October 1944. State recognition for this new denomination was such that by the 1950s it could claim 5,400 churches and 512,000 members, with the number of adherents reportedly "many times greater" (Sawatsky 1981, 67; see also Brandenburg 1974, 198; Newton 1990, 83). At the same time, Roman Catholicism within Soviet borders managed a new lease on life, not from Kremlin concessions, but simply through the absorption after World War II of western Ukraine, Belorussia, Lithuania, and Latvia that included many more Catholics than could be completely eliminated.

Eastern-Rite Catholicism, however, Moscow once again destined for total annihilation with, once again, the willing collaboration of the Moscow Patriarchate. In 1946 in those portions of western Ukraine seized from Poland and in 1949 in Transcarpathian Ukraine seized from Czechoslovakia, Eastern-Rite Catholicism once more ceased any legal existence. Russian Orthodoxy thereby gained millions of unwilling adherents and thousands of churches. In the process thousands of Eastern-Rite priests were "converted" to Russian Orthodoxy, went into hiding, or were arrested and deported to Siberian labor camps (Bociurkiw 1996, 148–228;

Chaplitskii and Osipova 2000, liv–lv; Elliott 1985, 214–16; Solchanyk and Hvat 1990, 54–56). All seven of the church's bishops were arrested and dispatched to Soviet camps with only one, Cardinal Joseph Slipyi, ever leaving Siberia alive (Chaplitskii and Osipova 2000, lvii; Elliott 1985, 214; Pelikan 1990, 169).

Stalin's wartime compromise with religion, which did not extend to Eastern-Rite Catholics, did not apply to the newly annexed Baltic states either. Rather, following their reoccupation by the Red Army in 1944, Estonia, Latvia, and Lithuania experienced systematic religious repression. Closure of churches, arrests, brutal interrogations, executions, mass deportations to Central Asia and Siberia with high rates of death in transit: these were the lot of Baltic Catholics, Lutherans, and smaller Protestant communities as well. In 1940 a strong Lithuanian Catholic Church numbered 1,180 churches, just under 1,500 priests, 1,530 monks and nuns in 158 monasteries and convents, and 4 seminaries. By 1979 only 574 churches still functioned; by 1969 only some 700 priests still celebrated Mass; and by 1982 all monasteries and convents had been closed and only 1 embattled seminary remained open in Kaunus (Beeson 1982, 120, 125–26; Bourdeaux 1979, 152, 166)). In Latvia after World War II the number of Catholic churches fell from 500 to 179 in 1964 (Pospielovsky 1988, 152; Solchanyk and Hvat 1990, 59).

Nikita Khrushchev, one of Stalin's chief lieutenants in the postwar suppression of armed resistance and religious opposition in Ukraine, ultimately succeeded his mentor in the Kremlin. His antireligious campaign of 1959–64 accounted for the second-most intense persecution of Christianity in the Soviet era, surpassed only by the even more repressive 1930s. Of the 13,325 functioning Orthodox churches in 1959, only 7,600 remained open in 1964, a drop of 47 percent (Davis 2003, 126; see also Tsypin 1994, 160). State actions reduced the number of Orthodox priests from 12,000 in 1950, to 10,237 in 1960, to 6,800 in 1966 (Davis 2003, 130–31; Tsypin 1994, 160, gives slightly lower numbers). The number of Orthodox seminaries fell from 8 in 1955 to 3 in 1964 (Davis 2003, 181–82; Ellis 1986, 120), while Orthodox monasteries and nunneries fell from 64 in 1957 to 18 in 1964 (Davis 2003, 165). Paralleling Orthodox losses, evangelical Christian-Baptists saw their functioning churches reduced from 5,400 in 1960 to 2,000 in 1964 (Steeves 1990, 84).

Khrushchev's antireligious campaign involved not only widespread utilization of the country's administrative and police apparatus in wholesale closure of churches, monasteries, and seminaries, it entailed mass mobilization of the media, schools, universities, even psychiatric hospitals, in the denigration of largely defenseless believers. Nevertheless, what most clearly set Khrushchev's repression apart from Stalin's assault on the church was the emergence of Orthodox and Protestant opposition movements that the Kremlin proved incapable of eliminating.

Even before Khrushchev's campaign, Eastern-Rite Catholicism had set the precedent, from 1946 on, by refusing to disappear. In western Ukraine a defiant catacomb church competed vigorously with state-imposed Russian Orthodoxy. In a remarkable challenge to a police state, Eastern-Rite Catholics participated in clandestine worship, supported—and were supported by—underground monks and nuns, operated secret seminaries, and circulated protests against the multiple violations of freedom of conscience they endured (Elliott 1985, 216–18; Zugger 2001, 443–44). The same can be said for Lithuanian Catholics who, despite grievous state attacks, organized determined opposition to Soviet antireligious campaigns, fueled by a fusion of longstanding Russophobia and faith, much as in neighboring Poland.

Significant Orthodox and Protestant dissident movements began to emerge in the early 1960s. On the one hand, the Kremlin instructed the Russian Orthodox Church and some of its other churches to join the World Council of Churches (1961–62), requiring these captive bodies to extol abroad the peaceful intentions of Soviet foreign policy and "freedom of religion" in the USSR. On the other hand, opponents of state manipulation of religion began speaking out. Among brave Orthodox souls who decried the passivity and compromises of the Moscow Patriarchate (with their year of arrest) were: Anatoly Levitin-Krasnov (1949, 1969, 1972), Archbishop Yermogen (forcibly retired to a monastery, 1965), Father Nikolai Eshliman (forcibly retired, 1965), Alexander Solzhenitsyn (1974), Alexander Ogorodnikov (1978), Father Gleb Yakunin (1979), Lev Regelson (1980), Father Dmitri Dudko (1980), and Irina Ratushinskaya (1982).

Similarly, opponents of state domination of Protestant church life began to defy church and civil authorities. In 1960 Soviet officials pressured cowed evangelical Christian-Baptist (ECB) leaders to issue a Letter of Instruction to local congregations barring children from worship and advising against "unhealthy missionary tendencies" (Sawatsky 1981, 139). The reaction was an outright revolt leading to a denominational split in August 1961 (Bourdeaux 1968). Dissident Baptists, also known as *Initsiativniki* (the Initiative Group), faced fierce state persecution and prison for its leaders and activists including (with the year of arrest): Peter Rumachik (1961), A. F. Prokofiev (1962), Aida Skripnikova (1962), Georgi Vins (1966), Gennadi Kriuchkov (1966), and Lydia Vins (1969). Seventh-day Adventists experienced a similar schism with identical results, including imprisonment for its leaders, with Vladimir Shelkov (1895–1980) becoming particularly well known for his courageous defiance and twenty-five years of total imprisonment (Beeson 1982, 96–97; Elliott 1983; Pospielovsky 1988, 158; Sapiets 1990, 68–134).

Most Pentecostals had long since refused legal recognition under the umbrella of the state-recognized ECB Union. As a result, they too regularly suffered harassment, arrest, imprisonment, and church closures during Khrushchev's antireligious campaign, but before and after it as well. Representative of the Pentecostal plight was the persecution endured by the "Siberian Seven" (Peter and Augustina Vashchenko and their daughters Lida, Lyuba, and Lila; Maria Chmykhalova and son Timothy). Various members of these longsuffering families fell victim to arrest, imprisonment, forced psychiatric treatment, even state abduction of children. In 1978, in desperation, eight members of these Pentecostal families traveled to Moscow, with seven managing to break through Soviet guards to enter the American Embassy compound. There they remained in limbo until their ultimate emigration to the US in 1983 (Hill 1991, 25–40; Pollock 1979).

One remarkably successful form of dissent, employed not only by the Siberian Seven but by all Christian confessions, especially from the 1960s on, was *samizdat*, "self-published" protest literature produced and distributed by clandestine means. Outstanding examples include Alexander Solzhenitsyn's April 1972 *Lenten Letter to Patriarch Pimen*, the long-running *Chronicle of the Catholic Church of Lithuania* (1972–88), the 1975 protest of Fathers Gleb Yakunin and Lev Regelson to the World Council of Churches, and the prodigious production of dissident Adventist Vladimir Shelkov and the dissident Baptist Khristianin Press (1971–), which printed over 1 million books and brochures by the late 1980s (Nikol'skaia 2009, 289–91; Rowe 1994, 172).

Soviet religious policy under Leonid Brezhnev (1964–82), Yuri Andropov (1982–84), and Konstantin Chernenko (1984–85) may best be described as a mixture of "carrot and stick." This differentiated strategy meant token concessions to legally recognized church bodies, such as state permission for the Orthodox to appoint additional bishops, the launching of a seminary correspondence course for Baptists, and the printing and importing of some Bibles and hymnals for both. At the same time, the Kremlin was unyielding in its repression of catacomb Orthodox, Catholics, and Protestants. But state recognition provided scant protection as the number of legally registered Orthodox parishes fell from 7,600 in 1964 to 6,754 in 1985, and the number of Orthodox priests dropped from 6,800 in 1966 to approximately 6,000 in 1988 (Davis 2003, 126, 131–32; see also Sawatsky 1992, 247–48).

In March 1985 leadership of the Soviet Union passed to fifty-four-year-old Mikhail Gorbachev. His campaigns of *glasnost* (openness) and *perestroika* (restructuring) introduced a new day, not only in the political and economic realms, but in church-state relations as well. New freedoms to celebrate the millennium of Christianity in Ukraine and Russia in 1988 were accompanied by the release of all prisoners of conscience (1986–89), an end to religious censorship, large-scale importations of Bibles, an end to jamming of shortwave religious broadcasts, and permission for some persecuted believers to emigrate (Elliott 1989; Elliot 1990). In 1989 the Eastern-Rite Catholic Church gained legal status. In 1990 the Soviet Parliament (October 1) and the Russian Republic Parliament (October 25) adopted laws on freedom of conscience as generous as any worldwide. And in 1991 the Kremlin abolished its malevolent Council of Religious Affairs (Ellis 1996, 157–63, 166).

However, just as Nicholas II's Edict of Toleration shortly gave way to renewed restrictions upon non-Orthodox believers, so too in the 1990s did Orthodox, nationalists, and Communists make common cause to impinge upon the free expression of faith by non-Orthodox churches and missionaries. As early as 1992, Patriarch Aleksei II called for legislation to curtail foreign missionary work in Russia (Elliott 1997b).

Finally, in 1997 the Moscow Patriarchate's concerted efforts to restrict the activities of missionaries and "nontraditional" faiths were rewarded in legislation that, if enforced as the Orthodox hierarchy hoped, would have dramatically reduced religious liberties previously granted by the 1990 laws on freedom of conscience. However, an unintended loophole in the legislation permitted churches to join "centralized religious associations" that exempted them from the law's most onerous provisions. In addition, a 1999 Russian Constitutional Court ruling set aside other discriminatory provisions of the law. However, the intent of Russian law and court rulings has never meant as much as the bias and whim of administrators charged with their implementation. As a result, the climate of suspicion of non-Orthodox faiths, fueled by the Moscow Patriarchate and the press from the 1990s on, spelled harassment and arbitrariness on the part of federal and local officials in their dealings with Catholics and Protestants (Elliott 1997a; Elliott 1999; Elliott 2000).

In the early twenty-first century non-Orthodox believers must once again suffer increasing infringements upon freedom of conscience. The Orthodox Church, the state, and the press charge that the loyalty and patriotism of non-Orthodox believers are suspect and that they and their missionary friends harbor spies working for foreign powers (Uzzell 2003). Current assaults on the religious liberties of Russia's non-Orthodox citizens—with a familiar ring from times past—include frequent difficulties in purchasing, renovating, and renting property for worship, increasing impediments to missionary residency, discrimination in employment, and increasingly, the exclusion of Catholics and Protestants from the public square, the military chaplaincy, and from ministry in orphanages, schools, and homes for the aged (Elliott 2005).

Following the breakup of the Soviet Union in 1991, all fifteen former Soviet republics adopted constitutions and legislation guaranteeing freedom of conscience. However, while some successor states have for the most part honored their citizens' civil liberties (Estonia, Latvia, Lithuania, and Ukraine), many others have not. The most egregious violators of freedom of conscience have been Turkmenistan, Uzbekistan, Tajikistan, and Belarus, with persecution of unwelcomed faiths comparable in many respects to some of the darker days of Soviet repression. Russia, Kazakhstan, Kyrgyzstan, and Moldova occupy a middle ground: for the most part not as oppressive of out-of-favor faiths as was common in the Soviet Union, but in practice falling far short of their own domestic and international commitments to protect the religious liberties of their citizens (Forum 18; Lunkin 2011; Marshall 2008).

The persecution of Christians in Russian, Soviet, and post-Soviet experience has been so vast and, despite occasional respites, so persistent that sympathy can be muted by the numbing statistics. Individual believers who faced oppression with courage or who perished holding fast to their hope in Christ may move us more than the martyred millions beyond our capacity to comprehend.

In 1967 the antireligious journal *Nauka i Religiia [Science and Religion]* complained of the case of a stubborn second-grader from a Christian home. Her teacher had explained in class that Soviet cosmonauts had traveled 300 kilometers into space with no sign of God above. This educator singled out her believing pupil, asking her if this evidence from the cosmos convinced her that there was no God. In a most intimidating setting, standing by her desk as her classmates looked on, this eight-year-old child had the God-given presence of mind to respond, "I do not know if 300 kilometers is very much, but I do know very well that only those who are pure of heart see God" (Powell 1975b, 155; Matt 5:8). Need we ever wonder again how little children will teach us?

Lydia Mikhailovna Vins endured over three years of imprisonment (1970–73) for her role in founding and managing the Council of Prisoners' Relatives, a remarkable enterprise that kept the West abreast of all manner of Soviet violations of the religious rights of dissident

Baptists. The weight of suffering for her faith that she was forced to bear can hardly be comprehended: her husband, Peter, a Baptist pastor, was arrested three times (1930, 1936, and 1937) and died in a Siberian labor camp in 1943; her son, Georgi, a leading dissident Baptist pastor, served two terms of imprisonment for his faith (1966–69 and 1974–79); her daughter-in-law, Nadezhda, with a university degree in philology, could find employment only as an ice-cream vendor; and her grandchildren, because of their faith, faced harassment in school and unemployment afterwards. Notwithstanding her "three generations of suffering," Lydia Vins could write her son in prison (October 4, 1967): "Believe in man. Believe that everyone has a place beneath the surface of evil feelings where the true face of their divine origin can be seen. People feel this to be impractical and often … laughable and stupid, but it is a fine thing to remain unembittered by life's sufferings" (Vins 1975, 90–91; see also Vins 1976, 89–97).

In 1974 the KGB arrested Nijole Sadunaite for typing carbon copies of the underground *Chronicle of the Catholic Church in Lithuania*. Interrogated, tortured, and convicted in a closed trial to three years of strict regime labor camp followed by three years of Siberian exile, she never surrendered the names of fellow Catholic dissidents. Her spiritual autobiography, smuggled to the West and aptly published under the title *Radiance in the Gulag*, provides profound testimony to indomitable faith. Broken in the flesh but with undaunted spirit, she confounded her captors with longsuffering love: "This is the happiest day of my life. I am being tried for the truth and the love of my fellow man…. My sentence will be my triumph! … How can one not rejoice when Almighty God has guaranteed that the light will conquer darkness and the truth will overcome error and falsehood!" After Nijole's trial her young Russian guards, who could not understand Lithuanian, said to her: "For two years we have been escorting those on trial, and we have never seen anything like it. You were the prosecutor, and all of them were like criminals condemned to death! What did you speak about during the trial to frighten them like that?" (Sadunaite 1987, 57–58).

On February 16, 1960, at a Kremlin-sponsored international "disarmament" conference, Russian Orthodox Patriarch Aleksei I gave a speech that very likely was written for him by Metropolitan Nikolai. In it the patriarch, in the first throes of the dire Khrushchev antireligious campaign, declared boldly that "the gates of hell will not prevail against the church of Christ" (Fletcher 1968, 188; Matt 16:18). Rather than wreak its wrath upon the all-too-visible Aleksei, the Soviet regime instead inflicted its retaliation on Nikolai, the patriarch's first lieutenant. The metropolitan was not seen again in public after February 1960. Nikolai "resigned" his post as chairman of the Russian Orthodox Department of External Relations on June 21, 1960. Then the church accepted his "request" to be relieved of his duties as metropolitan on September 15, 1960. His death on December 13, 1961, followed hospitalization in isolation so strict that not even his sister, an Orthodox nun, was permitted to see him. Suspicions of an unnatural death have persisted ever since (Fletcher 1968, 199–201).

Stalin and his League of the Militant Godless are history. Khrushchev, who failed in his promise to parade the Soviet Union's last Christian on TV, and his antireligious Znanie (Knowledge) Society are also history. But the church (Russian Orthodox, privileged to its detriment; and Protestant and Catholic, restricted to no good end), nevertheless, endures. Indeed, the gates of hell have not prevailed.

## QUESTIONS FOR REFLECTION

1. Contrast the Russian government's treatment of Russian Orthodoxy before 1917 and in the interwar period, 1917–39.
2. Compare and contrast the Soviet antireligious campaigns of the 1930s and 1959–64.
3. What similarities may be drawn from Orthodox, Catholic, and Protestant dissident activities from the 1960s through the 1980s? How were the church bodies at times manipulated against each other?
4. What advantages and disadvantages do Orthodox, Catholic, and Protestant Christians experience in the post-Soviet period?
5. What was similar and what was unique in the sufferings experienced by Lydia Vins, Nijole Sadunaite, and Metropolitan Nikolai?
6. Elliott refers to the waves of repression of Christianity during the Soviet era (1917–89) as the deadliest in all of history until that period. What is the significance of the well-documented persecution of Christians in Russia both long before Communism and well after its demise? Why, in spite of promises of more freedom after the fall of the Soviet Union, does the experience of many non-Orthodox believers "have a familiar ring from times past"?

## REFERENCES

Beeson, T. 1982. *Discretion and valour: Religious conditions in Russia and Eastern Europe,* rev. ed. London: Collins.

Beglov, A. 2008. *V poiskakh "bezgreshnykh katakom:" Tserkovnoe podpol'e v SSSR [In Search of "Sinless Catacombs:" The Underground Church in the USSR].* Moscow: Izdatel'stvo Sovet Russkoi Pravoslavnoi Tserkvi "Arefa."

Bociurkiw, B. R. 1996. *The Ukrainian Greek Catholic Church and the Soviet State (1939–1950).* Edmonton: Canadian Institute of Ukrainian Studies Press.

Bourdeaux, M. 1968. *Religious ferment in Russia: Protestant opposition to Soviet religious policy.* London: Macmillan.

———. 1979. *Land of crosses: The struggle for religious freedom in Lithuania, 1939–78.* Chulmleigh, UK: Augustine.

Brandenburg, H. 1974. *The meek and the mighty: The emergence of the evangelical movement in Russia.* London: Mowbrays.

Chaplitskii, B., and I. Osipova. 2000. *Kniga pamiati: Martirolog Katolicheskoi Tserkvi v SSSR. [Book of memorials: The martyrdom of the Catholic Church in the USSR].* Moscow: Serebrianye Niti.

Davis, N. 2003. *A long walk to church: A contemporary history of Russian Orthodoxy*, 2nd ed. Boulder, CO: Westview.

Elliott, M. R. 1983. Seventh-day Adventists in Russia and the Soviet Union. *Modern Encyclopedia of Russian and Soviet history*, vol. 34. Gulf Breeze, FL: Academic International Press.

———. 1985. Uniates. *Modern Encyclopedia of Russian and Soviet History*, vol. 40. Gulf Breeze, FL: Academic International Press.

———. 1989 and 1990. Bibles east, letters west: Religious glasnost and the availability of Scriptures in the Soviet Union. *Occasional Papers on Religion in Eastern Europe* 9 (November), 10 (February).

———. 1997a. New restrictive law on religion in Russia. *East-West Church and Ministry Report* 5, no. 3 (Summer): 1–2.

———. 1997b. The Protestant missionary presence in the former Soviet Union. *Religion, State and Society: The Keston Journal* 25 (December): 333–51.

———. 1999. The 1997 Russian law on religion: The impact on Protestants (with Sharyl Corrado). *Religion, State and Society: The Keston Journal* 27 (March): 109–34.

———. 2000. The church in Russia: Between the law and administrative practice. *East-West Church and Ministry Report* 8, no. 1 (Winter): 1–3.

———. 2003. All-union council of evangelical Christians-Baptists (AUCECB). *Encyclopedia of Protestantism*. New York: Routledge.

———. 2005. Russian restrictions on missionary visas. In *Mission in the former Soviet Union*, ed. W. W. Sawatsky and P. F. Penner, 188–205. Prague: International Baptist Theological Seminary.

Ellis, J. 1986. *The Russian Orthodox Church: A contemporary history*. London: Routledge.

———. 1996. *The Russian Orthodox Church: Triumphalism and defensiveness*. New York: St. Martin's.

Emel'ianov, N. E. 2004. Otsenka statistiki gonenii na Russkuiu Pravoslavnuiu Tserkov' (1917–1952 gody) [Evaluation of statistics of persecution of the Russian Orthodox Church, 1917–1952]. http://www.goldentime.ru/nbk_31.htm.

Fletcher, W. C. 1968. *Nikolai: Portrait of a dilemma*. New York: Macmillan.

Forum 18. http://www.forum18.org.

Hefly, J. C., and M. Hefly. 1979. *By their blood: Christian martyrs of the twentieth century*. Grand Rapids, MI: Baker Books.

Hill, K. R. 1991. *The Soviet Union on the brink: An inside look at Christianity and glasnost.* Portland, OR: Multnomah.

Lunkin, R. 2004. The Russian security service versus Western missionaries. *East-West Church and Ministry Report* 12, no.4 (Fall): 1–3.

———. 2007. Protestanty i politicheskie konflikty v Evrazii: spasenie dushi i upravliaemaia demokratiia. [Protestants and political conflicts in Eurasia: Salvation and managed democracy]. *Rossiiskaia Politicheskaia Entsiklopediia,* 208–21.

———. 2011. The status of and challenges to religious freedom: In Russia. In *Constituting the Future: Religious Liberty, Law, and Flourishing Societies,* ed. Allen D. Hertzke. West Conshohocken, PA: Templeton Foundation.

Marshall, P. A. 2008. *Religious freedom in the world.* Lanham, MD: Roman and Littlefield.

Newton, M. 1990. Antireligious propaganda in USSR. In *Modern encyclopedia of religion in Russia and the Soviet Union,* vol. 2, 87–92. Gulf Breeze, FL: Academic International Press.

Nikol'skaia, T. 2009. *Russkii protestantizm i gosudarstvennaia vlast' v 1905–1991 godakh [Russian Protestantism and state power from 1905–1991].* St. Petersburg: Izadetel'stvo Evropeiskogo Universiteta v Sankt-Peterburge.

Pelikan, J. 1990. *Confessor between East and West: A portrait of Ukrainian Cardinal Josyf Slipyj.* Grand Rapids, MI: Eerdmans.

Pollock, J. 1979. *The Siberian Seven.* Waco, TX: Word.

Pospielovsky, D. V. 1984. *The Russian church under the Soviet regime, 1917–1982,* vol. 1. Crestwood, NY: St. Vladimir's Seminary Press.

———. 1988. Soviet anti-religious campaigns and persecutions. In *A history of Soviet atheism in theory and practice, and the believer,* vol. 2. New York: St. Martin's Press.

Powell, D. E. 1975a. *Antireligious propaganda in the Soviet Union.* Cambridge, MA: MIT Press.

———. 1975b. Rearing the new Soviet man: Anti-religious propaganda and political socialisation; in the USSR. In *Religion and atheism in the USSR and Eastern Europe,* ed. Bohdan R. Bociurkiw et al., 151–70. Toronto: University of Toronto Press.

Robson, R. R. 1995. *Old believers in modern Russia.* DeKalb, IL: Northern Illinois University Press.

Rowe, M. 1994. *Russian resurrection: Strength in suffering; A history of Russia's evangelical church.* London: Marshall Pickering.

Sadunaite, N. 1987. *Radiance in the Gulag: The Catholic witness of Nijole Sadunaite.* Manassas, VA : Trinity Communications.

Sapiets, M. 1990. *True witness: The story of Seventh-day Adventists in the Soviet Union.* Keston, Kent: Keston College.

Sawatsky, W. 1981. *Soviet evangelicals since World War II.* Scottdale, PA: Herald.

———. 1992. Protestantism in the USSR. In *Protestantism and politics in Eastern Europe and Russia,* ed. Sabrina Ramet. Durham, NC: Duke University Press.

Shkarovskii, M. V. 1999. *Russkaia Pravoslavnaia Tserkov' pri Staline i Khrushcheve (Gosudarstvenno-tserkovnye otnosheniia v SSSR v 1939–1964 godakh) [The Russian Orthodox Church under Stalin and Khrushchev (Church-state relations in the USSR, 1939–1964)].* Moscow: Krutitskoe Patriarshee Podvor'e Obshchestvo Liubitelei Tserkovnoi Istorii.

Simon, G. 1974. *Church, state, and opposition in the USSR.* London: Hurst.

Solchanyk, R., and I. Hvat. 1990. The Catholic Church in the Soviet Union. In *Catholicism and politics in Communist societies,* ed. Pedro Ramet, 49–92. Durham, NC: Duke University Press.

Steeves, P. D. 1990. Antireligious campaigns in USSR. In *Modern encyclopedia of religion in Russia and the Soviet Union,* vol. 2, 81–87, editor unknown. Gulf Breeze, FL: Academic International Press.

Stroyen, W. B. 1967. *Communist Russia and the Russian Orthodox Church, 1943–1962.* Washington, DC: Catholic University of America Press.

Tsypin, V. 1994. *Istoriia Russkoi tserkvi, 1917–1990 [History of the Russian church, 1917–1990].* Moscow: Moskovskaia Patriarkhiia Izdatel'skii Dom "Khronika."

Uzzell, L. 2003. Review of *Ekspansiya [Expansionism]* by N. Trofimchuk and M. P. Svishchev (Moscow: Akademiia Gosudarstvennoi Sluzhby, 2000) in *East-West Church and Ministry Report* 11, no. 1 (Winter): 12.

Vins, G. 1975. *Georgi Vins: Testament from prison.* Elgin, IL: David C. Cook.

———. 1976. *Three generations of suffering.* London: Hodder and Stoughton.

Zugger, C. L. 2001. *The forgotten: Catholics of the Soviet Empire from Lenin through Stalin.* Syracuse, NY: Syracuse University Press.

**Mark R. Elliott** holds a PhD in modern European and Russian history from the University of Kentucky. He is the founding and current editor of the *East-West Church and Ministry Report* (www.eastwestreport.org). A retired professor of history, Dr. Elliott previously served as director of the Institute for East-West Christian Studies, Wheaton College, and as director of the Global Center, Samford University.

# CHAPTER 25

# PERSECUTION OF CHRISTIANS IN THE SOVIET UNION

*Johannes Reimer*

For most of the twentieth century, Russia was understood among the church in the free world as a synonym for persecution of Christians. Millions of Christians died under the "first godless regime," which began with the Communist Revolution in October 1917 and ended with the *perestroika* (restructuring) program of the general secretary of the Communist Party of the USSR, Mikhail S. Gorbachev, and the dismantling of the USSR in 1991. Historians estimated that Christians have never before been as severely persecuted as under the Soviet regime (Emelyanov n.d.). The Soviet state followed an atheist ideology, militantly committed to the destruction of religion (Sundgren 1978; Froese 2005) and to this effect, it destroyed churches and church structures, imprisoned and executed religious leaders, and forced Christians out of the public into deep private underground. Communism required the abolishment of all religion (Sundgren 1978; Froese 2005). Religion was considered to be unscientific and, therefore, an obstacle to the construction of the Communist society, to be replaced with atheism (Anderson 1994, 3) as the only scientific truth (Pospielovsky 1998, 291; Anderson 1994, 3). It was a fundamentally important ideological goal of the state. At the same time the official Soviet Constitution always guaranteed the human right to believe. Holding on to a religion was never outlawed but the atheist system was designed to hamper religious activities, to control religious bodies, and to interfere with them with the ultimate goal of total destruction.

The persecution of religion *in toto* and Christianity in particular was carried out through massive antireligious propaganda and atheist education and indoctrination, following secret instructions that remained unofficial. Any resistance to atheistic indoctrination was viewed as resistance to the state and consequently punished with legal measures. Such measures included confiscation of church property, ridiculing and harassing believers, torture of active Christians (especially ecclesiastic leaders) sending Christians to prison and labor camps. Many of them were subjected to psychological torture in mental hospitals. Christian parents were even compulsively deprived of their parental rights (see details in Sundgren 1978).

There were three major waves of church persecution in the Soviet Union: 1917–28; 1929–40, 1954–64. The first antireligious campaign (1917–28) began right after the October

Revolution 1917. And it primarily targeted the Russian Orthodox Church (ROC). Having enjoyed enormous privileges during the centuries of tsarist Russia, the ROC massively opposed the revolution and soon became a major counterrevolutionary force. Metropolitan Tikhon, who was in November 1917 elected patriarch of the church, openly anathematized the Soviet government and called on believers to fight against the new regime. In its appeal entitled "To the Orthodox People," the leadership of the ROC encouraged Orthodox believers: "It is better to shed one's blood and to be awarded a martyr's crown than to let the enemies desecrate the Orthodox faith" (Barmenkov 1983). The new rulers of Russia reacted promptly. Within weeks after the revolution, in November 1917, the People's Commissariat for Enlightenment was established, which a month later created the All-Russian Union of Teachers-Internationalists for the purpose of removing religious instruction from school curricula (Pospielovsky 1987, 29). A few months later Lenin's decree "On the Separation of the Church from the State and the School from the Church" deprived the formerly state church of its status of legal person, the right to own property, or to teach religion in both state and private schools, or to any group of minors (Academy 1958, 7–8). The decree abolished the privileges of the church and, thus, ended the alliance between church and state. An open war between the Soviet regime and the ROC began. Patriarch Tikhon excommunicated the Soviet leadership on January 19, 1918 for conducting this campaign. In retaliation the regime arrested and killed dozens of bishops, thousands of the lower clergy and monks, and multitudes of laity (Pospielovsky 1984, ch. 2). The seizing of church property over the next few years would be marked by a brutal campaign of violent terror. The church claimed that 322 bishops and priests had been killed during the revolution (Pospielovsky 1987, 27).

Parallel to the destruction of the power base of the ROC, the Soviet Regime began an unprecedented anti-religious propaganda campaign which was centrally consolidated underneath the Agitation and Propaganda Department of the CP Central Committee (Agitprop) in 1920 and aimed, according to the guidelines of article 13 of the Russian Communist Party adopted by the 8th party congress, "at the complete destruction of links between the exploiting classes and … religious propaganda, while assisting the actual liberation of the working masses from religious prejudices and organizing the broadest possible education-enlightening and anti-religious propaganda." This article has been very important in anti-religious policy in the USSR in later years. The main means of antireligious legislation in those years became the public debate (KPSS 1970–1972, 49).

The war against the ROC intensified after the tenth CPSU (Communist Party of the Soviet Union) congress in 1921 which passed a resolution calling for "wide scale organization, leadership, and cooperation in the task of anti-religious agitation and propaganda among the broad masses of the workers, using the mass media, films, books, lectures, and other devices" (Powell 1975, 34; KPSS 1970–1972, 242). Russia experienced famine. Using the famine as an excuse, the government decreed on February 26, 1922, that surplus church valuables should be expropriated in response to the people's requests. Under the decree, part of the gold and silver articles were to be confiscated from the property, placed at the disposal of believers by the state free of charge. The church leadership protested. Lenin encouraged, in his letter of March 19, 1922 to the party leadership, literally "to eliminate as many clergy as possible" (Archivy 1997, 143). The secret police began systematically to arrest and execute bishops, priests, and devout worshipers, such as Metropolitan Veniamin in Petrograd in 1922, for refusing to accede to the demand to hand over church valuables (including sacred relics). Archbishop Andronik of Perm, who worked as a missionary in Japan, was buried alive, Bishop Germogen of Tobolsk, who voluntarily accompanied the tsar into exile, was strapped to the paddlewheel of a steamboat and mangled by the rotating blades. In 1922, the first Russian concentration camp in a former Orthodox monastery was established in the Solovki Islands in the White Sea. Eight metropolitans, twenty archbishops, and forty-seven bishops of the Orthodox Church died there, along with tens of thousands of the laity. Of these, ninety-five thousand were put to death, executed by firing squad (see Yakovlev 2002).

The war against religion did not mean the ROC only. However, other Christian churches, especially Protestant ones, experienced this period as their "Golden Years" of growth (Kahle 1976, 394–406; Kasdorf 1991, 113–44). To weaken the ROC, the Soviet state allowed the activity of the sectarians and Orthodox renovationists. The state changed its position on them and began to increasingly see them as an independent threat in the late 1920s due to their great success in attracting people to their communities (Davis 2003, 7).[1] With the death of Patriarch Tikhon, who died in 1925, and the declaration of his successor Metropolitan Sergius (Stragorodsky 1887–1944) to accept the Soviet authority over the church as legitimate in 1927, the first period of massive Soviet persecution came to an end (Pospielovsky 1987a, 41).

The second wave of persecution began in 1928. Despite all persecution and atheist propaganda, the numbers of active Christian believers, especially in Protestant circles, grew constantly. The church seemed to successfully compete with the ongoing and atheistic propaganda. Its success prompted Stalin and his regime to adopt new laws in 1929 on "Religious Associations," as well as amendments to the constitution, which forbade all forms of public, social, communal, educational, publishing, or missionary activities for members of religious organizations. The Stalinist persecution began. This time it meant all religious bodies, including all Christian churches. The closing of churches, mass arrests of the clergy and religiously active laity, and persecution of people for attending church reached unprecedented proportions (Pospielovsky 1987a, 41). The main executor of the persecution became The League of the Militant Godless (LMG). The regime assigned all legal powers to this organization to fight and completely eliminate all religious expression in the country (Dixon 1945). The clergy and active believers, especially intellectuals, were accused of subversive activities against the Soviet state as foreign spies and were sentenced to prison, labor camps, and often death (Pospielovsky 1987a, 66). From 1932–37 Stalin declared the "five-year plan of atheism" with the aim of destroying all religion in the country.

> But recall the former days when, after you were enlightened, you endured a hard struggle with sufferings, sometimes being publicly exposed to reproach and affliction, and sometimes being partners with those so treated. For you had compassion on those in prison, and you joyfully accepted the plundering of your property, since you knew that you yourselves had a better possession and an abiding one.
> *Hebrews 10:32–34*

---

1    See in this regard: Kröcker 1931; Prochanov 1933; Kahle 1978; Kasdorf 1991, 157–86 and others.

The ROC, as well as the different Orthodox sects, became again the prime targets for the state terror. Many of its members were killed or sent to labor camps. Church buildings were confiscated and often demolished. In the period between 1928 and 1940, the number of Orthodox Churches in the Russian republic fell from 29,584 to less than 500. In 1937 and 1938 church documents record that 168,300 Russian Orthodox clergy were arrested. Of these, over 100,000 were shot. In 1939 only three bishops remained in office (Yakovlev 2002, 165; Emelyanov n.d.). The situation of the Protestants was not different. By the year 1937 most Protestant church activity had crashed and the active church leadership imprisoned or killed (Sundgren 1978).

The Soviet state changed its militant antireligious politics during World War II (see Chumachenko 2002). The state needed the support of the church, and Stalin allowed the Orthodox as well as Protestant churches to restore their activities. Between 1945 and 1959 the official organization of the ROC was greatly expanded, although individual members of the clergy were occasionally arrested and exiled. The number of open churches reached 25,000. By 1957 about 22,000 Russian Orthodox churches had become active. Many Protestant churches opened their doors (Sawatsky 1981, ch. 1). The exemptions were those churches with foreign influence. German believers, both Roman Catholic as well as Protestant, were not allowed to hold any religious meetings (Reimer 1996, 53–70). All those church bodies who supported German occupants came under attack in Western territories, namely the Lutheran Church in the Baltic, the Reformed in Carpatia, and the Ukrainian Greek Catholic Church in western Ukraine (Riho 2002). Many active believers from those denominations were arrested after 1945 and sent to labor camps in Siberia.

Stalin's new tolerance for religion was limited. The state did not tolerate any missionary activity and public promotion of religion. Wherever these happened, harsh reactions of the authorities followed. The relative religious tolerance ended with the death of Stalin. The new strong men in the Kremlin criticized the liberal attitude of the authorities in the postwar years. On July 7 and November 10, 1954, the CPSU Central Committee noted the enormous growth of church activities in the country and criticized the state of antireligious propaganda, appealing to all public institutions to intensify the atheistic education (Pospielovsky 1987a, 73). An enormous wave of antireligious propaganda covered country between 1954 and 1958. A new period of persecution began.

Nikita Khrushchev, general secretary of the CPSU and successor of Stalin, personally declared he would extinguish all religion in the Soviet Union in less than a decade (Anderson 1994, 2). Church buildings and institutions such as seminaries or monasteries were closed again. From the 22,000 active ROC churches, only 7,000 were left in operation by the year 1965 (Pospielovsky 1987a, 83). All churches were forced to conduct all their services inside of church walls and record the personal identities of all adults requesting church baptisms, weddings, or funerals (Lane 1978, 34). Children were banned from any church activity and religious education, even parental. Nonfulfilment of these and other regulations was legally persecuted. And again many faithful believers went to prison. Large parts of the church went underground.

Khrushchev lost his power in 1964. The mass persecutions stopped, the antireligious propaganda changed direction and became less militant. The Brezhnev administration decided on a more subtle and indirect battle against religion. The growing underground religious activity seemed to be more dangerous. Consequently only those activities were officially under threat. Starting in mid-1970, the state aggressively began to force the underground operating churches into official registration. Initially Baptist, Pentecostal, Mennonite, and other denominations refused. Between 1975 and 1985 many of their active members were sentenced to prison and hard labor work. Among those included especially were many young men, who had refused to join the Soviet Army.[2]

The Soviet war against religion ended in the late 1980s, under General Secretary Mikhail Gorbachev. His program of *perestroika* and *glastnost* introduced new political and social liberties (Reimer 2009, 66–236) and Christian churches began a process of restoration after decades of persecution.

## QUESTIONS FOR REFLECTION

1. How does Reimer's mind-numbing summary of Christian persecution in the Soviet era illustrate the importance of "witnessing from within"?
2. What ideological twists and historical pressures drove the Soviet Union's Marxist leaders to implement the waves of severe persecution?
3. The Soviet system ended by "dismantling," according to Reimer. What are the implications of this for the remaining Communist states? Is it possible for them to be humanized by reform?
4. From the church demographics given in the article and other factors, how would you describe the long-term effects of severe persecution on the churches in the Soviet Union?

## REFERENCES

Academy of Sciences. 1958. K istorii otdeleniia tserkvi ot gosudarstva i shkoly ot teserkvi v SSSR. In *Voprosy Istorii Religii i Ateizma* 5 (1958): 7–8. Moscow: Publications of the Academy of Sciences of the USSR.

Anderson, John. 1994. *Religion, state and politics in the Soviet Union and successor states.* Cambridge: Cambridge University Press.

Archivy, K. 1997. *Politbüro i cerkov (1922–1925)*, vol. 1. Moscow/Novosibirsk: Sibirski Chronograph.

Barmenkov, A. 1983. *Freedom of conscience in the USSR.* Moscow: Progress Publishers.

---

2    See in this regard Grant 1976; Reimer 2005.

Chumachenko, T. A. 2002. *Church and state in Soviet Russia: Russian Orthodoxy from World War II to the Khrushchev years.* Ed. and trans. E. E. Roslof. Armonk, NY: Sharpe.

Davis, N. 2003. *A long walk to church: A contemporary history of Russian Orthodoxy.* Oxford: Westview.

Dixon, P. 1945. Religion in the Soviet Union. First published in *Workers International News.* http://www.marxist.com/religion-soviet-union170406.htm.

Emelyanov, N. E. n.d. *Ocenka statistiki goneni na Russuyu Pravoslavnuyu c (1917–1952).* http://userroma.narod.ru/goneniya.htm.

Grant, M. 1976. Gib nicht auf, Wanja. *Die Geschichte des Wanja Moissejew.* Wuppertal: Brockhaus.

Kahle, W. 1976. Renovatio und Reformatio im ostslawischen Protestantismus 1917–1939. In *Traditio- Krisis-Renovatio aus theologischer Sicht,* ed. W. Zeller. Marburg: Elwert.

————. 1978. *Evangelische Christen in Rußland und der Sovieunion. Ivan Stepanovic Prochanov und der Weg der Evangeliumschristen und Baptisten.* Oncken: Wuppertal und Kassel.

Kasdorf, H. 1991. *Flammen unauslöschlich. Mission der Mennoniten unter Zaren und Soviets 1789–1989.* Bielefeld: Logos.

KPSS. 1970–1972. *KPSS v rezolutsiiakh i resheniiakh S'ezdov, Konferenstii i Plenumov TsK.* Moscow: Izdatel'stvo politischeskoi literatury.

Kröcker, J. 1931. *Bilder aus Soviet-Russland.* Striegau: Theodor Urban.

Lane, C. 1978. *Christian religion in the Soviet Union: A sociological study.* New York: University of New York Press.

Froese, P. 2005. "I am an atheist and a Muslim": Islam, Communism, and ideological competition. In *Journal of Church and State* 2005/47.3.

Peris, D. 1998. *Storming the heavens: The Soviet League of the Militant Godless.* Ithaca, NY: Cornell University Press.

Pospielovsky, D. 1984. *The Russian church under the Soviet regime, 1917–1983.* Crestwood, NY: St. Vladimir's Seminary Press.

————. 1987. *A history of Marxist-Leninist atheism and Soviet antireligious policies.* New York: Palgrave Macmillan.

————. 1987a. A history of Soviet atheism in theory, and practice, and the believer. *Vol 1: A history of Marxist-Leninist atheism and Soviet anti-religious policies.* New York: St. Martin's Press.

———. 1998. *History of the Orthodox Church in the history of Russia.* Crestwood, NY: St. Vladimir's Press.

Powell, D. E. 1975. *Antireligious propaganda in the Soviet Union: A study of mass persuasion.* Cambridge, MA: MIT Press.

Prochanov, I. S. 1933. *In the couldron of Russia.* New York: All-Russian Evangelical Christian Union.

Reimer, J. 1996. *Auf der Suche nach Identität.* Lage: Logos.

———. 2005. *Der verweigerer. Glaube im schmelztiegel der roten armee.* Basel: Brunnen.

———. 2009. *Ende einer Supermacht.* Brunnen: Basel.

Riho, A. 2002. "Religious cults," particularly Lutheranism, in the Soviet Union in 1944–1949. In *Trames* 2002/6.1.

Sawatsky, W. 1981. *Soviet evangelicals since World War II.* Scottdale, PA: Herald.

Sundgren, N. 1978. *Gottes volk in der Sowjetunion. Ein Überblick über sechs Jahrzehnte sowjetischer religionspolitik.* Witten: Bundes-Verlag.

Yakovlev, A. N. 2002. *A century of violence in Soviet Russia.* Yale: Yale University Press.

**Johannes Reimer** is professor of mission at the University of South Africa and the Theologische Hochschule Ewersbach, Germany. Reimer grew up in the former Soviet Union and after his conversion to Christ spent years in labor work. He is married to Cornelia and lives in Germany.

**No. 714 – I will follow after Christ**
Songs of Renewal (Minsk, Belarus, 1990)[1]
Translation by Robin P. Harris

1. За Христом пойду я ... Боже милосердный,
Кто мне сил дарует оказаться верным?
В страхе и бессильи я Тебе молюся:
Помоги идти мне по следам Иисуса!

I will follow after Christ … most gracious God,
Who will give me strength to stay faithful?
In fear and powerlessness I pray to You:
Help me to walk in the steps of Jesus.

2. За Христом пойду я ... Чувствую влеченье
Крест и скорбь земную принимать в смиреньи.
Сила Божья слова разорвала узы,
И пойти готов я по следам Иисуса.

I will follow after Christ … I feel the call.
I will accept with humility the cross and earthly oppression.
The power of God's word destroyed the shackles,
And I am ready to walk in the steps of Jesus.

3. За Христом пойду я ... бодро и свободно,
Дух мой укрепляет дар любви Господней.
Смело отвергаю ветхой жизни вкусы,
С радостью шагаю по следам Иисуса.

I will follow after Christ … invigorated and free,
My spirit is strengthened by the gift of the Lord's love.
I boldly turn away from the tastes of my old life,
With joy, I will stride on in the steps of Jesus.

4. За Христом пойду я ... Он мой Искупитель,
И от всех недугов - верный Исцелитель.
Смерть Его дала мне жизнь, и я стремлюся
В край давно желанный по следам Иисуса.

I will follow after Christ … He is my Redeemer,
And from all afflictions – my faithful Healer.
His death has given me life, and I press on toward
That far land I have long desired, in the steps of Jesus.

5. За Христом пойду я к Родине прекрасной,
Хоть кругом бушует ураган ужасный.
Благодатью Божьей каждый день креплюся...
Он идти поможет по следам Иисуса.

I will follow after Christ to my marvelous homeland,
Although all around me a dreadful whirlwind rages.
I am strengthened every day by the grace of God …
Helping me to walk in the steps of Jesus.

---

1   Accessed at http://hvep.z16.ru/song.php?id_st=2233

# CHAPTER 26

# POST-COMMUNIST PERESTROIKA RUSSIA

## A Personal Narrative

*Eugene Bakhmutsky*

An interview with questions from Dr. William Taylor in conversation with Reverend Eugene Bakhmutsky, Russian Baptist pastor and vice-chair of one of the Baptist denominations of Russia.

*Tell our readers something about yourself, your family, your ministry, and the changes that have recently taken place in your life.*

My name is Eugene Bakhmutsky. I'm a fourth-generation Russian evangelical believer. Both of my great-grandfathers were evangelical Christians. Two of my grandfathers were ministers, one in a Baptist church and another in a so-called Evangelical Christian church. These two groups later joined together to form the Evangelical Christian Baptist Union of Russia. By God's grace I'm now a minister in a Russian Bible church of Moscow and also serve as a vice-chairman of the Russian Union of Evangelical Christians and Baptists. The Lord has blessed me with a wonderful wife, Tatyana, and three children.

*When we recently met, you stated that your great-grandparents had been "sent to Siberia." Can you explain the background to this "sending," what happened, and what this meant to your family? What price was paid by your extended family for the sake of the gospel of Jesus?*

My great-grandfather, Moisey Sikorsky, was shot because of his faith. His children were repressed and most of them were sent into exile to Siberia. Another grandfather, Pyotr Bakhmutsky, was also exiled to Siberia for forced labor in mines of different sorts. This meant constant pressure from the government. He was tossed from one job to another with only one stated reason—"a believer."

So, persecution and rejection were no strangers to my family. But I never witnessed any ill will towards the authorities, no hatred towards people around us, no "pity me" image among other relatives. Instead, they were joyous and happy Christians amidst constant need and humiliation.

*How did these events affect your grandparents and your own parents? How has it affected your own thinking, life, and spirituality?*

My grandparents were well aware of the price they had to pay for their public confession of Christ. Their lives were filled with him to overflowing and they made the most of every hour of their freedom by thanking God for salvation, both physical and spiritual.

My parents also suffered many restrictions because they were believer's children. They were ridiculed and purposefully given lower grades at school. Later they were blocked from getting a college education or a job. Rejection of every kind was their constant companion through their childhood and teenage years. They were told that by believing God they were second-rate people, but if they trusted in Lenin and other Communist theorists, then they would become superior ones.

All this has greatly influenced my life. Since I was a toddler I was taught to memorize Scripture because of the serious lack of printed Bibles among Christians. Knowing "the Book" by heart, I was told, would be especially vital in case I got imprisoned without a Bible. I learned to survive even when everyone was against me. I was also taught to love and be kind-hearted in spite of all the evil I might encounter. In essence, I was encouraged very early to accept Christ, cherish him more than life, and keep his Word as the greatest treasure I will ever have.

*Is there any idea of the numbers of Christians who were martyred during the seventy years of the Soviet System? Include nominal Christians as well as true disciples of Jesus from all streams of our faith.*

We often speak about hundreds of thousands, but here are some startling statistics: By the end of 1926 there were about 2 million evangelicals in a newly declared Soviet Union. By the year 1959 the numbers were reduced to a mere 200,000! In Russia itself (apart from other republics) only 45,000 remained alive.

It was not by accident that our leader, Nikita Khrushchev, optimistically promised to show the nation the very last Christian survivor by television during his time in office!

*What happened to church buildings during the seventy years? Where and how did Christians meet? How were evangelism and discipleship carried out?*

By the year 1935, each and every building or rented meeting place was confiscated from Christian congregations, with the single exception of the Central Evangelical Christian and Baptist Church of Moscow. However, Christians kept meeting, though illegally and secretly. They often met in their own homes or in the forest. Any meeting held carried the risk of persons being arrested or killed on the spot. Evangelism and discipleship were done discreetly through personal witnessing on the job or among extended family members. Favorite occasions were weddings and funerals, when people could be public with their faith without fear of being scorned.

*When did you really believe that true change would be coming to Russia as we approached 1988? What role did Mikhail Gorbachev play in the religious liberty changes? Who else in the political arena played a key role in religious liberty for Russia?*

Yes, the year 1988 was a turning point, when Mikhail made a decree in the USSR that the nation should celebrate the Millenary of the Baptism of Russia. By the way, the last prisoner of conscience was released in 1986. It was this decree in 1988 that marked the dawn of a new time of freedom in the former Communist empire.

Mikhail Gorbachev, no doubt, played a key role in the coming of such freedom of faith. He made his decision and he announced it, just like that. Unfortunately, the nation was unprepared for a drastic change. Many destructive and dangerous religious cults and groups took over the country unopposed. At the same time, huge numbers of believers emigrated to the West. No one knows the exact number, but tens of thousands of evangelicals deserted the country, seeking refuge in USA, Germany, and Australia.

Another man who was a prominent agent of religious liberties in Russia was Alexander Yakovlev, known also as a "spiritual father of *perestroika*." In the summer of 1985, Yakovlev became the head of the Agitprop Department of the Communist Party. In 1986 he was appointed as Central Committee Secretary. Along with Egor Ligachev, he was in charge of national ideology, information, and culture. Most of the critics blame him for treachery against the Soviet Union by deliberately weakening and hastening the breakdown of the Soviet regime and Communist Party. It was he who, as a Secretary of Communist Ideology, changed his view of religion and prepared most of the corresponding bills.

Then in 1993 under Boris Yeltsin's government, a Religious Liberty Law was issued which proved to be one of the most liberal throughout the post-Soviet territory.

*How would you describe the changing religious liberty scene in Russia during the years 1988–2000 (more or less)?*

This period must be split up into two distinctive parts:

1. From 1988–96, freedom of faith generated enormous interest among the Russian population. Congregations swelled with newcomers and lots of churches were planted.
2. In the years 1997–2000 there was a plateau period as excitement died down. The Russian Orthodox Church gained power over the nation's religious views. The government began to openly oppose evangelicals in many regions of Russia and actively promoted social antagonism in the media toward any non-Orthodox Christian group.

In 1997 a new Religious Law was issued, its the main purpose to cut out many liberties and rights secured by the 1993 law. For instance, its enacting clause declared the special significance of the Orthodox Church, while the law itself hardened the policy of legitimation of religious groups. Those religious organizations that had existed in Russia for less than fifteen years were no longer recognized, creating many legal problems.

*And from then to now? What recent laws have been passed that change the picture today?*

There are many legislative discrepancies. On one hand, the situation is gradually improving. A law was passed concerning property restitution to the churches and then a social-oriented institutions law which allowed churches to legally conduct their social projects. A law enacting no-charge transfer of property to the religious organizations was passed recently.

On the other hand, the government makes efforts to put limits on missionary work in the Russian Federation territory, creating difficulty for both foreign and native ministers. For instance, certain visa restrictions have been introduced to match rules of international law, especially European law. Thus, a foreign missionary cannot stay in the country for more than ninety days without going through an extensive, year-long process to obtain a residence permit. So religious organizations were the ones who suffered most from these visa restrictions.

Another series of laws, the Counteraction of Extremist Activity Laws, were passed that can be used to violate the rights and freedoms of religious groups. These cause an unfortunate return to religious discrimination and violation of rights of religious organizations in modern-day Russia. Out of many reasons that this law is dangerous, I would single out top three:

- The "antiextremist" law's imperfections and lack of objective legislative regulations concerning the activity of religious groups.
- The general nature of the law and lack of expert recognition of what constitutes extremist materials and groups. This leaves open the possibility that the law could be used against legitimate churches and other religious organizations.
- Legal and religious bias of the government officials, which hinders the execution of the existing laws. For example, an official that deems himself Orthodox regards anyone from another group as a menace and a proselyte. Accordingly, he imposes obstacles with a purpose to "protect" his faith and nation. Even public prosecutors defy the law. Thus, Russia greatly needs improved legal service, religious literacy, and institutions to protect religious liberty.

*How would you candidly evaluate "the Co-mission," where (primarily) Americans sent thousands of young adults to "teach values" in the schools, but the real purpose was evangelism?*

This project is not bound to either positive or negative estimation. When Russia had a high interest in the West—in particular during 1994–96—the Co-mission had definite success. But soon it became ineffective as the nation swayed back to the rejection of everything from the West.

The project itself had at least two strategic errors: First, it was done without concern for Russian culture. Most of the Co-mission people had little or no cross-cultural missionary training and didn't bother to try to learn the Russian language. Second, there was never any attempt to integrate believers from existing local evangelical churches into this ministry or to cooperate with Russian churches themselves. So the long-term impact was quite limited. For example, I never heard anything about it while living in Siberia.

*What do you see as the future of religious liberty in Russia?*

That is hard to say. It largely depends on the future attitude and policy of the Russian Ortho-dox Church. The position of the West plays a big role as well: if its cooperation with Russia worsens or stops, this could cause increased hostilities in our country; especially toward evangelical churches. In fact, during previous conflicts with the Western world, Russian Baptists were often called German spies (WW I) or American espionage agents (Cold War).

*What is the attitude of the Russian Orthodox Church towards Protestant evangelical Christianity?*

It changes under the influence of international relations as well as inside processes. We have a warm relationship with the Russian Orthodox Church on the highest level. But out in the countryside, you may still meet bitterly negative attitudes. In general they put up with us, but still count us as foreign to the Russian land and often blame us for proselytism.

*Are doors opening, closing, or revolving in relation to the presence and longer-term service of expatriate (foreign) missionaries in Russia?*

The doors are far from closed. New forms of foreign missionary involvement will emerge. Mission strategy must change. Perhaps Russia should be viewed as one of the "closed" coun-tries and at the same time one of the more civilized ones. Take the most effective missionary to Russia in the beginning of twentieth century—Vasily Fetler. He was kicked out of the country for his evangelistic efforts, but kept ministering in other ways. While in Europe, he spent six years equipping about two thousand Russian-speaking missionaries, mostly former POWs who were taken to Europe from Russia during WW I. Then he sent them to Russia. As a result, hundreds of churches were planted. During the following ten years a very wide-scale evangelism movement emerged and evangelicals multiplied ten times!

We need to work together in finding new ways and methods of ministry. Opportunities abound for the expatriate missionaries who come with the right attitude and who work with us to develop effective ministry strategies.

*What evidence do you see in Russia of a vision for cross-cultural mission that goes beyond the traditional Russian world?*

- There are a growing number of churches composed of mainly indigenous small people groups or migrant workers.
- There is a rearrangement of the Russian nationalities map as we experience mass immigration of people from former Soviet republics; especially from Central Asia, the Caucasus, as well as from China and North Korea. This has noticeably changed the population makeup of many Russian cities.
- A growing number of Russian missionaries are going abroad to a large variety of places, from Africa to India.

*How can the rest of the world pray for, serve alongside, and support the church in Russia today and tomorrow? What does "partnership" mean to you in Russia?*

Keep doing what you did before—pray! For seventy years people prayed for the USSR—and the Communist colossus came crushing down. At this time we really need prayer and financial support for the local ministers of different nationalities. There are 189 people groups in Russia, but only 7 have a translated Bible. There are 25 million local Muslims and 2 million Buddhists! Much still remains to be done.

*Is there anything else you would like to say to our global readership about true Christianity in Russia, and the world?*

Please, remember that Russia is largely influenced by the Eastern (Byzantine) branch of Christianity, which greatly differs from the Western.

The Orthodox Church has a rich Christian tradition and history that affects the people in general and evangelism in particular. Since our country is mainly Orthodox, we must maintain a good relationship with the Orthodox Church.

It seems Russia is the only European country that wasn't impacted by the Reformation movement by Luther, Calvin, and other prominent preachers. So, our time is yet to come!

## QUESTIONS FOR REFLECTION

1. Bakhmutsky recounts heavy discrimination and persecution against four generations of his Christian family, yet is able to say he witnessed no ill will against authorities or hatred of neighbors, nor any "pity me" complex. "They were joyous and happy Christians amidst constant need and humiliation." How is this possible?

2. The author describes current Russia as a "closed" or perhaps heavily restricted country, yet in need of and open to a certain kind of foreign missionary work. What are the mission tasks and challenges? What does he recommend concerning the kind of missionaries and methods needed?

3. Russians, say the author, were ill-prepared for the drastic changes that accompanied the collapse of Soviet Communism and also for the return to limitations and repression only eight years later. In retrospect, how might Russian Christians have been better prepared for both?

**Eugene Bakhmutsky** is the pastor-teacher of Russian Bible Church of Moscow, and professor at Moscow Theological Seminary. He graduated from Kuzbass State Technical University in Siberia, has an MDiv from Novosibirsk Biblical Theological Seminary, and is currently working on his doctorate. His grandparent's family was exiled to Siberia because of their faith. He has worked extensively with youth in a ministry of thousands of new believers with a strong leadership-training vision. He is now first vice-president of the Union of Evangelical Christian-Baptist churches of Russia.

# CHAPTER 27

# THE MODERN SECULAR WEST

## Making Room for God

*Janet Epp Buckingham*

The Peace of Westphalia in 1648 first established the "secular state" as a response to the wars of religion that raged across Europe for decades. At the time, it seemed like a great innovation. Previously, the religion of the sovereign dictated the religion of the citizens. Many citizens, on pain of death, had been forced to oscillate between Roman Catholic and some form of Protestant religion.

The "secular state" was not what we have today. The sovereign retained the right to determine the state religion but other religious minorities were granted a measure of religious freedom. When you consider that this new system replaced the Holy Roman Empire, with one religion enforced by the Inquisition, this was a major step.

No one at the time envisioned what has become the modern secular state. The French Revolution in the 1790s initiated the modern secularist state. Because the Roman Catholic Church was seen as part of the "establishment," it was persecuted along with the aristocracy; churches were closed, church lands were confiscated by the state and sold, and priests were made employees of the state. The revolution established a separation of church and state that went beyond what even the Americans had done during their revolution a century earlier.

Some defend the secular state on the basis that in its ideal form, it is neutral towards religion. Unfortunately, that is not how it works in practice. Secularism has become a religion in itself, and it brooks no rivals. So-called experts doomed religion to the dustbin of history, pronouncing that Western civilization was now a post-Christian society (Norris and Ingelhart 2004). Human rights protection for freedom of religion became freedom from religion.

The modern secular state has no room for God, therefore no understanding of religion. When the state officially separates itself from any established religion, it cannot acknowledge that God is sovereign. Thus, the state itself becomes the only place both it and citizens can turn to for answers. It therefore must deny the place of religion. I am not arguing that the state should be aligned with religion, that has its own set of problems, but one must understand the driving force behind the modern secular state in order to understand the place Christians can take in it.

Another feature of the modern secular state is that in order for diverse individuals and groups to coexist in society, the state must be "difference blind." However, given that individuals and groups in society have different needs, being difference blind does not work. The secular state forces everyone to strip themselves of what forms their identity. This, of course, means that they cannot express their diverse needs because that would reveal their unique identities.

There is an alternative approach. Whether you call it "principled pluralism" (The Center for Public Justice) or "multiculturalism" (Habermas 2008, 5), the approach is similar; recognize the differences we all have as individuals with identities centered in our communities, but commit to mutual respect and dialogue with a view to peaceful coexistence.

## RESTRICTIONS CHRISTIANS FACE

The kinds of restrictions Christians face in the secular West range from the mild to severe, but they are usually couched in the language of "tolerance." The restrictions are also usually duly passed laws by some level of government and are therefore enforced by the courts. Given that there are constitutional and international agreements that protect religious freedom, this is all the more insufferable. The very courts that Christians relied on to protect their freedoms are undermining them.

### RESTRICTIONS ON EXPRESSION

The first set of examples involve public expression of religion, including preaching, evangelism, and free expression. These are all core expressions of religion, particularly Christianity.

The case of Swedish pastor Åke Green was well publicized internationally. Pastor Green faced criminal charges for preaching a sermon in his church on the biblical view of homosexuality. He was initially found guilty and sentenced to one month in jail for expressing "disrespect" to homosexuals, equivalent to "hate speech" in English-speaking countries. In 2005, this was overturned on appeal in light of the European Convention on Human Rights, which offers strong protection for religious freedom (Riksåklagaren v. Åke Green 2005).

Jehovah's Witnesses are well known for door-to-door evangelism. A Greek Jehovah's Witness was convicted of the crime of proselytism for engaging in this practice, and sentenced to four months in jail. The European Court of Human Rights overturned this in a 1993 ruling (*Kokkinakis v. Greece*). The court strongly affirmed religious freedom as one of the foundations of a democratic society. It also affirmed that the right to "manifest" one's religion by talking to others is a fundamental right.

While these are two high-profile cases that were decided at a very high level, there have been numerous similar issues in every Western country. These two legal cases involved criminal charges, leaving the religious adherent no choice but to defend himself in court. Many similar issues are resolved by religious adherents backing down, or by decisions being made at a lower level but the accused not having financial resources to pursue an appeal.

From the perspective of a Canadian, I can point to dozens of situations where Christians have been excluded or marginalized. While religious adherents generally, be they Muslim, Jewish, or Christian, are often marginalized, Christians have been singled out for particular exclusion. A pastor on the east coast of Canada requested the use of a public park stage in the center of town for a play. He was rejected on the basis that religion is controversial. When his church put on the play regardless of having a permit, the pastor was charged with trespassing. He successfully defended his actions on the basis that he had attempted to get a permit and brought a successful complaint against the municipality for discrimination (Gilliard 2004).

One common feature of many religious legal cases is that they involve interaction with human rights codes or charters. These kinds of national and international human rights protection (*International Covenant on Civil and Political Rights; International Covenant on Economic, Social, and Cultural Rights*) were introduced following World War II as a response to newly sensitized consciences following the Holocaust. People understood that discrimination, when tolerated, can lead to persecution, torture, and even genocide. Legal protection for human rights serves an important function; Christians would do well to be aware of this kind of protection, both locally and internationally.

Unfortunately, legal protection for human rights has been a double-edged sword. In Canada, the policies have been used against Christians as well as for them. For example, a human rights complaint was made against a Roman Catholic bishop in western Canada alleging that his pastoral letter was "likely to expose homosexuals to hatred or contempt." While Pastor Green in Sweden was charged under a similar sounding law, he was charged with a criminal offense while the case in Canada was a violation of part of a human rights code. The complaint was ultimately dismissed on the basis that Bishop Henry enjoys religious freedom and the pastoral letter was a religious perspective on same-sex marriage.

One of the most disturbing trends is the censorship and punishment of Christian university students. University professors seem to be the vanguard of the militant secularists. They try to indoctrinate students with an antireligious or, even more targeted, anti-Christian ideology. Students who stand up for their beliefs are humiliated and sometimes punished with lower grades. In extreme cases, Christians expressing certain beliefs, like pro-life or concerns with homosexuality or same-sex marriage, have been expelled from the university or not permitted to graduate. Students have even been arrested for erecting graphic pro-life displays on campuses. Universities were once the bastions of free expression of ideas, but they have become enclaves of political correctness.

## RESTRICTIONS ON RELIGIOUS PRACTICES

The secular West protects private religious practices but tends to limit public expressions of religion. This has been most evident in the USA, which has a high percentage of its population who are practicing Christians, but also one of the most strident secularist organizations in the American Civil Liberties Union (ACLU). Other countries have had similar issues, but to a lesser degree, or they have been framed differently.

The USA seems to have one of the highest levels of public religiosity of any Western country. Presidents have long called for national days of prayer and are regularly photographed in churches and with religious leaders. American churches publicly display national flags and mix nationalism with religious fervor. Yet many court battles have been fought over student prayers at sporting events and graduation ceremonies. They have even been fought over children's stories and classroom work that mention Jesus or Christianity. Judges have been forced to remove displays of the Ten Commandments from their courthouses. This is similar to the European Union's refusal to recognize its Christian heritage.

Schools have been a battleground in North America regarding religious content, and Christian student clubs have even been excluded. Ostensibly, the exclusion has been on the basis of "separation of church and state." That principle was articulated in a letter from a former US president to a church to assure it that it was protected from state interference (Jefferson 1802). It is not a constitutional principle in the USA and certainly not anywhere else in the world. Even in the USA the principle was never meant to stop young people from freely meeting to pray when a wide variety of other clubs are free to meet. That is clear discrimination against religion.

In Canada, state schools had religious instruction and public prayers until a Charter of Rights was introduced in 1982. It is ironic that a human rights document was used to limit religion in schools. It was excluded because it focused on the Christian religion even though Canada is over 80 percent Christian. Since that time, private religious schools have flourished. There have been several attempts to control the curriculum at these religious schools as well, forcing them to teach certain curricula about sexuality or evolution. So far, these attempts have not been successful.

France has been in the vanguard of restricting religious clothing. It was the first Western country to ban the wearing of conspicuous religious symbols in public schools (*Loi de laïcité*) in 2004. While it technically places the same restrictions on Christians as on Muslims, it is popularly referred to as the "headscarf ban" by the international press. Canada's francophone province has considered a similar ban—it would only limit the *niqab* but would restrict it in a broader range of public areas. In fact, women wearing the *niqab* would not be able to access any government services.

Many of the issues related to restrictions on religious practices arise in relation to minority groups. But as society has changed, and increasingly secularized, practicing Christians have become a minority group. Where once it was Seventh-day Adventists and Jews seeking exemption from requirements to work on Saturday, Christians must seek the same exemption in many countries where retail shops are open on Sundays. Once Muslims sought exemptions to wear the *hijab* or Sikhs to wear the *kirpan* but now Christians are curtailed in wearing a visible cross.

Christian professionals have been seeking conscientious objection to allow them to refuse to participate in abortions or euthanasia. In countries like Canada, where marriage has been redefined to include same-sex couples, officials solemnizing civil marriages have been denied exemption and must marry same-sex couples even if it violates their religion. Christian professionals have been restricted in expressing their religion in a variety of ways. Nurses and professional caregivers in Britain have faced professional discipline for offering to pray for patients and clients.

Christian organizations have also been threatened and restricted in some of their practices. In the 1990s a private Christian university in Canada was denied accreditation for its education program because the university had a community standards policy in which students agreed to refrain from sexual relations outside of marriage. This was considered discriminatory against homosexuals. The university took this through several levels of appeal and was eventually successful at the Supreme Court of Canada. (*B.C. College of Teachers v. Trinity Western University*). A Christian ministry that cares for mentally challenged adults faced a human rights challenge that questioned its ability to preferentially hire Christian staff (*Christian Horizons* 2010).

## HOW OUGHT CHRISTIANS TO RESPOND

Christians in the West have many means of influencing law and public policy to gain a wider acceptance of religious freedom. These countries are democracies so Christians have opportunities to run for public office and participate directly in the policy-making process. Christians may engage in advocacy to politicians as individuals or through organizations. All Western countries abide by the rule of law so justice can be pursued through the courts. As well, there is freedom of press, so Christians may get their message out through the media. It is crucial that those who engage in any of these types of advocacy understand the process and speak and act appropriately.

Many Christians in the secular West are complacent about their religious freedom. They believe that so long as church worship itself is not in jeopardy, religious freedom is protected. It is also widely believed that those who end up in court on religious freedom issues are "troublemakers." Neither of these is true.

Remember those who are in prison, as though in prison with them, and those who are mistreated, since you also are in the body. *Hebrews 13:3*

There are constant restrictions on Christians' ability to publicly express their faith. Some Christians also experience restrictions on even their private religious practices. To restrict the practice of our religion only to what happens in church or at home is very narrow indeed. Religious communities have historically engaged in a broad range of societal issues, not confining themselves to worship and pastoral care. Christian ministries exist the world over to care for the vulnerable, feed the hungry, clothe the naked, and give tools to the poor to lift them out of poverty. They provide schools, hospitals, and orphanages. But beyond that, Christians also are motivated to share the gospel through a variety of forms of evangelism: printed word, multimedia, and personal encounters. Christians should not have to limit themselves to traditional "religious" functions just because the broader society professes offense at being exposed to Christianity.

The conflict resolution strategy set out in Matthew 18, while established for resolving conflict between Christians, is a good starting point for resolving issues of religious conflict as well. Western society is pluralistic, meaning that there are many religions and cultures living side by side. We must get along because we live together. If there is a problem, the first step should always be to try to meet with the person or group that makes decisions to discuss why allowing such expression or practice of religion would be good. One must be careful in such circumstances not to use religious language; rather use the language that will resonate with that person. Often, human-rights language is best understood by many in secular society.

If the initial meeting does not produce positive results, it is time to either make a show of strength by having a larger group meet with the decision maker or makers, or contact someone in a higher level of authority, such as a supervisor. This step requires prayer and discernment. Either approach could backfire in that the decision maker feels threatened and hardens his or her stance. The decision maker may be trying to meet the concerns of another person or group and we may have to compromise, so long as we are not compromising our beliefs.

Only if dialogue fails should we move to a more confrontational approach. Christians should take this step only after considerable prayer and reflection. It should never be used to puff ourselves up. In Acts 25:10, Paul appealed to Caesar, but only after he had been in jail for years with no serious charge being laid against him. Paul knew the legal remedies available to him, he was trained in the law, and he used them. For Christians in modern secular society, this kind of appeal could be to politicians, to the courts, to the media, or to all three. Christian politicians can open doors in politics and government to assist those whose rights have been violated. Christian lawyers can assist them in making arguments to the courts. Christians in the media can use their influence to place positive and well-timed stories or opinion pieces in prominent media.

There is a variety of critiques to the proposal that Christians use the political and legal systems to ensure religious freedom. Some Christians object that Jesus commands us to "turn the other cheek." (Matt 5:39). After all, we are to love our enemies and pray for those who persecute us. (Matt 5:44) Others object that Paul says to obey those in authority over us. (Rom 13:1–5). Still others misinterpret Paul's instruction to the church, "Why not rather be wronged?" (1 Cor 6:7) This statement was in the context of the injunction against taking other believers to court. Christians should not rush to court the minute they are wronged, but when all other approaches fail, political or legal action should be considered. The secularist West prides itself on protecting human rights, and religious freedom is a protected human right. An advantage of using lawsuits and the courts is that a positive result in one case sets a precedent that can benefit the whole community.

The challenge Christians face is to make room for God in a culture that tries to exclude him. Christians, and other religious adherents, should not have to leave their religious beliefs and practices at home, but rather should be able to bring the richness of our faith into the open. I have argued that Christians must engage the secularists using common language, but at the same time, we must be wary of watering down our beliefs. As Ludin warns, "Christians are in danger of selling their rich birthright—their saving vocabulary of sin and grace, judgment and forgiveness, death and resurrection—for a cold pottage of jargon and obscurity" (Ludin 1993, 30). As Jesus cautions, "Be as shrewd as snakes and as innocent as doves" (Matt

10:16). In order to make room for God, Christians must take advantage of opportunities to speak truth into the political and legal process in ways that are winsome and appealing.

## QUESTIONS FOR REFLECTION
1. Are the religious freedom challenges Christians face in the secular West different than those faced in other parts of the world?
2. Why are Christians in the West at an advantage compared with those in other countries when it comes to addressing violations of religious freedom?
3. Are there positive steps Christians and/or churches can take to create a more positive environment for religious expression in Western society?
4. Discuss the approach you think is most likely to succeed in addressing a violation of religious freedom in the secular West.

## REFERENCES

Habermas, J. 2008. Notes on a post secular society. www.signandsight.com. Posted June 18, 2008.

Jefferson, T. 1802. *Letter to the Danbury Baptist Association.* January 1.

Ludin, R. 1993. *The culture of interpretation: Christian faith and the postmodern world.* Grand Rapids, MI: Eerdmans.

Norris, P., and R. Inglehart. 2004. *Sacred and secular: Religion and politics worldwide.* Cambridge: Cambridge University Press.

## REFERENCES TO COURT CASES AND POLICY

British Columbia College of Teachers v. Trinity Western University. 2001. 1 SCR 772 (Supreme Court of Canada).

Gilliard v. Pictou (Town). 2005. NSHRBID No. 2.

International Covenant on Civil and Political Rights. 1976. GA Res 2200A (XXI), 21 UN GAOR Supp (No. 15) at 52, UN Doc. A/6316, (1966), 999 UNTS 171, 1976 CTS, No. 47, signed at New York, December 19, 1966, entered into force 23 March 1976.

International Covenant on Economic, Social, and Cultural Rights. 1976. GA Res 2200A (XXI), 21 UN GAOR Supp (No. 16) at 49, UN Doc. A/6316 (1966), (1966), 993 UNTS 3, 1976 CTS, No. 46, signed at New York, December 19, 1966, entered into force January 3, 1976.

Kokkinakis v. Greece. 1993. Judgment of May 25, 1993, Series A No. 260–A. European Court of Human Rights.

Loi n° 2004–228. 2004. Du 15 mars encadrant, en application du principe de laïcité, le port de signes ou de tenues manifestant une appartenance religieuse dans les écoles, collèges et lycées publics, 2004–228 of March 15, 2004.

Ontario Human Rights Commission v. Christian Horizons. 2010. ONSC 2105. Ontario Divisional Court.

Riksåklagaren v. Åke Green. 2005. Judgment of November 29, 2005, case number B 1050–05. Supreme Court of Sweden.

**Janet Epp Buckingham**, LLD, is an associate professor at Trinity Western University and the Director of the Ottawa-based Laurentian Leadership Centre. She previously served as director of law and public policy for the Evangelical Fellowship of Canada and executive director of the Christian Legal Fellowship. Her doctorate in law from the University of Stellenbosch focused on religious freedom in Canada and South Africa. She has been honored with the Good Samaritan Award from Advocates International.

"*All who want to live a godly life in Christ Jesus will be persecuted.*" 2 Tim 3:12

Paul declares that in the last days people will be "lovers of self, lovers of money, proud, arrogant, abusive, disobedient to their parents ... lovers of pleasure rather than lovers of God." Paul calls Timothy to follow his example (v. 10–11), showing that persecutions and sufferings which will come as a result, and declaring that "all who want to live a godly life ... will be persecuted."

This persecution comes from the confrontation between contrasting lifestyles. "To live a godly life in Christ" is to manifest a counterculture which denounces the evil of society, and will cause a negative reaction. "Suffering and persecution" will come to those who commit themselves unconditionally to the Truth. The world did not accept Jesus, the Incarnated Truth, condemning him to the cross, and will reject his followers. True disciples will face persecution!

'Reflection by: Edilson Ribeiro Gomes Filho, Brazil

# CHAPTER 28

# ANGOLA

## A Missionary Experience
*Antonia van der Meer*

Angola was a Portuguese colony until November 1975. Several groups had been fighting for independence since 1961. Most of the revolutionary leaders came from evangelical families, which caused fierce persecution of the church by the Portuguese government. One group fighting was the MPLA (with a Marxist ideology), which received support from the Soviet Union and Cuba. Another group was UNITA, from the south, which received support from the USA and the Republic of South Africa. In 1975 the MPLA proclaimed themselves leaders of the new national government, which sparked a number of inner wars.

From 1975 to 1991 the war spread over the countryside, with some major attacks on cities. The roads became very dangerous and millions of land mines were planted. Life continued somehow and many people fled to the cities. There was one year of peace, the first elections, and then a more violent war from November 1992 to 2002.

The Marxist government did not persecute Christians too harshly, but there were restrictions and some cases of persecution. After 1991 Angola became more democratic, with growing religious freedom and a switch to a capitalist economy, which enriched a few but kept most people very poor.

Brazilian missionaries were well received. In the 1980s the number of missionaries slowly grew from just a few to about thirty. In the 1990s, after the most violent war, the number started to grow again. These missionaries came from several denominations and agencies. Once on the field, missionaries from different agencies would become friends and support each other.

I served in Angola from 1984–95 with the Evangelical Alliance (AEA) to help establish a student movement. I lived in a flat on the fifth floor. Sometimes water came in through the taps (during the night). I would get up and fill every bucket I had, because nobody knew when the water would come again (it could take months). Often we had to fetch the water from downstairs and carry the buckets up the stairs. Once there was a fire in the basement and the firemen were working to extinguish it throughout the whole night. I had nowhere to go so I stayed in the flat, praying. The next morning the ground floor was still burning hot.

The general secretary (Pr. Octávio) was a leader with vision, and slowly the work of the AEA grew and served the churches. I helped to establish contacts between ministries in Angola and Christian organizations abroad.

## STUDENT WORK

My student work involved visits to four provinces. In 1986 ministry started smoothly, but pressure began to build. Students in Lubango asked me not to visit in 1987. "When you arrive at the airport they will know you have come, it is not the right moment." A faithful remnant of eight students in the ministry were called before authorities three times and asked to choose between their studies or their faith. They said: "We want to serve our country, but we cannot deny our Savior." So they were expelled from the university. They were forced into the army. One escaped service because he had a lame foot. The others were taken and sent first to Luanda (with political accusations), then to several fronts. After two years the accusations were withdrawn and they returned, free to study and work.

> "Whoever hates me hates my Father also. If I had not done among them the works that no one else did, they would not be guilty of sin, but now they have seen and hated both me and my Father. But the word that is written in their Law must be fulfilled: 'They hated me without a cause.'"
> John 15:23–25

In Benguela/Lobito I had about one hundred young people ready to learn as much as I could teach them. During meals or free time I always had a few of them around me, asking questions. Only a few pastors had any training, and at school their faith was questioned. Evangelical books were not available. I started to take them some books, which I bought with my salary in Brazil. I became their "walking Christian encyclopedia."

Once they asked me to speak on "Philosophy and Christian Faith." I read some books about Marxist philosophy and some Christian books. My talk was planned for Sunday afternoon in a big unfinished church. The church was crowded. One minute before my talk I received a little slip of paper: "The Director of Religious Affairs is here." He was the person in charge of controlling the churches. I prayed very much during my talk, and even more during the questions afterwards: "Lord, give me wisdom!" Afterward there was tea for the visitors and I ended up sitting next to him. He said, "Thank you, sister, I learned a lot from you." I was very surprised. We continued to talk and later he said, "I am still a materialist, but certainly I am no longer an atheist."

After 1991 the political environment started to change, and slowly new opportunities arose for witnessing to students—at their residence halls, and even at the university.

## MINISTRY IN THE HOSPITALS

With some friends I visited a hospital and fell in love with this ministry of encouragement, evangelism, and practical service. We visited the Centre for Rehabilitation and Physical Medicine, where patients were lame or had lost legs or arms. We visited other hospitals as well. People were hurt, suffered from hunger, and lacked the most basic commodities. They were lonely and hopeless. They loved receiving visits. Some wanted to become Christians on our first visit. Many knew too little about God, Jesus, or the Bible and it took them several months to understand the gospel message. Others were Marxists, but their barriers were lowered through friendship and many came to believe.

José Gomes was a young man who became a quadriplegic when he was sixteen years old through a diving accident. He was a Marxist and thought the Bible was for ignorant people. His mother came from the countryside to help, but she was hit by a car and died. José was desperately sad. I became his friend; he started to ask questions about the Bible. This went on for a few months until he wanted to believe. He became a Christian, full of life and joy. People who came to the hospital stopped at his bed, and he had a word of encouragement for all. He wanted to learn to write with his mouth. After some time he wrote a beautiful poem. I encouraged him to write his own life story, I typed it for him, and its second edition has been printed in Brazil.

## QUESTIONS FOR REFLECTION

1. How can missionary work and witness have success in the context of Marxism/war/violence?
2. How does God change the saddest contexts and bring joy and new life?
3. In what ways do we need to be wise and careful in order not to cause unnecessary harm and persecution to the people we want to serve?

**Antonia Leonora van der Meer**, Brazilian with a Dutch background, served with IFES for many years in Brazil and Angola. Now at the Evangelical Missions Center in Brazil, she is development coordinator, dean, teacher, and mentor. She has a master's in theology at the Baptist Brazilian Theological Faculty in São Paulo and a doctorate in missiology at the Asia Graduate School of Theology in the Philippines. She has published several articles in *Connections: The Journal of the WEA Mission Commission*, in *Global Missiology for the Twenty-first Century*, in the Brazilian version of *Perspectives*, in *Doing Member Care Well*, in *The Dictionary of Mission Theology*, and in the *Atlas of Global Christianity*. She wrote several books in Portuguese: an inductive Bible study (*ABUEditora*), a personal missionary story (*Eu, um Missionário?*), and a book on caring for Brazilian missionaries in contexts of suffering (*Missionários Feridos*).

## WHERE SIN ABOUNDS, PEACE AND HOPE OVERFLOW

In the long history of Latin American conflicts, the Shining Path struggle of the 1980s and 1990s was particularly vicious. Yet out of the ashes and pain, Peruvian Christians created something remarkable.

More than three hundred pastors and lay workers were killed, including many women. Christian students at the universities were targeted. Sometimes government forces were the murderers. For example, naval infantry burst into a church during a Sunday worship service, held the congregation hostage, took six worshipers outside, and shot them, leaving the corpses for their families to stumble over as they streamed out.

Responding to the crisis, the national evangelical church gathered corn, lima beans, flour, oil, and medicines for Christians who had to flee their homes. Temporary housing in small and simple churches was organized. Impromptu clinics for the sick and the pregnant were established. Long-term care for widows and orphans was arranged. Eventually the national church helped the refugees pioneer new communities, clearing the jungle and building new villages.

Meanwhile the National Association of Evangelicals (CONEP) circulated a Declaration to government authorities, media, and citizens. It stated the facts. It called for the authorities to act. It also gave a theological framework for what was happening. "Sin, in all its manifestations, causes disunity: self-centeredness, pride, lies, violence, murder—and racism against indigenous peoples.... All Peruvians regardless of ideology, uniform, or religion are guaranteed human rights"(3).

The Declaration quoted Genesis 1 when it affirmed that God created people in his image.

It quoted 2 Chronicles 7:14: "If my people, who are called by my name, will humble themselves and pray and seek my face and turn from their wicked ways, then will I hear from heaven and will forgive their sin and will heal their land."

It quoted the commandment "Thou shall not kill—" and added "—neither with ideologies, nor bullets, nor lies, nor hunger." It quoted God's question to Cain, "What have you done? Listen! Your brother's blood cries out to me from the ground" (Gen 4:10).

It quoted Jesus' words, "Blessed are the peacemakers" (Matt 5:9). It quoted great Peruvian thinkers.

To do all this, church leaders formed the Peace and Hope Commission, so named when one of them was encouraged by Romans 15:13, "May the God of hope fill you with great joy and peace as you trust in him, so that you may overflow with hope by the power of the Holy Spirit." Twenty years later, this Commission continues in sustainable ways to help Peruvian Christians in need.

Miriam Adeney, *Kingdom without Borders: The Untold Story of Global Christianity* (2009, 88–93), citing John Maust, *Peace and Hope in the Corner of the Dead* (Miami: Latin American Mission, 1987)

# CHAPTER 29

# BRAZILIAN MISSIONARIES

## In Contexts of War and Extreme Poverty

*Antonia van der Meer*

When we consider that the present world situation of varied and extreme suffering is likely to continue and that evangelical missionaries face intense suffering in the different regions of the world where they serve, we realize there is a need to improve the way we prepare them and care for them. The following study sought to listen to missionaries themselves.

## THE MAIN NEEDS OF THE PEOPLE THEY ARE SERVING

Research was conducted among missionaries who were serving in countries which had recently gone through devastating wars, starvation, droughts, and floods. The destruction and poverty were still shocking, as were the diseases, physical handicaps, and lack of available services. The main concerns of the missionaries were not related to their own needs, but to the suffering of the people they had come to serve and to love.[1]

Malaria was still a serious problem in such poor and war torn countries and continues to kill many people because there is a growing resistance to the more common available drugs and many people have a low resistance to any disease.

The prolonged wars in these countries, allied to general poverty, have caused the lack of structure in houses and schools. There are houses without basic sanitary conditions; made of plastic, straw, cardboard, grass, and mud. Up to twelve people may share one small room. There are schools with no roof, no blackboard, no desks, and where students arrive carrying an empty tin on which they sit, writing on their laps.

Fear of witchcraft is a problem. The venom from snakes is used in attempts to manipulate evil spirits to kill or harm others. But even worse than the actual practices are fears of accusation, for when circumstances become unbearable, people will deduce that someone has practiced witchcraft against them and begin to seek out the culprit. Families become divided, people (even children) are rejected and punished, without the possibility of proof of either culpability or innocence.

---

1    See figure 1 on "Needs of the people as seen by the missionaries according to their occupation" in the "Attachments" section at the end of this chapter.

AIDS is a grave problem, but often still a taboo subject. A number of patients are abandoned by their families. Some missionaries are reaching out to them.

## THE NEEDS OF THE MISSIONARIES THEMSELVES

*What do the missionaries see as their own main needs?*[2]

Workers of denominational agencies did receive pastoral care; even so, 38.7 percent expressed this need. They suffered fewer problems in the areas of loneliness and doubts related to their calling. However, they felt a lack of privacy (19.4 percent), were concerned with the lack of available aid (58.1 percent), and also expressed concerns about the security of their children (54.8 percent). Most of these missionaries were families.

The needs expressed by missionaries of interdenominational agencies were usually below average, but they felt the lack of time for leisure (33.9 percent), the need for pastoral care (53.6 percent), loneliness (19.6 percent), and expressed struggles in relationships with colleagues (19.6 percent). They are less concerned with appropriate aid for crises (23.2 percent).

The independent missionaries (with no agency support) felt a greater need for support. They were concerned about pastoral and psychological support (respectively 56 and 64 percent), orientation for ministry (40 percent), and the studies of their children (20 percent). Another difficulty expressed by 32 percent was their relationship with national leaders (a figure way above the general percentage). The whole process of their going to the field is informal.

"But the one who endures to the end will be saved. And this gospel of the kingdom will be proclaimed throughout the whole world as a testimony to all nations, and then the end will come." *Matthew 24:12–13*

Agencies and churches are learning to give special care to missionary children. Security issues are difficult to deal with in unstable contexts, but when missionaries know that their leaders stand beside them, they are encouraged to persevere.

Visits to missionaries on the field are helpful when the visitors have a pastoral concern. Some missionaries serving for many years in very stressful situations received a short visit from leaders who were concerned about ministry possibilities, but had no time to sit with them, listen to them, and pray with them.

Missionaries of all agencies felt assured of prayer support, which is vital for those serving in contexts of suffering.

*How do missionaries react to the context of intense and continuing suffering?*

Loneliness, depression, and sadness in contexts of suffering is a common problem of single female missionaries and of married women with small children who are unable to become involved in mission work. Feeling useless and incapable in contexts of great suffering happens to many.

---

2        See figure 2 on "Needs of the missionaries according to their agencies" in the "Attachments" section at the end of this chapter.

Very few mentioned the difficulty of living in a context of violence and war. They are ready to face these painful contexts, serving with love.

It is encouraging to observe that missionaries care for the needs of the people and serve them lovingly, even though this means great stress to the point of near burnout and fear for the lives of their children.

Appropriate member care, a more focused training, and a biblical understanding about suffering in missionary service can help in dealing with these issues.

## HOME ASSIGNMENT AND REENTRY

Home Assignment is not an easy time for missionaries. Usually they do not expect to have problems in adapting back home, but they discover how much they have changed, how foreign and insecure they feel, and how little people at home understand their struggles. Dealing with great challenges on the field was expected, but when they return they hoped to be cared for, to rest, to be renewed. Some churches cut their support ("if you are at home you are no longer a missionary"); other churches and agencies organize a loaded agenda, not leaving time for rest or medical care. Even more difficult is the reception when the church just ignores their return and does not offer opportunities to share their experience.

There are some basic needs: How to shop (things have changed at home and were different on the field)? What kind of clothing is appropriate for adults and for children or teenagers? What are the new rules in financial issues? It is important to offer assistance to missionaries, helping them in their reintegration, and to give loving support to missionary children, who feel even more like strangers in their passport country.

## FAMILY ISSUES

Families need support and guidance to feel free to serve, knowing that their children are well cared for. Most children cope well and grow through their cross-cultural experience, but some families may not be able to cope with the struggles and need to return home (temporarily) to receive special care.

There is a need to care for couples during periods of stress in their relationship. It may be desirable to send the couple back home for a time of restoration. There are some times in a family's life when there is more stress and vulnerability, for example during childbirth (especially if it is a first baby) or when children become teenagers. They need to be listened to and know that they will be allowed to go back home when they need it.

## PASTORAL AND PSYCHOLOGICAL CARE

There is a need to invest in the spiritual growth and emotional stability of missionaries before sending them to contexts of suffering. This can be done through mentoring and discipleship, through pastoral care, group activities with psychologists, and Bible studies on suffering and perseverance.

Sending people to contexts of extreme suffering is a great responsibility. With proper training and member care, people who have a calling will usually be able to cope and be a blessing.

Missionary attrition is a tragedy in the lives of those who go to the mission field hoping to be a blessing and who come back discouraged. It is also a tragedy for their churches, which will have greater hesitation about investing in missions in the future.

Few agencies and churches understand what life looks like in a context of violence and war. This makes it hard for missionaries to share their needs, but these missionaries need much prayer and, if possible, communication, guidance, and specific pastoral help, especially when they are forced to leave their field of service and arrive home emotionally broken and burned out.

## NEEDS OF SINGLE WOMEN

Single women are a significant contingent of those who serve in all fields where there is great suffering.

The main advantage of single women is that they have a greater freedom to serve, to travel, to interact with local people, and even to face dangerous situations if they are willing to pay the price. They usually integrate sooner, learn the language more quickly, develop good relationships, and find satisfaction in their ministry and friendships. Because they do not belong to a family they may be seen as easily available women (like prostitutes). So they have to be careful and respect local rules.

There is often a concern about sending single women to contexts of stress and suffering, but often they cope well and serve well. An experienced leader who has offered member care to many said:

> Single women usually do well and are able to do more than the families; the community cares for them; they suffer loneliness, but things are more difficult for single men, and especially for married women.

The issue of going alone and remaining single is a challenge for many women, for most have the desire to find a husband with a similar calling. Some will get married to another missionary or to local Christians. Cross-cultural marriage can be a blessing, but we need to prepare our single missionaries not to enter into such relationships hastily, they need to know the culture well before considering such a decision.

## CONCLUSION

I would like to affirm the need for churches, training institutes, and mission agencies to recover a biblical perspective on suffering. In some churches suffering is viewed as the result of a lack of faith, or as due to sin. In such contexts it becomes very difficult for missionaries going through personal hardships and being overburdened by the pains of their context to receive understanding and support. A return to a more balanced biblical understanding of suffering and of the cost of discipleship will help churches to offer their missionaries mercy, understanding, and support.

Missionaries are facing difficult contexts and some complain that their leaders are not giving them the necessary opportunities to express their needs. I have heard them asking, "When will people start to listen to us?" So I decided to help them to express their needs and pain.

Churches, agencies, and training institutes must learn how to prepare their missionaries, not only academically but by helping to form their character and by a deep commitment to a continuing discipleship. They must learn to listen to their missionaries, to understand their contexts, and to offer member care, practical guidance, and involvement in their projects. Our sensitive response can help these missionaries to persevere with joy.

## QUESTIONS FOR REFLECTION

1.  Do missionaries from your country face similar painful contexts? How do they react to the suffering of the local people and what are the needs of their own families?
2.  How has your church or agency received missionaries on home assignment or after finishing their service? How did you care for their needs, including both practical support and pastoral care?
3.  What kind of support has your church or agency offered missionaries living in very difficult contexts? Who is listening to them? How can you improve your member care?

## ATTACHMENTS

*Figure 1. Needs of the people as seen by the missionaries according to their occupation.*

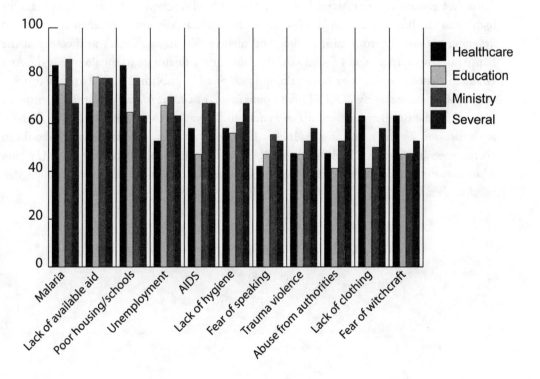

*Figure 2: Needs of missionaries according to their agencies.*

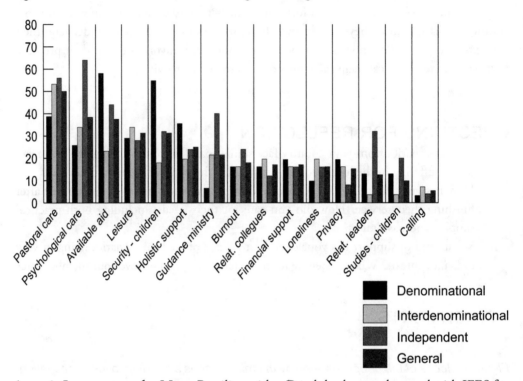

Denominational

Interdenominational

Independent

General

**Antonia Leonora van der Meer**, Brazilian with a Dutch background, served with IFES for many years in Brazil and Angola. Now at the Evangelical Missions Center in Brazil, she is development coordinator, dean, teacher, and mentor. She has a master's in theology at the Baptist Brazilian Theological Faculty in São Paulo and a doctorate in missiology at the Asia Graduate School of Theology in the Philippines. She has published several articles in *Connections: The Journal of the WEA Mission Commission*, in *Global Missiology for the Twenty-first Century*, in the Brazilian version of *Perspectives*, in *Doing Member Care Well*, in *The Dictionary of Mission Theology*, and in the *Atlas of Global Christianity*. She wrote several books in Portuguese: an inductive Bible study *(ABUEditora)*, a personal missionary story *(Eu, um Missionário?)*, and a book on caring for Brazilian missionaries in contexts of suffering *(Missionários Feridos)*.

# CHAPTER 30

# TRAINING OUR MISSIONARIES TO DIE

## A Case Study of Nigerian Church and Missions

*Reuben Ezemadu*

## THE CONTEXT OF LIVING AND WITNESSING FOR CHRIST IN NIGERIA

As I pondered the messages the Lord sent to the seven churches in chapters 2 and 3 of the book of Revelation, I began to notice some similarities in the focus and context of his assessment of each of the churches, representative of the global church with its various experiences of living and witnessing for Christ in the different contexts of our existence. The Lord said to five of those representative churches, "I know your deeds," which described more of what they were doing or not doing—the witnessing aspect of the church's existence. But to the church in Smyrna he said, "I know your afflictions and your poverty," emphasizing more of what they were "experiencing"—the persecutions, imprisonments, martyrdoms, and many other challenges they were facing. To the church in Pergamum he said, "I know where you live—where Satan has his throne," emphasizing the context of the existence and witness of the church.

The context of living and witnessing for Christ in Nigeria today fits into what the Lord said to the churches in Smyrna and Pergamum: afflictions and poverty, persecutions, martyrdom, where Satan has his throne. The phenomenal destruction of lives and properties of Christians in the northern part of Nigeria at the slightest spark, the burning down of church buildings, the denial of places for building houses of worship in certain Muslim-dominated areas, the discrimination against Christians for employment or promotion by Islamic bigots in government establishments, etc., indeed spell out the above description of the context in which the church in Nigeria exists and witnesses for Christ.

Also, the context within which we carry out our missionary endeavors in Nigeria and Africa is described by the Lord in Matthew 10, which contrasts the challenges, dangers, and hazards of the missionary enterprise with the blessings, securities, and insurances provided by the Lord of the harvest himself. Most of our fields are located in the highly resistant Muslim areas of west and central Africa or the war-torn regions of countries like Liberia and Ivory Coast. Our missionaries have been operating in the face of dangers and in environments and situations fraught with hazards. The Lord himself warned of this when he gave an orientation to the Twelve and the Seventy, respectively, before sending them on their missionary assignments. He described the fields (whether at home or abroad) as fraught with dangers and warned about obvious costs to be paid by those who have chosen to heed his call and be engaged in his work. He sent them as "sheep in the midst of wolves" (Matt 10:16). He also painted a picture of "a continuum of hazards," from denial of access, to persecution, arrest, detention, imprisonment (including kidnapping), and ultimately death (Matt 10:14–39). These aptly describe what it is about living and witnessing for him in the context of afflictions and poverty, persecutions, and martyrdom, "where Satan has his throne" (Rev 2:9,10,13).

In his priestly valedictory prayer for his followers in John 17, Jesus also reminded his disciples that the world into which he was sending them was full of dangers and ministry hazards, and he asked the Father to protect them while doing their ministry in the world—not to remove them from the world or even to shield them from those possible attacks (John 17:6–18).

## RECEIVING MISSIONARIES IN THESE CONTEXTS

The early missionaries from Europe and North America came into Nigeria at a time when Africa was regarded as "a dark continent" as well as "the white man's graveyard." Many of them died due to hostile and harsh environmental conditions, tropical diseases they were not immune to, the savagery of the native Africans, and as victims of intertribal wars. Their toils and tears, sweat and blood watered the soil from which the seed of church germinated and began to grow.

The rise of the spirit of nationalism and revival of traditional religion, coupled with the rise of fundamental Islamic fervency has fueled more recent antagonism and aggression against Christianity. As the fundamentalists and traditionalists gained control of government, they used such opportunities to devise measures and policies which targeted the missionary efforts from outside Nigeria, restricting the number of expatriate missionaries that could come into Nigeria, reducing the validity period of visas granted to those who were already in the country, refusing to extend the validity of expiring visas, deporting some missionaries on false accusation or minor incidences, delaying or totally denying approval for fresh applications for entry and residence visas. These measures, coupled with the dwindling economies of countries from where the expatriate missionaries were coming, led to the exodus of expatriate missionaries and the decline in the number that arrived. Some of the institutions the missionaries had set up (e.g., schools, hospitals, Bible translation centers) were either taken over by the government (and in some cases converted to Islamic institutions in Muslim-dominated areas of Northern Nigeria), or closed down (like the Summer Institute of Linguistics in Jos).

The fallout of these developments had a huge impact on the fledging church. Pioneer church-planting efforts among the remaining unreached peoples of Nigeria either slowed down or were entirely halted. There was a shortage of well trained and adequately equipped workers to continue to nurture the growing church and manage the institutions the national church inherited. The flow of aid and support from sending churches abroad diminished with the continued exit of the expatriate missionaries who were the trusted channels by which they sent resources. This forced the national church to begin to look inward. It was in this environment that indigenous mission agencies like Evangelical Missionary Society of ECWA, Calvary Ministries (CAPRO), Christian Missionary Foundation (CMF), etc., began to spring up.

For us, the teachings, admonitions, orientation, and insight into the realities of the mission fields and the hazard-fraught context of ministry that the Lord Jesus presented to the disciples in Matthew 10 and Luke 10 were a sufficient manual for training, equipping, and preparing our people to live and witness for Christ in a country, like the churches of Smyrna and Pergamum in Revelation, are full of afflictions and poverty, persecutions and martyrdom—where Satan has his throne.

## SUSTAINING THE MISSIONARY ENTERPRISE IN THE CONTEXT OF LIMITED RESOURCES AND POVERTY

We also found Jesus' teachings on "zero-budget" missionary enterprise, God trusting, and faith-based missions support in Matthew 10:9–10, as well as the "feeding and housing" schemes he recommended in Luke 10:5–8 as "antipoverty" measures that sustain our witnessing in the context of poverty. In practice and principle, these have helped our missionaries to continue to reach remote areas and survive very severe poverty conditions. Therefore, we emphasize such measures in the training and equipping of the missionary personnel we deploy to the fields.

## INEVITABILITY OF PERSECUTIONS AND MARTYRDOM

The Lord also indicated the inevitability of persecutions and martyrdom (Matt 10:17–23), but assured us the grace to face it all and divine protection. The reality of spiritual warfare is a result of living "where Satan has his throne." There is no way you can live in and witness for Christ in Nigerian society without encountering principalities and powers which operate in so many forms to oppose the work of the gospel. This happens through traditions, customs, traditional rulers, government, institutions, media, etc. These are the wolves among which we are called to live and witness for Christ in the country; hence the need to continue to heed the injunction by the Lord Jesus Christ "to be wise as serpents and harmless as doves" (Matt 10:16 NKJV).

## TRAINING TO DIE

Our policies concerning the dangers of being a missionary under the Christian Missionary Foundation, whether on a short-term or career basis, derive from the Lord's own policies as contained in the tenth chapter of Matthew as well as that of Luke.

Since the ultimate price of being in a military institution is death, we too have identified that as the highest price to be paid by any missionary (whether on short-term or career missionary assignment). We "train our missionaries to die" (apologies to Canon Bayo Famonure's book, *Training to Die*). As part of the training, orientation, and commitment to our missionaries, we emphasize the fact that missionary assignments involve risks and hazards and could ultimately lead to death.

Therefore, it is not only that we have built these principles into curriculum for the training of a new crop of missionaries, we have also formulated policies around such concerns, one of which is the "Statement of Commitment to and Affirmation of CMF Policies" which every prospective missionary signs and communicates to their relatives. This statement reads, "A missionary must be prepared to die and be buried in the field of his/her assignment except his/her relatives opt for the retrieval of his/her corpse for burial in their own place of preference, and on their own account." Such disclaimers are extended to other areas of social responsibilities in light of the complicated and sensitive family issues in our African culture with regard to marriages, extended family relationships, number of children to be born by a couple, etc., as well as the responsibilities for generating and disbursing support.

## FACING AND SURVIVING THE HAZARDS OF MINISTRY

In his message to the churches in Smyrna and Pergamum, the Lord encouraged them to be steadfast in the midst of the dangers they faced each day. In the admonitions he gave to the disciples in Matthew 10 and Luke 10, Jesus stressed the fact that poverty, persecutions, sufferings, and martyrdom are the realities of living and witnessing for him in the hostile environments in which they would find themselves always, and he advanced many measures they would employ in order to overcome and survive such. These included the examples cited in the preceding paragraphs: sources of their support, what to eat, where to stay, ministering in teams, connecting with the man of peace, moving away from hostile spots, "being wise as serpents and harmless as doves." In his valedictory prayer for the disciples and believers in John 17, he reminded the Father about the hostilities and danger the disciples over the ages were going to face in the world that was antagonistic of the purpose for which he came and had sent his followers. He prayed that the Father should not remove them from the world nor provide immunity from the sufferings and persecutions and possible martyrdom they would face. Rather he prayed for their sustenance and unity in the face of all these hazards of their living and witnessing for him in the world "where Satan has his throne."

> "O Jerusalem, Jerusalem, the city that kills the prophets and stones those who are sent to it! How often would I have gathered your children together as a hen gathers her brood under her wings, and you would not!" *Luke 13:34*

We inculcate these measures and principles to our missionaries as we admonish, train, and equip them for ministry in our danger-fraught environments. We encourage them to teach and help new believers to imbibe the same measures and principles, since they face similar dangers just for changing their religious affiliation. We also emphasize a holistic approach to ministry that targets the "whole man" with the whole word of God, which totally liberates and empowers the believer. In many cases the holistic approach creates access to people as well as engenders "peace" and neutralizes hostile postures. We do not ignore the realities of the spiritual battles. We teach and infuse in our people the need to be combat ready and to "fight the good fight of faith" through all manner of prayer and intercession.

## EMERGING NEW DIMENSIONS OF THE BATTLE

The progenitor of the hostilities never gives up. In Nigeria, new dimensions of his tactics emerge every day. As the Christian faith grows, he has sown the seed of discrimination and divisions within the body of Christ. Many denominations have arisen along lines of doctrinal differences and tribal lineages. These engender more severe rivalries and even worse persecutions. The harvest fields have become battlefields for denominational bigots. In certain cases, territories have been declared "occupied" by various groups even before they set their feet on such places. The unity of the body is undermined. The common enemy takes advantage of such to unleash further afflictions, persecution, and sufferings on the battle-weary church "militant."

The domination of the Islamic faith in certain parts of Northern Nigeria has been exploited by radical Muslims to take over government and stifle the rights of Christians to practice and share their faith in society. Persecution, discrimination, abuse, and affliction of various indescribable dimensions have been unleashed on Christians in many parts of Northern Nigeria. Events that concern the Islamic faith in any other part of the world trigger anti-Christian sentiments there, leading to the wanton destruction of lives and properties of Christians in those areas where Muslims are in majority. The Muslim-dominated security forces and concerned government agencies turn their eyes the other way. Many Christians have been displaced or forced to abandon completely their traditional places of abode due to fierce and sustained attacks. The "Boko Haram" (Islamic anti-Western sentiment) "religious cleansing" wind, that started from the northeastern city of Maiduguri, is spreading in such a ferocious manner that the whole country is under very serious threat. Each day, church buildings and Christian individuals receive their deadly blows through targeted bombings. In it all, the Lamb triumphs and his church will continue to march on!

## QUESTIONS FOR REFLECTION

1. How does Ezemadu describe the context of the church living and witnessing in Nigeria itself and of the fields where their missionaries are being sent? Do our churches face any similar hazards, and do we send our missionaries to such costly contexts of poverty and persecution?

2. Describe the transition from foreign missionaries to Nigerian missionary vision and commitment? How were the Nigerian missionaries trained for facing very difficult contexts in their mission work? What can we learn from them?

3. The situation of Christians in Nigeria has not become any easier lately. What are their main challenges today? How do they face them? How can we support them?

**Reuben E. Ezemadu** of Nigeria is the international director of the Christian Missionary Foundation as well as continental coordinator of the Movement for African National Initiatives (MANI). He authored *Sending and Supporting African Missionaries in the 21st Century* (2005) and contributed an article titled "Financing Missions in a Depressed Economy" in *The Church Leader in Africa* magazine.

## RAISING THIRTY-TWO GRANDCHILDREN ALONE ON A SMALL PLOT

"I had twelve children," a Zimbabwean woman told Esme Bowers, when Esme came to conduct a workshop for the women's program of the Africa Evangelical Alliance. "All my children were all married. But they all died of AIDS. All their spouses died too. Now I'm left with thirty-two grandchildren to support on a little plot of ground."

Yet, in spite of horrendous burdens, this woman came to Esme's workshop to be trained as a thoughtful Christian leader.

Miriam Adeney, *Kingdom without Borders: The Untold Story of Global Christianity* (2009, 37)

# CHAPTER 31

# THE RWANDAN MARTYRS OF ETHNIC IDEOLOGY

*Antoine Rutayisire*

Israel Havugimana,
Lived what he preached,
Died for what he believed,
Reconciliation.

This is the epitaph on the tomb of Israel Havugimana, former team leader of African Evangelistic Enterprise-Rwanda, gunned down on April 7, 1994, the beginning date of the infamous genocide against the Tutsis of Rwanda. Israel was not a Tutsi, he was a Hutu who, out of his Christian convictions, dared to stand against and challenge ethnic hatred and divisions. Israel is a real martyr, "a witness" who lives what he preaches and is "killed because of his religious or other beliefs." And he is one case among many other courageous Rwandan Christians who were persecuted but still refused to bow down to the idol of ethnicity. Some were threatened and verbally abused, others were beaten and even killed. Some gave up, others stood their ground and faced the consequences. The aim of this case study is to survey how those martyrs resisted the divisive ideology of ethnicity from its beginning in the 1960s up to its culmination in the infamous genocide of 1994, where more than 1 million Tutsis and moderate Hutus were killed in less than a hundred days between April 7 and July 4, 1994. A short introduction is given to explain the context and causes of that madness, then different cases of Christian bravery are presented, and finally lessons are drawn to inspire the way we do mission in different contexts of ethnic, tribal, and racial coexistence and conflict.

## UNDERSTANDING THE MADNESS

Rwanda is a small country, landlocked in the heart of Africa with a population of around 10 million people made up of three social groups: the Hutus, the Tutsis, and the Twas. The Tutsis were predominantly cattle raisers, the Hutus worked the land, and the Twas were hunters and clay potters. From the ninth century, Rwanda expanded into a large kingdom under the leadership of Tutsi kings originating from the Banyiginya clan. The power stayed in their hands until 1959 when, under the instigation and support of the Belgian colonial powers, the Hutus turned against the Tutsi leadership and overthrew it in a bloodshed that saw more than thirty thousand people killed and more than 300,000 sent into exile in the neighboring countries where they would stay in refugee settlements until 1994. It was the second generation of these exiles (the children who grew up in the settlements) who, tired of living without a country, formed the Rwanda Patriotic Front and attacked the country in 1990, sparking off a domino process that would eventually culminate in the 1994 genocide against the Tutsi. This is a brief contextualization to set the scene for our discussion of the central issue of this chapter.

Calling the Hutu, Tutsi, and Twas "ethnic groups" or "tribes" is a misnomer because the three groups have lived together from times immemorial and they share the same skin color, the same language, and the same culture, living next to each other all over the national territory. There is no such a thing as a Hutu, Tutsi, or Twa village, there is no such a thing as a Hutu, Tutsi, or Twa dialect or custom. This kind of situation defies all scientific and anthropological definitions of ethnic group, race, and tribe. For reasons of convenience I will use the word "ethnic group" throughout this paper. Some people have often asked how the genocide could happen in such a situation where it is not easy to distinguish people from each other by their physical or linguistic characteristics. First, Rwanda is a predominantly rural country and people who have lived next to each other in the same village can easily trace their ancestries. Moreover, the colonial system introduced ethnically marked identity cards, a system that was kept even after independence and was most instrumental in helping to identify who to kill and who to let go during the genocide.

## CHRISTIANITY AND THE PROBLEM OF ETHNIC IDENTITY

Christianity came to Rwanda in the beginning of the twentieth century, and by the time the genocide happened in 1994, Rwanda was 90 percent Christian with the majority being Roman Catholic (63 percent of the total population) and a nonnegligible Protestant presence of 27 percent. The contradiction of a genocide in a country that is predominantly of Christian allegiance has raised many questions about the type of Christianity we had in the country. How can ethnicity become more powerful than the Christian faith? How can Christians turn against other Christians in the name of ethnic belonging? Were there Christians who lived their faith and did not negate their Lord? Were there Christians who accepted to die with and for their brothers and sisters? What motivated them? What strengthened them? What lessons can we learn from them? These are the main questions this paper tries to answer.

It is well documented that the early Catholic missionaries came with the clear mission philosophy of "converting the indigenous chiefs so as to reach their subjects more easily." They decided to openly favor the Tutsi chiefs and their children in their education programs, hence Bishop Leon Classe, the first Roman Catholic primate, came to be known as the "father of ethnicity in Rwanda" (Muzungu 2010, 54). This calculated policy yielded its fruit when King Mutara Rudahigwa desired to be baptized in 1941 and under the inspiration and guidance of the very same Bishop Leon Classe, he dedicated the country to Christ the King in 1946. These two factors sparked off the "national conversion" a la Constantine, with a majority of the chiefs and subchiefs following suit and getting baptized. Then a great number of the ordinary people toed the line without much of a change in character or lifestyle. Some of the missionaries themselves did see the danger and questioned the move but they could not dam it (De Lacger 1962). Nominal Christianity became the norm, with a lot of syncretism. The Hutu, Tutsi, and Twa identity was not challenged but rather transferred into the church. It was (and is still) not uncommon for instance to hear of a Tutsi family refusing to give their daughter in marriage into a Hutu family, although both families attend the same church. It was—and is still—inconceivable for some to think of sharing from the same Holy Communion cup with a Twa brother or sister.

The greatest failure of the church, however, manifested when ethnicity was slowly and progressively becoming a national ideology and was used as a foundation stone for the political system when the Hutus took power in 1959. What Bishop Classe had been to King Mutara Rudahigwa, the new catholic primate, Bishop Andre Perraudin, became for the new Hutu leader, Gregory Kayibanda, who was first his personal secretary, then his political protégé and mentoree. It is amazing to read some of the racist and divisive lines that came from the pen of that man of the church! The ethnic ideology that later on culminated into genocide was hatched under the wings of church leadership (Gatwa 2005; Muzungu 2010). When ethnicity was moving from being a social reality to becoming a political ideology, those who opposed it in the name of human rights or Christian faith were persecuted and even killed.

As the Roman Catholic Church had cut a lion's share with the political system, the other churches did not have a say and we do not see many of them raising their voices to fight and oppose the unjust system that was developing. Those Roman bishops who did not support the trend suffered tremendous persecution (Muzungu 2010). Already in the early 1960s, Bishop Aloys Bigirumwami had shown his strong opposition against the

> "See, we are going up to Jerusalem, and the Son of Man will be delivered over to the chief priests and the scribes, and they will condemn him to death and deliver him over to the Gentiles. And they will mock him and spit on him, and flog him and kill him. And after three days he will rise."
> Mark 10:33–34

new ethnic ideology developments, but his superior, Bishop Andre Perraudin who was in collusion with the colonial powers and the new Hutu regime, managed to keep that opposing influence at bay. Bishop Bigirumwami never gave up his strong stand and he was eventually forced to go into premature retirement and died a broken-hearted man, living in his isolated countryside retreat house on the shore of Lake Kivu. The most appalling case is that of Bishop Bernard Manyurane who was apparently assassinated by the same leadership of his own church. "The semi-official opinion had it that he was poisoned since he refused to follow the path traced.... A Hutu bishop who was not in favor of the ideology of his ethnic group was unbearable" (Muzungu 2010, 58).

The situation became worse when ethnic identity became the center of conflict in 1990 when the already mentioned RPF from the refugee settlements decided to use the power of arms when their peaceful pleas to return to their homeland fell on deaf ears. The RPF never used ethnic propaganda but the Hutu government in place in Kigali mobilized all resources to polarize the population along ethnic lines. The propaganda of hatred was preached in papers, in public speeches, and even in churches! Here the Christian identity of all of us was put to the test and that is when a great number of real martyrs emerged. Tutsis were persecuted and killed because of their ethnic belonging and will not be considered as martyrs in this context. A large number of Hutus suffered because they rejected the ideology of ethnic hatred and division, some doing it out of personal convictions, others because of their adhesion to political parties that were against that line of thought, and others out of their

Christian faith. In my book *Faith Under Fire: Stories of Christian Bravery* (Rutayisire 1996), I have collected and documented testimonies of Christians who put their lives at risk to save others from the killings during the genocide. Here are two case studies excerpted from the book:

> Israel was a man who lived what he preached … and he often preached against ethnic divisions and hatred. In the 1972/73 massacres against Tutsi students, he protected a Tutsi fellow student at Shyogwe Secondary school, covering him with his own body and receiving all the beating until he managed to get him out of the reach of the attackers. During the 1990–94 ethnic tensions that led to the genocide, Israel stayed equal to his Christian commitment, spearheading a reconciliation ministry throughout the country. But his position and his undying friendship with Tutsi brothers and sisters were resented by the extremist Hutus, and the ethnically mixed Bible study group that met at his home every Tuesday night was misinterpreted to be a political reunion to raise support for the Tutsi rebels (RPF). In February 1994, a hand grenade was thrown into the living room of his house as a warning. We then met to discuss the possibility of stopping our Bible study meeting so as not to compromise him any further. "What Christian testimony would that be?" he asked us. "To shy away from my brothers and sisters in Christ because they are targeted! I have preached reconciliation and I will live it even if I have to pay for it with my blood." Two months later, he paid with his blood! The very first day of the genocide against the Tutsis, he was gunned down with his three daughters, his father who was visiting, his house boy, and another guest who has not been identified.

> Father Jean Bosco Munyaneza was the curate of the Mukarange Roman Catholic Parish when the genocide started. Most of the Tutsis in the area decided to take refuge at the parish, as in previous massacres those who had taken refuge in church compounds and buildings had never been bothered. But this time it was different! The soldiers and the militias attacked the compound of the church and as Father Bosco was a Hutu, they asked him to leave the place. They begged him but he was adamant. "These are sheep the Lord has given me to look after. If they must die let me die with them. And if you want to save my life, save theirs with mine." The militias, angered by his firm stand, backed away and threw a hand grenade into the crowd where he was standing. Many people were wounded, the Father died some minutes later.

A close observation of the different stories in the book shows that there are different reactions among the Christians when they are faced with social injustice and ethnic violence: (1) At the far negative side, there are church leaders and Christians who will abandon their faith and side with their "ethnic group." In most cases, these are people whose ethnic identity has been reinforced and never been challenged by their faith. They are Christian on the outside but inside they are more members of their ethnic group than of the holy nation of God. (2) In the middle stand a big crowd who out of fear, do not take part but do not try to help either. The bystanders will flee when the time comes and the best weapon of wicked people is to turn good people into passive bystanders (Staub 1989). (3) The third group is made up of those people who take active steps to denounce the ideology and acts of violence or who silently side with those who are oppressed and help them to hide or to flee. The martyrs of faith will always come from this last group. And it is from such groups that comes the saying that "martyrdom is an act of love." Fired by their love of neighbor and their faith in God, they dare challenge the system even unto death. A close scrutiny of this group shows a common denominator: these are people who know their God, know their calling as witnesses of Jesus Christ even in dangerous situations, and who have articulated a clear definition of their identity in Christ.

## CONCLUSION

Many lessons can be drawn from the Rwanda case. First, tribal or ethnic violence in a predominantly Christian context should be taken as a failure in mission! When people come to Christ without having a sense of becoming "a new creation," when people become Christians without becoming citizens of the holy nation of God where there are no Greeks nor Jews, no Hutus, Tutsis, or Twas, then something has gone wrong in the mission process. It is easy to rejoice over the number of converts and baptisms while overlooking the quality of character that Christ expects from his disciples. When the blood of our ancestry runs deeper than the blood of Christ, then we are living a failed Christian identity. Ethnicity, tribalism, racism, and other "-isms" are symptoms of a Christianity without a clear Christian identity. When we do not use the message of the cross to heal the divides in our communities, we are failing our mission as Christians. Second, people should be taught and trained to articulate a theology for their new identity and mission in the society (Frost 2006). Third, shaping a message of reconciliation that is well contextualized should be part of mission. Healing the wounds of the past that often underlie the ethnic ideologies is the only way to prevent the future explosion of ethnic violence.

## QUESTIONS FOR REFLECTION

1. How was the church influenced by the national ideology based on ethnicity? What were some of the causes of this unbiblical understanding? How did church leaders contribute to this unhealthy development?
2. How did Christians respond to the development of induced ethnic hatred and violence? What marked the lives of those who became martyrs because of their Christian commitment? What price were they ready to pay for their convictions?
3. What lessons should we, who are committed to mission, learn from this tragic story where Christians murdered Christians because of their ethnic belonging? And from those who remained faithful to their Christian calling?

## REFERENCES

De Lacger, L. 1962. *Rwanda*. Kabgayi: Imprimerie de Kabgayi.

Frost, M. 2006. *Exiles: Living missionally in a post-Christian culture*. Peabody, MA: Hendrickson.

Gatwa, T. 2005. *The churches and ethnic ideology in the Rwandan crises 1900–1994*. Oxford: Regnum Books International.

Muzungu, B. 2010. Eglise Catholiques pendant le genocide. In *Cahiers Lumiére et Société* 43 (March).

Rutayisire, A. 1996. *Faith under fire: Stories of Christian bravery*. Buchurst Hill, Essex: African Enterprise.

**Antoine Rutayisire** is pastor of St. Peter's Anglican Church in Remera, Kigali. He is married to Penina and together they have four children. He has served on the Rwanda National Unity and Reconciliation Commission from 1999 to 2011. He holds MA in global leadership and is completing a doctorate in missiology at Fuller Theological Seminary.

# CHAPTER 32

# THE RWANDAN MARTYRS

## A New Definition of Persecution and Martyrdom

*Célestin Musekura*

The complexity of understanding the Rwandan persecution and martyrdom has been alluded to by my friend Antoine Rutayisire because it has been tied to political and tribal turmoil happening in the country. In addition to this contextual situation, the traditional definition of Christian persecution and martyrdom has been challenged by the changes in levels, forms, methods, intention, perpetrators, etc. Some persecutions have been equated or confused with human-rights violation without considering the religious impact and influence in the context.

A certain level of persecution in Rwanda has existed during tumultuous times in Rwanda such as during the days of revolution (1959–63), the times of tribal wars between Tutsi-dominated rebels known as the Rwanda Patriotic Front and the Hutu-dominated army (October 1990 to March 1994), the days of genocide against Tutsi and moderate Hutus (April 7 to July 1994), and the period of massacres of thousands of Hutus and Congolese inside Rwanda and in refugee camps and the remote regions of eastern Congo (April 1994 and 2008). Persecution and martyrdom have happened because of what leaders said (whether right or wrong) or what they failed to say. The interpretation of what they said or what they meant depended on both the interlocutor and the listener/interpreter. For the sake of this article, I will address three kinds of Rwandan martyrs: those pastors and church leaders who were persecuted and killed just because of their faithful witness, those who were martyred because of standing for the truth and therefore posed a challenge to their perpetrators, and those martyrs who died because they felt the obligation to protect their congregants and later were killed together. We must make it clear here that those priest, bishops, pastors, and church leaders who are being rightly and genuinely jailed because of their participation in the genocide and killings before, during, and after the Rwanda genocide are not considered martyrs or victims of religious persecution.

Before embarking on the first category of Rwandan martyrs, it is important to clarify that martyrdom, in the traditional definition, is considered to be related to the forces outside the church that seek to destroy the church. Unfortunately, the Rwanda case is different. Those who persecuted and continue to persecute the church and those who murdered Tutsi and Hutu priests, bishops, and lay leaders were in most cases members of both the Catholic and Protestant churches. Ours in Rwanda is more of a political persecution, assassination, and martyrdom whose goal was not necessarily to wipe out Christianity but rather to silence the voice of the church or to remove credible witness to murder, genocide, and massacres by different armed groups, tribes, and political groups. What has happened to Rwandan church leaders, bishops, priests, pastors, and lay leaders redefine the meaning and intention of persecution and martyrdom.

## MARTYRS OF FAITHFUL WITNESS

In the years that followed Rwandan independence from the Belgians and especially during the time when the political powers in Rwanda were controlled by strong men from the northern region. Any bishop, church leader, or clergy who dared to speak against the policies of the Hutu regime was intimidated, persecuted, and in some cases mysteriously disappeared or found dead. Every time I visit the Nyamata Church genocide memorial, I stop by the grave of Sister Tonia Locatelli, an Italian nun who was murdered by the Hutu regime in 1992 when she tried to alert the international community about the imminent danger of the extermination of Tutsi in Bugesera in the eastern province of Rwanda. Sister Locatelli is a good reminder of a faithful witness and servant to God and people.

Other church leaders have been persecuted, murdered, and tortured just because they belong to the "wrong group/tribe" without necessarily doing or failing to do, saying or failing to say something wrong. The compiler of "Today's (unofficial) Martyrs of the Roman Catholic Church"[1] makes an interesting observation on those Rwandan martyrs who were killed by "gunmen, unidentified attackers, Hutu gunmen, militants, etc." Because the Rwandan political leaders have played Christian and have identified themselves as Christians, they do not want to be seen as persecutors and torturers and murderers of religious leaders. They prefer to use other means to intimidate, silence, annihilate, and make disappear those bishops, priests, pastors, and lay leaders—not because of what they have done but only because they belong to the undesirable tribe. They are treated like the rest of their tribe. If the Hutu government is killing the Tutsis, then Tutsi bishops, priests, pastors, and lay leaders have to be killed. The leaders killed because of ethnic motives are not martyrs in the real sense of the word. However, among these leaders, there are those who were killed because they decried and denounced the acts of injustices perpetuated by political leaders against innocent Rwandans publicly in their sermons, homilies, and speeches. They were harassed, intimidated, imprisoned, and killed because of performing their duties faithfully. Because they refused to be persuaded to side with their tribes or any tribe, they lost their lives—some mysteriously and others openly. These are the ones we will call Rwandan martyrs.

Father Marcel was a Hutu priest at Mubuga Roman Catholic Church in the Western Province of Rwanda who was killed by a Hutu soldier because of his conviction as a priest. In the report "Rwanda: Cases for Appeals," Amnesty International reports of a conversation between the victim and a soldier as narrated by an eyewitness:

—You, the priest, leave! The others are going to die.
—But these people are Christians! Like you, like me . . .

1    http://www.catholicdoors.com/news/martyrs2.htm.

—It's an order of the government.

—You are not going to let the blood of Catholics flow, not in a church! (Amnesty International 2004, 10)

The dialog ends when Father Marcel, who had fallen on his knees pleading for the lives of the Tutsis, was stabbed to death. The following day, it is estimated that around four thousand Tutsis were massacred by a group of about five hundred men armed with guns, grenades, and machetes. A Christian leader was assassinated because he did not want to do what was against his belief. He chose to die rather than give up "the sheep" to be slaughtered. Instead, the blood of the shepherd and the sheep were mingled at the altar.

Father Marcel is a martyr because of his faithful witness. In today's world and especially in sub-Sahara Africa, persecution and martyrdom will continue to result not in the refusal to recant or deny one's faith or belief, but more so in the refusal to act against one's Christian convictions. Father Marcel became a martyr of his convictions while many priests were giving up people to be killed or even involved in the killing.

## MARTYRDOM AND POLITICAL ASSASSINATION

The killing of Rwandan church leaders, bishops, pastors, priests, nuns, and lay leaders by both Hutu- and Tutsi-dominated governments and armies before, during, and after the genocide have caused students of religious persecution and human rights to wonder whether these killings can be categorized as persecution or just political assassination. A closer look at the number of Tutsi bishops, priests, pastors, and nuns killed before the genocide in their homes, parishes, convents, churches, cars, etc., will reveal a deliberate target of religious leaders given the fact that even during the past worst tribal violence of 1959 and 1963, bishops, pastors, priests, and nuns were not killed. Killers never pursued their victims inside the churches.

In investigating the killings of many such Tutsi priests, pastors, nuns, and other religious leaders by Hutu government and armed men, human-rights activists and researchers Rakiya Omaar and Alex de Waal state that in the years that preceded the genocide:

> There [was] a disproportionately high number of Tutsi priests, and many Tutsi children who were denied a state education under the quota system instead joined seminaries. As priests have a certain influence, they could say in church what Tutsis could not say elsewhere. The church remained the only place that remained open to Tutsis to speak freely. Therefore the perception was growing that priests had a privileged social status. Since 1990, a number of priests used the pulpit to denounce many injustices. But some have paid a heavy price. (1994, 14)

Omaar and de Waal went on to list specific priests, nuns, and clergy who were killed in the Kigali areas as well as in the prefectures (provinces) of Gisenyi, Butare, and Kibungo.

The Catholic Church in Rwanda has qualified the killings of her clergy and lay leaders as persecution and martyrdom. The writers of "Rwanda: The Persecuted Church; The Forsaken Nation" state that "The Catholic Church in Rwanda has millions of reasons of being alarmed by the persecution, murders, and slaughters of its clergy in Rwanda. The rate at which priests and nuns are assassinated by the Rwandan leaders is unprecedented" (AfroAmerica Network 1999). The writers went on to list Catholic bishops (Rwandan and foreigners) killed in Rwanda between 1994 and 1998:

> His Eminence Vincent Nsengiyumva, Archbishop of Kigali, killed by the Rwandan Patriotic Army (RPA), in Gakurazo on June 5, 1994. His Eminence Joseph Ruzindana, Bishop of Byumba, killed by the Rwandan Patriotic Army (RPA), in Gakurazo on June 5, 1994. His Eminence Innocent Gasabwoya, Vicar-General of Kabgayi, killed by the Rwandan Patriotic Army (RPA), in Gakurazo on June 5, 1994. His Eminence Thaddee Nsengiyumva, Bishop of Kabgayi, killed by the Rwandan Patriotic Army (RPA) on June 5, 1994. His Eminence Phocas Nikwigize, Bishop of Ruhengeri, killed by the Rwandan Patriotic Army (RPA) on November 30, 1996 in Goma, the Democratic Republic of the Congo. His Eminence Jean Marie Rwabirinda, Vicar-General of Kabgayi, killed by the Rwandan Patriotic Army (RPA), in Gakurazo on June 5, 1994. His Eminence Andre Sibomana, Acting Bishop of Kabgayi, mysteriously killed (apparently by the RPA secret services) in Kabgayi on March 9, 1998. Chaplain Antoine Hategekimana, killed in Bukavu in November 1996, by the Rwandan Patriotic Army, along with His Eminence Christopher Munzihirwa-Mwene-Ngabo, Archbishop of Bukavu, the Democratic Republic of the Congo. Chaplain Fidel Gahonzire, Chaplain of the Kabgayi Hospital, killed by the Rwandan Patriotic Army in Gakurazo on June 5, 1994. Father Guy Pinard, a Canadian, killed by the Rwandan Patriotic Army in February 1997, while conducting a Mass. His Eminence Boniface Kagabo, Acting Bishop of Ruhengeri, killed by the Rwandan Patriotic Army on May 26, 1998. Father Vjeco Curic, a Friar priest from Croatia, mysteriously killed by his passenger (apparently from the RPA secret services) in front of the Holy Family Church of Kigali on January 31, 1998.

Following this list of bishops and foreigners killed, the reporters proceeded with another extended list that gives the distribution of slaughtered priests and nuns by diocese. Apart from these lists that present mainly the Catholic martyrs, there are many Protestant bishops, priests, pastors, evangelists, and lay leaders who have been persecuted, tortured, intimidated, exiled, and murdered because of their roles and influence. One hopes that the Rwanda Protestant Council or the Alliance of Evangelicals of Rwanda will collect the list and names of the victims of the political assassination, persecution, and martyrdom in Rwanda before, during, and after the 1994 genocide.

However, the majority of Rwandan Christians will say that in most cases, these killings and torture were not just political but were also religious in nature. The killings were not directed at Christians or any religious groups in the country, but rather to members of clergy and Christian leaders because of their stand on political and moral issues that the political leaders were facing. If these leaders opposed (rightly or wrongly) the popular agenda of the political powers and ruling party, persecution and assassinations ensued. Other religious leaders were singled out for intimidation, torture, assassination, and martyrdom because they belong to a certain tribe and therefore either "deserved" the same treatment as their fellow tribesmen or needed to be silenced because they could speak on behalf of the people or could become eye-witnesses of atrocities perpetuated against members of their communities and congregations. The goal of this sort of persecution was to intimidate, silence, assimilate into political ideology, hide the truth, erase evidence, revenge, persecute, and assassinate. A nation devoid of a national conscience, prophetic voices, custodians of moral values and social justice, and voices against cruelty, human-rights violations, ethnic cleansing, massacres, and genocides would allow government and politicians to do what seems right in their eyes. The Rwandan Christian persecution and martyrdom sought to rid the society of its eye, voice, and soul.

## MARTYRS OF VENGEANCE AND RETALIATION

There are those who argue that the killing of many Catholic and Protestant bishops, pastors, priests, and nuns was mostly motivated by vengeance. The RPF troops and fighters did not expect to find in churches dead bodies of Tutsi relatives they sought to save. Even members of the clergy who hid people in their churches did not expect militia and armed men to violate the church. Historically and in the Hutu-Tutsi violence of 1959 and 1963, those who found refuge in the church were saved in most cases. What was very inhuman and more repugnant in the 1994 genocide is that not only did the militia enter the sanctuaries to murder Tutsis but also some members of the clergy invited the murderers into the church to kill those they had lured or hidden inside the church building. Unfortunately for the Catholic Church, the majority of these churches were Catholic, since these were more solid, well protected, and somehow historically more respected by the political leaders of the time, since the majority of the Hutu leaders attended the Catholic Church.

> Repay no one evil for evil, but give thought to do what is honorable in the sight of all. If possible, so far as it depends on you, live peaceably with all. Beloved, never avenge yourselves, but leave it to the wrath of God, for it is written, "Vengeance is mine, I will repay, says the Lord."
> *Romans 12:17–19*

The number of Catholic bishops, priests, nuns, and lay leaders killed by the Tutsi-dominated Rwandan Patriotic Front is higher in proportion, speed, and extension than the number of Protestant bishops persecuted, tortured, imprisoned, and killed. The places where the majority of these bishops, priests, and nuns were killed leaves one to wonder whether this was a retaliation or a calculated and intentional decimation of the power and influence of the Catholic Church that had dominated and influenced politics in Rwanda and also had played a role in the 1959 revolution that brought the Hutu to power and sent many Tutsis into exile. Jerome Karabayinga and Clarisse Mwambali of the *World News Journal* reported of a priest in Kabgayi, Rwanda, who, during the celebration of Pentecost on May 24, 1999 "described how the leadership of the Catholic Church, once the undisputed dominant of the Rwandan spiritual life, is being slowly but steadily decimated" (Karabaying and Mwambali 2008). The priest continued his sermon by saying, "Before we conclude, let us remember that at this very moment His Eminence Augustin Misago, Bishop of Gikongoro is impris-oned in filthy conditions by our leaders; that His Eminence Thaddee Ntahinyurwa, Bishop of Cyangugu and many, many, many more religious and laity are persecuted by our political leaders" (Karabying and Mwambali 2008).

The martyrdom by vengeance was advanced in the case of the killing of thirteen Hutu cler-gymen, including the Roman Catholic archbishop of Kigali and two bishops, by the four rebel soldiers assigned to guard them. The Rwandan rebel radio Muhabura reported that "the guards believed the clergymen had taken part in massacres of their relatives" (Associated Press 1994). This incident being one of the earliest in a series of killing and murdering of clergy members makes one ask the question if such vengeance was limited to these low ranking soldiers among the Tutsi dominated rebel group or if there was a higher order to intentionally kill bishops and priests. Did finding dead bodies in the churches motivate or encouraged the killings of those who were not able to protect them or those who were seen to be traitors and agents of the Hutu-killing machinery? These are questions that may not find answers in this life.

The most advanced reasons for discrediting and sometimes demonizing the Rwandan church and especially the Roman Catholic Church is the close relationships that senior clergy men had with the former government accused of planning and executing the genocide. It was known that before the genocide, some bishops and denominational leaders were very close to the Hutu regime. The Catholic archbishop of Kigali, Dr. Vincent Nsengiyumva, served on a committee of senior members of the ruling party MNND until 1990. He later was an official confessor to the president's wife, Agatha Habyarimana, who is accused of being one of the masterminds of the genocide.

Those who see the assassination of members of the Rwandan clergy as political assassination not as persecution and martyrdom use this close tie between the church and the state. However, the estimated number of "about 320 priests, nuns, and seminaries died in the genocide" (Walsh 2004) does not support this line of thoughts because most of them were lower level clergy that probably had no direct contact with political leaders. Probably some of these priests and nuns did not have any voice in who among their leaders would serve on government committees or commissions. The revenge should have been limited to top church leaders, not village and parish priests and nuns.

The paradox of the close relationships between the government and the church of Rwanda continue to defy the minds of church historians even today, sixteen years after the genocide. A close observation of the current relationship between the Rwandan government, the ruling party, and the bishops of the Anglican Church show some similarities or even deeper relationships than those that existed between the Hutu government and the Roman Catholic Church during the years leading to the genocide. Phillip Cantrell observes that "the Anglican Church leaders of Rwanda have elicited great support from wider evangelical community in America, even while taking part in the Rwandan Patriotic Front's (RPF) campaign to confirm its legitimacy by obfuscating Rwanda's, and its own, complex history.… Moreover, the churches' relationship to Kagame's regime has disturbing parallels to the Catholic, and Protestant church's relationship to the pre-genocide government" (Cantrell 2007, 334–35).

In a country where politicians are not openly anti-Christian and in fact profess to be Christians, the temptation of the top leaders of the church to be too close to the regime is a reality. On the other hand, political leaders are aware of the influence the bishops and church leaders have and therefore seek their support by drawing them closer through favors, gifts, positions, and material gains. One hopes that the murdering of Catholic bishops and the embracing of the Anglican bishops will not be construed or interpreted as a maneuver or as a tactic to replace one powerful and influential church and her leadership with another one. Will another period of persecution, martyrdom, and assassination of members of clergy take place again when a new "Pharaoh who does not know Joseph" ascends to power in Rwanda? Will the current church in Rwanda avoid persecution and martyrdom by conforming to political agendas and embracing wholesale the policies of the regime or ruling party? Or will the church of Rwanda, both Catholic and Protestant (including Anglicans) continue to be the voice, the eye, and the soul of the nation through their prophetic and priestly roles while at the same time submitting to the governing authorities and honoring them when they do what is right (Rom 13:1–7; 1 Pet 2:17).

## CONCLUSION

The context, nature, forms, modes, level, intensity, and extent of persecution and martyrdom in Rwanda defy the traditional definitions of persecution and martyrdom. Nowhere in the history of the church in Africa were such a large number of bishops, priests, pastors, nuns, and lay leaders killed intentionally and in many cases tortured, persecuted, and murdered by members of their congregations who professed to be Christians.

Was the killing of bishops, pastors, priests, and nuns considered normal just like the rest of the killings of innocent Hutu civilians due to vengeful Tutsi who were overcome by the grief of the loss of their loved ones in the hands of Hutu killers? Or was the killing of the Hutu clergymen a persecution against the church that had been seen as an ally of the Hutu government that committed the genocide? Was the persecution or martyrdom of these bishops and priests a way of getting rid of potential opposing voices of Hutu bishops in order to install a different church leadership of Tutsi bishops to be allies of the Tutsi regime just as Hutu bishops were to the Hutu regime? Timothy Longman observed that in postgenocide Rwanda, "the RPF-dominated government has been careful to prevent an independent civil society from re-emerging. The government has even intervened in the selection of church leaders" (1999, 354).

Were some of these bishops killed because of their convictions and because they called the regimes to account for threatening the people? Did some of the bishops and priests die because of the messages they preached or because of what they said or failed to say? Persecution and martyrdom in Africa is taking on a new image and a new definition. Political assassination, mysterious deaths, disappearance, intimidations, forced exile, false accusations, criminalizing, dehumanizing, and demonizing—all these are being used to persecute the leaders of the African church. And the persecutor is from within the church—a brother and a sister in Christ!

## QUESTIONS FOR REFLECTION

1. How does Musekura define martyrs in the Rwandan context of genocide? What influence did their faith and Christian witness (including ethical behavior) have on their being persecuted?
2. Martyrdom in Rwanda happened in a so-called Christian society. Musekura says that perpetrators were not trying to make people deny their faith. Why then were these Christian leaders persecuted and killed and how can they be defined as martyrs?
3. Musekura writes that since 1994 several Roman Catholic clergy have been killed by the RPF. How can we help to prevent yesterday's victims to become today's perpetrators? What active and positive role can the international Christian community play, serving with the local Christian community in this context?

## REFERENCES

Amnesty International. 1994. *Rwanda: Cases for Appeals.* November 1:10.

Associated Press. 1994. Thirteen Rwandan clergymen slain by rebels. *Los Angeles Times,* June 9. http://articles.latimes.com/1994–06-09/news/mn-2199_1_rebel-radio.

Cantrell, P. A. 2007. The Anglican Church of Rwanda: Domestic agendas and international linkages. *Journal of Modern African Studies* 45: 334–35.

Karabayinga, J., and C. Mwambali. 2008. A list of clergymembers killed in Rwanda 1994–1998. *World News Journal.* June 13. http://africannewsalaysis.blogspot.com/2008/06/list-of-clergymembers-killed-in-rwanda.

Longman, T. 1999. State, civil society, and genocide in Rwanda. In *State, conflict and democracy in Africa,* ed. R. A. Joseph. Boulder, CO: Lynne Rienner.

Omaar, R., and A. de Waal. 1994. Rwanda: Who is killing; who is dying; what is to be done—A discussion paper. *African Rights* (May), 14.

Walsh, D. 2004. The long road to redemption: How did Catholic priests in Rwanda end up in prison on murder charges? An Irish missionary priest talks to Declan Walsh about the legacy of genocide. *The Irish Times.* July 17. http://www.highbeam.com/doc/1P2-24752823.html.

**Célestin Musekura** is the president and founder of African Leadership and Reconciliation Ministries (www.alarm-inc.org). He is an ordained Baptist minister who was born and raised in Rwanda. Musekura is the author of *An Assessment of Contemporary Models of Forgiveness* (Lang, 2010), a contributor to the *Africa Bible Commentary: A One-volume Commentary Written by 70 African Scholars* (Zondervan, 2010) and a coauthor of *Forgiving as We've Been Forgiven* (InterVarsity Press, 2010).

# CHAPTER 33

# GOD AND RED CAESAR

## Church and State Relations in Contemporary China
*Xiqiu "Bob" Fu*

For many modern China church observers in the West, one of the most difficult questions is not about whether China has religious persecution but how and why the persecution exists. On the one hand, it is reported that a Western evangelist was able to preach to ten thousand people at a megachurch located about 120 miles south of Beijing in 2009 (*Christian Post* 2009). On the other hand, in May 2011 the Beijing government seemed determined to crush a one-thousand-member congregation, the Beijing Shouwang Church (Jacobs 2011). Are these cases happening because of different locality or different timing administered by different Party cadres, or is there a pattern of church-state relations that leads to what has been seen? This short essay attempts to use the angle of the broad scope of church-state relationship in modern China to explain why the conflicts between the two are inevitable and how they happen. The author will then state a few future options to address how the situation might develop for Christian churches in China.

Ever since the first group of Nestorian Christian missionaries was sent to China in AD 635, the conflicts and clashes between church and state authorities in China have almost never ceased.[1] The renowned modern Chinese church historian Jonathan Chao discovered that the traditional relationship of church and state in China has always been one of supremacy of the state over religion (Chao 1989, 8).

Chinese religious history after 1950 is broadly seen as "tightly intertwined with the theme of state and Communist Party control, interference, and repression" (Bays 2004, 34). The pattern of state supremacy and official orthodoxy persists in China under a Communist totalitarian state. The church must operate under the religious policies of the Chinese Communist Party (CCP) and under the legal ordinances of the state. The state has its own

---

1     In the history of Christianity in China there have been three brief periods of time when church and state enjoyed relative harmony. The Nestorians experienced broad acceptance in China for 210 years until being totally wiped out in AD 845 after the heavy persecution against Buddhism by the Confucianists in political power during the Tang Dynasty (618–907). The second peaceful period happened when the Jesuit missionary Matteo Ricci (1552–1600) moved into China in the late sixteenth century, after which Catholicism flourished for nearly a hundred years. And the last short period of harmony occurred when the Republic of China was established by Sun Yat-sen's revolutionaries (1911) until the CCP took power in mainland China in 1949. (See Chao 1999, 10–17.)

official orthodoxy; namely, Marxism, Leninism, and the Thought of Mao (after the fifteenth CCP congress, the Thought of Deng Xiaoping and Jiang Zemin Theory were added to it), which the Party seeks to propagate. All other ideologies and beliefs are considered heterodox (Kindopp 2004, 12).

World religions like Christianity, Catholicism, Buddhism, Taoism, and Islam are considered "heterodox" in relation to Marxist "orthodoxy." Yet they are allowed to conduct their religious activities so long as such activities are under the supervision and control of the state. The apparatuses of control include the United Front Work Department of the Party, the Religious Affairs Bureau of the state, and "patriotic religious organizations." Church activities that are conducted within this sphere of control are called "normal religious activities" and are given legal status. Only eight major patriotic religious organizations are allowed to operate legally under the CCP's control.[2]

Religious activities carried out outside of state control, that is, outside the patriotic organizations, are not only considered heterodox in ideology, but also "illegal religious activities," and hence are subject to prosecution, which can be seen as a form of legalized persecution. Protestant house churches and pro-Vatican unofficial Catholic churches that refuse to register with the state (and hence conduct their activities outside the Three-Self Patriotic Movement (TSPM) and China Catholic Patriotic Association (CCPA) come under this category of "illegitimate religious activities." Some of the organized house churches that are active in evangelistic expansion are labeled as "cultic groups," and these have become the state's primary target of attack.[3]

> Therefore we ourselves boast about you in the churches of God for your steadfastness and faith in all your persecutions and in the afflictions that you are enduring. This is evidence of the righteous judgment of God, that you may be considered worthy of the kingdom of God, for which you are also suffering.
> 2 Thessalonians 1:4–5

## CHINA'S RELIGIOUS POLICY

Although the constitution of China declares that citizens of China shall enjoy freedom of religious belief,[4] its actual religious policy as revealed in state ordinances and secret documents and its implementation of these policies show its true intention: administrative control over all religious activities. Protestantism is a particular target because of its rapid expansion, which includes the work of itinerant evangelists and the founding of house

---

2    These are: China Daoist Association, Buddhist Association of China, Three-Self Patriotic Movement Committee for the Protestant Churches of China, National Christian Conference of China, Chinese Patriotic Catholic Association, Chinese Catholic Bishops College, National Administrative Commission of the Chinese Catholic Church, and Islamic Association of China. For more about this issue, see Leung (2005, 11).

3    A great deal has been written about religious persecution in the People's Republic of China (PRC), including material published by Amnesty International (1992); Richard C. Bush Jr. (1970); Ho Kai-lin (1990).

4    Article 36 of the constitution of the PRC states: "Citizens of the People's Republic of China enjoy freedom of religious belief. No state organization, public organization, or individual may compel citizens to believe in, or not to believe in, any religion; nor may they discriminate against citizens who believe in, or do not believe in, any religion. The state protects normal religious activities. No one may make use of religion to engage in activities that disrupt public order, impair the health of citizens, or interfere with the educational system of the state. Religious bodies and religious affairs are not subject to any foreign domination." Translated from *Constitution of the People's Republic of China* (1982).

churches throughout the country, two "hilltops" that the Chinese government cannot yet conquer (Fu 2003, 10). The constitutional guarantee of its citizens' religious freedom has degenerated into manipulative rhetoric (Newman 1991, 112).

## "DOCTRINAL ADAPTATION WITH SOCIALISM": THE PLACE OF THE PATRIOTIC CHURCH AND THE PLACE OF HOUSE CHURCHES

In 1990, President Jiang Zemin launched a new campaign on managing religions. One of the three basic strategies on religion is to "make religion adaptable with socialism."[5] While Chinese national religious affairs leaders maintain that this adaptation does not necessitate the changing of fundamental beliefs, one must wonder how religion can be adapted to a philosophy that, at its core, holds that "Marxism is incompatible with any theistic worldview"[6] and will lead to the eventual demise of all religions. Regarding the goal of the campaign, CCP scholar Luo Shuze said:

> By religion adapting itself to the socialist society, we mean that … it is necessary, through the patriotic religious groups and personages, to expound and interpret the religious doctrine and canon in such a way as to be in the interests of socialism, and inspire and guide the religious believers gradually to modify their negative ways detrimental to national development and social progress. (1996)

In response to the political call, the so-called "construction of ideologies" movement was launched by the officially sanctioned organizations TSPM and China Christian Council (CCC) in 1998. The Chinese Christians are asked to remove "conservative and negative factors" that are deemed "cynical, illiberal, irrational, and anti-humanity theological ideologies"(Lao 2004, 133). Bishop Ding Guangxun was specifically praised for his contribution of combining "Christian belief with reality to form a theory that is both rational and transcendent"(135). Ding's distinctive theology of "justification by love" instead of "justification by faith" and assimilation of the Chinese "human nature is good" ideology as well as the suggestion of God's acceptance of some CCP martyrs into heaven are all part of the encouraging the construction theology in this movement (136–37).[7] This is one of the fundamental elements of conflict between the independent church and the government using the TSPM/CCC for control (Lambert 1991, 281).

---

5     The other two initiatives are: (1) wholly and correctly implement religious freedom policy; (2) use legal means to strengthen administration of religious affairs. (See Xiaowen 2000, 4–9.)

6     Britsch, supra note 7 (Cox 372). In addition, the white paper states: "Religion should be adapted to the society in which it is prevalent. This is a universal law for the existence and development of religion. Now the Chinese people are building China into a modern socialist country with Chinese characteristics. The Chinese government advocates that religion should adapt to this reality."

7     Accordingly, Ding's book entitled *Collected Works of Ding Guangxun* was published in 1998 and distributed within the TSPM churches and seminaries as the textbook for this theological adaptation construction movement. In one of the articles, Ding uses a rhetorical question asking how our loving God could be so narrowminded and intolerant that CCP's martyred heroes like comrades Lei Feng and Zhang Side who have done so many good deeds for the people would end up in Hell. (See Ting 2004, 621.)

## LEGALIZED PERSECUTION BY CRIMINALIZING RELIGIOUS ACTIVITIES: REGISTRATION OR THE "EVIL CULT" CHARGE

Within the above framework of church and state relations and China's religious policy, the only legitimate sphere for Christian activities is the sphere of the Three-Self Patriotic Movement[8] as one of the "patriotic organizations." Independent churches that have developed through itinerant evangelism or spontaneous growth of the church are considered illegal.

According to Spiegel, the primary method used by the Chinese government to exercise control over religion is a registration process administered by the State Council's Religious Affairs Bureau (RAB) through which the government "monitors membership in religious organizations, locations of meetings, religious training, selection of clergy, publication of religious materials, and funding for religious activities" (Spiegel 1997, 1).

Usually when a house church registers with the RAB, it must join the TSPM. Since 1999, growing out of its concern about the emergence of the Falun Gong sect[9] the Chinese government has used a new tactic against independent religious believers and organizations in the name of cracking down on "evil cults." The People's Congress and the People's Supreme Court as well the People's Supreme Procurate have passed new interpretations, definitions, and procedures on arresting, prosecuting, indicting, and sentencing "evil cult" leaders and practitioners.

China's new tactic of cracking down on so-called "evil cults" is in great part a smokescreen for persecuting believers whose only "crime" is to keep their distance from government-controlled religion (Shixiong and Fu 2002, 4). This tactic of labeling religious groups as "evil cults," and thus punishing them under the criminal code if they refuse to register (or are unable to register even if they attempt to do so (Peng 2009, 380) was increasingly employed in the late 1990s. It enabled government spokespersons to maintain the useful fiction that arrested and jailed believers are not falling foul of restrictive religious laws, but are mere criminals disrupting public and social order laws (380).

## A HARMONIOUS FUTURE

The pattern of church-state relations in both traditional and modern China can be summarized as the state authority having supreme dominance over the church. As professor Daniel H. Bays states:

> Looking back over a thousand years of Chinese history, one finds little new about today's pattern of relations between the state and religion in China. Government

---

8        Three-Self means "self-supporting, self-propagating, and self-governing." The TSPM was established after the outbreak of the Korean War in 1951. For a brief history of the TSPM and the CCC, see Chao (1989, 39–43).

9        Falun Gong (also called Falun Dafa) is a quasireligious sect founded in China by Li Hongzhi in 1992. Falun Gong practitioners responded to critics through peaceful protests, attempting to address perceived unfair media treatment. In April 1999, after one such protest in Tianjin, some ten thousand practitioners gathered at Zhongnanhai, the residence compound of China's leaders, in silent protest. In July 1999, the Chinese Communist Party (CCP) banned Falun Gong and began a nationwide crackdown and multifaceted propaganda campaign against the practice; in October 1999 it declared Falun Gong an "evil cult."

registration and monitoring of religious activities, although irregularly exercised, has been a constant reality of organized religious life in both traditional and modern times. (Bays 2004, 25)

This pattern of state dominance is the primary source of conflict between church and state in contemporary China. Through both religious policy and practice, the CCP has established a systematic legal and structural mechanism both inside and outside the church in order to exercise its administrative control over religious bodies. By overstepping its boundaries of authority, the Chinese government has severely impaired the freedom of religion guaranteed by both China's own constitution and international norms (Peerenboom 2005, 71, 100–103).

Having said this, besides the option of continuing the current escalating clashes and conflicts between church and state in China, if the Chinese CCP leaders are serious about the so-called "harmonious society building," the author lists three possible options for the CCP's leaders' consideration:

Option 1: "Neutralized Harmony Model." An example of this model is seen in how the Falun Gong spiritual movement has been persecuted and crushed in China.[10] The Chinese government can choose to declare all the unofficial churches including Catholic churches as "evil cult" organizations. Then ban them and jail anyone who defies the edict.

Option 2: "Forced Merger Harmony Model." The Chinese government can choose to execute a policy by demanding all the unofficial churches "either to join the official church or to die."

Option 3: "Principled Pluralism Harmony Model." The Chinese government can choose to treat both official and unofficial churches as well as other religious institutions equally, according to the legal standard of registration in the government social organization management system. All the churches will be invited to register voluntarily as equal religious entities. In order to establish this model, the government has to dissolve both the State Administration for Religious Affairs (SARA), its religious affairs bureaus in local levels, and disavow its protective role for the official patriotic associations.

Given what has happened in the history of the church both in China and the world, the price will be too big for China to continue the current model and the first two models listed above. We certainly pray the Chinese government will make wise decisions by considering the third option. This essay closes with a quote from the recent petition on religious freedom to China's National People's Congress submitted by a group of Chinese house church leaders They quote a common slogan of the current leadership to illustrate this appeal:

> We hope that by setting up a special investigation commission, the government will be able to handle the Shouwang incident in a rational and wise manner on the basis of the principles of "putting people first and ruling the country by law" and in the gracious spirit of serving the citizens, so as to avoid the escalation of the conflict between state and church. (Jacobs 2011)

---

10    Falun Gong at http://en.wikipedia.org/wiki/Falun_Gong.

## QUESTIONS FOR REFLECTION

1. What, according to Fu's analysis, are the main methods that China's authorities use to try to control the burgeoning house church movement? How successful are they?

2. Like Elliot documents about Russia, Fu shows that repression and persecution in China also long predate Communism. What are the implications of this for China's Christians today?

3. With some convincing documentation, Fu draws a stark contrast between the TSPM and the large house church movement. How might Fu's personal experiences have contributed to his views? Are there other views on the relationship between these two entities? Is there the possibility of healthy relationships between members of the two? How should foreign Christians relate to these two entities?

## REFERENCES

Amnesty International. 1992. *Freedom of religion in China*. Washington, DC: Human Rights Watch, Asia Watch Committee.

Bays, D. H. 1989. *Church and state in socialist China, 1949–1988*. London: Oxford Center for Mission Studies.

———. 2004. A tradition of state dominance. In *God and Caesar in China: Policy implications of church-state tensions*, ed. J. Kindopp and C. L. Hamrin, 25–34. Washington, DC: Brookings Institution.

Britsch, R. L. 1995. The current legal status of Christianity in China. *BYU Legal Revue*: 347.

Bush, R. C., Jr. 1970. *Religion in Communist China*. Nashville, TN: Abingdon.

Chao, J., ed. 1989. *The China mission handbook: A portrait of China and its church*. Hong Kong: Chinese Church Research Center.

Chao, J. 1999. The gospel and culture in Chinese history. In *Chinese intellectuals and the gospel*, ed. S. Ling and S. Bieler. 10–17. Phillipsburg, NJ: P and R Publishing.

*Christian Post*. 2009. Franklin Graham preaches to 10,000 at China megachurch. October 19. http://www.christianpost.com/news/franklin-graham-preaches-to-10-000-at-chinese-megachurch-41488.

*Constitution of the People's Republic of China*. 1982. Foreign Language Press. http://english. people.com.cn/constitution/constitution.html.

Cox, L. 2007. Freedom of religion in China. *Asian-Pacific Law and Policy Journal* 8, no. 2: 372.

Fu, X. 2003. Religion and public security in China, 1999–2002. *Chinese Law and Government* 36 (March–April): 10.

Information Office of the State Council of the PRC. 1997. *White Paper: Freedom of religious belief in China.* http://www.fmprc.gov.cn/ce/ceun/eng/zt/dqwt/t28618.htm.

Jacobs, A. 2011. Chinese Christians rally around underground church. *New York Times.* May 12. http://www.nytimes.com/2011/05/13/world/asia/13china.html.

Kai-lin, H. 1990. *Laogaiying zhong de taianju erleu* [Children of God in the labor camp]. Taipei: Guangqi Press.

Kindopp, J. 2004. Fragmented yet defiant: Protestant resilience under Chinese Communist Party rule. In *God and Caesar in China: Policy implications of church-state tensions*, eds. J. Kindopp and C. L. Hamrin, 12. Washington, DC: Brookings Institution.

Lambert, T. 1991. *The resurrection of the Chinese church.* Littleton, CO: OMF Books.

Leung, B. 2005. *China's religious freedom policy: The art of managing religious activity.* Hong Kong: Lingnan University.

Luo, S. 1996. Some hot issues in our work on religion. In *Theoretical Journal of the Chinese Communist Party.* Reprinted in *Spiegel*, supra note 9, app. I.

Luo, W. 2004. *Christianity in China.* Trans. Zhu Chengming. Beijing: China Intercontinental Press.

Newman, J. 1991. *On religious freedom.* Ottawa: University of Ottawa Press.

Peerenboom, R. 2005. Assessing human rights in China: Why the double standard? *Cornell International Law Journal* 38 (2005): 71, 100–103.

Peng, L., ed. 2009. Chu xiabai, jiating jiaohui mianlin de hefa xing wenti [The issue of legitimacy of house churches]. In *Zhongguo Jidujiao jiating jiaohui wenti yanjiu* [Chinese Christian house church issues studies]. Beijing: Pacific Social Science Institute.

Shixiong, L., and X. Fu, eds. 2002. *Religion and national security in China: Secret documents from China's security sector.* Bartlesville: VOM Publishing.

Spiegel, M. 1997. *China: State control of religion.* Human Rights Watch.

Ting, K. H. 2004. *God is love: Collected writings of Bishop K. H. Ting.* Colorado Springs, CO: Cook Communications Ministries International.

Xiaowen, Y. 2000. Shiji zhijiao zhongjiao gongchuo de Sikao [Reflections on the religious work at the change of millenium]. *Zhongguo Zhongjiao* [Religion in China] 20, no. 1: 4–9.

## WEBSITES FOR FURTHER ACADEMIC AND CHINESE GOVERNMENT POLICY READINGS:

Berkley Center for Religion, Peace and World Affairs: Religion in China and the United States: http://berkleycenter.georgetown.edu/projects/religion-in-china-and-the-united-states

CECC: http://www.cecc.gov

Center on Religion and Chinese Society at Purdue University: http://www.purdue.edu/crcs

ChinaAid: www.ChinaAid.org; www.MonitorChina.org

Holy Mountain Institute: http://shengshan.org (Chinese)

Pew Forum: Religion in China: http://pewforum.org/PublicationPage.aspx?id=971

Pushi Institute for Social Science: http://www.pacilution.com (Chinese)

USCIRF: http://www.uscirf.gov

## CHINESE GOVERNMENT RELIGIOUS POLICY:

http://english.people.com.cn/92824/92845/92875/6442436.html

http://www.chinadaily.com.cn/english/doc/2004-12/20/content_401602.htm

**Xiqiu "Bob" Fu** is president of China Aid Association, which he founded in 2002 to promote religious freedom in China and raise worldwide awareness of the ongoing persecution of Chinese Christians. Bob was a student leader of the 1989 Tiananmen Square democracy movement in Beijing before becoming a Christian. Considered a threat to the government for leading a house church, Bob and his wife, Heidi, were imprisoned for two months before escaping in 1996 and accepted as refugees to the USA in 1997.

# CHAPTER 34

---

# CHINA

## A Case Study
*G. Wright Doyle*

## HISTORICAL BACKGROUND

Chinese governments have restricted the practice of religion since the dawn of recorded history (Poceski 2009, 258). Though alternative faiths have usually been tolerated, there has always been only one "orthodox" worldview. In today's officially atheistic China, the state-sanctioned orthodoxy is Communism or "socialism with Chinese characteristics."

At all times, the central government has claimed supreme, total, and exclusive authority over its citizens with various freedoms granted as privileges, not rights. Both the bodies and property of China's citizens have been considered to be at the disposal of the state. China's rulers have assumed comprehensive sovereignty over all of life, including religion, with the brief exception of the Republican era (1911–49), and even then churches and Christian schools had to register with the government and abide by its regulations (such as voluntary, not mandatory chapel services). Though the extent of government interference has varied widely over the centuries, the prerogative of officials to control the practice of religion has never been in question (Kindopp and Hamrin 2004, 1–24). Furthermore, some religious groups have been denied toleration, and have been labeled "cults" [literally, "evil teachings"], meaning not so much that they deviate from acknowledged norms as defined within the major faiths (such as Buddhism, Daoism, Confucianism, Islam, or Christianity) but that they pose a risk to the security of the regime and a threat to social order. On those grounds, active—and often violent—persecution by the government has been employed to suppress these movements, some of which have, indeed, been revolutionary (Poceski 2009, 183–85).

## RELIGIOUS PERSECUTION IN THE PAST

At various times, Daoist and Buddhist monasteries and their properties have been expropriated by the state, depending upon the religious leanings of the current emperor. During the Great Cultural Revolution (1966–76), adherents of the five officially recognized religions, as well as devotees of popular religion, were actively persecuted: churches and temples were closed; clergy were imprisoned or secularized; and religious practices were completely forbidden (Charbonnier 2002, 425–43; Lambert 1994, 18–25).

Though tolerated at times, Christianity has encountered stiff opposition for much of its history in China. Missionaries of the Syrian Church of the East (sometimes called

"Nestorians") were welcomed when they first appeared in China, and even patronized by the Emperor, but their followers were later persecuted during the Tang dynasty, when Buddhists were favored (Moffett 1998, 288–95), and again when the Buddhists were also attacked (Moffett 1998, 302–4; Charbonnier 2002, 63–67). During the Mongol (Yuan) dynasty, both the Church of the East and the first Roman Catholic missionaries received a warm reception (Charbonnier 2002, 69–83).

When it was discovered that the Jesuits possessed useful technical skills and modern equipment, they were admitted even into the Forbidden City and allowed to propagate their faith. Thousands responded to them and to the Franciscans and Dominicans who followed them, but all were later proscribed as a result of the "Rites Controversy." The Pope's intervention in a dispute about whether Confucian rites venerating ancestors and the emperor would be allowed for Chinese Roman Catholics was utterly rejected by the emperor as a completely illegitimate interference in Chinese domestic affairs and a dangerous questioning of practices considered essential to social stability. Beginning in 1706, foreign Roman Catholic priests and then Chinese converts suffered intense persecution (Broomhall 2005, 1.19–25; Charbonnier 2002; Moffett 2005; Poceski 2009, 216–22).

Protestants fell under this ban and met with strong opposition when they tried to enter China in the early nineteenth century. Only after the First Opium War concluded in 1842 did they benefit from treaty provisions guaranteeing them freedom of travel and residence in China, first in a few designated ports and then, after several more wars and treaties, throughout the land. Even though protected by law, however, they ran into fierce local opposition from the local officials, who often instigated mob violence against them (Broomhall 2005, 2.12–13, 32–55, and often; Moffett 2005, 285–98).

There were several reasons for this hostility: First and foremost, Western missionaries and their followers were inescapably connected in the popular mind with the foreign powers which continued to humiliate and even occupy China (Poceski 2009, 224). Perhaps most repugnant of all was the natural association of foreign missionaries with the hated opium trade, which was forced upon China by treaties negotiated under duress by Western gunboats and bayonets, especially when some of them served as interpreters for the victorious foreigners (though they invariably tried to soften treaty provisions).

Western missionaries were also deemed socially dangerous because they brought a new religion, one that differed fundamentally from the Confucian worldview and which represented a challenge also to Buddhism, Daoism, and Chinese popular religion. In particular, Protestants generally taught that "worship" of ancestors constituted idolatry (though Confucianists deemed these rituals only veneration); this undermined the very foundation of Chinese notions of filial piety, a central support of the entire society. Educated officials also perceived that Confucian humanism was directly opposed to Christian theism.

Roman Catholics were the objects of special resentment because, under treaty provisions, their converts were exempt from some paying temple taxes and from prosecution by local magistrates; naturally, this exemption was liable to abuse by believers with unscrupulous motives. Nor did the officials appreciate the official governmental rank afforded to Roman Catholic bishops (Moffett 2005, 470, 472).

The climactic expression of Chinese anti-Christian hostility was the Boxer Rebellion (1899–1901) in which thousands of Chinese believers and hundreds of foreign missionaries were killed and foreign diplomats were besieged in Beijing. Military forces from eight nations lifted the siege and some of them wreaked havoc in the capital, deepening resentment against all things foreign (Charbonnier 2002, 334–35; Moffett 2005, 484–87).

The imperial system and the Confucianism which upheld it were repudiated in the Republican era, when Christians generally enjoyed freedom but were harshly attacked by intellectuals, some of whom later became prominent in the Communist Party (Charbonnier 2002, 384–87).

Beginning in the 1930s, Communists occasionally inflicted harm upon Christians; this tendency towards suppression emerged full-blown after the establishment of the People's Republic in 1949.

Since then, both Roman Catholic and Protestant Christians have experienced varying degrees of pressure, discrimination, legal limitations, and outright persecution. The reasons adduced have included charges that Christians, and the missionaries who taught them until they were forced to leave in the early 1950s, were (or are) agents of foreign governments (Poceski 2009, 262–63); purveyors of foreign ideas inimical to both Chinese culture and/or Communist doctrine; and potential instigators of organized resistance to the government.

Since the formation in the 1950s of the official "patriotic" Protestant and Roman Catholic bodies, those outside the system have been under constant pressure to join them or cease practice of the faith. Refusal to do so has often brought harsh reprisals, including arrest, fines, beating, torture, and even death. Meetings have been raided and leaders detained; milder treatment has included frequent visits for questioning or expropriation of property by security officials. Outstanding Protestant leaders, like Wang Mingdao, Allen Yuan (Yuan Xiangchen), Watchman Nee (Ni Tuosheng), and Samuel Lamb (Lin Xiangao) were subjected in the Mao era to accusation, interrogation, imprisonment, and harsh treatment (Aikman 2003; Anderson 1991; Harvey 2002; Kindopp and Hamrin 2004, 122–48; Lee 2001; Xi 2010), as were thousands of ordinary believers. For a while during and after the Cultural Revolution (1966–76) many Western observers believed that Christianity in China had been exterminated.

Beginning in 1979 under Deng Xiaoping's policy of opening up to the outside world, however, reports began to filter out, then grow to a flood, of a vast expansion of Christianity in China. This growth has only increased since the late 1980s, extending from the rural areas to the cities and from marginal groups to prominent elites (Aikman 2003; Lambert 1994; 1999; Lawrence 1985; Wallis 1986). Despite danger and great difficulty, Christians have continued to pray, to preach, and to evangelize. Miracles of healing and deliverance from danger emboldened them and awed their oppressors, as did the patient, joyful endurance of those who suffered terribly for their faith. Persecution became the catalyst for unprecedented growth in numbers and dedication.

Older house church leaders remember how the TSPM actively participated in the attacks upon those who would not join the official body (Harvey 2002) or held to theological differences. Even more recently, evangelical students and faculty were silenced or expelled from the Jinling Theological Seminary in Nanjing during Bishop K. H. Ting's "Theological Reconstruction" campaign begun in 1998 (Yamamori and Chan 2000; Xi 2010, 210). In general, however, the majority of local TSPM and "house" churches have enjoyed considerable harmony, and even cooperation in many places. Tensions were lessened greatly when the True Jesus Church and the Little Flock were "removed from the list of illegal organizations … [and] guaranteed a degree of recognition as distinct groups within the Three-Self structure" (Xi 2010, 211).[1]

## PRESENT SITUATION

Under the fundamental premise of the "leadership" (supremacy) of the Communist Party, the Chinese constitution guarantees freedom of religious belief (though not of practice) and five organized world religions are recognized: Buddhism, Daoism, Islam, Roman Catholicism, and Protestant Christianity. Each has its own "patriotic" association, which is under the control of the Communist Party and the government.

Regulations promulgated in 1994 and 2004 detail the current boundaries of legal religious practice in China (Burklin 2005, 219–39). Within specific limitations, believers within these associations may meet for worship and teaching; engage in religious education of adults; administer sacraments; educate, ordain, and support their clergy; and participate in certain charitable activities. The regulations have allowed, for example, the Protestant Amity Foundation press to print and distribute millions of Bibles in Chinese. Only religious venues may sell such "religious" materials as Scriptures and hymnals. But public and private bookstores in cities around the country sell a variety of other materials on religious topics published in China with legitimate ISBNs.

Restrictions on practice include: the "three designates" (church activities may only be held at designated places and times, and by leaders; e.g., those trained in China); a ban on evangelism outside the premises of the church; unauthorized receipt of resources including money or teaching from Christians outside of China; criticism of the government or of socialism, among other actions. Within these boundaries, Christians in official churches enjoy widening freedom. To some degree, there is even limited legal protection for recognized congregations; some have brought suits against local officials for expropriating property, for instance.

Technically, these rules outlaw all unauthorized religious activity, which would include meetings, etc., by unregistered religious groups including Protestant house churches and members of Roman Catholic groups who, out of loyalty to the Pope, refuse to participate in the

---

1        Such as the revolts of the Daoist Yellow Turbans, the Buddhist White Lotus Society, and the semi-Christian Taiping Rebellion in the nineteenth century; as well as the role of Christians in the overthrow of Communist regimes in Eastern Europe in the late twentieth century.

Catholic Patriotic Association. Since about 2005, and as of early February 2012, even these groups have, however, been allowed to carry on almost all normal functions with relative impunity, although greatly hampered by lack of access to bank accounts and difficulties renting or buying property. They have operated openly, and have even gained a substantial presence on the Internet. With a few rare exceptions, there has been no "persecution" of Christians for Christian beliefs or practices—despite widespread perception to the contrary in the Western media.

Academic study of religion, including Christianity, has flourished in recent years in universities where there are more than thirty institutes for the study of religion, including Christianity alone, as well as in government think tanks. Scholarly conferences about Christianity, even about religion and politics or law, are convened, and journals and books are regularly published.

According to state regulations (Burklin 2005, 203–07), unless they have been formally invited by one of the official church bodies, foreign Christians are not allowed to propagate their faith in China in any public way. They may not address Christian meetings, other than those for expatriates which must be led by designated Chinese pastors; train leaders; "develop followers, … engage in other missionary activities" (206); donate money to Christian groups; publish or distribute literature; or carry out evangelism. Those who violate these provisions may be summarily expelled from the country and forbidden to return for several years. The sporadic enforcement of these rules does not mean that the religious activity of foreigners is either unknown or acceptable to the government, which tolerates them temporarily for reasons of expediency. In fact, a number of foreigners have been ordered to leave China in the past few years because they violated these regulations.

> Yet if anyone suffers as a Christian, let him not be ashamed, but let him glorify God in that name. For it is time for judgment to begin at the household of God; and if it begins with us, what will be the outcome for those who do not obey the gospel of God? *1 Peter 4:16–17*

Hundreds, perhaps thousands, of foreign Christians such as teachers, charitable workers, and business people, however, have been allowed to live in China and quietly testify to their faith. Some enrolled in Chinese language study have spent much of their time evangelizing university students without very much government intervention.

Such widespread freedom has led some foreign observers to state flatly that Christians in China virtually have total freedom to practice and propagate their faith. They point especially to the wide latitude given the official Roman Catholic and Protestant bodies and to foreigners who work with them, and some even assert that house church believers and leaders are punished only when they break the law (76–77). Others speak of the "myth" of persecution of Christians in China, admitting its existence but calling it "sporadic and occasional" (Falkenstine 2008, 78).

Recent exceptions to this unofficial practice of toleration have involved large congregations, especially those renting or owning buildings, and particularly the Shouwang Church in Beijing, which tried to buy property; large congregations with a very public presence (like a loudspeaker broadcasting the worship service into the street); large churches or "networks" engaging in training involving leaders from elsewhere, especially across provincial lines; smaller networks with influence in a major city; Christian groups with extensive connections to foreigners, especially Americans; Christian attorneys engaging in human-rights advocacy, especially when they represent Falun Gong practitioners, Tibetans, or civil rights activists, and particularly when they appear to have relations with foreign governments. (More than two hundred Chinese Christians were probably prohibited from attending the Lausanne Congress in Cape Town for a variety of reasons, including some cited above.)

Furthermore, all unregistered churches, and especially millenarian and messianic sects, which remind the government of previous religion-inspired uprisings, are under constant government surveillance and suspicion.

Religious groups additionally suffer from government unfriendliness towards any growth of civil society, which has produced increasing restrictions on NGOs, including Christian charities and churches, since 2005. On the local level, individual congregations frequently face harassment by corrupt officials seeking bribes or valuable property. Job and employment discrimination in state institutions, including universities, is common; openly proclaiming one's Christian allegiance can be a barrier to advancement or even a cause for being fired. And, of course, no Christian voice is allowed on the state's public radio or television (with the notable exception of two documentaries about a Protestant and a Roman Catholic missionary who made significant contributions to society).

When Western Christians have protested, and especially when they have urged their governments to speak out in support of Chinese Christians, they have been accused of interference in Chinese internal affairs. Indeed, some believe that well-intentioned gestures (such as welcoming Chinese Christians to the White House) and State Department statements or programming by Voice of America, though sometimes perhaps temporarily successful, have generally backfired, for they often are perceived as confirming the suspicion that local Christians are, in fact, subversive tools of anti-Chinese powers.

The situation changed dramatically in April 2011, when the leaders of Shouwang Church, having been denied continued access to the restaurant where they had been meeting, decided to hold worship meetings outdoors in a public place. Repeated attempts to gather resulted in temporary detention of hundreds of church members, house arrest for the leaders, and the threat of criminal action against them. Leaders of other churches elsewhere in China were criminally detained; most seem to have been part of the group that had tried to go to the Lausanne Congress. In May, leaders of twenty house churches around China signed and sent a petition to the National People's Congress, standing with Shouwang Church and asking the central government to review and revise regulations regarding the practice of religion. Foreign Christians living in China have been denied visas to return, and many conferences and meetings with foreigners were cancelled. If continued, this trend, which is part of a larger crackdown on dissenting voices in China, could mark a significant reversal of the freedoms enjoyed by Christians in China in recent years.

Implications for missions: Under these conditions, foreign Christians should probably focus on prayer; the evangelization and training of Chinese living or studying overseas; and the development of a cadre of mature disciples who are fluent in the Chinese language, knowledgeable of Chinese culture, and committed to long-term "faithful presence" in China rather than short-term evangelism.

## QUESTIONS FOR REFLECTION

1. Compare and contrast G. Wright Doyle's description of the historical and current situation for Christians in China with Xiqiu "Bob" Fu's.
2. What, according to Doyle, are the reasons China's authorities have been suspicious of and/or repressive toward missionaries and local Christians throughout history? Were/are some of these reasons avoidable?
3. Doyle's second to last paragraph describes recent disturbing developments and fears that China may in 2011 be backsliding on improvements conceded to Christians in recent years. What might be the reasons for these developments? And how might Chinese Christians respond?
4. Doyle's final paragraph includes recommendations for foreign mission intervention. Reflect on these.

## REFERENCES

Aikman, D. 2003. *Jesus in Beijing: How Christianity is transforming China and changing the global balance of power.* Washington, DC: Regnery.

Anderson, K. 1991. *Bold as a Lamb: Pastor Samuel Lamb and the underground church of China.* Grand Rapids, MI: Zondervan.

Broomhall, A. J. 2005. *The shaping of modern China: Hudson Taylor's life and legacy,* 2 vols. Pasadena, CA: William Carey Library.

Burklin, W. 2005. *Jesus never left China: The rest of the story. The untold story of the church in China now exposed.* Enumclaw, WA: Pleasant Word (a division of WinePress Publishing).

Charbonnier, J. 2002. *Christians in China: AD 600 to 2000.* San Francisco, CA: Ignatius Press.

Falkenstine, M. 2008. *The Chinese puzzle: Putting the pieces together for a deeper understanding of China and her church.* Maitland, FL: Xulon.

Harvey, T. A. 2002. *Acquainted with grief: Wang Mingdao's stand for the persecuted church in China.* Grand Rapids, MI: Brazos.

Kindopp, J., and C. Hamrin, eds. 2004. *God and Caesar in China: Policy implications of church-state tensions.* Washington, DC: Brookings Institution.

Lambert, T. 1994. *The resurrection of the Chinese church*. Wheaton, IL: Harold Shaw Publishers.

_____. 1999. *China's Christian millions: The costly revival*. Grand Rapids, MI: Monarch Books.

Lawrence, C. 1985. *The church in China: How it survives and prospers under Communism*. Minneapolis, MI: Bethany House.

Lee, L. 2001. *A living sacrifice: The life story of Allen Yuan*. Tonbridge, Kent: Sovereign World.

Li, Xinyuan. 2003. *Theological construction—or destruction?: An analysis of the theology of Bishop K. H. Ting (Ding Guangxun)*. Hong Kong: Christian Life Press.

Moffett, S. H. 1998. *A history of Christianity in Asia. Volume I, Beginnings to 1500*. Maryknoll, NY: Orbis Books.

———. 2005. *A history of Christianity in Asia. Volume II, 1500 to 1900*. Maryknoll, NY: Orbis Books.

Poceski, M. 2009. *Introducing Chinese religion*. New York: Routledge.

Wallis, A. 1986. *China miracle: A silent explosion*. Columbia, MI: Cityhill.

Wang, D. 2010. Happy birthday, Chairman! *Gospel Herald*. December 8, 2010. http://www.gospelherald.net/article/opinion/46849/happy-birthday-chairman.htm.

Yamamori, T., and K. Chan. 2000. *Witnesses to power: Stories of God's quiet work in a changing China*. Waynesboro, GA: Paternoster.

**G. Wright Doyle** is director of Global China Center (www.globalchinacenter.org) and general editor of the *Biographical Dictionary of Chinese Christianity* (www.bdcconline.net). Publications include *China: Ancient Culture, Modern Society* (coauthor). He is also director of China Institute (www.chinainst.org).

# CHAPTER 35

# SRI LANKA

## Religions, Ethnicity, and Politics in Relation to Christian Suffering, Persecution, and Martyrdom

*Godfrey Yogarajah and Roshini Wickremesinhe*

"I want them to see Jesus," he says; "If I retaliate, they will not see anything different in me. So I will bear up until the day they see Jesus." The speaker of these words is a pastor serving in a village in the Southern Province of Sri Lanka. With him are his wife and three small children. They live in a small hut with a broken tin roof that lets the rain through during the Monsoon and soaks their few belongings. For the past five years, poverty has been the least of their problems. Their home was stormed by thugs who tossed and broke the few pieces of furniture they owned, the pastor was threatened with death if they did not leave the village, the well from which they drank water was deliberately contaminated to cause sickness, the pastor was publicly humiliated as a beggar by his persecutors. Yet this faithful servant of God refused to leave and continues to preach the gospel in the place where the Lord called him to serve.

## RELIGIOUS DIVERSITY

Sri Lanka is home to 20 million people comprising all of the world's major religions—Buddhism, Hinduism, Islam, and Christianity. The constitution of Sri Lanka accords Buddhism "foremost place" and accordingly, casts upon the state a duty to "protect and foster" Buddhism (1979, Article 9). Introduced to Sri Lanka in 247 BC, Buddhism remains the majority religion (70 percent of the population) and a dominant influence which shapes culture, language, government, and almost every sphere of Sri Lankan life. Christianity was introduced by the Portuguese, Dutch, and British who invaded the country between 1505 and 1948. Although the Christian population has declined since the time of colonial rule and—according to the last national census—remains at 6.89 percent of the population,[1] Christianity is still viewed as a tool of colonialism and a "Western" religion. This negative perception of Christianity, promoted by Buddhist nationalists, is influenced by atrocities and discrimination suffered by the locals under colonial rule. Since the 1990s the country has witnessed an upsurge in anti-Christian sentiments, violence, and actions preventing Christian worship.

---

1    Mostly Roman Catholics with less than 1 percent Protestants.

## ETHNICITY IN RELIGION

While the majority of Sinhalese (who are the main ethnic group) profess Buddhism, the majority of Tamils (who are the largest minority ethnic group) are Hindus. Christianity is the one religion which brings together both ethnic groups, with almost equal numbers of Sinhalese and Tamils professing Christ. In the context of the war fought on ethnic lines, which lasted over twenty years until 2009 and cost the lives of hundreds of thousands of Sri Lankans from both ethnic groups, this uniting factor among the followers of Christ is unique and important in healing wounds and bringing about reconciliation between individuals and communities.

Although religion was never a factor in the war, the colossal damage to property, loss of life, and suffering touched the lives of adherents of every religion. The Tamil Christian community living in the north endured the horrors of war, shelling, bombing, and mass displacement. At the end of the war in May 2009, hundreds of churches in the war-torn areas were destroyed and among the dead were more than ten clergy and pastors and many Christian civilians. Many of the pastors and clergy who lived through the war as well as those who died, chose to stay behind in the war-torn area without fleeing in order to minister to their flock who had no way of escaping. While the war raged on in the north, there were abductions, forced disappearances, and killings reported in other parts of the country. The victims were mostly Tamils, while Sinhalese who expressed dissenting views too were targeted, including journalists, lawyers, and aid workers. For many Christians from both ethnic groups who strongly believed in the biblical principles of justice, equality, and peace, it was a difficult and heartbreaking time to live through, where speaking up was a risk and voices of dissent were silenced.

## POLITICIZING RELIGION

As mentioned earlier in this paper, Buddhism in Sri Lanka influences and shapes all aspects of life, and in recent years the influence of religion in politics has been very conspicuous. The twenty-first-century political leaders recognized religion as a powerful and emotive issue which could win or lose votes. The past decade witnessed the formation of the first Buddhist political party in Sri Lanka, the *Jathika Hela Urumaya* (JHU) (national heritage party), led by a group of Buddhist monks who campaigned for their first election in 2005, promising to establish a Buddhist nation and to enact laws prohibiting religious conversions. For the first time in Sri Lanka's election history, the election manifestos of the main presidential candidates of 2005 and 2010 addressed the issue of religion.

## DISCRIMINATION

Many rural church congregations in Sri Lanka are compelled to meet together for worship in small groups in their homes. According to new rules introduced by the government, construction of new places of worship requires prior approval from the Ministry of Religious Affairs. Applications from nontraditional evangelical churches are routinely rejected by the Ministry. In many areas, the local government authority and the police demand that even existing church communities stop worship services, misapplying the government's directive. In early 2010, the government announced that five new Acts would be introduced in

Parliament to preserve Buddhism; including a proposal to create committees comprising leading Buddhist clergy to advise the government on matters related to Buddhism, as well as clauses dealing with religious conversions which resonates as a novel method of reintroducing anti-conversion laws under the guise of laws to protect Buddhism and religious harmony.[2]

## MARTYRDOM

All of the above illustrate the complex position of Christianity in Sri Lanka. This complexity is experienced on a daily basis by the followers of Christ, in all forms of persecution, discrimination, violence, and even death.

Pastor Neil Edirisinghe and his wife, Shiromi, lived in a small, half-built house while serving in the village of Ampara on the eastern coast of Sri Lanka. They endured tremendous economic hardship and faced numerous threats and opposition. However, this did not discourage or deter them from their commitment and passion for the gospel. On the night of February 17, 2008, while the family prepared to retire for the night, they heard someone approach their house. The intruder pointed a gun at Pastor Neil and shot him several times. As he slumped to the ground, the attacker turned on Shiromi who was desperately trying to shield her toddler son who was in her arms. She was shot twice and lay on the ground, unable to get up or go to her husband who was lying motionless in a pool of blood while their terrified son watched in fear, bewildered and helpless.

Pastor Neil was killed instantly. He was laid to rest in Ampara where he lived and served, while Shiromi lay unconscious in the hospital, unaware that her husband had died a martyr's death. Almost one month later Shiromi, who was not expected to survive, regained consciousness. She recalled how Pastor Neil had once commented, "What a wonderful privilege it would be to die a martyr for Christ."

O death, where is your victory? O death, where is your sting? *1 Corinthians 15:55*

Although doctors were certain that she would never walk again, Shiromi experienced a second miracle in response to fervent prayer by millions around the world. In the midst of personal tragedy, prolonged medical treatment, several surgical procedures, excruciating physical pain and sadness, Shiromi demonstrated tremendous courage and commitment to the God who saved her and her son. "God has a purpose for saving my life and I will return to the place where my husband laid down his life and continue the work he started for the Lord," she said.

Almost three years later, Shiromi lives with a bullet lodged in her spine. But, her faith and commitment to the Lord remain whole and unshaken. She ministers to the congregation in Ampara, building on the blood, sweat, and tears of her husband. God has blessed her faithfulness with revival and growth.

In Hambanthota in the Southern Province stands a vibrant church, with about three hundred members. The pastor in charge is Pastor Lalani, whose husband was Sri Lanka's first martyr, killed in 1988. Pastor Lionel Jayasinghe was a former Buddhist monk who came to

---

2    There were two pieces of legislation proposed to restrict religious conversions: the prohibition of forcible conversion of religions in May 2004 and the freedom of religion bill in June 2005.

know the Lord through a gospel tract. After graduating from Bible school, he was sent to serve in Tissamaharama, which is in the deep south of Sri Lanka, and an area where there was no Christian presence. He and his wife, Lalani, faced tremendous hardship and persecution but would not give up.

Five years later, as Pastor Lionel, Lalani, and their eleven-month-old baby were in their home preparing to have their evening meal, two men walked into their modest home. They thrust a shotgun in Pastor Lionel's mouth and shot him at point blank range in the presence of his distraught wife and baby.

The week before Pastor Lionel was murdered, those who instigated his murder had said, "We should have cut down this vine (his ministry) with our finger nail while it was small, but now we have to use an axe."

Lalani decided to stay on with her infant son and serve the cause of the gospel for which her husband gave his life, refusing to be evacuated to a safe place. She faced attacks, death threats, an arson attack on their home, and a plan executed to set off five bombs in her church that could have killed the entire congregation. But God was with her.

In John 12:24, our Lord Jesus Christ says, "Unless a kernel of wheat falls to the ground and dies, it remains only a single seed. But if it dies, it produces many seeds." Today, no human can cut down this mighty tree that God has nurtured through this courageous and faithful woman. The simple ministry of her martyred husband has today grown to over one thousand church members in the district with several branch churches. It has grown beyond the power of human effort or demonic influence.

The common thread running through these and the hundreds of other untold stories of the suffering church in Sri Lanka is the unwavering faith, passion, commitment, and courage of these servants of the Lord who toil tirelessly in the face of persecution and suffering. They have not and will not deny Christ.

## CONCLUSION

Centuries of Christian history drawn from all over the world also show that some churches withstand horrendous persecution and flourish in spite of it, while others facing persecution cease to exist. What distinguishes one from the other? A church which is built on the solid rock of proper teaching and is discipled in Christ is prepared for persecution. They will stand strong and grow in spite of persecution. However, a church built on a sandy foundation of superficial teaching is not prepared to face persecution and will be swept away by its tide.

The faithful men and women who face poverty, violence, suffering, and even death—simply because they profess that Jesus Christ is Lord and persevere in carrying out his Great Commission—are living examples of Christ's promise, "and on this rock I will build my church and the gates of death will not overcome it" (Matt 16:18).

## QUESTIONS FOR REFLECTION

1. Discuss the effect of combining history, analysis, and story in the chapter.
2. Is the "politicization of religion" unique to Sri Lanka or is this a wider trend?
3. How can one account for the incredible courage of the martyrs' widows in this chapter? What is the result?
4. Does the chapter support the explanation in the conclusion as to why some severely persecuted churches flourish and others disappear?

## REFERENCE

Constitution of the Democratic Socialist Republic of Sri Lanka. 1978.

**Godfrey Yogarajah** is the executive director of the Religious Liberty Commission of the World Evangelical Alliance and also the general secretary of the Sri Lankan Evangelical Alliance. A graduate of the Union Biblical Seminary in Pune, India, he was honored with the Good Samaritan's Award by Advocates International and the Pro Fide Award by Friends of the Martyrs Finland.

**Roshini Wickremesinhe** studied law at the University of Colombo in Sri Lanka and is a lawyer. She is the director of advocacy and law at the Sri Lankan Evangelical Alliance, where she has served for the past eleven years. She also serves as director of the Religious Liberty Commission of the Asia Evangelical Alliance.

**In the Midst of Severe Times**[1]
In the midst of severe times
Am I able to train myself.
In the midst of severe times
Am I able to grow.
Behold the tall pine trees on the mountain
Receiving the four faces of the wind (wind from all directions),
Enduring long ages,
Persevering the scorching heat and bitter cold.
Spring, summer, fall, winter:
Still rooted and standing,
Still tall and upright.
Never yield; never bend;
Ever green from age to age.

This is an English translation of one of more than a thousand hymns composed by Xiao Min, a house church Christian from Henan. Often considered the hymnal of the house churches in China, these songs are collectively known as the Canaan Hymns. Xiao Min wrote this song from prison, setting into song her understanding of the purpose of suffering. In this song she evokes an image of the pine tree, which, in scorching heat and bitter cold, demonstrates its integrity by its unwillingness to yield and be bent.[2] This hymn exhorts Christians to endure and remain loyal in the midst of adversity. Among Chinese believers, Christianity is often referred to as "the way of the cross." Suffering is a means of remembering Christ and imitating his actions. In their own broken bodies, Christians remember Christ's body that was broken for them; in their bleeding, they remember Christ's blood that was shed for them. They suffer "in remembrance of him." —*Irene Ai-Ling Sun*

---

1 Canaan Hymn 51, "In the Midst of Severe Times." Translation and commentary on this song comes from *Songs of Canaan: Hymnody of the House-Church Christians in China*, by Irene Ai-Ling Sun, published in *EthnoDoxology Journal* 4, no. 3 (2010). Used by permission.

For more information and to listen to some of these hymns, google "Canaan Hymns." Here is a sampler. Note how the music is combined with dance.
http://waysoflife.info/Canaan%20Hymns.html
http://www.youtube.com/watch?v=7dMpFofjzq8
http://www.youtube.com/watch?v=G2-gpTSaYx4

2 According to Confucius, "When the year grows cold, then one knows that the pine and cypress are the last to lose their leaves" (Analects 9:28). While the author probably did not intentionally allude to the ancient sage, nonetheless, her appropriation reflects the continuation of this ethnic metaphor.

# CHAPTER 36

# INDIA

## A New Kairos Moment for the Church in India
*Richard Howell*

The early church knew they were stewards of the gospel of Jesus Christ; they were genuinely conscious that the gospel is destined for all time and for the whole world and not just for one time, place, or people. Consequently the church very soon crossed boundaries and became a non-Jewish faith. It also reached, as per the tradition, the shores of India. The first encounter of the Christian faith with India was the coming of Saint Thomas the apostle to South India, especially to south of Malabar in AD 52, where many Christian communities were established. A church stands as tribute to his life of faithful witness to Christ in the place where Saint Thomas suffered martyrdom in AD 72 (cf. Brown 1982). The church in India is as old as Christianity itself, and so is its story of suffering and persecution.

## TRANSLATING THE GOSPEL MESSAGE
God revealed on the day of Pentecost that the gospel is to be communicated to all in their own mother tongue, as the gathered people declared, "We hear them declaring the wonders of God in our own tongue" (Acts 2:11). The non-Christian religions still consider the language of their scriptures as untranslatable. For example, Muslims still pray in the Arabic language, the Brahmanical Hindu social order still recites the mantras in Sanskrit, while Sikhism uses Gurumukhi, and Pali is the language of Theravada Buddhism. It is a special characteristic of only the Christian faith that it is translated in the language of the people it addresses, because the Christian faith believes in the incarnation of God. The faith was propagated not in the language of its founder Jesus Christ. Jesus spoke Aramaic; the Scripture was inspired by the Holy Spirit in the Greek language. That God understands and speaks all languages is a revolutionary teaching in the context of the plurality of religions and cultures of India. "Christianity acquired a worldwide cultural and geographical orientation" (Sanneh 2008, 3).

The first Protestant missionaries, Bartholomäus Ziegenbalg and Heinrich Plutschau, landed in a small Danish settlement called Tranquebar in South India on July 9, 1706. Ziegenbalg was publicly critical of some members of the Brahmin caste, accusing them of disregard for lower castes in Hindu society. For that reason, at least one group plotted to kill him. However, his work did not generally encounter unfriendly crowds. The first copies of the New Testament came out of the little mission press in Tranquebar in 1714. The pioneer missionaries were of German origin, Lutheran by confession, sponsored by a pious Danish king, and supported by the Society for Promoting Christian Knowledge (SPCK), which was an English organization. The next great missionary pioneer, the English Baptist William Carey, landed on November 11, 1793. He also started work in a Danish settlement of Serampore. He translated the Bible into Bengali, Sanskrit, and numerous other languages and dialects. Carey's sermon, using Isaiah 54:2–3 as his text, repeatedly used the epigram which has become his most famous quotation: "Expect great things from God; attempt great things for God."

With its 4,635 distinct people groups and numerous linguistic groupings, India is a nation of diversity in unity. About three hundred plus people groups have a Christian presence; mostly come from the Dalit and tribal people groups. Laing writes:

> Prior to the mass movements, the Indian church existed as a tiny elite group of high caste converts. The entrance, in their thousands, of illiterate villagers had a profound impact on the demographics within the church. The heart of the church moved from the cities into the villages. (2001, 92)

## TRIBAL RESPONSE TO THE GOSPEL

The advent of Christianity in northeast India goes back to the nineteenth century. The missionaries encountered innumerable challenges to reach remote and treacherous terrains to witness. Lakshom Bhatia writes, "the practices of head hunting, inter-tribal raids, animal sacrifices, and varieties of feasts were presented as sin by missionaries, the first step towards their atonement was their confession before the Holy Spirit" (2010). The confessions led to massive growth in the followers of Jesus Christ. Christian faith took deep roots in other states of northeast India as well. The Bawi system of slavery prevalent in traditional Mizo society was abolished and it was replaced by the Christian ethos of equality, brotherhood, and mutual love and respect. The mission introduced script for the Dhulian dialect of the Mizos, which became the lingua franca; as a result literacy and education made rapid strides.

## DALIT ENCOUNTER WITH CHRISTIANITY

The traditional focus of caste Hinduism within the Brahmanical frameworks tends to put Dalits on the periphery. They are considered outcasts, the impure ones. Caste system is based on the principle of discrimination and inequality, that all humans are not born equal. It is one of the most rigid and institutionalized instrument of brutality of the Hindu society. Caste as a conceptual category was seriously challenged only after the arrival

And Jesus cried out again with a loud voice and yielded up his spirit. *Matthew 27:50*

of the Christian missionaries, who initiated the radical idea of extending education to the Dalits. Although the Indian society advocates toleration, it maintains an otherwise intolerant cruel society. Who can leave the caste hierarchy and claim the benefits of toleration? Who can vertically challenge and aspire for a higher caste in the hierarchy and expect accommodation? On Christmas Day 1927, Dr. Ambedkar, a Dalit leader, publicly burned Manu Smiriti, the most sacred and basic document Brahmins used to justify caste and ascribe untouchability. The movements to Christ represented an effort on the part of the Dalits to gain dignity, self-respect, and the ability to choose their own identity. The Dalits who begin to worship Christ are denied reservation benefits which the government provides to only Hindu Dalits. This is discrimination. Vengal Chakkarai, a high-caste Hindu convert to Christ, advocated that the church should "confront Hinduism on the plains of life." By this he meant confronting the caste oppression and exploitation.

The nineteenth-century growth of Christianity was in the context of colonial India and in the midst of a rising national awakening, led by established, foreign-funded Western missionary societies that were in control of the transmission and direction of the missions. The mission birthed what we call the mainline churches, which continue to imitate Western church structures and liturgy; termed as the Latin captivity of the church (cf. Boyd 1975).

## CONTEMPORARY GROWTH OF THE CHURCH

With the contemporary growth of the church in India, the emphasis now is on the local church, which does not import and imitate the lifestyle, law, liturgy, and theology of the European churches. The churches are increasingly culturally rooted in their contexts. It is indeed a new *kairos* moment for the church in India. The indigenous cultures have discovered Christianity and Jesus Christ. The fact that Indians are responding in the midst of militant resurgence of anti-Christian forces suggests a degree of indigenous compatibility with the gospel. The contemporary growth of the church is postcolonial, encountering a militant Hindu nationalism, and is happening without Western organizational structures. And this growth is occurring amid widespread instability. It needs to be termed as the growth of Indian Christianity. Unconventional religious gatherings of new believers continues to take place. The church is attempting to define itself afresh.

## PERSECUTION OF CHRISTIANS

History bears witness to ample religious conflicts in the Indian society. Religious language is most effective in adding fuel to the fires of ethnic or religious conflict. The warfare religious language is often used as a motivational tool for political ends, for nothing better unites and mobilizes people and resources for action than war. For religious language to lead to conflict it is essential for the pious to believe that the cosmic struggle is realizable in human terms. "By identifying an earthly struggle with the cosmic struggle of order and disorder, good and evil, light and darkness, justice and injustice, political actors and religious leaders utilize the readily available way of thinking that justifies the use of violent means" (Juergensmeyer 1991, 386).

Religious intolerance is not alien to Hinduism "despite the nineteenth century myth that the Hindus are by instinct and religion a nonviolent people. The genesis of this myth was partly in the romantic image of the Indian past projected, for example, by scholars such as Max Müller" (Thapar 1994, 19ff.).

However, Christians did not become a political target until 1998, when India had its first Hindu nationalist government—through a coalition led by the Bharatiya Janata Party (BJP). The Independent India witnessed its first large-scale, indiscriminate attack on Christians in the Dangs district of Gujarat in December 1998. In January 1999, an Australian missionary, Graham Staines, and his two underage sons were burned alive in Orissa's Keonjhar district.

After the confessions of Sangh Parivar's Swami Aseemanand who had reportedly taken upon himself the task of targeting Christian missionaries working in the Dangs district of Gujarat ever since he arrived there in late 1995, the Vishwa Hindu Parishad and the Bajrang Dal organized a rally on Christmas Day in 1998 in Subir to prevent Christmas celebrations. In 2006, Aseemanand organized a Shabri Kumbh in the Dangs. The slogan was, "Every single person converted to Christianity adds one more enemy to the country." The pattern followed by Aseemanand in the Dangs was replicated in Kandhamal by Swami Laxmanananda Saraswati. After Saraswati's death at the hands of the Maoists, Sangh Parivar workers unleashed violence against Christians for forty-two days, killing nearly 100 people, burning 147 churches, leaving nearly 48,000 people homeless, and raping a nun. The state government totally failed in its duty to protect innocent Christians who were unable to defend themselves. The police stood by and occasionally joined the Sangh mobs in the violence. The atrocities against Christians in Orissa were the worst ever in the recorded history of Christianity in India.

The story is the same in Karnataka. The state is under an unprecedented wave of Christian persecution, having faced more than 1,000 attacks in 500 days. On January 26, 2010, the day we celebrate India's Republic Day, Karnataka's thousandth attack took place in Mysore city. In the past few years, the number of attacks on Christians, recorded by the Evangelical Fellowship of India, has been more than one thousand a year. The Freedom of Religion Bills in seven states of India require an individual to get permission from the designated government officers before deciding to worship Christ and become his follower.

The Christian community in India does not have a history of involvement in religious violence, even though they are victims of violence. They work to alleviate human misery and injustice because they believe God loves all people equally and desires justice for all.

## SUFFERING AS PART OF CHRISTIAN IDENTITY

The church must integrate suffering and pain as part of the church's life story. The overwhelming biblical language for mission, for promoting the faith, reflects the notion of blessing rather than warfare, reconciliation and peace rather than violence and hatred. Those traumatized and wounded by violence require healing of their memories. How should the church remember and respond to the suffering, persecution, and martyrdom? Should we harbor cold and enduring anger, thirst for revenge, and react like wounded animals? In order to respond as free human beings we must value feelings, even the desire for revenge, but we must also follow moral requirements implanted by God into the framework of our humanity. As the church we must be determined not to lose sight of the command to love one's neighbor, even if the other acts as our enemy. The victim might question whether the perpetrators who are truly guilty be dealt with as they deserve to be treated with the strict enforcement of retributive justice. The state is a gift of God's common grace and is granted authority to maintain law and order and restrain evil in society (Rom 13:1–7). However, it needs to be stated that Christian love of the enemy does not exclude concerns for justice but goes beyond it, to forgiveness and reconciliation.

## QUESTIONS FOR REFLECTION

1. Does the "translatability" of the Christian Scriptures have wider than linguistic applicability?
2. Discuss the elements and consequences of the inevitable clash between the caste system and the Christian gospel.
3. Consider Howell's observation, "The fact that Indians are responding in the midst of militant resurgence of anti-Christian forces suggests a degree of indigenous compatibility with the gospel."
4. Summarize Howell's description of Christian's response to increased persecution in India today.

## REFERENCES

Bhatia, L. 2010. Contradiction and change in the Mizo society. In *Margins of faith: Dalit and Tribal Christianity in India,* eds. R. Robinson and J. M. Kujur. Thousand Oaks, CA: Sage Publications.

Boyd, R. 1975. *India and the Latin captivity of the church.* New York: Cambridge University Press.

Brown, L. 1982. *The Indian Christians of St. Thomas.* Cambridge: Cambridge University Press. First published in 1956.

Laing, M. 2001. The consequences of the "Mass Movements": An examination of the consequences of mass conversion to Protestant Christianity in India. *Indian Church History Review* 35, no. 2 (December).

Sanneh, L. 2008. *Disciples of all nations.* Oxford: Oxford University Press.

Thapar, R. 1994. Syndicated Hinduism. In *Hinduism reconsidered,* eds. G. Sonteimer and H. Kilke, 19. New Delhi: Manohar.

**Richard Howell** of New Delhi / India is the general secretary of Evangelical Fellowship of India (EFI) and Asia Evangelical Alliance (AEA). He is a member of the Global Christain Forum (GCF) and was principal of the Allahabad Bible Seminary in Uttar Pradesh, India, from 1990 to 1996. He holds a BA (Hons), MA, and BD from India, a ThM from Canada, and a PhD from Netherlands.

*"While they were stoning him, Stephen prayed … 'Lord, do not hold this sin against them'"* Acts 7:59–60

After Stephen's death, the persecution of Christians became more violent, but the apostles were able to continue to preach and to witness about Jesus responding to all human needs and reaching all people from Jerusalem to the ends of the earth. Through their witness, many came to believe in the name of Jesus and to receive him as their Lord and Savior.

The book of Acts makes it clear that the early Christians, and especially the apostles, suffered several threats, but not even the imminence of death or prison could stop them proclaiming the name of Jesus. Stephen suffered his martyrdom proving his faith in Christ, faithful to his calling until the end, not abandoning his faith, because in Jesus he was more than conqueror.

Reflection by: Aron Rodrigo Batista, Brazil

# CHAPTER 37

# GRAHAM STAINES (1941–1999)

## Missionary Turned Martyr

*Abhijit Nayak*

*"The blood of the martyrs is the seed of the church."* —Church Father Tertullian

On January 23, 1999, Australian Baptist missionary Graham Staines and his two sons Philip and Timothy were sleeping in their station wagon in the village of Manoharpur in Orissa, India. It was early morning when an angry mob surrounded their vehicle, poured gasoline over it, and burned the three to death. Unfortunately, Staines' martyrdom has remained just a heroic story, while his three decades (1965–99) of sacrificial work among the poor, destitute, lepers, and outcasts in rural villages has been forgotten. Most of the media, human-rights activists, and Christian organizations got excited over the martyrdom of the Staines, but then lost interest after a few days. The result is that in subsequent writings about the event, the impact of the Staines' work and martyrdom is not taken into consideration.[1] The thesis of this essay is to evaluate the changes in Christian witness that have taken place, both within the Christian community and in the Indian society, either directly or indirectly as a result of the Staines' martyrdom.

## QUEENSLAND TO MAYURBHANJ

Graham Stuart Staines was born in 1941 in Palmwoods, Queensland, Australia. Graham yielded his life to Christ at the age of ten during an evangelistic meeting conducted by the late Alan Cunningham at his local church. During different stages of Graham's early teenage years, he felt God's call to missionary service and he was sure of God's purpose in his life but he did not know where in the world that call would take him. At the age of fifteen, Staines, while still in Australia, saw the photograph of Josiah Soren, a Mayurbhanj boy his age, who had severe leprosy. Staines' connection with Orissa became stronger when he became the pen-pal friend of Baripada resident Santanu Satpathy in 1956 (Satpathy 1999, 8).

---

1    For instance, literature published on Graham Staines: Vishal Mangalwadi, *Burnt Alive* (1999), V. P. Mathaikutty, *From Golgotha to Monoharpur* (2000), Voice of Martyrs, *Hearts of Fire* (2003), and an unpublished research by Niranjan Sahu, *Commitment and Service: A study of the life and works of Graham Stuart Staines among the Santhal Tribe in Mayurbhanj District of Orissa* (2005). These works have attempted to present the life and work of the Staines in an impressive manner but have ignored to assess the impact of the Staines' martyrdom on Christian missions and society from people's perspectives. My attempt to assess the impact of the Staines' martyrdom in this essay is mainly based on emic (insider's opinion).

For six years Graham worked as a clerk before entering Queensland Bible Institute. While there, he prayed and felt a sense of peace and a strong sense of God's call to the village of Orissa, India. The confirmation of God's call came through a Bible passage from Mark 1:35–42. Because of this call, along with his continued compassion for those suffering from leprosy, in 1965 he applied to the Evangelical Missionary Society in Mayurbhanj (EMSM) to be a missionary in Orissa. Staines was known as a "pillar of strength" at EMSM and a faithful servant in whatever he did, whether he was serving leprosy patients, preparing accounts, involving himself in serving at the Rotary club, or caring for animals (Rolley 1996, 63).

Staines met his wife, Gladys, in 1981 while she was working with Operation Mobilization in India. They fell in love and were married in Australia on August 6, 1983. Their daughter Esther and two sons Philip and Timothy were born in Orissa. Gladys committed herself, and later their children, to work side by side with him in caring for lepers, the destitute, and orphans in the remotest part of the Mayurbhanj district of Orissa.

Today, Gladys lives in Australia with Esther (who is studying medicine). She continues to provide support to EMSM in Orissa. Graham's life had one purpose and he diligently kept to that goal: to be salt and light to the people (Cameron 1999, 5). Even after he and their two boys died, Gladys is still passionate, enthusiastic, and energetic about fulfilling Graham's vision and mission for the remote villages and people of Orissa. Graham's vision was to see the lives of the destitute, lepers, and poor be transformed and to see them cared for.

## THEN AND NOW

The All Indian Congress on Mission and Evangelism predicted the rise of persecution and martyrdom decades before the Staines' deaths: "We predict increasing persecution because of the revival in religious fundamentalism.… Many of our dear ones will be called to martyrdom" (AICOME 1988, 147). There is no doubt that persecution has always had some negative effects on the evangelization and expansion of the church: including the expulsion of many missionaries and fear and distrust of Christianity. At the same time, the prospect of martyrdom kept commitment high and this in turn attracted many more to the faith. The author himself carried out empirical research to find out the impact of the Staines' martyrdom during May–December 2008.[2]

Indian evangelists, Christians, and people of other faiths have all been impacted by the Staines' martyrdom. Even in the wake of persecution in Orissa, the evangelists are firm in their faith and feel more responsible for preaching the gospel. According to a study conducted by the author, more than 97 percent of indigenous missionaries responded; "Indigenous missionaries are enthusiastic for the gospel work now and they are not living in fear of persecution." More than 70 percent of people of other faiths said, "Graham Staines' life is an example of a true Christian." Graham did not get the opportunity to publicly confess

---

2      A convenience sample of 105 informants was chosen. The following categories of respondents were chosen: Staines' organization workers, board members, church pastors, other local mission heads, and people of other faiths. The interviews and questionnaires were carried out using structured questions in personal and group interviews, all recorded on a digital MP3 recorder. For more details, see Nayak (2009).

his faith at the time of his death, but his martyrdom itself is a witness and testimony to the people of other faiths.

In spite of continuous attacks on churches and Christian missions during the last ten years, church growth is identified in Orissa.[3] One of Graham's former pastors and associates said, "There is significant growth in evangelistic effort and people are coming to the Christian faith. Recently, nine people of other faiths accepted the Christian faith in our church." The influence of the Staines' martyrdom is enormous, and it is a more powerful witness than all his activities that he did for more than three decades.

The martyr's life and death teaches us that suffering patterned after the life and death of Christ is intrinsic to the cultivation of Christian virtue. Swami Agnivesh, a key Hindu leader of *Arya Samaj*,[4] stated, "The murder of Dr. Graham Staines and his two sons in Manoharpur has justly pricked the conscience of the nation. Very few events in recent history have evoked such strong, spontaneous, and universal indignation as this inhuman deed has" (Agnivesh 1999, 217). Staines' martyrdom was a storm that was permitted to scatter the seed of the Word, and it has dispersed the Sower and reapers over many fields. This shows that the blood of the martyrs is the seed of the church: it is God's way of expanding his Kingdom. Persecution often accompanies mission, for "mission leads to martyrdom and martyrdom becomes mission. Martyrdom and mission—so experience teaches us—belong together" (von Campenhausen 1974, 71). In other words, martyrdom and mission are inseparable. The influence of the Staines' martyrdom on local Christians, foreign missionary strategy, and Indian society is enormous. Lessons are many from the martyrdom of the Staines for witness in the Indian context.

Graham was a popular figure among the deprived, underprivileged, and the lepers in Orissa. He is remembered now for his commitment to uplift the poor, heal the sick, and treat the lepers. He could not see lepers on the roadside and do nothing, but would instead rescue them and treat them in the Leprosy Home. He loved everyone regardless of caste, religion, or status. He didn't go out and "convert" people, but let his life and work be his witness and attract people to Jesus. Graham's martyrdom and Gladys' message of love and forgiveness has transmitted the message to indigenous Christians that they must be ready to suffer for the gospel, and take the gospel of Jesus to people of other faiths.

> Some of his children God blesses with happiness; he lets everything that they set out to do succeed; he is with them, he gives them the goodwill of people, success and recognition in what they do, yes, he gives them great power over other people and lets his work be fulfilled through them. Certainly most of them must also go through times of suffering and testing, but whatever evil people try to do to them God always lets turn out for good. Others of his children God blesses with suffering that leads to martyrdom.
>
> D. Bonhoeffer in Andachtshilfe zu "1 Mose 39,23" (May 24, 1944) (1996b, 653f)

---

3     According to *Operation World* 2010, "Church growth has multiplied despite great opposition. The census numbers Christians as 2.4% in Orissa (2.0% in 2001), but some groups (both Christians and Hindutva claim 28% or more." For more details on Christianity in Orissa and challenges, see Mandryk (2010).

4     One of the oldest and most prominent Hindu religious fundamental groups in India originally inaugurated on April 10, 1875, by Swami Dayananda Saraswati in Bombay. Basically, this organization is involved in intrareligious reform, interreligious confrontation, social work, and advocating Hinduism. For more description on its work and ideology, see Matthew (2001, 63–107).

## QUESTIONS FOR REFLECTION

1. Briefly define the terms "martyr" and "martyrdom" and explain what causes martyrdom today.

2. Tertullian says, "The blood of the martyrs is the seed of the church." In what ways is this true? Does it ever contribute to the demise of the church? Explain.

3. What difference does it make that Staines was a foreign missionary who was killed? Would the witness have been different if it was a local Indian Christian pastor or missionary who was killed? If there would be a difference, how might it have been interpreted differently in the Western world and in India?

## REFERENCES

Agnivesh, S. 1999. Hailing the spirit of Gladys Staines. *Vidyajyoti* 63, no.3: 217–18.

*AICOME.* 1988. *Persecution in missions.* Pune, India: EFI.

Cameron, R. 1999. Tribute to Graham Staines. *AIM* (March).

Mandryk, J. 2010. *Operation world.* Colorado Springs, CO: Biblica.

Matthew, C. V. 2001. *The saffron mission.* New Delhi: ISPCK.

Nayak, A. 2009. The impact of the Staines' martyrdom on Christian mission and society in the Mayurbhanj District of Orissa. MTh diss., Union Biblical Seminary, Pune, India.

Rolley, A. 1996. *Mayurbhanj messengers.* Chermside, Australia: EMSM.

Satpathy, S. 1999. Graham Staines: My pen friend. *AIM.*

Von Campenhausen, H. 1974. Das martyrium in der mission. In *Die Alte Kirche*, ed. H. Frohnes. Kaiser: Munchen.

**Abhijit Nayak** is from Orissa, India, and is a PhD student in the School of Intercultural Studies at Fuller Theological Seminary in Pasadena, California. He was a cross-cultural missionary with Operation Mobilization India from 1997–2003 and on the faculty of Calcutta Bible College from 2005–2007. He is author of the forthcoming book, *Walking through the Blazing Fire: Australian Missionary Graham Staines' Life, Work and Martyrdom Revisited* (Secunderabad: OM Books, 2011).

# CHAPTER 38

# VIETNAM

## Not an Accidental Advocate
*Reg Reimer*

Advocacy for persecuted Christians in Vietnam has been my passion for over thirty years. It has also been a constant activity even as I have served various international ministries.

It was not an accidental development. As a boy I heard my father recount with horror his first living memory. As a five-year-old he witnessed the assassination of his grandfather and uncle in their home by anarchistic marauders who terrorized southern Russia (now the Ukraine) in the wake of the 1917 Communist Revolution. What followed the shooting was equally memorable. His devout grandmother came out of hiding, fell on the bodies of her husband and son, screaming, "There is no God, there is no God!" The next day the two men were hastily buried and the entire village fled.

This part of our family story made a deep impression on me, even though I was to learn that religious persecution was not the whole story. As in other persecutions, the causes were complex.

To learn more I studied Russian history at my university in the 1960s. This led me to discover the remarkable work of Michael Bourdeaux. Through a journal published by Keston College in the UK, he tirelessly documented the terrible persecution of Christians in the USSR during the Soviet era.

In 1966 our family went to serve in Vietnam as missionaries. Eight years later, after the Communist victory (1975), we were forced to leave the country. Both my family history and my study of the ruthless persecution of Christians in the Soviet Union told me Christians in Vietnam would face very hard times. Indeed, they did.

Shortly after the fall of Vietnam to Communism, we were assigned by our mission organization to Thailand to work with refugees fleeing newly Communist Vietnam, Laos, and Cambodia. Our contacts with arriving refugees, among them Christians, gave us a window into the dark decade which had descended on these countries. It was a story of deep deprivation for all—and heavy persecution for Christian believers.

We gave ourselves to help those fortunate enough to survive perilous flights across treacherous land borders and pirate-infested rough seas. Refugees came regularly but in numbers manageable by the Thai government with the support of mostly Christian NGOs, until late 1979 that is. Then Vietnam, angered by attacks on its border villages by the Khmer Rouge, overthrew the murderous Khmer Rouge regime. Hundreds of thousand of desperate, starving and dying Cambodians poured into Thailand, for a time overwhelming us all.

In July 1980, over breakfast coffee, I read in the *Bangkok Post* an advertisement for the first Western group tour to the Socialist Republic of Vietnam. I jumped to join. There were eight of us and an embarrassingly impolite British guide. However, not one of us was a tourist. Among us were a journalist, a Red Cross representative, a couple of intelligence agents, and a missionary.

Sunday was a day off on our highly supervised tour. Our government minder looked puzzled when I informed him I wanted to worship with Christians, but he did not say no. There were a few hundred people at worship when I arrived at the large evangelical church on Tran Hung Dao Boulevard. I recognized a significant number of friends and acquaintances. None acknowledged me! During the distribution of the communion elements, I managed through a server to exchange notes with the pastor who preached that day. I knew him well. His return note to me said simply, "Come to the side street beside the church at dusk and follow the directions of an old lady who will be watching for you."

When I came as instructed, I was guided through the back door of the big building, up narrow stairs into a room where four pastors awaited me. After an emotional reunion, I listened as they poured out their hearts concerning the suffering of persecuted Christians throughout the country. Many leaders were in prison, some had died, and many shepherdless Christians were living in fear. When the room fell silent, I asked, "What do you want me to do?"

Immediately, the president of the Evangelical Church of Vietnam, the Reverend Doan Van Mieng, said, "Please, raise our voice in the outside world; we cannot speak for ourselves!"

This request proved to be a seminal moment. It burned into my mind and heart. I knew then and there that I had received another calling, though I had little idea how consuming and complicated it would become. The very next day, I "accidentally" spotted the wife and children of Pastor Mieng's son, a close friend of mine, who was in prison. They stood on a low balcony of a flat as I passed by in a pedicab. Our eyes met, but the situation was such that I could only move my hand in acknowledgement.

That moving moment contributed to my first response. I knew I must help the families of those in prison, so I began to raise money for this purpose. To my consternation, neither my own mission nor a relief organization that I served were willing to pass these donations through their books. They deemed this activity "political." I knew beyond a doubt that I was obliged to help the suffering families and contribute to the care packages they were occasionally allowed to give their prisoner husbands and fathers. I found ways. That experience foreshadowed other evangelical ambivalence and misunderstanding about advocacy that I would encounter.

During the thirty years since that first visit, I have made at least one hundred more to Vietnam. I have learned, often by trial and error, what it is required of an advocate for the voiceless. I have also come to understand that what I have learned in Vietnam has application for others who would understand advocacy or wish to become advocates.

## GRADUAL IMPROVEMENT

Before discussing advocacy, let me paint the religious liberty situation in Vietnam. The first decade in a Vietnam united under Communism (1975–85) came to be called "the dark decade." All Vietnamese ethnic minority pastors were imprisoned, their churches disbanded. Ethnic Vietnamese Christians also suffered hardships and imprisonments. Many Christians ceased gathering for public worship. Small denominations voluntarily were subsumed into the largest, the Evangelical Church of Vietnam South. The situation improved marginally toward the end of this period. Importantly, through intense prayer and a spiritual revival many fearful Christians were emboldened.

During the sixteen years from 1986–2004, religion was ruled in Vietnam by a series of decrees. In 1986 Vietnam announced a period of *Doi Moi* or "Renovation," which included the decision to abandon much of Marxist economics and to engage the outside world for trade. This political change of perspective helped expose and modestly ameliorate some of Vietnam's harsh policy and practice regarding religion.

This period also saw the birth and dynamic growth of the house church movement. Denominations multiplied. In Vietnam's Central Highlands and Northwest Mountainous Region, where Protestant Christianity virtually exploded among ethnic minorities in the 1990s, the authorities devised comprehensive plans to "eradicate" the growing faith, including government programs of brutal, forced renunciations of faith.

The third period may be dated from 2005. Strong international pressure helped usher in some new religious legislation. One policy change promised a greater measure of freedom by registering churches. The new laws also made illegal the large, systematic measures taken to force renunciations of faith. Mercifully they were stopped. By 2010 the nine church organizations that were able to convince the government they had roots before 1975 achieved registration. However, dozens of other organizations representing many hundreds of congregations remain unregistered. The situation has improved, but all churches, registered or not, currently remain under close scrutiny by Vietnam's large religion management bureaucracy.

> Rejoice in hope, be patient in tribulation, be constant in prayer. Contribute to the needs of the saints and seek to show hospitality. Bless those who persecute you; bless and do not curse them.
> *Romans 12:12–14*

Vietnam's Christians affirm that international advocacy was the biggest contributor to positive changes. They plead for it to continue.

In spite of it all, the Protestant movement grew from 160,000 in 1975 to an estimated 1.4 million by 2010. That is 900 percent growth in thirty-five years! In Vietnam it is more accurate to say that persecution came (and still comes) to where churches grow, rather than that persecution caused growth.

## ADVOCATING SUGGESTIONS

Following are some strategies and methods for advocating learned over thirty years. I begin with work inside the country, based on the assumption that the advocate has access to it. Next I will explain advocacy in the international arena. Finally I will share personal lessons learned—some perhaps surprising.

## IN COUNTRY

1.  Establish solid trust relationships with the persecuted believers themselves or those closest to them. This enables an advocate to secure accurate information. Accuracy and detail are absolutely necessary. Nothing derails advocacy or undermines the reputation of an advocate faster than giving out information which becomes readily exposed as sloppy or false. If at all possible, cross-check information with multiple sources.

2.  Train local people to be able to discreetly gather information on persecution. Reputable advocacy organizations have developed helpful codes of conduct and model questionnaires.[1]

3.  Ideally, an advocate should secure the permission of the persecuted Christians themselves before publicizing their cases. In reality this is often not possible. The next best recourse is to secure the permission of family members and/or the local church. Always one should strategize with local Christian leaders who have oversight responsibility.

4.  Find international allies in the country. This includes the political officers of Western embassies who are charged with monitoring human rights, as well as international news correspondents of wire services (e.g., Reuters) and TV (e.g., BBC). Sometimes it involves helping set up meetings and interviews for journalists with the victims or families of the persecuted, both for those based in country or who visit from abroad. This work is not for the faint-hearted or impulsive! Great discretion and wisdom is required.

5.  International allies can also include Christian business people or missionaries on "creative platforms" who are willing, and indeed must, act with utmost discretion. All such contacts hold more potential if the advocate develops a personal relationship with them. The frequent rotation of international personnel makes this a special challenge. I have over the years oriented many diplomats on persecution issues.

To summarize, the main and difficult tasks in country are to gather accurate information about the persecuted and wherever possible to direct it to people and organizations that can either publish it or use it to apply pressure on the country to change its behavior.

## IN THE INTERNATIONAL ARENA

1.  Accurate information about the persecuted should be brought to churches worldwide, both for prayer and for other advocacy actions. This can be done through news agencies such as Compass Direct which specialize in persecuted church issues, through

---

1       Organizations such as Christian Solidarity Worldwide, Open Doors, Voice of the Martyrs, and others have such codes of conduct and questionnaires. Additionally, Lausanne Occasional Paper 32, *The Persecuted Church*, has a section called "Guidelines on Reporting for Publicity and Advocacy" (95–99). This paper may be downloaded at the website www.lausanne.org.

denominations related to the persecuted Christians, through organizations which specialize in ministry to the suffering and persecuted church (e.g., Open Doors, Voice of the Martyrs, Christian Solidarity Worldwide), and through international organizations such as the World Evangelical Alliance, which has a Religious Liberty Commission and sponsors an International Day of Prayer for the Persecuted Church (IDOP).

2.  The Religious Liberty Partnership, with member organizations from more than a dozen countries, can also be very helpful in the important task of internationalizing advocacy causes.

3.  Information can also be provided to secular human-rights organizations such as Human Rights Watch and Amnesty International. Given solid and verified information they will take up Christian persecution cases. Again, personal relationships will greatly help.

4.  Information on individual cases, carefully supplemented by perspective and analysis, is appreciated by departments of foreign affairs of Western countries. These may be provided in writing, but it is even better if one supplements reports with personal visits and builds relationships with country desk officers. The credibility of a field advocate's long experience and regular grassroots contacts is given considerable weight by diplomats.

5.  There are professionals in the persecuted church advocacy community with legal expertise and relationships with key people in intergovernmental organizations (IGOs) such as relevant United Nations and European Union offices. Such advocates are skilled in taking the raw material of field-based advocates and professionalizing its presentation for maximum effect.[2]

## LESSONS LEARNED—SOMETIMES THE HARD WAY

1.  An advocate who would speak for the persecuted must first listen carefully. Only when advocates have understood the situation should they offer strategies to the victim or their family members, who may then chose to let their case go forward. Always respect that it is the victims and their families who take the most risk.

2.  It is better for an advocate to have a connecting mind-set rather than a centralizing, controlling, or self-promoting one. Trust and discretion among the concerned parties are essential, but when such are established it is best for the advocate to connect the players directly and get out of the middle. This makes practical sense because at any time key advocates may be discovered by the persecutors, or even betrayed from within, hence limiting their work.

3.  There is a wide spectrum of advocacy strategies and methods and there is often tension between the extremes. Those who specialize in exposing the evil of persecution can be suspicious of advocates committed to befriending and respectfully engaging the persecutors. The "engagers" can be upset with the "exposers" because exposing by itself is insufficient and can make engagement more difficult. Both strategies are necessary and useful, as are the variants in between. An effective advocate will learn to

---

2   The UK-based Christian Solidarity Worldwide organization is a good example.

understand, respect, and employ the various advocacy philosophies and methods and not be owned by any one of them.

4. It is hard but necessary to confront those in the advocacy community who publish factually inaccurate, sloppy, or overly sensational reports about persecution. Such reports, which by their nature often get wide traction quickly, tar the whole advocacy community and can severely harm responsible, long-term advocacy efforts.

5. Advocates will encounter nay-sayers and critics. Critics are often elusive and will spread rumors rather than confront the advocate directly. Most are not close to the situation and can be safely ignored. But advocates should be open to legitimate concerns brought to their attention. Even harder than gratuitous criticism is the ever-present possibility of outright betrayal. Betrayers, sadly, can include compromised Christians who have been seduced by authorities with a promise of personal gain if they report an advocate.

6. There is a small but vocal minority in the evangelical community which holds romantic views of persecution and actually opposes advocacy. They argue that because persecution can build faith in the persecuted, and that sometimes persecuted churches grow, that to advocate against persecution is to interfere with God's way of deepening and expanding his church. Such thinking, it seems to me, fails to understand the "image of God" basis for upholding human dignity. Should we passively tolerate evil because God is able to turn evil to good? Would such thinking also wish cancer on people, because sometimes the extremity of cancer causes people to turn to God or deepen their faith?

7. I have found that the severely persecuted themselves, those who have learned deep and salutary spiritual lessons in that experience, are among the first to ask for advocacy intervention for others who are persecuted. They do not wish on others the cruelties they have experienced.

## WHAT ARE THE OUTCOMES OF CONSISTENT ADVOCACY?

Here are some outcomes that I have experienced and observed:

1. Advocacy work quickly becomes an exchange. One begins with the noble intention of helping; i.e., advocating, for the persecuted. From my first encounters with the persecuted I always come away humbled and blessed—often feeling I have gotten more than I gave. I have come to believe that we in the West really need to consider and absorb the spirituality that comes out of persecution and suffering, at least as much as the persecuted need our intervention.

2. The advocate can be a bridge builder, helping the church in nations with religious freedom to actualize Hebrews 13:3, "Remember those in prison as if you were their fellow prisoners, and those who are mistreated as if you yourself were suffering." More than a call to cognitive remembering, this means the advocate must be able to guide people toward concrete actions on behalf of the persecuted, not just stir them up to thankfulness for their freedoms.

3. The "ministry of presence," showing solidarity with the persecuted just by making the effort to be with them, is highly significant. Some years ago some friends in Vietnam were honoring me for my work. I will not forget the words of a brother who said, "Thank you for daring to come to be with us during the hardest times." I had "done" many things; it was the "being" that was remembered.

4. We were able to put Vietnam on the radar of a range of churches around the globe for prayer, a prime advocacy activity, and for other advocacy work.

5. As a direct result of my contributions to sustained and persistent advocacy, some persecuted Christians were released from prison and others from a mental hospital where they had been falsely detained. The fact that most of these did not know of the role I played in their release did not decrease my joy and satisfaction.

6. Painstaking research, reporting, and analysis over a long time has contributed to diplomatic pressure by Western countries on Vietnam which, as a result, has caused some of its harsh policies and practices toward Christian believers to be modified. It is too early to discuss the details.

7. Some of the same analysis also made its way to Vietnam's top authorities. Truth was spoken to powerful leaders, and it was apparently helpful to moderates in the Party and government who understand that repression of religion is unhelpful to Vietnam's goal of becoming a more respected member of the international community.

8. Long and consistent advocacy in one location and the reputation it builds eventually allowed me to help coordinate various organizational advocacy efforts for optimum effect.

Advocacy is long project. It is not a matter of staging one big battle, but rather picking a thousand small ones to contribute to the goal of winning that most precious freedom—to choose one's beliefs.

## QUESTIONS FOR REFLECTION

1. What are some of the factors that turned the author into a passionate advocate for persecuted Christians in Vietnam?

2. How is one of the author's conclusions, that "advocacy is a long project," supported by his experience?

3. What, according to the author's testimony and experience, are some of the important characteristics of an effective advocate?

4. Are there lessons here to be learned by missionaries who may not be strongly called to specific advocacy activity, but who want to be supportive of the advocacy cause where they minister?

**Reg Reimer**, a Canadian, has worked internationally in evangelism, relief and development, reconciliation ministry, promoting collaboration, and advocating for religious freedom. He describes himself foremost as a missionary to Vietnam where he began ministry in 1966 and remains deeply involved. He is considered an authority on the Protestant movement there. His book *Vietnam's Christians: A Century of Growth in Adversity* was released in July 2011. Reg was president of World Relief Canada from 1984 to 994. He then served as senior staff member of the World Evangelical Alliance. He currently serves as international partnership advisor with the Evangelical Fellowship of Canada and South East Asia coordinator for International Partnering Associates. He is regularly called on by organizations for advice on promoting religious freedom in Vietnam. Reg is a long-time participant in the WEA Mission Commission. He is married to LaDonna, a social worker. The Reimers live in Abbotsford, BC, Canada. Their two children serve in Cambodia and South Korea.

## WE LOVE OUR NEIGHBORS AS OURSELVES

Jesus called his disciples to obey this commandment as the second greatest in the law, but then he radically deepened the demand (from the same chapter), "love the foreigner as yourself" into "love your enemies." [31]

Such love for our neighbors demands that we respond to all people out of the heart of the gospel, in obedience to Christ's command and following Christ's example. This love for our neighbors embraces people of other faiths, and extends to those who hate us, slander and persecute us, and even kill us. Jesus taught us to respond to lies with truth, to those doing evil with acts of kindness, mercy and forgiveness, to violence and murder against his disciples with self-sacrifice, in order to draw people to him and to break the chain of evil.

We emphatically reject the way of violence in the spread of the gospel, and renounce the temptation to retaliate with revenge against those who do us wrong. Such disobedience is incompatible with the example and teaching of Christ and the New Testament.[32] At the same time, our loving duty towards our suffering neighbors requires us to seek justice on their behalf through proper appeal to legal and state authorities who function as God's servants in punishing wrongdoers.[33]

[31] Leviticus 19:34; Matthew 5:43-4
[32] Matthew 5:38–39; Luke 6:27–29; 23:34; Romans 12:17–21; 1 Peter 3:18–23; 4:12–16
[33] Romans 13:4

Cape Town Commitment, Part I, Section 7. We love God's world, Paragraph D. www.lausanne.org/ctcommitment

# CHAPTER 39

# SURVIVING EVIN PRISON

*Maryam Rostampour and Marzieh Amirizadeh*
*Interview by Sam Yeghnazar*

They had to overcome the fear of life imprisonment and the possibility of execution because they loved and followed Jesus Christ. They had to remain strong through weeks in solitary confinement and endless hours of interrogation by Iranian officials and religious leaders. They had to endure months of harsh living conditions and debilitating sickness.

In their first interview since their 259 day-ordeal in Tehran's notorious Evin Prison in 2009, Maryam Rostampour (29) and Marzieh Amirizadeh (32) tell Sam Yeghnazar what life was like in prison and how they survived their ordeal.

## THE SHADOW OF EXECUTION

*SY: What was the worst thing that happened to you?*
*Marzieh:* One of the worst things was the execution of two of my fellow prisoners. I had never experienced such a thing. One of those killed was my roommate. We had spent a lot of time together. And one day they took her to be executed. For a week I was in shock that killing a human being was so easy. She lived among us, a fellow human being; I saw her every day, and we said, "Hello." The next day she was not there. After these executions, the spirit of sorrow and death hung over the prison. There was deadly silence everywhere. We all felt this. There was nothing we could do. Everyone was under pressure. The sadness was overwhelming. We stared at each other but had no power to speak. This was the worst experience. It was horrifying and tangible.

*Maryam:* The worst thing for me was the execution of Shireen who had become a close friend in prison.

*SY: Did you ever fear execution?*
*Maryam:* I never thought about execution. I thought we might be sentenced to life imprisonment because that is the punishment for women convicted of apostasy. I just thought this was something we would have to bear.

*Marzieh:* Before prison we talked about execution, but when we got to prison and experienced the fear of it—our way of talking changed. The very first night that we were arrested, when they threatened us, we were really frightened. We never imagined we would be so frightened; we had talked about these things before. But the atmosphere there and what happened to us frightened us beyond our expectations. We were confined to a dark and dirty room and paralyzed with fear. We could see the fear in each other's faces. We prayed, and what calmed us was the presence of God and the peace that he gave us.

I just want to add, it is easy to say that I would give my life for the Lord and I would do anything for him, even die. I always thought it would be a privilege to give my life for the Lord. You say these things. I know for sure that if this would happen to us, we would rejoice ultimately. But human fears gripped us. The power the Lord gave us helped us to overcome these fears, just as when we prayed in the police station, God banished our fear and renewed our strength.

## FROM "UNCLEAN APOSTATE!" TO "PLEASE PRAY FOR ME"

*SY: How did the guards treat you?*
*Maryam:* When we were arrested most of the guards treated us badly, especially when they knew we had been involved in evangelism. They would curse us and would not let us drink water from the public tap or use the wash basin. But this changed and eventually they asked us to pray for them.

*SY: How did the other prisoners treat you?*
*Marzieh:* Some called us "dirty, unclean, apostates," but their opinion changed and they asked for forgiveness. We had become an example to them and they would take our side.

*Maryam:* At Evin Prison the well-educated political and business prisoners called us *mortad kasif* (unclean apostates). In less than a month everything changed. As they got to know us, they were curious about our faith, they respected us and called upon us to sort out arguments they had among themselves.

*SY: Did any other prisoners come to faith?*
*Marzieh:* Yes. There were those who accepted Christ. When we were in Vozara (the first prison the women were taken to), we prayed the sinner's prayer with many of the prostitutes. They prayed themselves and we prayed for them. But there were others who were too frightened to confess their faith. There were many who were impacted.

## LETTERS "GAVE US HOPE"

*SY: What message do you have for the thousands who prayed for you when you were in prison?*
*Marzieh:* I would like to thank them for their prayers and support and for the letters they sent us. During this time it wasn't just Maryam and Marzieh who were imprisoned, but all these prayer warriors. This was a great encouragement for us. We felt their presence alongside us. So please keep praying for those who are in prison for their faith, believers in Afghanistan and Pakistan and other places. Don't think that your prayers are unimportant.

*SY: What happened to the thousands of letters you were sent?*

*Marzieh:* We heard that people sent us letters in prison, but we didn't get any of them: Just hearing that people sent us letters was a great encouragement to us. And what's interesting is that the guards who opened our letters read the Bible verses and the prayers and were impacted. We know this because they told us and mentioned some of the verses from the gospel. I can't acknowledge those who prayed and sent letters adequately; I can just say "thank you" with all my heart.

*Maryam:* I thank them. It's true we didn't see the letters they sent, but we knew there was a large group supporting us. This was a huge encouragement to us and helped us to stand firm. We heard from our guards that forty to fifty letters were coming every day. They saw how Christians stood together to support their own. This was something that gave us hope.

## QUESTIONS FOR REFLECTION

1. How does this very realistic appraisal of their fears and suffering help us to understand and support brothers and sisters in similar situations? How do you react to the things that these women shared?
2. Think about the impact their presence and witness had on the guards and fellow prisoners. What do you think caused the radical change in their attitudes? What can we learn from them?
3. How did the assurance of receiving many letters help the prisoners and influence the guards? How can we serve Christians in prison better?

**Sam Yeghnazar** is the founder and director of Elam, a ministry to train and equip Iranian Christians to reach and disciple their countrymen.

**Maryam Rostampour** and **Marzieh Amirizadeh** are two Iranian women who were imprisoned because of their witness to Christ.

Discipleship means allegiance to the suffering Christ, and it is therefore not at all surprising that Christians should be called upon to suffer. In fact it is a joy and a token of his grace. The acts of the early Christian martyrs are full of evidence which shows how Christ transfigures for his own the hour of their mortal agony by granting them the unspeakable assurance of his presence. In the hour of the cruellest torture they bear for his sake, they are made partakers in the perfect joy and bliss of fellowship with him.

D. Bonhoeffer in *The Cost of Discipleship* (1976, 96)

## BLOODY ARMHOLES AND A PEACEFUL FACE

Blood spurted in great gouts where Qazi Abdul Karim's right arm should have been. Jagged flesh quivered from his gaping armhole. Against the wall the bailiff lounged, his sword dripping. Qazi wobbled.

"Recite the creed: 'There is no God but Allah and Muhammad is his prophet,'" the judge commanded.

Through waves of pain, Qazi held on to one truth. Jesus was the center of his life.

"Jesus is everything," he breathed.

"Off with his left arm," the judge snarled at the bailiff.

Son of an Afghan Muslim judge, Qazi had found a job in a hospital just across the border in Pakistan. There he became a Christian. When he had spare time, he witnessed about Jesus all along the frontier. Eventually he was arrested.

Since he would not deny Jesus, a seventy-pound chain was placed around his neck and a bridle put in his mouth. He was marched three hundred miles from Kandahar to Kabul, and abused all along the way.

It was in Kabul that he lost first his right arm, then his left. When, armless, he still refused to recite the creed, his captors beheaded him.

Twenty-five years later, an Afghan man visited a Christian home in Iran. "I was there in the court that day," he said. "I was a boy of ten or twelve at the time, but I have never been able to forget it. I saw a man tortured and hounded to death for his faith in the streets of Kabul. He was a Christian. The remembrance of the light of the peace on his face remains with me to this day. I can never forget it. Tell me the secret of it."

This man committed his life to Jesus and returned to Afghanistan.

Twenty-five years after his death, Qazi's life still was speaking.

Miriam Adeney, *Kingdom without Borders: The Untold Story of Global Christianity* (2009, 253–54), citing J. Christy Wilson, *Afghanistan: The Forbidden Harvest* (Elgin, IL: David C. Cook, 1981, 121)

# CHAPTER 40

# THE KOREAN HOSTAGE INCIDENT

## Seven Lessons Learned

*David Tai Woong Lee and Steve Sang-Cheol Moon*

## INTRODUCTION

Twenty short-term workers from Sammool Church left the Incheon International Airport like any other similar team leaving the country to serve in different parts of the world. Since there already had been a number of short-term mission trips taken by the Sammool Church, it seemed to be no different from prior ventures. There were a number of other short-term teams representing different parties operating within Afghanistan and there seemed to be no imminent danger. There was one single woman worker sent from the same church situated in one locality for almost a year and a number of other NGO workers who had been there for some time—not many could blame them for having a sense of false security. Nonetheless, it is necessary to revisit the incident to assess what lessons could be learned from each stage of the incident: pre-hostage stage, the hostage-taking stage, and finally, the post-hostage stage.

## SUMMARY OF THE HOSTAGE CASE

### PRE-HOSTAGE STAGE

Sammool Church belongs to the Koshin Presbyterian denomination. It was formed after Korean liberation from Japanese annexation after World War II. During the occupation, Korean Christians were forced to take part in so-called "emperor (Japanese emperor) worship." There were some that resisted bowing to the emperor at the risk of their lives. Koshin was formed among those who refused to bow to the emperor's image. Sammool Church has been one of the leading churches in that denomination, well known for social service both within and without the country. Pastor Un-Jo Park, a staunch evangelical, is considered by many to be one of the preeminent pastors in Korea. Sending out short-term workers was an expression of their philosophy of ministry for the local church—an emphasis on both evangelism and social service.

### THE HOSTAGE-TAKING

The twenty-member team left Incheon International Airport on July 13, 2007. They arrived in Kabul on the following day. It was reported that the twenty-member team successfully carried out their educational and medical service July 14–18 in the northern region of

Afghanistan, where it was comparatively safe. However, on July 19, they were joined by three medical team members that were already in Afghanistan and they then moved from Kabul to Kandahar. These three were supposed to act as guides. It was during this journey that the hostages were taken.

They should have been suspicious when the bus driver exchanged places with a new driver, and more suspicious when the bus driver picked up a stranger on the road. The rest we already know. The twenty-three were taken as hostages and it was not until forty-two days later that the final hostages were released. Two persons died; twenty-one returned home safely, but not without physical and mental scars that are bound to haunt some of them for a long time.

"They will put you out of the synagogues. Indeed, the hour is coming when whoever kills you will think he is offering service to God." *John 16:2*

On July 21, the president of Korea, Mr. Moo Hyun Noh, publicly pleaded to the Taliban through CNN, a global news network, that they release the hostages as soon as possible. By then, the matter was out of control and it became a national affair. All the Korean cabinet members, including the president, acted as a sort of contingency committee. The whole nation was in suspense and terror as the news alternated from bad to worse. The Korean government banned all travel to Afghanistan on July 21. After long hours and days of negotiation, the Taliban finally agreed to let the rest of the hostages loose on two conditions: One, that the noncombat Korean troops stationed in Afghanistan would be withdrawn by the end of 2007. Two, that all of the Christian workers, including NGO personnel, would leave Afghanistan as soon as possible. There have been rumors that the Korean government negotiation team paid a large ransom in exchange for the hostages. There is, however, no way to confirm this. The Korean government has denied these allegations.

Let me turn our attention to the responses of various factions during and after the hostage situation. The secularists are at one end of the continuum of those voicing their opinion about the post-hostage and mission by the Korean church, and the conservatives in theology but radical in their mode of mission are at the other end of the continuum. The secularists have launched the severest attack against Christian mission and the church. Sammool Church suffered from harsh criticism, and it is not completely over yet. The following are samples of the reactions by different groups over the hostage incident, particularly toward the Sammool Church and the Korean church in general.

There is almost unanimous agreement from all spectrums that the hostage situation has affected future hostage negotiations, both nationally as well as internationally. The loss is almost incalculable. Existing rules for hostage negotiation in the past were violated, whereby more frequent hostage-taking may occur by terrorists around the globe. The Korean church must take responsibility for this outcome and back off from confrontational and aggressive mission and mobilization of masses in demonstrative forms, particularly in sensitive and dangerous countries such as Afghanistan and other Islamic countries with similar hostilities.

The leaders of Yong Dong Presbyterian Church and like-minded progressive pastors have declared that the days of sending mission workers are outdated. The majority of the Korean church will not identify with this view, though.

Perhaps the declaration made by Dr. Han Hum Ok (recently deceased), the former pastor of Love Church and Dr. Myung Hyuck Kim, chairman of the Korea Evangelical Alliance, and others seem to mirror the position of the majority of the evangelical Korean church. They equally protest against aggressive and demonstrative mission methods while agreeing that evangelism and social responsibility are still the core curriculum of mission. They have, in essence, been most accurate in their description of the situation. They renounced a few radical groups who have staged demonstrative outreaches of thousands of people in spite of strong protests by the Afghanistan government, major daily media, and even the local mission workers.

## POST HOSTAGE STAGE

Nineteen released hostages finally arrived at the Incheon International Airport on September 2, 2007. Two had previously arrived. Of twenty-three hostages, two were killed and twenty-one finally released. They were taken to the Sam Hospital in An Yang, a satellite city adjunct to Seoul, where a debriefing team was ready to meet the former hostages. They spent ten days being debriefed and counseled in a safe environment. Subsequently, they were taken to a remote town in Kang Won Province for a week of group therapy. Most of them have now returned to normal life, but not without scars. For some of them, the scars will remain for a long time. At least two couples have married among them. Several have changed jobs. Eight family members have become Christians. The families of the two members who were killed were the hardest hit among them.

## MISSIOLOGICAL LESSONS OF THE HOSTAGE CASE

This hostage case provides us with important lessons in the midst of suffering and damage. We must remember that the incident happened in God's providence, and we must find lessons from it to improve the practice of world mission, especially from the Majority World.

**Lesson One:** We learned that passion and pure-mindedness are not enough for good practice of missions. The abducted team members and the involved churches and agencies were all pure-minded and passionate, reflecting the zealous mission mind of the Korean church. However, a pure passion is not enough for missions. We need wisdom, too. What we lack in cross-cultural missions is often wisdom rather than purity. We assume our local experience and knowledge within our own culture will work in another cultural context, but it is not true. We need to be wise as snakes in God's work, especially when we cross cultures for the gospel. Korean Christians are known for their passion and zealousness for the cause of the Kingdom of God, but must learn what it means to be wise and strategic in cross-cultural ministries. Old missionary sending countries need to help young missionary sending countries with wisdom and expertise for ministry, especially in security sensitive locations.

**Lesson Two:** We learned that understanding local cultural context is a prerequisite for missionary activities. An environmental scan must be a necessary part of cross-cultural ministry. We need accurate information and in-depth research on the local situation and environment before embarking on a serious engagement in the mission fields. Pure missionary motivation should lead to in-depth research on the cultural characteristics, social changes, and potential risks in the target areas. Activism and excessive optimism may neglect this need. Research into missions has not been emphasized enough among Korean churches and missions over the years. The activistic tendencies of Korean missionaries who pursue visible outcomes of ministry are in the way of strategic development of the missionary movement. Churches and missions need to create a corporate learning environment for mature missionary activities across cultures.

**Lesson Three:** We learned that we need to pursue qualitative instead of quantitative growth in this developmental stage of the missionary movement in Korea. The Korean missionary movement marked phenomenal growth over the last thirty years quantitatively, but it did not grow qualitatively as much as was required. It is not a matter of either/or, but of both/ and. However, qualitative growth seems to be more urgent at this developmental stage because of the imbalance. Without proper systems for member care and training, the numbers of missionaries and short-termers cannot be a reason for self-content. Qualitative growth means pursuing global standards in missions in this ever-globalizing world. There are national cultural traits reflected in a national missionary movement, but we need to pursue true globalism as well as localism for the sake of glocalization of the missionary movement.

Partnership and networking across cultural and organizational boundaries is desirable for qualitative growth in this global age. Many Korean churches and missions are not connected enough with other entities for missions. We can make right decisions when we are connected properly. Consequently we can prevent many more unnecessary dangers, particularly in hostile situations like Afghanistan.

**Lesson Four:** We learned that we need to invest in expertise development for the maturation of the missionary movement. There are approximately twenty thousand Korean missionaries in over 170 countries globally, but there are less missionary experts than what is needed to prevent a repeat of this crisis. We need expertise in information networks, research and development, strategic coordination, mobilization, member care (including counseling services), missionary training, and administration. For a balanced development, local churches in Korea need to see and invest in expertise development among mission agencies. Along with expertise development, expertise sharing is needed. There are limited but substantial sources of expertise available among Korean mission communities, but expertise is not shared widely because of self-centeredness in big local churches.

**Lesson Five:** We learned that massive rallies in the field have serious negative side effects. The hostage crisis in 2007 had something to do with the massive rallies with missionary purpose in Kabul in 2006. The big mission events were planned and performed with good intention, but without regard to the opposition of Korean missionaries in Afghanistan. In the sensitive Islamic context, massive events of such a nature can be seen as a religious demonstration by foreigners. A rally can raise the tension level rapidly; so much wisdom is needed when missioners plan such a program. It is a spiritual myopia if missioners think they should drive out demons and evil spirits in haste to facilitate and guarantee the fruitfulness of missionary activities in the target countries. A long-term perspective is needed and desirable to fight the spiritual warfare well. We are concerned about the short-term mentality of some massive rally programs, particularly in hostile countries, such as Afghanistan. We wonder if they are based on the wrong worldview perspectives. We need to recover the biblical balance between the extremes.

**Lesson Six:** We learned that short-term "vision" trips need to focus on educating participants rather than on direct evangelism in the creative access areas. It is widely agreed that we cannot expect too much from a vision trip, especially in a creative access area. Fewer and fewer countries permit direct evangelistic activities of foreigners. We need to be realistic in setting the goals of short-term trips to sensitive areas. We need to learn first before engaging in any serious mission activities. We can think and pray about what to do and how to serve the local people from a missional perspective as we gather information and knowledge about the local people. One temptation on the part of sending churches and short-term visitors is to leave visible results of their activities. There are too many unwanted buildings and facilities which were not initiated from a thorough needs assessment. Physical artifacts not based on actual needs may serve to self-satisfy the sending churches and short-termers, but may not serve the local people. Short-term visitors can focus on learning what it means to live as Christians in this ever-globalizing world. They can learn to pray, give, and do more in this way for reaching the unreached in God's salvific will.

**Lesson Seven:** We learned that we need to make more efforts to care well for missionaries. There are dangers and risks involved in missionary activities, both with long-term and short-term prospects. Missionaries are more vulnerable than ever to various kinds of potential dangers and risks. Korean churches and missions need to emphasize member care for a balance between a sacrificial life and well-being. It is the obligation of pastors of sending churches and mission leaders to care well for their members. Sometimes people overemphasize martyrdom and neglect their obligation to care for members. As pastors, fellow missionaries, mission leaders, and supporters, our part is to do our best in caring for missionaries. According to my own survey directed to Korean mission executives, member care is regarded as one of the weakest points of Korean missions. We need nationwide awareness and orchestrated efforts in promoting member care.

Whether in long-term or short-term ministries, we need incarnational approaches which highlight unity in the midst of diversity, humility and self-emptying, contextualization, soft power, and the presence of the Holy Spirit. The hostage crisis of August 2007 may turn out to be a disguised blessing for the maturation and development of Korean missions as we commit to incarnational ministry.

## QUESTIONS FOR REFLECTION

1. This article contains the refreshingly frank reflections of two Korean missionary leaders. Discuss the statement, "There is almost unanimous agreement from all spectrums that [this] hostage situation has affected future negotiations, both nationally and internationally. The loss is almost incalculable."

2. Discuss the wider implications of the statement that "national cultural traits are reflected in the national missionary movements."

3. In what specific ways might "older missionary sending countries" help "younger missionary sending countries"? What would be required for this to work?
4. In what ways might more "incarnational approaches" mentioned in the final paragraph mitigate potential future crises?

**David Tai Woong Lee** has been training Korean cross-cultural missionaries for the past twenty-five years. He is the founding director of Global Missionary Training Center, and the chairman of the WEA Mission Commission (1994–2002). His MDiv and DMiss are from Trinity Seminary. He is currently the director of the Global Leadership Focus.

**Steve Sang-Cheol Moon** is director of the Korea Research Institute for Mission, based in Seoul, South Korea. He is married to Mary Hee-Joo and they have two children who are now university students. Steve is the foremost researcher and voice on church and missions in Korea. He earned a PhD in intercultural studies from Trinity Evangelical Divinity School.

# CHAPTER 41

# THE REFUGEE HIGHWAY PARTNERSHIP

## Offering Hope on the Journey

*Heidi Schoedel*

Their journey began with a whispered warning. "Get up. You must leave. They are coming to kill your son." Father and mother scrambled to grab whatever valuables could be carried and hurried their family off into the night. After traveling long miles, they finally reached their country's border. Safety lay on the other side, out of reach of the ruling authorities who targeted them for persecution.

This particular journey is described in Matthew 2:13–14, when Jesus and his parents fled to Egypt. But countless refugee families from Afghanistan, Burma, Colombia, Iraq, Serbia, Somalia, Sudan, and other countries around the world experience similar trauma.

According to the latest statistics from the United Nations High Commissioner for Refugees, more than 42 million refugees and displaced persons currently travel the "refugee highway." Some embarked on this painful journey only recently, while others have spent twenty, thirty, or even sixty years searching for a safe place to call home. Refugees are warehoused in isolated refugee camps surrounded by guards and fences. Some hide in the alleys and parks of major cities, surviving as best they can without work authorization or permission to stay. Still others struggle with new languages and unfamiliar cultures after being resettled in host countries.

Although every story is unique, individuals along the "refugee highway" share common experiences of suffering. The pain of loss runs deep, as refugees lose material possessions, beloved friends and family members, and their homeland with its familiar sights, sounds and smells. Feelings of loneliness and abandonment are strong. Refugees were violently and forcibly rejected by their former neighbors and are often viewed with hostility and suspicion by their new neighbors. Refugees are acutely aware of their vulnerability, as they depend on others for protection, legal status, food rations, medical care, and basic necessities.

Scattered along the "refugee highway" are Christians living out the biblical mandate to love the alien among us. Churches located in refugee transit and receiving countries open their doors in welcome, missionaries and parachurch organizations reach out to help, and vibrant refugee-led churches take root in refugee camps. The challenges they face are complex and overwhelming, and include meeting spiritual needs, dealing with emergency crises, providing physical necessities, healing emotional trauma, and advocating for justice.

The Refugee Highway Partnership (RHP) works to connect these different, and often isolated, leaders and organizations involved in refugee ministry. The goal of the RHP is to create a global community of Christians that collaborates together to implement more effective ministry, stimulate strategic initiatives, and envision and equip the church. Under the coordination of a team of leaders from Africa, Europe, the Middle East, North America, South Asia, South East Asia, and the South Pacific, the RHP facilitates regional networks and issue groups, hosts regional and global roundtable consultations, sponsors and promotes World Refugee Sunday, and offers resources, tools, and connecting points through the RHP web page.

> By this we know love, that he laid down his life for us, and we ought to lay down our lives for the brothers. 1 John 3:16

We pray that one day every person journeying along the "refugee highway" will be welcomed and embraced by the church.

## QUESTIONS FOR REFLECTION

1.  Jesus' refugee journey was described in the book of Matthew. What other refugee stories are found in the Bible?
2.  What Old and New Testament passages describe how God expects his people to care for the alien and stranger among us?
3.  Do you have any refugees living in your community? If so, what are their needs?
4.  Project Idea: Celebrate World Refugee Sunday at your church! Visit the Refugee Highway Partnership web page at www.refugeehighway.net for ideas and resources.

**Heidi Moll Schoedel** is cofounder and executive director of Exodus World Service, a ministry that mobilizes and equips churches to welcome refugees. She serves on the global leadership team of the Refugee Highway Partnership. Prior experience includes work in refugee resettlement at the local, state, and national level in the United States.

# CHAPTER 42

# SUFFERING IN MISSION AMONG THE POOR IN INDIA

*Iris Paul*

## POWER ENCOUNTER

Walking through the deep forest area with my husband, Paul, we smell incense. As we move toward a village we hear the loud chanting of the witchcraft man (*thisari*) using his witchcraft to cure a very sick, almost comatose young man. We watch him brand the forehead and stomach area of the sick man with red hot iron rods, then he waves leaves over the man, chanting all the time, and starts to bite his face and parts of his hand and legs. He then spits out many small particles with force—bits of bones, bits of strings, bits of dried twigs, etc.

The ceremony suddenly stops and the witchcraft man moves his hand and asks us to leave— as no witchcraft can work when we are near and have Jesus in us. So we both walk away to a distant tree and start praying that the witchcraft will be broken, but at the same time to heal the young sick man. It may take anywhere between half an hour or more till the Thisari comes out of the hut to drink his booze. He drinks heavily, instructs the people to bring him a goat, chicken, rice, money, and liquor, and walks away. Then Paul and I walk to the sick man's hut again. I touch him and know that he has a high fever and most probably cerebral malaria—so I ask his relatives whether I can pray in Jesus' name and treat him. Many times the people will emphatically say no. If so, Paul and I walk away, claiming the promises of God and praying that the areas where our legs have trod will become Jesus' land.

But if the relatives say yes, a miracle occurs every time; the man usually becomes conscious, his fever lowers, and he asks for food to eat—wow!! What power there is in Jesus' name! The people know a miracle has happened and they are then willing, in the following weeks, to listen to Jesus stories and start literacy classes—and the nucleus of a church is born. What an awesome God we have.

## SUFFERING OF CHRISTIANS IN INDIA

It was a cool Sunday morning. The early sun-rays were trickling into the village. The birds were chirping and fluttering from tree to tree. There was peace and quiet. Friends David and Irema were getting ready to go to an interior village for the Sunday morning worship. The village is about two hours away and one must travel through thick forest to get there. David and Irema prayed together and committed the day to Jesus. Then they rode off into the thick forest area on their motor bike. They chit-chatted to each other as they drove the motorbike through a six- to nine- inch clearance on the forest footpath. Forty-five minutes passed when suddenly they were waylaid by police with guns. They manhandled David and Irema. They pulled them off the motorbike and started to beat them mercilessly, saying that they were terrorists.

David and Irema were taken aback at the sudden onslaught and dumbfounded. Finally David, unable to bear the pain, started to shout that they were missionaries and not terrorists. The police continued to beat them and tell them that they must renounce their faith in Jesus. The police dragged them into the forest. Irema was too frightened and continued to bear the beating without answering questions. He was blindfolded and dragged into the forest.

It is said that forests have "many eyes and ears." The news of the arrest reached David's village. There are no phone lines or mobile phones in this village, so the villagers sent out runners to me and I received the news in the late afternoon. I rushed to the Superintendent of Police (SP) and I was able to get an audience with him. I explained to him that David and Irema are my staff and not terrorists. The SP remarked that they would be kept by the police for questioning and then would be released.

I hired a jeep and left for David's village. This village takes five hours by rough road to reach. Late in the evening, the jeep pulled into David's village. The people came running to me. We all cried out for God to protect David and Irema. After about an hour we saw David come into the village on the motorbike. David was beaten up and asked to renounce his faith in Jesus. But he refused. By God's grace after much beating he was released.

I continued on in the village—two days passed by and there was no news of Irema. In the forest area if anyone is killed or torn by animals the news will trickle in, so as there was no news of any death we knew Irema was still alive. On the third afternoon Irema dragged himself in. He said that the police had kept him blindfolded and without food or water for the whole time and had often beaten him, asking him to turn to his tribal religion or become a Hindu. If he did, they promised to immediately release him and give him a police job. Irema, with a bright face, related that he had refused to renounce Jesus who had saved him and given him joy and peace. He said that even if they killed him he would not renounce Jesus. Oh, what joy the family had to see Irema alive and to know that Jesus had helped him to endure beating and starvation for Jesus!

> For we who live are always being given over to death for Jesus' sake, so that the life of Jesus also may be manifested in our mortal flesh. So death is at work in us, but life in you.
> 2 Corinthians 4:11–12

Yes, even death cannot kill Irema as he is always alive in Jesus.

## CHILD SACRIFICE

It was dusk and a few people were busily digging a four foot by five foot pit in the deep, deep forest. The witchcraft man was getting ready for his act. He started to chant. Opposite the pit was a young lady looking rather frightened. The witchcraft man was mesmerizing her and she went into a trance with a fixed stare. Within a couple of minutes, a boy of about four years was brought into this deep forest, gagged, blindfolded, tied, and dragged by two tribal men to the pit. The witchcraft man first cuts off the tongue of the child, chants, and throws the tongue into the pit. The blindfolded and tied-up boy struggles and then the witchcraft man pulls out both of the boy's eyes, chants again, and throws the eyes in the pit. The boy continues to struggle and bleed profusely as part by part each pieces of the boy are cut off, chanted over, and thrown into the pit.

Even in this twenty-first century, people fully believe that the witchcraft man knows the way to make an infertile lady pregnant by this gruesome, heartless procedure. The people fully believe that the cut parts of the boy will enter part by part into the womb of the infertile woman in a trance and she will bear a son the following year.

This horror scene is seen by someone in the forest and the news slowly trickles to the police. The witchcraft man and the woman are arrested and put in jail. There, they learn about Jesus and the woman receives God's forgiveness. So far the witchcraft man has not softened to the Lord as the satanic influence on him is strong. Please pray for all witchcraft men and women to be touched by Jesus' love and for God's deliverance to come into this area.

## DEATH THREATS

The village had retired for the night. Except for the movements of the leaves in the gentle breeze there was almost pin-drop silence in the village  There is no electricity for miles around and the new moon meant no moonlight as well!

It is said that if you truly want to enjoy the moonlight—a beautiful creation of God—you have to be in such a village. It is no exaggeration that a full moon lights up the whole village as though with a million lights and everything is sparkling and beautiful. Full moons are the time when the young try to find their life partners!

However, on this night everyone in the village had retired to bed by seven in the evening due to the pitch darkness.

Around 9 p.m., a paper arrow suddenly whizzed through the crack in the bamboo door of Samuel's hut. The paper arrow landed on Samuel's face and he woke with a start, turned on the night lamp, and read, "You will all be dead if you are here in the hut tomorrow morning." For a few seconds Samuel was paralyzed. The note had the tell-tale evidence of having been sent by Maoists. Besides the terrors from the Hindu fanatics, active Christians also have to face the terrors of the Maoists. The Maoists kill people in broad daylight if their demands are not met and have also been fighting the government for a part of the state as their own. They harass Christians if they become more popular in a village than them.

Samuel cried to Jesus for help and woke up Rita, his wife. His ten-month only son Joy was fast asleep, cuddling near his mother.

Rita had undergone a tiring day and was not willing to be woken up. She turned to the other side of the bed and said, "Please wait until the morning to tell me whatever you want to tell." She pulled the sheet over her and was about to go back to sleep. With fear in Samuel's voice he cried, "Rita, the Maoists will kill us if we stay till the morning!"

Rita sat up with a start, quickly packed a bag with whatever was absolutely necessary, and loaded this on to their cycle. She carried Joy on her shoulder and Samuel opened the hut door and pushed the cycle outside in the pitch darkness. They just had a torch light to light up the way.

They had to push the cycle for nearly two miles in a thick forest area to reach the next center where other missionaries were staying.

The forest is infested with every poisonous snake you can think of, including the big black king cobra which roams freely at night. Add to this danger, bears and huge wolves too.

Their journey felt like eternity as they walked the thick jungle path. By God's immense grace, Samuel and Rita finally reached the safety of the next village and the following morning traveled to the main missionary center, which is only forty miles away but takes five hours by jeep—there is no bus service to any of these interior villages.

All gathered for special prayer at the main center. After a week, the chief executive collected all the rest of their belongings and the hut was abandoned. It is indeed sad for the local tribal people who said that they missed Samuel and Rita—who had been their friends, who had been teaching them to read and write, and whose son Joy really brought Joy to them.

But life goes on. When one center closes another is opened until persecution knocks at the new door.

One wonders whether this persecution is God's way of pushing us out to further interior areas with no outside accessibility so that all of his creation will know his love and hear Jesus' name at least once in their lifetime.

## QUESTIONS FOR REFLECTION

1. How do you react to the power encounter story? Why do you think these experiences are so real in Dr. Paul's ministry? Have you faced any similar challenges? How has your faith helped you to respond?
2. The suffering of Christians, especially those who are poor and live in villages, continues in India. How does the experience of David and Irema encourage us to trust God in similar situations and dangers? What can we do to support and serve those faithful servants?
3. How do you react to the story of the death threats? How can the church continue to develop in such difficult contexts? How can we encourage each other to remain faithful and not to lose hope or the willingness to continue to serve?

**Iris Paul**, MD, together with her late husband, Paul, pioneered gospel and medical missions among the remote tribal Bondo people of Orissa, India. After Paul's death, Dr. Iris established the Reaching Hands Society, which brings medical, literacy, and development programs, as well as the gospel, to many villages and unreached peoples. *Pioneering on the Pinda,* authored by Dr. Beulah Wood, tells of the Pauls' life story. Her son, Remo, and daughter-in-law, Dr. Susan, MD, have joined Dr. Iris to work in the same area.

# PART FOUR

# PREPARATION, SUPPORT, AND RESTORATION

How do we anticipate and prepare? How do we recover and heal? We juxtapose these two themes in this major section of the book. Jesus very clearly prepared his apostles and other followers for their future with blunt and realistic words. He knew what he was doing. And so must we. Too many believers in the Global North and, rather surprisingly, in Latin America say, "But persecution and martyrdom do not happen here." Aha, perhaps not yet or in the same way as in other countries. How do we identify and learn from the suffering church around the world? How should we prepare our cross-cultural servants for their future ministry in an uncertain and violent world? Do Christians in the wealthier North have a theology of suffering, persecution, and martyrdom? What are their particular heresies and weaknesses?

However, the deficiencies are not only in the North. They are also found in much of the South, especially where a "thin gospel" has been preached or where the heretical theology of the prosperity gospel has taken hold. This has permeated large swaths of the churches of Africa, Latin America, Asia, and the Caribbean.

In the following chapters we present a cross section of voices from both South and North committed to preparing both the local church as well as its missionaries for the near future. We listen to a global conversation of mission leaders and then another of missionary trainers. We examine codes of best practices for short-term and longer-term ministry in troubled areas. We learn from persecuted believers and become advocates and strategic engagers. We include resources for those seeking healing from the trauma of suffering and persecution. We come to understand the role of academics and research related to our core topics.

There is so much more that we could have included in this section, and in the book. But grapple now with this sampler, and ask yourself, "What can I learn? What can my family learn? What can my church, my mission, my team, my ministry, my seminary, my missionary training center learn as we cast our vision and reset our preparation into the future?"
—*William D. Taylor*

# CHAPTER 43

# A PASTORAL THEOLOGY OF SUFFERING IN MISSION

*Antonia van der Meer*

Missionaries need to work in difficult and hard situations where the least reached and poorest people of the world live today. But these missionaries are normal human beings and, as such, need to be encouraged and enabled to continue their ministries through faithful support.

## A THEOLOGY OF SUFFERING IN MISSION

According to Gärtner (1986, 724), "Christ's vicarious suffering means ... for his followers not deliverance *from* earthly suffering, but deliverance *for* earthly suffering.... He is our pattern and example. His suffering requires us as his followers to tread a similar path (1 Pet 2:21)." This vision is not understood by many evangelical Christians today, who feel they have the right to be delivered from suffering. Unless we adopt a more Christlike commitment to do the will of our heavenly Father, whatever the cost, it will be difficult to find those willing to go to places of great risk and suffering.

"To suffer 'as a Christian' means to share in the sufferings of Christ (Phil 3:10) ... their sufferings may be identified as one and the same (2 Cor 1:5)" (Gärtner, 1986, 724). Our suffering in mission has a meaningful and eternal purpose. Christ's disciples have experienced a special intimacy in their fellowship with him in their obedient service and consequent suffering.

Gärtner (1986, 725) encourages suffering Christians, writing:

> In Romans 8:18 Paul emphasizes that the sufferings of the present time bear no comparison with future glory, so that suffering may be regarded as a precious gift (Phil 1:29).... Again and again in the New Testament suffering and glory (Rom 8:17; 1 Pet 5:1,10) ... are mentioned in the same breath.... Thus the Christian awaits not the *end* of suffering but its *goal*.

It is encouraging to know that suffering for Christ has a definite goal, it is temporary, and we are promised future glory incomparably greater than any suffering. We can suffer with courage and even with joy because we suffer for our Lord and we will be glorified eternally with him.

This does not mean that missionaries are those called to endure suffering while their churches continue to live in comfort and may even have a condescending attitude towards them when they return broken-hearted. Those who go, and those who stay behind, are equally called to pay the price, supporting each other. Jesus was not insensitive to the suffering of his disciples but offered encouragement and loving care. "And surely I am with you always" (Matt 28:20); "Simon, Simon, Satan has asked to sift you.... But I have prayed for you" (Luke 22:31); "I have told you these things that in me you may have peace, in the world you will have trouble, but take heart" (John 16:33).

According to Morris (1990, 86):

> We regard suffering as something evil and do what we can to avoid it. It seems to make people doubt if God is good. Paul went through a lot of suffering, but he calls us to exult in it. For Paul suffering is evidence that God loves us (Rom 5:3–5). There are qualities of character that only develop in us through suffering. So God uses trials to make us better. Paul's sufferings were also evidence of his love for his Lord and for the people he is reaching out to.

We have grown used to believing that we have the right to live in comfort, and to overcome suffering. When we face hardships it is common to question, "Where is God when it hurts?" The Bible explains that God loves us, but that in order to restore his creation he suffered in our place and he invites us to become his followers and carry our cross. And it is true that suffering will purify us (while others are hardened by it because they reject it).

The early Christian church had a very different attitude to suffering for Christ.

> In his *Letter to the Ephesians* Bishop Ignatius wrote thanking them.... His desire is to "attain the grace to receive my fate without interference," being afraid that in their love they might seek to attain his freedom. "For if you remain silent ... I will be a word of God, but if you love my flesh, then I will again be a mere voice. Grant me ... to be poured out as an offering to God.... Let me be food for the wild beasts.... I am God's wheat, and I am being ground by the teeth of the wild beasts." (Lightfoot and Harmer 1990, 86, 102–3)

People understood the value of suffering for Christ and the power of Christian witness in the midst of suffering and martyrdom. Those who hate and despise Christians somehow are touched by their gracious attitude towards their tormentors and their trust and joyful response to their Lord.

Bosch (1991, 121) also writes about suffering as a necessary part of Christian mission. "One last ingredient of Luke's missionary paradigm: the fact that mission, of necessity, encounters *adversity* and *suffering*."

Jesus' disciples are called to suffer and carry their cross daily as his followers (Luke 9:23). In the book of Acts the disciples respond to adversity with boldness (Acts 4:27–30). From Paul's conversion it becomes clear that he "must suffer for the sake of my name" (Acts 9:16). Wherever Paul proclaims the gospel opposition arises. "Paul became the first Christian theologian precisely because he was the first Christian missionary.... His theology is a missionary theology and his mission flows from his theology" (Bosch 1991, 121–22).

Peskett and Ramachandra (2003, 194) write about suffering and mission:

> Jesus' primary call to his disciples is to be where he is.... And where is Jesus? He is about to die ... in utter ignominy and abandonment!

According to Bonhoeffer (1953, 123), "It is not some religious act which makes a Christian what he is, but participation in the suffering of God in the life of the world." And Peskett and Ramachandra write:

> But the suffering Jesus invites his disciples to is a suffering like his that is freely chosen.... Christians deny themselves in order that they may give themselves fully to God for his purposes in the world. If Christians say "no" to their own lives, it is so that they may affirm the lives of others. (2003, 195)

In following Jesus' missionary call we no longer live to please ourselves, but to please God and to bless others. It is a wholehearted humble service, in grateful response to Jesus suffering for us.

When Jesus spoke clearly about his suffering and Peter rebuked him, he showed that

> the Church of Christ ... does not like to have the law of suffering imposed upon it.... Peter's protest displays his own unwillingness to suffer.... Jesus must make it clear ... that the "must" of suffering applies to his disciples no less than to himself ...the disciple is a disciple only in so far as he shares his Lord's suffering and rejection and crucifixion.... To deny oneself is to be aware only of Christ and no more of self, to see only him who goes before and no more the road which is too hard for us.... To endure the cross is not a tragedy, it is the suffering which is the fruit of an exclusive allegiance to Jesus Christ. (Bonhoeffer 1967, 96–97)

What a tremendous challenge. This may explain why Christians grow in their faith and why the church grows stronger where people are forced to suffer for their Lord. People in democratic capitalist societies have grown used to think that "freedom of religion" is normal, but it may not be the healthiest environment for the church.

## SUFFERING FOR THE NAME OF JESUS

Suffering should not be sought or glorified, as if it were proof of superior holiness. Sometimes such mistaken ideas surface in contexts of suffering: those who were imprisoned, were tortured, those who died—these are seen as the really holy ones, while those who survived and who continue to serve faithfully are often seen as second-class citizens of the Kingdom of God.

The Bible makes it clear that suffering due to a lack of wisdom or insensitive behavior does not glorify God, for it is deserved suffering (1 Pet 2:18–20; 4:14–16). Some people are bold in an unwise way, and provoke negative reactions by disrespect for the government or the majority faith. This kind of suffering does not glorify God. We need to be wise and learn to witness in appropriate ways, times, and places.

According to Gärtner (1986, 724):

> Not all suffering is fellowship with the sufferings of Christ. For suffering to be in this category, the apostles and the church must suffer for the sake … of their Christian calling.…True suffering in this sense is called suffering "according to God's will" (1 Pet 4:19); "in the name" of Jesus Christ (Phil 1:29), "for the gospel" (2 Tit 1:8).

Suffering for the name of Jesus is the suffering we face when we have done the very best we could, faithfully serving him, As a result we are despised, threatened, tortured, imprisoned, or killed. This suffering brings a deep fellowship with Christ and a new form of joyful service, even though those who suffer often are in lonely situations. So it is important for them to know that others care and pray for them.

Suffering for the name of Jesus may also mean that missionaries serve in contexts of violence and may be hurt physically, become traumatized, or need to be evacuated. Some will allege that the missionary who is "really called" will never leave his post, but this depends on the local situation. It is important to listen to advice from local Christians and not to force people to stay if they are unable to cope with the stress at that moment or if their presence may cause greater danger to national Christians. Maybe some need to go home, be cared for, and return when it is appropriate and when they are ready.

Those who suffer serving Jesus and spreading his Kingdom may be very sure that they are never alone, for Jesus promised to be with us always, everywhere, and he will keep his promises (Matt 28:18–20; Heb 13:5–6). We may not always feel his presence, because our suffering does hurt and sometimes nearly crushes us, but he will not allow our sufferings to exceed our strength to bear them (1 Pet 5:10; 2 Cor 4:7–11). This is a great encouragement for missionaries on the field, especially in times of danger or extreme pressure.

## SELF-DENIAL, A SERVANT ATTITUDE

These values are the very opposite of what the world teaches. But these were the values of Jesus' life and teaching, and they will help us to persevere in difficult situations. Sadly, most Christians have values similar to those of the world and development of a Christian character is not being taught in our churches. We need to recover this essential dimension of Christian discipleship, for missionary training does not start in the mission schools but in the churches. However, mission training programs should develop a process of growth

"Remember the word that I said to you: 'A servant is not greater than his master.' If they persecuted me, they will also persecute you." *John 15:20–21*

in Christian character, through godly models, biblical teaching, and living in community, seeking the Lord together and being open to mutual correction. This process never ends. And no training will produce the desired effect if trainers are not open to learn and to be molded as well.

The qualities of self-denial and humility will be important in relationships with the agency, with colleagues, and with local leaders, for conflicts will arise but can be overcome and the process of dealing with them can result in a growing godliness. Jesus' way of dealing with evil and suffering is the way of the cross—of self-giving love, obedience, and service unto death. The result may be that we receive hatred for love. Some missionaries and local Christians have the experience of serving humbly and receiving a response of misunderstanding or hatred, sometimes from local people or even more painfully, from missionary colleagues or from those who sent them. We need to keep our eyes on Jesus, trust, and serve him, for he knows what we are doing.

## LEARNING TO PERSEVERE

Missionaries need to understand how important perseverance is in the development of a Christian character, especially for those called to serve in contexts of suffering. Churches, agencies, and training institutes need to prepare biblical training on this subject, so that missionaries will understand that persevering is essential, and that all Christians will go through times of testing and pain. The logical human reaction to such situations would tell us to give up, but the Bible teaches us that we should keep going, trusting God and knowing that he will bring good fruit in the midst of the most difficult experiences.

The church and training institutes can offer opportunities to serve in tough ministries in less distant cultures, in situations in which the missionary's ability to persevere will be tested and strengthened. But we also need to discern the limits of what people can endure, and bring workers back home for a time of renewal when they are no longer coping well. It is important, in such cases, that the home church, agency, and field leaders decide together about the most appropriate course of action.

## LEARNING FROM PAUL'S SUFFERING IN MINISTRY

Soon after his conversion, Paul was told that he had been chosen to carry Jesus' name before Gentiles and the people of Israel, and that this mission would involve much suffering. Paul never sought suffering or provoked it unnecessarily through lack of wisdom. He used his rights as a Roman citizen to protect himself from being flogged by the Romans and from being lynched by the Jews (Acts 22:25–29; 23:16–24; 25:9–11). But he was willing to suffer when it was necessary to fulfill his calling.

Paul was ready to suffer for the proclamation of the gospel and was not ashamed of the consequences, for it was an honor to suffer for Christ. He wanted Timothy to follow his example and to be ready to suffer, because no one can preach Christ faithfully and escape persecution (2 Tit 1:11–12; 3:12; Kelly 1983, 154–55).

Paul showed that a biblical theology of glory is inseparably linked to a theology of the cross. God's way of action is through weakness, suffering, and self-sacrifice, and this applies to Christians as well. Christ was humiliated and despised. So was Paul and so will be Jesus' servants (Prior 1985, 65–66). Paul understood that God had determined that the apostles should be willing to die as martyrs, something not to be seen as a tragic event, but as a commission given by Jesus (Ton 2000, 148, 156, 165). As martyrdom is becoming a present reality for many Christians, we need to face this possibility and its implications. Tension and suffering are part of the body of Christ today.

Paul expressed his deepest humiliation in the context of his experience of highest exaltation. About the precise nature of the "thorn in the flesh" it is probably best that God decided to leave us in ignorance. It was very painful and humbling. So we can identify the thorn with our own deepest humiliation and pain. Paul's thorn crippled his life, draining his energies. But it was permitted and overruled by God for his servant's good. Its purpose was to keep Paul humble and dependent on God, and it taught him the secret of Christ's power manifest in weakness (2 Cor 12:7; Barnett 1988, 177-78; Carson 1984, 175).

Paul accepted the suffering that came to him from his Lord, because he knew that human weakness provided the opportunity for divine power. Paul never sought suffering to receive merit. We learn from Paul to discern God's hand in painful circumstances, knowing that he remains in control. The answer to Paul's prayers was the promise of more abundant grace to be able to live with his painful thorn (2 Cor 12:9b–10; Hughes 1977, 452–54).

> Paul triumphs over suffering in faith despite the most adverse circumstances. Joy is cheerful, victorious: "Death, where is your sting?"
>
> D. Bonhoeffer in "'Freude' im Urchristentum. Festgabe für Adolf von Harnack" (1986, 427)

In 2 Corinthians 4, Paul described how unbelieving people have their minds blinded by the god of this age and how God may enable them to believe, making "his light shine ... to give [them] the light of the knowledge of the glory of God in the face of Christ" (4:6). This is the treasure, which Paul carries in a weak earthen vessel. His tribulations and daily dying are for Jesus' sake in order to spread the grace of God. As he suffers for the gospel, the truth shines, penetrating the blinded eyes of unbelievers (Ton 2000, 145–47). The way Christians react to suffering is a powerful witness.

Paul was a true servant of Christ, a shepherd with a loving heart, a man conquered by Christ's great and undeserved love. He was the apostle who worked most, took the gospel to many new lands. One of the secrets of his continuing perseverance in ministry and of his unbroken spirit was his willingness to suffer for Christ.

## WHAT DOES THIS MEAN TO MISSIONARIES TODAY?

If we consciously follow Jesus' model, we will learn to bear difficulties in team relationships with patient endurance, be ready to forgive and not to hold onto hurts in our heart, and be able to love those who are less lovable, asking the Holy Spirit to pour out his love in our hearts. We will be able to pray for those who persecute us. We will not seek our own glory, but God's glory. We will express our hurts and pains to our loving Father, but continue to be submissive to his will, knowing that he is sovereign, and our present pains for the name of Jesus will bring us a reward of glory beyond all understanding.

If we follow Jesus we will be sensitive to the needs and hurts of others, listen to them with love and respect, identify with them, and speak words of comfort and encouragement, serving according to their needs in a culturally sensitive way, according to our possibilities.

## QUESTIONS FOR REFLECTION

1.  What are the most common reservations against sending missionaries to the more difficult fields today?
2.  What kind of biblical teaching is necessary to help us understand our responsibility to reach the more resistant peoples and contexts and to motivate us to commit ourselves?
3.  How do your church leaders and members react when one of them feels called to such a difficult context?
4.  How can we best help those servants who feel called to serve in such contexts: before they go, while they are in such a context, and when they return?

## REFERENCES

Barnett, P. 1988. The message of 2 Corinthians. *The Bible speaks today.* Leicester: InterVarsity Press.

Bonhoeffer, D. 1953. *Letters and papers from prison.* London and Glasgow: SCM.

———. 1967. *The cost of discipleship.* 9th printing, New York: Macmillan.

Bosch, D. J. 1991. *Transforming mission.* Maryknoll, NY: Orbis Books.

Carson, D. A. 1984. *Del triunfalismo a la madurez.* Trans. D. Menezo. Barcelona: Publicaciones Andamio.

Hughes, P. E. 1977. Paul's second epistle to the Corinthians. *The new international commentary on the New Testament.* Grand Rapids, MI: Eerdmans.

Kelly, J. N. D. 1983. I e II Timóteo e Tito: Introdução e comentário. In *Série cultura bíblica* 14, trans. G. Chown. São Paulo: Vida Nova and Mundo Cristão.

Lightfoot, J. B., and J. R. Harmer. 1990. *The apostolic fathers,* 2nd ed. Ed. and rev. M. W. Holmes. Leicester: Apollos.

Morris, L. 1990. *New Testament theology.* Grand Rapids, MI: Zondervan.

Peskett, H., and V. Ramachandra. 2003. *The message of mission.* Leicester: InterVarsity Press.

Prior, D. 1985. The message of 1 Corinthians. *The Bible speaks today.* Leicester: InterVarsity Press.

Ton, J. 2000. *Suffering, martyrdom and rewards in heaven.* New York: Romanian Missionary Society.

**Antonia Leonora van der Meer**, Brazilian with a Dutch background, served with IFES for many years in Brazil and Angola. Now at the Evangelical Missions Center in Brazil, she is development coordinator, dean, teacher, and mentor. She has a master's in theology at the Baptist Brazilian Theological Faculty in São Paulo and a doctorate in missiology at the Asia Graduate School of Theology in the Philippines. She has published several articles in *Connections: The Journal of the WEA Mission Commission*, in *Global Missiology for the Twenty-first Century*, in the Brazilian version of *Perspectives*, in *Doing Member Care Well*, in *The Dictionary of Mission Theology*, and in the *Atlas of Global Christianity*. She wrote several books in Portuguese: an inductive Bible study *(ABUEditora)*, a personal missionary story *(Eu, um Missionário?)*, and a book on caring for Brazilian missionaries in contexts of suffering *(Missionários Feridos)*.

# CHAPTER 44

# GLOBAL DIALOGUE SUMMARY

## Pastors, Mission Pastors, Agency and Network Leaders Reflect on Policies in Sensitive Fields

Editors' note: this is a short summary from a much more extended article that appeared in *Connections: The Journal of the WEA Mission Commission*.[1] In that issue of *Connections*, you will find threads of a global communication between mission societies, mission movements, and mission leaders as they respond to questions on mission in contexts of suffering, violence, persecution, and martyrdom.

Some responded briefly to the questions given; others in a more narrative format; some sent copies of their written policies. Some leaders, due to the delicacy of the issues, asked that they not be included in this issue of the journal, or gave permission to quote but only without attribution. One said that he could write very little because their agency at that very time was in delicate negotiations to seek the release of one of their recently kidnapped missionaries.

## THE CORE QUESTIONS

1. What policies does your national mission movement, sending agency, or church have when sending first, short-term, and second, longer-term missionaries to dangerous contexts? What are some of the specific guidelines?
2. Do you have a written summary statement giving a biblical theology of persecution or martyrdom? If so, please share it with us.
3. What guidelines do you have (or feel you must develop) in case a missionary, or a child of missionaries, is kidnapped?
4. What guidelines do you have (or feel you must develop) regarding monetary ransom of a kidnapped missionary?
5. What post-trauma care is given to your mission force family that has gone through a situation of violence, illness, death?
6. What kind of pre-field missionary training do you give or encourage for contexts of danger, violence, persecution, or martyrdom?
7. What more ought we to be saying to our churches and future missionaries in this area?
8. Please include a short example or case study if you can.

## SUMMARY OF RESPONSES

Suppose you are the leader of a church or agency that places personnel in dangerous places, as many inevitably do. How should you prepare your people for such assignments? What should you do if and when danger changes from being a possibility to actual experience? What preparation, plans, and policies should you have in place ahead of time and understood by all who might be involved? How can you act responsibly, while also recognizing that some of the places most acutely in need of committed gospel witness are also those most hostile to it? And how will you care for people after such an event?

What follows is an amalgam of twelve extended responses to the questions. There was significant consensus, but with some individual details.

The first two questions relate to policies and guidelines for sending (1) short-term and (2) longer-term missionaries to dangerous contexts. It is rare to send short-termers into dangerous or isolated situations, and where it is countenanced at all it is only where there is a mature team already in place to whom the short-termer will go. That team could be from a partner agency rather than the one sending the short-termers, but it must be stable and experienced, affirming in their willingness to receive the person, and able to provide appropriate guidance and mentoring. One agency specifies that short-termers are required to take personal responsibility to have travel insurance with evacuation provisions, whereas long-termers are more likely to be covered by their agency in such an eventuality. Several emphasize that the short-termer must obey instructions from the team leadership, but this too is also required of long-termers. This is especially important in order to protect local believers when there is trouble.

Many agencies have quite stringent recruiting procedures, especially for those wanting to go to dangerous or difficult places. They explore general maturity, emotional and physical health, and spiritual resilience, which are essential for such placements. They will also insist on attendance at an orientation training, where specifics relating to each destination are spelled out. One organization includes simulation training. For both short and long-term service, the agency must give careful, honest briefing about the situation into which the person will go, so that if there is the potential for danger, the worker will fully understand it, as well as their immediate family and home church. Some agencies have detailed manuals, frequently updated as situations change, to cover basic principles of handling crisis situations such as armed robbery or attack, and all serving staff are required to know this information thoroughly. Most agencies also observe advice from the national embassies of their personnel, especially in relation to evacuation when general danger levels escalate for some reason such as the outbreak of civil war.

Of course, what is perceived as a high-risk situation will vary from one part of the world to another, and indeed some contexts may pose greater risks for people from some people groups rather than others. This is especially complicated for international agencies, as their personnel come from backgrounds with different expectations about what constitutes "reasonable risk," about what hardships are acceptable, and even what the legal requirements may be of different countries from which people come. So for instance an Indian respondent comments that Indian missionaries, most of whom work cross-culturally within India, are more likely to face health hazards in remote areas than martyrdom. Many become sick with malaria, typhoid, jaundice, brain fever, and other diseases. By contrast, many Western missionaries would expect to be evacuated to expert medical care far sooner than our Indian brethren, and in any case may be covered by medical insurance not financially viable for many from the Global South.

Surprisingly, despite most agencies having documents and training on practical responses to dangerous situations, only one, the "umbrella" German organization DMG, has a specific summary statement giving a biblical theology of persecution or martyrdom. Perhaps this reflects evangelical activism, but several leaders, surprised by the question, commented that this is something they need to act on. Kirk Franklin, of Wycliffe International, sadly comments that missions originating in the West do not have such a theology of suffering because culturally in recent decades there has been a focus on harm reduction, risk avoidance, and personal comfort. At the same time, most agencies have some general statements which could be a good starting point, and indeed represent some fundamental truths. So for instance, Patrick Fung of OMF International affirms that "our dependence is upon God for our safety and security."

> And he began to teach them that the Son of Man must suffer many things and be rejected by the elders and the chief priests and the scribes and be killed, and after three days rise again.
> Mark 8:31

There is strong consensus that in the event of a kidnapping, including of children of missionaries, no ransom should be paid, as this endangers everybody else. This of course is agonizing for the family of the kidnapped person, so that special care is given to support them and provide ongoing counseling. In most cases the family would be evacuated to their home country, or at least to a place of safety. Since this is agreed policy, the kidnapped person would be comforted to know his or her family were safe and being cared for. Sometimes a kidnapping incident is an indication that a whole team should be evacuated, at least for the time being, but this too is a very difficult decision and emotionally demanding. Advice about wider evacuation is sought from local believers, particularly where they will be directly affected by potential further action by the kidnappers. Where possible, experienced negotiators are brought in, and local government authorities are informed as necessary. If the situation is very sensitive, it may not be wise to circulate information widely, but where the incident is already in the public domain Christian networks are mobilized to pray for all involved and for a safe resolution. Agencies will seek to reach close relatives and home churches to inform them of what is happening before the media, Christian or otherwise, publishes news.

Any traumatic experience—kidnap, rape, armed robbery, murder, and many more—can deeply affect the person or persons at the heart of it, but also team members. Most agencies have systems in place to provide counseling by professionals and good debriefing, but inevitably that varies from place to place in quality and adequacy. None of the respondents commented on counseling for local believers who may also be badly affected; there wasn't an explicit question relating to that, but we do have a responsibility of care not only to our own members but also to those among whom we serve. Also, most respondents spoke of immediate crisis care, for which there is now considerable experience in many parts of the world, but little was said about long-term support. Both adults and children often struggle with the aftermath of trauma for many years after the event.

Good post-trauma care is expensive, and makes heavy demands in poorer constituencies. Bob Lopez of the Philippine Mission Association writes, "There are times, depending on the need, when we try to raise financial support for the family," an important reminder that more and more of the world's missionary force come from countries where general state support (free health care, pensions, cheap public housing, etc.) is limited or absent; here the mission agency may have a long-term very practical responsibility to help those bereaved or injured. From India comes the observation that at the present time there is very little available care, and very little budget for post-trauma care; at the same time, there is growing awareness that this needs to be tackled.

Along with professional care, of course there is the crucial support of a loving community. So, the church family, both where the missionary is serving and also his or her sending church, play an important role. However, in both cases there may be limited understanding of what the hurt person is going through. Often the traumatized person cannot explain adequately, and very deep wounds are not easily expressed in words. Those who wish to help may not have the skill or imagination to know how best to do that. Nonetheless, both agency leaders and praying friends can surround the person with love and patient support.

## QUESTIONS FOR REFLECTION

1. Is it possible to anticipate every crisis that might arise? How can the individual, his sending church, and the agency, work together to provide reasonable training? If the individual claims to have a strong sense of call to a potentially dangerous place, how should the church and agency handle the situation if they consider him to be unsuitable?

2. Growing numbers of cross-cultural missionaries come from poor economies, or places where the sending church is small and/or poor. What special challenges face them? Should the global church provide funds for health care for them, for instance? What would be the positive impact and what would be the negative impact of such action?

3. Refusal to pay ransom money for a kidnapped person often leads to their death. Is this policy of refusing to pay ransom a right one? Why? Why not? Are there circumstances when it might be right to pay? What would be the likely consequence?

# CHAPTER 45

# MISSIONARY TRAINING

## In the Context of Suffering, Persecution, and Martyrdom
*Rob Brynjolfson*

## IN HARM'S WAY

Ministry trainers take the task of preparing people for God's service very seriously. We are conscious of the implications and inherent risks, each life a gamble, and fret over the potential tarnishing of the ministry when a poorly trained workforce is launched into service. Of course, our concern should be for people, not just the ministry, but sometimes we fret more over our institutional reputation, or perhaps, our own. Training in and for the context of suffering, persecution, and martyrdom (SPM) raises a different spectre, potentially a very real and long nightmare, filled with shadows that haunt our conscience, because we might find ourselves asking, "Did we do all we could to prepare that person to be placed in harm's way?"

The Mission Commission of the World Evangelical Alliance (WEA-MC) from the outset invested significant resources to address the concerns of missionary training, especially with the emergence of the Global South as a missionary force. Missionary training benefited through WEA-MC sponsored research focusing on causes of attrition and factors in retention of field workers. This resulted in a commitment to develop training that intentionally addressed these causes and factors. We hope that the missionary training emphasis shifted from being content driven to results driven, and that it focuses on character and spiritual qualities as well as acquiring job-ready skills for cross-cultural service. Integral training, or training that focused on the whole person, emerged as the rallying cry for those committed to the pursuit of excellence in missionary training. Now it is time to ask if the training we offer adequately prepares people to serve in the contexts where suffering, persecution, and martyrdom are realities.

A well-known homiletics instructor humbly expressed his strongest credential for training preachers when he quipped, "I might not be the best preacher, but I have listened to thousands of sermons, and I know what a good sermon is." I approached the task of researching and writing about missionary training in the context of SPM conflicted, or at least, afflicted with the consciousness that this has never been a focus of any of the training programs in which I have been involved. I can offer no credential of expertise in training in and for the context of SPM. All I can bring to this topic is the blessing of having good and sometimes intimate knowledge of different training programs around the world. As such, over a decade and a half of reviewing and collecting many dozens of missionary training outcome profiles expressing institutional or programmatic training goals, I cannot remember ever seeing a learning outcome that was directed specifically and intentionally to the area of SPM. Intuitively (before initiating any research) I proposed that we would be hard-pressed to find any significant training for this area. Immediately, I knew this void must be filled, this inadequacy addressed. In the course of writing this article I have been enlightened, but too many of our programs do not intentionally address this needy training area with explicit learning outcomes or goals.

## A BIBLICAL MODEL

The New Testament is rich with examples of effective training, usually on-the-job and strongly interpersonal. Our Lord himself departed from existing school-type training methods and chose a training model that forced the small community of disciples to walk and breathe his mission. His mission was fraught with danger and would ultimately end with suffering, persecution, and martyrdom. The Sermon on the Mount, one of the few recorded formal educational lessons of Jesus, spoke of blessings to be found in persecution, but that those persecuted for following Jesus would find themselves in line with the faithful prophets of old (Matt 5:11–12). Again the Lord warned the disciples of coming hardships when he sent the

"Blessed are you when people hate you and when they exclude you and revile you and spurn your name as evil, on account of the Son of Man!" Luke 6:22

disciples out to complete ministry internships, saying, "I am sending you out like sheep among wolves" (Matt 10:16; cf. Luke 10:3). There is a hint from amongst the disciples that danger lurked in Judea. The Apostle John records their objection: "But Rabbi," they said, "a short while ago the Jews tried to stone you, and yet you are going back there?" (John 11:8). And minutes later it was the sinister, dark, and brooding comment of Thomas that suggested they were all walking into a potentially fatal encounter. The apostle writes, "Then Thomas (called Didymus) said to the rest of the disciples, 'Let us also go, that we may die with him'" (John 11:16). These were not mere accidental encounters with suffering, persecution, or potential martyrdom. The Lord, who we presume was anything but accidental, intentionally used these opportunities to prepare the disciples for the future.

Enoch Wan and Mark Hedinger, in *Missionary Training for the Twenty-first Century: Biblical Foundations* (originally published in Spanish), identified several aspects of the methodology and content of the Apostle Paul's missionary training practices. This article points to 2 Timothy 2:2 as one of the critical passages alluding to the hands-on method of training used by the apostle. Implied in this training of trainers injunction is, as Wan and Hedinger see, a list of the many things that Timothy and others were witnesses to and which needed to be passed on in the training of others. In this list, Wan and Hedinger see persecution (with the examples of being jailed, beaten, and suffering for the gospel—Acts 16:22) and preaching under difficult circumstances (Acts 18:5) (Wan and Hedinger 2010, 6). The article concludes that missionary training strategies, following the example of the Apostle Paul, must include six strategies, one of which is "an emphasis on how to minister during persecution and opposition." So, now we might ask, how are we doing at this important task in missionary training?

In his own dissertation project entitled "Towards a Paradigm of Integrated Missionary Training" (2006), Mark Hedinger looked for themes found in the Apostle Paul's missionary training. One of the stronger themes was "the missionary as defender against opposition" and he listed four examples of defending against opposition, including persecution using the passages 2 Timothy 2:9,10,14 and Titus 1:11 (93). In a further analysis he proposes that, based on the apostle's training examples, missionary training content needs to include confronting opposition by looking at rejection, desertion, the abuse by government or other authority, and religious persecution (154f). He also finds that the missionary should be trained to react to opposition by realizing "that God rewards endurance (2 Tim 4:8)" and by a willingness to "suffer for the sake of the gospel and endure (2 Tim 1:8–12)" (172).

## SCOPING OUT THE PANORAMA

From the beginning there was a consciousness in WEA Mission Commission publications regarding the need to prepare people for suffering or worse. Lois McKinney, in her chapter "New Directions in Missionary Education" from the early MC publication *Internationalising Missionary Training* (Taylor 1991), headlined one of the foreseen needs of missionary training and said:

> Many missionaries from both the North Atlantic and the Two-Thirds World come from social positions of relative affluence. They will often be working in the midst of political turmoil, economic chaos, and religious persecution. They must learn how to minister to the poor and the oppressed through a moderate lifestyle, loving deed, and social action. (McKinney 1991, 244)

It is noteworthy that she assumed missionaries would come from the more affluent countries. The twenty-first century began with the explosion of missionary activity that in many ways no longer fits this paradigm. We have witnessed how nationals of countries with little political influence or economic power have been denied their rights, mistreated, or did not enjoy access to due process under the rule of law. The new mission force around the world is in greater jeopardy of a denial of protection and legal rights. Her observation that new workers will be serving in the midst of political turmoil, economic chaos, and religious persecution was accurate and valid. The last statement, about ministering "through a moderate lifestyle, loving deed, and social action" is not entirely representative of the present situation. This is a valid statement, but it assumes that the missionary needs to be prepared for those suffering privation and injustice, and makes no mention of the explicit risk to missionaries who serve in dangerous circumstances. This assumption, that missionaries will not necessarily be the target of suffering, persecution, and martyrdom needs to be dispelled.

The allusion of ignorance in the last paragraph of the introductory section "In Harm's Way" demonstrated that, though I suspected little was being done in our missionary training programs to prepare people to serve in the context of SPM, more research was obviously needed. A brief questionnaire with five questions was prepared and sent to a list of experienced missionary trainers who were in a position to comment on the state of missionary training in their own countries and regions. Indeed, the questions were general, inquiring about any programs and not just the program in which the trainer was involved. Respondents, though few in number, provided representation from five continents: Brazil, South Africa, West Africa, Korea, the Middle East, and North America.

## AVAILABLE TRAINING – POSING FIVE QUESTIONS (Q) AND A SERIES OF ANSWERS (A)

*Q 1:* The first question we advanced simply asked respondents to describe what training (planned learning experiences) is available in their area to help people serve in the context of suffering, persecution, and martyrdom. One respondent questioned whether this was even the right approach, appealing for the topic of SPM to be covered with greater theological integration.

### A: Theological Integration

Recalling early missionary trainer experiences in a country where Christians were persecuted for their faith, one respondent pointed out, "We didn't have any specific courses in 'Persecution,' but EVERYTHING we talked about in class was deeply rooted in the context, which was a context of Eastern Orthodoxy/Islam/Communist persecution (a powerful and fascinating dynamic!)." This respondent was deeply concerned that a subject like persecution needs to be fully integrated into a theological framework.

> My main take-away from those nine years (nineteen years total in the country) is that ALL theological education must be thoroughly integrated between theory and practice. I would be very suspicious of a program that had a specific course in persecution, because it would hint that courses in Bible, theology, etc., might not be adequately interacting with the real world.

In subsequent correspondence, this contributor admitted that theological integration is next to impossible to achieve in circumstances where there is no "context" of persecution. Many Western countries lack courses or planned learning experiences to train missionaries going into these difficult contexts presumably because persecution is not known. Perhaps, now is the time to work towards some form of theological integration, and if that is not possible, to address this need more directly with planned learning experiences so that missionaries leaving the Americas, Europe, or other parts of the world devoid of persecution, can receive some preparation for the task ahead of them.

### A: Implicit Training

A well-established missionary training program in Asia was able to point to some isolated planned learning activities that were defined as "direct training experiences" relating to SPM. Examples given were courses in crisis management, as well as case studies and the use of debriefing. This same program described more abundant planned learning activities that were semidirect or indirect training experiences. Semidirect training experiences included: cross-cultural evangelism, cross-cultural discipleship training, cross-cultural church planting, and cross-cultural ministry strategy, where the challenges of ministering in SPM contexts would be addressed. Perhaps the strongest contribution then, was from the indirect training experiences. These were more informal and affective in nature. Examples given were: ministry philosophy, life formation, tutorial meetings, missionary life and work, and devotions.

As in the example of the training program from Latin America, a strong emphasis is placed on Bible studies that relate to the subject, usually in smaller groups or individually with mentors. Added to this is a strong emphasis on prayer for the suffering church and missionaries.

Both of these examples share the approach that the subject of SPM as a training topic is neither absent nor explicit. These spontaneous learning activities are powerful tools that can transform lives and prepare people to face difficult circumstances. However, an educational technologist would persistently ask, how can we make this intentional, and therefore, something that can't be missed?

### *A: Generalized and Theoretical*

The lack of theological integration was highlighted as a challenge for training people outside of the context of SPM. Another very serious obstacle to training in the absence of the context of SPM is the tendency to approach the subject in a manner that is both generalized and theoretical. Out of the African south comes a response that admits that few people can truly grasp what persecution means. The lack of exposure to real life suffering or persecution unavoidably restricts learning to a more superficial level. This respondent wrote:

> The concept of persecution and martyrdom is not well understood due to the lack of worldview and understanding as well as exposure to the realities out there. In our training school we do talk about it and go into some level of depth, but still we note that due to the lack of exposure it stays a theoretical concept rather than a reality.

In Brazil, programs try to place students into internship experiences that are very challenging to familiarize them with real challenges.

> Our students go to practical mission placements, which are not the easygoing church life ones, but in the very poor northeast semi-desert; among the tribal peoples and those living at the margins of the Amazon rivers; among the very poor in slum communities, with children living on the streets and marginalized inner city dwellers; as well as in other countries. The students have a mentor who accompanies them during their placement and does debriefing when they return.

Like cross-cultural adaptation or language acquisition, our programs must strive to provide learning experiences that expose students to the realities of SPM in some way or other. Our efforts will not be perfect if our context is far removed from the realities of SPM, but here we must become creative and help students to engage emotionally with the topic. Simulations and case studies can make the subject emotionally real and dynamic. Too easily we view these techniques as games and diversions, but experiential learning might be the only way for students to engage these subjects emotionally. We do well to remind ourselves here that research demonstrates that when subjects are learned with emotional detachment, little life-transformation (significant affective learning) occurs.

## ABSENCE OF LEARNING OUTCOMES

*Q / A 2:* When asked to provide learning outcomes that addressed training for SPM, most respondents admitted that their institutions did not target these areas with expressed learning goals. A couple of programs provided examples of learning outcomes that relate to SPM. For example, trainees would "accept God's purpose of mission," or "recognize God's sovereignty," which are valid and important learning outcomes. Yet, we are not assured that a trainee will be ready to meet persecution or suffering unless some competencies are created and addressed more explicitly.

In some instances, the topic is addressed directly with learning outcomes. One example comes from a well-established training program in Asia where a learning outcome is expressed directly. Trainees would "learn how to deal with specific suffering, persecution, and martyrdom cases." Or in another example from Nigeria, where many missionary trainees anticipate serving in the conflicted northern regions of that country, arguably twelve outcomes address training needs for missionaries serving in the context of SPM. These twelve outcomes are listed below under the headings of know, be, and do.

"I tell you, my friends, do not fear those who kill the body, and after that have nothing more that they can do. But I will warn you whom to fear: fear him who, after he has killed, has authority to cast into hell. Yes, I tell you, fear him!"
*Luke 12:4–5*

Several of these learning outcomes are very striking. How many institutions and programs from affluent and well-protected countries would say they train missionaries to be "ready to pay the price" or "ready to die"? I know a missionary who packs a 45 (calibre pistol), but I don't think this is what our respondent intended by the outcome "art of self-defense." This example of learning outcomes coming from a context where trainees expect to face persecution highlights how training needs are vastly different from one context to another. However, in this we cannot equivocate, unless our institutions create and target explicit learning outcomes focused on the training needs of people serving in the context of SPM, we shall fail to prepare people adequately for life threatening challenges ahead.

## SETTING PRIORITIES

*Q / A 3:* When asked, "What do you think is the greatest priority in training for people preparing to serve in the context of suffering, persecution, and martyrdom?" respondents made similar assertions: the greatest priority was in spiritual formation. Some respondents expanded their replies identifying a number of aspects of this spiritual formation that are urgently needed. Trainees need to understand God's ultimate goal for the lost and to perceive God's sovereign purpose in SPM. Also, trainees need to grasp the incarnational spirit and sacrificial life of missionaries, while learning how to protect one's self and others' lives. Finally, the need to be fortified with ongoing spiritual growth was highlighted.

From the Middle East, a respondent questions whether people are aware of the "rich theological framework of sharing in Christ's sufferings." He went on to tell a story about a conference for emerging youth leaders where the participants were asked if they were able to secure a visa, who would emigrate? Everyone raised their hand. He then asked, "How can we address the training needs of those who do not have a choice but to serve in the context of SPM?"

# FACING CHALLENGES

*Q 4:* Another question asked the respondents to identify the greatest challenges they faced in the training of missionaries to face SPM. The variety of answers could be categorized under two areas: Lack of experienced trainers and lack of exposure to realities.

### A: Lack of Experienced Trainers

There are few resources for people to draw upon, and even if there were, experience is critically important for training missionaries. As one respondent from the Middle East stated, "Words on suffering are empty from those who themselves have not suffered." One of the challenges we face is the "lack of adequate time and professional advice on the issues of suffering, persecution, and martyrdom in the various contexts and situations."

### A: Lack of Exposure to Realities

Most respondents lamented that isolation from a context of SPM meant training would be generalized and theoretical. Respondents recognized the difficulty of training people to face SPM outside of the context where these realities are faced. This was indicated by a respondent who simply said that contextualized missionary training curriculum is lacking. Training is reduced to a classroom or chapel experience and people cannot synthesize theory and praxis.

One of the aspects of this challenge is that people living in affluence or comfort face a wider learning gap than those people who are on the front lines. Someone training close to a context of SPM still identified this as a problem and mentioned that "church members are not well discipled, and so are not well prepared for missions training." In some cases, like the Korean context, this is also seen as a generational issue. Previous generations of missionaries grew up with stories of affliction and survival from the war. Younger missionaries come to training accustomed to affluence and protection. In Latin America, a respondent mentioned that a particular challenge is the emphasis on success and prosperity teaching, where people have little understanding of how suffering is a natural part of our Christian witness. From the Middle East came the comment that "the rapidity with which missionaries are pulled out by their agencies at any sign of trouble communicates a very clear message." Training missionaries in this context is challenging when the models of historical mission movements react to persecution or suffering with flight.

# A BETTER FUTURE

*Q 5:* The last question probed for new ideas, and asked, "What do you think could/should be done to help prepare people to serve in the context of suffering, persecution, and martyrdom?" Here the responses were dynamic and enthusiastic. In the case of a training program from Nigeria, we were invited to use and improve a missionary training profile in and for the context of SPM. After taking the liberty to make a few adjustments, I have included this document as an appendix. Readers will find an electronic version at www.WEAResources. org in the section for mission articles.

### A: Theology of Suffering

Respondents almost unanimously expressed the urgent need to develop and teach a genuine theology of suffering, persecution, and martyrdom. From the Middle East, we are told that this should be taught in parallel with inspirational stories of faith heroes who were willing to pay the price. Concern was expressed from Asia that missionaries would need assistance to contextualize this teaching for their context of service. In Latin America, this accompanied a suggestion that the theology of suffering needed to filter down into the church as well. A strong theology of suffering would serve church and mission well in facilitating the acquisition of a greater sacrificial attitude. The Johannine version of the great commission should be prominent, for who cannot consider the sacrificial implications of Jesus' words, "as the Father has sent me, so I am sending you" (John 20:19 NLT).

### A: Theory and Praxis

Because many training programs serve trainees in areas not afflicted with persecution, respondents saw the need to connect trainees to people and contexts where suffering and persecution are realities. Classroom learning is an obviously inadequate technique to prepare people to face persecution. Programs and institutions must creatively develop learning activities that integrate theory and practice. Trainees need to see and feel the realities of suffering and persecution. This critical exposure is certainly difficult to manage. Perhaps through carefully planned internships or experiential learning techniques trainees can be impacted by the emotional realities of service in the context of SPM. One respondent suggested that we challenge missionaries to lead by example and have outsiders who are willing to stay in times of suffering.

### A: Growing Spiritually

Though many skills are needed to be an effective witness in the face of persecution, we intuitively feel that the overwhelming and singular training need is in the area of spiritual growth and character formation. One respondent pointed out:

> Since it is now evident that many unreached peoples in the world have become more volatile than ever, it is pertinent that the mission enterprise must begin to raise die-hard missionaries who are well equipped in the KNOW-BE-DO training philosophy, where the major emphasis is on character and spiritual formation.

By *KNOW-BE-DO training philosophy*, we might presume the respondent meant a holistic or integral approach to training where we address the training needs of the whole person, and not merely focus on the acquisition of knowledge or academic skill.

## IMPLICATIONS FOR MISSIONARY TRAINING FOR BOTH NORTH AND SOUTH

Participating in research is itself a learning activity that creates awareness and encourages the discovery of solutions. In most instances participants in this five question survey made comments that a greater emphasis on training for SPM was needed. It makes this writer confident that, along with the recent interest in this topic, we will begin to see a growing emphasis on this previously ignored training need. Programs and institutions will begin to create learning outcomes to address this area of training.

However, this emerging training would profit from the counsel of our respondents by ensuring that it is firmly rooted in a strong theology of suffering, that the theory is integrated with praxis, and that it be characterized by a strong emphasis on spiritual and character formation.

This final appeal is directed to our brothers and sisters who learn about serving God in the context of suffering, persecution, and martyrdom as a way of life borne out of the reality of faithful service in a desperate context. Those of us who train in contexts of relative comfort, security, and affluence must look to you to take the lead and show us what this training must become. Give us examples of clear and finely honed learning outcomes. Help us to begin to acquire needed skills that will make our witness effective and might even save lives. Attend to our deficiencies so that we might grow in spirit and enjoy the qualities that are characteristic of effective and faithful servants in the contexts of suffering, persecution, and martyrdom.

## QUESTIONS FOR REFLECTION

1. One of the missionary training challenges identified was that of the integration between theory and practice—why is this a problem and how could theory and practice be integrated in the context where you intend to train missionaries?

2. Read through the Nigerian example "Outcomes Profile for Missionaries Serving in the Context of Suffering, Persecution, and Martyrdom" (in the appendix of this chapter), and reflect on the following: What is your first impression as you read this list of training outcomes? What caught your attention, and what do you think is missing?

3. What would you propose to do in your context of training that would intentionally address the training outcomes that are focused on character and spiritual qualities? (You can use the outcomes profile found below to remind yourself of the "Be" character and spiritual qualities.)

4. In your context of training how would you propose to address the needed skills? (You can use the outcomes profile found in the appendix to remind yourself of the "Do" skills and competencies.)

## APPENDIX: OUTCOMES PROFILE FOR MISSIONARIES SERVING IN THE CONTEXT OF SUFFERING, PERSECUTION, AND MARTYRDOM

Missionary Training Partners International
Nigeria Graduate School of Intercultural Studies
P.O. Box 2723, Jos Plateau State
E-mail: mtpinigeria@yahoo.com

Adapted from the "Competencies Profile for Missionaries Serving in the Context of Suffering, Persecution, and Martyrdom, Especially in the Islamic Context," by Segun Adekoya.

## KNOW

1. Understands the field of advocacy
2. Can describe the characteristics of good governance
3. Conversant with the history of Islam
4. Able to express the causes of crises and conflict resolution
5. Understands the fundamentals of living and coping in hostile environments
6. Familiar with the Arabic language and Qur'an
7. Can describe principles for the prevention and management of crises
8. Grasps the fundamentals of contextualization and church planting in Northern Nigeria
9. Is familiar with the Sharia legal system
10. Understands principles of evangelism within a Muslim worldview
11. Can thoroughly answer the question, What is jihad?
12. Understands the similarities between the Bible and Qur'an
13. Answers the question, What has the Bible and the Qur'an to say about Isa al-Masiu?

## BE

1. Enjoys a friendly disposition
2. Lives a simple lifestyle
3. Demonstrates a life disciplined with obedience
4. Has a courageous attitude
5. Is not easily discouraged
6. Hears and listens to God
7. Not afraid to take risks
8. Serves God fearlessly
9. Relates to others with a genuine love
10. Relates to others with a generous spirit
11. Does not seek revenge when wronged
12. Models a forgiving heart
13. Lives and guides others with true wisdom
14. Models tolerance with grace and truth
15. Expresses a sacrificial attitude willing to pay the price
16. Possesses an attitude of readiness to die
17. Relies on God for protection

## DO

1. Skilled in animal husbandry (e.g., cow herding)
2. Demonstrates the ability and discipline to learn the language
3. Skilled in post-crisis counseling (trauma) and rehabilitation of victims of trauma
4. Adapts well to the northern culture (dress, appearance, food, communication, etc.)
5. Demonstrates skill in the art of intercession and spiritual warfare techniques for evangelism
6. Skilled in relevant business networking with Muslims and other Christian organizations
7. Able to defend oneself appropriately

8.  Interprets and discerns the context and immediate environment
9.  Able to see and respond appropriately to early warning signs of trouble or persecution
10. Skilled in target reduction techniques
11. Improves safety by choosing appropriate living environments
12. Skilled in ministry for women
13. Able to teach

## REFERENCES

Agron, D. 2002. *Learning objectives and instructional methods for competency based missionary training.* Ann Arbor, MI: Proquest Information and Learning Company.

Harley, D. n.d. *Equipping for ministry and mission.* http://www.oikoumene.org/fileadmin/files/wcc-main/documents/p5/ete/Equipping%20for%20ministry%20and%20mission%20-%20David%20Harley.pdf.

Hedinger, M. 2006. *Towards a paradigm of integrated missionary training.* http://www.globalmissiology.org/english/resource/Hedinger_missionary_training_2006.pdf.

Lewis, J. P. 1992. *International stakeholders' perceptions of missionary competencies training profile.* Fort Collins, CO: Colorado State University.

McKinney, L. 1991. New directions in missionary education. In *Internationalising missionary training,* ed. W. D. Taylor, 241–250. Grand Rapids, MI: Baker Book House.

Sauer, C. 2008. *Between advocacy and readiness to suffer: Religious liberty and persecution of Christians as topics at the World Evangelical Alliance General Assembly and its Mission Commission Consultation.* http://worldevangelicals.org/pdf/Christof%20Sauer%20Pattaya%202009.pdf.

Wan, E., and M. Hedinger. n.d. *Missionary training for the twenty-first century: Biblical foundations.* http://ojs.globalmissiology.org/index.php/english/article/view/616/1550.

**Rob Brynjolfson**, a Canadian, is the director of the World Evangelical Alliance Leadership Institute and former director of the Mission Commission International Missionary Training Network. He coedited the manual *Integral Ministry Training Design and Evaluation* (William Carey Library, 2006) and specializes in outcome-based curriculum design and missionary training.

## BESIDE THE PROSTITUTE'S BED

Kidnapped and forced into prostitution, Elizabeth wrote verses from Psalm 27 on the wall beside her bed.

> The Lord is my light and my salvation. Whom shall I fear?
> The Lord is the stronghold of my life. Of whom shall I be afraid?
> When evil men advance against me to devour my flesh,
> When my enemies and my foes attack me,
> They will stumble and fall.

Elizabeth looked to God for rescue, and it came. The International Justice Mission discovered her and set her free. Today she is a college graduate who quotes from Psalm 34:

> I sought the Lord and he heard me,
> And delivered me from all my fears.

Miriam Adeney, *Kingdom without Borders: The Untold Story of Global Christianity* (2009, 257-58), citing Sharon Cohn Wu, "RSVPrayer: Answering God's Invitation," *Prism* 15, no. 6 (November–December 2008): 23

# CHAPTER 46

# PREPARING CHURCH AND MISSION AGENCIES

## For Suffering, Persecution, and Martyrdom
*Stephen Panya Baba*

## THE NEED TO PREPARE

Tremendous progress has been made over the years in taking the gospel to unreached people groups and for this we give God the glory. However, like God told Joshua in Joshua 13:1, there is so much land yet to be possessed. According to *Operation World*, of the world's 16,350 people groups in the Joshua Project list, 6,645 are counted in the least reached and unreached category, which is about 40.6 percent of the groups. Furthermore, the total population of individuals from unreached people is 2.84 billion, or 41.1 percent of humanity. Of great interest and special relevance to our subject is that the vast majority of the unreached originate from the "10/40 Window."

The 10/40 Window is the rectangular area of North Africa, the Middle East, and Asia lying between approximately 10 degrees and 40 degrees latitude. All fifty of the world's least Christian and least evangelized countries are located within this region. It contains more than 90 percent of the unreached people groups in the world—more than five thousand tribes and ethno-linguistic groups with little or no gospel witness.

This region is highly resistant to the gospel, a region of strong satanic strongholds. According to John Piper, reaching them, as Jesus commands, will be dangerous and costly. Some of us, and some of our children, will be killed. It is therefore not surprising that this region has the least number of missionaries. The cost of being a witness for Christ in this vast unreached region is very high and for many, it is a cost that they are either unprepared for or unwilling to bear. If the task of world evangelization is to be accomplished, then the church and the missionaries the church sends out must be prepared to pay the price for reaching the remaining unreached people groups, especially in the 10/40 Window. This will definitely involve suffering, persecution, and even martyrdom. This requires that the church and its missionaries be purposely prepared.

## THE READINESS OF CHURCH AND MISSION AGENCIES

Missionaries are sent to the field to be witnesses for the gospel from various church denominations. These denominations have, over the years, developed certain peculiarities which may include theological and doctrinal beliefs, the religio-socio and even economic environments of their operations, etc. Some churches and missionaries may therefore be more prepared to face suffering, persecution, and martyrdom because of their deliberate biblical emphasis and correct theological and doctrinal perspective of them. For example, many churches in the two-third majority of the world were founded by Western missionaries who sacrificed much in terms of suffering, persecution, and martyrdom. Consequently, they emphasized biblical teachings on the same, primarily in order to make the churches being established mission-minded who would send out indigenous missionaries that were well prepared to sacrifice and endure in taking the gospel to many other unreached areas. In fact, many such misunderstood denominations, including my own denominational church, have been wrongly accused of having preached poverty as a spiritual virtue or having equated poverty and suffering to spirituality.

Reverend Dr. Panya Baba stated that one of the then Sudan Interior Mission (SIM) principles in the beginning was planting missionary-minded churches. This was done through literary work, Bible teaching, and apprentice methods, whereby the young converts practiced what they learned as they participated in the ministry of the gospel. This was the practice of SIM from the beginning of their work in Nigeria. The natural outcome of their methods and practices ensured the establishment of indigenous missionary-minded churches ready to take gospel to other areas at great sacrifices.

Yusuf Turaki recalled the attitude of the pioneering missionaries of SIM, which was passed on to the established church, by quoting a letter written by Mr. Gowans to his mother in which he said:

> Our success in this enterprise means nothing less than the opening of the country for the gospel; our failure, at most, nothing more than the death of two or three deluded fanatics. But if we fail, it will be our fault from lack of faith. God is faithful—he faileth not. Still, even death is not a failure. His purposes are accomplished. He uses deaths as well as lives to the furtherance of his cause. After all, is it not worth the venture? Sixty millions are at stake! Is it not worth even risking our lives for so many!

Turaki concluded that there is no doubt that these pioneer missionaries were spiritually prepared to face any difficulty or danger on their way as they embarked on reaching the Sudan with the gospel. Indeed, they were, for in less than a year, two of the first three pioneer missionaries died in what later became today's Nigeria. God, however, providentially spared Roland Bingham, who pressed on with the work against all odds, and which eventually resulted in the establishment of the then SIM churches, now Evangelical Church Winning All (ECWA) churches, which has over five thousand local congregations and pastors and well over 6 million members worldwide.

Above all, the Evangelical Missionary Society (EMS) of ECWA's missionaries have continued to minister in disease-infested remote areas and in the fanatically volatile Islamic core north of Nigeria. This is a legacy that was inherited from the pioneer missionaries and which has continued to be passed on to subsequent generations. Recently, during the April 2011 Muslim uprising against Christians in Northern Nigeria, one of our EMS missionaries, Isma

Dogari, was abducted, forced into the mosque, and compelled to renounce Christ and accept Islam. When he refused, they gouged his eyes out and then killed him.

Some of the denominations established by pioneer Western missionaries that were engulfed in suffering, persecution, and martyrdom early in their ministries consequently developed a very strong resilience. This not only helped them to survive the fiery furnace, but helped best prepare them to be missionary witnesses of the gospel in similar situations of affliction. For example, when the Chinese house churches planned to embark on the "Back to Jerusalem Vision," a movement that was begun in hopes of taking the gospel to the unreached nations neighboring China all the way to Jerusalem, they first required that their best workers be sent. When deciding who these best leaders were, they looked for those who had been in leadership positions within the house churches for at least ten years, who had suffered much hardship for the Kingdom of God, and whose ministries have produced much fruit over time. These were necessary criteria, as twenty-nine out of the first thirty-six workers sent out were arrested in their first few days as missionaries! They therefore had encountered a situation they anticipated and were prepared for well in advance.

> You, however, have followed my teaching, my conduct, my aim in life, my faith, my patience, my love, my steadfastness, my persecutions and sufferings that happened to me at Antioch, at Iconium, and at Lystra—which persecutions I endured; yet from them all the Lord rescued me. Indeed, all who desire to live a godly life in Christ Jesus will be persecuted. *2 Timothy 3:10–12*

Most denominations who were the fruit of sacrificial missionary ventures or who have grown and thrived in the midst of suffering, persecution, and martyrdom would naturally be more prepared and adapted to reach out to similar areas of hardship. Unfortunately, many churches planted out of modern denominations have not had the privilege of developing from these difficult backgrounds, but are a product of modern showmanship evangelism or the so-called prosperity gospel—a gospel that is propagating Christianity mainly to those already evangelized, and which is devoid of the requirement of the believers to take up their cross and, like Paul, fill up in their flesh what is still lacking in regard to Christ's afflictions for the sake of his body the church (Col 1:24). Thus they are not prepared and willing to pay the price of taking the gospel to the unreached or least evangelized people groups.

Other churches, especially in the western hemisphere but also in some of the regions of the Majority South of the world, have become comfortable and complacent over the years. They have lost evangelistic fire and missionary zeal and certainly are reluctant to venture out of their comfort zone, to risk anything for the sake of spreading the gospel which they profess is the only means and power for salvation of souls. In 1 Chronicles 12:32 the men of Isaachar were reputed to be men who understood the times and knew what Israel should do. In times like these, there is definitely a need to consciously reawaken and prepare the church and mission agencies to face the challenges of missions in the twenty-first century. This necessarily entails preparing them for suffering, persecution, and martyrdom.

## A TWOFOLD APPROACH

Generally, preparing the church and mission agencies for suffering, persecution, and martyrdom can be considered from two major perspectives:

## THE THEOLOGICAL, DOCTRINAL, AND SPIRITUAL PERSPECTIVE

It was the correct biblical, theological, doctrinal, and spiritual perspective that inspired the great William Carey, reputed father of modern missions, to reawaken the entire church of Christ to its divine responsibility to take the gospel to the unreached people groups of the world. In the present age, it is the correct biblical, theological, doctrinal, and spiritual view of suffering, persecution, and martyrdom that is needed to spur the church into reaching out to the remaining unreached people groups who are in so-called closed countries. It will require sacrifice, even the sacrifice of our lives, to take the gospel to them.

The church needs to be awakened to the gospel truth that, in the words of Pastor Tson, "Christ's suffering is for our propitiation, our suffering is for propagation." Suffering, persecution, and martyrdom, as a necessary price to pay in the propagation of the gospel, are emphasized in the Scriptures. These need to be taught and emphasized in the church and mission agencies. Mission agencies need to ensure that the missionaries being sent out are most acquainted with these particular Scriptures, a few of which are set out below:

- The Lord Jesus said those who would follow him must take up their cross. By this, he was referring to following in the foot path of his suffering, persecution, and even death if it be God's will (Matt 16:24).
- The Bible makes it clear that "we must go through many hardships to enter the kingdom of God" (Acts 14:22).
- The Lord Jesus warned us that "a time is coming when anyone who kills you will think he is offering a service to God" (John 16:2–3). How true indeed it is for many who are being martyred by Islamic fanatics today in the name of carrying out the injunction of Allah their god.
- Peter said, "Dear friends, do not be surprised at the painful trial you are suffering, as though something strange were happening to you" (1 Pet 4:12).
- James said, "Consider it pure joy, my brothers, whenever you face trials of many kinds, because you know that the testing of your faith develops perseverance. Perseverance must finish its work so that you may be mature and complete, not lacking anything" (James 1:2–5).
- Speaking about the end times that we are in, Revelation 13:5–7 says, "The beast was given a mouth to utter proud words and blasphemies and to exercise his authority for forty-two months. He opened his mouth to blaspheme God, and to slander his name and his dwelling place and those who live in heaven. He was given power to make war against the saints and to conquer them." Thus, martyrdom is definitely God's will for some believers.

Church and mission agencies should not, however, encourage believers and missionaries to wish or seek for persecution, suffering, or martyrdom for the cause of the gospel. Writing on wishing for persecution, Gordon Heath emphasizes this point, saying early Christians were wary of those seeking after persecution. The early church learned quickly that those who sought after it were usually the ones unable to stand it. He went on to say that persecution needs to be seen as it really is—"bloody, painful, and a tragedy." Christians should expect and be ready for persecution, but should not seek or wish for it. If it comes and cannot be avoided, then suffer. But if it does not come, do not wish for it or bring it about.

Except the church and indeed mission agencies are prepared to accept suffering, persecution, and martyrdom as part of the divine plan and purposes of their calling, it could be their greatest undoing. Adoniran Judson lived on the great hills of God's sovereign grace. He faced so much adversity on the mission field, including losing his wives and children and becoming psychologically depressed, he confessed, "If I had not felt certain that every additional trial was ordered by infinite love and mercy, I could not have survived my accumulated sufferings."

A renewed emphasis on developing believers' personal relationship and fellowship with the Lord needs to be made in the church and by mission agencies if believers and missionaries are to cope and thrive in an atmosphere of sufferings, persecution, and martyrdom. In many cases, missionaries end up ministering in isolated and very harsh situations so that it is the inner spirituality, built up and sustained through the missionary's habit of personal prayer and fellowship with the Lord, that would sustain him. It is not uncommon for missionaries to be arrested and caged in prisons and subjected to very hard labor. In such instances, their only survival resource is their inner spiritual strength, as they are often stripped of all human fellowship and help. Believers and missionaries can only thrive in situations of suffering, persecution, and martyrdom if they pay enough attention to developing these inner spiritual resources. This is the general experience of the church in China and in most other countries of similar circumstances. The brutal persecution of the church in China resulted in the church being stripped of all the external things associated with Christianity. Church buildings were confiscated and either demolished or used as houses, gymnasiums, or storage facilities. Bibles and hymnbooks were burned, while almost the entire church leadership was removed. However, despite living in the midst of a system dedicated to destroying them, churches in China have learned to have no fear—not because they enjoy persecution and torture, but because they have met God and have been deeply transformed. They have experienced God's deep intimate love and come to personally know the truth of his promises.

## PHYSICAL PREPARATION

Nowhere is the truth of Matthew 10:16 more applicable than with regard to how the church and mission agencies should handle the issue of suffering, persecution, and martyrdom. There is need to be as shrewd as snakes but innocent as doves. While the church needs to prepare believers and missionaries for any eventuality and indeed, as earlier stressed, to be ready to suffer and if necessary die because of their Christian witness, there is a theological basis for the church to take reasonable steps in preparing believers and missionaries physically for a practical response.

Some sufferings and persecution can actually be induced by ignorance, insensitivity, and even blatant disregard to the culture, tradition, and dominant religion of the community or mission fields. Therefore, missionaries need to be properly oriented to minister within the cultural and socioreligious context of their fields, to avoid self-inflicted suffering.

There also has been a major shift in the attitude of many (certainly not all) of today's missionaries from Western countries compared to the veteran missionaries of old, at least in the eyes of an ordinary African observer.

The "old veterans" were definitely more prepared for very adverse circumstances. This showed in the very scanty material possessions they brought along with them to the mission field. Furthermore, they were more willing to live at a basic subsistence level with their indigenous mission populace for their whole lifetime. Some missionaries actually started to practice how they would live on the mission field while still in their home country by living with far less luxury and less sumptuous meals. On the contrary, many of today's missionaries come with varied and heavy equipment, imported food stuffs, and other conveniences to make their lives as comfortable as possible on the so-called mission field. Unlike before, their mission field base is often restricted to towns and cities, because of, as it is often reasoned, "security and health concerns." Many of today's missionaries operate from their comfortable bases in towns and cities, paying occasional visits to indigenous missionaries who are laboring in very dangerous and difficult terrains. Such missionaries also normally stay on the mission field only for as long as it is convenient for them. They often fly out at the slightest hint of danger or conflict. This kind of attitude is one of the chief reasons that has promoted the idea, wrongly or rightly, that Global South mission agencies only need financial support from Northern partners. The idea is that this financial support can sponsor many more indigenous missionaries already accustomed to hardship and so be more effective, at a fraction of the cost, than a Western missionary.

> Jesus must therefore make it clear beyond all doubt that the "must" of suffering applies to his disciples no less than to himself. Just as Christ is Christ only in virtue of his suffering and rejection, so the disciple is a disciple only in so far as he shares his Lord's suffering and rejection and crucifixion. Discipleship means adherence to the person of Jesus, and therefore submission to the law of Christ which is the law of the cross.
>
> D. Bonhoeffer in *The Cost of Discipleship* (1976, 96)

Missionaries coming from developed counties, especially the West, need to be oriented to the need for them to be witnesses to the indigenous mission people groups in their context and to be ready to suffer a reduced standard of living, persecution, and even martyrdom with the sheep that the Lord gives them to take care of and not behave like hirelings that would flee once there is the slightest threat.

Although missionaries should be prepared to be willing to suffer and even die if it be God's sovereign will, the experience of Christ after his birth (Matt 2:13) teaches us that there may be times to actually run away from persecution. When King Herod ordered that children of two years old and under should be killed, God ordered the parents of the baby Jesus to run to Egypt until the reigning king died. Also, Paul's experience is a very good illustration of the need to be open to God's leading and directive in such situations. Early on, when he was being persecuted by the Jews, he was let down through the wall window in a basket. Another time, however, he was warned of the danger of death he faced but he responded that his life was worth nothing to him if only he could complete the task of spreading the gospel (Acts 20:24).

The Chinese church has made missionaries prepare to be able to run and escape if the Lord so leads. They say, "We know that the Lord sends us to prison to witness for him, but we also believe that the devil sometimes wants us imprisoned to stop the ministry God has called us to do. We teach the missionaries special skills, such as how to free themselves from handcuffs in thirty seconds and how to jump from second-story windows without injuring themselves." This kind of preparation is not out of place for the church and especially for missionaries who would serve in persecution-prone countries, like the 10/40 Window countries.

Although a mission agency may need to put in place emergency evacuation plans in case of danger to the missionaries, decisions as to whether the missionaries should stay or flee should be taken by the missionaries and not forced on them as a matter of general policy.

Drawing from the experience of our denominational (ECWA) church, the church needs to take the following measures in order to prepare for suffering, persecution, and martyrdom:

### Prayer
The church should be highly mobilized to consistently pray against further occurrence of violence and for the comfort and encouragement of victims of violence.

### Sensitizing church leaders and members on early warning signs of conflict and how to get help
From our experience, Christians have been reactive to conflicts rather than proactive. Church members need to be properly sensitized and taught how to detect impending attacks and how to get to safety during such attacks.

### Providing immediate reliefs
The church must be prepared at all times, because of the increasing frequency of attacks, to move into affected areas to check on the conditions of its members and to offer immediate relief in terms of resettlement for displaced persons, food, clothing, medical care, blankets, mattresses, and other essential items to affected families. A network should be established which would make it easier to mobilize church members and Christians to crisis-free areas, states, zones, or even countries and to send help to affected brethren in need immediately and on long-term bases.

### Supporting members to rebuild their homes and churches
The church must establish a crisis relief fund from which it can draw upon to help its members rebuild their homes and places of worship. This should be done as a means of ameliorating their suffering, but also in ensuring that the presence of Christian witness is maintained in those areas.

### Investigation, report compilation, and the presentation of church position before the commissions of enquiries and the media
There is a need for the church to objectively analyze each crisis situation (its causes, damage level, and its intents) in order to come up with a comprehensive report to the church

leadership. In a country like Nigeria, the government traditionally commissions enquiries into the crisis. The report of the church can be sent to the commission as the voice of the affected members.

### Legal representation for arrested members

As often is the case during religious violence, members of the church are often wrongly arrested by religiously biased law enforcement agents, thereby compounding the suffering for families whose breadwinners in most cases are detained. The church should be able to have free legal services they can turn to in order to ensure that such members get justice and are released.

### Appeal for calm and to shun violence

Unlike most religious bodies in the country who often use their places of worship to incite and inflict pain and launch violence against Christians, the church should use its pulpit and the media to appeal to its members and Christians alike to remain calm in the face of persecution against them by avoiding violence and seeking peace by all means necessary.

### Consultation with other religious groups and government

The church should continue to meet with government authorities where possible to consult and proffer useful suggestions that would help stop further crises in the country due to increasing religious intolerance.

### Working with security

Where possible, the church should be in constant touch with the military, police, and other security agencies to help bring the violent situation under control and if possible to prevent the violence before it occurs.

On a last note the question arises, should Christians and mission agencies be prepared to defend themselves using weapons of war? This is a very difficult question that would need separate consideration. However, it is certain that, unlike Muslims who consider jihadists who kill, get killed, or commit suicide in the course of spreading Islam as martyrs, no Christian can be such considered as a martyr except that he dies willingly as a necessary sacrifice he has to make because of his Christian witness.

## QUESTIONS FOR REFLECTION

1. What were the principles of pioneer SIM missionaries in terms of willingness to pay the cost of establishing churches in the interior of Africa? What was the fruit of their attitude and dedication? How does their example inspire us in our work?

2. How, according to Baba, can churches learn to be prepared for suffering and martyrdom, and what would be inadequate attitudes in response to such struggles? How does your church respond to such questions: both in the local and the global church of Christ?

3. What do you think about the measures the ECWA churches have developed to relate to their crisis and persecution? How can we adapt their guidelines to our own and other contexts?

## REFERENCES

Abu, S. n.d. *ECWA's response to the religious conflict in Plateau and other northern states of Nigeria.* Paper presentation to the ECWA conflict response secretary.

Baba, P. 2009. *A vision received, a vision passed on.* Jos, Nigeria: ACTS.

Hattaway, P. 2003. *Back to Jerusalem.* Tyrone, GA: Authentic Media.

Heath, G. L. 2010. Wishing for persecution? *International Journal for Religious Persecution* 3 no. 1, 15–22. www.iirf.eu.

Mandryk, J. 2010. *Operation world.* Colorado Springs, CO: Biblica.

Piper, J. 2009. *Filling up the afflictions of Christ.* Wheaton, IL: Crossway.

Turaki, Y. 1993. *An introduction to the history of SIM/ECWA in Nigeria 1893–1993.* Jos, Nigeria: ECWA Publications.

**Stephen Panya Baba** holds a university degree in accounting and a master's degree in biblical studies (MABS) from ECWA Theological Seminary, Igbaja, Nigeria. He had twelve years experience as a church planter and pastor in Abuja, Federal Capital Territory of Nigeria, before assuming his present office as the director of Evangelical Missionary Society (EMS) of the Evangelical Church Winning All (ECWA) in January 2009. He is based in Jos, Central Nigeria.

Song 1-14
I Refuse, I Refrain
*Tesfaye Gabbiso*

መዝሙር 1-14
እምቢ አሻፈረኝ
በተስፋዬ:ጋቢሶ

1. A friend of the dead
   A sinner was I;
   Believing the Lord, I was saved from loss.
   Though I'm forced to deny now
   This life of mine.
   I will not deny my Jesus
   And worship an object.
   I refuse, I refuse, I refuse.

1: የሙታን ባልንጅራ
   ኃጢአተኛ ሳለሁ
   ጌታን ብማመኔ ከጥፋት ድኛለሁ
   የሕይወቴን ጌታ እንድክድ
   አሁን ብገደደም
   ኢየሱሴን ክጄ
   ግሉዝ አላመልክም

CHORUS:
   I refuse, I refrain.
   I will not worship the image.
   Nor kneel down before a man-made thing.
   From the burning anger of Nebuchadnezzar,
   My Lord, whom I serve, will surely deliver
   me.

አዝማች:
   እምቢ አሻፈረኝ
   እምስሉ አልሰግድም
   ለሰው እድ ሥራ አልገበረከክም
   ከናቡክደነጾር የቁጣ ነበልባል
   የማመልከው ጌታዬ በርግጥ ያድነኛል
   እምቢ እምቢ እምቢ

2. I can see the furnace.
   I can feel the heat.
   I'll not hate it because of fear.
   It will purge and cleanse me;
   It will make me fit for His heavenly kingdom.
   It would never bring hurt as people might
   think.

2: አቶኑ ይታየኛል
   ግለቱ ይሰማኛል
   በአጄ አልጠላውም
   እንጸት ያጠራኛል
   ለሰማያዊው መንግስት ብቁ ያደርገኛል
   ሰው እንደሚያስበው መቼ ይነዳኛል

3. Those who were in the fire—
   Even the smoke hasn't affected them.
   But to those who tied them up and cast
   them into the fire,
   The flame of the fire consumed them.
   Since I have such a powerful Lord
   Let the fire burn seven times hotter.
   What does it matter to me?

3: በእሳት ውስጥ ያሉትን
   ጭሱ ሰይነካቸው
   አስረው የጣልዋጨውን
   ወናፈልን ፈጀቸው
   እንደዚህ የሚሥራ
   ኃያል ጌታ ካለኝ
   እኔ ምን ቸገረኝ

During the Marxist years in Ethiopia (1974–91), many of the churches in Ethiopia went underground for survival. Also, in the 1960s and 1970s, a wellspring of new indigenous songs, by both soloists and choirs, sprang up throughout the nation. Prominent among the many soloists, Tesfaye Gabbiso was incarcerated for seven years because of his songs and public faith. Thus the songs became even more powerful. They were played on cassettes throughout both Christian and Muslim music shops, public markets, and homes. "I Refuse, I Refrain," the song included here from Cassette #1, is the testimony of the young men in the story of Nebuchadnezzar and the fiery furnace, an Old Testament story which surfaces in at least five of Tesfaye's songs. Currently pastor in Awasa, Ethiopia, Tesfaye has recently published an Amharic autobiography, *At That Time*, covering the years of his persecution, and soon to be released in Addis Ababa is a *diglot* (English and Amharic) of 104 of his songs. Pastor Tesfaye is frequently invited to preach and sing at Ethiopian diaspora conferences around the world. —*Lila Balisky*

*Additional references:*

Balisky, Lila. 1997. Theology in song: Ethiopia's Tesfaye Gabbiso. *Missiology: An International Review* 25, no. 4, October: 447-56.

———. 2011. *Afewerk Tekle: Mother Ethiopia.* September 4. www.artway.eu, (This meditation includes a prayer song by Tesfaye Gabbiso.)

Gabbiso, Tesfaye. 2002. በዚያን ጊዜ *[At That Time].* Addis Ababa: Ethiopian Full Gospel Believers' Church.

———. Seven cassettes presenting a total of 104 songs.

# CHAPTER 47

# PREPARING BOTH CHURCH AND MISSIONARIES: GLOBAL NORTH

*Paul Estabrooks*

In January 2004, I was leading a group from my home church in Canada on a mission trip to Cuba. The church in Cuba had experienced a significant revival movement and the fast-growing house church movement was overflowing with new believers.

In Havana we visited the Baptist Seminary and were delighted to have some time with its elderly president, Reverend Dr. Vegilla. He spoke perfect English and shared with us how he had spent five years in Castro's prison system in the 1960s just because he was a Christian pastor. He further itemized the pressures the church had experienced at the hand of the Castro regime over the past forty-five years. Then he smiled and in his very positive and gentle manner concluded, "But we have learned three things through all these years. We learned not to fear, not to hate, and not to harm!"

I have meditated on this statement for some time and concluded that it expresses very succinctly the biblical essence of standing strong through any storm. Learning "not to fear" infers developing boldness and courage. Learning "not to hate" implies focusing on love, forgiveness, and grace. And learning "not to harm" indicates commitment to the biblical principles of nonviolence and aggressive love. Three valuable insights.

Ministering to persecuted Christians in Communist countries during the Cold war years, Brother Andrew and his Open Doors teams quickly developed awareness of the need for preparatory training in regions where Christians were threatened by the prospect of persecution. Years of listening and observing principles of victorious Christian living—as well as the failures—in restricted-access countries produced a basic framework for such training.

Dr. Everett Boyce, of the Open Doors-Asia team, produced the first training manual titled *More than Conquerors*. He taught these lessons to Christians of varied denominations throughout South East Asia in the early 1980s. They primarily centered on biblical and practical methodology in preparing for and responding to the threat of Communism.

As the challenges of militant Islam and religious intolerance in Hindu and Buddhist nations increased, it was soon apparent that the preparatory training program needed expanding.

This was the origin of the training manual, *Standing Strong through the Storm* (SSTS). A committee of talented Open Doors field staff from South East Asia, the Gulf, Latin America, China, and Africa worked together for years to make sure the final product was biblical, practical, and teachable. I was privileged to be the curriculum text writer. Dr. Jim Cunningham, now with Canada Institute of Linguistics at Trinity Western University, produced a student and teacher's manual.

Though successful field testing was carried out in Sri Lanka and northeast India, it was a Muslim-Christian conflict in Ambon, Indonesia, that brought the first significant opportunity to truly see results. In 1998, two Open Doors workers met with leading pastors on the island recommending the SSTS seminar. Their response was not unexpected: they felt that the rising conflict with extremist Islam might affect Jakarta, the capital, but would not likely challenge their island where Muslims and Christians had lived together peaceably for centuries.

Indonesia has been described as a "meeting place of the world's religions." It contains the world's largest Muslim community, as well as three other major religions: Christianity, Buddhism, and Hinduism. Though the majority of the population is Muslim, Indonesia is not a religious state. Under the national motto "unity in diversity," the state philosophy of *Pancasila* is based on five principles, namely:

1. Belief in a singular and omnipotent almighty God;
2. A just, fair, and civilized humanitarianism;
3. A democracy guided by wisdom and representation;
4. A social justice for all; and
5. A united Indonesia.

In early 1999, the extremist Muslim group known as Laskar Jihad, with the help of foreigners from Afghanistan, began stirring up the Muslim community in Ambon City on Ambon Island, provincial capital of Maluku Province. An unfortunate incident between a Christian bus driver and a Muslim passenger triggered the first act of violence. The Christian community was attacked with churches burned and homes destroyed, leaving many refugees and Christian people killed.

The Christian community responded immediately. Their thinking was influenced by a concept held widely around the world—especially in countries like Sudan and Nigeria—which articulated says, "We must show those Muslims that our God is stronger than their God!"

They armed themselves and destroyed mosques, Muslim homes, and people. This ignited a flame of violence that grew larger with every incident. Soon thousands were dead, on both sides, and tens of thousands were left as homeless refugees. Police and military seemed impotent to stop the fighting. In fact, they were often charged with siding with the Laskar Jihad.

In the midst of the violence, however, were reported incidences of strong Christian witness. One such story surrounds a fifteen-year-old Christian boy named Roy Pontoh who submitted himself to martyrdom. In the summer of 1999, he attended a Christian camp on

Ambon Island where the Bible studies were from 2 Timothy on the theme of "Soldiers for Jesus Christ." An armed mob of Muslims attacked the camp and found young Roy holding his Bible. They made an example of him in front of the others, posing threatening questions which he answered with respect and gentleness. He was butchered to death with a machete and his last spoken word was "Jesus."

The cycle of violence had developed to such a severe level by late 2001 that church leaders almost gave up hope for a peaceful solution. They decided it was now time to invite Open Doors to share the SSTS seminar. Needless to say, there was violence and destruction occurring all around us as we met with fifty church leaders in Ambon City. One of the saddest scenes we witnessed was a Muslim mosque with only the blackened wall facades standing. On the walls written in red spray paint in English—not Bahasa Indonesian—were the words, "I love Jesus!" We knew Jesus was weeping as he observed the Ambon situation.

> And the soldiers led him away inside the palace (that is, the governor's headquarters), and they called together the whole battalion. And they clothed him in a purple cloak, and twisting together a crown of thorns, they put it on him. And they began to salute him, "Hail, King of the Jews!" And they were striking his head with a reed and spitting on him and kneeling down in homage to him. *Mark 15:16–19*

Response to the seminar was reserved at first but later very positive—especially to the persecution stories from other countries and the biblical teaching on forgiveness and prayer. Feedback comments included, "The question is, will I live for Jesus now? It is more difficult to live for Jesus every day than to die for him once." Another said:

> The teaching of forgiveness has been a tremendous blessing to me. The reminder of forgiving even those who have deeply hurt us and caused so much destruction has touched my life. I acknowledge that in my heart at times I want to quit forgiving. Yet I know I cannot change what Jesus had commanded us to do and that is to forgive even our enemies. I want to be more committed and put this into practice.

One memorable confession came from a respected pastor who told the group:

> The hardest teaching of this seminar has been the teaching on forgiveness. It is easy to quote Luke 23:34 where Jesus said, "Father, forgive them; for they know not what they do," but I have told myself I cannot forgive these Muslims because they *knew* what they were doing when they burned my house. They *knew* what they were doing when they murdered my wife. And they *knew* what they were doing when they burned my church! I have been unable to forgive until today. By God's grace I now do forgive them—and will forgive them.

His comments began a series of conversations at the end of the seminar about "What steps do we take next?" The seminar had affected the pastors deeply and they were now seeking wisdom on how to respond. Reverend Dr. Iman Santoso, leader of the Indonesian National Prayer Movement, was one of our team members. He proposed to the pastors that they spend the remainder of that first day of Ramadan in prayer together. This led to amazing results!

After praying together on their knees before the Lord and asking for forgiveness, healing, and reconciliation, they agreed to return to their pulpits on Sunday and make this request of their church members: Stay home for the next three days if you can; go to work only if you have to; but set aside this time for prayer and fasting before the Lord. Then like Esther, after you have fasted and prayed for three days, we will go to the Muslim leaders and seek a peace agreement (Bohm 2005, 201–2).

Unknown to the pastors and their parishioners, while they prayed and fasted, the Afghan jihad-advisors began leaving the island for Kabul to prepare for the anticipated invasion by the American army in response to 9/11.

The following week a small delegation went to the leaders of the Muslim community and asked for forgiveness and peace. The Ambon Muslim leaders accepted the peace apology and by Christmas of 2001, a peace agreement brokered by the government had been signed, the barb wire roadblocks were down and Christians and Muslims were once again purchasing from each other's shops.

A group of Christians decided to establish a 24/7 prayer tower on the top floor of the hotel where the SSTS seminar and prayer meeting was first held. The prayer vigil continues to this day.

SSTS is now being taught as a three-day seminar in more than twenty-seven languages in many parts of the world where Christians live under pressure. It is comprised of six sections following the introduction:

1. *The way of the cross.* The uniqueness of Christ is the starting point, with Isaiah's prophecy of Jesus being the "Suffering Servant" as its basis. Jesus also repeatedly pointed out that if he was persecuted, so would be his followers. A biblical definition of persecution from Luke 6:22 leads to the various biblical bases for suffering in the world and how as a Christian you respond to that suffering and persecution. The bottom line is to walk "the way of the cross" versus "the way of the culture."

2. *The victorious church and family.* The simplicity of the church requires understanding of its essence, functions, and forms leading to a flexible, unstoppable, and growing church, enabling it to be victorious in a world of antagonism and opposition.

3. *Knowing our enemy.* (Satan's strategies against believers.) Our enemy Satan's tactics against us are both internal and external but all can be categorized by deceit and intimidation. Victory comes when we resist him—especially his favorite tactic, the fear of death.

4. *Provisions for victory.* God has provided us with effective resources to stand strong: the whole armor of God, the Bible, prayer and the Holy Spirit.

5. *Training in righteousness.* (Developing a servant spirit.) The Christlike one acts as salt and light in community showing love to everyone. Each also encourages others as each one perseveres. The bottom line is living a life of forgiveness and grace as a servant of Jesus Christ.

6. *The victory.* (Victorious overcomers.) The secret of standing strong is not in affluence and prosperity nor the absence of problems, but obedience in the midst of trials and troubles.

Some churches in Western countries feel this teaching is also significant for their people. Satan just uses different tactics against those of us living in so-called free countries. One pastor in Norway told me, "We are not persecuted here. We are just seduced!" So SSTS is also taught as a seminar in Western countries and the textbook is also available for small group study sessions. A booklet titled *Red Skies @ Dawn: The Coming Storms* (Estabrooks and Cunningham 2005) was produced to introduce these opportunities.

Then the request from countries using SSTS came for training future pastors and church leaders at the seminary academic level. Dr. Jim Cunningham has visited seminaries in countries such as Sri Lanka and Bangladesh to help develop a curriculum for a *Theology of Persecution and Discipleship* course. Today as I write, he is back in Ambon, Indonesia, with eight of eleven theological schools on Ambon Island, each wanting to add this to their curriculum.

The main texts are *Standing Strong through the Storm* (Estabrooks and Cunningham 2004) and the doctoral dissertation about suffering, persecution, and martyrdom of Romanian pastor Josef Ton (2000), Glenn Penner's *In the Shadow of the Cross* (2004) and Open Doors' noted author, Dr. Ron Boyd-MacMillan's *Faith that Endures: The Essential Guide to the Persecuted Church* (2006). Dr. Cunningham and I have taught the course once in 2010 as an intensive elective at ACTS Seminary on the campus of Trinity Western University in Langley, British Columbia, Canada. Other seminaries are now also requesting it.

In the Upper Room discourse, just days before his crucifixion, Jesus told his disciples, "If the world hates you, keep in mind that it hated me first" (John 15:18). Hatred of Jesus Christ is foundational to the persecution, however intense, of Christians. Today, evangelical Christians in free societies are hated by many because of their faith in the supernatural Jesus—even though Jesus in the form of jewelry worn around the neck, movies, music, and even tattoos has become somewhat trendy. As well as attacks against our faith in Jesus, there are also attacks against the Bible, the church and its mission—evangelism. The winds of these storms are beginning to gust.

How then do Christians living in Western societies respond to these storms? Do we cower in paralyzing fear and lose energy for doing good works to help others before, during, and after the storm? Do we flee the coming storm and try to hide? Do we become verbally and physically aggressive, lashing out in righteous indignation to change a system that is out of control? Do we complacently smile and say, "Things have to get worse before our Lord Jesus Christ returns to earth as *King of kings and Lord of lords.* Therefore, persecution is good because it separates the sheep from the goats and allows the church to grow, so 'Don't worry, be happy, everything will be OK!'"?

These options are neither biblical nor realistic. Based on our observations of Christians in other countries who have endured—or are currently experiencing—persecution, we must prepare ourselves intellectually, practically, and spiritually for today's storms as well as for the coming storms.

## QUESTIONS FOR REFLECTION

1. Read Mark 4:35–41. What principles of surviving storms do we learn from this passage?
2. Read Revelation 12:11 in its context. Explain how the blood of the Lamb, the word of testimony, and sacrificial love (martyrdom) can counter Satan's accusations.
3. Can you love your enemy and fight with him too? Explain your answer with biblical support.
4. Identify the primary biblical reasons why we must forgive others. Why is forgiveness such a hard action to implement?

## REFERENCES

Bohm, C. J. 2005. *Brief chronicle of the unrest in the Moluccas: 1999–2005.* Ambon, Indonesia: Crisis Centre Diocese of Amboina.

Boyd-MacMillan, R. 2006. *Faith that endures: The essential guide to the persecuted church.* Grand Rapids, MI: Revell.

Estabrooks, P., and J. Cunningham. 2004. *Standing strong through the storm: Victorious living for Christians facing pressure and persecution.* Santa Ana, CA: Open Doors International.

———. 2005. *Red skies @ dawn: The coming storms.* Santa Ana, CA: Open Doors International.

Penner, G. 2004. *In the shadow of the cross: A biblical theology of persecution and discipleship.* Bartlesville, OK: Living Sacrifice Books.

Ton, J. 2000. *Suffering, martyrdom and rewards in heaven.* Wheaton, IL: Romanian Missionary Society.

**Paul Estabrooks** has completed more than thirty years of ministry among persecuted Christians with Open Doors International, and currently serves as Senior Communications specialist. He is the author of four books, the most recent being *Night of a Million Miracles,* in which he describes his coordination of Project Pearl, the 1981 secretive delivery of 1 million Chinese Bibles.

# CHAPTER 48

# PREPARING BOTH CHURCH AND LOCAL MISSIONARIES: GLOBAL SOUTH

## A View from Brazil

*Paulo Moreira Filho with Marcos Amado*

## THE RIGHT PLACE TO START IN THE (NOT SO) GLOBAL SOUTH REALITY

Labels can be quite misleading. Hence, to speak of the church in the so-called Global South without conceding the vast differences therein can lead to gross generalization. Churches in Latin America, Africa, Asia, and the South Pacific are a multicultural manifesto of God's creative sovereignty and universal grace. On the other hand, one can affirm biblically that true discipleship is costly wherever it is fleshed out, whether individually or corporately. In our view that is a fair approach to discuss the task of preparing local churches and missionaries for suffering for Jesus' sake.

New Testament missionaries modeled suffering in mission. After Paul and Barnabas encountered very tough opposition in Pisidian Antioch, Iconium, Lystra, and Derbe—where Paul was stoned—they returned and encouraged the young local churches in each of these cities by telling them, "We must go through many hardships to enter the kingdom of God" (Acts 14:21–22). Such hardships Paul experienced again in Philippi in the company of Silas:

> The crowd joined in the attack against Paul and Silas, and the magistrates ordered them to be stripped and beaten with rods. After they had been severely flogged, they were thrown into prison, and the jailer was commanded to guard them carefully. When he received these orders, he put them in the inner cell and fastened their feet in the stocks. About midnight Paul and Silas were praying and singing hymns to God, and the other prisoners were listening to them. (Acts 16:22–25)

That was a momentous night: a violent earthquake shook the town and the jailer with his whole family ended up saved and baptized. The next morning Paul and Silas were released from prison by the magistrates with an apology and a request to leave town. But, there was one very important piece of business still to take care of before they left. Paul and Silas went straight to Lydia's house (Europe's first house church), and met there with the brethren to encourage them. *Then they left* (Acts 16:40).

The pattern is quite clear: as they went about making disciples of all peoples, missionaries expected to suffer. When persecuted, rather than lamenting, they rejoiced and blessed the Lord for the privilege of suffering for the sake of the gospel. Moreover, this pattern they passed on by word and deed to the young churches made up of new followers of Jesus, even as Paul later wrote to the Philippians:

> For it has been granted to you on behalf of Christ not only to believe in him, but also to suffer for him, since you are going through the same struggle you saw I had, and now hear that I still have. (Phil 1:29–30)

To be sure, we have all been blessed by the examples of dedicated servants today who have considered their life worth nothing to them if only they might finish the race and complete the task of testifying to the gospel of God's grace (Acts 20:24). Strangely, their number seems to be shrinking in reverse proportion to the exuberant growth of the church in the Global South. There may be an explanation for this.

## EMERGING COMFORT

Globalized consumerism and a craze for comfort are fostering in our societies a pursuit of happiness in terms of welfare, pleasure, and safety; Brazil is an example of this reality. Entire populations of emerging economies are riding a seemingly endless wave of material accumulation, giving them access to superfluous goods once a privilege to few. "I have, therefore I am (happy)." This notion of happiness based on well-being and wealth leads some to the extreme of exorcizing the demons of suffering as abnormalities and annoyances of life. It dialogues with the animistic roots of many of our peoples and finds echo in the popular dualistic spirituality found in our urbanized societies.

"The Son of Man must suffer many things and be rejected by the elders and chief priests and scribes, and be killed, and on the third day be raised." *Luke 9:22*

Unfortunately, this trend to reject suffering, contrary to New Testament teaching, has already cast a spell upon large segments of the church through the widespread preaching of the prosperity gospel. Suffering is seen as necessarily bad, an omen of the curse rather than a sign of blessing, and a means of punishment instead of purification. This theological distortion had a devastating effect upon how many churches perceive their mission. Scores of local churches are offering people ways and resources to be happier in this life. Accordingly, their effort and investment concentrate on local programs to make the church experience more exciting, and interesting. The world out there is dismissed, because it is doomed to destruction anyway. Very little focus, if any at all, is given to the evangelization of unreached or unengaged peoples. The reason is, bluntly, that to reach them requires greater levels of intentionally breaking out of the comfort zone, and requires a higher degree of cost, risk, and suffering.

To make things worse, mission recruiters, trainers, and executives are under a lot of pressure to make mission work more palatable to an emergent generation not too keen on breaking too far away from the comfortable sphere of life around home and within their social networks. Little is said about cost and sacrifice. Some mission organizations go out of their way to assure potential candidates that they will be cared for adequately and that there is an escape route when the road gets rough.

## EDUCATING A FIERCE MISSIONARY FORCE FROM THE BOTTOM UP

Local churches in the Global South present an urgent need for consistent teaching on both the cost of discipleship and the value of perseverance under persecution in the pursuit of mission.[1] Without changing the core of our perspective with regard to suffering and persecution, we risk seeing missionary zeal dwindling in churches where it once used to be aflame. In Brazil, for instance, there is a growing tendency for missionary prospects to approach the call with a "what's in it for me?" attitude, resulting in fewer commitments to reach or engage people groups located in riskier and more difficult situations.

The solution, we propose, starts at educating disciples at the root level, meaning, within the local church life and context. A number of initiatives can be implemented in order to rekindle missionary zeal in local churches and challenge local disciples to look to the world beyond their comfort zone:

1. Include both in the preaching calendar and the Sunday school curriculum consistent teaching on the theology of suffering, persecution, and martyrdom in church and mission. By sowing the seeds of a theology of suffering throughout the core curriculum of Christian education in the local church, we will reap the sort of commitment to the Christian faith that won't waver before antagonism and persecution.
2. Show and tell regularly in public church gatherings stories of men and women who persevered in the face of persecution when taking the gospel to both unengaged and engaged peoples, and encourage families to do the same at home. It is imperative to expose the lie that being a hero equals outsmarting the competition. True heroes are plain individuals who dare to believe that God can use them against all odds to live and proclaim the gospel among people who have never heard of God's love for them.
3. Encourage and plan for regular seasons of prayer for the suffering church, as well as unreached and unengaged peoples, especially those that pose a greater challenge to engage. Prayer connects us to God's heart. Our spiritual understanding of God's mission will grow deeper as we ask him to open our eyes to see the world as he sees it and love the world as he loves it.
4. Encourage families, groups of friends, cell groups, Sunday school classes, and whole churches to join the support network of missionaries working as pioneers in risky fields. This will create channels of blessings going both ways between missionaries and supporters. During the last 150 years God has been using this type of connection to call generations of missionaries to the harvest.
5. Partner with sister churches in other countries already involved in reaching peoples that pose a challenge to the gospel in their region. This kind of partnership may

---

1    For a detailed outline of the theology of suffering in mission and a discussion of its implications for mission and theological education, see Sauer (2010).

require some hard work to develop, but where it does it will serve as a true testimony of God's boundless love and a source of enormous encouragement to sister churches in those fields.

6. Train and lead church groups in ministry trips and projects targeting areas closer to home, but where some risk is involved as they cross-cultural and socioeconomic boundaries. Usually there are clear opportunities near any one church to experience serving outside its comfort zone. In urban areas, this will most likely be a mission to an impoverished neighborhood where crime rate is higher and ill feelings against people from middle class neighborhoods run high.

7. Train and lead church people in educational mission trips designed to expose them to the realities and risks of the mission field. A well-planned, prepared, and coordinated trip with the missionary in the field can change lives forever and increase the mission knowledge base of the local church. This will prove invaluable in the decision-making process and the ongoing involvement of the church in reaching an unengaged people.

8. Partner with and learn from experienced mission organizations already working in fields antagonistic to the gospel when looking to train, place, and support missionaries in such fields. Local churches will be wise to do this because this is a highly specialized field within mission work. A partner with a proven track record will spare the church from unnecessary mistakes and pain.

There is yet another crucial key in the preparation of missionaries to be sent to regions where there is persecution. If the local church is the starting point of this preparation, then sending agencies, missionary training centers, and theological seminaries must build on that foundation by also retooling their curricula to equip missionaries for adversity and suffering in mission. Instructors should speak from their own experience, not just from textbooks on missions. The content of the program should cover, among other topics, simple and sacrificial lifestyle, servant leadership, cultural sensitivity and observation, modest behavior and self-restraint, functioning under pressure, team work, communication in high security environments, and issues of security involving team members and national converts.

Due to the specialized nature of some of these subjects, agencies and training institutions should seek to cooperate and pool their expertise in order to offer trainees the best possible prefield learning experience. Finally, upon arrival in the field, missionaries should still be considered in training and each be assigned a field coach to walk him or her through the initial adaptation. This extra layer in preparation will significantly contribute to the missionary's ministry longevity.

## BLESSING IN THE FUTURE

These are unprecedented times. We live longer and more people are younger. Collaboration between experience and innovation can go a long way if we focus on both mission and task. We need not fear our ever-changing reality or the current institutional instability. Disciples of Jesus are best equipped to lead the way for a lost generation, provided they stick to the commanding orders of the King of kings. One thing, though, is necessary, and that is the commitment to live and die for Jesus Christ. This must be genuine. We won't be followed if we fake it. There remains one blessing to the ebullient, multifaceted church in the Global South:

> Blessed are those who are persecuted because of righteousness, for theirs is the kingdom of heaven. Blessed are you when people insult you, persecute you and falsely say all kinds of evil against you because of me. Rejoice and be glad, because great is your reward in heaven, for in the same way they persecuted the prophets who were before you. (Matt 5:10–12)

## QUESTIONS FOR REFLECTION
1. Do you agree with Moreira and Amado that the number of servants willing to dedicate their lives without any restraint and to complete the task of preaching the gospel to all peoples is diminishing? How does this challenge affect your local church situation? How do you respond?
2. How does global consumerism and the effects of the prosperity gospel as described by Moreira and Amado affect your churches and mission candidates? How have you sought to recover a more biblical attitude to serving in mission?
3. What can you learn and how can you adapt Moreira and Amado's suggestions to the local church and training institutions concerning the creation of a greater missionary zeal and commitment, including a willingness to suffer for our Lord?

## REFERENCE
Sauer, C. 2010. Mission in bold humility. *International Journal for Religious Freedom* 3, no. 1: 65–79.

**Paulo Moreira Filho** joined an urban mission project that birthed the Morumbi Baptist Church and daughter churches. In the late 1980s Paulo and family moved to Austria, serving for ten years throughout Eastern Europe as an itinerant teacher for pastors, church planters, and leaders. He was coordinator for the Baptist Mission Board (JMM), with 130 missionaries from the Baltics to Central Asia. Paulo is active in shepherding, training, and mentoring candidates and missionaries.

**Marcos Amado** serves as the Lausanne international deputy director for Latin America. For more than twenty years he worked, alongside his wife, Rosângela, among Muslims; they initially lived in North Africa and later in southern Spain. Marcos became the international director of PM Internacional, a Latin American mission agency that trains and deploys Latino workers to different parts of the Muslim world. He is presently taking the first steps in starting a missiological center in São Paulo, Brazil, and is the missions pastor of Morumbi Baptist Church.

# CHAPTER 49

# PREPARING A MISSION AGENCY

## A View from the USA

*S. Kent Parks*

Is what we are currently doing worth suffering for?

- What is a goal worth suffering for?
- What is legitimate suffering?
- Is how believers face suffering a tool God uses to show his glory?

Most of the global mission community would quickly agree that old colonial models of mission compounds and missionary visas are not legitimate in today's world. Yet, practices based on the cultural overhang of this era continue to hold sway in some common mission wisdom. Training for incarnational ministry is often focused on serving years in the same place in order to be effective, learning a single culture well, and maintaining a visa. Sometimes success becomes what programs can one start so the government and society will accept the outsider. Sometimes success is based on how many church institutions can be initiated rather than how to start the organic, reproducing body of Christ. Sometimes success becomes how close to the edge of suffering can one come without actually suffering. Thus, the following questions:

## IS EVERYTHING CALLED "MISSIONS" WORTH THE SUFFERING?

Many mission efforts use a minimum definition: the church doing good things. The goal of many efforts has been generally defined as transformation, or being the presence of Christ, or doing good in the name of Jesus. With such unmeasurable definitions, any activity or the mere ability to exist is defined as "missions." Many mission efforts do not hold either to professional standards of effectiveness or to biblical standards (which may be more similar than some might think). A commitment to biblical excellence requires paying full price rather than the bargain price many seek.

Is it worth suffering for a humanitarian project which has no clear definitions of how to measure community transformation in both physical and spiritual ways? Is it worth suffering for a program that may lead to random witness and a few believers and only a limited, subsidized temporal result? When success is defined by "deed only," while accepting government or religious restrictions on telling the story of Jesus (under the guise of being "wise as serpents"), does it logically follow that (1) people will really "see" Jesus in a way to lead them into a personal relationship and (2) will the few that do change allegiance to Jesus be enough of a threat for anyone in that society to care enough to make the suffering worth it?

Is it worth suffering for building a building and reaching a small number of people who live in this aquarium? Is it worth suffering if all one is doing is setting up a vocational training school called a seminary to train people to run these institutions of a few people? Is it worth suffering for creating a good secondary or higher education program with the hope (but no real plan) that people will experience Jesus by osmosis?

Frankly, it is not worth suffering for a farming project, or a school (of secondary or higher education, either one), or for starting a strange colony of one's home country (called a "church" with a building, degreed pastor, etc.), whether Korean, North American, Singaporean, or Ibero-American.

## WHAT GOAL IS WORTH THE SUFFERING?

The question really is, "Why did Jesus and the apostles suffer?" The answer is that the inherent nature of the overt words and works and wonders (word, deed, miraculous signs) of the Kingdom was quickly recognized as a complete threat to and contradiction of the power structures of government, religion, philosophy, and society's whole way of life. Jesus, the apostles, and the early church suffered because they unapologetically asked people to change all their allegiances from earthly kingdoms to Jesus' Kingdom.

> When we heard this, we and the people there urged him not to go up to Jerusalem. Then Paul answered, "What are you doing, weeping and breaking my heart? For I am ready not only to be imprisoned but even to die in Jerusalem for the name of the Lord Jesus." And since he would not be persuaded, we ceased and said, "Let the will of the Lord be done." *Acts 21:12–14*

Ironically, when a huge goal is seen as achievable, even if it requires a high price, people will sacrifice to reach that goal. A goal worth suffering for is to see reproducing groups of "obeyers" ("disciples") of Jesus Christ who start reproducing groups of obeyers who start reproducing groups of obeyers who... These reproducing groups are taught to obey everything they read in Scripture under the guidance of the Holy Spirit (thus removing the need for a long-tenured and "trained" outsider). Having learned to be guided by Jesus' Spirit, these groups of obeyers—the true *ekklesia*—begin to feed the poor in their neighborhood, tear down virgin houses to free their teenage girls from sexual oppression, help the widows, and love their enemies (personal and ethnic). They become a full blown embodiment of Jesus within their culture with enough critical mass to not require outside maintenance. They change the balance of allegiance in their society. They join in completing the Great Commission. Such a shift into the Kingdom of God is worth any suffering.

The workers and the organization must be prepared to face the Gethsemane moments (Matt 26:36ff.) when, like Jesus, the workers realize they must also drink the cup of suffering in order to achieve God's plan. Where real movements have occurred, the cross-cultural witnesses who bring the change message and the leaders of these multiplying groups will suffer. The outsider must decide if it is more important to keep a visa and avoid suffering, or help start a movement of thousands into personal, abundant, and eternal relationship with Jesus —and pay whatever price for the suffering.

C. T. Studd, a well-known mission leader from another century summed it up: "If Jesus Christ be God and died for me, then no sacrifice can be too great for me to make for him."

## UNDERSTAND WHAT SUFFERING FOR THE GOSPEL IS AND WHAT IT IS NOT

When one asks a society to change allegiance to Jesus, suffering at the hands of government and political or cultural leaders in a society will occur (e.g., beatings, imprisonment, loss of visa). Yet, sometimes suffering happens because someone uses foolish methods (such as barking through a loud speaker as Muslims exit evening prayers in the capital of Malaysia). Other times, when one knowingly chooses *not* to follow legitimate laws, such as getting a required legal work permit, one needs to be willing to suffer the consequences rather than writing a prayer letter talking about how this corrupt Asian government is persecuting them. Suffering for being bold in the right way and suffering for being stupid are totally different.

Further, missionaries must be equipped to be aware that suffering can come in the form of attacks from the evil one and his followers. This suffering can take the form of a series of illnesses, family crises, etc. The purpose is not to have people blaming every difficulty in this broken world on direct attack by an evil spiritual being. The purpose is to help our teams understand that every need can and must be taken to the Lord for his solution. When several teams serving among an unreached people group began to experience a strange wave of illnesses, a few in the group sensed a pattern beyond normal. They invited all the teams and all the prayer supporters to join in praying for relief from the illnesses. The series of illnesses suddenly stopped. The confidence to go to the Lord for help in any manner of suffering must be developed in all workers.

## UNDERSTAND THAT HOW BELIEVERS FACE SUFFERING IS A POWERFUL WITNESS ABOUT JESUS AND FOR GOD'S GLORY

Sometimes, God heals on this earth to show his power. Sometimes, this God of all comfort (2 Cor 1:3–4) helps people walk with peace that passes understanding through suffering and death. Sometimes, the healing is eternal after death on this earth. If being a follower of Jesus meant that one was always healed or never faced suffering, many might take this cheap option to follow Jesus rather than following out of love for him.

A more complete understanding of suffering for the sake of the gospel brings meaning to why mission organizations will not pay ransoms, beyond just the effort to avoid making missionaries a lucrative target. It changes whether missionaries ask if they should flee or stay in the middle of violence in a country. It changes whether or not to launch "God-lobbying" efforts rather than government-lobbying efforts to get someone out of jail. It changes whether to rush in to help new believers escape from trial.

In a country hostile to Christianity, six key believers/leaders were put on trial for their lives on charges of heresy. They called the outsider (church planter) for advice. Rather than launching rescue efforts, the outsider urged them to ask God for wisdom. They called back to say God had told them to stand trial and not flee. As the trial began, with an impressive panel of religious judges and a packed courtroom, a demon began to manifest violently through a woman. These religious leaders—including some powerful shamans—failed in every effort to stop or remove this woman. The judges announced they would have to adjourn the trial for a later time.

The Lord impressed the six leaders to ask the panel of judges if they could try to solve the problem. The panel skeptically agreed. The men quietly but audibly began to pray in Jesus' name that the demon would leave. The demon was cast out and the woman became quiet, and a stunned silence fell across the whole court. Many came to faith in Jesus, including some of the judges.

If, as is often the common wisdom, these believers had been smuggled to safety because of the suffering they faced, God could not have shown his power to change lives in such a visible way.

Are they servants of Christ? I am a better one—I am talking like a madman—with far greater labors, far more imprisonments, with countless beatings, and often near death. Five times I received at the hands of the Jews the forty lashes less one. Three times I was beaten with rods. Once I was stoned. Three times I was shipwrecked; a night and a day I was adrift at sea; on frequent journeys, in danger from rivers, danger from robbers, danger from my own people, danger from Gentiles, danger in the city, danger in the wilderness, danger at sea, danger from false brothers; in toil and hardship, through many a sleepless night, in hunger and thirst, often without food, in cold and exposure.

*2 Corinthians 11:23–27*

This kind of commitment is evident through how Hudson Taylor (leader, China Inland Mission) faced suffering. While he was in Europe recruiting workers and also sick, he heard the news of the rising missionary death toll in the Chinese Boxer Rebellion (c. 1900). He could only say, "I cannot think, I cannot pray, but I can trust."

One hundred eighty-eight missionaries died in the Boxer Rebellion, and although the CIM had suffered the greatest losses (seventy-nine), Hudson Taylor refused to submit any claims or accept any compensation (which the Western powers had required China to offer). He considered such actions contrary to the gospel. The mission's work did not diminish after the rebellion. Rather, it was pursued with greater vigor. The number of workers quadrupled in the next decades (Hefley 1994).

He was able to face this terrible tragedy because he had already wrestled with the Lord in 1865, at Brighton Beach, about the risk and suffering he was asking new recruits to face. "Eventually, a shaft of light broke over his mind and he exclaimed, 'If we are obeying the Lord, the responsibility rests with him, not with us.' Straightway he wrote in his Bible: 'At Brighton, June 25, 1865, prayed for twenty-four willing, skillful laborers for China'" (http://www.wholesomewords.org/missions/biotaylor3.html).

## CONCLUSION

As an organization, we are working *not* to train our personnel for suffering, but to help whole societies shift their allegiance to Jesus. If/when that happens, they will suffer.

Suffering for programs and institutions or visas is not worth it. Suffering to see the birth of the dynamic, obeying body of Christ is worth it.

Being safe physically is not the goal. A phrase "The safest place for you is in the middle of God's will" is false when it implies death, rape, beatings, imprisonment, etc. will not happen. Jesus was in the very center of God's will and he was killed. This statement is true if safety is understood as spiritual vibrancy, and close fellowship with God and effectiveness.

Most significantly, how dare we ask the peoples to whom we go to follow Jesus—to risk being alienated and persecuted by society—if we are not willing to face exactly the same?

## QUESTIONS FOR REFLECTION
1. Is what we are currently doing worth suffering for?!
2. What is a goal worth suffering for?
3. What is legitimate suffering?
4. Is how believers face suffering a tool God uses to show his glory?

## REFERENCE
Hefley, J., and M. Hefley. 1994. The Boxer Rebellion—1900. *By their blood: Christian martyrs of the twentieth century*. Grand Rapids, MI: Baker House Books.

**Kent Parks** has been a pastor, a seminary professor, and a church planter for twenty years among Muslim unreached people groups in South East Asia. In 2008 he began serving as the president of Mission to Unreached Peoples, which focuses on stimulating holistic movements to Christ among the 27.9 percent of the world which still has no access to see or hear the good news.

*"I have learned the secret to be content in every situation. I can do everything through him who gives me strength"*
Philippians 4:12,13

Are we, Christians of the twenty-first century, ready to learn from Paul about the virtue of contentment, even when we are facing suffering caused by persecution? Paul teaches his disciples, by his own example, to understand that a Christian lifestyle does not presuppose a lack of troubles, but includes certainty that God is in control of everything, including our tribulations. As missionaries prepare themselves to face the hardest parts of the missionary task, we need to be totally dependent on Christ, hand over all our dreams and worries to him, and count on his strength to face every challenge. He promises to strengthen us in every circumstance, which gives us a different perspective on the world, including its injustice and evil.

Reflection by: Lícia Rosalee Santana, Brazil

# CHAPTER 50

# MISSIONARY FAMILIES

## Preparing, Supporting, and Restoring
*Laura Mae Gardner*

People are suffering around the world, and mission workers may suffer to the point of martyrdom as they live out their faith in dangerous places. How can we best prepare, support, and restore families engaged in such dangerous ministry?

Suffering, persecution, and martyrdom are overlapping experiences in the lives of many Christians today. Yet there are differences.

Suffering may have little to do with our faith but everything to do with our circumstances. It may be temporary or sustained, vicarious, or secondary. Suffering may be caused by our own actions, or we may be the innocent recipient of malicious acts. Suffering may be the result of our associations, or it may have to do with our location. Suffering may be confined to individuals or spread over large groups—i.e., whole populations struggle with the impact of AIDS and HIV, genocide, or disaster.

Persecution is likely to have a spiritual connection and be sustained or even increase in intensity. Persecution is directed toward persons or groups (ethnic or religious) and is usually motivated by ideological malice. It often results in material loss, curtailed freedoms, or hostile injustice.

Martyrdom includes the element of witness. The death that results is final, personalized, and related to one's faith. The only choice a martyr has is to recant or die.

## PREPARING MISSIONARIES FOR INTENSE HARDSHIP

Four things can be helpful to prepare missionaries for intense hardship. All should be encouraged by the sending organization and all four must be actively pursued by the individual worker.

First, formulate your own theology of suffering. Articulate your stance on suffering in a progressive, experiential document that will change as you increasingly understand yourself, your faith, and your circumstances.

Additionally, it is helpful to ask yourself the hard questions: Am I at peace with God's silence and his unpredictability? With his seeming "tardy" justice and capricious mercy? Have I come to terms with his apparent lack of response to evil in my world? Do I believe strongly in God's sovereignty and his loving presence? Do I believe God is good? Can I tolerate ambiguity and mystery? Am I moving toward positive responses to these questions?

Second, one should pursue relational transparency and integrity in specific areas. There is no known sin between you and God. Your relationships with organizational authorities are trusting and communicative, free from conflict. You enjoy good spousal relationships, open and supportive. You share age-appropriate information with your children yet without sparing them difficulties that will increase their hardiness. And with your colleagues, you are respectful, communicative, and caring.

Third, it is important to engage in intentional preparation. You can prepare your mind and heart by reading biographies of past missionaries and stories of current pioneers of the faith. (See this chapter's suggested reading list.) You can also become familiar with the history, culture, and current events shaping the environment you are in. This includes staying abreast of events taking place around the world. Finally, listen to godly, experienced missionaries.

> In this you rejoice, though now for a little while, if necessary, you have been grieved by various trials, so that the tested genuineness of your faith—more precious than gold that perishes though it is tested by fire—may be found to result in praise and glory and honor at the revelation of Jesus Christ. *1 Peter 1:6–7*

Fourth, build and maintain resourcing relationships. Such relationships include local trustworthy friends who will give you reliable information. And cherish your relationship with your sending churches by finding discreet ways to tell them the truth about your situation, and inviting informed prayer. If possible, worship locally and find spiritual strength with indigenous believers.

## SUPPORTING MISSIONARY FAMILIES IN THE MIDST OF GREAT HARDSHIP

Emotional upheaval and mood swings are often the response to aloneness, bewilderment, helplessness, and frustration. "How can this be happening? Where is God? Why isn't our leadership doing something about this?" The biblical writer Mark records about the disciples, "They were overwhelmed with sorrow to the point of exhaustion" (14:34). In supporting missionary families it is helpful to remember the person's interconnectedness—mind, emotions, body, will: physical pain saps energy; churning emotions sabotage clear thinking; frustration hinders perspective. All of these complicate the making of good decisions in the midst of trouble and loss. One can seek to maintain equilibrium through the mechanisms of health, life routines, and spiritual practices.

It is also very important that organizations and sending churches be aware of and responsive to the worker's situation. Leaders must communicate, guide, pray for, and be attentive to beleaguered workers. The silence of these in difficult times will exacerbate the worker's sense of aloneness, helplessness, bewilderment, and frustration.

Connectivity is a lifeline. Connectedness to God, to colleagues, and to leaders conveys hope and strength. Peter refers to this connectivity in his first letter (5:9), "You're not the only ones plunged into these hard times. It's the same with Christians all over the world, so keep a firm grip on the faith." Paul's second letter to the Corinthian church is filled with the record of his hardships, it is also sprinkled throughout with a list of his relationships and how they were sustaining to him. Paul's prayer for the Colossian Christians asked that they "be strengthened for all endurance" (1:11). He prayed for others and told them so and asked to be prayed for himself (Eph 6:19).

Disaster often leaves its victims with increased sensitivity that makes them especially responsive to gestures of attention, helpfulness, and care. If you are the victim of a disaster, in the midst of your trials seize the opportunity to minister to those around you; they also may be devastated, perplexed, and needy. The comfort we receive from God is intended to be used to help others (2 Cor 1:4). And in comforting others, we are comforted.

Satan is our enemy and he is *good* at his work. Sometimes he may even seem to be victorious. Therefore we must look beyond the apparent instigator of the current suffering to the real enemy and resist him with spiritual weapons and spiritual armor (Eph 6:10–18). These tools of spiritual warfare equip and support the worker.

## RESTORING FAMILIES AFTER GREAT HARDSHIP AND LOSS

Restoring families after difficulties is critical and there are very practical and helpful things to do. Colleagues, friends, and family can participate with agency leadership in the process. The family too must be active in the recovery process.

It's not over when it's over. Memory lasts longer than the event. And unprocessed memory tends to lean in a given direction. It is important that one's memory of the facts be as accurate as possible. No single participant in a tragedy has all the facts. Retelling the story together (debriefing) assures that one's information is accurate by putting the pieces of the story together. Processing what happened with others who went through the same experience builds and clarifies perspective. Weeping together over the losses; rejoicing together over the goodness that surprised and sustained—these spiritual activities build unity and increase understanding and compassion.

The organization must take initiative to make debriefing events happen. This includes encouraging the process by funding and staffing it. All those who went through the event should attend the debriefing because not processing difficulties like these contributes to "sealing over" the emotional part of the experience and burying those feelings. Intentional absence from the debriefing sends a message of disregard for colleagues, possible superiority, or resistance to authority. How people were cared for or not cared for stays with suffering families.

Help the person engage in intentional personal assessment. "I didn't know what I thought until I heard myself say it...." Verbalizing the experience breaks the power of the grip of pain. "What did you do well? What weak places in your faith or your attitudes showed up during this trial? Were there energy drains in your life; e.g., unresolved relational problems? Were there inadequacies in your practices of health or spiritual disciplines? What will you change as a result of what you've been through?"

Help individuals understand that they must guard against bitterness and anger at perpetrators or toward those who minimize loss. They must resist the temptation to withdraw. Encourage them to revisit their call. When God calls us to a task, he does not promise safety or success. Jesus reminded his disciples, "You will have suffering in this world. Be courageous! I have conquered the world" (John 16:33). He did not deceive you. He promised to be with you—Matthew 28:19–20.

People are meaning-seekers. Why did this happen? That was Job's question too, but God never answered it. It is always the question, but it is seldom answered. However, Job was a different man after his multiple trials and because of them.

## CLOSURE

The words above may sound formulaic or trite. However, there is nothing trite about the stories I've heard from colleagues, the tears I've shed with someone who bears emotional and spiritual scars, or the sorrow in my heart as I read the last verses of Hebrews 11 about those who endured without vindication or rescue. Thank God that justice, exoneration, and peace will be realized in eternity. Until then, we must lovingly care for those who are suffering and call on God's help when our own times of suffering come. With Paul we say:

> For I am convinced that neither death nor life, neither angels nor demons, neither the present nor the future, nor any powers, neither height nor depth, nor anything else in all creation, will be able to separate us from the love of God that is in Christ Jesus our Lord. (Rom 8:38–39)

## QUESTIONS FOR REFLECTION

1.  How can organizations and sending churches become aware of and responsive to the worker's situation, struggles, and pain? What will be the results of a lack of response in very difficult times in the worker's life? What are some very important responses?
2.  What kind of results can unprocessed memories cause in the lives of missionaries and other victims of severe tragedies? What are some of Gardner's insights in how debriefing may help those who went through severe suffering?
3.  Discuss how the following questions might help your missionaries to deal with their pain: "What weak places in your faith or your attitudes showed up during this trial? Were there energy drains in your life; e.g., unresolved relational problems? What will you change as a result of what you've been through?"

## RECOMMENDED READING

Hiney, T. 2000. *On the missionary trail.* New York: Atlantic Monthly.

Ilibagiza, I. 2006. *Left to tell: Discovering God amidst the Rwandan holocaust.* Carlsbad, CA: Hay House.

Roseveare, H. 2007. *Living sacrifice*. Fearn, Tain, UK: Christian Focus Publications.

Van der Meer, A. 2008. Biblical reflections on ministry and suffering. *Connections* 7, nos. 1 and 2: 6–9.

Yancey, P. 2010. *What good is God?* New York: Faith Words.

**Laura Mae Gardner** has served fifty years at Wycliffe in the areas of translation, administration, counseling, member care, leadership, and board service. She has written many articles and coauthored a three-volume series with Lois Dodds on *Care of Global Servants*. She is an international personnel consultant and trainer for SIL and WBT.

Suffering has to be endured in order that it may pass away. Either the world must bear the whole burden and collapse beneath it, or it must fall on Christ to be overcome in him. He therefore suffers vicariously for the world. His is the only suffering which has redemptive efficacy. But the Church knows that the world is still seeking for someone to bear its sufferings and so, as it follows Christ, suffering becomes the Church's lot too and bearing it, it is borne up by Christ. As it follows him beneath the cross, the Church stands before God as the representative of the world.

D. Bonhoeffer in *The Cost of Discipleship* (1976, 102)

## PALESTINIAN POWER

Rami Ayyad directed the Palestinian Bible Society's office in Gaza. He was known for his friendliness. Yet on the evening of October 6, 2008, just as he was closing his office, he was abducted. The next day his body was found, brutally murdered.

In the months before Ayyad died, threats had arrived at his office. But he had stayed at his post because he believed the work deserved to be continued.

Miriam Adeney, *Kingdom without Borders: The Untold Story of Global Christianity* (2009, 257)

# CHAPTER 51

# A STORY OF MISSIONARY MARTYRS' CHILDREN

## Experiencing, Recovering, and Returning

*Dave Thompson*

My parents were killed by Communist soldiers in the Central Highlands city of Banmethuot, Vietnam, during the infamous 1968 Tet Offensive.

I was a nineteen-year-old student at Geneva College in Pennsylvania. I had resumed classes after a dreary Christmas break at my uncle's house near New Kensington, PA.[1] Getting back to my dorm, my friends, and my books was a relief.

My older sister, a junior at Nyack College near New York City, had just returned to college after a pleasant Christmas break with renewed vision to become a missionary.

As for my three youngest siblings in Vietnam, my parents, just three days before being killed, had kissed them goodbye and put them on a plane bound for boarding school in Malaysia.

Our parents knew trouble was brewing in the Central Highlands, but certainly didn't anticipate death. They had, however, fulfilled the mission's requirement and prepared a last will and testament. I vaguely recall talk about going to my aunt and uncle (my mother's sister and her husband) should a catastrophe occur. But my aunt and uncle had not been consulted. None of us were prepared for what happened.

On February 1, 1968, I was a happy, second-year premed student. The next morning I was wolfing down breakfast in the cafeteria when another student announced I was wanted in the dean's office. Mystified, I hastened to the office. There I found the dean, my favorite professor, and several others. They broke the horrible news to me. A mission executive had called them during the night and had asked them to inform me before the news went public.

---

1    He and my father were the only two sons of an alcoholic coal miner who committed suicide during the Great Depression. Their mother had remarried badly. But she found Jesus and was so transformed that my father followed her example. To his older brother's great displeasure, Dad became a pastor, married my mother, and became a missionary to Cambodia and Vietnam.

The school officials wept with me, comforted me, prayed with me, and hugged me. I remember little else except that it was decided I should take a train to New York City to meet my sister.

Tearfully, I headed to my dorm to pack. Alone in my room, I locked the door and broke down. I wept bitterly, crying out to God for answers. I was furious that he had not protected my parents who were doing what he asked of them.

Something extraordinary happened in that room. In the midst of my cries for an explanation I heard God's still, quiet voice urging me to trust him. The sense of his love was so overwhelming that my anger subsided and I fell in love with him. The eight-hour train ride to New York City seemed endless, but already I felt my heart had begun to heal.

> When he opened the fifth seal, I saw under the altar the souls of those who had been slain for the word of God and for the witness they had borne. They cried out with a loud voice, "O Sovereign Lord, holy and true, how long before you will judge and avenge our blood on those who dwell on the earth?" Then they were each given a white robe and told to rest a little longer, until the number of their fellow servants and their brothers should be complete, who were to be killed as they themselves had been.
>
> Revelation 6:9–11

My older sister's experience was similar, though she did not sense God speak to her as I had. Friends of our parents had helped her through the terrible first day. Now they lovingly took care of our needs. My sister and I assumed that we would soon be seeing our siblings overseas to grieve together.

My younger siblings had a very different experience. Their dorm parents did their best to comfort them. But they later described being bewildered and devastated. Eight-year-old Tommy understood that Mom and Dad had gone to be with Jesus and he would not see them again. Eleven-year-old Laurel understood that during a terrible battle her parents had been killed by Communist soldiers and had been buried in the back yard of their home.

Fifteen-year-old Dale understood more, but couldn't fathom why his older siblings didn't show up. For the three boarding school siblings the events were surreal. The descriptions of their parents' deaths were vague. There was no funeral. Nothing about the irrevocable separation from their loving parents was tangible.

During the days I visited my sister the decision about what to do with our parent's bodies hadn't yet been made. It was several days before the security situation permitted missionaries to visit the bunker-cum-grave where they lay. When they arrived, missionaries found the bodies too decomposed to move so they interred them where they had fallen. My older sister and I were not consulted about this, though we could hardly have objected. My siblings and I have no regrets that our parents were buried where they fell.

What I do regret is that at the time I had no sense of how to properly honor and mourn my parents' death. I don't even remember if I was asked to attend the memorial service our mission had arranged. In any case, I had no money to make the trip. I had powerfully met God, but was living in an emotional fog. The only things I knew to do were to trust God, try to put the terrible event behind me, and work doubly hard to finish my studies well.

Our aunt and uncle who inherited us were also missionaries to Vietnam. As our two families were close this involved minimal disruption. Our adoptive parents visited my younger siblings at their boarding school shortly after our parents' death. They loved and comforted them, and they tried to offer them a secure new family.

It seems that in the late 1960s our culture believed the best way to help children overcome grief and loss was to keep them from dwelling on it. My two youngest siblings fell right in step. For the next twenty-five years my youngest brother closed off that part of his memory so completely that he didn't remember anything about his first eight years.

About three months after my parents' death, I wrote to our mission's leaders to ask for tickets for my older sister and me to go to spend the summer in Vietnam with the rest of our family. Shockingly they said no. I am not bitter about this now, but this refusal was almost as painful as the news of my parents death. I rudely awoke to the fact that my siblings and I had lost not only our parents, but lost our sibling relationships as well.

Right after Mom and Dad's death, many people blessed us with love, understanding, and encouragement. But as the weeks turned into months, my life became a long, confusing tunnel of loneliness. During holidays I was welcomed into the homes of other families, but I did not belong to them. I only borrowed them. It wasn't until five years later when I married that I realized how acutely I had missed belonging, and how solitary my existence had become.

I did not see my middle brother until two years after the event. It was four years before I saw my youngest sister and brother. By that time we had become strangers. My relationship with my middle brother, then seventeen, to whom I had felt close, had completely changed. To my bewilderment he could scarcely bear to be in the same room with me.

This brother turned his back on God and on me for thirty-one years. Ten years after the death of our parents we attended his wedding. There he told my older sister and me that he would never forgive us for abandoning him while we pursued our careers. We were stunned and broken, but this confrontation eventually opened the way for mutual forgiveness and reconciliation.

My youngest sister became a true daughter to her adopted mother. Her adjustment seemed the healthiest, but later she too experienced brokenness. For her it was a crisis of trust. She recently wrote that twenty-three years after her parents' death she "was looking up from the bottom of the deepest pit of despair, close to insanity, to reach for a tiny speck of light." At that point she began the long road to spiritual and emotional recovery. My youngest brother became a man of the world and lived a stranger to the rest of us for twenty-five years. After he came back to Christ he rejoined our family. Not long after, his childhood memories came back in a flood.

In December 2009, forty-two years after our parents' death, my siblings and I were finally allowed to visit our parents' grave in Vietnam. This journey of clarification was a miracle of God's grace. The Vietnamese government had previously denied us. In November 2009 we met at my brother's house in Wisconsin to make our final plans. We pooled our money but came up $6,000 short. So, as Mom and Dad had taught us, we bowed and asked God to provide. The next weekend medical school friends invited my wife and me to dinner in San Francisco. They asked if we had any special needs. When we explained they wrote us check for the full amount!

On Sunday, December 20, 2009, we stood together at our parents' grave for the first time since their death. What remained of the original gravesite was a low perimeter wall and a pillar with a plaque listing the names of six missionaries killed there in February 1968. Strangely, we were not overcome with emotion. In fact we felt slightly perplexed about what to do. We posed for pictures and made a rubbing of the names on the pillar.

The most emotional time for us came while visiting a small church crammed with some six hundred people. We learned there were now many such churches in the tribal areas where our parents had invested their lives.

We also got permission to drive past the leprosy hospital where my wife, Becki, had last seen her father in 1962. Here, as a young girl, she had witnessed Viet Cong soldiers tie him up and march him into the jungle. He became a martyr too. Becki's mother remained to serve with Becki and two siblings.

This is the truth. We left Vietnam filled with joy. We had seen that our parents' sacrifices had turned into the triumph of a rapidly growing body of believers, and we were overwhelmed.

Today, all five of us are in love with Jesus Christ. The seeds of our faith were planted by our parents' teaching, yes, but even more by their love for Christ, for each other, and for us children. That heritage of faith was the single, greatest preparation they could have given us. Following that our aunt and uncle's unqualified love, and the church of Jesus Christ brought us through.

In the years to come many more missionaries and Christian believers will be required to give their lives for their faith in Jesus. My hope is that our story will help churches and missionary organizations do better in helping the children of martyrs recover from their inestimable loss. We strongly recommend that provisions be made for survivors to stay together in their remaining family bonds to help them best experience the immeasurable love and grace of God and to heal.

## QUESTIONS FOR REFLECTION

1. Discuss the challenge given by Dr. Thompson in the last paragraph. How might he and his siblings been better cared for and guided to recover from their "inestimable loss"?
2. Surely none of the concerned parties would have wanted to add injury to the children of martyred missionaries, but some did. What factors might have hindered or prevented the mission organization, concerned churches, and friends from doing more right things or things right?

3.  In spite of the loss by martyrdom of both Dr. Thompson's parents and his wife Becki's father (Archie Mitchell) in Vietnam, this couple became effective and long-serving medical missionaries in West Africa. On the other hand, some siblings admit to long struggles with issues of faith and relationships. By the grace of God the family is now united in faith and reconciled in relationships. Does the information provided here give any clues as to why their experiences were so different?

**David Thompson, MD**, serves as the director for Africa of the Pan-African Academy of Christian Surgeons and has served for over thirty years as a missionary surgeon at the Bongolo Hospital in Gabon. He is the author of *On Call, Beyond the Mist*, and *The Hand on My Scalpel*. His parents were martyred in Banmethuot, Vietnam, in 1968.

For who knows who will stand in the hour of final trial—therefore—"blessed are the dead who die in the Lord from now on"—"blessed are the dead"—that we must understand—not from fatigue, from aversion, but from the fear of not keeping faith and in the joy of having kept faith—"blessed are the dead"—"from now on"—beginning with such times as those in which the power of Babylon and the Beast become tremendous—not all the dead are blessed—but "those who die in the Lord"—who have learnt how to die at the right time, who have kept the faith, who have held to Jesus to the last hour, whether suffering public martyrdom or persevering in a life of silent, solitary martyrdom.

D. Bonhoeffer in "Predigt zu Apokalypse 14,6-13" (1996, 917)

# CHAPTER 52

# CODE OF BEST PRACTICES

## Cross-cultural Visits to Restricted Nations
### *Voice of the Martyrs Canada*

## PREAMBLE
We believe that everything we do and say has the potential to build or undermine the trust of our team members and our international partners. It is with this understanding that we commit ourselves to following these Best Practices for Cross-cultural Visits to Restricted Nations.

## PRIOR TO THE VISIT
1.  Prior to departure all team members will be involved in a comprehensive and formal briefing that will address issues such as:
    *   Security
    *   Objectives and expectations
    *   Team roles (leader, finances, devotions, contact person, etc.)
    *   Medical issues
    *   Cross-cultural issues
    *   Ethical concerns
    *   Communications issues
    *   Political/historical/religious environment
    *   Spiritual well-being
    *   Other relevant issues; e.g., paying for our own meals, covering internal travel expenses, not asking to use personal telephones, Internet, etc.
2.  We aim that all team members come together prior to the trip for this briefing. In exceptional circumstances it may be possible to do this briefing by Skype conference and Powerpoint, at the discretion of the team leader.
3.  Prior to each trip a security rating will be assigned to each country by mission executives and the appropriate practices to be employed. The security ratings will be Green (unrestricted), Amber (restricted), or Red (very restricted).
4.  Each trip will be approved by the mission executive only after prayer, a definite benefit to the mission and our partners is identified, and the trip's purposes can be clearly stated.

## DURING THE VISIT

1.  We will endeavor to be good guests while in country. We endeavor not to be a burden to our hosts. This is, in fact, very difficult. We cannot avoid being a burden on their time and schedules, but we can exercise prudence and modesty by, for example, avoiding being a financial burden to them.

2.  We will clearly express our expectations and objectives for the visit to our hosts/partner, while exercising sensitivity to their needs, concerns, and aspirations which may differ from our own. If an agreement cannot be reached, the judgment of our host/partner will prevail.

3.  On-field activities of the visit will be aligned to long-term partnerships and priorities. Long-term partnerships and priorities will always take precedence over short-term needs or aspirations. For example, we will not endanger a partner or a project for the sake of a photo or interview.

4.  All nonproject gifts should be given by the team leader on behalf of the mission through our local partners only after consultation with them as to its appropriateness. Ideally, gifts should be anonymous with the understanding that this is not precedent setting. All gifts must align with the mission, purpose, and values of the mission. They must be receipted and reported upon.

5.  We will be careful not to make unauthorized promises or raise expectations that we cannot guarantee fulfilment of. We will endeavor to clearly explain the decision-making processes of the mission that precludes individual staff from making such commitments. These include requests for finances, photos, videos, services, and projects.

6.  We commit to meet together as a team each day of the trip for prayer and Bible reading.

7.  We commit to meet together daily to assess the progress of the trip objectives, team dynamics, the present security situation, and emerging issues and to determine corrective action.

8.  We commit to follow our partners' directives and guidance as to what can be reported on and how it can be publicized. In principle, we will say less than what is approved by partners in the country but we will not say more than what they have approved. We will always confirm the appropriateness of the use of photos and interviews with trusted leaders/partners in the country, even if the interviewee has already given approval.

9.  We will endeavor to maintain as low a profile as possible when in country. We will inform our partners/hosts of this desire and ask for their assistance and advice on how to carry this out appropriately and especially when it involves invitations to preach, visiting homes, arranging interviews, etc.

## AFTER THE VISIT

1.  Within a week of the conclusion of each trip, each team member and the team will be verbally debriefed by the mission executive. We aim that all team members come together after the trip for this debriefing. In exceptional circumstances it may be possible to do this debriefing by Skype conference at the discretion of the mission executive.

2.  Within a month of the conclusion of the trip, each team member will submit a written report including how the trip purposes have been fulfilled, what were the team dynamics, how the partnership is functioning, financial accounting, and what follow up is needed.

## QUESTIONS FOR REFLECTION

1.  What are the main underlying values and motives for these commendable best practices for sending people to visit Christians in restricted nations?
2.  How might these best practices clash with the "spirit of the age" which has also affected many Western Christians?
3.  Based on your own experiences, are there any issues in cross-cultural visits not addressed in this code of best practices?

**The Voice of the Martyrs Canada** stands alongside persecuted brothers and sisters worldwide. They help Christians who are, or have been, persecuted for their involvement in spreading the gospel by giving their testimony a voice and informing Christians in Canada to know how to help.

## FIVE BONUS YEARS

"I wish I could give you better news," the doctor said, "but unfortunately your disease is incurable.

"Isn't there something more you can try?" Steven sputtered.

"No. I'm very sorry. I advise you to go home and put your affairs in order. You don't have very long."

In his anxiety, Steven listened to a gospel witness, and responded. To everybody's surprise, Steven's disease disappeared. He was healed completely. Overflowing with gratitude, he told people his story. He was a poor farmer, but in the winter season when the ground lay fallow he had free time. He began to travel and preach. Although he was illiterate, he soon had an oral command of biblical teaching and spoke with authority. He established four small house churches.

It was not long before he was arrested and sentenced. The prison was in the Muslim region of China. In the jail was a Muslim who had been sick for a long time. Steven prayed for him, and he was healed. Shortly after that, ten Muslim prisoners put their faith in Jesus as their Lord.

To keep this movement from spreading throughout the prison population, the officials released Steven early. However, they escorted him out of the prison at midnight into bitter cold, four degrees below zero. Steven was wearing thin clothes. Without transport, he started walking, crunching one foot in front of another through snow and ice. Nine miles later he arrived at the home of a Christian. To his surprise, the house was packed with people who had gathered to pray for him that very night.

Steven planted two more churches before he was rearrested. This time he was beaten so badly that he died. But in five years—five extra years of life that he had never expected to see—Steven planted six churches, won 150 Chinese to Jesus, and encouraged many more.

Miriam Adeney, *Kingdom without Borders: The Untold Story of Global Christianity* (2009, 54), citing Paul Hattaway, *China's Book of Martyrs* (Carlyle, UK: Piquant, 2007, 587)

# CHAPTER 53

# BEST PRACTICES FOR FOREIGN TEAMS VISITING THE PERSECUTED CHURCH

*National Christian Evangelical Alliance of Sri Lanka*

1. Culture shock
   It will be most helpful for the sending organization to conduct a brief orientation for visitors and staff, prior to arrival in Sri Lanka. This will help them grasp the local situation and be culturally sensitive. Such orientation is essential to the safety of visitors and local pastoral workers serving in hostile environments.

2. Objectives
   Most visitors from organizations have set objectives for their visits to the persecuted church. It will be most helpful to communicate your trip objectives to the local partner well in advance of the visit, giving time for any adjustments, and setting a suitable date for the visit that is acceptable to both parties.

3. Itinerary
   When making travel arrangements, etc., we, the local partners, have to work within certain limitations. For example, some parts of Sri Lanka are not easily accessible and can require eight hours of road travel. Travel to some other areas requires prior clearance from the Ministry of Defense. It is essential for visitors to consult with the local partner in preparing an itinerary. A sudden visit to a given location may not be realistic.

4. Local wisdom
   It is always best to follow guidelines set by the local partner when making field visits. Your host will have a better understanding and experience of the ground situation and is in a better position to make good decisions and assessments.

5. Enthusiasm vs. good sense
   While we appreciate the efforts of visitors to capture on film and highlight the plight of the persecuted church in Sri Lanka, it should also be born in mind that while visitors leave our shores after a brief visit, the local pastors, staff, and workers continue to live here amidst persecution and are vulnerable to danger. For example, a very visible and loud reporter or video crew invariably attracts attention and places

the local pastor in danger. It must be remembered that most places you will visit are often watched and monitored by interested parties.

6. Camera shy

Most victims of persecution are from very humble circumstances. To them, facing a foreign journalist, interviews, posing for video filming, etc., are strange and alien experiences. Many of them feel uncomfortable "acting" for the camera. This situation needs sensitive handling.

7. Taking no for an answer

It is our culture to show hospitality to visitors. This is particularly so in rural villages. Most local Christians will accommodate the requests of a guest, even if it is inconvenient, dangerous, embarrassing, or uncomfortable. For example, requesting a persecution victim to act out a traumatic scene from an attack or repeat a painful experience several times. In such instances, it is our responsibility as the local partner to intervene on behalf of the victims and deny the request. Please trust our judgment in such instances, even if the victim may "appear" to be willing to comply with the visitor's request.

8. Gifts

The churches or victims you visit may have many material needs and often a visitor's heart will be moved to help. It is best to consult with your local partner as to the appropriateness of a gift or a promise of help before making such a commitment to the victims. Ideally, any gift from the visiting organization should be given through the local partner. As local partners, we will in turn issue proper receipts and reports of such gifts.

9. Attire and conduct

There may be places that you visit where being clad in appropriate clothing is a way of showing courteousness to your hosts. For example, if you are invited to speak or share at a meeting or visit a business office, dressing in shorts is not appropriate. Most places of cultural interest which are also places of Buddhist worship require modest dress. Similarly, behavior which may be normal and acceptable in the West may also not be acceptable in very conservative, rural areas. Seek guidance from your host as to what is appropriate.

10. Reporting

There may be times when publicizing sensitive information can endanger the local Christians or hinder the work of the church. It is best to follow the guidelines set by the local partners and always cross-check reports, scripts, and copy before it is publicized.

11. Our commitment
    As partners and hosts, we are committed to making your visit fruitful and mutually beneficial, subject to our paramount duty to protect and ensure the safety and best interest of local pastors, believers, and churches. In this context, we advocate that visitors follow the advice of our staff as to what actions and behavior are acceptable when making field visits.

*Formulated by: Roshini Wickremesinhe, advocacy and legal officer, National Christian Evangelical Alliance of Sri Lanka, 2003, updated 2007.*

# 10 WAYS TO REDUCE TENSION WITHIN THE COMMUNITY YOU SERVE

And twisting together a crown of thorns, they put it on his head and put a reed in his right hand. And kneeling before him, they mocked him, saying, "Hail, King of the Jews!" And they spit on him and took the reed and struck him on the head. *Matthew 27:29–30*

1. Be sensitive to sound levels during meetings and services.
2. Integrate in to the village without alienating yourself from the community.
3. Be culturally sensitive in your conduct, especially when dealing with youth.
4. Avoid high publicity programs on special religious holidays.
5. Do not use relief or social programs as "bait" for evangelism.
6. Adopt a simple lifestyle consistent with the village.
7. Promote unity among Christian leaders in the area.
8. Gather in a small congregations if hostility persists.
9. Avoid promoting foreigners or outsiders to a prominent role in the village or church.
10. Avoid disrespectful comments towards other religions at all times.

*Used with permission from the Religious Liberty Commission of the National Christian Evangelical Alliance of Sri Lanka.*

## QUESTIONS FOR REFLECTION
1. From the sending organizations' point of view, are these best practices formulated by a host church reasonable? Which are the hardest to implement in actual practice?
2. Are there legitimate sending agency concerns not listed in these best practices?

**The National Christian Evangelical Alliance of Sri Lanka** (NCEASL) serves the national church of Sri Lanka. NCEASL's membership consists of five Christian denominations and seventy-four churches and Christian organizations, representing more than 200,000 evangelical Christians.

# CHAPTER 54

# GUIDELINES FOR CRISIS MANAGEMENT AND PREVENTION

*Global Connections, in association with the Global Mission Network*

## INTRODUCTION TO GUIDELINES

The Global Connections Guidelines for crisis management and prevention are designed to assist dealing both with critical incidents and also when working in high-risk situations. They are designed to apply to any UK-based organization or church sending staff or volunteers overseas. The principles should be applied to all types of staff, such as mission partners, volunteers working overseas, national staff, and UK staff visiting field locations.[1] Agencies and churches should also apply them in all contexts, both long and short term, although different procedures might be needed in each context. Some of these guidelines have been formed specifically with high-risk areas in mind, but most of the principles can also be useful in lower-risk situations and wherever or whenever crises arise.

No area of the world or working situation is completely risk-free. Crises and accidents can happen in any location. However, some mission partners live in areas of the world where they could be susceptible to insecurity, violence, and even kidnapping. They do not normally carry weapons or have guards and this can add another dimension to any proposed response.

Quite obviously, if an attack on mission partners were to be successful, with money being handed over or political demands being conceded, cross-cultural work in some areas of the world might become more impracticable.

Anticipating and preparing for crisis situations is an essential first step to dealing with them. Safety and security is extremely important and therefore Global Connections has formulated these guidelines in consultation with its members. Safety and security must be the responsibility of all staff and they must be equally committed to the process to ensure success.

---

1     The use of the term "staff" throughout this document is a generic word, which is used to include all categories of people working overseas, including volunteers and those who are self-supported. Also, note that these guidelines remain in their original form, orientated to UK-based organizations.

It is impossible to provide "off the shelf" policies and procedures that fit the locations, circumstances, and needs of all groups. This set of guidelines has therefore been developed to help agencies and churches think through and create their own policies and procedures.

All UK agencies should appoint a representative (or team) who is responsible for the management of a crisis situation. Agencies should also ensure that there are crisis management policies and procedures in place and implemented, consistent with the standards set out in these guidelines. An agency that is part of an international structure should ensure its head office has appropriate policies and procedures in place and that its local office is an integral part of any procedures.

## SECTION 1
## AIMS AND OBJECTIVES OF A CRISIS MANAGEMENT POLICY

A Crisis Management and Prevention Policy is a statement of intent that demonstrates a responsibility and commitment to staff and national workers of agencies and churches who send staff or volunteers overseas. It helps to create the safest and most positive environment for staff and to show that the agency/church is taking its responsibilities seriously.

1. All UK agencies and churches should have a Crisis Management and Prevention Policy regardless of whether or not they work in a high-risk area, as situations can happen unexpectedly. Policies and procedures should be written with a holistic approach, keeping in mind all departments.
2. The policy should be written clearly and should be easily understandable. It should be integrated with all other personnel and member care policies.
3. The policy should be given to all staff and volunteers who work in or visit overseas locations. It should be an integral part of the staff handbook, orientation, and training program.
4. Crisis management and prevention issues should be an integral part of personnel and member care practice. It should also be an integral part of an agency's risk management analysis. Therefore the policy should be reviewed on a regular basis, preferably every year in view of continual changes in legal legislation. The policy should always be revisited when there is a significant change in the UK agency/church.
5. In situations where a staff member is seconded to a local partner, the local partner should also be encouraged to develop crisis management and prevention policies and procedures.
6. Clear, overall procedures should be developed and then adapted as appropriate for each overseas location and be based on the overall policies.
7. One of the aims of the policy should be to identify clear management structures so that everybody knows who should be informed and involved so that the best standards of member care can be offered.

## SECTION 2
## SELECTION AND APPOINTMENT, INDUCTION AND ARRIVAL, AND ONGOING SUPERVISION

Taking potential crisis situations into account during selection, induction, and supervision of staff is important in all settings. However, in high-risk situations especially, where there are serious external risks as specified in appendix 2, it is especially important. As a result each agency/church should:

- Appoint a crisis management coordinator who has overall responsibility for developing, completing, and implementing its Crisis Management and Prevention policies. In each location, a local crisis management officer should be appointed.
- The crisis management coordinator should keep knowledge, policies, procedures, and best practice requirements up to date and ensure local crisis management officers are adequately trained.
- Agree about and ensure that there is clarity on whom to contact overseas and in the home country.
- Review regularly security procedures at staff meetings and ensure all changes in the security situation are communicated to all staff.

### PROCEDURES RELATING TO SELECTION AND APPOINTMENT
- All potential personnel and volunteers working overseas should be informed of any possible risks associated with a placement at the start of any recruitment, appointment, or redeployment process.
- The application process should ensure basic health screening of applicants.
- During the interview process, applicants should be asked about previous high-risk areas and crisis situations in which they have been involved as appropriate.
- Any additional criteria relating to a person's suitability for being appointed to work in a high-risk area should be clearly set out in the selection process.
- The Crisis Management Policy should be integrated into the staff handbook or appropriate document and all personnel should be required to acknowledge in writing that they have received and understood the Crisis Management Policy.

### PROCEDURES RELATING TO ORIENTATION, INDUCTION, AND ARRIVAL
- Orientation should be provided for all categories of staff and volunteers relating to crisis management.
- People working in high-risk areas should be provided with appropriate specialist training, including personal security training.
- Induction relating to specific situations should be provided on site on arrival.
- Relationships with embassies should be established and all staff members and families should be registered. Their guidance should be sought for those working in high-risk areas.
- Advice should also be sought from local Christian leaders and other agencies including international bodies. Appropriate use should be made of any UN traffic-light system for entering restricted areas.

## PROCEDURES RELATING TO ONGOING SUPERVISION

- Staff working in stressful situations should have regular periods of rest and refreshment away from their work place. This should be in addition to normal holiday entitlement.
- Reporting mechanisms should be in place for work-related injuries, sickness, accidents, and fatalities and should be monitored to help assess and reduce future risk to staff.
- Anticipation of a crisis:
  - *External:* External crises can be predicted by regular monitoring of media, both international and local. Staff can alert their crisis management officer of potential crises.
  - *Personal:* Personal crises may be detected early by observation and interaction. Consistent pastoral care at various levels should facilitate this process. Individuals who observe behavior which may lead to individual crises should make their concerns known to their crisis management office. Staff should be expected to use their common sense with regard to health and travel. Travel routes should be secure and others be advised of routes taken.
  - *Ministry:* It should be made clear to staff that their behavior can affect their own ministry and the ministry of others. Staff may sense that their movements are being monitored. If so, they should inform the crisis management coordinator, not use a home phone, and be discreet in their contact with other personnel.

# SECTION 3
## BEING PREPARED

It is easy to assume that everyone knows what is appropriate in a situation of crisis or potential crisis. This is rarely the case and there is often an absence of specific expectations. Clear guidance needs to be given to staff on many issues.

The following is a checklist for staff:

- All staff should be made aware regularly of security, travel, and health risks together with evacuation procedures for the specific country or region.
- Agency obligations and individual responsibilities in relation to possible risks should be clearly communicated to staff.
- Agencies/churches should provide adequate health and evacuation insurance cover. Local insurance options for local staff should also be sought.
- Each staff member or family should appoint a current power of attorney for every adult family member.
- Each staff member should have an up to date will and its location should be known by their power of attorney.
- Each staff member or family should notify their agency/church about the details of whom to contact in an emergency.

- Each staff member or family should notify their agency/church of their wishes in the event of a death overseas, including guardianship of children.
- All staff should establish access to funds that will be adequate for emergencies. In the case of married couples, both partners should be able to access the funds in the event of an emergency.

# SECTION 4
## CRISIS PROCEDURE

Mechanisms must be put in place for actions to be taken when a crisis happens. While some procedures depend on the particular nature of the event, the following general procedures should be included:

- A verifiable source will identify the crisis.
- A list should be made of all key stakeholders to be involved, both at field office, home office, and head (international/regional) office level.
- A person should be appointed (normally by default the crisis management officer or team leader) to coordinate the situation on the field. Delegation should be made to specific people regarding specific tasks so that everyone is aware of who does what and when and where to report back.
- Clear lines of communication should be established to ensure reliable and confidential channels are used.
- Depending on the crisis, the crisis management coordinator may take overall charge on behalf of the whole agency. It is important that there are clear decision-making processes over who has full overriding authority and whether it is the head office or remains at local level.
- The person taking the lead will be responsible for the following as necessary:
  - Maintaining a chronology of events, during and after the crisis or critical incident
  - Keeping a log of phone calls and notes of all relevant meetings
  - Collecting relevant signed statements or testimonials
  - Overseeing funds of team members if appropriate
  - Overseeing return or burial arrangements for any deceased staff, including liaison over autopsies
  - Seeing to the honorable discharge of any of the team's liabilities
  - Overall liaison with:
    - trustworthy legal counsel
    - local government
    - embassy
    - family

# SECTION 5
## COMMUNICATIONS PROCEDURE IN A CRISIS

It is important to have clear procedures in the event of a crisis situation. The following may be helpful examples of some of the areas that should be covered.

## OVERALL COMMUNICATION

- For security purposes, consideration should be given regarding what is the best communication channel to use in the case of emergencies.

## COMMUNICATION WITH THE FAMILY

- Contact should only be made with the contact specified by the staff member. There should be clarity about who is to be contacted depending on the crisis and its likely impact on the family.
- Ensure that the crisis management team or responsible person has decided exactly what information is to be passed on and that possible responses of the nominated contact are considered and prepared for:
  - How much information can be passed on and why?
  - Should the family go to the site or stay where they are?
  - Who can they inform and what can they say?
  - How to handle media?
  - How to try to affirm trust?
- The family will want time and attention and must feel that all is being done.
- Be aware that the family may take action themselves.

## COMMUNICATION WITH THE AUTHORITIES

- A decision must be made as to how to deal with local and national authorities as well as the home authorities of the person/people involved.
- Complications may arise if they are not informed or if they are informed.
  - They will want to be seen to be assuming their responsibilities.
  - They may distrust mission/aid agencies.
  - They may accuse mission/aid agencies of not seeking their security advice.
  - They may not want mission/aid agencies to negotiate with their "enemies."
  - They may try and resolve rapidly by using violence.

## COMMUNICATION WITH THE EMBASSY

- Keep in touch with the relevant embassies. However, the extent to which they are involved depends on the nature of the crisis.

## COMMUNICATION WITH THE MEDIA

- Generally try and exclude media as it may complicate matters.
- If the story is in the public domain, ask the media to limit what they say.
- Answer questions with minimal information (only facts).
- It may be necessary to use media at a later date so be aware of who they are and what they are reporting.
- Always use one focal person. Head office should share with the field exactly what has been said (and vice versa).

## COMMUNICATION WITH OTHER AGENCIES

- Incidents may increase risk, information needs to be shared, but with strict confidentiality.
- Risk control may then be further discussed to ensure safety of others.

## SECTION 6
### DEBRIEFING AND POSSIBLE COUNSELING

When staff members and their families come through a crisis, appropriate counseling must be given. It is routine that staff should receive debriefing and counseling, regardless of their apparent emotional well-being. This should not be at the discretion of the supervisor or the staff member.

- Staff should be aware of how to access emergency member care and this should be facilitated by the agency/church.
- Debriefing following an emergency situation should take place within at least seventy-two hours of the crisis.
- Affected colleagues may also require counseling, for example in the event of the death of a colleague.
- It is common to attempt to shelter children from distress by trying not to mention concerns in front of them. Ensure that children are included in any debriefing.

## APPENDIX 1
### SOME DEFINITIONS

**Kidnapping:** Forced capture and detention for the specific purpose of obtaining some sort of payment (or political aim) from them, their organization, or a government. Release and safety are usually dependent on certain criteria being met. The cause may be political in nature or economic (extortion or ransom). Because of the negotiation skills needed in this, a specialist will probably be needed.

**Hostage-taking:** This is more a situation of siege, where abductors take a person(s) as part of their strategy for escape.

**Abduction:** This is the forced taking of a person(s) but with no demand made. (For example, young men forced into the army.) When there is no demand there may be another reason, often political statements to make an example of someone. These situations are very serious—response may be only to give high level media coverage. It may also require negotiation with advocacy groups and human-rights groups.

## APPENDIX 2
### DEFINITION OF A CRISIS

A crisis may be external, individual, or ministry related.

### EXTERNAL
- Kidnapping
- Civil unrest, accelerated military activity or war
- Terrorism
- Hijacking/carjacking
- Natural disaster

External crises can often be predicted by regular monitoring of media, both international and local.

## INDIVIDUAL

- Disagreement between members in conflict
- Missing persons
- Serious accident
- Violence including murder or accidental death
- Major health problem (physical and psychological)

Individual crises may be detected early by observation and interaction. Consistent pastoral care at various levels can facilitate this process. Individuals who observe behavior which could lead to an individual crisis should make their concerns known to their team manager. Early intervention may diffuse a larger crisis.

## MINISTRY

- Imprisonment or expulsion
- Refused reentry
- House arrest

Individuals may sense that their movements are being monitored. If so, they should inform their team leader, not use a home phone, and be discreet in their contact with other team members.

# APPENDIX 3
## USEFUL RESOURCES

*People in Aid*
  Regent's Wharf, 8 All Saints Street
  London N1 9RL
  Phone: 020 7520 2548
  E-mail: info@peopleinaid.org
  www.peopleinaid.org

*RedR London*
  1 Great George Street
  London SW1P 3AA
  E-mail: info@redr.org
  Phone: 020 7233 3116
  www.redr.org/london

*International Health Exchange*
  1 Great George Street,
  London SW1P 3AA
  E-mail: info@ihe.org.uk
  Phone: 020 7233 1100
  www.ihe.org.uk

*Crisis Consulting International*
  E-mail: tmercer@cricon.org

Tel: 02891 457689

www.cricon.org

*Member Care*

Mrs. Marion Knell

Tel: 015 0989 0268

E-mail: marion@knell.net

*List of UK Embassies*

www.fco.gov.uk

## QUESTIONS FOR REFLECTION

1. Many of the procedures recommended here are influenced at least in part by the requirements of British law. How could you adapt this document for your context?
2. Western cultures have become "risk averse." When should we take risks for the sake of the gospel? What biblical principles would you turn to, both for taking risks and for avoiding harm?
3. What is the responsibility of the individual, of his sending church, and of his sending agency? If there is an established church to which the person is to go, what would be reasonable care to expect from them?

**Global Connections** is a network of over three hundred UK agencies, churches, colleges, and support services linked together for resources, learning, and representation toward the common goal of mission outreach.

**Global Missions Network** is a connecting place providing exposure, inspiration, and identity to New Testament missions, ministries, and church growth in South East Asian countries.

# CHAPTER 55

# POLICY RECOMMENDATIONS

*Crisis Consulting International*

Crisis Consulting International (CCI) has identified the need for a core set of twelve policy guidelines addressing four critical areas of crisis management. Although the circumstances of specific organizations may create the need for additional policy guidelines, these twelve core areas are considered the foundation necessary for adequate crisis management preparation.

CCI has developed a set of "model policy" recommendations for each of these twelve circumstances. We are making these model policy recommendations available to interested Christian organizations. However, we emphasize that these model policies should serve as a starting point for consideration and evaluation, and should not just be adopted as presented.

## CHARACTERISTICS OF POLICIES
- Policies should be consistent with and reflect the organization's core values and standards.
- Policies should be value driven.
- Policies should apply throughout the organization.
- Policies describe what you will do, not how you will do it.
- Compliance should be mandatory throughout the organization.

## USING THIS MATERIAL
CCI authorizes any nonprofit organization to use this material as necessary, including reproducing and distributing it within the organization.

## MODEL POLICY: PAYMENT OF RANSOM, YIELDING TO EXTORTION
This organization recognizes that payment of ransom, acquiescing to other demands in kidnapping and hostage-taking cases, and making concessions in the face of extortion are all actions that contribute to the probability that similar future events will occur. Put another way, we understand that payment of ransom or similar actions that make the underlying event a "success" in the minds of the perpetrators will create incentives to encourage the same perpetrators, or others, to commit similar acts in the future.

This organization also places a high value on the safety of its members, staff, and families, and in cases of kidnapping or hostage-taking desires to take all reasonable steps to secure the safe release of the hostage(s).

*It is the policy of this organization that in cases of kidnapping, hostage-taking, or other extortion, no ransom or concession that is reasonably likely to cause or contribute to the probability that future similar events will occur shall be paid (or made).*

In specific cases, it shall be the responsibility of the crisis management team to determine whether or not a proposed payment or concession complies with both the letter and spirit of this policy. If the crisis management team cannot reach a consensus on this policy as it applies to a specific proposed concession, or if a proposed concession would likely be viewed by the broad Christian community as violating the spirit of this policy, the proposed payment or concession shall be reviewed by the authority that convened the crisis management team prior to the proposed payment of concession being agreed to or made.

## MODEL POLICY: NEGOTIATION WITH KIDNAPPERS AND HOSTAGE-TAKERS

This organization recognizes the distinction between negotiations and payments or concessions in cases of kidnapping and hostage-taking. We understand that negotiations can be conducted without necessarily obligating the organization to make payments or concessions that violate our values and policies. We also understand that negotiations, if they can be effectively and competently conducted, are the strategy of first choice in cases of kidnapping and hostage-taking.

This organization also recognizes that hostage negotiations are a very specialized and a potentially dangerous activity.

*It is the policy of this organization that in cases of kidnapping or hostage-taking of our members, our staff, or members of their families, their safe return shall be a priority of the organization. All reasonable efforts consistent with our policies and core values will be made to achieve their safe return. These efforts include hostage negotiation as a strategy of first choice. In cases where this organization has the opportunity to negotiate for the safe return of hostages, we will seek assistance from professional hostage negotiators.*

A source of hostage negotiation consultation and assistance is CCI, a nonprofit organization providing support to international Christian organizations:

Crisis Consulting International
PMB 223, 9452 Telephone Road
Ventura, CA 93004
USA
Phone: 805-642-2549, Fax:805-642-1748
E-mail info@CriCon.org, Internet: www.CriCon.org

## MODEL POLICY: FAMILY RELOCATION

Experience has shown that in cases of kidnapping and hostage-taking, rapid relocation of family members away from the area of the event is strongly advised. Having such a policy is a significant comfort to hostages, who report that uncertainty about the location and status of their families was the primary worry and source of anxiety during their captivity. Experience has also clearly demonstrated that such an action is in the best interest of these families (especially ones with younger children). Lastly, experience has shown that the presence of family members at the immediate site of crisis management and hostage negotiation efforts can create distractions and situations that divert the attention and energy of those responsible for resolution of the event away from that primary responsibility.

*It is the policy of this organization that in cases of kidnapping and hostage-taking, family members will be relocated from the country of occurrence as soon as possible. This relocation will normally take place to the home country of the family. In specific cases, the crisis management team may waive this policy if doing so is in the best interests of the crisis management effort.*

In cases where this policy is invoked, this organization will make ongoing support and assistance to the family a priority. This will include, but not necessarily be limited to, support in finding appropriate housing, school transfers, ongoing financial support, and similar matters. This will also include establishing a regular system of providing timely and accurate information to the family on the status of the case and the work of the crisis management team. This support will also include insuring that adequate pastoral, emotional, and psychological support, including that of trained professionals, is provided as indicated.

## MODEL POLICY: NOTIFICATIONS TO GOVERNMENTS IN KIDNAPPING AND HOSTAGE-TAKING

In cases of kidnapping and hostage-taking, this organization understands that the local (host) government has authority and responsibility for such crimes that occur within the country. We are also aware that the home government (government of citizenship) of the hostage(s) has a legitimate interest, and perhaps even legal jurisdiction, in these foreign kidnappings or hostage-takings of their citizens. However, we recognize that in some of these cases in some countries, the involvement of governments may create a conflict with our objectives and values.

*It is the policy of this organization to cooperate with legitimate government inquiries and activities in cases of kidnapping and hostage-taking, when doing so is judged to be in the best interest of the hostage(s) and the organization. The decisions of when and how to make these notifications to government agencies shall be made by the crisis management team.*

## MODEL POLICY: RISK ASSESSMENT

Accurately and adequately understanding risk is the essential foundation for all contingency planning and security preparation and management. A commitment to understanding risk is an essential component of our overall member care and security management efforts. Such a commitment requires the use of a disciplined and structured protocol of risk assessment.

We also recognize that it is important that measures or descriptions of risk and danger be in a form that is as objective and quantifiable as possible, and that the descriptive criteria used be as standardized as possible (so the same term or description applied to one situation or country means essentially the same thing in another situation or country).

Finally, we realize that there are two distinct types of risk assessment: tactical assessment, which analyzes the present situation and identifies threats and vulnerabilities that are here and now; and strategic risk forecasting, which forecasts future risks and predicts both the probability and consequences of unwanted events occurring. We appreciate that both types of risk assessment are necessary for the most comprehensive and accurate understanding of risks and dangers facing the organization.

*It is the policy of this organization to require all field entities to conduct and maintain adequate and timely tactical and strategic risk assessments. Strategic risk assessments are to follow CCI's "Strategic Risk Forecasting" protocol, and are to be conducted at least every two years (see next paragraph). Field Vulnerability Assessments are to follow CCI's "Tactical Risk Assessment" protocol, and are to be conducted at the beginning of a new project and at least every two years thereafter (see next paragraph).*

*The frequency of both strategic and tactical risk assessments are to be increased if:*
- *There is a significant change in the environment (change of government, substantial political shift, threat or outbreak of war, etc.).*
- *The assessed risk/threat level is such that field, regional, or headquarters leadership determines that a more frequent risk assessment schedule is appropriate.*

## MODEL POLICY: CONTINGENCY PLANS

This organization recognizes the need for contingency planning as a major component of security and crisis management. Contingency plans assist the organization not only in responding to events that have occurred, but also assist the organization identify and implement proactive steps that seek to reduce both the probability of unwanted events occurring and the consequences and impact of those events should they in fact occur.

Risk assessments done by local entities will determine specific threats and situations requiring advance contingency planning. However, there are some areas that are sufficiently common and foreseeable that all entities need corresponding contingency plans.

Finally, there is significant benefit in the use of contingency plan formats that are consistent throughout the organization.

*It is the policy of this organization that each entity prepare and maintain current contingency plans for threats and dangers that are reasonably foreseeable and potentially threaten the safety of staff or the disruption of our work. As much as possible, given local conditions and circumstances, contingency plans shall be written in CCI's recommended format and shall identify proactive measures to reduce both probability and consequences (if possible) as well as response protocols.*

*All entities shall complete and maintain current contingency plans for the following situations:*
- *Evacuation of staff (both local and country-wide)*

- *Establishing and operating an entity crisis management team*
- *Information management during a crisis*

*In addition, each entity shall complete and maintain current contingency plans for any event for which a Tactical Risk Assessment results in a "critical" or "high" rating; and for any event for which a Strategic Risk Assessment results in a forecast rating of "critical" or "high."*

*"Current" contingency plans are those that remain consistent with the threat, environment, and organizational conditions and resources. Contingency plans are to be reviewed at least every two years and either modified as necessary or certified as still current. Increased risk and dynamic local conditions may require more frequent review and modification.*

## MODEL POLICY: TRAINING

The most effective security and crisis management activities are those that prevent unwanted occurrences or reduce the impact/consequences of unpreventable events. Training of personnel is one of the most valuable and effective proactive steps an organization can take. Trained personnel are the most successful at minimizing their own exposure to danger, and trained personnel assist the organization avoid dangerous, disruptive, and compromising situations.

"And now, behold, I am going to Jerusalem, constrained by the Spirit, not knowing what will happen to me there, except that the Holy Spirit testifies to me in every city that imprisonment and afflictions await me. But I do not account my life of any value nor as precious to myself, if only I may finish my course and the ministry that I received from the Lord Jesus, to testify to the gospel of the grace of God." *Acts 20:22–24*

*It is the policy of this organization to provide security and crisis management training to all personnel. The type and degree of training shall be commensurate with the assessed risks and dangers the member is exposed to, and also commensurate with the member's organizational responsibility for the safety and security of other staff and organizational assets.*

*All personnel shall receive training in (at least) the following areas:*
- *The organization's policies*
- *Evacuation procedures*
- *Basic personal safety and security*

## MODEL POLICY: CRISIS MANAGEMENT TEAM

Experience teaches that in the event of a crisis or emergency, the existence of a predetermined and structured response speeds resolution and recovery and also minimizes the overall disruption to the organization. Experience also teaches that the absence of such a plan not only hinders the organization's ability to resolve the crisis, but also may create new and additional crises that can ultimately be more disruptive than the original event.

We also recognize that even in the face of a significant crisis or major emergency, the primary objective of the organization is to continue its work and to be as productive as possible in the accomplishment of its objectives.

For these reasons, we acknowledge the importance and need of a predetermined organizational response plan for crises and emergencies.

*It is the policy of this organization that in the event of a crisis (or emergency), a crisis management team (CMT) will be formed to manage that event through resolution and recovery. The CMT will be formed and structured on models consistent with those described in the literature and in professional training for corporate and government entities (such as the model taught by Crisis Consulting International).*

*For purposes of this policy, a "crisis" is understood to include events that threaten the organization, that present a danger to the safety of staff or the potential for significant organizational disruption, that are likely to be extended in time, and are likely to require an abnormal commitment of resources.*

*A CMT can be established by field leadership for any event within that field, and by regional or headquarters leadership for any event whose foreseeable organizational impact is likely to extend beyond the local entity.*

*When a CMT is established, it is to be the only component of the organization "working" on that crisis. All other components and members of the organization shall refer all information and suggestions to the CMT. No action related to the crisis is to be taken without the authorization of the CMT. No public statements related to the crisis are to be made without the authorization of the CMT.*

## MODEL POLICY: INFORMATION MANAGEMENT

It is the intention of this policy that information flow during a crisis be carefully and strictly directed and controlled. Incoming information such as background information, suggestions about resources and assistance, ideas for resolution, etc., need to be received by the crisis management team. Outgoing information must be monitored and controlled to prevent the release of confidential information, to prevent exacerbation of the situation or the creation of secondary crises and to control the spread of rumors.

*It is the policy of this organization that all information, intelligence, ideas, suggestions, etc., relating to a crisis be directed to the crisis management team at the earliest possible time. Any member of the organization with such information or with suggestions for the crisis management team shall forward the information or suggestions immediately to the CMT.*

*It is further the policy of this organization that during a crisis all information released and all public statements about the crisis be made by (or with the specific approval of) the crisis management team. No member of the organization outside the CMT is authorized to make any statement that relates in any way to an ongoing crisis. This includes statements to internal constituencies (other members, families, etc.) as well as external constituencies (the media, extended family, home churches, government agencies, etc.).*

## MODEL POLICY: MEMBER CARE

It is the intention of this policy to recognize that individuals who undergo traumatic events, and others associated with these events, can suffer emotional reactions that may become destructive if untreated. It is the intention of this policy that those involved in traumatic events receive evaluation and, if necessary, intervention from mental health professionals.

It is the also intention of this policy that this evaluation and intervention be conducted confidentially with the objective being the treatment of existing trauma and the prevention of future trauma associated with the crisis.

*It is the policy of this organization that those personnel who are directly involved in a crisis receive an initial and follow-up evaluation from a qualified Christian mental health professional. These evaluations shall occur as soon as possible following a crisis and again six to twelve months following the crisis (unless otherwise specified by the mental health professional).*

*These evaluations and any treatment are confidential between the member of the organization and the mental health professional. Costs associated with this policy shall be paid by the organization. Although the individuals who should receive evaluation as described herein may vary from incident to incident, in each case at least the victim, the immediate family, and the crisis management team shall receive this evaluation.*

*In situations involving large numbers of members, such as group evacuations, the use of a supervised Critical Incident Stress Debriefing (CISD) may fulfill the requirements of this policy (providing the CISD incorporates a mechanism for recognition of the need and provision for accomplishing follow-up counseling or therapy as needed).*

## MODEL POLICY: EVACUATION AUTHORITY

The intention of this policy is to address those components of evacuation planning and decision making that can be identified before a crisis occurs. One of the most critical (and potentially divisive) elements of evacuation decision making is determining who has the authority to mandate an evacuation. Experience has demonstrated that those on the field and close to the situation will have perspectives that tend to prioritize different factors than those in leadership roles and more geographically removed from the events. Experience has also shown that in some cases, those closest to the scene will have access to the best information to support an evacuation decision, but in other cases this information will be denied to them and will only be available to those more removed from the event.

*It is the policy of this organization that decision-making authority regarding evacuation exists at the individual or family level, at the local entity level, and at the headquarters leadership level. In different circumstances, each of these levels may have access to information that makes evacuation an appropriate decision; so, each is authorized to act on such information and make a decision. The remainder of the organization will respect such a decision. This policy is multilateral: Just as headquarters will support an individual family's decision to evacuate, so will individuals and families support a directive from local leadership or regional or headquarters authority to do so.*

## MODEL POLICY: EVACUATION CRITERIA

The intention of this policy is to address those components of evacuation planning and decision making that can be identified before a crisis occurs. Experience shows that training and contingency planning ahead of time will often times make the difference between successful and safe evacuations and those that endanger members and result in unnecessary organizational disruption.

*It is the policy of this organization that each local entity will prepare evacuation plans for all personnel serving under its jurisdiction. Copies of these plans shall be submitted to headquarters leadership where a reference copy will be maintained. These plans shall be reviewed, updated, and revised as needed, at least every two years. At a minimum, these plans shall include:*

- *A description of how the local entity will determine whether an evacuation is necessary; specifically identifying the decision-making authority and criteria to be used to make such a decision.*
- *A description of the notification system that insures all personnel receive necessary information before and during an evacuation.*
- *A description of the procedures the local entity will use; such as, means of transportation, evacuation routes and alternates, staging and destination sites, and communications procedures.*

*Each member or member and family shall prepare for two types of evacuation scenarios by identifying what would be taken with them and how they would accomplish an evacuation (e.g., method of transportation, routes, staging areas, and destination) for each of these circumstances:*

- *An evacuation with at least twenty-four hours' advance notice and in which a carload (persons and belongings) could be taken.*
- *An evacuation with one hour's notice and in which only those items that could be hand-carried could be taken.*

*Each member/family's plan will be submitted to the local entity and maintained as an annex to that entity's evacuation plan.*

## QUESTIONS FOR REFLECTION

1. Do you feel any dissonance between the concerns of this chapter and the thrust of the book? If so, why? If not, why not?
2. Are the concerns addressed in the suggested policies in this chapter adequately handled by your mission (or one you know well)? If not, what are the priority areas for improvement needed by your mission?
3. Does the missionary movement emerging in the Global South view missionary security in the same way this Western organization does? Should it?
4. Is there a point at which concern for missionary security becomes such a preoccupation that it conflicts with risks promised and inherent in biblical mission as described by Jesus and historically experienced by his followers?

**Crisis Consulting International** provides security and crisis management services and training to the Christian missionary, humanitarian, and church sending communities.

# CHAPTER 56

# BEST PRACTICES FOR MINISTRY TO AND WITH THE PERSECUTED CHURCH

## *The Religious Liberty Partnership*

The Code of Best Practices for ministry to and with the persecuted church around the world is designed as a benchmark document to guide the policies and practice of organizations in their involvement. It is not intended to establish legal standards or liability. Rather the motivation for the development of this code is based upon the responsibility toward all participants and partners in religious liberty work so that they are served with the highest standards possible.

The code does not necessarily reflect current practice, but encourages aspirations toward excellence. However, minimal standards are implied and therefore these principles should be seen as steps in the process rather than an end in themselves. It is also recognized that the code may not be applicable to all situations in religious liberty ministry.

Please recognize that no document or agreement on principles can reflect the attitude and relationships from which they were birthed. We have attempted, however, to do so.

These issues were identified by the membership of the Religious Liberty Partnership (RLP) as needing to be somehow addressed in this document:

- Problems of market or donor-driven ministry
- Common understanding of the needs of the situation
- Doing no harm
- Cross-cultural value and appreciation
- Long-term thinking that is proactive as opposed to reactive
- The tendency to see money/technology/resources as the primary responses to need
- Possible disagreements over the root causes of persecution
- Ministry preparation, biblical and theological training, knowing and applying biblical principles concerning persecution

- Communication integrity
  - Between organizations
  - Within own organization/network
  - Between nationals and international
  - Encouraging partners abroad
- Respect a body of Christ relational viewpoint
- Partnering and collaboration
- Accountability among RLP ministries
- Recognizing the centrality of the local church; i.e., providing funds through and the capacity building of the local church to render aid and counseling
- Concept of working with persecuted church leaders as equals as opposed to primarily seeing them as victims
- Equal access to opportunity, including those without a knowledge of English
- Danger of overprofessionalism

## PRINCIPLE 1: COLLABORATION AND PARTNERSHIP

The persecuted church is best served by ministries working together and cooperating while maintaining ministry distinctives. This includes the reduction of duplication; wisely sharing information; growing a common understanding of problems and root causes of persecution; strong relationship and trust; and accountability (information, money, etc.).

### KEY INDICATORS

- We are making the time to develop relationship and trust with one another.
- We are seeking to avoid duplication of ministry in a given area whenever possible.
- We are seeking to develop our collective intellectual capital by appropriately sharing information, knowledge, and lessons learned.
- We are seeing that attitudes of competition are being reduced.
- We are speaking well of each other and making direct contact with each other in the case of any disagreements.
- We are seeing more joint projects launched.
- We are learning how to share success with each other.

## PRINCIPLE 2: DOING NO HARM

Ministry to the persecuted church should operate under the core value of ensuring that we actively work to never do harm to those we are trying to serve. This includes cross-cultural consideration and appreciation; equal access to opportunity; support of local leaders; long-term thinking and sustainability; and the examination of possible exploitation.

### KEY INDICATORS

- We are respecting local culture, language, and practices.
- We are learning when to take no for an answer in avoiding the exploitation/overexposure of persecuted believers for the sake of publicity/promotion.
- We are promoting unity and not feeding disunity among local Christians by providing broad access to resources, consultation on possible projects, and evaluation of past and present projects, especially as it relates to sustainability.

# PRINCIPLE 3: EDUCATION AND TRAINING

As learning entities we are continually trying to learn from our mistakes, as well as the mistakes of other ministries, and willingly embrace the opportunity to do so in order to serve the persecuted church more effectively. This includes preparation for future possible persecution; training on biblical principles and theology; orientation and teaching to workers in countering dependency; and promotion of local church leadership.

## KEY INDICATORS

- We are providing orientation and training on key issues such as dependency, partnering, cultural sensitivity, etc., to our staff and workers.
- We are promoting the understanding and awareness of different levels of persecution.
- We are providing appropriate preparation to our leadership, staff, and partners as to the biblical and missiological principles of persecution.

# PRINCIPLE 4: COMMUNICATION

We strive to demonstrate integrity in all of our communications. This includes integrity in promotions; integrity in information gathering; integrity in dissemination; and integrity in the use of statistics.

## KEY INDICATORS

- Organizations are providing effective communication without exaggerating the needs, the statistics, and the plight of persecuted Christians.
- Accurate and verifiable statistics and research are being used.
- Appropriate sourcing, acknowledgements, and permissions are being practiced.
- Sensitivity is being shown to the impact on persecuted believers in our information gathering.
- We are following the directives and guidance of a variety of local leaders in what can be reported and publicized.
- We seek agreement to use the same numbers regarding the number of those being persecuted and the number of martyrs.

# PRINCIPLE 5: ACCOUNTABILITY

Mutual accountability leads to more effective ministry and faithful stewardship of our shared calling to the persecuted. This includes financial standards, information, and evaluation.

## KEY INDICATORS

- Adherence to nationally agreed upon financial standards, including certified audited accounting, is occurring.
- Organizations are open to receiving input from other RLP members as to our faithfulness to and our fulfillment of the best practices.
- Significant concerns on accountability are being expressed face to face.
- Where there is failure to resolve disputes among us, they are handled by Matthew 18 principles and possible mediation.

## PRINCIPLE 6: ADVOCACY

We will raise awareness of persecuted believers as well as seek to influence socioeconomic and political policies and structures. This includes: advocacy being done with the benefit of persecuted believers in mind, and advocacy being done collaboratively with other ministries.

### KEY INDICATORS

- Neglected peoples are receiving appropriate attention.
- Whenever it is possible, public advocacy is being done cooperatively with other organizations.
- Campaigns and public advocacy are being done with the participation and agreement of their families and local church leadership whenever possible.

## PRINCIPLE 7: OPERATIONAL STRATEGIES

Ministry to the persecuted church must go beyond "marketable" strategies. This includes attitudes of participating with persecuted church leaders and understanding that there may be differences in opinion among local believers on how to handle a given situation.

### KEY INDICATORS

- We try and see that our work is never only donor driven.
- Money, technology, and resources are not being seen as the only "answer." When looking to address the needs of the persecuted we are looking beyond monetary, technical, or other material resources.
- Organizations are growing in their heart motivation for the persecuted, not merely by secular management standards.
- Organizations are looking to determine long-term considerations and impact as part of their overall strategy rather then mere expediency.
- Branch offices are established with sensitivity to local culture, context, and economic realities (salary, personnel) as well as avoided when national organizations are doing the required work.
- Organizational involvement is building the capacity and self-sufficiency of national leaders and churches.
- We make available our vision, mission, and long-term strategies to each other.

## PRINCIPLE 8: FUND-RAISING

Raising funds for ministry to the persecuted church needs to exemplify integrity.

### KEY INDICATORS

- Accurate and verifiable statistics, facts, and testimonies are used in fund-raising materials with the avoidance of sensationalistic approaches.
- The needs of the persecuted are presented truthfully, respectfully, and in such a way as not to exploit their plight for material gain or further endanger them through publicity.

We view these best practices as a "living document," originally drafted by a multi-organizational task force from the Religious Liberty Partnership in August 2007. This is the seventh incarnation, dated March 2011.

Questions, comments, and additional information requests should be sent to:

Brian F. O'Connell, RLP Facilitator
Phone: 1-425-218-4718
E-mail: brian@RLPartnership.org
www.RLPartnership.org

## QUESTIONS FOR REFLECTION

1.  How does writing down a Code of Best Practices help to achieve organizational goals?
2.  Why is revisiting these codes important?
3.  Which of the seven principles is a strength for your organization? Which needs improvement?

**The Religious Liberty Partnership** is a collaborative effort of over thirty organizations focused on serving the persecuted church around the world to address advocacy and raise awareness of religious persecution globally.

"And take up his cross." Jesus has graciously prepared the way for this word by speaking first of self-denial. Only when we have become completely oblivious of self are we ready to bear the cross for his sake. If in the end we know only him, if we have ceased to notice the pain of our own cross, we are indeed looking only unto him. If Jesus had not so graciously prepared us for this word, we should have found it unbearable. But by preparing us for it he has enabled us to receive even a word as hard as this as a word of grace. It comes to us in the joy of discipleship and confirms us in it.

D. Bonhoeffer in *The Cost of Discipleship* (1976, 97)

The Martyrs of Uganda were a group of forty-five Anglican and Roman Catholic believers killed for their faith under Mwanga, ruler of Buganda (now in Uganda), from 1885 to 1887. Their numbers included Protestant and Catholic missionaries, young pages who were receiving religious instruction, an assistant judge, an Anglican Bishop, an advisor to the king, and others. Each of these martyrs were either burned alive, castrated, speared, dismembered, bludgeoned, or beheaded for their faith.

Rather than hindering the spread of Christianity, their martyrdom sparked a period of church growth, illustrating the words of Tertullian that "the blood of the martyrs is the seed of the church." Today, Christianity (in its various expressions) is now the dominant faith in Uganda. The twenty-two Catholic martyrs were canonized by Pope Paul VI on October 18, 1964, during the Vatican II conference. This was a first for modern Africa and a source of pride throughout the continent. A national holiday is celebrated in Uganda on June 3rd every year, when the bulk of the martyrs were killed. Above is a portrait of the twenty-two canonized Catholic martyrs.

*The Christian Martyrs of Uganda.* http://www.buganda.com/martyrs.htm.

Martyrs of Uganda. 2011. *Encyclopædia Britannica.* http://www.britannica.com/EBchecked/topic/612654/Martyrs-of-Uganda.

# CHAPTER 57

# WHAT DO WE LEARN FROM THE PERSECUTED?

*Ronald R. Boyd-MacMillan*

There are at least three ways our faith can be transformed by an encounter with persecuted Christians. They can be for us a *faith model,* a *faith warning,* or a *faith boost.* Indeed, they can be all three at once. Each forces us to ask a particular question of our own walk with God:

*Faith boost* – "Is my God big enough?"
*Faith warning* – "Am I in enough trouble for Jesus?"
*Faith model* – "Am I walking the way of the cross?"

Let us start with the last of these first.

## FAITH MODEL: AM I WALKING THE WAY OF THE CROSS?

The ultimate challenge of the persecuted church is that they teach us things about God which we can incorporate into our daily walk. If all we do is pray for the persecuted, support the persecuted, march for the persecuted, then we are still operating in the mode of "us helping them." We have not actually allowed the persecuted to change our lives.

Here, let me focus on one insight from the persecuted that will help us specifically with the Western challenges of living the Christian life. I call it *the way of the cell.*

In the West each of us is influenced by the information revolution. New technologies driven by the silicon chip have resulted in an explosion of information, which in theory should make us better informed. But we are realizing that while the total amount of information has vastly increased, good information is harder to find. We can't see the truth for the "data smog."

Worse, to search for truth in the information age is incredibly stressful. Voice mail, e-mail, Internet—all were supposed to make our lives easier. Yet they have added hours to our working day. The computers seem to mock us because we can't keep up. We are valued in the marketplace only if we can do five things at once. We almost wish we were a computer.

The persecuted church has an answer—build yourself a cell! At least that's what Wang Ming Dao said.

Born at the turn of the century, Wang Ming Dao was China's most famous house church pastor and evangelist and, until his death in 1991, received famous religious VIP's like Billy Graham. Wang was the genuine article. Released in 1980, his steadfast faith during twenty-three years of imprisonment inspired millions of Chinese Christians. Said one Shanghai pastor, "Wang Ming Dao proved that God existed—no one goes to jail for that long and comes out with their faith still intact if God is not real."

Yet his visitors often found him unattractively trenchant and fierce. He was fond of wagging his finger and saying to his guests, "You do not have revival because you do not walk the hard road." For Wang, revival could only come upon those who knew that walking the way of Christ would be hard, requiring courage, determination, and sacrifice.

But what does the hard road look like for the Western Christian, where (thank God) we will not spend twenty years in jail for our faith? In three separate interviews with Wang Ming Dao, I gained a little inkling into what his answer might be.

The first time I met him he asked me suddenly, "Young man, how do you walk with God?" I listed off a set of disciplines like Bible study and prayer, to which he mischievously retorted, "Wrong answer … to walk with God you must go at walking pace."

Frankly I had no idea what he was talking about, and let it go as the ramblings of a slightly senile old man in his late eighties.

The next time I visited he was sharper from a good night's sleep. I remember looking at him and confessing that I was finding it hard to relate his experience to mine. I said, "I will never be put in jail like you, so how can your faith have any impact on mine?"

He thought for a minute, and then replied by asking me a series of questions: "When you go back home, how many books do you have to read this coming month? How many letters do you have to write? How many people do you have to see? How many articles do you have to produce? How many sermons must you preach?"

He kept up the questions and I answered each time. After about fifteen of these questions I was beginning to feel panicked at the amount of work ahead. I mopped my brow and looked gloomily at the slice of watermelon on the plate in front of me.

He seemed to sense this, despite his virtual blindness, and said these words that have meant so much to me since:

"You need to build yourself a cell!"

He explained, "When I was put in jail I was devastated. I was sixty years old, at the peak of my powers. I was a well-known evangelist and wished to hold crusades all over China. I was an author. I wanted to write more books. I was a preacher. I wanted to study my Bible and write more sermons. But instead of serving God in all these ways, I found myself sitting alone in a dark cell. I could not use the time to write more books. They deprived me of pen and paper. I could not study my Bible and produce more sermons. They had taken it away. I had no one even to witness to, as the jailer for years just pushed my meals through a hatch. Everything that had given me meaning as a Christian worker had been taken away from me. And I had nothing to do."

He stopped, and his eyes moistened again. "Nothing to do except get to know God. And for twenty years that was the greatest relationship I have ever known. But the cell was the means."

His parting advice was, "I was pushed into a cell, but you will have to push yourself into one. You have no time to know God. You need to build yourself a cell, so you can do for yourself what persecution did for me—simplify your life and know God."

The third time we met was shortly before his death. I referred back to our first talk and asked, "Why did you say to walk with God you must go at walking pace? Surely God can walk, run, go at any pace he likes. Why would God choose to walk and ask us to walk?"

His answer haunts me still: "Because he loves his garden!"

Wang Ming Dao never explained, but I think I got his drift. Eden is where God comes walking, looking to speak with Adam and Eve. The whole world is a fellowship garden. And the aim of human life was, and still is, to walk in this wonderful garden with this wonderful God! If we work, as we must, but do not walk, as we might, we lose the meaning and joy of life, and no amount of religious freedom will compensate.

In this exchange is one of the keys to the faith of the suffering church. God does things slowly. He works with the heart. We are too quick. We have so much to do. So much in fact we never really commune with God as he intended when he created Eden, the perfect fellowship garden. For Wang Ming Dao, persecution, or the cell in which he found himself, was the place he returned to "walking pace," slowing down, stilling himself enough to commune properly with God. Revival can only come to those who make room for God.

The Japanese missiologist Kosuke Koyama talks of the "three-mile-an-hour God" of the Bible, leading the Israelites out into the desert for a forty-year walk at three miles an hour so they would learn "that man does not live by bread alone, but by every word that comes from the mouth of God" (Deut 8:3). Three miles an hour—the pace at which we walk. Forty years ... to learn a nineteen-word truth. It's hardly a productivity rate we would be satisfied with, but then, if a great truth is to be properly learned, maybe we have to redefine spiritual productivity. It seems to be a lesson we can only learn at three miles an hour. God is more interested in how deep the truth goes than in how much we know.

For those who want God to be more real, perhaps a slice of the answer is to slow our lives down to a spiritual walking pace—imposed on the persecuted by circumstances—so that we can know God instead of merely serving him. It may take a cell if we follow Wang Ming Dao's advice, but then, if he is right, the cell becomes a garden. And so this is an example of how persecuted Christians can be faith models. But they can also provide a faith warning.

## FAITH WARNING: AM I IN ENOUGH TROUBLE FOR JESUS?

The biblical scholar William Barclay famously described a New Testament Christian as having three characteristics: "One, they were absurdly happy; two, they were filled with an irrational love for everyone; and three, they were always in trouble!" Persecuted Christians also are constantly in trouble. As a Palestinian pastor put it, "If you speak truth to power, power always reacts." An encounter with the persecuted reveals the incendiary nature of this gospel we follow, and if our witness does not provoke some sort of explosive reaction, we have to check whether our gospel powder is damp or dry. We should be in trouble for Jesus! If we aren't, something is wrong. This is what is meant by a faith warning.

Of course, it is the gospel itself that gets us into trouble, not ourselves. We live in a world of idols, and if we refuse to worship those idols, the idols—ironically—always hit back. A good definition of an idol is: "something that becomes more important to you than God." Like it or not, we live in an arena of conflict, though some of us prefer to keep our "eyes wide shut" to this fact. We have to fight, because every day we receive a thousand messages asking us to be more self-centered and to love Christ less, asking us to put the idol first and Christ second.

> Some were tortured, refusing to accept release, so that they might rise again to a better life. Others suffered mocking and flogging, and even chains and imprisonment. They were stoned, they were sawn in two, they were killed with the sword. They went about in skins of sheep and goats, destitute, afflicted, mistreated—of whom the world was not worthy—wandering about in deserts and mountains, and in dens and caves of the earth. *Hebrews 11:35–38*

Persecuted Christians are not tempted into the illusion that the world is actually a friendly place that does not mind our identifying with Christ. The world for them is unmasked in its hostility to Christ.

Perhaps the key to the faith warning is to realize that it can be our culture that is hostile to Christ, at root idolatrous and leading us away from Christ, even though the rhetoric may be quite Christian. It was a young artist in Shanghai that brought this home to me.

Her name was Ping An, and she was a Chinese landscape painter. In the course of her training at a very prestigious academy she became a Christian. A traditional Chinese landscape painting depicts sheer mountains rising into mist covered summits, streams falling spectacularly into wide shimmering lakes. Any human figure in such a painting is always tiny, reflecting a belief that humans are insignificant relative to the glories of nature.

But Ping An was reading Genesis chapter 1, and her eyes widened when she suddenly realized how radically different the Christian view of creation was to the one she depicted in her traditional canvases. She recalls, "What amazed me was that the story of creation culminates with the creation of Adam and Eve, not the mountains, seas, or heavens. We Chinese find mountains and rivers a lot more impressive than human beings. But God turns that upsidedown, and values a fragile life more than a mighty rock."

The next day, she sat in the classroom and drew a landscape in its traditional form, then placed two figures at the center, drawing them much larger than usual. It was a break with tradition to say the least. She returned from her lunch and was told, "The governors have asked to see you." She made her way along to a room where six stone-faced men sat in a row. To the right of them hung her new painting. "What is the meaning of this?" they asked.

Ping An tried to explain, but a very distinguished professor interrupted her. He said patiently, as if to a child, "Look, if I thrust a branch into you, blood flows out and you die. But if I poke a branch into a mountain, the mountain makes it into a tree. How then can you possibly say we humans are more significant than mountains? They go on forever. We are here for a fleeting moment. That's why we paint human figures so small."

"No, we are not insignificant," she flashed back, and quoted the words of Jesus in Luke 21:33 to the astonished committee: *"Heaven and earth will pass away, but my words will never pass away.* Don't *you* see, it's God's words that make things significant. He doesn't talk to the mountains. He talks to us. He has made the mountains for us! Isn't it incredible?"

The governors did not agree. She was expelled from the school, barred from any further artistic training and now ekes out a living as a teacher, doing portraiture in her spare time. But it was her traditional Chinese culture that was at odds with her new Christian convictions. Her clash had little to do with the fact that she lived in a Communist country where the worship of God was restricted.

In the same way, we all have to awaken to the same clash of values in our own culture. Brother Andrew puts it this way, "Persecution is because of the radical life, not the other way around. Why are we not having persecution? Because we are dodging it. There are many Bible verses like 2 Timothy 3:12, 'All who want to live a godly life in Christ will be persecuted.' We go around that because we don't like that verse, and we interpret it so that it becomes meaningless. Or we apply it only to the time of the Apostle Paul. If we are radical in our Christian walk we will be persecuted."

That is why we must also take a *faith boost* from the persecuted.

## FAITH BOOST: IS MY GOD BIG ENOUGH?

Most of us usually encounter the persecuted church by hearing or reading a story of someone who has suffered greatly for God but has been triumphant. Testimonies of triumph travel fast, and missions have served us well to circulate these testimonies. One pastor I knew described the effect of reading stories from the persecuted: "It felt like I had been living in a closet, and these saints came to me and led me out saying, *actually you live in a mansion, let us show you some of the rooms!"*

This is what we mean by a faith boost. It is when Christians reading of these persecuted believers realize that the God who delivered or strengthened the persecuted saint loves them just as much and will help them as much; and so faith is boosted. We are reminded of how big our God is.

But why do we need to be reminded of this? Perhaps it is because as comfortable Western Christians we do not have enough emergencies—situations so hopeless that all we can do is pray. The persecuted face emergencies every week. They are always crying to God for deliverance, because so often that is all they can do. No wonder they know more about God than us. It is through their stories, through their testimonies of God's power and love, that our faith can be fortified.

The stories themselves tend to come in two main forms: *deliverance* stories that testify to the rescuing power of God and *endurance* stories that testify to the faithfulness of God over time.

## DELIVERANCE STORIES

At their most robust, deliverance stories make us marvel at the power of God, reminding us that miracles are just as much a part of daily life today as in Bible times. I heard of an evangelist who went to Tibet to evangelize Buddhists. He was caught and actually given a famous sky burial ... alive! He was sown into a yak skin and left to die in the baking sun. His Tibetan tormentors—fearful of the spirits—left him alone, not even watching from a distance. It would be a slow and excruciating death.

But this was not his lot. He later told his story to a Henan evangelist, "I think maybe on the second day I began to notice large birds around me. Vultures I think they were. And they began pecking at me. I was so far gone I hoped they would peck my eyes out all the way into my brain and make death come quickly. But after a while I began to realize that their attempts to eat me had only pecked through the sewing, and it was loosened to such an extent that I was able to emerge out of it like a butterfly from a cocoon."

A man who heard that story said that it turned his life around. A Hong Kong securities dealer, he was about to take his own life after running up gambling debts he had no hope of paying back. His wife left him, taking his child, and—last and least—his Mercedes was stolen, all in one week. He went upstairs to his flat and put his head in the oven. As he twisted the knobs to turn the gas on, he suddenly thought of that story, picturing the bird beaks slicing through the sewing. Then he stopped and said to God, "Why don't you save me too?" He fiddled with the knobs for twenty minutes, but nothing happened. The gas had been turned off that afternoon because of an overdue bill. He saw that as another deliverance, and went on to confess to the police his addiction. He has not paid his debts yet, but he does have his wife and child back, so impressed were they with his new attitude.

## ENDURANCE STORIES

Yet it has to be said that deliverance stories—though they tend to grab the headlines—are not the norm. A dear old Christian in Beijing used to say to me, "Remember, for every deliverance story you hear, there are ten endurance stories." He was right. The story of the persecuted is primarily one of endurance. It has been so since New Testament times. Paul warns that only those who endure with Christ will reign with him (2 Tim 2:12). And this is surely right—after all, the things we are "delivered" from come back to take us. The disease that threatened to take our life may have passed, but another will come along and take our life eventually.

God delivers through endurance. If Jesus had been delivered from the pain of the cross and miraculously released, we would not be delivered from our sins. He endured so that a deeper, greater deliverance could take place.

I never saw this principle better illustrated than in the story of an old Christian lady in China. A doctor in Beijing, she was well known for her bright Christian witness. She never married in order to look after a sick brother. Her family was wealthy. They lived in a large house in the center of the capital.

All that changed abruptly in 1949. Her large house marked her out as one of the landlord class. She was evicted from her house and her Christian convictions meant she became an object of suspicion. When the Cultural Revolution broke out, she was stripped of her doctor's post and sent to work shoveling sand in a work gang. But the final indignity was when the Red Guards—teenagers who were given power to direct the revolution—began to visit her, beating her up, parading her in the streets, and forcing her to wear a placard with her so-called crimes written on them.

"Therefore I send you prophets and wise men and scribes, some of whom you will kill and crucify, and some you will flog in your synagogues and persecute from town to town, so that on you may come all the righteous blood shed on earth, from the blood of innocent Abel to the blood of Zechariah the son of Barachiah, whom you murdered between the sanctuary and the altar."
*Matthew 23:34–35*

So thorough were the Red Guards that they erected a large sign outside her house declaring her a pariah because she had distributed "imperialistic literature in praise of anti-Mao factions," which meant that she had given out Bibles in the "mistaken" belief that religion was helpful. For the Red Guards, there was only one "god" allowed, that was Mao, and only one "bible" allowed, his little Red Book.

Mabel descended into hell. Shunned by neighbors, victimized daily by her work gang, and beaten up regularly by the Red Guards, she came back one night into her little shed and said to God, "I've had enough." She reasoned, "I'm in my sixties now, I've lived a good life, and God will not mind me coming to heaven early." So she took a large chopper, held it over her wrists, and issued one last prayer before bringing it down, "Lord, if this is wrong, help me."

She never brought the chopper down. She put it away, sat down, burst into tears, and endured another eight years of the beatings, isolation, and victimization. She said, "Somehow, God gave me the strength to endure, but I never knew how."

## LATER, MANY YEARS LATER, SHE KNEW WHY

In the late seventies, after Mao died and Deng returned to power, China began to put the excesses of the Cultural Revolution behind it. The hated Red Guards were disbanded, the little Red Book fell into disuse. But Mabel was not restored to her house. However, she began to receive a stream of visitors. To her astonishment, these visitors were all rather high-ranking members of the Communist Party. Even more astonishingly, they asked her for Bibles.

"Why come to me—out of all the people in Beijing, why do you come to the house of a seventy-year-old?" she would ask. Each would answer the same: "Well, during the Cultural Revolution there was a large sign outside your house full of your crimes. One of them was that you had distributed Bibles. I'm here on the chance that you might have some left."

Amazingly, that sign which made her life such a misery became the means of a new ministry. It kept people away from her during the Cultural Revolution, but afterwards, after she had endured, it drew them. Mabel was able to contact a Western mission who smuggled Bibles to her and became the first conduit of Scriptures into China's capital. She became a vital supplier, and a number of high-ranking members of the Communist Party in China today owe their faith to her endurance.

She reflected, "It's been nice to know why. It helps my faith. But it was hard. Every day was hard. I can't say I saw Jesus or even felt him close most of the time. I just got the strength to keep going, and that was enough."

Not all get to see why either, but press forward in faith that through their endurance, God will work out his triumphant will, just as he did for Christ on the cross.

Thus in these ways at least, an encounter with the persecuted church—no matter how slight or indirect—can transform our spiritual lives. They can be a faith model, a faith warning, and a faith boost if we have the eyes to see and the ears to hear.

## QUESTIONS FOR REFLECTION

1. How does this article refute the idea that ministry involving the persecuted is a one-way street in which the non-persecuted help the persecuted?
2. Churches and Christians in the nonpersecuted world often know little about the persecuted. How can they/we more effectively learn the valuable lessons readily available from the persecuted?
3. Summarize in your own words the three ways Boyd-MacMillan suggests we ought to learn from persecuted Christians.
4. In what ways will faithfully following Jesus get us "in trouble" in our respective societies?

**Ronald R. Boyd-MacMillan** is currently the chief strategy officer for Open Doors International. He has enjoyed contrasting careers as a Bible smuggler in Cold War Eastern Europe, a pastor in Bristol, England, a journalist in Hong Kong, and a trainer of underground preachers in China. He has over twenty-five years experience of ministering among persecuted Christians on three continents. He is the author of *Faith that Endures: The Essential Guide to the Persecuted Church* (Baker Books, 2006).

# CHAPTER 58

# HUMAN RIGHTS AND PERSECUTION

## The Framework for Mission and Freedom of Religion

*Thomas Schirrmacher and Thomas K. Johnson*

The United Nations Universal Declaration of Human Rights (1948) proclaims that all human beings possess equal dignity (article 1) and forbids discrimination due to race, color, sex, language, religion, or political conviction (article 2). All people have the right to be treated "as persons." And what is the ultimate basis of equal human dignity, if not that all are created in God's image? "God created man in his own image, in the image of God he created them; male and female he created them" (Gen 1:27). And why are such protections needed, if not like with Cain, "sin is crouching at the door" (Gen 4:7) so that we easily become murderers, especially over religious frustrations? And how did it come about that there is a public recognition of human rights (and corresponding duties to protect those rights) if not for God's common grace, which not only led to the covenant of the rainbow but also to the public duty to protect justice by law enforcement (Gen 9:6)?

Missionaries and activists engaged on behalf of persecuted Christians can be strengthened and guided by considering the interaction between human-rights protections and the gospel, between common grace and saving grace. Dignity is a gift of God's common grace to all people, the basis for freedom of religion and all human rights, which must be protected by all common grace institutions; that common grace is also God's call to repentance and faith in the gospel. Proper mission work can also promote a wider protection of human rights, including a differentiated understanding of the state's role in protecting life.

## GOD AND HUMAN RIGHTS

The idea of human rights given to protect the individual developed largely within the Christian world, from which it then contributed to wider political cultures.[1] The fact that some branches of the church did not fight for human rights earlier does not argue against this claim. The UN Declaration of Human Rights echoes the Christian roots of some of the authors as well as moral concerns brought into society by Christians. The bans on slavery

---

1      Some of the earlier discussions of human rights were in medieval Christian philosophy, though some similar discussions occurred in ancient Greek and Roman thought. On the multiple relations of the Word of God to cultures, see Johnson (2011, 4–16). An older version of these principles is available online at www.bucer.eu/international, MBS Text 79.

and torture, the principle of equality before the law, and the right to rest and recreation (referencing Sunday observance) come from Christian traditions and reflect God's concerns. It is no accident that the governments which first confirmed these rights in their constitutions were influenced by Christians.[2] God's common grace is at work.

When people defend human rights from inside other worldviews, it is a good which should be endorsed by Christians; we can also ask if their human-rights concerns should not lead them to Christian convictions.[3] It is no surprise that most countries with a significant Christian heritage (excepting some Orthodox countries) have become democracies which attempt to protect human rights. Conversely, the development of better systems of human-rights protection (including responsible governments) teaches something about human nature (both our dignity and our sinfulness) that points to also knowing God, for the knowledge of human nature can lead to knowing God, as knowing God leads to knowing human nature. Common grace follows as a cultural result of the gospel, but it also prepares the way for the gospel.

No legal system develops without a minimum of moral values; a legal system assumes a moral/cultural value system. The law is derived from moral standards which exist prior to and outside itself, which are metaphysically based, coming from without, both through general and special revelation. The legal protection of human dignity assumes that the *human* is more than he directly perceives about himself, something not comprehended by means of natural science; humanity is open to transcendence. A responsible legal system depends on requirements that it cannot itself guarantee.

> For it is better to suffer for doing good, if that should be God's will, than for doing evil. For Christ also suffered once for sins, the righteous for the unrighteous, that he might bring us to God. *1 Peter 3:17–18*

Human dignity and rights are part of man's being as God's creation. The state does not create human rights; it merely codifies and protects them. The right to life belongs to the very essence of humanness; man does not receive it from the government; no government owns the life of its citizens so they may be assaulted at the ruler's whim. Our other fundamental rights follow directly from how God created us, despite some denials of those rights and despite frivolous claims which call mere desires "rights."

## SEPARATION OF CHURCH AND STATE

The decisive Scripture about the state is Romans 13:1–7. Paul teaches clearly that no one who foundationally opposes the state can appeal to God's authorization. On the contrary: he is opposing God's law and is rightly liable to arrest (Rom 13:2). Since the state has the duty to restrain and punish evil, Christians must do good if they wish to avoid conflict. If a Christian does wrong, he is justly punished by the state. For the government, as God's minister, has the duty of justice (13:4). As a result, the Christian pays his taxes and gives government officials proper respect (13:6–7).

---

2    Before 1948, some streams of virulent atheism, especially those influenced by Karl Marx and Friedrich Nietzsche, regarded human rights as a distinctly Jewish or Christian moral doctrine which atheists should reject.
3    See Johnson (2008, 29–50).

From Paul's statement we derive three principles:

1.  The government can judge only what people do, not what they think, believe, or feel. It is responsible for good or evil "works," with actions. It is not the duty of the state to control all sin, only those sins whose activity can be observed and damage public order, which the state must protect.

2.  The state may not distinguish between Christians and other people; i.e., between believers in different faiths, as long as they pursue their beliefs in a peaceful manner. Since God forbids partiality in legal matters, Christians must be punished just as severely as unbelievers when they break the law. The state cannot distinguish between Christians and members of other religious groups, for it may judge only on the basis of deeds.

3.  The state is an institution of common grace, not a gospel preaching institution. Just as the state may not dominate a church or a religion, it may not itself be subject to any church or religion nor take on churchlike functions. The separation of church and state does not contradict the Christian faith but arises naturally out of it. For the Bible makes it the duty of the state to enable people to live in peace and justice, whatever they believe, while it is the duty of the church to preach the gospel and nurture people in the faith.

Historian Eugen Ewig described the Old Testament "Doctrine of Two Powers." Eduard Eichmann observed about this biblical division of powers between priest and king: "Along with the sacred Scriptures, such Old Testament views have become common property of the Christian West" (1928, 6, 8). Jesus confirmed this separation in the words, "Render to Caesar the things that are Caesar's, and to God the things that are God's" (Mark 12:17). This rule comes from God: religious institutions are not above the emperor, but there is a certain realm that is under God and not under the emperor. God determines and limits what belongs to Caesar; Caesar has no authority to determine what belongs to God. This does not mean that the ruler is dependent on the church, for God has given him responsibility for all the people in his realm, not only for the members of one religious group. The separation of powers in society has biblical roots; it does not imply a war against Christianity unless the state forgets its primary obligations and begins to persecute the faith (see Rev 13; Johnson 2009, 33–38).

## FREEDOM OF RELIGION: STEPCHILD OF THE REFORMATION[4]

Early modern demands for religious freedom and freedom of conscience arose in English seventeenth-century radical Protestantism. In a comprehensive study of the sources of religious freedom, Michael Farris notes that Sebastian Castellio, a student of John Calvin, spoke out against Calvin in 1554, advocating a rudimentary form of religious freedom (which would still punish the "godless"; Farris 2007). The English Baptist Thomas Helwys (1550–1616) subsequently wrote the first known tract calling for complete religious freedom in 1611 (Helwys 1611); the English Baptist Leonard Busher produced a similar tract in

---

4       For more on this topic, see Schirrmacher (2009, 73–86).

1614 (Busher 1614). The idea spread among Baptists and other "dissenters" in England and the Netherlands. Later, in the United States, Roger Williams (1604–1685), cofounder in 1639 of the first American Baptist church with a Congregational structure, called for complete religious freedom in 1644 (Williams 1644). He established Rhode Island with the first constitution in which church and state were truly separated in a manner assuring religious freedom for Jews and atheists, while he also supported Christian mission. Rainer Prätorius hits the nail on the head: "Not in spite of the fact, but rather because he was deeply religious, Williams called for a separation of politics and religion" (2003, 35). The same applies for William Penn's (1644–1718) subsequent "holy experiment" in Pennsylvania.

The important historian Ernst Troeltsch[5] noticed that the codification of human rights was not due to the established Protestant churches, but rather to Free Churches, sects, and spiritualists—from the Puritans to the Quakers—who were driven to the New World. "At this point the stepchildren of the Reformation finally had their moment in history" (Troeltsch 1911, 62). In the United States of America several factors combined and merged: the hard-earned freedom of religion and conscience that had been pioneered by the deeply religious Williams and Penn, the separation of church and state, the constitutional texts (initially without freedom of religion) developed further by the Puritans and other Reformers, and the implementation of democracy for the territorial states by enlightened and deistic politicians who translated religious guidelines into secular law. The birth of religious freedom, with a little exaggeration, was the struggle for freedom by Christian minorities against the Christian majority churches. This explains the initial ambivalence of established churches with regard to democratic developments, "the ambivalence of Christian tolerance" which makes it impossible to draw a straight line historically from Christianity to democracy with human-rights protection (Forst 2006). Nevertheless, freedom of religion became a gift of God's common grace to the global political culture that came through the evangelical faith.

## HELPING OTHER RELIGIONS[6]

Religious persecution is not only a call for Christians to demonstrate their discipleship by loving fellow Christians; it is also a call to love all our neighbors at the same time in a similar manner. Whenever we love Christians by seeking their religious liberty, there should also be a benefit for all religions and all people. Support of persecuted Christians in Iran (or for converts who seek asylum in foreign countries) should also help the Baha'i, who share the brutal persecution in Iran. Their cause for religious liberty is far less known around the world, since they have practically no lobby. And whoever helps India and Indonesia remain secular states and not give in to the pressure of religious nationalists (who might persecute Christians) is also supporting adherents of all religions.

Involvement for the rights of Christians often directly helps adherents of other religions. Engagement for the converts to Christianity from Islam in Afghanistan, for example, draws worldwide attention to the fate of many Buddhists and Muslims in that country. Assistance

---

5      Cf. Graf (2002, 42–69).
6      For more on this topic, see Schirrmacher (2008).

in the difficult situation of Philippine Roman Catholics in Saudi Arabia also draws attention to the suffering of Philippine Muslims in Saudi Arabia.

## RELIGIOUS CONVERSION AND RELIGIOUS LIBERTY

The classic definition of religious liberty is Article 18, UN Universal Declaration of Human Rights:

> Everyone has the right to freedom of thought, conscience and religion; this right includes freedom to change his religion or belief, and freedom, either alone or in community with others and in public or private, to manifest his religion or belief in teaching, practice, worship, and observance.

Note that religious liberty especially contains the right to change one's religion and world-view! Religious conversion within Christianity itself, as a result of inner conviction, was the primordial origin of modern religious liberty. The question is what to do if out of inner conviction, I no longer hold the beliefs which were previously taken for granted or which had been instilled in me?

I (TS) have often discussed this with journalists who oppose mission work. They say, "You can't be surprised if there are problems in Iran when Muslims become Christians. Just leave the Iranians in peace." I immediately reply, "In Iran it has long been the case that it is indigenous people, not Western missionaries, who evangelize. As a result of their efforts, Iranians leave Islam for the Baha'i religion or become Christians. Who may prevent that?" Secondly, "Should we also reinstate in Western law the principle that whoever leaves the church loses his job and has to suffer civil consequences?" This used to be the case in Europe, that religious affiliation and civic life were closely related. I am glad we changed this.

It is a complete illusion to think that real religious liberty means simply keeping the religion in which one is raised without speaking with adherents of other religions. This is a form of prescribed and forced religion that few will accept for themselves; we should also not want it for anyone else. Religious liberty means to uncouple religious affiliation from civic status. Where this is the case, individuals can stand in public and propagate their beliefs, without their employer, who happens to pass by, being able to fire them for it. This benefits Christians, atheists, and Muslims.

## PEACEFUL MISSION WORK AND HUMAN RIGHTS

Peaceful mission work is organically linked to several other human rights, in addition to freedom of religion. The right to conduct missions can be derived from the right to freedom of expression embedded in the 1948 Declaration on Human Rights. Just as political parties, environmental groups, and even advertisers may publish their views, so also religions. The Declaration on the Elimination of All Forms of Intolerance and of Discrimination Based on Religion and Belief (Resolution 36/55 of the General Assembly of the United Nations, November 25, 1981, article 6, paragraph d) describes religious liberty as embracing the right "to write, issue, and disseminate relevant publications in these areas." The freedom of expression includes the right to present one's belief to the general public, not only that one may pray in private. Peaceful mission work is also tied to the right to assemble and the right to travel; these rights show the legal legitimacy of mission, and mission work should be conducted in a manner that promotes the wider protection of these rights.

There have been missionary activities in the past that prepared the ground for violence and oppression. Christian and Islamic crusades and colonialism come to mind. The problem in these instances is not the public propagation of one's own views. Rather, it is the suppression of human rights.[7] The problem is one of violence, and the term "mission" is certainly out of place. We should also not forget that the majority of encounters between Christianity and Islam have taken place peacefully within a mission setting which included intellectual and cultural exchange.

## TO DO

The modern protection of human rights is a gift of God's common grace given partly through Christians, partly through other people. Christians should carry out their mission work with gratitude and in a manner that seeks to further extend this great gift. And we should always say that all of God's gifts are a call to repentance and faith.

## QUESTIONS FOR REFLECTION

1.  What, according to the authors, is the fundamental basis for human rights? Which church organizations have contributed the most toward the modern development of human rights and why?
2.  What is the significance of the extensive use of the terms "common grace" and "saving grace" in the arguments about human rights?
3.  What is the relationship of religious freedom to other fundamental human rights?
4.  Discuss the "to do" of the article which appears in the final paragraph. "Christians should carry out their mission work with gratitude and in a manner that seeks to further extend great this gift [human rights]."

## REFERENCES

Busher, L. 1614. *Religious peace.* London: Sweeting, 1644.

Eichmann, E. 1928. *Königs und bischofsweihe.* Sitzungsberichte der Bayerischen Akademie der Wissenschaften: Philosophisch-philologische und historische Klasse Jahrgang. Abhandlung. Munich: Verlag der Bayerischen Akademie der Wissenschaften.

Farris, M. 2007. *From Tyndale to Madison.* Nashville, TN: Thomas Nelson.

Forst, R. Original bibliographic unknown. Quoted in Manfred Brocker/Tine Stein, eds., *Christentum und demokratie,* (Darmstadt: Wissenschaftliche Buchgesellschaft, 2006).

---

7    For further analysis, see Schirrmacher and Johnson (2010, 23–37).

Graf, F. W. 2002. Puritanische sektenfreiheit versus Lutherische volkskirche. *Zeitschrift für Neuere Theologiegeschichte* 9, no. 1: 42–69.

Helwys, T. 1611. *A short declaration of the mystery of iniquity.* London. Reprint. London: Kingsgate, 1935.

Johnson, T. K. 2008. *Human rights: A Christian primer.* WEA Global Issues Series, vol. 1. Bonn: VKW.

———. 2009. *What difference does the Trinity make? A complete faith, life, and worldview.* WEA Global Issues Series, vol. 7. Bonn: VKW.

———. 2011. Christ and culture. *Evangelical Review of Theology* 35, no. 1 (January): 4–16. An older version of these principles is available online at www.bucer.eu/international, MBS Text 79.

Prätorius, R. 2003. *In God we trust: Religion und politik in den USA.* Munich: CH Beck.

Schirrmacher, T. 2008. *The persecution of Christians concerns us all.* WEA Global Issues Series, vol. 5. Bonn: VKW.

———. 2009. Christianity and democracy. *International Journal for Religious Freedom* 2, no. 2: 73–86. www.iirf.eu.

———, and T. K. Johnson. 2010. Why evangelicals need a code of ethics for mission. *International Journal of Religious Freedom* 3, no. 1: 23–37. www.iirf.eu.

Troeltsch, E. 1911. *Die bedeutung des Protestantismus für die entstehung der modernen welt.* Munich/Berlin: Oldenbourg.

Williams, R. 1644. *The bloody tenent, for cause of conscience.* London. See also *Christenings make not Christians.* London: 1645.

**Thomas Schirrmacher**, German, is director of the International Institute for Religious Freedom (Bonn, Cape Town, Colombo) and serves as chair of WEA's Theological Commission. Based in Germany, he holds extensive professorial and presidential roles across Europe as well as in Shillong, India, teaching sociology of religion, theology, global ethics, and international development.

**Thomas K. Johnson**, American, is a church planter who, as a Christian apologist, spent nineteen years teaching philosophy and ethics in six secular universities in four countries, including work among the anti-Communist dissidents in the former USSR. He is now based in Prague and serves the International Institute for Christian Studies, the Comenius Institute, Martin Bucer European School of Theology and Research Institutes, and Olivet University.

## TO STAY AND BE A LIGHT IN THIS IRANIAN CITY

"The children will be placed in Muslim homes," the court decreed.

Nadia was eight years old. Her parents had just been imprisoned for their Christian faith. Nadia and her siblings were separated and placed in Muslim homes.

But as she grew up, she remembered the Scripture verses sealed in her heart. "My parents did not suffer in vain," she determined. "They stuck to their commitments. I'm not going to throw that away."

After she married Hafez, the couple began to minister quietly to neighbors and workmates. "So many are desperate for something more. What a privilege it is to be able to share Jesus with them," Nadia commented.

One night uniformed men knocked loudly on their door.

"Oh God, is history repeating itself?" Nadia cried.

It seemed so. Nadia and Hafez were pulled apart. Later, in their court appearance, the judge was harsh. "You have broken the law of the land," he thundered. "You have introduced a foreign religion, and induced Iranians to turn away from their true faith. You have led them into apostasy. This is a crime worthy of death."

Hafez and Nadia were jailed, he in one prison and she in another.

In time, for unknown reasons, they were released. "We are free from prison, but we are not free from persecution. They still have a file against us stating that we work with foreigners to blaspheme Islam and the penalty is death," Nadia says. "Miraculously until today we are alive. We do not know what the future holds but we believe God has chosen us to stay and be a light in this Iranian city."

Miriam Adeney, *Kingdom without Borders: The Untold Story of Global Christianity* (2009, 142–44)

# CHAPTER 59

# ADVOCATING FOR THE PERSECUTED

*Reg Reimer*

## THE ISSUE

Advocacy is here defined narrowly as appealing for religious freedom to persecutors and/or those who can influence them for the elimination or reduction of persecution of Christian believers. Sometimes the persecuted can advocate for themselves but often advocacy must be done by others.

I will postulate a biblical basis for advocacy, summarize the God-ordained role of governments, describe how various Christian views on the relationship between church and state affect readiness for advocacy activity, and finally, describe some common advocacy strategies and intervention methods. While I cannot anticipate every scenario in such a short space, what I discuss here has wide geopolitical application.[1]

## THE BIBLICAL BASIS FOR ADVOCACY

Religious freedom is integral to fundamental or natural human rights, also understood as self-evident and universal. We speak here of freedom of thought, of conscience, of religion, of expression, of assembly, and so on.

It is common for Christian thinkers to consider that freedom of religion is the first freedom or the mother of human rights.[2] Religious freedom is considered part of "customary international law" and incumbent even on states which have not signed international treaties (Thames, Seiple. and Rowe 2009, 1).[3] In chapter 60 of this book Chris Seiple says, "We ... think about religious freedom as the greatest gift, after grace, from a gift-giving God." To put it negatively, what could be worse than to deny fellow human beings the right to seek and serve their Creator, and to search for ultimate meaning?

---

1      It will be useful to compare this chapter with my two other chapters in this book on closely related topics (chapters 3 and 38).

2      See works of George Weigel, contemporary Catholic ethicist, theologian, and author of a best-selling biography of Pope John Paul II.

3      This book, *International Religious Freedom Advocacy: A Guide to Organizations, Law and NGOs,* is an indispensable help for religious freedom advocates to understand the labyrinth of organizations that can help them in their work.

On what basis do we stand up for human rights, including religious freedom for ourselves, and advocate for those denied it? We do it based on the human dignity derived from our creation in the image of God.

From Cain and Abel (Gen 4:1–14) we see God's extreme displeasure with one who murdered someone made in the image of God. "Your brother's blood cried out to me from the ground. Now you are under a curse."

As we shall see, God ordains even civil governments to work for justice among their subjects. And in the church we are to consider each other as members of the same body (1 Cor 12:12–31). If so, how can we not stand up when members of our one body are persecuted? "Remember those in prison as if you were their fellow prisoners, and those who are mistreated as if you yourselves were suffering" (Heb 13:3).

The consistent call in both biblical testaments to live justly, and the warnings against injustice, also form part of our mandate to advocate for the persecuted.

Missionaries have historically stood against injustices such as suttee, infanticide, and slavery, and may do so against religious persecution on the "image of God" argument.

Charles Taber's 2002 article, "In the Image of God: The Gospel and Human Rights," is a landmark in this regard. He points out that the idea of universal nondiscriminatory rights is of quite recent origin. He argues convincingly that while this idea may have some roots in ancient Greece and in the Hebrew Scriptures, it was Jesus who set the benchmark.

> Do not repay evil for evil or reviling for reviling, but on the contrary, bless, for to this you were called, that you may obtain a blessing.
> *1 Peter 3:9*

He "alone among all religious founders and leaders rejected all forms of discrimination and insisted that all human beings ought to be treated in exactly the same way. His own dealings with women, with children, with lepers and other ritually polluted people, and with foreigners radically undermined all the distinctions that human societies of his day unanimously institutionalized. He extended the category of 'neighbor' to all humankind and insisted that the two Great Commandments applied to all" (Taber 2002, 99). That is a view of humankind that can provide the basis for universal human rights, including religious freedom.

An excellent discussion synthesizing Christianity with human rights is ethicist and theologian Thomas K. Johnson's *Human Rights: A Christian Primer* (2008). He couples the "image of God" argument with a keen understanding of the reality of human evil which makes it necessary for humans to be protected from one another (Johnson 2002, 43–47). Johnson concludes with an appeal to evangelical Christians to make advocacy for fundamental human rights a matter of Christian ethics and a response to God's grace (102).

Likely the most valiant human attempt to capture human dignity was the 1948 Universal Declaration of Human Rights (UDHR).[4] While it and the elaborations it inspired are admirable documents, they are often impotent. Some nations signatory to these conventions routinely violate religious freedom and other human rights. International organizations and governments must ever aspire to live up to the UDHR ideal.

> But when all is said and done, there is only one resource available to Christians to bring non-Christians to see human dignity as Jesus did. It is the intrinsic credibility and persuasiveness of the gospel, since the truth of human dignity is a component of the gospel and has no secure existence apart from the gospel. That truth ought to be presented to the whole world, first of all, by the life of the church, inspired, empowered, and directed by the Holy Spirit; second, by its proclamation of the gospel and its invitation to the world to submit to the rule of God; third, by its sacrificial service to the hurting and suffering people of the world, to the least and the poorest; fourth, by its prophetic confrontation and denunciation of all those principalities and powers that abuse human beings. (Taber 2002, 102)

## WHAT ARE GOVERNMENTS FOR?

I once spoke with a Communist official in Vietnam on the touchy subject of the church and the political order under Communism. He quickly quoted Romans 13:1, "Everyone must submit himself to the governing authorities." I have heard Christians make the same unqualified statement, as if that is the end of the story. It is not. The New Testament establishes a role and a standard for governments.

The passage from which these commonly quoted words are excerpted, Romans 13:1–7, goes on to explain that governments are God-established, and further, "For rulers hold no terror for those who do right … For he [the ruler] is God's servant to do you good." And "the authorities are God's servants." Some regimes fall far short of this biblical standard when they routinely terrorize those who do what is right and do evil instead of good.

The New Testament teaches that governments are established by the sovereign God to both restrain evil and to promote the common good (Rom 13:1–8; 1 Pet 2:13–17). John Redekop, a Mennonite political scientist, in *Politics under God* (2007) derives twenty "God-pleasing tasks" of government from his study of Romans 13:1–7. Christians can and should support government to fulfill these tasks (69–81). Another purpose of a peaceful social order is to contribute to evangelism. Saint Paul urges prayer for "kings and all those in authority" so that all "may live peaceful and quiet lives," which in turn will contribute to people coming to a "knowledge of the truth" and "men to be saved" (1 Tim 2:1–4).

What should the Christian do when governments not only fail to meet God's standards but act completely contrary to them? For example, some governments themselves become persecutors of Christians or become silent, compliant bystanders when nonstate actors violently

---

4    Refer to *Christianity and Human Rights* (Adeney and Sharma 2007) for a variety of insightful articles on the contribution of Christianity to the UDHR and the critique from some quarters that it is only Western.

suppress Christians. Some governments are dominated by the major engines of persecution, such as Communism, radical Islam, and religious nationalism.

The nature of Christians' submission to the state is tempered by how much a state fulfills its God-given mandate. Christians will be constructively critical even of a state which largely fulfills its biblical responsibility, urging fuller justice. But on the other far extreme, the renowned theologian Dietrich Bonhoeffer came to believe it was required of him to participate in the demise of the head of a patently evil nation which had turned the biblical mandate completely on its head and indulged in monstrous evil.

A Christian's ultimate allegiance is to the Kingdom of God, but the Christian will support a government which governs justly, and will challenge and confront one which does not. In my view the persecution of Christians, whether committed or permitted by the state, requires advocacy and confrontation.

## VARIOUS VIEWS

In reality, however, Christians' readiness for advocacy is greatly affected by how they perceive their relationship with their world and culture, including government.

All followers of Christ historically have had to reconcile their allegiance to Christ, his church, and his Kingdom with the demands of whatever earthly government they lived under. Different Christian understandings of church and state relations, and widely varied manifestations of government mean there are not simple, universal formulas for advocating for persecuted Christians.

An "enduring problem" was what American theologian and ethicist H. Richard Niebuhr called the relation of church and state, or of Christians to their government. His analyses of this in *Christ and Culture* (1951) has for sixty years been a classic categorization of the ways Christians relate to their cultures. These were: *Christ against culture; Christ of culture; Christ above culture; Christ and culture in paradox;* and finally Niebuhr's recommended *Christ transforms culture.* This final category would find resonance with Kingdom of God theology from George Eldon Ladd to N. T. Wright.

One problem with Niebuhr is that his categories have largely been overcome by events. A timely critique and updating of Niebuhr is provided by evangelical scholar Craig Carter in his *Rethinking Christ and Culture: A Post-Christendom Perspective* (2006). Carter points out that in the 1950s Niebuhr was still writing from within a Christendom paradigm. Carter is particularly critical of the church's embrace of Christendom and the rationalization of state violence. He expands and refines Niebuhr's categories and argues that the demise of Christendom offers new opportunities for the church, unfettered by the burdens of Christendom, to again engage non-Christian cultures in a more New Testament way.

All this has broad implications for how Christians live in the world. Significantly for advocacy it means learning to advocate from a position of weakness rather than power, quite contrary to the earlier Christendom model.

Niebuhr's original typology and Carter's rethinking each concentrate more on Christian attitudes and behavior than on government attitudes and behavior toward Christians. Both factors determine whether or not advocacy can and will occur, and if so what kind of advocacy it will be.

First, some current Christian attitudes. There remains a tension in the evangelical mission world between those who view the chief task of the church as verbal proclamation of the gospel, and those who focus more on the totality of God's purposes in human history. It is the tension between Jesus' final instruction to "go and make disciples of all nations" (Matt 28:19) and the prayer he taught us, "Your kingdom come, your will be done on earth as it is in heaven" (Matt 6:10).

The one school expresses Kingdom of God theology. It holds that Jesus announced that the Kingdom has come and calls his followers to live it and extend its boundaries here and now even as they wait for future ultimate fulfillment. This view is reflected currently in *missio dei* and *missional church* concepts which include working for justice and freedom for the oppressed, providing food and healing for the poor and the sick, all as integral to God's plan. Advocating for persecuted Christians flows out of this view (see D'Souza and Roger 2007).

This same urgency for advocacy is not always felt by those who prioritize verbal proclamation of propositional truths, who hold a more dualistic view of the primacy of spiritual over temporal, and who emphasize getting saved as a rescue mission for the future more than "to act justly and to love mercy" (Mic 6:8) here and now.

Second, the attitude a state has toward religion (especially Christianity) will determine who can advocate and the likelihood of advocacy success. Local Christians are hardly able to advocate for themselves in hard-line North Korea or Iran. Likewise, outside advocators will have little success here too as such governments are virtually impervious to world opinion. In another example, Communist Vietnam and Islamic Indonesia are both more and willingly integrated into the global community. These countries have constitutions and laws on religious freedom, and are signatories to international conventions promising the same, but fall far short of keeping them. In such places it is possible and desirable, though risky, that local Christians advocate their authorities to abide by their own laws and commitments. Christians in such places, however, emphasize the need for international advocacy as a necessary complement to their own.

## ADVOCACY STRATEGIES AND INTERVENTION METHODS

First, advocates must respect and support the decisions of the persecuted, whether to flee persecution, to patiently endure it, or to stand up to fight and advocate against it—and support them accordingly.

Advocates often take risks to come alongside those found worthy to suffer for his name's sake to help carry their load. Their very presence is an encouragement, reminding the persecuted that they are not forgotten.

The role of frontline missionaries or Christians in advocacy is often unnecessarily considered controversial. There can be a division of labor. Those living on the front lines of persecution may choose to discreetly share information they often uniquely have with others who will do the private and public work of advocacy. Without the support of frontline people taking some risks, advocates will be at a great disadvantage.

Advocacy is at once a highly spiritual and practical response. Ron Boyd-MacMillan helpfully summarizes and assesses seven advocacy "intervention tactics" in *Faith that Endures: The Essential Guide to the Persecuted Church* (2006, 254–83). I list them here with some support from his book, supplemented by my own experience.

1. **Prayer/intercession.** I have found in asking the persecuted what outsiders can do that prayer is the first request. The persecuted know the power of prayer. We can intercede in prayer with perseverance for those who are persecuted, suffer, and are found worthy to be martyred. This is advocacy to the highest authority who is still able to blow off prison doors as he did for Paul and Silas (Acts 16:16–40).

2. **Truth-telling/publicity.** This is sometimes described as shaming the persecutors and forcing persecutors to deal with their misdeeds in the court of public opinion. Also the prophetic denunciation of the principalities and powers which demean and desecrate Gods' children through persecution involves shining the light on their evil, appealing to laws—national and international, providing information for and engaging world opinion on the side of justice.

3. **Private representation.** The opposite of public shaming, this method employs people of influence, political or economic, with access to the persecuting government to appeal quietly to release Christian prisoners of conscience or otherwise ameliorate persecution. Importantly, it saves face. Those who advocate privately must be content with receiving no public credit when they succeed. Another form of this tactic is for ordinary Christians to write specific and respectful advocacy appeals to officials of governments which persecute.

4. **Legal intervention.** This is the appeal to the rule of law. This involves holding persecuting authorities to their own laws which are often much better than their practice. Legal appeals require the painstaking assembly of accurate documentation in specific persecution cases. Even small successes in this approach can give Christians a feeling of empowerment. Legal intervention also involves holding persecuting authorities accountable to the international conventions their governments have signed.

5. **Illegal intervention.** This tactic refers more to helping the persecuted than to advocating for them. Peter declared to the Sanhedrin, "We must obey God rather than men!" (Acts 5:29). There are times when it is necessary to break laws and act contrary to the desires of persecuting governments in order to help persecuted Christians. Brother Andrew gives a spirited defense of this in *The Ethics of Smuggling* (1974).

6. **Political pressure.** When representatives of country A with potential influence on country B try to positively influence the religion policy of country B, they employ political pressure. This can happen between influential individuals. It can also happen government-to-government.

7. **Positive contribution.** Christians sometimes intentionally work to build up a society where persecution is taking place. By their good works, done as Christians, they hope to influence a persecuting country to change its views about Christians and adopt more moderate polices. Teaching, doing social work, or establishing a commercial business are some methods. Boyd-MacMillan points out that this necessarily involves close contacts and agreements with authorities of the persecuting country and thus runs the risk of compromise and even co-option. He feels few have the skill, perseverance, and savvy to use positive contribution to make serious gains for religious freedom (Boyd-MacMillan 2006, 279–82).

To this list I would add an eighth method called **"constructive engagement."** This involves building strong relationships and trust with the members of the persecuting government and then appealing to their self-interest to stop oppressing believers.[5] While the constructive engagement approach holds considerable promise, the risks are also high.

I would argue that all of these methods are necessary and complementary in the difficult and complicated calling of advocating for persecuted Christians.

## QUESTIONS FOR REFLECTION

1. Compare the basis of religious freedom and other human rights cited by Reimer to the arguments in the chapter by Schirrmacher and Johnson on human rights in this book.
2. Does the injunction in Romans 13:1 for Christians to submit to governing authorities have any qualifications?
3. Is it legitimate for frontline missionaries who are nonspecialists in advocacy to support the advocacy cause for the oppressed and persecuted where they minister? If so, how might they do this?
4. Why do fighting for religious liberty and other kinds of human-rights advocacy remain controversial in the evangelical mission community?

## REFERENCES:

Adeney, F., and A. Sharma, eds. 2007. *Christianity and human rights.* Albany: State University of New York Press.

Boyd-MacMillan, R. 2006. *Faith that endures: The essential guide to the persecuted church.* Lancaster, UK: Sovereign World.

Brother Andrew. 1974. *The ethics of smuggling.* Wheaton, IL: Tyndale House.

---

5    The theology, strategy, and application of constructive engagement are described by Dr. Chris Seiple of the Institute of Global Engagement in chapter 60 of this book.

Carter, C. 2006. *Rethinking Christ and culture: A post-Christendom perspective.* Grand Rapids, MI: Brazo.

D'Souza, J., and B. Rogers. 2007. *On the side of the angels: Justice, human rights and Kingdom mission.* Hyderabad, India: Authentic Media.

Johnson, T. K. 2008. *Human rights: A Christian primer.* WEA Global Issues Series, vol. 1. Bonn: Culture and Science Publishers.

Niebuhr, H. R. 1951. *Christ and culture.* New York: Harper and Row.

Redekop, J. H. 2007. *Politics under God.* Scottdale, PA: Herald.

Taber, C. R. 2002. In the image of God: The gospel and human rights. *International Bulletin of Missionary Research* (July): 89–102.

Thames, H. K., C. Seiple, and A. Rowe. 2009. *International religious freedom advocacy: A guide to organizations, law and NGOs.* Waco, TX: Baylor University Press.

**Reg Reimer**, a Canadian, has worked internationally in evangelism, relief and development, reconciliation ministry, promoting collaboration, and advocating for religious freedom. He describes himself foremost as a missionary to Vietnam where he began ministry in 1966 and remains deeply involved. He is considered an authority on the Protestant movement there. His book *Vietnam's Christians: A Century of Growth in Adversity* was released in July 2011. Reg was president of World Relief Canada from 1984 to 1994. He then served as senior staff member of the World Evangelical Alliance. He currently serves as international partnership advisor with the Evangelical Fellowship of Canada and South East Asia coordinator for International Partnering Associates. He is regularly called on by organizations for advice on promoting religious freedom in Vietnam. Reg is a long-time participant in the WEA Mission Commission. He is married to LaDonna, a social worker. The Reimers live in Abbotsford, BC, Canada. Their two children serve in Cambodia and South Korea.

National Socialism has brought with it the end of the Church in Germany, and carried that out consistently.... That we are confronted by this clear state of affairs seems to me to be beyond any further doubt.... And although I am doing all I can to work along with the Church opposition, it is quite clear to me that this opposition is only a very preliminary stage before a quite different opposition.... I believe that the whole of Christendom must pray with us that "resistance to the point of having to shed blood" [Heb 12:4] takes place and that people will be found who will suffer it.... You know: I believe ... that the whole question will come to a head around the Sermon on the Mount.... The issue is always the keeping of the commandment and not evading it. To follow Christ [Nachfolge Christi], what that means is what I want to know....

D. Bonhoeffer in a comment to his Swiss friend Erwin Sutz on April 28, 1934 (1994, 128f)

# CHAPTER 60

# REFLECTIONS ON THEOLOGY, STRATEGY, AND ENGAGEMENT

*Chris Seiple*

The challenges of the twenty-first century can be distilled into a single question: how do we live with and work across our deepest differences? Every challenge is foremost an issue of how we choose to engage one another.

Mere tolerance is not enough. But with engagement across divides, based on respect and reconciliation, there is a chance for constructive candor—to name differences, identify common values and interests, and build solutions to address root causes of complex issues.

Though there is nothing distinctively Christian about this logic, Christians and the church should be the first to embrace this reality—as ambassadors of reconciliation (2 Cor 5:16–21).

Determining if one is ready to be an ambassador of reconciliation depends on three questions:

1. What is the theology of engagement?
2. What is the strategy of engagement?
3. How is engagement implemented?

These are the questions that we at the Institute for Global Engagement (IGE) have wrestled with for a decade as we have sought to be obedient to our call to build sustainable religious freedom worldwide through local partners.

The following are some thoughts I've had as I try to trust Jesus a little bit more everyday and as I have come to understand that my faith is real and relevant in the most fragile and complex places in the world.

## A THEOLOGY OF ENGAGEMENT

As I've worked in the Muslim-majority world and in Communist East Asia, six principles are daily revealed to me. I believe that understanding their practical impact is the precursor to constructive engagement and reconciliation, no matter one's vocation or location.

*God is sovereign.* If God is sovereign, then there are no intractable problems. If it is his world, and he is at work in it, then we should expect to find him working in the most difficult situations. For his good purposes he uses good people, bad people, and those who don't acknowledge him (Isa 45). His mystery and majesty are things we can only pretend to name. "I am who I am" (Ex 3:14). We are wise to put no other gods before him, including our own religion, country, and our methodologies of advocacy.

*We were made to glorify him.* During the Hebrews' exodus from Egypt, God gave his people guidelines on how to glorify him. The Ten Commandments (Ex 20:3–17) made clear that we humans are to worship God alone, honor our parents (Jer 1:5), and respect our neighbors who are made "in his own image" (Gen 1:27).

*We glorify him by loving our neighbor.* "The One of Sinai" (Judg 5:5; Ps 68:8) receives glory when we love our neighbor. C. S. Lewis certainly understood. "The load, or weight, or burden of my neighbor's glory should be laid daily on my back, a load so heavy that only humility can carry it.... There are no *ordinary* people.... Next to the Blessed Sacrament itself, your neighbor is the holiest object presented to your senses" (quoted in Dorsett 1988, 369–70).

*That neighbor is foremost the alien.* God is clear, telling his people that because he is sovereign, and because he made them to glorify him, they should love those not like them: "The alien [someone not of Israel, not of the majority culture] living with you must be treated as one of your native-born. Love him as yourself, for you were aliens in Egypt" [where Israel had been an ethnic minority in the Egyptian majority culture] (Lev 19:34, cf. Ezek 47:22–23).

Like Father like Son, Jesus tells his disciples: "If you love those who love you, what reward will you get? ... And if you greet only your brothers, what are you doing more than others" (Matt 5:46–48). In engaging a despised and shunned prostitute at midday amidst a patriarchal society—a cultural, religious, and gender no-no if ever there was one—Jesus gave a crystal-clear example to his followers (John 4:4–42).

*If we live this love, we are alien.* By believing that Jesus died and rose again to overcome our own alienation from God, we now become alien to this world. Because we are made new in Christ, we will no longer be "foreigners and aliens, but fellow citizens ... and members of God's household" (Eph 2:19). But because our ultimate loyalty now resides with Jesus, we are now "aliens and strangers in the world" (1 Pet 2:11)—a world that will treat us the same way it treated Jesus (John 15:18; 1 Pet 2:21). In living out this love, the more our identity is rooted in our neighbor's, the more we become fully human and more fully citizens of heaven called to steward our global and national citizenships.

*Show up and shut up.* With the above theological understanding, we come alongside what God is doing in a particular country context. Some ask, "What would Jesus do?" The real question is, "What is Jesus doing?" The answer we get from those who live there is that God is present and working, often through his local church, long before we arrived and will remain long after we leave (Job 38).

God doesn't need us to accomplish his purposes (Gen 18:14; Num 11:23), but he invites us to join him in what he is doing. Jesus was clear about the nature of the call and the consequences: "I am sending you out like sheep among wolves. Therefore be as shrewd as snakes and as innocent as doves" (Matt 10:16).

In sum, God is sovereign and made us to glorify him. We glorify him by loving our alien neighbors, including enemies. We learn to love in different contexts by discerning how Jesus is already at work there. Only then can we love our neighbor appropriately and become ambassadors of reconciliation.

There is no greater joy than obeying this call, but in my experience it can have unpleasant consequences. Well-intentioned Christians and nonbelievers will categorize and stigmatize you, some saying that you're too "liberal" and others "too conservative." Overseas, some will call you a spy for America, while back home some Americans say that you're not "American" enough.

> Then Jesus told his disciples, "If anyone would come after me, let him deny himself and take up his cross and follow me." *Matthew 16:24*

I recommend guarding a right relationship with God and obeying what he is asking you to do. Second, be in relationships of candid accountability with key people who can help you discern what is from God and what is not. Finally, be sure to pray with your eyes closed so that the "facts" in front of you do not cause you to shirk from the task, for that is the definition of unfaithfulness (Heb 10:36–39).

## A STRATEGY OF ENGAGEMENT

There is no major challenge in this world that can be solved by one entity. The defining characteristic of the twenty-first century will be coalitions and communities of the willing that work at the nexus of the public and private spheres toward sustainable solutions to seemingly intractable problems. For Christians, every global challenge is an opportunity to demonstrate the reconciling love of Christ.

Christians are the body of Christ perfectly pre-positioned in every vocation and location to be intentional ambassadors of reconciliation. We are good neighbors who use our vocation—from Bible translation to electrical engineering to military service to nursing—as an opportunity to be ambassadors of reconciliation.

My call is to work for religious freedom at two levels. First, there is its basic definition, recognized in international human-rights covenants and most national constitutions. Religious freedom is the opportunity to choose or not choose faith freely, to share and change one's faith, or to have no religious beliefs at all.

As a Christian organization, however, we also think about religious freedom as the greatest gift, after grace, from a gift-giving God. I cannot love my alien neighbor who bears the image of God—I cannot glorify God—if I do not respect my neighbor's freedom to accept or reject him. Accordingly, IGE tries to communicate and embody religious freedom as the responsibility to respect, and be reconciled with, our (alien) neighbor.

If we are to be as "shrewd as snakes and as innocent as doves," we should feel free to ask what the need or self-interest of our neighbor is. Doing so can catalyze a relationship that otherwise might not develop.

At IGE we had to discover how religious freedom serves the interests and needs of states and societies as consistent with the best of the local social-cultural-religious context. For example, people who can practice the core of their identity—belief in a particular faith system—are less likely to rebel against the state (Jenkins 2004, 2007). They are also more likely to have integrity in word and action, acting as a moral bulwark against the corruption that comes with the transition to a market economy (as more than one Communist official has shared with me).

These believers are also more likely to be good citizens, living out their faith by serving the less fortunate around them. This can alleviate the financial responsibilities of governments. In such environments stability is built, helping attract foreign investment so necessary to enable the people and land to prosper.

In developing this "case" for religious freedom—combining theology and self-interest—we found a strategy of engagement. Rooted in the example of Jesus with the Samaritan woman, we call this strategy "relational diplomacy."

IGE's relational diplomacy has three primary characteristics. First, relational diplomacy transparently engages the state and society, working simultaneously from the top down (government) and the bottom up (grassroots).

We call it "Track 1.5" diplomacy as we work in the space between traditional, government-to-government diplomacy (Track 1), and nontraditional, people-to-people diplomacy (Track 2). This approach requires practitioners to listen diligently, to research, and to strive to comprehend local social-cultural-religious contexts.

Over time, with patience and persistence, relationships develop, but not without difficulty and messiness. Space is created where differences can be named and common values discovered. Conversations with partners at the national and provincial levels yield a consensus about the role of religion in their society, and eventually about how best to promote religious freedom.

Second, the consensus achieved by relational diplomacy is defined by signed agreements that promote religious freedom in a contextual manner. These "road maps" demonstrate a tangible strategy of measurable and mutually accountable steps. The approach of mutual respect creates a "win-win" for all parties, promoting the interests of marginalized religious communities as well as governments concerned about security and social cohesion.

Finally, and most importantly, these agreements enable a public transparency whereby all parties can hold each other accountable and celebrate the implementation of agreement goals. Such dignity-based engagement of nations and cultures—through partners at the governmental and grassroots levels—can have positive, long-lasting impact.

IGE seeks to create a space for practical dialogue about how a state and society can both protect and promote the alien minority in its midst as a full neighbor. It is a "radical middle" where citizens can be respectfully honest and agree to disagree (when necessary) while maintaining relationships.

## RELATIONAL DIPLOMACY APPLIED

It has not been easy to be a Christian in the countries of Laos and Vietnam since the establishment of Communist governments in 1975. Only ten years ago, Christians were put in wooden stocks in Laos, and in 2001 and 2004 several Vietnamese Army divisions cracked down on the Central Highlands—where Christianity has been growing rapidly among ethnic minority groups.

However, with more than half of their populations born since 1975, the need to provide education and jobs, compete in a global economy, and balance the large northern neighbor, both countries intentionally began to seek a relationship with the United States.

The US responded with concern about the human-rights situation in each country, especially religious freedom. In fact, the US put Vietnam on the worst religious freedom violations list in September 2004 and threatened to put Laos on as well.

In 2011, amidst uneven progress, the religious freedom situation is considerably better than ten years ago. Many issues and individuals enabled this change, particularly hard-working people in governments on both sides who want a strong bilateral relationship.

IGE has worked in that middle ground between Track 1 and Track 2 diplomacy, building trust and contributing to more religious freedom. IGE is the only nongovernmental international religious freedom organization that has signed agreements with both Vietnam and Laos towards this end. These agreements include IGE in the religious freedom training of local religious and government leaders in provinces where the worst persecution had previously taken place.

Remarkably, a ten-person *Christian* NGO has signed agreements with the *Communist* governments of Laos (population 6 million) and Vietnam (population 87 million). It is as if a Muslim NGO from Iran came to the most evangelical district in Texas and advised their local Parent Teacher Association on education. How did this happen?

Several factors were at play. First, my father had flown three hundred combat missions from Danang, Vietnam, twenty-five of them over Laos in the "secret war." Later God gave him a heart for reconciliation with these countries. As the founder of IGE, along with my mother, they were obedient to the call to engage. (For other accounts, see references.)

They focused on Laos while I focused on Vietnam, an engagement introduced to us by a Vietnamese official who we later learned fought against Dad in Danang (Seiple 2008). God is sovereign, he has a plan. He uses our family for his purpose.

Second, we continued to show up, seeking to understand before we engaged. In many ways, especially in the first trips to Laos and Vietnam, it didn't matter what we said or did. It was simply that we returned. Our "yes" was "yes" and our "no" was "no." We could be trusted. We found similar people in both governments, people who wanted what was best for their country and who saw that working with IGE was in their government's best interest.

Third, we understood the geopolitical-economic context and the resulting points of leverage. After seeing tangible religious freedom progress in places that other human-rights organizations did not visit, we were able to present a more comprehensive understanding of religious freedom than the simple, black-and-white version offered by some NGOs.

As a result we were able to advocate "win-win" suggestions to both governments. Critically, we were always transparent, saying the same thing to everyone involved—be it the US ambassador, the Vietnamese president, a house church leader, a Congressman, or the governor of a province (please see references in my testimony to the US Senate, Seiple 2006b).

Statements of two senior Vietnamese officials summarize why we have been blessed with some "success." That the relationship took place at all is the direct result of Vietnamese officials visiting our home. One said, "You are the first Americans who did not first give me a list and tell me what to do." As the relationship evolved and matured, we were told in Hanoi, "Whether we like it or not, we recognize religious freedom as a permanent US national interest."

## CONCLUSION

Between the human desire to be respected as an equal neighbor and the sometimes unyielding logic of self-interest there is a space for constructive engagement in a way that is "shrewd as snakes" and "innocent as doves," and to be ambassadors of reconciliation in the most complicated places. Not because of us, but because we chose to come quietly alongside what Jesus was already doing through those whom he had appointed (non-Christians) and anointed (Christians) for such a time.

We followers of Christ are called to be bridge builders, practical ambassadors of reconciliation. This calling is not a question of debate but of obedience. Obedient bridge-building requires a long-term commitment, discernment, and a willingness to "take fire" from all sides—theologically and politically. By such obedience, significant and sustainable impact for religious freedom can be made, and our sovereign God is glorified.

## QUESTIONS FOR REFLECTION

1. Jesus intentionally demonstrated his love for the person most unlike him (the Samaritan woman), crossing every geographic, theological, social, and gender boundary to do so. Can we do any less?
2. How can you love someone completely different than yourself? What are the practical steps you need to take, personally and professionally?
3. Do you have a theology and strategy of engagement at your church? What does that look like locally? Globally?

# REFERENCES

Dorsett, L. W., ed. 1988. *The essential C. S. Lewis*. (C. S. Lewis, The weight of glory, origi-nally preached as a sermon on June 8, 1941.) New York: Macmillan.

Galli, M. 2007. Good morning, Vietnam. *Christianity Today* (May): 26–32.

Jenkins, P. 2004. The politics of persecuted minorities. In *Religion and security: The new nexus in international affairs,* ed. D. Hoover and R. Seiple. Landham, MD: Rowman Littlefield. (This chapter later adapted as an article, Repression and rebellion, in *The Review of Faith and International Affairs* 5, no. 1 (2007): 3–12.)

Seiple, C. 2005. Religious freedom and reconciliation. September 6. https://www.globa-lengage.org/pressroom/ftp/475-from-the-president-religious-freedom-and-reconcilia-tion.html.

———. 2006a. The gate at Bethel: Building religious freedom in Vietnam. July 6. https://www.globalengage.org/pressroom/ftp/469-the-gate-at-bethel-building-religious-free-dom-in-vietnam.html.

———. 2006b. Vietnam, religious freedom, and PNTR. Testimony before the US Senate Committee on Finance, July 12. http://finance.senate.gov/sitepages/hearing071206.htm.

———. 2007. Religious freedom in Vietnam: An update. Testimony before the Congres-sional Human Rights Caucus (CHRC), the CHRC Taskforce on International Reli-gious Freedom, and the Congressional Caucus on Vietnam, December 6. http://www.globalengage.org/WorkArea/showcontent.aspx?id=9080.

———. 2008. The road to reconciliation. November 5. https://www.globalengage.org/pressroom/ftp/775-the-road-to-reconciliation.html.

———. 2009. Case study II: Vietnam. In *International religious freedom advocacy: A guide to organizations, law, and NGOs.* H. K. Thames, C. Seiple, and A. Rowe, app. 8. Waco, TX: Baylor University Press.

———. 2010. Miracle on the Mekong. March 30. https://www.globalengage.org/press-room/ftp/1148-miracle-on-the-mekong.html.

**Chris Seiple, PhD,** is president of the Institute for Global Engagement (www.globalen-gage.org) and founder of *The Review of Faith and International Affairs.* He is coauthor of *International Religious Freedom Advocacy* (2009) and the forthcoming *Religion and Security Handbook* (2012).  He serves on the Council on Foreign Relations, the International Insti-tute for Strategic Studies, the WBT board of directors, and the Federal Advisory Committee to Secretary of State Hillary Clinton's "Strategic Dialogue with Civil Society," where he also acts as a senior advisor to the committee's "Religion and Foreign Policy" working group.

## LOVE CALLS FOR SOLIDARITY

Loving one another includes especially caring for those who are persecuted and in prison for their faith and witness. If one part of the body suffers, all parts suffer with it. We are all, like John, "companions in the suffering and kingdom and patient endurance that are ours in Jesus."[51]

We commit ourselves to share in the suffering of members of the body of Christ throughout the world, through information, prayer, advocacy, and other means of support. We see such sharing, however, not merely as an exercise of pity, but longing also to learn what the suffering Church can teach and give to those parts of Christ's body that are not suffering in the same way. We are warned that the Church that feels itself at ease in its wealth and self-sufficiency may, like Laodicea, be the Church that Jesus sees as the most blind to its own poverty, and from which he himself feels a stranger outside the door.[52]

[51] Hebrews 13:1–3; 1 Corinthians 12:26; Revelation 1:9
[52] Revelation 3:17–20
Cape Town Commitment, Part I, Section 9. We love the people of God, Paragraph C

# CHAPTER 61

# JESUS CHRIST'S COMFORT AND HEALING FOR TRAUMATIC WOUNDS

*Kyle Miller*

## THE HARD QUESTIONS

"They killed my wife and children! I was gone and they rode in and killed them!" Ibrahim[1] looked intently in my eyes with sadness and anger as we spoke one hot afternoon in October 2008. Ibrahim's eyes filled with tears as he told me the details of his family's death at the hands of the militia during a raid that destroyed his African village the previous year. His grief was compounded by guilt because he hadn't been home. Ibrahim's heartbreaking story ended with, "And I am still very, very angry and I do not know what to do about it!" What could God possibly help me say to Ibrahim? How could any words begin to touch the deep suffering that he was experiencing? How could I help him, especially since I was fairly certain that he was not a believer in Jesus Christ as God's Son?

"How can I believe that God is good and loves me when all these horrible things have happened to me?" Olga asked me in June 2011. She spoke through a staff translator as I counseled the residents at Freedom Home in Chisinau, Moldova. Through her desperate hopelessness, Olga, like Ibrahim, was asking me seemingly unanswerable questions. Olga had been neglected and abused in a poor, rural Moldovan family before being sold to gypsies. She ended up in a nearby capital where she experienced unrepeatable atrocities at the hands of sex traffickers and johns. When I was talking with Olga and her fellow residents, most spoke with blank dissociation when describing the horrors of being sex slaves, constantly living under the threat of torture or death for them or a friend if they were not compliant or attempted to run away.

How could I respond to these things since I have had such a different life? How could I say anything, however true, and it not seem ridiculously trite and uncaring in comparison to the evil genocide of Ibrahim's family and the dozen rapes a day and torture to Olga? God showed me that all I can do is to be poor in my spirit so that I can be rich in God's Spirit and not try to explain it all. After a lifetime of counseling people, I am learning in each holy

---

moment to weep with those that weep (Rom 12:15) and not be overcome by the evil that was done to them, but rather overcome evil with good (Rom 12:21).

## THE BODY OF CHRIST AND THE MINISTRY OF RECONCILIATION

In a world full of suffering, persecution, and martyrdom it is difficult to imagine a more important role in the body of Christ than offering Christ's compassion, comfort, and healing to those who have survived great evils. The great discipleship commission that Jesus gives us in Matthew 28:19–20 seems easier to explain when sharing with someone in an air-conditioned Western coffee shop than in a secret Chinese house church, a crumbling Soviet-era apartment, or an African village that could be attacked at any time. But when we look at these same verses through the lens of the trauma ministry of reconciliation that God gave Jesus Christ in Isaiah 61 and through him to us, then by faith the invisible becomes seen (Heb 11:1) and the impossible begins to happen (Matt 19:26). Pray through Isaiah 61 to your heavenly Father and tell him that you want to fulfill his calling upon your life as he gives you more opportunities:

> The Spirit of the Lord God is upon me, because the Lord has anointed me to bring good news to the afflicted. He has sent me to bind up the brokenhearted, to proclaim liberty to captives and freedom to prisoners; to proclaim the favorable year of the Lord and the day of vengeance of our God; to comfort all who mourn, to grant those who mourn in Zion, giving them a garland instead of ashes, the oil of gladness instead of mourning, the mantle of praise instead of a spirit of fainting. (Isa 61:1–3 NASB)

I am following Jesus in this ministry of trauma reconciliation (2 Cor 5:18). As overwhelming as the evil is, as people's grief may feel, and as inadequate as I might feel—God is greater (1 John 4:4). That is why I am going on mission trips with my church, pursuing a seminary PhD, and even why I am writing this chapter—so I can entrust to you what God has taught me (1 Tim 2:2). I am following Jesus and becoming who I need to be to reach the Ibrahims and Olgas in my life. Let us follow Christ in his "more excellent way" (1 Cor 12:31 NASB) so that together across the world we may "be called oaks of righteousness, the planting of the LORD, that he may be glorified" (Isa 61:3c NASB).

To prepare for this calling, two of God's truths will help us. First, we need to receive and share transformation, not information, so that as we offer Scripture, hope, and spiritual authority God will transform people in the same miraculous way that he has transformed us. Second, we do not need to have survived genocide or sex slavery to help someone who has. If you have, then God's redemption means that he will be able to use you in ways that he cannot use me. Either way, for you to be effective, God is calling you to face your own trauma. Jesus teaches in Luke 16:10 that we are responsible to face our own trauma with him, even if it seems like "a very little thing" in comparison to the trauma of genocide or sex trafficking. "He who is faithful in a very little thing [your own traumas] is faithful also in much [someone else's severe trauma]; and he who is unrighteous in a very little thing is unrighteous also in much" (NASB).

If you and I are: (1) not approaching God and all those in our lives with poor in spirit humility; (2) not facing the pain, trauma, and suffering of our past; (3) not receiving the hard things of life—even the smallest ones—as opportunities from God to become like him; and therefore (4) not noticeably growing in Christ, then we will be unprepared when we face these trials firsthand or attempt to assist someone else secondhand. Proverbs 24:10 says, "If you are slack in the day of distress, your strength is limited" (NASB). To use an analogy, if I as a basketball coach have no practice sessions for my team, when game time comes my unprepared players will probably lose.

I would like to put this principle into practice right now: I am praying now for everyone who will read this. I ask that you pray for the other readers and for me, that all of us will grow in Christ, that we will become poorer in spirit so that we can become rich in God's Spirit, and that we will see and feel the pain and trauma around us just as Jesus would.

Three elements are needed in order for transformative healing discipleship relationships to happen: (1) a biblical model, (2) humility and teachability on the part of the worker, and (3) humility and teachability on the part of the subject. Teachability is a key component of the Beatitude Trauma Model. When Jesus leads a teachable worker, the worker's life will be transformed and the worker's own wounds will be healed (1 Pet 2:24). Then the worker will have personally experienced Jesus' process and power. The worker will then be more aware and equipped to minister to the deep wounds of those he or she is serving and to have the faith and patience with a traumatized person to help bring about transformational healing, just as God did for the worker previously (2 Cor 1:2–4).

An Old Testament verse cautions us about not being teachable. Ecclesiastes 4:13 states, "A poor yet wise lad is better than an old and foolish king who no longer knows how to receive instruction" (NASB). This king once was wise and could receive instruction from others, but presently his value is less than that of a poor adolescent, who is wise in that he will still receive instruction. We can connect this proverb to a powerful yet not well-known attribute of Jesus Christ—his teachability through suffering. Hebrews 5:8 illustrates the good news of teachability. It clearly describes Jesus as not only having learned obedience—but having learned it through suffering. "Although He was a Son, He learned obedience from the things which He suffered" (NASB). Christ models ongoing maturity through learning, and further ongoing learning through life and suffering. This is true of Christians in a developed country—we all must face our own suffering and through it come to hunger and thirst for God's righteousness (Matt 5:6) in order to have spiritual authority in both our personal relationships and our professional lives. However, it is even more necessary for those in developing countries working with survivors of atrocities, natural disasters, and war.

## THE BEATITUDE TRAUMA MODEL

Jesus Christ said in Matthew 5:3–5, "Blessed are the poor in spirit, for theirs is the kingdom of heaven. Blessed are those who mourn, for they shall be comforted. Blessed are the gentle [meek], for they shall inherit the earth" (NASB). Based on the Beatitude Counseling Model that I have used since 1984, I developed the Beatitude Trauma Model (BTM) in 2008 to reach out to genocide survivors in Africa. The BTM is a transformational and relational process model—not a short-term performance model; a humility model—not an expert model; an exegetically biblical model—not a topically biblical model; and a core spiritual model—not a conceptual psychological model. The Beatitudes in Matthew 5, especially the first three in verses 3–5, gives us a scriptural and spiritual kick-start to begin talking and praying with someone who is in grief and distress. The BTM gives us an approach to: (1) know God (poor in spirit) in order to become free from one's old self, (2) become free of the pain of the past and of present sin (mourn), and (3) learn how to relate to others in peace and power and not victimize or be victimized by others (meek). Beatitude Trauma Model is a paperless approach (three principles for each of the three Beatitudes). It was developed to be presented to a not-yet saved audience; presentations do not include culture-bound references, but do include culture-specific references; and the missional approach is similar to the medical missions model (Build relationships→Offer medical care→Continue relationships→Share Jesus Christ as possible, and not require a profession of faith to receive medical care).

In our 2008 outreach to the African village, we were able to teach or talk with eight hundred of the two thousand villagers in small groups. The Beatitude Trauma Model and the story of Joseph were compelling to present, yet it was very painful to talk, pray, and mourn with the people, half of whom (many of them surviving children) had witnessed their family members' torture and deaths in the genocide. Words cannot describe what my new friends like Ibrahim were feeling as they talked, but they were actually quite eager to talk. They told our church that since the latest attack a year before, they had been grateful for the medical care and the food that other NGOs were providing, but that until we had come, no one had asked them specifically what had happened to them nor would they sit and listen to their stories.

Following that life-changing experience in 2008, I was invited by Andy and Nancy Raatz, the founders of Freedom Home in Moldova, Chisinau, to teach a three-day Beatitude Trauma Model training for their staff in May 2010. The BTM was thus adapted to be effective for the young, female, Christian, Romanian or Russian-speaking Moldova Freedom Home staff workers. This event was followed the next year by monthly Skype training sessions for the staff. The staffs began using the BTM with the residents, and hundreds of people around the world supported Freedom Home through an eight-week spiritual warfare prayer campaign in the Spring of 2011. Then in June 2011, a team from our church, Great Hills Baptist Church in Austin, Texas, went to Moldova to provide more Beatitude Trauma Model training to the staff. It was a blessing to counsel the staff individually, as well as the young women residents who are recovering from being trafficked for sex.

The nine transforming principles of the BTM that are taught, modeled, and applied are as follows:

### Poor in spirit (Matthew 5:3)

1. Realize that we cannot meet our own needs; we must become poor continually in our spirit and rich in God's Spirit (Isa 57:15; Matt 11:28–30; 2 Cor 8:9; Phil 2:1–7; Jas 4:6; 1 Pet 5:5–7).

2.  Increase in the true knowledge of God by becoming poor in spirit (Col 2:2; 3:10; 2 Pet 1:2–4,8).
3.  Receive and walk in your true identity in Christ by putting off the old self and putting on the new self of who you really are in Christ (Col 3:9–11).

### Mourn (Matthew 5:4)

1.  Understand and change your Sad→Mad→Bad reactions to life (Mark 3:5; Eph 4:26).
2.  Become willing to give forgiveness to those who have wronged you; repent from your sins and ask for and receive forgiveness from Jesus Christ (Matt 6:12; Eph 4:32).
3.  Learn how to mourn out your pain, guilt, fear, sadness, trauma, and anxiety, thus creating a vacuum that God can fill with his comfort (Matt 5:4; 2 Cor 1:2–4).

### Meek (Matthew 5:5)

1.  Understand that Christlike meekness is not weakness, but divine power under divine control (Gal 5:22–23; Matt 19:26; Phil 4:13).
2.  Learn to yield and stop the demand for your mythical "personal rights." By emptying themselves of personal rights, trauma survivors stop trying to become whole and powerful on their own and instead accept that Jehovah Rapha is the healer and that the Lord of Hosts can empower them to stand firm in Christ (1 Cor 8—9, esp. 9:4–6).
3.  Transform from being a victim to being a victor (1 Cor 15:57) in Christ, a soldier (Phil 2:25; Phlm 1:2), an overcomer (1 John 2:13; 4:4; 5:4–5), and a conqueror (Rom 8:37).

### Blessed

"Blessed" is one of the least understood words of Jesus. Blessed does not mean happy, lucky, or fortunate; its root word means large, thus it means big, fulfilled, and purposeful. Blessed does not mean easy circumstances or a pain-free life. Blessedness instead captures the benefit of having growing purpose and peace as one matures while walking with Christ. John Stott provides an excellent synopsis of the Beatitudes:

> The Beatitudes paint a comprehensive portrait of a Christian disciple. We see him first alone on his knees before God, acknowledging his spiritual poverty and mourning over it. This makes him meek or gentle in all his relationships, since honesty compels him to allow others to think of him what before God he confesses himself to be.... Such is the man or woman who is blessed, that is, who has the approval of God and finds self-fulfillment as a human being. (quoted in Greenman et al. 2007, 258–59)

Through all of his trials, Jesus had this blessed purpose and peace since he knew that he was doing what his Father was telling him to do (John 14:10). It was this lifetime of blessedness from his Father that prepared him to bear the world's sins—"who for the joy set before Him, endured the cross, despising the shame, and has sat down at the right hand of the throne of God" (Heb 12:2 NASB).

There is nothing quick, easy, or painless about the Beatitude Trauma Model for healing. For example, discussing blessed with the young women in Moldova is difficult—it needed to be recognized that their lives have been anything but blessed. But many of our conversations about their years in trafficking started with me sharing what Jesus meant by this word. In fact, just like the villagers in Africa, they also were more than ready to talk; I never once had to ask them, "What happened to you when you were trafficked?" After a few minutes of talking about their childhood, God, and their life at Freedom Home, their experiences in trafficking would start to pour out. When we are poor in spirit, God gives a "greater grace" (Jas 4:6)—both for the person who is healing and for the worker that is helping him or her heal. I am now over a half century old. I have lived in five countries, visited twenty-five, and counseled thousands of people. However, the things that I heard from the genocide survivors in Africa and the sex-trafficking survivors in Moldova were evil and heartbreaking beyond writing or imagination. Yet, God is calling us to help survivors to receive beauty for ashes so that the "Lord GOD will cause righteousness and praise to spring up before all the nations" (Isa 61:3,11 NASB).

> And after you have suffered a little while, the God of all grace, who has called you to his eternal glory in Christ, will himself restore, confirm, strengthen, and establish you. To him be the dominion forever and ever. Amen.
> *1 Peter 5:10–11*

Traumatized people experience Jesus' new blessedness in equal parts of "uncomfortable" and "hopeful." It is uncomfortable, not because God's Spirit is not drawing them with his love, but because not only have they been traumatized hundreds of times, but in the case of the trafficked girls they have also been deceived and tricked many times. Combining traumatized and tricked makes them naturally very suspicious, both of God's love and the love of caring staff women. But by becoming poor in spirit, by realizing they cannot meet their own needs and must rely on God's Spirit, the "greater grace" grows and they gradually become hopeful and their anxiety and depression can begin to decrease. By slowly realizing that they are not alone and by receiving God love and a new family, they can let down their guard in the present, reversing their anxiety and depression into expectancy and joy.

"Blessedness" for the staff at Freedom Home Moldova occurs as they respond to God's call on their own lives, allowing their heavenly Father to heal their traumas and to mature them with the resurrection power of Jesus Christ through the work of his Holy Spirit. Blessedness for the eight residents and their children occurs as they are healed and as they receive God's redemptive vision for their lives. Some of them will be in sex-trafficking ministry. As they do this work they are able to be the hands and feet of Jesus as Paul explains in 2 Corinthians 1:2–4, comforting those as we have been comforted by God. Blessedness will occur for the eight hundred adults and children we talked with in Africa when they begin to follow Jesus Christ as their Savior and Lord. We were able to subtly but sufficiently share his "grace gospel" of transformation with them.

## CLOSING

I do not know where Ibrahim is now, but God was working on him. The last thing he asked me was, "Are you telling me that I must forgive the people who killed my wife and children?" Grateful for translation time to pray, I said, "No, Ibrahim, I am not telling you that. God is telling you that." He nodded, smiled, and accepted the thought. He understood, as we had discussed, that if he did not forgive them then his hate would cause him to become just like them. In February 2009, the village where we had been was again attacked and looted, but everyone had escaped first. From the times that I talked and prayed with Ibrahim, I know that he heard that grace gospel of Jesus Christ, and I continue to pray for him and all the people from his village.

In contrast, I do know where Olga is, and she is doing well, as are the other residents. The huge difference is not only that Olga is now saved by Jesus Christ, but also that the Raatzes, the staff, and the residents are together working on the Beatitude Trauma Model principles by God's grace and good humor. God uses his Word, through his people and by his Spirit, in the most extremely traumatic situations to accomplish his loving will and purpose for people's lives. I plan to return to Moldova next year. I pray to be able to return to Africa as soon as it is possible. I ask you to pray for all these people that I care for and serve and I will pray for you and the people that God calls you to care for and serve.

## QUESTIONS FOR REFLECTION

1. Share one area of pride (self-sufficiency) in your life and how it holds you back in your ministry. Tell the group that you sense God's conviction to repent from pride and that you want to be poor in your spirit and become rich in God's Spirit. Think of one way that your ministry to people will be more effective as you become more humble.
2. Share one trauma in your life that God has shown you he wants to heal so you can be whole and can more powerfully help others heal from their traumas. In addition to sharing this new determination with a person or group, share what the next step of healing for you will be (i.e., forgiving someone or asking someone for forgiveness).
3. Share one traumatized group of people that God has burdened your heart to serve; share what you feel and discern when you think and pray about them. Explain the changes in your life that you would have to make to be prepared to help them heal and be transformed; ask for prayer.

## REFERENCE

Greenman, J. P., T. Larsen, and S. R. Spencer. 2007. *The Sermon on the Mount through the centuries: From the early church to John Paul II*. Grand Rapids, MI: Brazos.

**Kyle Miller** grew up in Asia as a missionary kid. He is married to Terri and they are blessed with their children Nathan, Kevin, Kristin, and Katherine. Kyle has a BA and two master's degrees from the University of Texas, Austin, in psychology/counseling. Since 1984 Kyle has been a professional biblical counselor and later executive pastor of his church. He now leads Global Care and Response, a worker care and trauma ministry based in Austin, TX, USA that responds to urgent needs around the world.

## THE GREATEST MUSIC IN THE USA

African-American "spirituals" were born in the hell of slavery. Some scholars have criticized spirituals for keeping slaves' minds on heaven so they would not agitate for justice in this world. Others, like theologian Paul Jewett, argue that these songs express an "inner freedom (which enabled the singers to) be truly human even as slaves. Even though they were treated as 'niggers,' these early black Christians knew they were not niggers but rather children of God; even though they were treated as things, they knew they were not things but persons. Ultimately this faith in themselves was rooted in their faith in God."

Furthermore, they expected God to get involved in their lives. In their songs they testify that God rescued the Hebrew slaves from the Egyptians. He protected the prophet Daniel from the lions. He liberated Daniel's three friends from the fiery furnace. Surely a loving God would not merely free folks in other eras. Surely that was not reserved for heaven. Surely God would transform their condition in this world too. Therefore they looked for concrete liberation: "Let my people go!"

Jewett concludes, "Rather than saying that the black singers borrowed their thoughts from white Christianity, one might better say that the slaves redeemed the Christianity which their masters had profaned."

Miriam Adeney, *Kingdom without Borders: The Untold Story of Global Christianity* (2009, 216-17), citing Paul Jewett, "America's First Black Christians and Their Songs," *Bulletin of Systematic Theology* 3 (Pasadena, CA: Fuller Theological Seminary 1983, 14)

# CHAPTER 62

# COUNSELING VICTIMS OF HUMAN-INDUCED TRAUMA

*Patricia Miersma*

She stared at the verse. "Thou wilt keep him in perfect peace, whose mind is stayed on thee." (Isa 26:3, KVJ). But it doesn't work, she thought. I *am* putting my mind on God. I *am* praying. I *am* memorizing Scripture. I *am* going to church. Why can't I feel any peace? And why do I feel so angry, so enraged. I don't want to be this way.

She had been a nurse in a war zone and had seen terrible things. Babies died in her arms. Children screamed in agony and fear. They lost their parents. Young men and women suffered horrific wounds. And when she asked God to stop it, to at least spare the innocent children, nothing happened. The evil continued. She still believed in God. She even knew he would not abandon her. But there were whole parts of her that didn't agree or couldn't feel anything at all. Even though she taught the Bible to others, when she read verses about God's peace and joy it only made her angry and frustrated. It wasn't working for her. What was wrong? It had been ten years since the war.

## THE COST OF UNHEALED TRAUMA

Many people think that the passage of time or not looking back will make the pain of traumatic events die out. But it often only allows living wounds to go on damaging lives. To be clear, in the case of single critical events such as natural disaster, accident, or even a series of traumas, many people (80–85 percent) can gradually recover with the love and support of others.

But without special help, people who have suffered from persecution and other human induced events such as war, rape, abductions, slavery, village burnings, imprisonments, torture, or even more subtle acts of intimidation, may go on suffering for a lifetime as they try to "forget it and go on," to "just get over it," or to "go forward with life."

Lingering along a painful path of thoughts, behaviors, emotions, and relationships now broken, they may feel confused and even blame themselves for being bad, unspiritual, or weak. They might realize their experience was a turning point yet still not realize the profoundly deep connection it has to the ongoing brokenness in their life. In some cases they may develop post-traumatic stress disorder (PTSD) or other conditions that exacerbate and prolong the pain.

And in the case of religious persecution and/or ethnic conflict, whole communities or groups of people with unhealed trauma can perpetuate ongoing cycles of violence and intractable states of fear, hatred, and suspicion. Even "peace" resulting from international intervention will be fragile and temporary. For where there is inadequate deep healing to the soul, true forgiveness and lasting reconciliation are unlikely. So facilitating deep and whole healing is not only good and right, it is critical for much broader reasons.

## DEFINITIONS

*Trauma* (the type discussed here) is serious and life-altering emotional and psychological injury caused by a single event or prolonged or repeated events that overwhelm a person's normal ability to cope. Normal reactions to trauma include shock, fear, sadness, a sense of helplessness, confusion, anger, and anxiety. Most people, with love and support, will recover over time. But severe, frequent, or ongoing trauma, especially human-induced trauma or accompanied by a lack of buffering factors such as social support, can result in some people developing post-traumatic stress disorder (PTSD) or other conditions.

*Post-traumatic stress disorder (PTSD)* is a severe anxiety disorder resulting from this type of trauma. A person with PTSD will experience the following symptoms:

1.  Repeatedly reliving the event in unwanted thoughts, nightmares, and "flashbacks."
2.  Constantly avoiding people, places, and other things that remind them of the event. This may include "psychic numbing" (inability to experience certain feelings) or inability to remember some of the event.
3.  Feeling hyperaroused and unable to rest or relax. Sleep disturbances, startle reactions, the inability to concentrate, and frequent anger or rage are common parts of this symptom.

This definition is helpful but it doesn't describe the full impact of trauma. For that reason, treatment approaches based on this definition alone may be found inadequate or ineffective. This is because it focuses primarily on the mind/body impact of trauma and does not directly address the effect of trauma on the soul.

## SOUL TRAUMA: SPIRITUAL LOSSES AT THE CORE OF WOUNDEDNESS

The soul, as defined by Willard (2002, 37), is that dimension of the person which organizes all other dimensions of the person into one life. Those dimensions are the heart, mind, body, and social contexts; all intricately related and influencing one another as well as the total well-being of the soul. So when any one of these is traumatized all will be affected to some degree. Effective care for traumatized people will base its approach on this model of intricately interwoven dimensions of the human.

As many trauma survivors will attest, the deepest, most enduring wounds are often not those to the body or mind, but to the heart, the place from which we live: "Above all else guard your heart, for it is the wellspring of life" (Prov 4:23). In many places, the Bible confirms the heart's capacity to be wounded: "My heart is wounded within me" (Ps 109:22). And a wounded heart will affect one's capacity to fully love God and neighbor as the Great

Commandment instructs (Mark 12:30–31). It is easy to see why this is so if we consider just a few of the deepest, most enduring, and most common spiritual losses of trauma felt by the heart, the center of emotion and will:

*Trust.* The trust-shattering, alienating, isolating impact of betrayal can result in a pervasive sense that no one, not others, not God, not even oneself, can be trusted.

*Intimacy.* Intimacy includes an innate vulnerability to loss. Repeated loss of loved ones and valued things, ideals, and hopes diminish one's openness to intimacy and caring. Someone said such loss makes establishing an intimate relationship more terrifying than walking into a moving bullet.

*Peace.* Sinclair (1993, 69) writes, "Their search is the endless search for rest, for peace. They have a terrible conviction that there is no peace until the past has been undone. Their fearful search is for ways to undo the past and to recreate it with a proper ending."

These are just three among many other potential spiritual wounds such as loss of hope, loss of innocence, loss of awe, and loss of wholeness.

# HEALING WOUNDS OF TRAUMA: A WHOLE PERSON APPROACH

Understanding core wounds to the soul can help make clear what core elements are needed for healing. Ministry to the wounded soul can be affected by directly engaging the dimensions of heart, mind, and body with which it is intricately connected. Of course, the practical outworking of this will vary depending on culture, conditions of trauma, and resources available. But including some basic contextual and healing elements can do much to foster conditions for heart, mind, and body that are congruent with tried and true biblical principles of human healing and thriving of the whole person.

## ESSENTIAL CONTEXTUAL ELEMENTS

*Safety.* Events which cause overwhelming feelings of powerlessness and lack of control require a context of safety before helpful processing of events can occur. Providing shelter, food, water, and medical care ministers to the body and helps reestablish a sense of control. Though conditions may never be ideal, as much as possible, safety for body, mind, and heart should be a primary contextual goal.

*Reunification with loved ones.* The first step in reconnecting people isolated by their trauma is reunifying them with loved ones as soon as possible. Research shows this one condition greatly reduces the risk of long-term negative effects of trauma such as PTSD. This provision is especially *critical* for children.

*Sensitivity to culture.* Experiences and understanding of traumatic experiences are culture-bound as are healing approaches and help-seeking behaviors (Drozdek and Wilson 2007, 7). Helping people examine cultural beliefs and practices in light of Scripture can encourage them to benefit from those that are helpful and to identify ways they may diverge from God's truth in ways that are unhelpful.

*Use of mother-tongue language.* Heart wounds are best healed in the language of the heart, the mother tongue. Wherever possible, teaching materials and trauma healing work should be provided in the heart language of those who are traumatized.

*Time.* The elements of healing described here are a place to begin. With patience and care, they can help. But for many deeply traumatized people, significant healing will take a long time. And this may be extremely difficult for some Christian families or communities to accept. They may be part of the voice saying, "Just trust God, just pray, just have faith." So it is critical that patience, hope, and care be provided from those who do understand the huge difficulty. This can begin sufferers on their journey to healing. And along the way, they will find riches of life they otherwise would not have known.

## ESSENTIAL HEALING ELEMENTS

*Community.* As injury to trust and intimacy indicate, traumatized people feel isolated. Herman (1992, 51) writes, "Traumatic events call into question basic human relationships. They breach the attachments of family, friendship, love, and community." Damage to relationships often most painfully reveal the true impact of trauma. Yet support from others is widely acknowledged as the single greatest determining factor in someone's ability to recover. So finding safe relationship contexts for people to begin healing is critical. This may be a family, a small group, or a community. According to Herman, "Recovery can take place only within the context of relationships, it cannot occur in isolation."

*Remembering and telling.* At their own pace and in their own way, people need to be able to tell and retell their story as often as needed. Science is now finding that the act of telling one's story can help "rewire" the neural pathways of the brain affected by trauma. During trauma ordinary connections between the right and left brain may diminish to help the person survive emotionally. In this way, the person functions via the left brain with the facts of what is happening but is not overcome by the feelings of fear or terror that would normally be associated with the event. But if this gap is not reestablished eventually, it leaves the person feeling alienated from their own feelings and feelings of others and of God. Storytelling can help rebuild the connection that is normal. Without that, attempts to "get better" or "forget it" will only lead to further despair. Thompson (2010, 137, 152) writes: "When we tell our stories or listen to another person's story, our left and right modes of processing integrate.... Isolating commands for right living apart from their storied context is at best neurologically nonintegrating and at worst disintegrating. This is why telling our stories is so vitally important." Storytelling requires a safe relationship with others who listen not just to the words but to the heart, without criticizing, judging, or interrupting. It is best if listeners can have some training in how to listen reflectively in ways that will not retraumatize people and in how to identify when people need professional help.

*Grieving.* Trauma involves significant losses. These may include loved ones, way of life, ideas, possessions, home, work, or health. Some studies show that traumatic loss of loved ones is a greater risk factor than the life threatening factor previously thought to most often lead to PTSD. Identifying what the losses are and taking time to mourn them is essential for the healing journey. Composing personal laments based on the biblical model is one powerful way sufferers can grieve well with both emotional honesty and spiritual victory.

*God's Word and prayer.* Many traumatized Christians, like the nurse in the introduction, find the most distressing impact of trauma is how it affects their understanding of and relationship to God. Their experience of communion with God may feel lost or numb. And they often feel a distressing gap between the truth of Scripture and their internal experience. It may take time for them to be ready, but Scripture engagement in a community of loving believers applying biblically sound mental health principles of caring can help people move beyond this to experience the reality of God's comfort, healing, and most importantly the nearness of God himself through Scripture. They can begin to know: "The nearness of God is my good" (Ps 73:28 NASB).

*The Cross.* Because of what Christ did on the cross our sins are paid for and our wounds can be healed (Isa 53:4,5). Coming to the cross is essential for cleansing of personal sin often entangled in events of trauma, but also critical for healing wounds inflicted by others. The profound impact on wounded hearts when sufferers bring their pain to the cross is not a matter of "getting over" the pain immediately. But the unexplainable mystery of God's response to even a whisper of trust or fragile faith helps sufferers begin to know their pain is fully accepted and understood by God and will begin to heal and bear fruit for good. Deeply traumatized people may need time and may even need to lean on the arms of others to get there. But the cross is the most important place on the journey. Sometimes the physical act of doing this with the company of others can help open the way for the heart.

> "I have said these things to you, that in me you may have peace. In the world you will have tribulation. But take heart; I have overcome the world." *John 16:33*

## ONE EXAMPLE OF A WHOLE PERSON APPROACH TO TRAUMA HEALING

In 2001, a Scripture-use tool incorporating the above approach to trauma healing was developed by some African church leaders and missionaries. Now translated into over one hundred languages, *Healing the wounds of trauma: How the church can help* (Hill, Hill, Bagge, and Miersma 2009) is being used by struggling churches in Africa, Asia, and elsewhere. Field reports indicate that this holistic, integrative approach can be beneficial even given differences in culture, country, language, and situation.

## CLOSURE

Healing from horrific trauma is possible. But deep and lasting healing will take time and occur only when the whole person—heart, soul, mind, and body—is engaged in the healing process. Significant healing may begin with the support and listening of others but more complete healing may take a period of years. Healing does not mean the person will be the same as before. But they can begin to integrate their experience into a meaningful place in their life. They can live with the truth of their experience without letting it control their life. They can learn to rebuild relationships and to love and be loved by others and by God.

They can experience forgiveness and be able to forgive others where once there was only fear, hatred, and revenge. They can find peace and become channels of God's peace to others.

Just ask the nurse.

## QUESTIONS FOR REFLECTION
1. If the fulfillment of the Great Commission (Matt 28:18–20) depends on our living out the Great Commandment (Luke 10:27), what are the implications of wounded hearts among those who suffer in your area?
2. What place might traditional spiritual disciplines have in helping heal wounds of trauma?
3. How can unhealed trauma affect people and communities that have suffered from religious persecution or ethnic conflict? What is needed to help them overcome their bitterness and the cycle of violence?
4. Why are the contextual elements, the sensitivity to people's culture (how they understand traumatic experiences), essential to the process of healing? How does the lack of such understanding and patience hinder any deeper healing?

## REFERENCES

Drozdek, B., and J. P. Wilson, eds. 2007. *Voices of trauma: Treating survivors across cultures.* New York: Springer.

Herman, J. L. 1992. *Trauma and recovery: The aftermath of violence—from domestic abuse to political terror.* New York: Basic Books.

Hill, M., H. Hill, R. Bagge, and P. Miersma. 2009. *Healing the wounds of trauma: How the church can help*, 3rd ed. Nairobi: Paulines Publications Africa.

Sinclair, N. D. 1993. *Horrific traumata: A pastoral response to the post-traumatic stress disorder.* New York: Haworth Pastoral Press.

Thompson, C. 2010. *Anatomy of the soul: Surprising connections between neuroscience and spiritual practices that can transform your life and relationships.* Carol Stream, Illinois: SaltRiver.

Willard, D. 2002. *Renovation of the heart: Putting on the character of Christ.* Colorado Springs: NavPress.

**Patricia Miersma** (MN, UCLA '84) serves as SIL International counseling consultant, specializing in community and cross-cultural issues related to trauma healing and post-traumatic stress disorder (PTSD). She is co-author of *Healing the Wounds of Trauma: How the Church Can Help,* and a senior consultant/trainer for its related workshops. She and her husband are RCA missionaries, seconded to Wycliffe Bible Translators as counselors since 1980, serving in Papua New Guinea and Africa, where they helped establish Tumaini Counseling Center in Nairobi.

# CHAPTER 63

# A REVIEW OF "HEALING THE WOUNDS OF TRAUMA"

*Patricia Miersma*

## HISTORY OF THE BOOK

In the wake of ethnic violence, civil wars, persecution of the church, HIV/AIDS, and other suffering in the 1990s, African pastors were facing whole communities of people in trauma. In 2001, a small group of church leaders from several countries worked with a few missionaries in East Africa (linguists and counselors) to develop simple lessons from Scripture that would help people begin to heal. The work resulted in a book *Healing the Wounds of Trauma: How the Church Can Help* (Hill, Hill, Bagge, and Miersma 2009).

## CONTENT OF THE BOOK

This interactive Scripture-use book addresses the issues of suffering, healing, forgiveness, reconciliation, and helping others. Developed for ministry among traumatized people and communities, the lessons include biblically sound counseling and caring principles congruent with the message of Christ's work on the cross (Isa 53). Holistic in approach, each lesson includes learning activities that engage the heart, mind, and body and promote sharing of personal stories within a safe and caring small community setting.

When asked what questions they most often heard from their people, the pastors responded with answers that would eventually define the lessons in the book.

Lesson 1: If God loves us, why do we suffer?
Lesson 2: How can the wounds of our hearts be healed?
Lesson 3: What happens when someone is grieving?
Lesson 4: How can we help children who have experienced bad things?
Lesson 5: How can we help women who have been raped?
Lesson 6: How can a church minister in the midst of AIDS?
Lesson 7: Care for the caregiver
Lesson 8: Response: Taking your pain to the cross
Lesson 9: How can we forgive others?
Lesson 10: How can we live as Christians in the midst of conflict?
Lesson 11: Looking ahead

## CHARACTERISTICS OF THE BOOK DESIGNED TO PROMOTE TRAUMA HEALING

1. The book promotes Scripture engagement and application to real life. Lessons focus on the connection between God's Word and pressing issues of the heart, mind, soul, and body. Application to the life of the believer is the intent.
   *Examples*: How to receive God's healing and comfort (Lesson 8)
   How to live in the midst of conflict (Lesson 9)

2. It integrates biblically sound mental health principles about suffering, trauma, and healing. This helps reduce fear and confusion, normalizes symptoms, encourages verbal expression, stimulates hope and energy to act, and equips people to help one another. Not intended as a substitute for professional counseling, it offers simple practical guidelines for promoting healing and helping others.

   *Examples*: How to listen well to help others (Lesson 2)
   How to help traumatized children (Lesson 4)

3. It aims to be culturally relevant by promoting discussion of cultural beliefs and practices and examination of these in the light of Scripture.

   *Examples*: Beliefs about the character of God and reasons for suffering (Lesson 1)
   Beliefs about causes of HIV/AIDS (Lesson 6)

   Culturally and situationally relevant stories at the beginning of each lesson (adaptable to other cultures/situations) encourage discussion of sensitive topics and help reduce fear or shame regarding cultural taboos about personal sharing.

4. Written in simple English and other languages of wider communication (e.g., French, Portuguese, etc.) it is intended to be translated into the mother tongue of suffering communities because heart wounds heal best in heart languages. So far it has been translated into over 120 languages in Africa, Asia, and elsewhere.

5. It uses an adult learning approach that facilitates the healing process and promotes understanding of the material. Some activities included are: discussion questions, skit writing and performing, writing and sharing personal laments, composing and sharing songs, art exercises, taking wounds to the cross, listening and sharing exercises, and opportunities for prayer.

6. It uses visual aids to convey complex concepts such as "wounds of the heart" (Lesson 2), "journey of grief" (Lesson 3), and "cycle of forgiveness" (Lesson 9). Graphs and pictures in the book were based on familiar symbols or ideas from the cultures of African colleagues. These are also adaptable for other cultures.

## HOW THE BOOK IS USED

*Translation Workshops.* Church leaders from several traumatized areas gather together for two weeks in a safe, central location. They work through one lesson each morning to understand the content and learn how to teach it. In the afternoon, the language teams present (usually six to ten languages per workshop; two or three speakers per team) and translate it into their mother tongues. In the evening they share their personal stories of suffering and are prayed for by the whole group. Following the workshop, they return to their churches to use and test the translation draft in local workshops as they have been taught. A year later they return to a second workshop for final consultation, revision of the draft, and preparation of the book for publication.

*Training Workshops.* Workshops five days in length are held several times a year in various locations, including the US, the UK, Africa, and elsewhere. The meetings train church leaders and missionary workers in the content and use of the book in their locations. No translation is done but discussion about how to adapt the book for use in their ministries is a main goal of the training.

> Jesus said, "Truly, I say to you, there is no one who has left house or brothers or sisters or mother or father or children or lands, for my sake and for the gospel, who will not receive a hundredfold now in this time, houses and brothers and sisters and mothers and children and lands, with persecutions, and in the age to come eternal life. But many who are first will be last, and the last first." *Mark 10:29–31*

## QUESTIONS FOR REFLECTION

1. How would the content of the lessons presented in this article and the way they are taught help people to overcome their trauma and learn to help others?
2. What are some of the aspects which make these lessons so useful and applicable in different contexts of violence?
3. What are some of the traumas people in your country (home country or country of service) are going through? How could you adapt and apply these lessons to your own context?

## REFERENCE

Hill, M., H. Hill, R. Bagge, and P. Miersma. 2009. *Healing the wounds of trauma: How the church can help*, 3rd ed. Nairobi, Kenya: Paulines Publications Africa.

**Patricia Miersma** (MN, UCLA '84) serves as SIL International counseling consultant, specializing in community and cross-cultural issues related to trauma healing and post-traumatic stress disorder (PTSD). She is co-author of *Healing the Wounds of Trauma: How the Church Can Help*, and a senior consultant/trainer for its related workshops. She and her husband are RCA missionaries, seconded to Wycliffe Bible Translators as counselors since 1980, serving in Papua New Guinea and Africa, where they helped establish Tumaini Counseling Center in Nairobi.

# CHAPTER 64

# THE PLACE AND FUNCTION OF ACADEMICS

*Christof Sauer and Thomas Schirrmacher*

## A MATTER OF PERSPECTIVES

> Violations of religious freedom worldwide are massive, widespread, and in many parts of the world intensifying.… Attention to and action on religious freedom have been comparatively weak; … the important role of religion in conflicts and in political orders has been comparatively neglected; … both these situations are now beginning to change. (Marshall 2008, 11)

> The fuller story of the contemporary persecuted church remains a tragically untold story.… We must understand the dynamics of contemporary persecution better to ensure more effective intervention and assistance.… Western Christians require an encounter with the persecuted church to recover essential insights into their own faith, especially the biblical truth that there is no such thing as a non-persecuted believer. (Boyd-MacMillan 2006, 13–16)

The above quotes stem from two seminal books on religious freedom and the persecution of Christians and represent two different perspectives on the same matter. The first quote comes from a human-rights and religious freedom perspective and is based on survey work. The second quote comes from a book subtitled *The Essential Guide to the Persecuted Church* and aims at educating the church.

This article on the place and function of academics in understanding mission in contexts of suffering, persecution, and martyrdom finds itself between these two poles.[1] With Marshall, we share the academic approach, a concern for scholarly methodology and an appreciation of the potential that research tools of various academic disciplines are able to contribute to the issue. With Boyd-MacMillan, we share a Christian theological perspective and a focus on the Christian church.

In order to better assess what academics and academic studies can contribute, let us reflect on the role of the International Institute for Religious Freedom (IIRF) of the World

---

1     Leading research is referenced in Sauer (2008, 26–48) and Schirrmacher (2008) on which this article is partly based. The *International Journal for Religious Freedom* (www.iirf.eu) is a good source for further research and reviews of current scholarly books.

Evangelical Alliance. This institute connects researchers globally who in some way or another are researching and teaching on religious freedom and particularly the suffering, persecution, and martyrdom of Christians. What is the distinguishing mark of this institute in comparison to other existing agencies (which provide help and advocacy to persecuted Christians) and networks (such as the Religious Liberty Partnership)? We would like to explain this using the "Three Worlds Framework" of sociologist Johan Mouton (2001, 137–42). From the perspective of the sociology of science, three different levels of reflection on the world can be distinguished. The scholar should distinguish in which "world" he is operating:

- *World 1* is the world of everyday life and lay knowledge guided by pragmatic interests.
- *World 2* is the world of science and scientific research interested in knowing.
- *World 3* is the world of metascience guided by critical interest: how can one do science?

The advocacy agencies and the Religious Liberty Partnership largely operate in World 1: how can we help persecuted Christians? Some of them might also touch on World 2; however, their guiding interest is not scholarly but that of documenting and reporting, in the way journalists do. The IIRF wants to complement this daily business of fund-raising advocacy agencies and non-fund-raising networks by researching the issues surrounding the suffering, persecution, and martyrdom of Christians. The IIRF, therefore, is operating in World 2 when asking, "What can we know abut it?" and in World 3 with the question, "Can it be researched at all?" and "How can it be researched?" So this article on the place and function of academics will focus on Worlds 2 and 3, on science and metascience.

## THEOLOGICAL STUDIES

Diverse academic fields and academics both in theology and secular sciences are involved or should be involved when it comes to understanding the persecution of Christians. The following are only some sample areas:

1. *Theology in general*
   Academic theology must make persecution of Christians an important subject in all classical disciplines of theology, ranging from exegesis, dogmatics, ethics, and church history to practical theology and missiology. Pastoral counseling must deal with people traumatized by persecution.

2. *Ethics*
   Many issues raised by situations of persecution unfortunately are not considered standard matter and are omitted from curricula of ethics classes and from discussion in textbooks. That has to change. Questions on the use of passive resistance, the justification of violence in the defense of one's family, various issues of religious freedom, recourse to legal means, and appeal to courts are significant ethical challenges that occur in real life. They are actually more important and occur more frequently than some other minor issues routinely dealt with in ethics textbooks. Topics of fundamental relevance in ethics are: the rationale and full definition of the concept of religious

freedom, freedom of persuasion and mission, the right to change one's religion, and the relationship of religions to the state.

3. *Missiology*

When researching mission in history and the present, one will discover that missionary work is encountering considerable resistance, that churches are being persecuted as a result of missionary work, and that persecuted churches themselves are engaging in mission. These topics must not be relegated to mission agencies and missionaries only, but must become standard components of teaching and research in missiology. Gathering the voices from the Global South on a theology of suffering and making them heard globally as a theological voice that needs to be taken seriously is another task of missiology.

4. *Other theological fields*

Biblical studies should link persecution and godly response to persecution to the experience of contemporary Christians. Systematic theology should examine all doctrinal aspects regarding persecution, including the relationship between the suffering of Christ and his exaltation to glory to the fate of his disciples throughout all times. Church history must uncover where the church has wrongly persecuted dissenting believers or drawn persecution upon itself by faults of its own. But it should equally

> Since therefore Christ suffered in the flesh, arm yourselves with the same way of thinking, for whoever has suffered in the flesh has ceased from sin, so as to live for the rest of the time in the flesh no longer for human passions but for the will of God. *1 Peter 4:1–2*

refute false allegations based on stereotypes and misperceptions. The phenomenon of the vanishing of whole Christian traditions and the withering of ancient churches in history equally needs to be well understood in order to react appropriately to phenomena like the exodus or expulsion of Christians of ancient traditions from the Middle East in the broader context of history.

# SECULAR SCIENCES

5. *Sciences of religion and sociology of religion*

When persecution of Christians occurs, it is always a matter of both spiritual and ecclesiastical aspects as well as of the relationship of religions and worldviews with each other and with the state. Expert knowledge of other religions and worldviews can be of help here, in order to understand what is happening and to assess what—if anything—can be done about it.

In light of the fact that a considerable portion of persecution of Christians emanates from fundamentalist movements in Islam, Hinduism, etc., their scholarly exploration is as important as raising a voice in the debate about fundamentalism itself.[2]

---

2    In our view fundamentalism is not simply a truth claim or an intensive spirituality, but is characterized by the attempt to enforce a truth claim by violence and coercion.

6. *Social sciences (I)*

Social Sciences provide definitions and research tools in order to explore the specific situation of societies when it is not obvious. For example, only a recent empirical study on the views of Muslim Turks about their non-Muslim neighbors revealed the whole magnitude of hostility against Christians in Turkey.

At the same time empirical research can provide checks and balances for Christian news reporting on persecution. In a world of electronic social networks, e-mail, and short message service (SMS), rumors and hoaxes easily rise to the status of true facts. It actually harms advocacy for persecuted Christians when half truths and nonverifiable descriptions of persecution events are circulated. Besides, there are unfortunately so many evident and clearly verifiable deplorable events that there is no need to add any that are poorly researched, based on guesswork, or which are simply rumors.

7. *Social sciences (II)*

The issue of persecution of Christians has grown to be a matter of interest beyond Christian circles, finding attention in the media, politics, and security. Therefore, the reliability of our reports and whether they are taken seriously by the non-Christian public has become increasingly important. Well-documented research of the phenomenon of religious persecution grows the trust of the media and politicians and gains a hearing for the matter in circles beyond the usual influence of churches and mission agencies. It is largely due to solid research reports that federal parliaments, the OSCE, the UN, and international symposia are now discussing the persecution of Christians.

Verifiable research is all the more important when the matters described are being disputed. Then often an engagement with the topic (e.g., in journals and conferences) will become necessary in order to influence mainstream thinking. We can and must not refrain from this and sometimes this will open up further opportunities. Reports like the World Watch List or annual martyr figures have long become the subject of global secular news reporting. We will do well to thoroughly research our output, so that it can be emulated and verified well. We should also practice self-critical reflection and be open to outside criticism of our research.

One of the strengths of social sciences is "ranking." One can assess and list by rank the freedom or lack of freedom in a country, its attitude toward democracy, or the spread of racism. In the same way, religious freedom can be ranked—both with respect to the attitude of the state as well as that of society. Christians are needed both for on-the-ground research as well as for discussion on the usefulness of the results.

8. *Legal sciences and human-rights studies*

The legal defense of persecuted Christians as well as the drafting and implementation of enforceable laws defending the human right of religious freedom are gaining in importance globally. Jurisprudence must increasingly deal with the ethics of religious persuasion, the age of religious maturity of children, religious freedom, etc. Christian legal scholars should take the lead and be available as experts for discussion. Jurists, in particular, are able to expose the continuing attempts of Islamic states within the realm of the UN to restrict or eradicate religious freedom.

All other scholarly disciplines that have a bearing on human rights are equally needed for engagement.

9. *Political sciences, international relations, and conflict and peace research*
Issues of the organization of state, of democracy, and of human rights closely relate to how the adherents of a country's majority religion see religious freedom and how religious minorities are treated. Religious minorities, among whom are often evangelicals, have played an important role in the past for the development of human rights and the development of religious freedom. They should continue to do so, particularly through competent academic representatives.

It is evident that peace studies must also include the question of how people of different religions can live together peacefully. It is our task to competently explicate that religious freedom produces peaceful societies, while countries without religious freedom and with a coercive religious majority or state religion usually have more violent revolutions and movements (Grim and Finke 2011).

10. *Other academic disciplines*
The phenomenon of persecution of Christians, as well as the persecution of other religious people, concerns hundreds of millions of people and therefore must be studied at universities.

The discipline of geography must explore spatial dimensions and produce maps, political sciences must explore concepts, and psychology must help those who are traumatized by persecution. All this will only happen if there are competent Christian academics who are studying these issues and who are taken seriously by their academic colleagues.

Academics and academic research can play an important role in drawing the right conclusions concerning persecution on the basis of facts and solid analysis. It must operate on the basis of a deeply anchored biblical understanding of suffering and martyrdom.

## QUESTIONS FOR REFLECTION
1. Can you describe situations in which the result of research could help the persecuted church?
2. Should we be in constant discussion with secular experts concerning persecution and religious freedom or will they never really understand the persecuted church anyway?
3. How and where in curricula should persecution studies be incorporated into theological training?

# REFERENCES

Boyd-MacMillan, R. 2006. *Faith that endures: The essential guide to the persecuted church.* Grand Rapids, MI: Revell.

Grim, B. J., and R. Finke. 2011. *The price of freedom denied: Religious persecution and conflict in the twenty-first century.* New York: Cambridge University Press.

Marshall, P. A., ed. 2008. *Religious freedom in the world.* Lanham, MD: Rowman and Littlefield.

Mouton, J. 2001. *How to succeed in your master's and doctoral studies: A South African guide and resource book.* Pretoria: Van Schaik.

Sauer, C. 2008. Researching persecution and martyrdom: Part 1; The external perspective. *International Journal for Religious Freedom* 1 no. 1: 26–48.

Schirrmacher, T. 2008. *Christenverfolgung: Die vergessenen märtyrer.* Holzgerlingen: Hänssler. [English translation pending.]

**Christof Sauer,** German, is co-director of the International Institute for Religious Freedom (Bonn, Cape Town, Colombo) and an editor of the *International Journal for Religious Freedom.* From Cape Town, South Africa, he supervises doctoral students in missiology and religious freedom studies at the University of South Africa. He is an associate professor extraordinary of the department of practical theology and missiology of the Theological Faculty at Stellenbosch University.

**Thomas Schirrmacher,** German, is director of the International Institute for Religious Freedom (Bonn, Cape Town, Colombo) and serves as chair of WEA's Theological Commission. Based in Germany, he holds extensive professorial and presidential roles across Europe as well as in Shillong, India, teaching sociology of religion, theology, global ethics, and international development.

# CHAPTER 65

# THE PLACE AND FUNCTION OF RESEARCH

*Steve Sang-Cheol Moon*

## INTRODUCTION

The notion of "reflective practitioner" posits the importance of combining reflection and practice in missions (Taylor 2000, 5–6). Reflection without practice is irresponsible abstraction. Practice without reflection is naive activism. To put reflection and practice together, research is needed. Research enables combining practice and reflection.

Reflective practitioners in the contexts of suffering, persecution, and martyrdom need to delve into what it means to be faithful and accountable in their contexts. Research certainly has a place and a function in these kinds of ministerial situations. It is more urgently required for reflective practitioners to invest their time and energy on research and development in those contexts.

In this chapter, we attempt to clarify the place and function of research in the uneasy ministerial contexts of suffering, persecution, and martyrdom. Difficult situations need to be approached with more caution, so we need even more research to address those contextual hardships. Purity and wisdom of mind are combined in and through research.

## THE PLACE OF RESEARCH

Research is not only involved in ministries in the contexts of hardship, but also plays important roles in every ministerial context (Nussbaum 2007, 148–49). In normal situations, research aims at promoting the effectiveness and efficiency of ministries. In difficult situations, research may also contribute to alleviating and coping in hardships.

The nature of missiology as a discipline between and betwixt text and context posits the necessity of empirical research. Empirical research is a good foundation for down-to-earth approaches in incarnational ministries (Hiebert 2008, 89–104). It reinforces a humble attitude toward the cultural contexts of ministries. It is only natural that missional theologies reflect and address context-specific issues and problems based on empirical findings. The empirical dimension of missiology should highlight the wholistic needs of mankind, one of which is related to human suffering. Environmental scan in this kind of situation is not a matter of choice, but of must.

The task of contextualization presupposes contextual research. Without solid contextual research, contextualization is merely an abstract process. Contextual research sharpens the focus of contextualization. Contextual research with a future perspective is envisioning. "Envisioning" is beginning with the end in mind, that is, beginning a ministry with the very end purpose of the ministry efforts and activities in mind (Felder and Bennett 1995, 35–39). Contextualization of churches, theologies, worship styles, leadership structures, organizational cultures, or other artifacts of faith is possible with envisioning or imagineering (or reimageneering) based on contextual research. The contextual research requires both historical and cultural understanding. Both of them should be combined with biblical understanding.

The core of contextual research is cultural exegesis. Cultural exegesis enables cultural understanding at a deeper level in a systematic way. Cultural exegesis also makes it possible for the cross-cultural workers to do needs assessment for ministries. Cultural exegesis lays the foundation for contingency planning. Contingency planning is an important part of ministry obligation, and it is even more so in the sensitive areas. Cultural exegesis, in this sense, is not a task of purely theoretical research, but one of applied research. It is also to be understood as a process to be continued and renewed for up-to-date and relevant situational understanding. This process is a spiral process, which is dynamically driven by ministry foci, purposes, approaches, and methods.

The limitation of empirical research is clear and evident in the sense that we cannot fathom the depth of the transcendental world in our experience through our sensing. Accordingly, we cannot control the environments of our ministry world with our knowledge and expertise. We must humbly acknowledge our finiteness and limitedness as human beings. We must confess that we cannot control the course of history. We must accept the historical givens that might lead to suffering, persecution, and even martyrdom sometimes. The scope of research is only whether we will accept, resist, or flee from those kinds of situations, not changing the course of given conditions. Nevertheless, the limitation of research does not prove that research is worthless, but only suggests the best possible way to serve the Lord in a faithful and wise way. For this reason, empirical research should be integrated with biblical and theological insights. The reference points are the biblical norms, which should precede the theological or cultural guidelines.

"And brother will deliver brother over to death, and the father his child, and children will rise against parents and have them put to death. And you will be hated by all for my name's sake. But the one who endures to the end will be saved."
Mark 13:12–13

The clash of worldviews is more serious in the global age than before. There are more cases of religious persecution in this phenomenon. This makes the cultural research more complex. A local perspective is not enough. We need a global perspective in our research. It is not just a matter of *emic* or *etic*, but of glocal. A glocal view can subtly differentiate and yet connect the local and global understandings at the same time. The ministry situation under hardship is both a local and global problem for the global church. Missional cultural exegesis or environmental scan should address this problem. The empirical research in the global age should be thoroughly up-to-date as relevant understanding needs frequent updates. Many reports of area studies and ethnographies are too outdated. We need to address new issues and research problems in this rapidly changing world. In order to do that kind of research more effectively and efficiently, we need to focus on the strategic information needed to understand the suffering contexts. We need to summarize the stories, not just the numbers of persecuted Christians and churches, and share them with the global church so that all parts of the body of Christ can share in the suffering, paying the price for being Christian.

The context of suffering, persecution, and martyrdom hastens empirical research even more than before, and calls for a sense of urgency in sharing real-life stories rather than any abstract discursion or idle collection of basic data. We need to gather strategic information for our decision making. Regardless of the limitations of empirical research, we need to invest in field-based research projects to get the right information. That is because the quality of the available Internet resources is not so good, the monographs are too out-dated, and the journals are too selective.

## THE FUNCTION OF RESEARCH

Research is not magic, but it plays an important function. The promise of research can be summarized in seven points. First of all, field-based empirical research clarifies the purpose of ministry. Secondly, it helps find appropriate ministry methods. Thirdly, it facilitates innovation in ministry. Fourthly, it makes the allotment of tasks possible for team ministries. Fifthly, it lays the foundation for contextualization. Sixthly, it raises the levels of effectiveness and efficiency of ministry. Seventhly, it helps avoid repeating the same mistakes in ministry. A well-done field-based research brings about the overall improvement of ministry performance. This observation is also true in real contexts of hardship.

In order for the research to perform these important functions, it should appropriate relevant research methods. Research methods include research design, data gathering, and data analysis. Research design should be realistic enough to be executed in missional contexts. Too rigorous research design hinders the actual execution of research by ordinary missionaries who need to understand such basic issues as validity and reliability. Simple methods that can lead to profound findings are the wisest strategy in research design in real missional contexts, especially in sensitive areas. Data gathering strategies should also adjust to missional conditions. Often times, questionnaire surveys are not possible in creative access countries, which guides us to consider qualitative approaches. Participant observation and ethnographic interviews are two important means of data gathering for a qualitative research. Even the interview questions should remain descriptive and open-ended instead of delving into the point hurriedly. Building rapport is a critical capability in this approach. It is all the more true in sensitive areas. Data analysis techniques have developed phenomenally over the last thirty years in qualitative research. The whole body of theory in cognitive anthropology seeks to overcome the traditional limitations of qualitative data analysis. Missionary researchers do not have to follow the whole discussions surrounding analysis of qualitative data, but it suffices here to comment that we need to focus our direction of analysis toward worldview exegesis. Worldview exegesis can be done more systematically as we attempt at semiotic analysis (Moon 1998, 308–13; Hiebert 2008, 97). Another recent strategy of schema analysis is also a concrete and useful suggestion.

The future of research is not bright considering the activistic orientation of missioners. There are certain stereotypes that have been accumulated in the history of missions, some of which need to be challenged in this ever-globalizing world. Following are several developmental issues for the future of field-based empirical research. Firstly, missionaries must understand research as a foundation of ministry. Secondly, seminaries and missionary training centers should be able to equip their students to write field-based dissertations, projects, theses, and reports. Thirdly, international research networks should be strengthened to the level of strategic alliance. Fourthly, qualitative research methods need to be developed and appropriated further in mission studies. Fifthly, missionary researchers need to update their understanding about research methods in both quantitative and qualitative approaches (Hiebert 2009, 162–64). Sixthly, a good teamwork between national and expatriate workers is necessary to escalate the level of empirical research. Seventhly, research grants should be established to encourage and promote researchers not only in the younger missionary sending countries but also in the older missionary sending countries. With these conditions met, the quality of research will be consolidated, and the breakthrough of mission will be visible.

In the contexts of suffering, persecution, and martyrdom mission research should be sensitive enough to reflect those realities in its whole process. The function of research in that kind of situation should be preventive and proactive rather than reactive. The task of environmental scan and envisioning should also address those questions and lay the foundation for such a function. In many contexts, the need for knowledge workers with expertise is great. The global missions community needs to find those experts and make the best use of research networks. Contingency planning needs expertise, too. Expertise in crisis counseling is much needed, but often neglected among the churches. Expertise for missionary deployment is also urgently needed for missionary sending countries. Expertise in the trends of world religions at both formal and folk levels is definitely needed. The global missions community needs to accumulate expertise and develop the knowledge base at the country, regional, and global levels.

## CONCLUSION

Research is related both to reflection and practice. A happy coexistence and combination of reflection and practice is possible with the function of research. A traditional understanding of the place of research could be expressed metaphorically as the root of a tree or the foundation of a building. In this globally contingent world, the place of research is not fixed on one part, but is more or less ubiquitous. The function of research in those contexts is multifunctional. The place and function of research cannot be overemphasized considering the orientation of activism among missioners, especially in the younger missionary sending countries. Activism is a sign of immaturity in the missionary movements. A mind-set of critical realism in the contexts of hardship should emphasize learning attitude, which will lead to the growth of research.

## QUESTIONS FOR REFLECTION

1. How can we integrate theological insights and empirical findings in missiological research?
2. How can missiologists and mission researchers cooperate with field missionaries for empirical research?
3. How can the global missions circle raise the level of quality for international research projects?

## REFERENCES

Felder, K., and S. Bennett. 1995. *Exploring the land.* Littleton, CO: Caleb Project.

Hiebert, P. G. 2008. *Transforming worldviews: An anthropological understanding of how people change.* Grand Rapids, MI: Baker Academic.

———. 2009. *The gospel in human contexts: Anthropological explorations for contemporary missions.* Grand Rapids, MI: Baker Academic.

Moon, S. 1998. *A hermeneutical model of urban religious symbols: The case of Konya, Turkey.* PhD diss. Trinity International University.

Nussbaum, S. 2007. *Breakthrough! Steps to research and resolve the mysteries in your ministry.* Colorado Springs, CO: GMI Research Services.

Taylor, W. D. 2000. From Iguassu to the reflective practitioners of the global family of Christ. In *Global missiology for the twenty-first century*, ed. W. D. Taylor, 3–13. Grand Rapids, MI: Baker Academic.

**Steve Sang-Cheol Moon** is director of the Korea Research Institute for Mission, based in Seoul, South Korea. He is married to Mary Hee-Joo, with two children who are now university students. Steve is the foremost researcher and voice on church and missions in Korea. He earned a PhD in intercultural studies from Trinity Evangelical Divinity School.

Suffering, then, is the badge of true discipleship. The disciple is not above his master. Following Christ means *passio passiva*, suffering because we have to suffer. That is why Luther reckoned suffering among the marks of the true Church, and one of the memoranda drawn up in preparation for the Augsburg Confession similarly defines the Church as the community of those "who are persecuted and martyred for the gospel's sake." If we refuse to take up our cross and submit to suffering and rejection at the hands of men, we forfeit our fellowship with Christ and have ceased to follow him. But if we lose our lives in his service and carry our cross, we shall find our lives again in the fellowship of the cross with Christ. The opposite of discipleship is to be ashamed of Christ and his cross and all the offense which the cross brings in its train.

D. Bonhoeffer in *The Cost of Discipleship* (1976, 100f)

# PART FIVE

# FINAL THEMES

## LESSONS FROM CELTIC CHRISTIANS

As we come to the last main section of our book, we wonder how to respond? We are called to pray; but what more can we do? We are now challenged to thoughtful advocacy and courageous action. We discover a beautiful liturgy to use in a celebration of the International Day of Prayer for the Persecuted Church (IDOP).

Briefly, let us mull over some lessons from Celtic Christianity and some of their leading voices: Patrick, Columba, Columbanus, Aidan, Hild, Ita, to name only a few. Celtic Christianity shaped Ireland and other areas of the British Isles particularly from the fourth to the eighth centuries. In a real sense they did "save" Western civilization by preserving education, libraries, art, and Scripture manuscripts. Their demise began during the ninth century when the Viking invasions destroyed many communities. Displaced, Celtic Christians were pushed to the margins of the British Isles. In 664 at the Council of Whitby, Roman Christianity officially trumped Celtic ecclesiology. Even so, revivals of Celtic Christian spirituality periodically surface and break out in Great Britain, spilling out to bless the world once again. We currently enjoy a revival of Christian Celtic studies, music, mission, and spirituality.

Celtic core values included a high view of and love for Scripture and trinitarianism, a deep interior life of prayer and holiness, a commitment to simplicity, a holistic respect for creation, importance placed on gathered community, engagement with spiritual warfare, a broader role for women in church and mission, the release of the visual and musical arts, the sending of both older and younger generations into mission, and mission that flowed from community and spirituality. Theirs was more of a relational rather than hierarchical social religious structure. Finally, they prepared, sustained, and sent teams into ministry—flowing out and returning back to community.

Over the years these lessons and values have become very meaningful personally as we have traveled the British Isles and Ireland, visiting key sites of historic Celtic missional communities, sites which even today retain a powerful spiritual presence.

These Celtic believers spoke of mission in the term *peregrinatio* (pilgrimage, or wanderlust to explore the unknown; hence mission). Their symbol for the Holy Spirit was the wild goose, untamable, coming and going, calling from afar, driven with or against the wind to unknown lands. This *peregrinatio* led them to evangelize the wild Picts (Scotland), Wales, much of north central and southwest England, and as far as Italy, the Ukraine, and Byzantium.

Celtic Christians developed a tricolored theology of martyrdom. White martyrdom spoke of the costly pain of leaving behind family, clan, and tribe to spread the gospel of Christ. Green martyrdom spoke of self denial and penitential acts that led to personal holiness. And red martyrdom spoke of persecution, bloodshed, or death.

There you have it: *peregrinatio* and the tri-colored martyrdom of mission and sacrifice.
—*Yvonne and William D. Taylor*

# CHAPTER 66

# PRAYER WITHOUT CEASING

## Lessons from the Persecuted Church

*Mindy Belz*

I have learned most about praying for the persecuted church by watching how the persecuted church prays for itself.

Insaf Safou had known me for about ten minutes when she asked me to pray with her. We were wedged into the back seat of a taxi dodging traffic in Amman on the way to Jordan's Queen Alia airport, luggage piled around us. It was 2003, nearly nine months following the US invasion, and she was making her first journey back to Iraq since escaping nearly a decade before. She had agreed to take me, a journalist she'd never met, along for the ride.

Insaf and her husband once had good jobs in Baghdad—she teaching physics at an elite high school, he working as a chef in one of Saddam Hussein's palaces. Insaf was born into a Catholic family but with her husband became a Protestant believer under the teaching she received at the Evangelical Presbyterian Church of Kirkuk. Together they could navigate some of the highest circles of the Iraqi ruler's Baath Party. That is, until Insaf decided after prayer and soul-searching that she could not show favoritism in the classroom to children of Baath Party members. Officials had asked her to give those students the highest grades. She lost her job and the couple, at the time parents of two young children, quickly realized their lives too were in danger.

The family made a dramatic escape, on foot, across the mountainous northern border of Iraq into Turkey. For seven years they lived in Istanbul as stateless refugees until Canadian authorities agreed to take them in. During that time, Insaf never stopped praying. She prayed for the churches in Iraq she'd left behind. She solicited lists of needy families in Iraq from pastors she knew and prayed for those strangers. Through her family that remained behind, she learned of new churches opened after the US invasion that sent Saddam into hiding in 2003.

A cousin became pastor for one of the fastest growing new churches in Baghdad and regularly sent her prayer lists from his congregation. With a new government and new freedom in Iraq, Insaf's prayers of compassion for the church in Iraq helped raise her courage along with the funds to return in late November 2003. By then she also had raised thousands of dollars from Iraqi refugees living in Canada to deliver to Christian families in Iraq. And that's why we had to pray in the taxi.

Between Amman's Ring Road and the airport, we prayed for the families in Canada who gave, and for the Iraqis—whom we did not know—who would receive. We prayed for the churches in Iraq. We prayed for the pastors by name. We prayed for our time together, for our families, our health and well-being so that we could help others. We prayed for the pilots who would take us there. It was the beginning of weeks of praying with Insaf that has stretched—she in Toronto, me in North Carolina—into years.

In Baghdad that year, we stayed together in a house rented only months before by an Iraqi Christian family just returned from exile in Jordan. The electricity was off more than it was on, and our host would drip wax from a candle onto the desk beside our beds, then plant the lit candle upright in the hot wax between us. By candlelight Insaf would slump to her knees on the floor, bent double like a child hiding her eyes, to pray softly in the dark.

Together with our hosts we endured gas lines and food shortages, heard bombs explode in the night, and saw needs in the neighborhood too great for us—bomb craters and sewage percolating from broken pipes beneath the street, children afraid to go to school, and adults who remained fearless about going to church. And we prayed on.

Insaf's prayers, uttered low and quiet but without hesitation, were much like those she posts daily on Facebook today: "Father, thank you for another day to worship you and become more like you. I submit my heart, mind, will, and emotions to you. I choose to treat others with love and respect, which shows that I honor you. Have your way in me and teach me to pray effectively for your glory, in Jesus' name. Amen."

The fearless testimonies of today's persecuted believers aren't so different from the record we have of Stephen, the church's first martyr. Before his death, Acts 6 says that church leaders chose him as one of the first deacons because he was "a man full of faith and of the Holy Spirit" who did "great wonders and signs among the people" (Acts 6:5,8). He was not a victim waiting for pity.

As the angry mob stoned Stephen, his face was like the face of an angel; gazing into heaven he was able to see the glory of God. To pray for persecuted believers, then, the rest of us can begin with joy because they find joy in their suffering and in their own prayers, too.

> Rejecting joy to stand in solidarity with the suffering doesn't rescue the suffering. The converse does. The brave who focus on all things good and all things beautiful and all things true, even in the small, who give thanks for it and discover joy even in the here and now, they are the change agents who bring fullest Light to all the world. (Voskamp 2010, 58)

What we can expect as we pray with joy for the persecuted is to find fruit. Strange as it seems, unexpected fruit awaits in the very bowels of suffering and hardship.

Sayed Musa is a forty-six-year-old Muslim convert to Christianity. Authorities in Afghanistan threw him into one of the harshest jails in Kabul after they discovered him taking part in a baptism and worship service. He remained jailed with militant Islamic captives, including Taliban members, who beat him and sexually abused him.

"They beat me by wood, by hands, by legs, put some things on my head, mocked me [saying], 'He's Jesus Christ,'" Musa wrote from his prison cell. Yet as months passed and a judge threatened him with death by hanging, Musa grew bolder in proclaiming the gospel to fellow inmates, leading three to saving faith in Jesus Christ.

Musa told the judge on his case that he wanted to be tried and hanged in public, "where I will introduce the Son of God to all people of the world, especially Afghan people." Instead he was freed in February 2011, eight months after his arrest. By that time his case was known in the halls of Congress and the White House; it had been raised in the highest diplomatic circles in Afghanistan and during at least one meeting between President Hamid Karzai and US commander General David Petraeus.

All the while, more and more people around the world heard of his case and prayed for Musa. I know because as I wrote stories about him, some wrote to me asking what they could do, longing for visible fruit. We never fully know what happens when the church prays for the persecuted, but expect fruit to grow, for both the one who prays and the one who is prayed for. I heard from Christians who got together in their churches to pray for Musa and ended up praying for all of Afghanistan, from Christians who prayed for Musa then wrote their congressman or other officials. One of those praying for Musa wrote me to say she'd asked a handwriting analyst to examine his published handwriting. "He is a truth teller," the expert wrote back. "See if you can find him help. Send to the State Dept."

After finding joy and finding fruit, those who pray best for the persecuted do so by finding hope, as Musa did. "Whether I prayed to be released or to die and be with Jesus, it is the same for me," he told me. Jesus teaches us to be thankful in all circumstances. Handed five loaves and two fish to feed five thousand, Jesus looked to heaven and gave thanks. At the Passover meal, Jesus proclaimed his betrayal and his broken body, but said a prayer of thanksgiving too.

Few of us think to begin our prayers for the persecuted with thanksgiving, but this is the model we have received from the Lord. It's rooted in hope that their suffering is working out a vast array of good.

> But I say to you, Love your enemies and pray for those who persecute you, so that you may be sons of your Father who is in heaven.
> Matthew 5:44-45

Praying with hope also means praying for the enemies of the persecuted, and the persecutors themselves. This we learn too from Jesus, and as we watch the persecuted pray for those who cause them to suffer.

Karachi is one of the most dangerous cities in the world, but I know a pastor who continues to preach despite having been arrested, having "enemies" infiltrate his services, and serving at funerals for those killed because they are part of Pakistan's Christian minority. One Easter morning he preached on the first words of Jesus on the cross: "Father, forgive them, for they know not what they do" (Luke 23:34). In addition to praying for the enemies outside the church, he said, "Most everyone in the church made confessions with their family and friends who they were not talking to or have some anger or grudge for in their hearts. People were thankful to know the power that the gospel offers."

Musa, locked in his Kabul jail cell, also found freedom in forgiveness: "This 'love your enemy like yourself,' to which other religion you find this word? Just in Christianity you find this word."

In Iraq, Insaf prayed with a member of the evangelical church in Kirkuk whose husband was killed by a roadside bomb. He left behind a thirteen-year-old daughter. The church itself has faced persistent bomb threats, even one dismantled by police just outside the entrance gate in 2011.

"She starts to cry and I hold her hand and she said, 'I'm burning from inside, Insaf. I feel I'm on fire.' Then I start to cry with her and I say, 'Can I pray with you?' And I pray for the power of the love of God to turn this fire to be like cold water to give her the peace of God. And after we prayed I feel her calm down. So she cried and we prayed, but in the midst of praying for her I feel the Holy Spirit coming in her, in me, and she said, 'Come back again.'"

And for both Insaf and this widow, that was the beginning of new answers to prayer. Insaf has gone back many times, and out of her visits helped to develop a women's ministry in the Kirkuk church, supporting women leaders who minister to other women. They in turn are supporting many needy women, including many widows. In 2011 they began an outreach to a local women's prison, the first of its kind.

Insaf later told me that she said to the widow, "My pocket is empty, my hand is empty, but I can pray for you and be your voice and be your heart and talk with my mouth and see how God provides." That is the way of prayer for the persecuted—praying with compassion, with joy, expecting fruit, and full of hope.

## QUESTIONS FOR REFLECTION

1. Discuss the importance and wider applicability of the chapter's first sentence.
2. The author helpfully develops and repeats several clear, key principles of prayer both by and for the persecuted. What are they?
3. At least twice, this chapter indicates how prayer for the persecuted can result in other action on their behalf. Discuss the significance of this.
4. A prominent persecuted Afghan Christian is described in this chapter as "not a victim waiting for pity." Discuss the ramifications of this observation.

## REFERENCE

Voskamp, A. 2010. *One thousand gifts*. Grand Rapids, MI: Zondervan.

**Mindy Belz** is the editor of *World Magazine*. As a journalist of twenty-five years, she has traveled to war zones in the Balkans, Sudan, the Middle East, and Asia. Her more recent writing has included coverage of the persecuted in the Middle East, Iraq, and Afghanistan. She is the mother of four children and is married to writer and editor Nat Belz.

# CHAPTER 67

# A CALL

## Accurate Information, Urgent Intercession, Thoughtful Advocacy, and Courageous Action

*Faith J. H. McDonnell*

Western Christians sing, "These are days of great trial, of famine and darkness and sword," (Robin Mark, "Days of Elijah"). But for Christians across the globe, this is not a song, but reality. In the persecuted church we confront both great suffering and vibrant faith. We embrace emaciated bodies, see scars and bruises, and hear the weeping of widows and orphans. Knowing their suffering, we can never again pretend to *not* know. We must commit in our personal lives and in the public arena to pray for, speak out about, and act on behalf of the persecuted church.

## ACCURATE, COMPREHENSIVE INFORMATION

Intercession and advocacy require accurate, comprehensive information. Today, facts are easily acquired over the Internet, but so are false or exaggerated reports. Stories should be confirmed through several sources.

Alternately, understated facts downplay a situation's severity. And sometimes euphemisms are used that create a sense of moral equivalency between the persecutor and the victim. Such is the case when Christian persecution is described simply as "ethnic conflict" or when statements such as "abuses have been committed on both sides" lack further explanation or justification.

Some church leaders believe that silence is the best policy. They think that speaking out will exacerbate hostilities. But we must honor the wishes of fellow Christians around the world. Some ask only for prayer. Some ask that we be their voice to the world. Still others publicly ask only for prayer, but privately ask that we raise awareness. These are people with a gun to their head—they cannot cry out. Do not accept silence as proof that all is well.

## URGENT INTERCESSION

Accurate, comprehensive information enables knowledgeable and urgent prayer for persecuted Christians. All advocacy should begin, end, and be infused with prayer. The late president of the Institute on Religion and Democracy, Diane Knippers, advised:

> Pray not only for a broken heart, but a big heart. Your heart will be broken. You will weep. Sometimes you will be tempted to pull away. You will feel guilty because you

have so much—materially and in terms of freedom—and the persecuted have so little. Pray for a heart big enough to obey the God of the nations. Big enough to embrace a child sold into slavery. Big enough to remember Chinese church leaders. Big enough to play your part in the household of faith.

Aids to intercession:

- Start a persecuted church prayer group and hold an all-night or all-day prayer vigil.
- Include the persecuted church during prayers at church every Sunday.
- Provide bulletin inserts with prayer points.
- During baptisms, pray for Christian converts from Islam and pastors who secretly baptize them.
- Read testimonies from the persecuted church.
- Carry crosses in worship, and pray for the Dinka and other Sudanese who carry crosses.
- Observe the International Day of Prayer for the Persecuted Church each year.
- Collect and frequently update materials on the persecuted church for a church prayer chapel.
- Use a globe, world map, or newspaper in family prayer time.

We pray for the persecuted church because God commands it, because they are our family, and because it works. God answers prayer. Finally, we pray because God changes our hearts and motivates us to action.

## THOUGHTFUL ADVOCACY

Today we are not limited to writing letters, as advocates once did to Christian prisoners, prison camp officials, and members of Congress or Parliament (or whatever system of government allows such). We receive and send messages almost instantaneously. And since the passage of the United States 1998 International Religious Freedom Act (IRFA), religious freedom has been enshrined in American foreign policy. Other advocacy resources include the US Commission on International Religious Freedom, created as a result of IRFA and the religious freedom office in the US State Department.

Thoughtful and effective advocates will utilize all of these tools. They will work for the persecuted with churches of all denominations as well as with concerned non-Christians. It was an American Jewish man, Michael Horowitz, who was the catalyst for increased US government awareness of global Christian persecution in the 1990s movement to defend the persecuted church. In addition, several Jewish organizations shared strategies from the campaign to free Soviet Jewry.

Effective advocates will also win the hearts and minds of young people. Start by teaching elementary school children to pray for persecuted Christians and inviting Christians from persecuted regions to come and speak to Sunday schools and youth groups. The message of the persecuted church should also be communicated increasingly through social networking, visual arts, literature, music, drama, dance, and film.

Many young people across America, Europe, and beyond are already active advocates, passionate about justice. American high school and college students have fueled the movement to rescue northern Ugandan children from the Lord's Resistance Army. They have raised awareness about international sex trafficking. And they have been stalwart in efforts to end genocide in Darfur and support peace and freedom in South Sudan. But global Christian persecution is a justice issue as well.

There is no dichotomy between spiritual warfare and political and social advocacy. To those uneasy about political involvement, the Right Reverend Munawar Rumalshah, former bishop of Peshawar, Pakistan exhorts Americans, "Keep on working on Capitol Hill. Keep on raising public awareness of the injustices suffered by Christians." After his congressional testimony, Rumalshah thanked America for fighting for global religious freedom, saying, "In our system I see this as the most effective way to help the persecuted."

## COURAGEOUS ACTION

The call for accurate information, urgent intercession, thoughtful advocacy, and courageous action is God's call for Western Christians to stand with the persecuted church. Courage to act comes when the Lord fills us with a passion for the persecuted, a passion exemplified by David and Nehemiah.

David was passionate in his response to Goliath's mockery of the army of Israel in the Valley of Elah, announcing that he had come "in the name of the Lord Almighty, the God of the armies of Israel, whom you have defied." He tells the giant that "the whole world will know that there is a God in Israel" and that all gathered will know ""that it is not by sword or spear that the Lord saves; for the battle is the Lord's" (1 Sam 17:45–47). To Saul and his cowering troops, David declares, "The Lord who rescued me from the paw of the lion and the paw of the bear will rescue me from the hand of this Philistine" (17:37).

Passion for the persecuted church is outrage—holy anger at the affront to the Lord when his people are persecuted. Persecution is evil, always an offense to God. Passion for the persecuted church is also zealousness to not only defend our brothers and sisters but to defend the Lord's honor. It does not honor God when Christians are so apathetic or self-focused that they cannot pray and act for those in his church body who are suffering. And passion for the persecuted church is confidence in the Lord who is able to rescue his people from today's vicious lions, bears, and giants.

Nehemiah's passion gave him boldness to ask King Artaxerxes for permission to go back to Jerusalem and rebuild it (Neh 2:5). Even more boldly, he asked the king for letters to the governors of the regions, permitting him to travel, and to the keeper of the king's forest, asking for free lumber! But Nehemiah had prayed before he made his requests and God directed his actions.

Passion did not cause Nehemiah to act rashly or imprudently, but strategically. He had received permission and provisions from the king. Then he recruited productive, creative people to assist him. His helpers were not fulfilling their usual functions (3:1–32). Priests, goldsmiths, perfume makers, and women all became construction workers and repairers in order to get the job done.

Passion for the persecuted church is boldness, to ask Western Christians, far removed from the realities in Sudan, Egypt, Burma, Indonesia, China, North Korea, and so many other places, to invest their time, money, energy, and emotions in those places. It means going outside our own comfort zones and helping others to move outside theirs.

Some people are called by God to do "nothing" but pray for the persecuted church. They really *do* pray, and their prayers move heaven and earth. Others, who protest that prayer is their only calling, God may actually be calling to move outside their comfort zone of prayer and act courageously, demonstrating outside an embassy or visiting their member of Congress. We are all called to pray, but our prayer should inspire most of us to courageous action—prayerful action, but action nonetheless.

> By faith Moses, when he was grown up, refused to be called the son of Pharaoh's daughter, choosing rather to be mistreated with the people of God than to enjoy the fleeting pleasures of sin. He considered the reproach of Christ greater wealth than the treasures of Egypt, for he was looking to the reward. *Hebrews 11:24–26*

Before the world and the church, the persecuted church is a testimony to God's grace. In his mysterious ways, God has given us the privilege of standing in solidarity with his persecuted ones through intercession, advocacy, and action. What will be our testimony before the world and the persecuted church?

## QUESTIONS FOR REFLECTION

1. What are some principles and some aids for effective intercessory prayer for the persecuted?
2. Discuss the sentence under the "Thoughtful Advocacy" heading which reads, "There is no dichotomy between spiritual warfare and political and social advocacy."
3. Recall some principles McDonnell draws from the narratives of David and Nehemiah for what she calls "courageous action."

**Faith J. H. McDonnell** directs the Institute on Religion and Democracy's Religious Liberty Program and Church Alliance for a New Sudan, Washington, DC, and is the coauthor of *Girl Soldier: A Story of Hope for Northern Uganda's Children* (Chosen Books, 2007). She has been an advocate for the persecuted church and other human-rights issues since 1993.

# CHAPTER 68

# A SERVICE OF THOUGHTFUL PRAYER FOR THE PERSECUTED CHURCH

## International Day of Prayer for the Persecuted Church

*Yvonne Christine DeAcutis Taylor*

## INTRODUCTORY NOTES AS YOU PREPARE FOR THIS SOLEMN CELEBRATION

1. As you consider the ideas used in this liturgy, feel free to adapt them in light of your own situation and goals. This liturgy focuses on prayer, forms of worship, and quiet meditation.
2. This service will last approximately 60–90 minutes, depending on whether or not you celebrate Holy Communion.
3. This service requires a committed team that will pray it into reality. It requires a lot of preparatory work, but we promise you that you and your people will not soon forget it.
4. I chose to incorporate as many of the senses as possible in the service, and we encourage you to do so as a way of engaging the total person in the total service. There are things to hear (music, Scripture), to see (flags of the nations, the setting itself, candles, visuals), to smell (candles or possibly incense), to touch (the bulletin, the flags, or candles to carry), to taste (if you conclude with the service of Holy Communion).
5. In some churches the service of Holy Communion may be included, but this lengthens the liturgy. It was not incorporated into this liturgy.
6. For special introductory and concluding points in the service, I have chosen music from the Russian Orthodox heritage. There is a solemnity and power about it. But feel free in different geographic and cultural contexts to use other forms of music. Well-played drums are primal and can serve the same points of the liturgy well.
7. We provide the master order of service for those directing the program, and at the end you will find paragraphs to introduce the bulletin handout for all. This services uses the New Living Translation (2003).

## GUIDELINES FOR THE COORDINATORS

1. Before people arrive, prepare the setting with lit candles in different sizes and colors, small candles for children and youth, larger ones for adults (representing the diversity

of the persecuted church). Red can refer to the persecuted and white to the martyrs of Revelation 6:11. Use flags from nations where Christians are persecuted today. The worship center lighting is dimmed.

2. As people enter they receive the handout, enter into the worship center, and sit in silence.

3. Images of the persecuted church around the world fade in and out on the screen.

## AS THE LITURGY BEGINS

1. The lighting dims and an image of a cross comes on the screen.

2. This cues the sound person to begin playing the solemn music.
   - We begin the service with the music of the Russian bells from the "Sacred Treasures: Choral Masterworks from Russia." Begin with "Russian Bells" [track 1, 22 seconds] and then play a good part of the "Song of the Cherubim" [track 4, 4:43 minutes].[1]
   - After the song ends, pause for 10 seconds.

3. A cantor (a man with a strong voice, either with or without amplification), speaks from the back of the auditorium and calls out: "The earth is the Lord's … (pause)… let the whole earth keep silence before him."

4. After 15–20 seconds of silence, the cantor speaks out, "The Word of God comes to us. Let us attend!"

5. Begin the reading of selected Scripture led by people who read well and have practiced the passages. These are the passages I chose, but you are free to utilize others that have the same content and power.
   Note: the lights remain low; screen images resume.

## READERS, CANTOR, AND CONGREGATIONAL READING SPEAK FORTH SCRIPTURES ON SUFFERING AND PERSECUTION

1. *Reader 1:* "And from the time John the Baptist began preaching and baptizing until now, the Kingdom of heaven has been forcefully advancing, and violent people attack it." Matthew 11:12.

2. *Reader 2:* "Then Jesus said to the disciples, 'If any of you wants to be my follower, you must put aside your selfish ambition, shoulder your cross, and follow me." Matthew 16:24–25.

3. *Congregation:* "When the world hates you, remember it hated me before it hated you. The world would love you if you belonged to it, but you don't. I chose you to come out of the world, and so it hates you." John 15:18–19.

4. *Reader 1:* "Then you will be arrested, persecuted, and killed. You will be hated all over the world because of your allegiance to me. And many will turn away from me and betray and hate each other. And many false prophets will appear and will lead many people astray. Sin will be rampant everywhere, and the love of many will grow cold. But those who endure to the end will be saved." Matthew 24:9–13.

---

1    Album available at http://www.amazon.com/Sacred-Treasures-Choral-Masterworks-Russia/dp/B000000X8J/ref=sr_1_1?s=music&ie=UTF8&qid=1314904455&sr=1-1.

5. *Cantor:* From the back of the auditorium; pauses for 15–20 seconds after the Matthew 24 passage, then cries out in a loud voice: "This calls for patient endurance and faithfulness on the part of the saints." Revelation 14:12.

6. *Reader 2:* "For we are not fighting against people made of flesh and blood, but against the evil rulers and authorities of the unseen world, against those mighty powers of darkness who rule this world, and against wicked spirits in the heavenly realms." Ephesians 6:12.

7. *Congregation:* "Dear friends, don't be surprised at the fiery trials you are going through, as if something strange were happening to you. Instead, be very glad—because these trials will make you partners with Christ in his suffering." 1 Peter 4:12–14.

8. *Cantor:* From the back of the auditorium; pauses for 15–20 seconds after the I Peter 4 passage, then cries out in a loud voice: "This calls for patient endurance and faithfulness on the part of the saints."

9. *Reader 1:* "Remember how you remained faithful even though it meant terrible suffering. Sometimes you were exposed to public ridicule and were beaten, and sometimes you helped others who were suffering the same things. You suffered along with those who were thrown into jail. When all you owned was taken from you, you accepted it with joy. You knew you had better things waiting for you in eternity." Hebrews 10:32–34.

10. *Reader 2:* "And when the Lamb broke the fifth seal, I saw under the altar the souls of all who had been martyred for the word of God and for being faithful in their witness. They called loudly to the Lord and said, 'O Sovereign Lord, holy and true, how long will it be before you judge the people who belong to this world for what they have done to us? When will you avenge our blood against these people?' Then a white robe was given to each of them. And they were told to rest a little longer until the full number of their brothers and sisters—their fellow servants of Jesus—had been martyred." Revelation 6:9–11.

11. *Cantor:* From the back of the auditorium; pauses for 15–20 seconds after the Revelation 6 passage, then cries out in a loud voice: "This calls for patient endurance and faithfulness on the part of the saints."

12. *Congregation:* "Then I heard a loud voice shouting across the heavens, 'It has happened at last—the salvation and power and Kingdom of our God, and the authority of his Christ! For the Accuser has been thrown down to earth—the one who accused our brothers and sisters before our God day and night. And they have defeated him because of the blood of the Lamb and because of their testimony. And they were not afraid to die. Rejoice, O heavens! And you who live in the heavens, rejoice!" Revelation 12:10–12a.

13. *Reader 1:* "I heard a loud shout from the throne, saying, 'Look, the home of God is now among his people! He will live with them, and they will be his people. God himself will be with them. He will remove all their sorrows, and there will be no more death or sorrow or crying or pain. For the old world and its evils are gone forever.'" Revelation 21:3–4.

14. *Cantor:* From the back of the auditorium; again pauses for 15–20 seconds after the Revelation 21 passage, then cries out in a loud voice: "This calls for patient endurance and faithfulness on the part of the saints."

Transition: A period of 15–20 seconds of silence follows the conclusion of the Scripture readings.

1. Now a segment of appropriate worship takes place, with historical and contemporary music selections that focus on the suffering church, about 15–20 minutes. God draws near as we worship. Lighting changes, but stays low.
2. The focus now moves to narrative, prayer, and intercession. Lights are dimmed again.
   • Ask someone to speak who has experienced persecution for his or her faith, preferably from another cultural or geographical context (6–8 minutes max).
   • Be sure to have the speaker write out what is to be said. This controls both the time and story, and allows the leaders to work with the speaker in an appropriate way.
3. The prayers of the people begin. This may require some explanation by the leader. The lights are still dim, and no images are on screen at present. Invest at least 20 minutes in prayer. Print out the prayer requests.
   • You can have prayer stations for people to gather around flags of nations where believers experience severe persecution.
   • You can have people go to other flags or other candle clusters (red and white, small candles for children and youth; larger ones for adults).
   • You can have selected people pray through a litany of requests that are current from the world of the persecuted church.

*Note:* At this point the service of Holy Communion may take place, if you wish. This depends on the amount of time allotted for the service and its place in the flow of worship at your church. Remember that the prime focus of this liturgy is prayer and quiet meditation.

## DRAWING TO A CLOSE
1. The leader invites people to return to their seats and together they pray the following two prayers.
   • All together, slowly and solemnly, from the *Book of Common Prayer:*
   "Almighty God who created us in your own image: Grant us grace fearlessly to contend against evil and to make no peace with oppression; and, that we may reverently use our freedom, help us to employ it in the maintenance of justice in our communities and among the nations, to the glory of your holy Name; through Jesus Christ our Lord, who lives and reigns with you and the Holy Spirit, one God, now and for ever. Amen."

   • All together, the Celtic prayer as we bless those for whom we have prayed:
   May God the Father surround them with his angels of light.
   May the Son surround them with his blood outpoured.
   May the Spirit surround them with his fire of power
   To save, to keep, to heal, to protect.

Each day, each night, each light, each dark, until their journey's end.
Amen.

2. The leader brings the service to a close with final comments, letting people know how the service will end, asking them to stay to pray and meditate or leave in silence. You may want to have informative material on the persecuted church on tables in the foyer or back of the worship center.

   • Then the leader asks for complete silence. Wait for 30 seconds. The lights are very dim; one strong image on screen.

3. The cantor then cries out from the back: "Blessed be God—Father, Son, and Holy Spirit—and blessed be his Kingdom, both now and ever, and unto the ages of ages. Amen!"

4. Pause, then the final selection from CD "Sacred Treasures" [track 12]. At end of selection, stop play. Then begin the CD at the beginning with lowered volume and leave playing.

5. People leave in silence or remain to pray quietly as the CD plays softly.

6. Final image of Celtic cross on screen, candles are burning, lights are low.

## PROGRAM HANDOUT NOTES

*A time of quiet reading and prayer for the persecuted church*
Welcome! Thank you for coming and joining with believers in scores of nations to pray for our suffering and persecuted brothers and sisters in Christ in other parts of the world. While it is good to gather information, set an agenda of needs, and then proceed to pray through the list as we often do in corporate prayer, we will be approaching our prayer time together a bit differently. The tone of this evening will be more focused on quiet listening to God, on worshiping him, and then responding to his Spirit's leading as we enter into intercession for those who suffer for his name's sake. Too often we rush into God's presence out of our scattered and fragmented lives and plunge into prayer where we do most of the talking and very little listening.

To that end we will use various means to aid us in quieting our hearts and coming into a place of attentive listening, humbly asking for a deeper identification with those who suffer and how best to pray for them. The visual images on the screen will bring to mind the suffering church and Christ's words in Luke 9:23,24 and 14:27, that we, too, must share in his cross. The candles, large and small, red and white, represent adults and children, martyrs and suffering ones from around the world. They also serve to remind us of "the prayers of the saints that rise up like incense before the throne of God" (Rev 5:8). The choral music written by Rachmaninoff and Tchaikovsky for church services in their native Russia not only calls us into a place of peace and quiet, but also reminds us of the glory that awaits us and the honor that will be given to those who suffer for Christ. We hear in this music hymns of praise to God as well as prayers for his mercy upon all Christians everywhere.

Ask God to attune your heart to the reading of his Word, to the time of worship, and finally to the time of prayer. Thank him that Christ who is seated at the right hand of the throne of

God ever intercedes for his own (Rom 8:34). And thank him for his Holy Spirit who dwells within each one of us and who, in and through us, "prays for the saints in accordance with God's will" (Rom 8:26,27).

After we have worshiped and prayed, we will conclude the service as we began, in silence. Some of you may want to linger to pray quietly and continue in a posture of worship. When you leave, please do so in complete silence and wait to enter into conversation until you are outside the worship center. Thank you for being with us this evening.

As you carry in your heart the persecuted and suffering ones, may the blessing of God be upon you "each day, each night, each step of the journey thou goest."

*Program handout can include the Scripture readings and liturgy.*

*Final notes:* I am grateful for the leadership of Cedar Springs Presbyterian Church, Knoxville, TN, USA, who allowed me to introduce and use this liturgy for the November 2003 International Day of Prayer for the Persecuted Church.

For further resources, go to www.IDOP.org. See also appendix C in this book, which lists a wealth of Internet sources as you select prayer requests.

Scripture quotations are taken from the Holy Bible, New Living Translation, copyright © 1996, 2004, 2007 by Tyndale House Foundation. Used by permission of Tyndale House Publishers, Inc., Carol Stream, Illinois 60188. All rights reserved.

**Yvonne DeAcutis Taylor** has ministered together with her husband, William, in cross-cultural mission since 1967. Her university degree is in the liberal arts and music. She is a classical musician and a long-time student of Christian spirituality in the various historic streams of Christianity. God's calling on her in ministry includes spiritual formation and spiritual direction/mentoring, as well as dedicated intercession. Additional areas of study and specific ministry are church history and Celtic Christianity.

And I heard a loud voice from the throne saying, "Behold, the dwelling place of God is with man. He will dwell with them, and they will be his people, and God himself will be with them as their God. He will wipe away every tear from their eyes, and death shall be no more, neither shall there be mourning, nor crying, nor pain anymore, for the former things have passed away."

*Revelation 21:3–4*

# CHAPTER 69

# APPROACHING THE FINAL DOOR OF OUR JOURNEY

## Engaging Another World

*William D. Taylor, Antonia van der Meer, Reg Reimer*

I believe [those] witnesses that get their throat cut. —*Blaise Pascal*

For the poor, the persecuted, the sick, and all who suffer; for refugees, prisoners, and all who are in danger; that they may be relieved and protected, we pray to you, O Lord. Lord, in your mercy, hear our prayer. —Prayers of the people, *Book of Common Prayer*

Congratulations for making it to the conclusion of this volume. This book is neither short, nor easy, nor is it another Christianity-lite chapter of soft gospel. It is strong meat.

You have surveyed global panoramas, examined key terms, listened to many personal stories. You have visited key Scripture, evaluated theological themes, and looked evil in the face. You have walked through history and evaluated case studies from around the world. You have grappled with how to prepare for and respond to suffering, persecution, and martyrdom. Surely you now know how to pray in a more informed and sustained manner, right?

What is left for your three editors to say? We want to underline that these themes cannot be mere tertiary or even secondary in our understanding of transformational discipleship, or for the way we prepare women and men for ministry and mission, or for our teaching and equipping of churches around the world. Of persecution too many Christians say, "But it can't happen here! After all, those things only happen with the Nazi, Communist, and Islamic regimes." Nothing could be farther from the truth.

This book has a wealth of illustrative material, first to guide Christians facing persecution, and second, to prepare Global North or Global South churches to deal with growing discrimination, harassment, facets of persecution, and even martyrdom.

We ask: when was the last time your pastor preached on persecution and martyrdom? When was the last time your church observed the International Day of Prayer for the Persecuted Church (IDOP)? Do our Bible colleges, seminaries, and missionary training schools offer curricula for these realities?

We are encouraged that we do have good examples of prefield equipping courses given by some agencies sending personnel into delicate and dangerous areas of the world. We are encouraged to see an emerging set of resources and challenges for the global church on the themes of our book. In the past, few theology of missions books written for the Global North dealt with persecution. One refreshing and new exception is Timothy C. Tennent's book *Invitation to World Missions: A Trinitarian Missiology for the Twenty-first Century* (Kregel, 2010). One of his final chapters is entitled "The Suffering, Advancing Church," a challenge in particular to the Global North, yet very relevant to the whole church of Christ.

## TWO FINAL ITEMS

First, we three editors have a few final words. Second, we invite you to engage with what this book has documented about suffering, persecution, and martyrdom in light of reflections on the remarkable life of Dietrich Bonhoeffer.

I, Tonica, believe in and am committed to serve the suffering church, wherever and whenever, and to create awareness in our more prosperous churches in relatively peaceful environments. We cannot just enjoy our happy Christian lives while others are suffering greatly. Our first decision should be to open our ears, our eyes, and our hearts to them and to understand what God wants us to feel and to do concerning them. We do not suggest a paternalistic way of serving, but faithfully praying and standing at their side, willing to share their burden.

Our commitment must be strong and faithful to those missionaries who have been sent to serve people living in these challenging realities. They need our support and our understanding. When I lived amidst war and Communism in Angola, the greatest need all of us missionaries and national Christians felt was for people to remember us and to pray for us.

This commitment also means that we will continue to send people and be willing ourselves to go to the most risky and resistant fields, to live out and proclaim the gospel, to serve, and to shine our light. We will learn with the early church to rejoice when we are persecuted for the name of our Lord. We will neither provoke persecution nor fear it to the point that we are unfaithful to our Lord's command.

I, Reg, am humbled to have had a part in this heavy exercise. No fluff and Christian *kitsch* here! "Coincidentally," I read *Bonhoeffer: Pastor, Martyr, Prophet* at the same time as our senior editor, Bill. It challenges me immensely.

While we speak much here of preparing missionaries and churches for hardship, in my experience we missionaries are uniquely equipped and positioned to mediate between persecuted and nonpersecuted churches to build strong bridges of mutual understanding and benefit. There is much to be gained in the reciprocity a thoughtful missionary can facilitate.

And finally, in reflection, I am strongly impressed that the whole content of this book is a rebuke of the many reductionist "gospels" that flourish and fade in the Christian world. I trust you found the deep satisfaction I did in coming closer to the biblical and historical realities of our suffering Christian ancestors and contemporaries. Let's keep leaning in that direction.

I, Bill, along with Reg, have just concluded reading the moving recent biography of Bonhoeffer. Just before penning this paragraph, I read the section on his hanging, which took place in 1945 just two weeks before the Allied forces liberated that part of Germany, and only three weeks before Hitler committed suicide and the Third Reich flamed out. How could this happen? Where was God? Yet those were not Bonhoeffer's concerns. His most penetrating writings on spirituality and community, discipleship, and the church were forged in the fires of the Nazi regime. We are deeply indebted.

## LESSONS FROM BONHOEFFER: FROM HIS DAY AND FOR OUR DAY

It is almost impossible to believe that this German Lutheran scholar-pastor wrote some of his most powerful essays and preached those prophetic messages when only in his mid-twenties. Right after Hitler came to power in 1933, democratically elected, he immediately began to address the "Jewish problem." German Christians were forced to ask themselves what their response would be. The majority of the nominal Lutheran church leadership capitulated to government pressures. But not Bonhoeffer and a body of committed Christians, who would soon form the "Confessing Church." In March 1933 Bonhoeffer, age twenty-seven, presented a Christian response to the "Jewish question," and articulated a threefold stance of church in relation to state. It was an extended understanding of Paul's teaching in Romans 13:1–7 on the relationship between believers and the state.

He affirmed that the church (in the historical context of Martin Luther's legacy and understanding of church and state) had a threefold responsibility. His premise was that "the church must 'continually ask the state whether its action can be justified as legitimate action of the state; i.e., as action which leads to law and order, and not to lawlessness and disorder.' In other words, it is the church's role to *help the state be the state*" (Metaxas 2010, 153–54).

What are the "three possible ways in which the church can act towards the state"? First, to "help the state be the state," and if necessary "to question the state regarding its actions and their legitimacy—to help the state be the state as God has ordained"(153).

Second, "to aid the victims of state action." Here Bonhoeffer took a huge, risky, and proactive leap. The church "has an unconditional obligation to aid the victims of state action." Clearly he was thinking of Jews in Germany, with the personal reality of two brothers-in-law of Jewish blood, though Christians by confession. Yet the personal sphere was simply a template for the national arena. The church "has an unconditional obligation to the victims of any ordering of society, even if they do not belong to the Christian community" (154).

> The third way the church can act toward the state, he said, 'is not just to bandage the victims under the wheel, but to put a spoke in the wheel itself' … At some point the church must directly take action against the state to stop it from perpetrating evil. This, he said, is permitted only when the church sees its very existence threatened by the state, and when the state ceases to be the state as defined by God. (154)

This inevitably meant opposition and resistance, leading to the conspiracy to assassinate Hitler as the only way to save Germany and Europe.

The "spoke in the wheel" metaphor is radical for many evangelicals, including your editors. Bonhoeffer's is one of various paradigms of church-state relations, some of which are discussed in chapter 3, "Christian Responses to Suffering, Persecution, and Martyrdom." You will find very helpful prescriptions for Christian action there. By holding Bonhoeffer's paradigm up as model, we don't intend to make his application of the third model a ready norm. However, we need to ask the hard questions regarding Christian responsibility when nations and churches fall as far short of God's ideal as they did in Nazi Germany. If we think this problem died with the Nazis, we have only to remember Rwanda in the mid-nineties.

## AND HOW DOES THIS APPLY TO US TODAY?

The German Confessing Church attempted to apply these three principles—and paid the price. So how might these three models apply to the global church today facing hostility, persecution, and even martyrdom? Regardless of what country or city we live in or what people group or context we serve in, we must be biblical; we must discern our own realities clearly, and we must prepare the church for the future.

To do this, we must first return to Scripture and reread it in the context of uncertainty, poverty, powerlessness, violence, opposition, persecution. We must evaluate the text and study its principles in light of first-century totalitarianism and in light of key passages, such as Romans 13:1–7 and 1 Timothy 2:1–4. We must see that as Paul writes to Timothy, the key as we pray is not to ask for peaceful, prosperous, democratic conditions, but rather a context where the gospel can advance, regardless of the political system.

Second, these biblical reflections and their implications must be studied in the context of the pastoral and theological community of each worshiping fellowship of Jesus. It cannot be the self-appointed assignment of radical individuals or solo prophets. It must come from the worshiping fellowship. We recommend a careful consideration of chapter 3 and the diverse responses devoted and wise Christians can take in these challenging days.

Third, this leadership community must consider where the church is in the spectrum of freedom to violent opposition and act accordingly. The spectrum ranges from total freedom to martyrdom, with levels in between:

1. Total freedom
2. Tolerance
3. Discrimination
4. Harassment
5. Persecution
6. Violent persecution
7. Martyrdom

Where do you find your context and church in this spectrum? Remember that these dynamics move back and forth along the two opposite poles.

Fourth, we may need to examine the relevancy of Bonhoeffer's three guidelines on church/state relationships, as well as other perspectives on the same. Germany had been indelibly marked by the legacy of Martin Luther, yet that was not enough to protect the Lutheran church under the Nazi regime. We live today in an incredibly diverse cultural, political, religious, and ideological world. The contexts of persecution today reveal profoundly different complexities and they in turn can easily create confusion in our modern world. How we need the thoughtful direction of the biblical shepherds and prophets, saturated in the Word, in deep spirituality, and in community!

And each context will produce variations on the Pauline and Bonhoeffer themes.

Can persecution and martyrdom happen "here," wherever "here" is? Only God knows. When? Well, in too many places it is today, now, here. In others it is imminent or dangerously looming in the future. In yet others it is a potential reality, even as legal and cultural pressures increase. Only God knows. Can we just live our normal lives and plan for a well-provided retirement? No.

> The cross is laid on every Christian.... As we embark upon discipleship we surrender ourselves to Christ in union with his death—we give over our lives to death. Thus it begins; the cross is not the terrible end to an otherwise God-fearing and happy life, but it meets us at the beginning of our communion with Christ. When Christ calls a person, he bids him come and die.
>
> D. Bonhoeffer in *The Cost of Discipleship* (1976, 98f)

We close with Bonhoeffer's prophetic poem, penned shortly after he heard of the failure of the plot against Hitler's life. He now knew what would happen. The two years of prison would come to an end. It was published in his posthumous book *Letters and Papers from Prison*.

### Stations on the Road to Freedom

*Discipline*

If you set out to seek freedom, then learn above all things
to govern your soul and your senses, for fear that your passions
and longing may lead you away from the path you should follow.
Chaste be your mind and your body, and both in subjection,
obediently steadfastly seeking the aim set before them;
only through discipline may a man learn to be free.

*Action*

Daring to do what is right, not what fancy may tell you,
valiantly grasping occasions, not cravenly doubting—
freedom comes only through deeds, not through thoughts taking wing.
Faint not nor fear, but go out to the storm and the action,
trusting in God whose commandment you faithfully follow;
freedom, exultant, will welcome your spirit with joy.

*Suffering*

A change has come indeed. Your hands, so strong and active,
are bound, in helplessness now you see your action
is ended; you sigh in relief, your cause committing
to stronger hands; so now you may rest contented.
Only for one blissful moment could you draw near to touch freedom;

then, that it might be perfected in glory, you gave it to God.

*Death*
Come now, thou greatest of feasts on the journey to freedom eternal;
death, cast aside all the burdensome chains, and demolish
the walls of our temporal body, the walls of our souls that are blinded,
so that at last we may see that which here remains hidden.
Freedom, how long have we sought thee in discipline, action, and suffering;
dying, we now may behold thee revealed in the Lord. (Metaxas 2010, 484–85)

The three of us—Tonica, Reg, and Bill—cry out triumphantly, "Maranatha!"


## REFERENCE

Metaxas, E. 2010. *Bonhoeffer: Pastor, martyr, prophet spy; A righteous Gentile vs. the Third Reich.* Nashville, TN: Thomas Nelson.

# PART SIX

# RESOURCES

## WALKING OUT

What further steps might we take on this journey, on this pilgrimage? This brief section provides some helps. The annotated bibliography presents a concise review of the literature on these urgent themes, and the Internet resources point you to a vast arena of information and investigation. We invite you to seriously consider the importance of the partnering platforms, vital samples today of how believers and groups converge in strategic cooperation for greater synergy. Finally, we conclude with some member care resources for you to consider in ministry to the wounded and suffering.

The next steps are now yours. —*William D. Taylor*

# THE BAD URACH CALL

## Toward Understanding Suffering, Persecution, and Martyrdom for the Global Church in Mission

### I. PREAMBLE[1]

By any definition of persecution, the worldwide Body of Christ can count many millions of Christians experiencing persecution today. Their sufferings range from violent death and martyrdom, to physical or psychological torture, to invasive rules confining their worship activities to church buildings, to lower-level forms of discrimination in countless other countries, including many with strong rules protecting religious freedom. Due to the massive rise in population and the explosion in the numbers of Christians, never in the history of the church have so many of Christ's followers experienced persecution as today, though the number of those who die as martyrs for the faith is not often so large. This situation gives three tasks to the Body of Christ:

1. **Remembrance:** The persecuted are not remembered, prayed for, and assisted by the general Body of Christ as well as they should be.
2. **Understanding:** There is a complex blend of ancient cosmic antagonisms and contemporary factors that drive persecution. These are not well enough understood, which results in ineffective intervention. While the persecution of Christians is ultimately due to the enmity between Christ and the fallen spiritual realm joined with human rebellion, four secondary forces deliver persecution to the church: religious extremism, totalitarian insecurity, religious nationalism, and secular intolerance. Thoughtless public statements or symbolic actions by Christians in contexts with substantial freedom of speech can unleash violent reactions against Christians in other contexts.
3. **Transformation:** Persecuted Christians have learned truths about God that Christians under less pressure need to hear in order to experience the fullness of God. The spiritual insights of the persecuted are vital to the transformation of the lives of the

---

1    This is a short, popularized summary of some of the points of the extensive *Bad Urach Statement* by evangelical leaders from many lands who gathered on September 16–18, 2009, in Bad Urach, Germany, on the invitation of the Religious Liberty Commission of the World Evangelical Alliance and other bodies, organized by the International Institute for Religious Freedom. The summary was edited by Pastor Dr. Thomas K. Johnson, Prague.

rest of the Body of Christ. One of these essential insights is that we will all be—if witnessing for Christ—in some sense persecuted. There is a grander, greater narrative of God's action underneath the stories of individual pain, suffering, deliverance, and endurance.

*Our call to the church of Jesus Christ:*
*We must willingly, actively, and corporately take up the cross of Christ in our time.*

## II. EXPLANATION

### 1. We need to respond to suffering appropriately.
We should distinguish between general human suffering, in which Christians partake, and the suffering of Christians for the sake of Christ. We recognize that much suffering has nothing to do with persecution, but obedience to God and allegiance to Christ lead to additional suffering. We must always respond to suffering with compassion, but suffering for Jesus requires additional responses.

The mature Christian knows that all suffering can become meaningful. No one wishes to suffer, but many Christians who have suffered do not regret it. God also suffers because the people he created suffer, and he suffers for their redemption. He suffers because he loves us. The suffering of God in Christ can shape our thinking on the suffering of the church. Christians should suffer in sympathy with others who suffer. Because Jesus commands us to love, we should voluntarily suffer to help others who are suffering, to reduce their suffering. We suffer as part of the general human condition and also because we must take up the cross as disciples of Jesus Christ. If we participate in the sufferings of Jesus, we will also share in his glory. Some of us must choose to make sacrifices and to suffer on behalf of fellow Christians who are being persecuted.

### 2. We need to properly understand religious persecution of Christians.
Religious persecution is an unjust action against a believer or group of believers of a certain religion or worldview. This may be by systematic oppression, genocide, discrimination, annoyance, or other means. Persecution may not prevent victims from practicing their beliefs. Religious persecution has religion (not ethnicity, gender, political persuasion, etc.) as its primary motivation, though other factors can be involved. Persecution of Christians is a form of religious persecution in which victims are targeted primarily because they are Christians. Victims may be of varying levels of commitment to Christianity and be subject to varying levels of animosity and harm.

### 3. We need to understand our place in history.
The persecution of Christians is rooted in our place in salvation history. A new age has been inaugurated by Christ, overcoming the age of sin and death which began with the fall. The second coming of Christ will visibly usher in God's rule and victory, making all things new. Until then the old age is still present, waging its war against the new age; the life of the Christian is marked by this tension. In this sense, suffering is a mark of the church. This suffering of the church was prefigured by the suffering of God's people in the Old Testament,

from Abel through the prophets, leading to Herod's pursuit of Jesus, reaching its high point in the murder of Jesus on the cross. Jesus' death on the cross was as a substitute for our sins, making full payment; by his death Jesus was also our representative, calling us to follow him to suffer in order to fight against sin and the devil.

### 4. We need to react properly to the conflict.

The nature of the conflict in which we are involved is characterized by the nature and methods of the two leaders in the conflict. Jesus reveals the character of Satan as evil, which brings forth the weapons of hate, lies, deception, falsehood, violence, and murder to bring destruction and death. Jesus confronted Satan's lies with the truth of God, Satan's evil with the goodness of God, Satan's hatred with the love of God, and Satan's violence and murder with God's self-sacrifice, out of which arise new creativity, healing, and restoration. This is the way in which Jesus fought and defeated evil, and this is the kind of war into which he sends his disciples. They must love their enemies, do good to those who hate them, and, like their heavenly Father, show goodness, mercy, and forgiveness to those who are evil and ungrateful. They must stop the chain of poisoning God's creation with Satan's deadly products by absorbing it in union with Christ, responding in love and goodness, thereby demonstrating God's character in the world. Jesus was sent as the Lamb of God to defeat the great dragon and to destroy his works. In the same way, he sends us as lambs to defeat wolves by transforming them into children of God. Christ's ultimate weapon is self-sacrifice, and our ultimate weapon must be the same, to draw people to Jesus.

### 5. We must remain faithful to Christ.

Jesus points out the seriousness of remaining faithful to him and confessing him in moments of trial. He warns his disciples that he would reciprocate their public acknowledgement or denial of him on this earth before his Father in heaven. While the love of many will grow cold, those who endure to the end and remain victorious will be saved. In order that his disciples do not fall away from him when persecution arises, Jesus has given advance warning and prays that God will keep them safe from the evil one.

### 6. We need to embrace suffering as part of our mission.

Jesus described suffering as a normal part of discipleship. Not all suffer equally; not all are persecuted equally, and only a relatively small proportion of Christians suffer martyrdom. In the mission that is the central purpose of the interim period in God's history of salvation, Christians must engage with their whole lives, including a readiness for suffering and martyrdom. Suffering is not just something that has to be endured passively, but it becomes a mode of mission, a mission that is done in weakness, focusing on service, and by its nature is accompanied with sorrow and affliction. The precious gospel treasure comes in perishable containers, in our weak bodies, so that everyone can see that the light that shines in us is not our own but God's. Martyrdom is the most radical form of discipleship and missionary witness. While Christians will not seek martyrdom, it is a risk of discipleship we must accept.

Witness to Christ can be a main cause of suffering, persecution, and martyrdom. The gospel certainly brings with it liberation from all kinds of slaveries and can lead to the improvement of the quality of living. This even may translate into material blessings. At the same time, it brings the hatred of the world, persecution, suffering, and martyrdom. We must keep these two aspects of the gospel in balance. The mission of God needs to be accomplished in spite of and through suffering, persecution, and martyrdom.

*7. We need to stand up for religious freedom and human rights.*
As a part of our proclamation of Christ we should always mention two truths about people, that people are both sinners in need of the gospel and also created in the image of God, carrying a God-given dignity. This dignity requires that we call on governments and all in positions of public authority to protect religious freedom and all fundamental human rights. When there is severe religious persecution, there is often a government that is failing to protect justice. Like the Apostle Paul, Christians should appeal to legal rights to protect themselves and their fellow Christians.

*We therefore call on the Body of Christ to take up the cross of Jesus actively, willingly, and corporately, in order to implement the mission of Jesus. This will include remembrance of those persecuted (with prayer and assistance), understanding (joined with informed efforts to reduce persecution), and transformation (so that the entire Body of Christ is renewed through the insights of those who are persecuted and martyred). May the grace of the Lord Jesus be with you all![2]*

---

2        The biblical and theological foundations, along with practical implementations, are developed in great detail in the extensive *Bad Urach Statement*, which can be found at www.iirf.eu and which is published as part of the compendium on the Bad Urach Consultation: *Suffering, Persecution and Martyrdom: Theological Reflections*, edited by Christof Sauer and Richard Howell (Religious Freedom Series, vol. 2, Kempton Park, South Africa: AcadSA Publishing; Bonn: VKW, 2010). See: International Institute for Religious Freedom, www.iirf.eu. and Religious Liberty Commission of the World Evangelical Alliance, www.worldevangelicals.org.

# SELECT ANNOTATED BIBLIOGRAPHY

## On Persecution, Suffering, and Martyrdom
*Samuel Chiang, Roberta Chiang, and Brian F. O'Connell*

The bibliography was selected with the following in mind:

A look at all parts of the world, including both Christian and non-Christian writings; a survey of global history, particularly including genocide and martyrdom; and intentional crossing of denominational, religious, and gender lines to include books from non-Protestant, female, and also non-Christian writers. Finally, we looked at different genres, including biographies/autobiographies, research, memoir, historical fiction, inspirational, factual, etc. When historical fiction is listed, it is only listed as a suggested "read along" for excellent flavor and context. For example, Khaled Hosseini's two well-known novels, *The Kite Runner* and *A Thousand Splendid Suns*, are listed within the annotation of another related book.

Aid to the Church in Need. 2011. *Persecuted and forgotten? A report on Christians oppressed for their faith*. Sutton, Australia: Aid to the Church in Need. http://www.aidtochurch. org. An excellent reference resource with global coverage.

Aikman, David. 2003. *Jesus in Beijing: How Christianity is transforming China and changing the global balance of power*. Washington, DC: Regenery. The former Beijing bureau chief for *Time Magazine* documents Christians living, thriving, and testifying in a hostile anti-Christian environment in China. A timeless book.

Ajak, Benjamin, Benson Deng, Alephonsian Deng, and Judy Bernstein. 2005. *They poured fire on us from the sky*. New York: Public Affairs. The real-life story of three "Lost Boys," who along with tens of thousands of young boys, fled from the massacres of Sudan's civil war. Read this book along with Dave Eggers' *What Is the What* (Doubleday 2006).

Akkara, Anto. 2009. *Kandhamal: A blot on Indian secularism*. New Delhi, India: Media House. A short but important book on anti-Christian violence in Orissa State.

Anderson, Ken. 1991. *Bold as a Lamb*. Grand Rapids, MI: Zondervan. Pastor Samuel Lamb's story of spending over twenty years in Chinese prisons.

Arnold, Duane W. H. 1991. *Prayers of the martyrs*. Grand Rapids, MI: Zondervan. A marvelous selection of prayers from the martyrs of the church throughout history.

Bergman, Susan, ed. 1996. *Martyrs: Contemporary writers on modern lives of faith*. New York: Harper Collins. A diverse and exceptionally well-written collection of essays documenting key faith leaders in the twentieth century. These range from Steve Saint writing on his father, Nate Saint, and Jim Elliot in 1956 Ecuador, to the highly acclaimed author Nancy Mairs on Janani Luwum's death in Idi Amin's Uganda.

Bonhoeffer, Dietrich. 1959. *The cost of discipleship*. Norwich, UK: SCM. An inspirational Christian classic written by a man who wrote well. It is a relevant reminder to all as to how to live in view of civic duty when evil is present.

Boyd, Andrew. 2006. *Baroness Cox: A voice for the voiceless*. Oxford: Lion Books. Biography of Carolyn Cox, one of the most public of religious liberty activists; detailing situations in Sudan, Myanmar, Nagorno Karabakh, and others.

Boyd-MacMillan, Ronald. 2006. *Faith that endures: The essential guide to the persecuted church*. Lancaster, PA: Sovereign World. Individual stories in the context of full analysis and how persecution is promulgated makes this book an important read. The personal application section sets this book apart to be timeless. Likely the best single source for the facts about persecution and the best religious liberty response strategies.

Brother Andrew, and Al Janssen. 2005. *Light force: A stirring account of the church caught in the Middle East crossfire*. Ada, MI: Revell. Inspiring true stories of the church in the Middle East; read along with the authors' *Secret Believers: What Happens When Muslims Believe in Christ* (Revell 2008).

Brother Yun. 2002. *The heavenly man*. Ed. Paul Hattaway. Chester, UK: Monarch Books. Inspirational autobiographical account of Brother Yun's China house church experience in the context of Communism and imprisonment, and God's dealings with him; read along with Brother Yun's *Living Water: Powerful Teachings* (Zondervan 2008). Paul Hattaway is an expert on the Chinese church and the author of *Operation China*.

Caner, Emir Fethi, and H. Edward Pruitt. 2005. *The costly call: Modern-day stories of Muslims who found Jesus*. Grand Rapids, MI: Kregel. Testimonies of men and women from seventeen countries on three continents who faced various religious persecutions in Muslim lands.

Chacour, Elias. 2003. *Blood brothers*. Grand Rapids, MI: Chosen Books. This is an important book by the archbishop of the Akko, Haifa, Nazareth, and All Galilee of Melkite Greek Church, who lives as a peacemaker to bring reconciliation to both the Israelis and the Palestinians. Highly recommended to read along with Susan Abulhawa's *Mornings in Jenin* (Bloomsbury 2010), historical fiction looking at four generations of Palestinians living through the birth of Israel, the wars that follow, and the lives of those who were born and raised in refugee camps.

Chumachenko, Tatiana A. 2002. *Church and state in Soviet Russia: Russian orthodoxy from World War II to the Khrushchev years.* Ed. and trans. Edward E. Roslof. Armonk, NY: Sharpe. The author gained access to previously closed archives and provides insight into the turbulent relationship between the church and the state from 1948 to 1957. Scholarly work accompanied by photographs. A contribution to knowledge!

Companjen, Anneke. 2007. *Singing through the night: Courageous stories of faith from women in the persecuted church.* Ada, MI: Revell. An inspirational book about eleven women in nine different countries who suffered through persecution. Read this along with *Hidden Sorrow, Lasting Joy: The Forgotten Women of the Persecuted Church* (Tyndale 2001), where the same author writes from the perspective of women around the world whose husbands were imprisoned or killed for their faith.

Conway, John S. 1997. *The Nazi persecution of the churches: 1933–1945.* Vancouver, BC: Regent College Publishing. Meticulous scholarship and excellent documentation drawing on material from Nazi archives, with detailed descriptions of measures taken by the Nazi government to limit the activities of the church.

Cormack, Don. 1997. *Killing fields, living fields.* London: Monarch Books. An inspirational story of church growth in Cambodia from the 1920s to the 1970s; then, what they endured under the Khmer Rouge. Recommended to read along with Kim Echlin's work of fiction *The Disappeared* (Grove Press 2009) which leaves the reader with a profound sorrow at the devastation of not only this country during the genocide years in the seventies, but at the tearing apart of almost every family.

Cunningham, Scott. 1997. *Through many tribulations: The theology of persecution in Luke–Acts.* Sheffield, UK: Sheffield Academic. A literary and theological examination of tribulation through Luke's writing in the New Testament.

Davis, Nathaniel. 2003. *A long walk to church: A contemporary history of Russian Orthodoxy.* Oxford: Westview. An updated edition that examines the Russian Orthodox Church during and after the Communist era.

Demick, Barbara. 2010. *Nothing to envy.* New York: Spiegel and Grau. Six defectors from North Korea and their personal journeys provide the reader further insights into the country.

Durie, Mark. 2010. *The third choice: Islam, dhimmitude, and freedom.* Australia: Deror Books. A very significant historical and sociological work with insights into evil, rejection, and suffering. Extremely highly recommended! Read along with Sidney H. Griffith's scholarly book *The Church in the Shadow of the Mosque: Christians and Muslims in the World of Islam* (Princeton University Press 2010).

Eide, Oyvind M. 2000. *Revolution and religion in Ethiopia 1974–1985.* Addis Ababa: Addis Ababa University Press. An important document of the church in revolutionary times.

Eitel, Keith E., ed. 2008. *Missions in contexts of violence*. Pasadena: William Carey Library. Nineteen conference papers from the (North American) Evangelical Missiological Society. Some interesting articles, like "Baptism in Cultures of Persecution."

Eshete, Tiebe. 2009. *The evangelical movement in Ethiopia: Resistance and resilience*. Waco, TX: Baylor University Press. A convert from the Ethiopian Orthodox Church to Ethiopian Pentecostalism, the author's excellent research shows the growth and conflict of the evangelical movement with the Orthodox Church and also the government. Highly recommended.

Fazzini, Gerolamo. 2009. *The red book of Chinese martyrs*. Trans. Michael Miller. Fort Collins, CO: Ignatius Press. Catholic suffering under Mao, based on actual diaries of priests and nuns who survived the gulag.

Fernando, Ajith. 2007. *The call to joy and pain: Embracing suffering in your ministry*. Wheaton: Crossway. The noted speaker and writer from Sri Lanka focuses the reader on why "suffering in all its aspects is an integral part of the Christian calling."

Foxe, John. 2007. *Foxe: Voices of the martyrs; 33 AD to today*. Alachua, FL: Bridge-Logos. A Christian classic from AD 1599, updated for the twenty-first century to include martyrdom across the globe.

Grdzelidze, Tamara, and Gguido Dotti, eds. 2009. *A cloud of witnesses: Opportunities for ecumenical commemoration*. Proceedings of the International Ecumenical Symposium: Monastery of Bose, October 29–November 2, 2008. Geneva: WCC Publications. Focuses on the commemoration of martyrs and makes an important contribution concerning the problem of intra-Christian persecution. For the open-minded and discerning reader who wants to learn from the perspectives of Christians from other creeds and denominations.

Harvey, Thomas Alan. 2002. *Acquainted with grief: Wang Mingdao's stand for the persecuted church in China*. Grand Rapids, MI: Brazos. An important examination of the role, life, and endurance of suffering by one of the fathers of the modern Chinese house church movement.

Hattaway, Paul. 2007. *China's book of martyrs: Fire and blood*. Carlisle, UK: Piquant. A biographical story of those who have been martyred in China from the beginning of the church in China to the present.

Hefley, James and Marti Hefley. 1979. *By their blood: Christian martyrs of the twentieth century*. Grand Rapids, MI: Baker Books. A well-researched book covering over fifty countries from all parts of the world.

Hunter, Harold D., and Cecil M. Robeck, eds. 2006. *The suffering body: Responding to the persecution of Christians*. Milton Keynes/Waynesboro, GA: Paternoster. Papers from a scholarly side conference to the International Charismatic Consultation on the topic

"The Suffering Church." Some theological contributions and reports from four continents by authors from various denominations.

Ilibagiza, Immaculee, with Steve Irwin. 2008. *Led by faith: Rising from the ashes of the Rwandan genocide.* Carlsbad, CA: Hay House. The book details the author's journey after the 1994 Rwandan genocide; read along with *Left to Tell: Discovering God Amidst the Rwandan Holocaust,* by the same authors (Hay House 2007). Inspirational.

*International Journal for Religious Freedom.* (Since 2008.) Provides scholarly articles on suffering, persecution, martyrdom, and religious freedom, mostly from a Christian perspective, twice a year. Includes many book reviews in every issue. Free online at www. iirf.eu.

Jenkins, Philip. 2009. *The lost history of Christianity: The thousand-year golden age of the church in the Middle East, Africa, and Asia and how it died.* New York: Harper-Collins. The title says it all, a *tour de force* tracing the church's history that the West usually misses. A must read.

Johnson, Todd M., and R. Kenneth Ross, eds. 2009. *Atlas of global Christianity.* Edinburgh, UK: Edinburgh University Press. This extremely important volume comes with an interactive CD and covers many topics, including religious violence done to Christians. This is an important reference book for any library!

Johnstone, Patrick. 2011. *The future of the global church: History, trends and possibilities.* Colorado Springs, CO: Biblica. This reference work is a must for libraries and will give you the big picture into which to place persecution, martyrdom, and mission. More popular than the *Atlas* by Johnson and Ross, with an inspirational edge.

Kiernan, Ben. 2007. *Blood and soil: A world history of genocide and extermination from Sparta to Darfur.* New Haven, CT: Yale University Press. An examination of atrocities in the last six centuries including Maoism in China, Rwanda in Central Africa, the activities of al-Qaeda, and many others.

Kidder, Tracy. 2010. *Strength in what remains.* New York: Random House. A beautifully written story of the struggle for survival in an American city while remembering scenes of genocidal massacre in Burundi. Highly recommended reading.

Kim, Esther Ahn. 1979. *If I perish.* Chicago, IL: Moody Publishers. An autobiography of the author's savage persecution during World War II in Korea.

Kreeft, Peter. 1986. *Making sense out of suffering.* Ann Arbor, MI: Servant Books. In this inspirational book, Kreeft guides those asking the question, "Why am I suffering?"

Lee, Lydia. 2001. *A Living Sacrifice: The Life Story of Allen Yuan.* Kent, UK: Open Doors International. Allen Yuan was one of the founding fathers of the house church movement in China. This book tells the story of his conversion to Christianity, persecution, and imprisonment for many years.

Lee, Young Kee. 2012. *God's mission in suffering and martyrdom*. Bonn: Culture and Science Publ. A missiological treatise from a Korean perspective for the educated missiologist.

Levi, William. 2005. *The Bible or the axe: One man's dramatic escape from persecution in the Sudan*. Chicago, IL: Lift Every Voice. From a Messianic Hebrew background, the author's memoir of Islamic persecution of Christians and his response is a worthwhile read.

Liao, Yiwe. 2011. *God is red: The secret story of how Christianity survived and flourished in Communist China*. New York: Harper-Collins. The author is a not a Christian. His perspective is fresh; documentary interviews are rich. His excellent research confirms how human beings tried to wipe out Christianity through desecrating burial sites, taking over land, and crushing the human spirit; but Christians did not waver. It is a must read.

Maass, Peter. 1996. *Love thy neighbor: A story of war*. New York: First Vintage Books. The author asked the questions, "Why did 250,000 Bosnians lose their lives" and "Why can't Christians and Muslims work their differences out after so long?"

Mandryk, Jason, ed. 2010. *Operation world*. Colorado Springs, CO: Biblica. The prayer guide on every country of the world from an evangelical missionary perspective that also takes note of persecution.

Marshall, Paul A. 1997. *Their blood cries out*. Dallas, TX: Word. Well researched; a call for Christians to wake up and accept the challenge to care about persecution.

———, ed. 2008. *Religious freedom in the world*. Lanham, MD: Rowman and Littlefield. Helpful surveys on many countries. Includes background essays on major regions and shows what questions to ask if one wants to assess the situation of religious freedom in a given country.

Marshall, Paul, and Nina Shea. 2011. *Silenced: How apostasy and blasphemy codes are choking freedom worldwide*. New York: Oxford University Press. A *tour de force* global survey of apostasy and blasphemy accusations in the Muslim world, the West, and in various organizations. The authors are experts in their field and are with the Hudson Institute.

Metaxas, Eric. 2010. *Bonhoeffer: Pastor, martyr, prophet, spy; A righteous Gentile vs. the Third Reich*. Nashville, TN: Thomas Nelson. This award-winning, well-researched book (608 pages) is a must read! The readers' guide and ending questions are highly reflective and should generate not only discussions but also individual and collective actions. Read along with *Love Letters from Cell 92*, a 1992 volume that contains Bonhoeffer's letter exchanges with Maria, to whom Bonhoeffer was engaged.

McGill, Arthur C. 1982. *Suffering: A test of theological method*. Louisville, KY: Westminster John Knox Press. Through an examination of the concept of power the author responds to the question, "How can an omnipotent God allow suffering and violence to pervade the world?"

Middleton, Paul. 2011. *Martyrdom: A guide for the perplexed*. London: Continuum. A more substantial example of the many smaller books that have appeared on martyrdom recently. The author is most familiar with early Christianity but includes chapters on the Christendom era, Judaism, and Islam.

Milton, Giles. 2008. *Paradise lost: Smyrna 1922*. New York: Basic Books. Engaging and well written, with acute insight into the British Levantines and the Greek and Armenian tragedies as the Ottoman Turks invaded Smyrna. Highly recommended!

Neill, Stephen. 1986. *A history of Christian missions*, 2nd ed. London: Penguin Books. The most comprehensive single volume source outlining the expansion of Christianity—the challenges, opportunities, and persecutions faced—from the beginnings of the church through the mid-twentieth century.

Newell, Marvin. 2006. *A martyr's grace: Stories of those who gave all for Christ and his cause*. Chicago, IL: Moody Publishers. An inspirational book of twenty-one Moody Bible Institute graduates who have been martyred while serving in the Middle East, China, Africa, South East Asia, and Latin America.

Noll, Mark, and Carolyn Nystrom. 2011. *Clouds of witnesses: Christian voices from Africa and Asia*. Downers Grove, IL: InterVarsity Press. A survey of seventeen individuals who withstood conflict and suffering. From 1880s to 1980s, they stood firm and contributed to the growth of the church today.

Nouwen, Henri. 2008. *Compassion: A reflection on the Christian life*. London: Darton, Longman, and Todd. A Christian life lives with compassion at the heart level and will embrace suffering and endure persecution; this timeless classic should be read by all.

Ohlrich, Charles. 1982. *The suffering God*. Downers Grove, IL: InterVarsity Press. An inspirational book focusing on the suffering of God and how we relate to him.

O'Malley, Vincent J. 2001. *Saints of Africa*. Huntington, IN: Our Sunday Visitor Publishing. Historical accounts from Africa including popes, church fathers, and thousands of martyrs.

Penner, Glenn. 2004. *In the shadow of the cross: A biblical theology of persecution and discipleship*. Bartlesville, OK: Living Sacrifice Books. A thorough biblical examination of persecution; inclusion of other experts and input have made this a timeless book to be read by all followers of Christ. Highly recommended.

Reimer, Reg. 2011. *Vietnam's Christians: A century of growth in adversity*. Pasadena, CA: William Carey Library. A rare glimpse into the history of the church, its persecution, and growth in Vietnam by a lifelong missionary and advocate for Christians in Vietnam.

Royal, Robert. 2006. *The Catholic martyrs of the twentieth century: A comprehensive world history*. New York: Crossroad. A well-researched book of twentieth-century Catholic martyrs, including both well-known and obscure accounts across the globe; an important reference.

Saberi, Roxana. 2010. *Between two worlds: My life and captivity in Iran*. New York: Harper-Collins. The author is an American-born daughter of an Iranian father and a Japanese mother. She arrived in Iran in 2003 as a journalist, was arrested by the secret police in January 2009 on trumped-up charges of spying, and was released on May 11, 2009. Ms. Saberi describes a country where lines between religion and politics blur, where the secret police rule much of society, and a place where there seems to be a "spiritual yearning" above and beyond the legalism of Islam. Worth reading for a good picture of modern-day Iran.

Sauer, Christof, and Richard Howell, eds. 2010. *Suffering, persecution and martyrdom*. Kempton Park, South Africa: AcadSA Publishing; also Bonn: Culture and Science Publishers, free online at http://tinyurl.com/sauer-howell. An extremely significant compendium of twelve contributors providing perspectives on the theology of suffering. This book is a result of a consultation which was organized by the International Institute for Religious Freedom, sponsored by the WEA Religious Liberty Commission together with the Theological Commission, the Mission Commission, and the Lausanne Theology Working Group. Exceptional resource!

Schlossberg, Herbert. 1991. *A fragrance of oppression: The church and its persecutors*. Wheaton, IL: Crossway. This timeless book examines the sources, motives, and tactics of persecution in the early church, then moves into modern times with a call for believers' action.

Schoenberner, Gerhard. 2004. *The yellow star: The persecution of the Jews in Europe, 1933–1945*. Bronx, NY: Fordham University Press. First published in 1960, this is a revised and updated version of the first photographic account of the Holocaust.

Seierstad, Asne. 2003. *The bookseller of Kabul*. London, UK: Little Brown Book Group. Well-written story of one man who braves persecution to bring books to the people of Kabul. For a rounded, updated picture, best read along with Deborah Rodriguez's *The Kabul Beauty School: An American Woman Goes Behind the Veil* (Random House 2007) and Khaled Hosseini's two well-known novels *The Kite Runner* (Riverhead 2004) and *A Thousand Splendid Suns* (Riverhead 2009).

———. 2006. *With their backs to the world: Portraits from Serbia*. New York: Basic Books. A true account and kaleidoscope portrait of a nation made up of so many different hopes, dreams, and points of view.

Shea, Nina. 1997. *In the lion's den*. Nashville, TN: Broadman and Holman. An account of persecution and martyrdom of both Protestant and Catholic Christians; read this along with Paul Marshall's *Their Blood Cries Out* (Word 1997).

Sookhdeo, Patrick, ed. 2004. *The persecuted church*. Lausanne Occasional Paper No. 32. www.lausanne.org. A collaborative report from the 2004 Forum held in Pattaya, Thailand. Its strength lies in its attempt of listening to the persecuted and in giving ample strategic advice on how to work alongside the persecuted.

Stark, Rodney. 1997. *The rise of Christianity: How the obscure, marginal Jesus movement became the dominant religious force in the Western world in a few centuries.* New York: Harper Collins. Chapter 8, "The Martyr's Sacrifice as Rational Choice," enriches our study with Stark's historical research and multiple illustrations.

Storm, Kay Marshall, and Michele Rickett. 2003. *Daughters of hope: Stories of witness and hope in the face of persecution.* Downers Grove, IL: InterVarsity Press. Inspirational stories of women, globally, who suffered persecution; comes with specific prayer points and suggested practical action steps.

Tieszen, Charles. 2008. *Re-examining religious persecution: Constructing a theological framework for understanding persecution.* Kempton Park, South Africa: AcadSA Publishing; also free online at http://tinyurl.com/tieszen. A thoughtfully presented book (short, only ninety-one pages with eleven pages of bibliography) that provides any layman or pastor a workable, biblical framework. Highly recommended.

Ton, Josef. 1997. *Martyrdom and rewards in heaven.* Lanham, MD: University of America Press. Second edition published in 2007, Oradea, Romania: Crestina (available in the US via the Romanian Missionary Society). An in-depth biblical study combined with historical doctrines of suffering for Christ. An excellent reference.

Totten, Samuel, ed. 2008. *Century of genocide: Critical essays and eyewitness accounts,* 3rd ed. London: Routledge. First-person accounts of genocides, holocausts, and massacres; updated to include Darfur and persecution against indigenous peoples.

Tutu, Desmond. 2000. *No future without forgiveness.* New York: Doubleday. A personal memoir of the Anglican Archbishop from Cape Town, South Africa, who served as chair of the Truth and Reconciliation Commission; documentation of horror, moving beyond apartheid's legacy, and lessons learned for the future.

Von der Heydt, Barbara. 1993. *Candles behind the wall: Heroes of the peaceful revolution that shattered Communism.* Grand Rapids, MI: Eerdmans. Documentation, even a martyrology, of the triumph of spiritual beliefs and of the leaders who brought down the Berlin Wall.

White, Andrew. 2011. *Faith under fire: What the Middle East conflict has taught me about God.* Oxford: Monarch Books. The "vicar of Baghdad" reflects on how the Middle East conflict has informed his faith. Detailed descriptions of Christians in Iraq, from death threats to church bombings.

Wiesel, Eli. 1960. *Night.* New York: Bantam Books. *Night* is a vivid memoir of a Holocaust survivor. Powerful narration. One will not forget the scene in which the entire concentration camp is forced to witness the hanging of a boy!

Windsor, Stuart. 2011. *God's adventurer: The story of Stuart Windsor and the persecuted church*. Oxford: Monarch Books. Tells the story of Stuart Windsor and the work Christian Solidarity Worldwide does on behalf of persecuted believers.

Witt, David, and Mujahid El Masih. 2009. *Fearless love. Rediscovering Jesus' spirit of martyrdom with meditations of Christ and his love*. Clarkdale, AR: Martus. A Pakistani believer and an American pastor team-teach about martyrdom; useful in small groups or Sunday schools.

Woehr, Chris, and Terry W. Whalin. 1993. *One bright shining path: Faith in the midst of terrorism*. Wheaton, IL: Crossway. The story of Romulo Saune, martyred because of his work translating the Scriptures into the Quechua language of Peru.

Wurmbrand, Richard. 1998. *Tortured for Christ*. Bartlesville, OK: Living Sacrifice Books. The founder of The Voice of Martyrs wrote his autobiography documenting his testimony and faith in God. If you have previously heard him speak, this book captures his intensity equally.

Yakovlev, Alexander N. 2002. *A century of violence in Soviet Russia*. New Haven, CT: Yale University Press. The author is both a participant and a transformer who brought about the change and downfall of Communism in Russia. Very unique perspective.

Ye'or, Bat. 1996. *The decline of Eastern Christianity under Islam: From jihad to dhimmitude; seventh–twentieth century*. Madison, NJ: Fairleigh Dickinson University Press. An excellent scholarly book tracing Islamic history, texts, renowned scholars, and the implementation of both jihad and dhimmitude in conquered lands through the centuries. An important reference!

**Samuel Chiang**, executive director of International Orality Network, along with his bride, **Roberta Chiang**, serve the global church; Rev. Chiang also serves on the board of The Seed Company. Mrs. Chiang is interested in the area of spiritual direction and the ancient church, and she loves to read. They have three children and have lived in Hong Kong since 1991.

**Brian F. O'Connell** is the president and CEO of REACT Services (www.REACTServices.com). He serves as the facilitator of the Religious Liberty Partnership (www.RLPartnership.org) and helped launch and establish the WEA Religious Liberty Commission. He has been involved in global partnership development and international missions for over twenty years, ministering in over one hundred countries.

# PERSECUTION INFORMATION ON THE WEB

*A. Scott Moreau and Mike O'Rear*

The Internet provides ample evidence that persecution of Christians is an extensive international tragedy. Google yields over 200,000 hits from a search for "persecution of Christians" (with the quotes). Searching for websites dealing with persecution of Christians in a particular country, such as India or China, further demonstrates the scope of the problem: entering the words "persecution Christian India" (without the quotes) into Google results in nearly 1.5 million hits; substituting China for India gives a similar result.

Wikipedia can often provide an initial introduction to an issue, its definition, and its context. The Wikipedia article on "Persecution of Christians" (http://en.wikipedia.org/wiki/Persecution_of_Christians) includes an extensive historical overview along with links to nearly two dozen related Wikipedia articles.

We highlight some of the key websites (in alphabetical order with one exception) that provide valuable online resources (see them all at www.mislinks.org/practical/persecuted.htm). We group the resources into three categories: (1) Christian organizations focused on ministering to the suffering church, (2) Christian news and information sources focused on persecution, and (3) major secular sites.

## CHRISTIAN ORGANIZATIONS

Because it serves such a broad constituency and has such significant links to resources, we want to highlight the *International Day of Prayer for the Persecuted Church (IDOP)* (www.persecutedchurch.org) site first. Sponsored by almost twenty persecution-focused organizations, IDOP has had significant impact on churches around the world through the annual event (on a Sunday each year in November) and the resources they provide.

*Barnabas Aid* (www.barnabasfund.org) offers "hope and aid for the persecuted church" and promotes prayer and advocacy ministries. Focused primarily on the Muslim world, its website provides daily prayer points, a news archive, and feature articles.

*Christian Freedom International* (www.christianfreedom.org) is "an interdenominational human rights organization that combines advocacy with humanitarian assistance for persecuted Christians on the front lines." The website offers news, Persecution Spotlight items, a few videos, and practical ways to get directly involved.

*Christian Solidarity Worldwide* (www.cswusa.com) is "called to stand with our persecuted brothers and sisters in Christ, giving voice to their cries of suffering and urging action on their behalf, by raising prayer support and emergency aid in partnership." The website provides profiles of several dozen countries, a newsletter, a daily prayer calendar, and government petitions.

*Christians in Crisis* (www.christiansincrisis.net), "a prayer advocacy ministry that prays for the persecuted church worldwide," offers online devotionals and stories from the field. The ministry emphasizes Islamic regions, but the online news section covers persecution of Christians around the world.

*International Christian Concern* (www.persecution.org) is an interdenominational human-rights organization dedicated to providing assistance, advocacy, and awareness for the suffering church. The site includes prayer profiles of countries where Christians are persecuted, current news stories, a semimonthly prayer bulletin, and petitions to sign.

*International Institute for Religious Freedom* (www.iirf.eu) is a network of Christian professors, researchers, academics, and specialists from all continents who work on background research about religious freedom and persecution worldwide. The website offers their own research in book length, the *International Journal for Religious Freedom* and other periodicals, as well as many shorter reports from various sources.

*International Justice Mission* (www.ijm.org) is "a human rights organization that rescues victims of violence, sexual exploitation, slavery, and oppression. IJM documents and monitors conditions of abuse and oppression, educates the church and public about the abuses, and mobilizes intervention on behalf of victims." The website includes monthly in-depth "Justice Briefings" and valuable articles by IJM staff.

*Iranian Christians International* (www.iranchristians.org), while primarily focused on evangelism and discipleship, also engages in assisting Iranians, Afghans, and other Persian-speaking Christian refugees fleeing persecution.

*Jubilee Campaign* (www.jubileecampaign.org) exists to, among other things, "advance the human rights and religious liberty of ethnic and religious minorities."

*Open Doors International* (www.opendoors.org), the ministry founded by Brother Andrew, focuses on Bible delivery programs, leadership training in restricted areas, and prayer mobilization. Its World Watch List, available free online, ranks countries according to a fifty-question set of criteria related to religious freedom.

*The Voice of the Martyrs* (www.persecution.com), founded by Richard Wurmbrand, is "dedicated to assisting the persecuted church worldwide." Sign up to access the audio/video media room, country profiles, weekly e-mail updates, and monthly newsletter. The related PrisonerAlert.com site (www.prisoneralert.com) profiles individual prisoners, encouraging writing letters to prisoners and sending e-mail to government officials. VOM's Persecution Blog (www.persecutionblog.com) provides good insight, and their extensive blog roll will lead you to many related bloggers.

*World Evangelical Alliance's Religious Liberty Commission* (www.worldevangelicals.org/commissions/rlc) monitors the religious liberty situation in more than one hundred nations, "defending persecuted Christians, informing the global church, challenging the church to pray (www.idop.org), and giving all possible assistance to those who are suffering." The website provides a weekly News and Prayer Bulletin. Additionally, the WEA offers an ever-growing list of resources related to religious liberty (www.worldevangelicals.org/resources/categories/index.htm?cat=42).

## CHRISTIAN NEWS AND INFORMATION SERVICES

*Assist News Service* (www.assistnews.net), providing "Aid to Special Saints in Strategic Times," produces multiple news articles on a daily basis, many of which deal with persecuted Christian communities. Use the search feature to find previous news items from Assist's extensive online database; for instance, searching for "Sudan" finds over 370 articles.

*Christian Monitor* (www.christianmonitor.org) provides news headlines focused on persecution of Christians around the world, along with related editorials, book reviews, and interviews.

*Christian Persecution Info* (www.christianpersecution.info), "a Christian news journal" provided by Worthy Ministries, specializes in tracking the latest news on Christian persecution. Regional tabs let you focus on recent news items in Africa, China, Russia, etc.

*Compass Direct News* (www.compassdirect.org) is a professional news service dedicated to providing "strategic news and information from the world's most difficult areas." Via an exclusive international network of news bureaus and correspondents, it provides paid subscribers with reports, interviews, and analyses of persecuted Christians worldwide.

*Project Open Book* (www.domini.org/openbook/home.htm) focuses on "documenting the persecution of Christians in the Islamic world." It provides online access to papers and articles documenting specific incidents of persecution.

## SECULAR ORGANIZATIONS

*Amnesty International* (www.amnesty.org) focuses on human rights in general and has multiple ongoing campaigns. You can search their extensive online library of over fifty thousand items: newsletters, reports, appeals for action, video and audio clips, stories, etc.

*Center for Religious Freedom* (crf.hudson.org), sponsored by the Hudson Institute, "promotes religious freedom as a component of US foreign policy by working with a worldwide network of religious freedom experts." The website provides online access to almost four hundred articles related to religious freedom.

*Human Rights Watch* (www.hrw.org) is "dedicated to protecting the human rights of people around the world." The site provides an online list of substantial publications (including HRW's annual World Report), a list of current campaigns, a set of photo galleries, and an array of video clips.

*The United Nations Refugee Agency* (www.unhcr.org) provides extensive textual information, statistics, databases, and maps describing the world's refugee population as well as a list of publications (www.unhcr.org/pages/49c3646c4b8.html). You can search their massive on-line database, Refworld (www.unhcr.org/cgi-bin/texis/vtx/refworld/rwmain), a collection of reports as well as policy and legal documents from countries around the world.

*The United States Department of State* publishes an annual report on international religious freedom (www.state.gov/g/drl/rls/irf/), which "contains an introduction, executive summary, and a chapter describing the status of religious freedom in each of 195 countries throughout the world."

Finally, we note that *Google* has continued to increase the sophistication of its search capabilities—and how it displays them. For example, *Google Trends* (www.google.com/trends) allows you to look at the number of searches on a given phrase over various spans of time. Type in "persecution" and you will see the traffic on Google's servers related to persecution as well as news stories over the past several years. You can limit your search by country or by month. *Google News* (news.google.com) lets you examine news related pages (which you can separate into stories, images, or blogs), and you can choose to limit your search by dates (e.g., all of 2009; one day in 2010).

To make your search easier, we've compiled these links (and more) on our MisLinks site at www.mislinks.org/understanding/persecution. We've also set up a list focused on persecution on our MisLinksOrg twitter account; those on Twitter can follow that list at twitter.com/#!/MisLinksOrg/persecution.

**Scott Moreau** served fourteen years on staff with Campus Crusade for Christ, ten in Africa. For the past twenty years he has taught at Wheaton College, where he is now professor of intercultural studies and missions. He also serves as editor of *Evangelical Missions Quarterly* and general editor of the Encountering Mission series (Baker Books).

**Mike O'Rear** served as president and CEO of Global Mapping International (GMI), dedicated to providing applied mission research, geographic mapping, and digital publishing services for international Christian ministries. He coauthored the MisLinks.org website and the "Missions on the Web" series in *Evangelical Missions Quarterly*. Mike passed away suddenly on January 14, 2012. While we know he is rejoicing in eternity, we miss his wisdom and insight on behalf of the missions community.

# PARTNERING PLATFORMS SERVING THE PERSECUTED

*Brian F. O'Connell*

Working together to serve persecuted believers is the most effective strategy that ministries have to raise awareness, mobilize prayer, and develop key projects that assist the persecuted church. Founded on a scriptural basis, partnering can reduce needless duplication, maximize financial and people resources, and enhance ministry effectiveness.

Of course, it also sends a positive message to those seeking to follow Christ in difficult situations—most of whom live in relational, people-focused cultures. Leaders with long experience in working among those being discriminated, harassed, and persecuted for their faith in Christ have regularly pointed out that those who suffer can often be quite dysfunctional. They have relational issues, physical challenges, often are alienated from their families (who may be hostile to them), and many times are spiritually immature. Serving the persecuted is always a challenge, but a worthy one.

Working together in networks and partnering efforts requires intentionality and often much time. The things these key leaders seek to do as they champion the cause can be summarized under four general categories:

- Convening agencies and ministries under a more neutral and competition-free atmosphere;
- Catalyzing specific work together by creating space and appropriate process to address the question of what can we do together that we cannot do by ourselves;
- Coordinating the collaborative projects identified as strategic and important (it is one thing to come up with the ideas and another to actually see results from them);
- Communicating to the wider community—and among the partners themselves— what is happening and how to join the effort.

Let me present three specific and relevant examples of collaborative platforms serving the persecuted church world: Middle East Concern, the Religious Liberty Commission of the World Evangelical Alliance (WEA), and the Religious Liberty Partnership. Successful results within these three collaborative platforms are multiple, but often they occur in countries and areas where security precludes speaking of specific examples. However, even by just sharing information with each other, by identifying best practices and emerging trends, they have provided substantial added value to those who participate and connect.

*Middle East Concern* (www.MEConcern.org) is an association of agencies and individuals advocating the human rights of Christian communities in the Middle East and North Africa, within the general human-rights context in the region. They have specialized in assisting believers in this broad and extensive Middle East region, through mobilizing prayer, public advocacy, and providing practical support to those fleeing persecution. They also seek to equip Christians in the region to prepare for and respond to persecution through theological and legal training.

*The WEA Religious Liberty Commission* (www.worldevangelicals.org/commissions/rlc/) monitors the religious liberty situation in the over 130 countries that are part of the WEA family. They seek to inform the global church through research, mobilizing prayer (www.idop.org) and giving possible assistance to those who are suffering for their faith in Christ. The RLC also organizes and makes occasional fact-finding trips, meeting with government officials on behalf of persecuted believers.

*The Religious Liberty Partnership* (RLP) is a collaborative effort of over thirty organizations focused on serving the persecuted church around the world. Current members come from eighteen countries and cooperate to provide assistance to persecuted believers as well as in public advocacy. The RLP website (www.RLPartnership.org) is a portal to most of their members and it also outlines some of the projects that the partnership is undertaking. One of their new initiatives is the development of an "early warning system" that can help determine where religious liberty challenges are newly emerging and are at risk.

**Brian F. O'Connell** is the president and CEO of REACT Services (www.REACTServices. com). He serves as the facilitator of the Religious Liberty Partnership (www.RLPartnership. org) and helped launch and establish the WEA Religious Liberty Commission. He has been involved in global partnership development and international missions for over twenty years, ministering in over one hundred countries.

# MEMBER CARE RESOURCES

## For those in the Context of Suffering and Persecution
*Harry Hoffmann and Pramila Rajendran*

## INTRODUCTION

A suicide in Thailand, abduction in Sudan, murder in Turkey, hostage-taking in the Philippines, imprisonment in Malaysia, team conflicts in Brazil, rape in Nigeria, etc. These and many others are among the situations to which member care responds. Member care addresses all aspects of the well-being of missionaries and their dependents, including spiritual, emotional, relational, physical, and economic matters. But, however strong the systems in place for everyday health and well-being, crises provide their own particular, acute challenges.

## RESPONSE

### Psychological trauma: overwhelming our ability to cope

Psychological trauma results from a single event, or repeated or sustained experiences, which completely overwhelm our ability to cope or to integrate the ideas and emotions involved. Being a witness to a traumatic event can cause secondary trauma. Both can lead to serious long-term psychological and physical changes within the brain and to brain chemistry, which damage the person's ability to cope adequately with stress. This can lead to depression, anger, fear, addictions, physical health breakdown, or questioning our core beliefs.

### Resources

There is no quick fix for people suffering from psychological trauma, and different people will react in different ways to similar situations. The Global Member Care Network (GMCN) has a helpful database of resources worldwide at www.globalmembercare.com. GMCN's core team includes regional networks of leaders who can provide current advice on Christian regional and local resources. Some regions have more resources than others, but an inquiry to info@globalmembercare.com will connect you to the best known resources in your region. Note: the GMCN tries wherever possible to serve people where they are and in their own language.

### Pyramid of support

People suffering a traumatic event need a good network of support. We sometimes use the image of a pyramid, its four corners being: (1) family and friends, (2) the safety of the church, (3) empathetic people helpers or a cell group to share and pray with, confidentially and personally, and (4) professional counseling. The top of the pyramid, connecting all four corners, is God and your developing relationship with him.

### Psychologists and psychiatrists
These professionals are specialists in trauma care and in post-traumatic stress disorder. GMCN can link you with the professionals in your region.

### Spiritual direction and prayer counseling
Spiritual direction and prayer counseling have become well-received among evangelicals in recent years. Many people have testified to finding healing and of restructuring their core beliefs and relationship with God after a traumatic experience left them with uncertainties and questions. For spiritual direction, initiate a Web search or contact the GMCN. Also look at Elijah House global network on www.elijahhouse.org or Theophostic Ministry's website on www.theophostic.com.

### Forums
Victims of trauma and caregivers can find peers to share and interact with on several online forums; e.g., www.ptsdforum.org.

### Seminars
Training seminars are available in many regions or can be accessed through the GMCN. For example, Crisis Response Training: Mobile Member Care Team (www.mmct.org/#/work-shops/crt); or Crisis and Trauma Response Seminar: Le Rucher (www.lerucher.org); or Healing the Wounds of Trauma: SIL Africa (margaret.hill@sil.org).

## PREPARATION AND PREVENTION

### The church and sending organizations
Good preparation, and prevention where possible, is essential. Risk assessments help with making informed decisions. The missionary is not simply an individual; missionaries have many relationships and many people involved in their calling, their placement, and their well-being. Foremost among these are families, sending churches, receiving churches, prayer partners, and sending organizations. In the event of a crisis, embassies and government officials are involved as well. Sometimes embassies will advise against going to a place of significant danger or will ask an NGO to review contingency plans regularly.

### Resources
*Crisis Consulting International* (www.cricon.org) provides security-related training and consultation services, assisting Christian organizations in areas such as event security, protection of personnel, investigation of hostile acts, etc. During crises such as kidnappings, they serve as consultants and hostage negotiators. CCI has a global network and works with individuals and organizations.

*The Code of Good Practice* (www.peopleinaid.org/code) is an internationally recognized management tool that helps humanitarian aid and mission agencies enhance the quality of their staff management. Principle 7 addresses health, safety, and security as a primary responsibility of organizations.

*Do-it-yourself resources:* Teams and families should visit the following:

- Earthquake: Do an Internet search on "What to do during an earthquake" and discuss.
- Hostage: Do an Internet search on "How to survive if you are taken hostage" and discuss.
- Risk analysis: Three core questions for risk analysis are: (1) What can go wrong? (2) How likely is it? and (3) What are the consequences? These questions and discussions should be revisited on a regular basis where contexts are changing.
- Contingency plan: Who has your home church or organization contact details, blood type, phone numbers, copy of your passport? Are you registered with your embassy? Is there an agreed meeting point in case of social unrest or natural disaster? Do you have medical insurance?
- High-risk and high-stress areas require personnel to leave the country on a regular basis in order to prevent burnout, blind spots, or irresponsible behavior. Some teams leave the country where they minister four times yearly for two to three weeks.

*Suffering Unseen:* Regular debriefings are especially helpful because some people are ashamed or afraid to share the emotional or relational suffering they are experiencing. Debriefing questions should purposefully address different aspects of missionary life, including personal, emotional, behavioral, relational, cultural, and organizational aspects. If a questionnaire is used, it is important to add personal discussion and/or coaching. Free debriefing questions and guidelines are available online, or you can use professional services such as the Cerny Smith cross-cultural adjustment assessment (www.cernysmith.com).

## RESOURCES

Baldwin, B. A. 1979. Crisis intervention: An overview of theory and practice. *The Counseling Psychologist* 8: 43–52.

Burgess, B., and L. Holmstrom. 1997. Rape trauma syndrome. *American Journal of Psychiatry* 131, no. 9: 981–86.

Carr, K. 1994. Trauma and post-traumatic stress disorder among missionaries. *Evangelical Missions Quarterly* 30 (July).

Figley, C. 1989. *Helping traumatised families*. San Francisco, CA: Jossey-Bass.

Greeson, C., M. Hollingsworth, and M. Washburn. 1990. *The grief adjustment guide*. Sisters, OR: Questar.

Hill, M., H. Hill, R. Bagge, and P. Miersma. 2009. *Healing the wounds of trauma: How the church can help*, 3rd ed. Nairobi: Paulines Publications Africa.

Langberg, D. 1998. The truth about rape. *Christian Counseling Today* 6, no. 1: 23–25.

Matsakis, A. 1992. *I can't get over it: A handbook for trauma survivors.* Oakland, CA: New Harbinger.

Meichenbaum, D. 1994. *A clinical handbook/practical therapist manual for assessing and treating adults with post-traumatic stress disorder.* Waterloo, ON: University of Waterloo.

Mitchell, J. T., and H. L. P. Resnick. 1986. *Emergency response to crisis.* Ellicott City, MD: International Critical Incident Stress Foundation.

O'Donnell, K., ed. 2001. *Doing member care well: Perspectives and practices from around the world* (especially pp. 117–26). Pasadena, CA: William Carey Library.

Prashantham, B. J. *Indian case studies in therapeutic counselling.* Vellore, India: CCC.

Slaikeu, K. A., and S. Lawhead. 1987. *Up from the ashes: How to survive and grow through personal crisis.* Grand Rapids, MI: Zondervan.

Wright, H. N. 1993. *Crisis counselling: What to do and say during the first 72 hours.* Ventura, CA: Regal Books.

———. 1999. *Why did this happen to me?* Ann Arbor, MI: Servant.

**Harry Hoffmann** is the coordinator of the Mission Commission's Global Member Care Network (www.globalmembercare.org) and founder of two member care centers in Asia, where he and his family have resided since 1996. He is German, received a master's degree in Chinese studies from Free University of Berlin, and likes to dream big and strategize accordingly.

**Pramila Rajendran**, India, worked with Operation Mobilisation for over twenty years in mission and leadership capacities in India and overseas. She initiated the Membercare Network for Indian Mission Association. Presently she serves with her husband, Dr. K. Rajendran, as staff of the WEA Mission Commission and the MC Global Membercare Task Force. Pramila has a BA in anthropology and criminology and an MA in pastoral theology and counseling. They are parents of daughter Preeti, a clinical psychologist, and son Pradeep, a freelance media consultant.

# GLOBALIZATION OF MISSION SERIES

## World Evangelical Alliance Mission Commission Publications

Taylor, William D., ed. 1991. *Internationalising missionary training: A global perspective.* Carlisle, UK: Paternoster, Grand Rapids, MI: Baker Book House.

Taylor, William D., ed. 1994. *Kingdom Partners for Synergy in Missions.* Pasadena, CA: William Carey Library.

Lewis, Jonathan, ed. 1996. *Working your way to the nations: A guide to effective tentmaking.* Downers Grove, IL: InterVarsity Press.

Taylor, William D., ed. 1997. *Too valuable to lose: Exploring the causes and cures of missionary attrition.* Pasadena, CA: William Carey Library.

Taylor, William D., ed. 2000. *Global missiology for the twenty-first century: The Iguassu Dialogue.* Grand Rapids, MI: Baker Academic.

O'Donnell, Kelly, ed. 2002. *Doing member care well: Perspectives and practices from around the world.* Pasadena, CA: William Carey Library.

Tiplady, Richard, ed. 2003. *One world or many: The impact of globalisation on mission.* Pasadena, CA: William Carey Library.

Brynjolfson, Robert, and Jonathan Lewis, eds. 2006. *Integral ministry training: Design and evaluation.* Pasadena, CA: William Carey Library.

Hay, Rob, Valerie Lim, Detlef Blöcher, Japp Ketelaar, and Sarah Hay. 2007. *Worth keeping: Global perspectives on best practice in missionary retention.* Pasadena, CA: William Carey Library.

Cook, Matthew, Rob Haskell, Ruth Julian, and Natee Tanchanpongs, eds. 2010. *Local theology for the global church: Principles for an evangelical approach to contextualization.* Pasadena, CA: William Carey Library.

Dowsett, Rose, ed. 2011. *Global mission: Reflections and case studies in contextualization for the whole church.* Pasadena, CA: William Carey Library.

Taylor, William D., Antonia van der Meer, and Reg Reimer, eds. 2012. *Sorrow and blood: Christian mission in contexts of suffering, persecution, and martyrdom.* Pasadena, CA: William Carey Library.

**Forthcoming**

Taylor, William D., and John Amalraj, eds. 2013. *Spirituality and mission: Global currents, spirit-empowered convergences.* Pasadena, CA: William Carey Library.

# INDEX

\* Check also appendices for references to these terms.